OUT OF
OUR PAST

The Forces That Shaped
Modern America

"Nor for the past alone—for meanings to the future."

WALT WHITMAN

OUT OF
OUR PAST

*The Forces That Shaped
Modern America*

CARL N. DEGLER

HARPER & ROW, PUBLISHERS

New York, Evanston, and London

To Catherine, who endlessly read it, and to Paul and Suzanne, who endlessly heard about it.

Contents

3. But All White Men Are Not Free   4. The American
Dilemma.

Preface

WHEN the historian sits down to write about the past, there are always several approaches open to him. The one most commonly taken might be called descriptive history, in which the story of what happened in the past is told as accurately and minutely as research, literary style, and the space available will permit. Insofar as it is possible, the events of the past are presented as they took place; small effort is made to distinguish between those events which have relevance to the present and those which have little. The primary purpose is to recreate the past as nearly as possible, not to draw morals or to uncover guides for the present.

That is not the approach taken here. To put it simply, this book seeks an answer to the question "How did Americans get to be the way they are in the middle of the twentieth century?" In other words, the multitudinous events of the American past are here seen through the lens of the present. Admittedly, much of the material usually included in the story of America is missing in such an approach. Readers should be warned that they will find nothing here on the Presidential administrations between 1868 and 1901, no mention of the American Indians or the settlement of the seventeenth-century colonies; the War of 1812 is touched upon only in a footnote.

History viewed through the eyes of the present is understandably different from history written from the standpoint of the past. Persons and events which in other treatments might remain un-noticed or unappreciated now spring into focus. Therefore, in this book events and developments usually ignored or subordinated in standard accounts of American history now move to the center of the stage. For example, the history of the Negro in America figures prominently in three chapters, the rise and influence of the city dominate two, and the beginnings of American nationality in the colonial period come in for extended discussion.

All written history, no matter how slow its pace or numerous its pages, is a selection from the infinite number of facts in the past. A history of a whole nation in one volume, like this, is of necessity even more selective. Therefore, in addition to confining myself to those aspects of the past which bear on the present, I have also limited myself to the history of Americans as a people. There is little in this book about great men or individual genius, except where such men embody the values and aspirations of the whole people. The work and thought of many American thinkers, artists, scientists, and statesmen are therefore ignored, not because they are unimportant, but because to have included them would have made this something other than a history of the shaping of the American people.

In current historical writing it is fashionable to look to economic and social forces for the explanation of the movement and direction of history. Certainly this approach is more sophisticated than attributing the course of history to the actions of a few great men. But at the same time it seems to ignore a force in history which this book seeks to emphasize—the role of ideas. And by ideas I mean the beliefs, assumptions, and values of the people rather than the great ideas of thinkers which form the basis of formal intellectual history. Because, for example, Americans cherished ideas like freedom, equality, and Christian justice, they acted to realize them; in doing so, they changed the course of their history.

Karl Marx and other writers of the nineteenth century made a luminous contribution to the understanding of human history when they were able to show that men's ideas bore a close relation to the socioeconomic context in which they flourished; that, for example, the poetry of a pastoral people is filled with pastoral imagery, that an industrial society extols free labor. But this insight is often betrayed by the careless conclusions drawn from it. It is one thing to see connections between ideas and the economy and quite another to assume that all ideas must necessarily be but pale reflections of economic interests and the mode of production. One cardinal assumption in this book is that ideas have a life of their own, regardless of their origin. And by "a life of their own" I mean that men defend or oppose ideas for reasons not always related to their immediate self-interest, or to the socioeconomic character of their society.

The truth of this, it seems to me, arises out of the nature of man himself. Admittedly, men are animals and, in common with other beasts, have powerful drives toward food, self-preservation, and sex, none of which can be easily denied or sublimated. On these indubitable facts rests the materialist conception of history. But man is more than an animal. He surrounds himself with ritual, ideal, and prejudice to such an extent that the essentials of life, like food-gathering, sexual satisfaction, and the urge to know the universe, are unnecessarily hedged about with obstacles to immediate gratification. No other animal is guilty of such illogicality. No other animal, for example, exposes himself to death in defense of vague, indefinable conceptions like national honor or the nature of God. Ideas are live forces in human history; often they are more powerful than the elemental drives. On an individual basis and in psychoanalytical language, this is to say that the superego can and does override the id.

Sometimes ideals derived from one social context are still vital in another. An example of this is the Progressive period, when Americans attempted to retain the ideology of Jefferson in the face of economic and social forces which ran counter to it. The ideology was not overwhelmed, however; for though economic and social pressure are potent, ideals are tenacious.

This toughness of men's ideals is part and parcel of the human condition. By nature man is moral; on all levels of culture and through all recorded time, men have labeled things as good or evil. And so long as men divide their world into good and bad, they will strive to make the world and themselves conform to their ideal of the good. Of course, they do not and will not always succeed. For, as this book tries to show, though Americans at times successfully imposed their ideals on the society, at other times they permitted the social relations they evolved to dictate what was morally good and bad. But wherever men have striven to realize their moral visions, they have demonstrated that ideas, as well as economic forces, can change the direction of history.

Recently, in *The Power Elite*, C. Wright Mills, the sociologist and critic of modern American society, called historians "the celebrants of the present." Perhaps this book places me in what Mr. Mills obviously intended to be an uncomfortable and unenviable category. By the standards of those who believe that criticism is synonymous with denigration, this book will indeed seem to celebrate the American past as well as the present. To those who are frustrated by and

discontented with the state of American culture, the criticisms of
that culture contained in this book will appear tepid and mild. In
reply I can only say that this is not an arraignment of American
society, but neither is it a panegyric. At the outset I freely admit
that I am somewhat awed by the 350-year history of the American
people. For even when one has discounted all the blessings bestowed
upon Americans by their fortunate separation from the turmoil and
destruction of Europe's wars and by the bounty of nature in the
soil, the achievement of Americans is still worthy of being ranked
with that of any people.

This is true, it seems to me, whether one measures that achievement in the scales of material wealth or in the balance of spiritual
values. Noble ideals like equality, opportunity, and democratic government are as American as big, flashy automobiles or indoor
plumbing. Moreover, the ideal of a wide distribution of wealth that
America has long represented and come closer to achieving than any
other people in the history of the world is something more than
dollar-chasing; it is truly one of the great humanitarian visions of
mankind. One basic assumption of this book is that one can stress
the positive achievements of America without descending into the
swamp of sycophancy or the desert of chauvinism. Only the reader
can judge whether this purpose is gained.

Another assumption upon which this book rests is that Americans
are different from other people, that their culture is unique. Undoubtedly, in the long perspective of world history, the United States
is but one of several variants of western European civilization. But
within the framework of that civilization, I believe, the Americans
are distinct and even unique. From time to time within these pages
these similarities and differences are a part of our story, for in them
can be discerned the outline of the American national character. Indeed, this book might well be called "An Exploration into the
Origins of the American Character." The word "exploration" is important. For, considering the magnitude of the subject, this venture
cannot be a definitive chart of American social topography; it can
be only exploratory. It is in that spirit that it is offered.

More than most books, this one is indebted to many people. In
this instance, they are not so much librarians and friends, though
they too figured in its making, but the scores of writers on American
society, past and present, who have quarried the material which
alone has made it possible to write a broad-swinging venture like this.

Today it is no longer possible to write an interpretation of American history directly from the sources; the documentation is too vast for one or even a dozen men to encompass in a lifetime. Hence, the great bulk of the material I have used in writing this book was first dug out of the sources by a myriad of scholars. Occasionally I have done some of the digging myself in order to try to get answers to questions which I thought vital to my story but which I could not find in the published literature. But it would be untrue to the facts if I left the impression that this book is a work of original research.

The Critical Bibliographical Essay at the end of the book attempts to discharge partially my overwhelming indebtedness to my fellow workers in the field of American culture. Needless to say, none of these writers is responsible for what I have written in this book since I have not always agreed with their individual interpretations, nor have I always used their facts as they did. For that reason the weaknesses and mistakes which inevitably must be found in this book are all due to me; the valuable things are largely the result of the work of those many scholars from whom I have shamelessly borrowed.

In common with all authors, I am deeply indebted in a variety of ways to a number of people who helped me write this book. Mildred Campbell, John Dydo, Clyde Griffen, and Charles C. Griffin of the Vassar faculty read several of the chapters and graciously gave me the benefit of their knowledge and criticism. Needless to say, they are in no way responsible for what here appears, though they often saved me from errors of fact and interpretation. John Appleton and Evan Thomas of Harper's gave me not only the benefit of their substantial editorial skills but, even more precious to any writer, that indispensable commodity—encouragement.

Though individuals are usually thanked in this place, an institution—Vassar College—also richly deserves mention. Though a small college, Vassar has given more than lip service to the ideal of encouraging scholarship and writing by its faculty. For a whole year, while I worked on this book, I was supported by a Vassar Faculty Fellowship in the style to which I was accustomed. No greater faith can a college display in its faculty.

I am also indebted to the several scores of students with whom, over the years, I discussed these ideas in History 265. With their criticisms and insights they helped me to hammer out the substance of this book. I should also like to thank Miss Sandra Suits for her careful checking of the Bibliography and Mrs. J. R. Churchill for her conscientious and accurate typing of the manuscript.

As is traditional, my wife, Catherine Grady Degler, appears last, but not least. Although she did none of the typing for which wives are usually commended, her assistance was of the kind none but a wife dare offer. Because she was impatient with vagueness, scornful of pomposity, and ruthless with verbiage, I am greatly indebted to her ; and so will the reader be.

Poughkeepsie, New York   C. N. D.

OUT OF OUR PAST

The Forces That Shaped
Modern America

CHAPTER I

The Beginnings

IN MORE ways than is often recognized, the one hundred years after the death of Elizabeth I in 1603 comprise the first century of the modern world. A number of developments peculiar to modern European thought cluster within these years: the true beginnings of modern science in the work of Galileo and Newton, Harvey and Boyle; the first expression of modern democratic ideas by the Levelers and in the Army Debates of the English Civil Wars; the decisive break in a millennium of religious dominance with the end of the wars of religion and the acceptance of the principle of religious tolerance; the achievement of lasting constitutional and representative government in England with the Glorious Revolution of 1688. It was also the time of the first permanent settlement of English colonists.

For America, its origin in this first century of the modern era was filled with meaning. In the New World, the future was still fluid. Europe's ways, both the new and the old, could be planted in America free of the choking weeds of outmoded habits. America would be a testing ground, but it would be difficult to predict what would happen. Some of the European ways would wither; some would strike root; still others would change and adapt to the new environment. For a good part of the century this plasticity was characteristic. But then, by the end of the century, the mold had hardened. In a number of ways what Americans would be for generations to come was settled in the course of those first hundred years.

1. CAPITALISM CAME IN THE FIRST SHIPS

To men coming from the "tight little isle" the vast land of America, though untamed and dense with forest, was remarkably like the old, both in the flora that covered it and in the crops that it

1

would yield. Although in a region like New England settlers would
soon discover the soil to be thin and unfertile compared with that of
the more southern colonies, it was not a desert, and from the beginning a well-organized group like the Massachusetts Bay people were
able to wring a comfortable, if not opulent, living from the lean and
rocky soil. The Chesapeake colonies had better soil and, as it turned
out, a climate conducive to the production of a staple of world-wide
appeal—the infamous weed, tobacco.

A land endowed with such promise could not fail to attract a continuous stream of men and women from the shops and farms of
Europe. For centuries the problem in Europe had been that of
securing enough land for the people, but in the New World the elements in the equation were reversed. "I hear . . . that servants
would be more advantageous to you than any commodity," wrote a
Londoner to a Virginian in 1648. For over three centuries, through
wars and revolutions, through economic disaster and plague, the
underlying, insistent theme of American history was the peopling of
a continent.

Though the pervasive influence which Frederick Jackson Turner
attributed to the frontier in the shaping of the American character
can be overestimated, the possibility of exaggeration should not hide
the undeniable fact that in early America, and through most of the
nineteenth century, too, land was available to an extent that could
appear only fabulous to land-starved Europeans. From the outset,
as a result, the American who worked with his hands had an advantage over his European counterpart. For persistent as employers and rulers in America might be in holding to Old World
conceptions of the proper subordination of labor, such ideas were
always being undercut by the fact that labor was scarcer than land.

The imagination of men was stretched by the availability of land
in America. Though land was not free for the taking, it was nearly
so. In seventeenth-century New England there were very few landless
people, and in the Chesapeake colonies it was not unusual for an indentured servant, upon the completion of his term, to be granted a
piece of land. Thus, thanks to the bounty of America, it was possible
for an Englishman of the most constricted economic horizon to make
successive jumps from servant to freeman, from freeman to freeholder, and, perhaps in a little more time, to wealthy speculator in
lands farther west. Not all men were successful in America, to be
sure, but, as the emigration literature reveals, enough were to en-

courage most men in the new land to strive hard for wealth and success.

In America the availability of land rendered precarious, if not untenable, those European institutions which were dependent upon scarcity of land. Efforts to establish feudal or manorial reproductions in the New World came to nothing. The Dutch, for example, tried to set up an ambitious system of patroons, or great land-owners, whose broad acres along the Hudson were intended to be worked by tenants. In keeping with the manorial practices common in Europe, the patroon was to dispense justice and administer in his own right the government of his little kingdom. But contrary to the popular tradition that sees these patroonships carrying over into the period of English rule after 1664, only two of the Dutch grants outlasted New Netherland, and of them, only one was in existence ten years later. Under English rule only Rensselaer retained his original grant; all the others returned or forfeited them to the Dutch West Indies Company. It is significant that the other land-granting policy of the Dutch, that of individual small holdings, was much more successful.

At the beginning, Lord Baltimore's attempt to erect manors in Maryland and to create a feudal aristocracy enjoyed more success than that of the Dutch. Some sixty manors were established in the province during the seventeenth century, the lords of which constituted a kind of new Catholic aristocracy. On at least one of these manors, that of St. Clement, manorial courts-leet (for tenants) and baron (for freeholders) were actually held, private justice being dispensed by the lord. But here too the experiment of transplanting European social ways to the free and open lands of America was to prove futile. Slavery and the plantation were much more efficient ways for utilizing land than the outmoded manor; moreover, tenants were restive in the face of free lands to the west.

The failure in New York and Maryland to reconstitute the manors of Europe did not prevent the founders of the Carolinas from making one more attempt. In the Fundamental Constitutions of 1669 provisions were included for "leet-men" who would not be able "to go off from the land of their particular lord" without permission. Moreover, it was decreed that "all children of leet-men shall be leet-men, and so to all generations." Atop this lowest stratum of hereditary tenants was erected a quasi-feudal hierarchy of caciques and landgraves, capped by a palatine. It seems hardly necessary to add that this design, so carefully worked out in Europe, was implemented in America only to the extent of conferring titles upon the ersatz nobility; the leetmen, so far as the records show, never materialized. Indeed, the Fundamental Constitutions caused much friction between the settlers and the proprietors. Even though the hereditary nature of leetmen was discarded in 1698, the popular assembly never accepted the revised Constitutions. By the opening years of the eighteenth century, the baronies which had been taken up ceased to exist, having become simply estates or farms, none of which enjoyed the anticipated array of tenants.

Thus in those areas where an attempt was made to perpetuate the social system of Europe, it was frustrated almost from the beginning. Quite early in the colonial period, great disparities of wealth appeared in the agricultural South, as elsewhere, but this was stratification resting initially and finally upon wealth, not upon honorific or hereditary conceptions derived from Europe. As such, the upper class in America was one into which others might move when they had acquired the requisite wealth. And so long as wealth accumulation was open to all, the class structure would be correspondingly flexible.

In New England there was no experimentation with feudal or manorial trappings at all. The early history of that region is a deliberate repudiation of European social as well as religious practices. As early as 1623, for example, William Bradford wrote that communal property arrangements had failed in Plymouth and that as a consequence the governing officials divided the land on an individual basis. Individual ownership of land, so typical of American land tenure ever since, was thus symbolically begun. The larger colony of Massachusetts Bay, in its first codification of laws, the Body of Liberties of 1641, made explicit its departure from feudal and manorial incidents upon landholding. "All our lands and heritages shall be free from all fines and licenses upon Alienations, and from all hariotts, wardships, Liveries, Primerseisins, yeare day and wast, Escheates and forfeitures. . . ." [1]

---

[1] Not all of the legal incidents and limitations on landholding then in practice in England were absent in America. Primogeniture, for example, obtained in the southern colonies and entail prevailed in all the English settlements. But it is also a fact that both institutions, all through the colonial period, were viewed as foreign to the tendency of American social development, to be abandoned completely by the end of the eighteenth century. "By the time of the Revolution, although much land throughout Colonial America was still held in fee tail estates,

The failure of America to inherit a feudal aristocracy carried implications for the future which transcended the mere matter of land tenure. The very character of the society was affected. As we have seen already, it meant that wealth, rather than family or tradition, would be the primary determinant of social stratification. Furthermore, the absence of a feudal past in America has meant that there are no classes which have a vested interest in the social forms of an earlier age. American society, as a consequence, has never split into perpetually warring camps of reactionaries and radicals in the way, for example, French society has been riven ever since the Great Revolution. Moreover, without a feudal past America offers only the thinnest of soils into which a conservatism of the European variety can sink its roots. Almost all Americans, regardless of class, have shared a common ideology of Lockean or Whig liberalism. The so-called conservatives of the American past have been only more cautious liberals. There has been in America no widely held tradition analogous to the conservatism of Edmund Burke. Burke's considerable doubts about the hopefulness of progress, the efficacy of reason, and the value of revolution have found few sympathetic ears in America. Only some ante-bellum Southerners like Thomas Dew and George Fitzhugh showed any signs of a Burkean conservative outlook. And those murmurings were killed off with the end of slavery.

There are economic as well as political consequences which flow from the fact that America was born free of the medieval tradition of aristocracy. These are seen in purest form if we contrast the attitudes of French and American businessmen of today. (It is not so true of Englishmen because participation in trade never carried the taint it did in France.) Recruitment into management has often been hampered in France, John Sawyer has shown, because of the tradition of family enterprises. Businesses, as a result, were confined to a limited group of potential entrepreneurs and managers, "much like hereditary fiefs." Instead of being able to draw upon the population at large for the best men available, French business enterprises

---

the practice of holding land in fee simple estates was widespread. Great strides had been made in barring fee tail estates by provisions in original grants to private parties, by private action in the making of wills, and by special acts of the colonial assemblies on behalf of individual cases." Marshall Harris, *Origin of the Land Tenure System in the United States* (Ames, Iowa, 1953), p. 373. By way of contrast, it might be recalled that primogeniture was not finally relinquished in England until 1926.

have often been handicapped by adherence to a feudal-like familism

Moreover, a feudally derived aristocratic disdain for trade and business still permeates French thought. As a consequence, the French businessman, unlike the American, is beset by a nagging feeling that success in business carries little prestige, and is perhaps a sign of unfashionable materialism. Hence he does not drive to expand his business or to make a lot of money; he is satisfied with a comfortable, gentlemanly living. As Sawyer concluded, "the French businessman has *himself* been unable to slough off the anti-capitalist sentiment in his social inheritance." Devoid of such an inheritance, America was also free of such inhibitory attitudes; from the beginning, if one may paraphrase a President of the United States, the main business of America has been business.

In place of medieval and aristocratic notions about the degrading nature of trade and business, seventeenth-century Englishmen brought to America two forms of that bourgeois spirit which Max Weber has called the Protestant ethic: Puritanism and Quakerism. It is possible to overemphasize the extent to which Puritanism departed from medieval conceptions of a just price, prohibitions on interest, and so forth, for such restrictions on unfettered capitalism also formed a part of Puritan economic practice in Massachusetts. But the general loosening of economic restraints which Puritanism unquestionably condoned, and its strong accent on work and wealth accumulation, bestowed religious sanction upon business enterprise. The backward-looking and forward-looking economic attitudes of Puritanism are both apparent in a Massachusetts statute of 1633. The first part of the law, in keeping with medieval practices, prescribed the proper wages for bricklayers, wheelwrights, and other skilled craftsmen, while the second part of the statute ordered "that noe person, hawseholder or other, shall spend his time idely or unprofflably, under paine of such punishment as the Court shall thinke meet to inflicte. . . ." The close connection the Puritans saw between godliness and worldly success is implied in a story told by Governor Winthrop in his *History*. The story concerns one Mansfield who arrived in Massachusetts poor but "godly." With the help of a local rich man, "this Mansfield grew suddenly rich, and then lost his godliness, and his wealth soon after."

The calling or occupation of a Christian was an important conception in Puritan thought; it also serves as an illuminating instance of the tight linkage between religion and economics. To the

Puritan, a Christian's work was a part of his offering to God. "As soon as ever a man begins to look toward God and the way of his Grace," the Reverend John Cotton taught, "he will not rest til he find out some warrantable calling and employment." No matter what the calling, "though it be but of a day laborer," yet he will make of it what he can, for "God would not have a man receive five talents and gain but two; He would have his best gifts improved to the best advantage." To work hard is to please God. As Cotton Mather, the grandson of Cotton, said at the end of the century, "Would a man *Rise* by his Business? I say, then let him Rise to his Business. . . . Let your *Business* ingross the most of your time."

Important, but often overlooked in the Puritan conception of the calling, was the idea of social obligation. For a calling to be "warrantable," John Cotton emphasized, a Christian "would see that his calling should tend to public good." Moreover, he continued, "we live by faith in our vocations, in that faith, in serving God, serves man, and in serving man, serves God." Cotton Mather at the end of the century put it even more succinctly. One should have a calling "so he may Glorify God by doing Good for *Others*, and getting of *Good* for himself." It was this cementing of social conscience to thoroughgoing individualism which saved Puritanism from degenerating into a mere defense of economic exploitation.

If the earliest New England divines, like John Cotton, had some doubts about the trader because—as the medieval schoolmen had contended—he bought cheap and sold dear, later Puritans easily accepted the new economic order. Cotton Mather, in good Calvinist fashion, argued that there "is every sort of law, except the Popish, to justify a regulated *usury*. 'Tis justified by the law of necessity and utility; humane society, as now circumstanced, would sink, if all *usury* were impracticable." By the end of the century the bulging warehouses, the numerous ships in Boston harbor, and the well-appointed mansions of the merchants bore ample testimony to the compatibility of Puritanism and wealth-getting.

Widely recognized as the dominance of Puritan economic ideals may be in New England, it is less often acknowledged that the thriving commercial center of Philadelphia owed much of its drive to a similar ethic among the Quakers. It was William Penn, not John Winthrop, who advised his children to "cast up your income and live on half; if you can, one third; reserving the rest for casualties, charities portions," Simple living, as the bewigged Cotton Mather reminds us, was more a trait of Quakers in the seventeenth and eighteenth century than of Puritans. Indeed, so concerned were the Friends over the vices of ostentation and vanity that they would not permit portraits to be painted of themselves. The only concessions to the ego were black silhouettes. "Be plain in clothes, furniture and food, but clean," William Penn told his children, "and the coarser the better; the rest is folly and a snare." Furthermore, he counseled, diligence "is the Way to Wealth: *the diligent Hand makes Rich. . . . Frugality* is a Virtue too, and not of little Use in Life, the better Way to be Rich, for it has less Toil and Temptation."

As early as the seventeenth century, "the legend of the Quaker as Businessman" was widely accepted. This view, which was very close to the truth, pictured the Friends as shrewd, canny traders, "singularly industrious, sparing no Labour or Pains to increase their Wealth," as one seventeenth-century observer put it. Much like the Puritans, the Quakers were eminently successful in the countinghouse, preaching and practicing that doctrine of the calling which united religion and bourgeois economic virtues in happy and fruitful marriage.

As New Englanders fanned out into the upper Middle West in the late eighteenth and early nineteenth centuries, the seed of Puritanism, now stripped of its theological skin, was planted across America. Furthermore, if one recognizes that the doctrine of the calling was Calvinist before it was Puritan, then the numbers of people imbibing that economic precept with their religious milk swells to impressive proportions. At the time of the Revolution, Ralph Barton Perry has calculated, one out of every two white Americans was a Calvinist of some persuasion.

Though no longer clothed in theological vestments, the virtue of work and wealth has remained with Americans. As Max Weber pointed out, the advice of Franklin's Poor Richard is but the Puritan ethic shorn of its theology; in Franklin the Puritan has become the Yankee. No longer anxious about unearthly salvation, but keenly concerned about a good bargain, the American still carries the telltale brand of Puritanism.

2. WERE THE PURITANS "PURITANICAL"?

To most Americans—and to most Europeans, for that matter— the core of the Puritan social heritage has been summed up in

Macaulay's well-known witticism that the Puritans prohibited bear-baiting not because of torture to the bear, but because of the pleasure it afforded the spectators.[2] And as late as 1925, H. L. Mencken defined Puritanism as "the haunting fear that someone, somewhere, may be happy." Before this chapter is out, much will be said about the somber and even grim nature of the Puritan view of life, but quips like those of Macaulay and Mencken distort rather than illumine the essential character of the Puritans. Simply because the word "Puritan" has become encrusted with a good many barnacles, it is worth while to try to scrape them off if we wish to gain an understanding of the Puritan heritage. Though this process is essentially a negative one, sometimes it is clarifying to set forth what an influence is *not* as well as what it is.

Fundamental to any appreciation of the Puritan mind on matters of pleasure must be the recognition that the typical, godly Puritan was a worker in the world. Puritanism, like Protestantism in general, resolutely and definitely rejected the ascetic and monastic ideals of medieval Catholicism. Pleasures of the body were not to be eschewed by the Puritan, for, as Calvin reasoned, God "intended to provide not only for our necessity, but likewise for our pleasure and delight." It is obvious, he wrote in his famous *Institutes*, that "the Lord have endowed flowers with such beauty . . . with such sweetness of smell" in order to impress our senses; therefore, to enjoy them is not contrary to God's intentions. "In a word," he concluded, "hath He not made many things worthy of our estimation independent of any necessary use?"

It was against excess of enjoyment that the Puritans cautioned and legislated. "The wine is from God," Increase Mather warned, "but the Drunkard is from the Devil." The Cambridge Platform of the Church of 1680 prohibited games of cards or dice because of the amount of time they consumed and the encouragement they offered to idleness, but the ministers of Boston in 1699 found no difficulty in condoning public lotteries. They were like a public tax, the minis-

[2] Joseph Crouch, in his *Puritanism and Art* (London, 1910), p. 350 n., attempted to even the score with Macaulay by quoting from the Puritan Stubbes, who wrote against bearbaiting in 1583: "What Christian heart can take pleasure to see one poor beast to rend, tear and kill another, and all for his foolish pleasure? . . . So, love God, love his creatures." And Increase Mather, father of Cotton Mather, condemned cockfighting by saying that "to delight in tormenting dumb creatures, and to make sport of their miseries, is a great inhumanity and a scandalous Violation of the 6th Commandment."

ters said, since they took only what the "government might have
demanded, with a more *general imposition* . . . and it employes for
the welfare of the publick, all that is raised by the *lottery*." Though
Cotton Mather at the end of the century condemned mixed dancing,
he did not object to dancing as such; and his grandfather, John
Cotton, at the beginning saw little to object to in dancing between
the sexes so long as it did not become lascivious. It was this same
John Cotton, incidentally, who successfully contended against
Roger Williams' argument that women should wear veils in church.

In matters of dress, it is true that the Massachusetts colony endeavored to restrict the wearing of "some new and immodest
fashions" that were coming in from England, but often these efforts
were frustrated by the pillars of the church themselves. Winthrop
reported in his *History*, for example, that though the General Court
instructed the elders of the various churches to reduce the ostentation in dress by "urging it upon the consciences of their people,"
little change was effected, "for divers of the elders' wives, etc., were
in some measure partners in this general disorder."

We also know now that Puritan dress—not that made "historical" by Saint-Gaudens' celebrated statue—was the opposite of
severe, being rather in the English Renaissance style. Most restrictions on dress which were imposed were for purposes of class dif-
ferentiation rather than for ascetic reasons. Thus long hair was
acceptable on an upper-class Puritan like Cromwell or Winthrop,
but it was a sign of vanity on the head of a person of lower social
status. In 1651 the legislature of Massachusetts called attention to
that "excess in Apparell" which has "crept in upon us, and especially amongst people of mean condition, to the dishonor of God,
the scandall of our profession, the consumption of Estates, and
altogether unsuitable to our poverty." The law declared "our utter
detestation and dislike, that men or women of mean condition, should
take upon them the garb of Gentlemen, by wearing Gold or Silver
Lace, or Buttons, or Points at their knees, or to walk in great
Boots; or Women of the same rank to wear Silk or Tiffany hoods,
or Scarfes, which tho allowable to persons of greater Estates, or
more liberal education, is intolerable in people of low condition." By
implication, this law affords a clear description of what the well-
dressed Puritan of good estate would wear.

If the Puritans are to be saved from the canard of severity of
dress, it is also worth while to soften the charge that they were

opposed to music and art. It is perfectly true that the Puritans insisted that organs be removed from the churches and that in England some church organs were smashed by zealots. But it was not music or organs as such which they opposed, only music in the meetinghouse. Well-known American and English Puritans, like Samuel Sewell, John Milton, and Cromwell, were sincere lovers of music. Moreover, it should be remembered that it was under Puritan rule that opera was introduced into England—and without protest, either. The first English dramatic production entirely in music— *The Siege of Rhodes*—was presented in 1656, four years before the Restoration. Just before the end of Puritan rule, John Evelyn noted in his diary that he went "to see a new opera, after the Italian way, in recitative music and scenes. . . ." Furthermore, as Percy Scholes points out, in all the voluminous contemporary literature attacking the Puritans for every conceivable narrow-mindedness, none asserts that they opposed music, so long as it was performed outside the church.

The weight of the evidence is much the same in the realm of art. Though King Charles' art collection was dispersed by the incoming Commonwealth, it is significant that Cromwell and other Puritans bought several of the items. We also know that the Protector's garden at Hampton Court was beautified by nude statues. Furthermore, it is now possible to say that the Puritan closing of the theaters was as much a matter of objection to their degenerate lewdness by the 1640's as an objection to the drama as such. As far as American Puritans are concerned, it is not possible to say very much about their interest in art since there was so little in the seventeenth century. At least it can be said that the Puritans, unlike the Quakers, had no objection to portrait painting.

Some modern writers have professed to find in Puritanism, particularly the New England brand, evidence of sexual repression and inhibition. Though it would certainly be false to suggest that the Puritans did not subscribe to the canon of simple chastity, it is equally erroneous to think that their sexual lives were crabbed or that sex was abhorrent to them. Marriage to the Puritan was something more than an alternative to "burning," as the Pauline doctrine of the Catholic Church would have it. Marriage was enjoined upon the righteous Christian; celibacy was not a sign of merit. With unconcealed disapprobation, John Cotton told a recently married couple the story of a pair "who immediately upon marriage, without

ever approaching the *Nuptial Bed*," agreed to live apart from the
rest of the world, "and afterwards from one another, too. . . ."
But, Cotton advised, such behavior was "no other than an effort of
blind zeal, for they are the dictates of a blind mind they follow
therein and not of the Holy Spirit which saith, *It is not good that
man should be alone.*" Cotton set himself against not only Catholic
asceticism but also the view that women were the "unclean vessel,"
the tempters of men. Women, rather than being "a necessary Evil
are a necessary Good," he wrote. "Without them there is no comfortable Living for Man. . . ."

Because, as another divine said, "the Use of the Marriage Bed"
is "founded in man's Nature" the realistic Puritans required that
married men unaccompanied by wives should leave the colony or
bring their wives over forthwith. The Puritan settlements encouraged marriages satisfactory to the participants by permitting
divorces for those whose spouses were impotent, too long absent, or
cruel. Indeed, the divorce laws of New England were the easiest in
Christendom at a time when the eloquence of a Milton was unable
to loosen the bonds of matrimony in England.

Samuel Eliot Morison in his history of Harvard has collected a
number of examples of the healthy interest of Puritan boys in the
opposite sex. Commonplace books, for example, indicate that Herrick's poem beginning "Gather ye rosebuds while ye may" and
amorous lines from Shakespeare, as well as more erotic and even
scatological verse, were esteemed by young Puritan men. For a
gentleman to present his affianced with a pair of garters, one letter
of a Harvard graduate tells us, was considered neither immoral nor
improper.

It is also difficult to reconcile the usual view of the stuffiness of
Puritans with the literally hundreds of confessions to premarital
sexual relations in the extant church records. It should be understood, moreover, that these confessions were made by the saints or
saints-to-be, not by the unregenerate. That the common practice of
the congregation was to accept such sinners into church membership
without further punishment is in itself revealing. The civil law, it is
true, punished such transgressions when detected among the re-
generate or among the nonchurch members, but this was also true
of contemporary non-Puritan Virginia. "It will be seen," writes historian Philip A. Bruce regarding Virginia, "from the various instances given relating to the profanation of Sunday, drunkenness,

swearing, defamation, and sexual immorality, that, not only were the grand juries and vestries extremely vigilant in reporting these offences, but the courts were equally prompt in inflicting punishment; and that the penalty ranged from a heavy fine to a shameful exposure in the stocks . . . and from such an exposure to a very severe flogging at the county whipping post." In short, strict moral surveillance by the public authorities was a seventeenth-century rather than a Puritan attitude.

Relations between the sexes in Puritan society were often much more loving and tender than the mythmakers would have us believe. Since it was the Puritan view that marriage was eminently desirable in the sight of God and man, it is not difficult to find evidence of deep and abiding love between a husband and wife. John Cotton, it is true, sometimes used the Biblical phrase "comfortable yoke mate" in addressing his wife, but other Puritan husbands come closer to our romantic conventions. Certainly John Winthrop's letters to his beloved Margaret indicate the depth of attachment of which the good Puritan was capable. "My good wife . . . My sweet wife," he called her. Anticipating his return home, he writes, "So . . . we shall now enjoy each other again, as we desire. . . . It is now bed time; but I must lie alone; therefore I make less haste. Yet I must kiss my sweet wife; and so, with my blessing to our children . . . I commend thee to the grace and blessing of the lord, and rest. . . ."

Anne Bradstreet wrote a number of poems devoted to her love for her husband in which the sentiments and figures are distinctly romantic.

> To my Dear and loving Husband
> I prize thy love more than whole Mines of gold
> Or all the riches that the East doth hold.
> My love is such that Rivers cannot quench,
> Nor aught but love from thee give recompense.

In another poem her spouse is apostrophized as

> My head, my heart, mine Eyes, my life, nay more
> My joy, my Magazine of earthly store

and she asks:

> If two be one, as surely thou and I,
> How stayest thou there, whilst I at Ipswich lye?

Addressing John as "my most sweet Husband," Margaret Winthrop perhaps epitomized the Puritan marital ideal when she wrote, "I have many reasons to make me love thee, whereof I will name two: First, because thou lovest God and, secondly, because thou lovest me. If these two were wanting," she added, "all the rest would be eclipsed."

It would be a mistake, however, to try to make these serious,[3] dedicated men and women into rakes of the Renaissance. They were sober if human folk, deeply concerned about their ultimate salvation and intent upon living up to God's commands as they understood them, despite their acknowledgment of complete depravity and unworthiness. "God sent you not into this world as a Play-House, but a Work-house," one minister told his congregation. To the Puritan this was a world drenched in evil, and, because it truly is, they were essentially realistic in their judgments. Because the Puritan expected nothing, Perry Miller has remarked, a disillusioned one was almost impossible to find. This is probably an exaggeration, for they were also human beings; when the Commonwealth fell, it was a Puritan, after all, who said, "God has spit in our faces." But Professor Miller's generalization has much truth in it. Only a man convinced of the inevitable and eternal character of evil could fight it so hard and so unceasingly.

The Puritan at his best, Ralph Barton Perry has said, was a "moral athlete." More than most men, the Puritan strove with himself and with his fellow man to attain a moral standard higher than was rightfully to be expected of so depraved a creature. Hence the diaries and autobiographies of Puritans are filled with the most torturous probing of the soul and inward seeking. Convinced of the utter desirability of salvation on the one hand, and equally cognizant of the total depravity of man's nature on the other, the Puritan was caught in an impossible dilemma which permitted him no rest short of the grave. Yet with such a spring coiled within him, the Puritan drove himself and his society to tremendous heights of achievement both material and spiritual.

[3] Winthrop provides an example of the rather trivial lengths to which this serious view of life could lead an otherwise worldly-wise Puritan. Early in his life in America he gave up toasting the health of fellow drinkers—though, significantly, not the drinking. Starting from the premise that "Every empty and ineffectual representation of serious things is a way of Vanity," Winthrop was led to the conclusion that toasting was vain. For it holds "forth love and wishes of health, which are serious things, by drinking, which neither in the nature, nor use, it is able to effect. . . ."

Such intense concern for the actualization of the will of God had a less pleasant side to it, also. If the belief that "I am my brother's keeper" is the breeding ground of heightened social conscience and expresses itself in the reform movements so indigenous to Boston and its environs, it also could and did lead to self-righteousness, intolerance and narrow-mindedness, as exemplified in another product of Boston: Anthony Comstock. But this fruit of the loins of Puritanism is less typical of the earthy seventeenth-century New Englander than H. L. Mencken would have us think. The Sabbatarian,[4] antiliquor, and antisex attitudes usually attributed to the Puritans are a nineteenth-century addition to the much more moderate and essentially wholesome view of life's evils held by the early settlers of New England.

To realize how different Puritans could be, one needs only to contrast Roger Williams and his unwearying opponent John Cotton. But despite the range of differences among Puritans, they all were linked by at least one characteristic. That was their belief in themselves, in their morality and in their mission to the world. For this reason, Puritanism was intellectual and social dynamite in the seventeenth century; its power could behead kings, overthrow governments, defy tyrants, and disrupt churches.

The Reformation laid an awesome burden on the souls of those who broke with the Roman Church. Proclaiming the priesthood of all believers, Protestantism made each man's relationship to God his own terrifying responsibility. No one else could save him; therefore no one must presume to try. More concerned about his salvation than about any mundane matter, the Puritan was compelled, for the sake of his immortal soul, to be a fearless individualist.

It was the force of this conviction which produced the Great Migration of 1630–40 and made Massachusetts a flourishing colony

---

[4] It is true that the Puritans insisted on proper behavior during the Sabbath, but so did other seventeenth-century communities. The law in Virginia, like the law in Massachusetts, compelled church attendance. Moreover, the records of seventeenth-century Virginia are filled with examples of indictments and convictions for breaking the decorum of the Sabbath. P. A. Bruce lists the following as examples of such infractions of Sunday in Virginia: shelling corn, hiring out a horse, carrying a gun, fishing, killing a deer, getting drunk, going on a journey, stripping tobacco, selling cider, driving a cart, fiddling and dancing, swearing, carrying wheat, and fighting. The greater rigidity of the Victorian age regarding the Sabbath is indicated by the nineteenth-century editor's comments on Winthrop's traveling on the Sabbath. "His example would justify the many others," wrote editor Savage in 1854. "Such instances are now almost unknown."

in the span of a decade. It was also, ironically, the force which impelled Roger Williams to threaten the very legal and social foundations of the Puritan Commonwealth in Massachusetts because he thought the oligarchy wrong and himself right. And so it would always be. For try as the rulers of Massachusetts might to make men conform to their dogma, their own rebellious example always stood as a guide to those who felt the truth was being denied. Such individualism, we would call it today, was flesh and bone of the religion which the Puritans passed on. Though the theocracy soon withered and died, its harsh voice softened down to the balmy breath of Unitarianism, the belief in self and the dogged resistance to suppression or untruth which Puritanism taught never died. Insofar as Americans today can be said to be individualistic, it is to the Puritan heritage that we must look for one of the principal sources.

In his ceaseless striving for signs of salvation and knowledge of God's intentions for man, the Puritan placed great reliance upon the human intellect, even though for him, as for all Christians, faith was the bedrock of his belief. "Faith doth not relinquish or cast out reason," wrote the American Puritan Samuel Willard, "for there is nothing in Religion contrary to it, tho' there are many things that do transcend and must captivate it." Richard Baxter, the English Puritan, insisted that "the *most Religious*, are the *most* truly, and *nobly rational*." Religion and reason were complementary to the Puritan, not antithetical as they were to many evangelical sects of the time.

Always the mere emotion of religion was to be controlled by reason. Because of this, the university-trained Puritan clergy prided themselves on the lucidity and rationality of their sermons.[5] Almost rigorously their sermons followed the logical sequence of "doctrine," "reasons," and "uses." Conscientiously they shunned the meandering and rhetorical flourishes so beloved by Laudian preachers like John

[5] One of the persistent myths about the Puritans is the assertion that they preached "hell-fire and damnation." The original source for this myth is undoubtedly Jonathan Edwards' timeworn sermon at Enfield, "A Sinner in the Hands of an Angry God." This sermon, however, is not only unrepresentative of the seventeenth-century Puritans—it was delivered in 1739—but it is extreme for Edwards himself. As a deliberate effort to ignite a revival in Enfield during the Great Awakening, it reflected neither Edwards' usual style of preaching nor the closely reasoned, decidedly unemotional sermons which were the usual fare of Puritan congregations in the seventeenth century.

Donne, and in the process facilitated the taking of notes by their eager listeners. One of the unforgivable crimes of Mistress Anne Hutchinson was her assertion that one could "feel" one's salvation, that one was "filled with God" after conversion, that it was unnecessary, in order to be saved, to be learned in the Bible or in the Puritan writers. It was not that the Puritans were cold to the Word—far from it. A saint was required to testify to an intense religious experience—almost by definition emotional in character—before he could attain full membership in the Church. But it was always important to the Puritans that mere emotion—whether it be the anarchistic activities of the Anabaptists or the quaking of the Friends—should not be mistaken for righteousness or proper religious conduct. Here, as in so many things, the Puritans attempted to walk the middle path—in this instance, between the excessive legalism and formalism of the Catholics and Episcopalians and the flaming, intuitive evangelism of the Baptists and Quakers.

Convinced of reason's great worth, it was natural that the Puritans should also value education. "Ignorance is the mother (not of Devotion but) of Heresy," one Puritan divine declared. And a remarkably well-educated ministry testified to the Puritan belief that learning and scholarship were necessary for a proper understanding of the Word of God. More than a hundred graduates of Cambridge and Oxford Universities settled in New England before 1640, most of them ministers. At the same date not five men in all of Virginia could lay claim to such an educational background. Since Cambridge University, situated on the edge of Puritan East Anglia, supplied most of the graduates in America, it was natural that Newtown, the site of New England's own college, would soon be renamed in honor of the Alma Mater. "After God had carried us safe to New-England," said a well-known tract, some of its words now immortalized in metal in Harvard Yard, "one of the next things we longed and looked after, was to advance learning, and perpetuate it to posterity; dreading to leave an illiterate ministry to the churches, when the present ministers shall lie in the dust." "The College," founded in 1636, soon to be named Harvard, was destined to remain the only institution of higher learning in America during almost all the years of the seventeenth century. Though it attracted students from as far away as Virginia, it remained, as it began, the fountainhead of Puritan learning in the New World.

Doubt as one may Samuel Eliot Morison's claims for the secular origins of Harvard, his evidence of the typically Renaissance secular education which was available at the Puritan college in New England is both impressive and convincing. The Latin and Greek secular writers of antiquity dominated the curriculum, for this was a liberal arts training such as the leaders had received at Cambridge in England. To the Puritans the education of ministers could be nothing less than the best learning of the day. So important did education at Harvard seem to the New Haven colony in 1644 that the legislature ordered each town to appoint two men to be responsible for the collection of contributions from each family for "the mayntenaunce of scolars at Cambridge. . . . "

If there was to be a college, preparatory schools had to be provided for the training of those who were expected to enter the university. Furthermore, in a society dedicated to the reading of the Bible, elementary education was indispensable. "It being one chief project of that old deluder Satan to keep men from the knowledge of the Scriptures" began the first school laws of Massachusetts (1647) and Connecticut (1650). But the Puritans supported education for secular as well as religious reasons. The Massachusetts Code of 1648, for instance, required children to be taught to read inasmuch "as the good education of children is of singular behoof and benefit to any Common-wealth."

The early New England school laws provided that each town of fifty families or more was to hire a teacher for the instruction of its young; towns of one hundred families or more were also directed to provide grammar schools, "the master thereof being able to instruct youths so far as they may be fitted for the University." Though parents were not obliged to send their children to these schools, if they did not they were required to teach their children to read. From the evidence of court cases and the high level of literacy in seventeenth-century New England, it would appear that these first attempts at public-supported and public-controlled education were both enforced and fruitful.

No other colony in the seventeenth century imposed such a high educational standard upon its simple farming people as the Puritans did. It is true, of course, that Old England in this period could boast of grammar schools, some of which were free. But primary schools were almost nonexistent there, and toward the end of the seventeenth century the free schools in England became increasingly tuition schools. Moreover, it was not until well into the nineteenth century that the English government did anything to support schools. Primary and secondary education in England, in contrast with the New England example, was a private or church affair.

Unlike the Puritans, the Quakers exhibited little impulse toward popular education in the seventeenth and early eighteenth centuries. Because of their accent on the Inner Light and the doctrine of universal salvation, the religious motivation of the Puritans for learning was wanting. Furthermore, the Quakers did not look to education, as such, with the same reverence as the Puritans. William Penn, for example, advised his children that "reading many books is but a taking off the mind too much from meditation." No Puritan would have said that.

Virginia in the seventeenth century, it should be said, was also interested in education. Several times in the course of the century, plans were well advanced for establishing a university in the colony. Free schools also existed in Virginia during the seventeenth century, though the lack of village communities made them inaccessible for any great numbers of children. But, in contrast with New England, there were no publicly supported schools in Virginia; the funds for the field schools of Virginia, like those for free schools in contemporary England, came from private or ecclesiastical endowment. Nor was Virginia able to bring its several plans for a college into reality until William and Mary was founded at the very end of the century.

Though the line which runs from the early New England schools to the distinctly American system of free public schools today is not always progressively upward or uniformly clear, the connection is undeniable. The Puritan innovation of public support and control on a local level was the American prototype of a proper system of popular education.

American higher education in particular owes much to religion, for out of the various churches' concern for their faiths sprang a number of colleges, after the example of the Puritans' founding of Harvard. At the time of the Revolution, there were eight colleges besides Harvard in the English colonies, of which all but one were founded under the auspices of a church. William and Mary (1693) and King's College, later Columbia (1754), were the work of the Episcopalians; Yale (1701) and Dartmouth (1769) were set up by Congregationalists not comforted by Harvard; the College of New Jersey, later Princeton (1747), was founded by the Presbyterians;

Queens College, later Rutgers (1766), by the Dutch Reformed Church; the College of Rhode Island, later Brown (1764), by the Baptists. Only the Academy of Philadelphia, later the University of Pennsylvania (1749), was secular in origin.

The overwhelming importance of the churches in the expansion of American higher education during the colonial period set a pattern which continued well into the nineteenth century and to a limited extent is still followed. Well-known colleges like Oberlin, Wesleyan, Haverford, Wittenberg, Moravian, Muhlenberg, and Notre Dame were all founded by churches in the years before the Civil War. By providing a large number of colleges (recall that England did not enjoy a third university until the nineteenth century), the religious impulses and diversity of the American people very early encouraged that peculiarly American faith in the efficacy and desirability of education for all.

When dwelling on the seminal qualities of the seventeenth century, it is tempting to locate the source of the later American doctrine of the separation of Church and State and religious freedom in the writings of Roger Williams and in the practices of provinces like New York, Maryland and Pennsylvania. Actually, however, such a line of development is illusory. At the time of the Revolution all the colonies, including Rhode Island, imposed restrictions and disabilities upon some sects, thus practicing at best only a limited form of toleration, not freedom of religion—much less separation of Church and State. Moreover, Roger Williams' cogent and prophetic arguments in behalf of religious freedom were forgotten in the eighteenth century; they could not exert any influence on those who finally worked out the doctrine of religious freedom enshrined in the national Constitution. In any case, it would have been exceedingly difficult for Williams to have spoken to Jefferson and the other Virginians who fought for religious freedom. To Williams the Puritan, the great justification for freedom of religion was the preservation of the purity of the Church; to the deistic Virginians, the important goal was the removal of a religious threat to the purity and freedom of the State.

3. RIGHTS OF ENGLISHMEN

For one who cherishes American political institutions, the manner in which representative government began in the seventeenth century might well make him shudder as well as wonder. The process was largely "accidental," arbitrary and hardly to be anticipated from the nature of things. This is especially true of Virginia, where the whole precedent of self-government in America was first worked out. When in 1619 the Virginia Company suggested that the colonists "might have a hande in the governinge of themselves," there was, as Charles Andrews has pointed out, "no sufficient reason, legal or other, why a popular assembly should be set up in Virginia." It was all that casual.

The precarious existence of this first representative assembly in America was emphasized in 1624, when the Crown, for various reasons, revoked the Company's charter, the King declaring that "the Government of the Colonies of Virginia shall immediately depend upon Our Selfe." Thus was terminated the legal authority for an assembly. Three times between 1625 and 1629 the planters held "conventions" for specific purposes, but these were neither regular nor legitimate assemblies. Beginning in 1630, however, and each year thereafter, without any encouragement from the Crown, the Virginians held an Assembly and presumed to legislate. Interestingly enough, in the light of the later Revolution, among their earliest laws was a prohibition upon the Governor and the Council—both of whom were appointed by the Crown—to "lay any taxes or impositions, upon the colony, theire land or commodities, otherwise then [*sic*] by the authoritie of the Grand Assembly." The legal authority for the Assembly, however, was still in doubt, for the King had not assented to its existence, and no one disputed his final and complete authority. Then in 1637 the royal instructions to the Governor contained a call for an Assembly, but the failure to provide for annual sessions indicated that the Crown was still undecided on the matter. Finally, the Governor's instructions in 1639 made it clear that the King had responded favorably to the colony's persistent requests for a continuing representative assembly.

The importance of this decision as a precedent can hardly be exaggerated. Virginia was the first English settlement to fall under the direct control of the Crown, and its forms of government could not fail to influence, if not determine, those of subsequent royal colonies—and, it should be remembered, in time all but four of the thirteen colonies would be royal.

The evolution of Massachusetts' government was somewhat different; the fact that the charter was brought with the settlers insured that events in America would be the determining factors.

The narrow limits of the charter, which was intended for the running of a corporation, not a community, came under attack in the first year, when over a hundred settlers applied for the rights of freemen. At that point the decision was made to open the coveted rank to "such as are members of some of the churches within the lymitts of" the colony. This broadening of the franchise signalized the transformation of the corporation into a true commonwealth, composed of citizens with rights and duties. In practice, confining citizenship to church members was not as restrictive as might at first be supposed, for this was, after all, a Puritan venture. There were towns like Roxbury in 1638–40, for example, which consisted of sixty-nine householders, of whom fifty-nine were church members and voters.

For the first four years Massachusetts was governed by the magistrates, who, in turn, were elected by the whole body of freemen; there being no representative assembly, the magistrates made the laws. It is more than coincidental, however, that at about the same time the Virginia Assembly was putting itself on record as opposing taxation by the executive, a similar remonstrance was afoot in Massachusetts. Early in 1632, Winthrop tells us, a group of ministers and elders of Watertown "delivered their opinion, that it was not safe to pay moneys" levied upon the people by the Governor and the assistants, "for fear of bringing themselves and posterity into bondage." The coincidence, of course, is not accidental, for it simply underscores the common English origins of the two widely separated colonies. For centuries Englishmen had jealously guarded their right to levy their taxes locally; they continued to do so in the New World. Moreover, in the first part of the seventeenth century the issue of taxation and representative government was before the eyes of the whole nation as King and Parliament carried on their struggle for supremacy. It was to be expected that history and current events would both be reflected in the two English colonies in America.

As the number of settlers in Massachusetts increased, thereby rendering it more and more difficult for all freemen to meet together, it became necessary either to abandon the meeting of freemen, a step which men like Governor Winthrop apparently urged, or else to elect deputies or proxies who would act for the general body of freemen. At the insistence of the freemen, the latter method was accepted at the same time that it was agreed that taxes would be levied only by the legislature. Thus, in May, 1634, the first representative assembly met in Boston, with each town sending three deputies. It was understood that they "shall have full power and voice of all and said freemen," except for the election of the magistrates.

The history of constitutional development in both Massachusetts and Virginia makes it quite apparent that the ordinary man's dogged insistence upon self-government in America was perhaps the most important single factor in the establishment of the representative government we esteem today. Even an opponent of popular government, John Winthrop, expressed grudging admiration for the people's ingenious if illogical pursuit of their own governance. Noting their appeal to the patent or charter in a recent dispute with the magistrates, Winthrop wryly commented that it "may be observed how strictly the people would seem to stick to their patent, where they think it makes for their advantage, but are content to decline it, where it will not warrant such liberties as they have taken up without warrant from thence."

If representative government can be said to have triumphed in the seventeenth century, it can also be said that the idea of democracy, defined as government by the consent of all the governed, was born in that century. The line to the present, however, is more tenuous, the traces fainter; not until the nineteenth century was democracy in full flower. But the beginnings of the democratic idea are already to be found in the Puritans' conception of the covenant. The idea of an agreement between the ruler and the ruled as the basis for government was very well understood in seventeenth-century Protestant America, not only because of the contemporary theological use of it, but because the extensive and close reading of the Bible among all classes made the idea common coin. The covenants with Adam, with Noah, and with Abraham were well-known Biblical agreements between God and men. Only by the agreement of all concerned, read the Cambridge Church Platform of 1648, could "we see . . . how members can have Church-power over one another mutually." It was natural that this religious or Biblical example should be extended to civil affairs,[6] especially in a new land where

---

[6] It is hardly accidental that the most democratic political document of the seventeenth century, the Agreement of the People, originated in the turmoil of the Puritan revolution in England. The very title of the document suggests the debt to the covenant idea, and its contents set forth a conception of popular participation in government which was not realized in any country before the nineteenth century.

the usual sanctions for government were wanting, Thomas Hooker
of Connecticut fame, for example, applied the covenant idea directly
to government when he wrote, "there must of necessity be a mutual
agreement . . . before, by any rule of God," men "have any right
or power, or can exercise either, each toward the other."

Since the Church, according to Puritan thought, could be brought
into existence only by the action of the whole membership, and the
minister was called and ordained by the congregation, it was hardly
to be expected that the state would long remain outside such popular participation. It was this germ of democracy which never ceased
to ferment within the hard shell of Puritan government. In a very
real sense, Puritanism, with its doctrines of individualism and the
covenant, contained the seeds of its own destruction as an authori-
tarian government.

"Nothing is more striking to a European traveler in the United
States than the absence of what we term the government, or the
administration," wrote Alexis de Tocqueville after his tour of the
United States in the 1830's. "Written laws exist in America, and
one sees the daily execution of them; but although everything moves
regularly, the mover can nowhere be discovered." The reason for
this, Tocqueville concluded, was the great importance and strength
of local government in America. Over a century later, in 1958, the
viability of local government in the United States is yet observable
in the South's adamant resistance to the desegregation of schools.

It is not to be doubted that the strength of local government in
America is due to the English heritage of the first settlers. Immigrants brought with them a long experience in local self-rule in the
shires and towns of old England. But the distribution of the two
primary forms of local government in the United States—the town
of New England and the county of Virginia—is largely the result
of geography and the motivations of the people who settled in the
two sections of English America. When the Puritans landed in Massachusetts, they laid out their settlements in a form that best secured the object of their coming—that is, the practice of ·their
religion. Instead of spreading out over the land in individual farms
—a procedure which would have hampered church attendance and
hindered control over the religious and moral life of the people—the
seventeenth-century settlements took the shape of compact villages,
with the farming land stretching around the periphery. Though
such a nucleated village was similar to those in England and on the

Continent, the fact that settlers in Virginia evolved a much different scheme of settlement makes it clear that religious and social aims, not the European inheritance, were the controlling factors.

The Englishmen who settled in Virginia, once the dangers of Indian attacks and starvation had been surmounted, spread themselves out on individual farms, forsaking the village settlement so familiar to many of them in England. (It is true that in the western part of England, especially in Devon, whence some settlers came to Virginia, separate farmsteads were well known, but even there the nucleated village was common.) The settlers in Virginia quickly found that large plantations situated along the great rivers of the tidewater were best suited to the growing of tobacco. These widely separated plantations became so typical of the colony that by the end of the century Virginian historian Robert Beverley was regretting they had ever gotten started. "This Liberty of taking up Land and the Ambition each Man had of being Lord of a vast, tho' unimproved Territory, together with the Advantage of many Rivers, which afforded a commodious Road for shipping at every Man's Door, has made the Country fall into . . . an unhappy Settlement and course of Trade." As a result, he continued, "to this Day they have not any one place of Cohabitation among them, that may reasonably bear the Name of a Town."

The forms of local government adopted in both Virginia and New England reflected the configuration of the settlements. With population spread thin by the centrifugal forces of geography and economy, the county, with its sheriffs, justices of the peace, and county court, all inherited from England, became the Virginian, and by extension, the southern form of local government. In New England, geographical forces were largely neutral—there were no navigable rivers to encourage the spreading out of population—while religion acted as a powerful cohesive force. Though as early as 1650 a Connecticut law spoke of the "great abuse of buying and purchasing home lots and laying them together, by means, whereof great depopulations are like to follow," the village or town, clustering around the all-important meetinghouse, was the typical New England form of local government, with town meeting and selectmen.

Since the church was self-governing in New England, it was to be anticipated that the town meeting, which was in some seventeenth-century towns indistinguishable in membership from the church, should be also. Indeed, it might be said with justice that the town meeting, so peculiar to New England and so remarkable to Tocqueville, was the natural offspring of the religion and geography of New England. In practice the town meeting was one of the most democratic features of seventeenth-century life. All residents of the Massachusetts town, whether they were church members or not, could speak at meeting, though before 1647 only "saints" could vote.[7] After that date and at the instance of the freemen, it was provided that all male residents over twenty-three could vote, be elected to town offices, and serve on juries, regardless of church membership. Recent investigations make it clear that all through the Puritan era most men in Massachusetts could participate in town government if they wished to. The New England town was truly a training ground for responsible and democratic government.

From what has been said up to now regarding the political institutions of the seventeenth-century colonists, it is apparent that they were formative for modern Americans. But the adaptation of English political ways to America, especially the representative assembly, exercised a further influence upon the course of American history. The very rhetoric and framework within which the revolutionary crisis of 1765–76 was carried out stemmed from the political forms which Americans had evolved in the wilderness. Indeed, without this particular development of representative assembly, local government, and political freedom, the Revolution, if it took place at all, would have had different goals and different slogans. For this reason, if for no other, this haphazard, often accidental, transfer of English political ways to America is suffused with a significance which origins otherwise rarely enjoy.

4. BLACK MEN IN A WHITE MEN'S COUNTRY

As the germ of the Revolution is to be detected in the political history of the seventeenth century, so the genesis of the Civil War is implicit in its social history. In late August, 1619, said John Rolfe, a Dutch ship dropped off "twenty Negars" at Jamestown. But, contrary to popular history, the American race problem did not begin then. It would be another half century before slavery, as it was to be known later, was established in America. As late as 1671 the

---

[7] That the tendency of these town governments was more democratic in practice than in law is shown by a statute of the New Haven colony in 1656. After calling attention to the fact that only freemen could vote in the towns, the General Court went on to observe that in some towns "others besides freemen have had liberties to vote in things of weightie trust and concernment."

Governor of Virginia estimated that Negroes made up less than 5 per cent of the population.

For most of the seventeenth century, Virginia society consisted largely of small, independent, landowning farmers; slave plantations as they would be known in the eighteenth century were not only few in number but their owners were relatively insignificant politically and socially.

Not until the opening years of the eighteenth century were land-holding yeomanry and indentured servants displaced to any appreciable degree by Negro slaves. Whereas in 1671, 5 per cent of the population was Negro, in 1715 the figure was up 24 per cent, and by 1756 Negro slaves accounted for over 40 per cent of the population. (By 1724, Negro slaves outnumbered whites more than two to one in South Carolina.) As slavery grew in importance, so did the great planter; by the end of the seventeenth century, the landed squire with his scores of slaves had superseded the sturdy yeoman in the political and social affairs of Virginia. The causes for this sharp shift in class power in the province do not concern us here. The reason for discussing it at all is in order to make clear that for most of the century neither the institution of slavery nor the Negro race was an important part of the life of Virginians.

Yet it must be said that slavery and racial discrimination began in the seventeenth century. Over a century ago, that most perspicacious student of America, Alexis de Tocqueville, pointed to slavery as the origin of the American prejudice toward the black man. Contrary to the situation in antiquity, he remarked, "among the moderns the abstract and transient fact of slavery is fatally united with the physical and permanent fact of color." Furthermore, he added, in the North "slavery recedes, but the prejudice to which it has given birth is immovable." More modern historians have also stressed this causal connection between the institution of slavery and the color prejudice of Americans. And it is patent to anyone conversant with the nature of American slavery, especially as it functioned in the nineteenth century, that the impress of bondage upon the character and future of the black man in this country has been deep and enduring.

But if one looks at other societies into which the Negro came as a slave, it is readily apparent that the causal relationship is not as pat as appears at first sight. The most striking examples of deviation from the American pattern are to be found in Brazil and

Spanish America. Like America, these areas have a history of large numbers of Negroes being introduced into the culture through the medium of slavery; but the "recession of slavery" there has not left an indelible mark of caste upon the former slave as it has in the United States.

Even in the days of slavery, Negroes in Brazil enjoyed an enormous amount of social equality. Gilberto Freyre, the Brazilian historian and sociologist, quotes a traveler in his country in the 1850's as seeing "black ladies in silks and jewelry, with male slaves in livery behind them. . . . Several have white husbands. The first doctor of the city is a colored man; so is the President of the Province." In Cuba and other parts of Latin America it was not uncommon for a slave to buy his freedom, doing so, often, in installments as he secured the money. Once outside slavery, the Negro was accorded a measure of social equality quite unknown in North America, for as early as the eighteenth century there were Negro priests and even black bishops in the Church south of the Rio Grande.

Contrary to the sentiment in North America, the Latin Americans did not attempt to impede manumission of the slave; in 1827, for example, there were 20,000 *more* free Negroes in Cuba alone than there were in all of the British Caribbean islands put together. The racist content of the two systems of slavery is clearly measured in these divergent attitudes toward the free Negro.

Today, Professor Freyre has said, Brazil stands out as an "experiment in ethnic and cultural bi-continentalism" in which "three-races and cultures are fused under conditions that, broadly speaking, are socially democratic. . . ." The Negro in Brazil today is very nearly a full citizen; he has successfully cast off the disabilities of slavery.

As much can hardly be said for the Negro in the United States. The question immediately arises: Why did slavery seem to produce such different consequences for the Negro in Brazil and in English America? Looking at the problem primarily from the Brazilian and Spanish American angle, Frank Tannenbaum has named three traditions or influences which have tended to prevent the stigma of slavery from being permanently placed upon black skin. They are the unbroken tradition of Roman law of slavery in Spain and Portugal from antiquity to the conquest of America; the Roman Catholic Church's insistence upon the baptism and Christianizing of Negro slaves at the same time that it proclaimed the equality of all Christians; and finally, the long history—by Anglo-American standards —of Spanish and Portuguese contacts with dark-skinned peoples in the course of the Moorish wars and the fifteenth- and sixteenth-century African explorations.

The uninterrupted persistence of Roman slave law is of prime importance because in that code the incidence of slavery was accidental, not racial, if only because all races were subject to slavery in practice. This conception of slavery as an unfortunate accident that might befall any luckless one was carried, through the medium of the law, to America. "The Negro may have been racially a new element," Tannenbaum concludes, "but slavery was a known and recognized institution—known especially to the law." Thus when the Negro became a slave, he "was automatically endowed with the immunities contained in the ancient prescription."

The considerable weight of the Church was in the same direction. Always conceiving of manumission as ennobling in the sight of God, the Church tirelessly reiterated the doctrine that all Christians, in the eyes of the Church and of God, were equal. As an institution, as Tannenbaum has put it, the Church was "biased in favor of freedom," thus helping to sustain a tone and an attitude favorable to the preservation of the Negro's humanity even while he was held in the degraded status of slavery.

Tannenbaum's argument is persuasive and sound as an explanation of the situation in Iberian America, but it does little to account for the fact that slavery in the English colonies was of such a different character. What we want to know is why slavery in the English colonies seemed to place a stigma of inferiority, of caste, upon the Negro. Tannenbaum makes it clear why this did not happen in South America; can it be explained why it did happen in North America?

Unfortunately, the matter is complicated by the fact that slavery was not written into the statutes of Virginia and Maryland until some forty years after the introduction of the first Negroes. Furthermore, two recent writers on the subject, Mary and Oscar Handlin, have gone so far as to conclude that before 1660 no essential distinction was made between Negroes and white indentured servants. Actually, as we shall see, it is this late development of slavery which holds the key to the explanation for the differences between the North and South American experiences with slavery.

In searching for the origins of racial discrimination, the usual procedure has been to argue that there was little or no discrimination against the Negro before slavery was legally defined in the 1660's. As a result, it was to slavery that investigators have looked for the origin of the racism in subsequent years. This conclusion, however, is contradicted, or at least weakened, by the South American experience, for we know from it that slavery does not always foster a caste place for Negroes. We can avoid this contradiction, however, if we reverse our assumptions as to which came first, slavery or discrimination. If, instead of assuming that discrimination is a consequence of slavery, we work on the assumption that discrimination preceded slavery and thereby conditioned it, then the contradiction disappears. Under this assumption American race prejudice originated in the discriminatory social atmosphere of the early seventeenth century, long before slavery came into legal existence. When slavery did become embodied in law, it could not help but reflect the folk bias within the framework of which it developed. Thus legal slavery in the English colonies reinforced and helped to perpetuate the discrimination against the Negro which prevailed almost from the beginning of settlement.

In the absence of restraining influences, it was not likely that men of the seventeenth century would accord Negroes an equal status with Englishmen. Even Irishmen, who were white, Christian, and European, were held to be literally "beyond the Pale," and some were even referred to as "slaves." The African, after all, was a heathen at a time when "Christian" was a title of import; moreover, he was black and culturally different. In Shakespeare's play, Brabantio's horror at his daughter's elopement with the black Moor Othello reflects the seventeenth-century Englishman's consciousness of the Negro's differences. "Damned as thou art, thou hast enchanted her," exclaims the outraged father, ignoring the fact of Othello's Christianity. Only in a bewitched state, he argues, would his daughter shun "the wealthy curled darlings of our nation . . . to incur a general mock" and leave her family in order to seek "the sooty bosom of such a thing as thou." Desdemona herself admitted that she perceived the Moor's "visage in his mind"—an acknowledgment that his difference in countenance would have been a serious obstacle to a love less profound than hers. In *Titus Andronicus* Tamora is reviled by Bassianus for loving the Moor Aaron. "Believe me, queen, your swarth Cimerian doth make your honour of his body's hue, spotted, detested and abominable." Why, he asks her, are you wandering in the forest "with a barbarous Moor"?

But a feeling that Englishmen and Negroes were different did not depend upon vague impressions gained from chance and rare contact with black men or Moors in England. The fact that Negroes arrived in English America as the cargo of the international slave trade unquestionably fostered a sense of superiority among Englishmen. If the noble and commanding Othello could be stigmatized as a "thing," how much more likely it was that degrading terms be applied to those wretches newly spilled out of the slave ships! It was to be anticipated that from the beginning a special inferior position would be assigned black men.

Such, indeed, was the fact even though the Virginia and Maryland records in the years between 1620 and 1660 rarely refer to "slaves" but speak mainly of "Negroes." The failure to use the term slave should not blind us to the real possibility that the status for which it stood was already in being. The legal definition of the inferior status which Englishmen in America—both in New England and in the Chesapeake colonies—were building for Negroes was imprecise in those early years. But that an inferior status was in the process of being worked out seems undoubted. Moreover, the treatment accorded another dark-skinned heathen people, the Indians, offers further evidence that enslavement was early the lot reserved for Negroes. Indian slavery was practiced in all the English settlements almost from the beginning; rarely were any distinctions made between Indians and Negroes when discriminatory legislation was enacted. But let us now turn to the beginnings of slavery in the English colonies.

The colonies of Virginia and New England had ample opportunity to learn of discriminatory practices against Negroes from island settlements of Englishmen like Bermuda and New Providence in the Caribbean. As early as the 1620's and 1630's these colonies provided a discriminatory or outright slave status for Negroes. In 1623, for example, the Assembly of Bermuda passed an act restraining "the insolencies of the Negroes," limiting the black man's freedom of movement and participation in trade, and denying him the right to bear arms. The Puritan venture of New Providence Island in the western Caribbean was notorious for its pirating of Negro slaves from the Spanish colonies in order to sell them or use them on its plantations. By the 1640's, according to the contemporary his-

torian Richard Ligon, Barbados, another Caribbean English settlement, was using Negroes as outright slaves.

There is evidence as early as the 1630's and 1640's that Virginia
and Maryland were singling out Negroes for discriminatory treatment as compared with white indentured servants. One Hugh Davis
in Virginia in 1630 was "soundly whipped before an assembly of
Negroes and others for abusing himself to the dishonor of God and
the shame of Christians, by defiling his body in lying with a Negro."
An act passed in Maryland in 1639 enumerated the rights of "all
Christian inhabitants (slaves excepted)." The slaves referred to
could have been only Indians or Negroes since all white servants
were Christians. Negroes were specifically denied the right to bear
arms in Virginia in 1640 and in Maryland in 1648, though no such
prohibition was put upon white servants; indeed, in statutes that
prohibited Negroes from being armed, masters were directed to arm
the white servants.

It is significant that though both Maryland and Virginia passed
statutes to fix limits to the terms for indentured servitude for those
who came without written contracts, Negroes were never included in
such protective provisions. The first of such statutes were enacted in
1639 in Maryland and in 1643 in Virginia. Three times before
1660—in 1643, 1644, and 1658—the Virginia Assembly included
Negro and Indian women among the "tithables," though white women
were never included in such a category. The discrimination was a
recognition of the fact that Negro and Indian women worked in the
fields, whereas white women, servants or no, usually did not.

Two cases for the punishment of runaway servants in Virginia
throw some light on the status of Negroes by 1640. The first case
concerned three runaways, of whom two were white men and the
third a Negro. All three were given thirty lashes, and the white men
had the terms owed their masters extended a year, at the completion
of which they were to work for the colony for three more years. The
other, "being a Negro named *John Punch* shall serve his said master
or his assigns for the time of his natural Life here or elsewhere."
It is obvious that the Negro's punishment was the most severe and
that his penalty, in effect, was reduction to slavery, though it is also
clear that up until his sentencing he must have had the status of a
servant.

The second case, also of 1640, suggests that by that date some
Negroes were already slaves. This one also involved six white men

and a Negro who had plotted to run away. The punishments meted out varied, but Christopher Miller, "a dutchman (a prince agent in the business)," was given the harshest treatment of all: thirty stripes, burned with an "R" (for Rogue) on the cheek, a shackle on his leg for a year "and longer if said master shall see cause," and seven years of service for the colony upon completion of his time due his master. The only other one of the plotters to receive the stripes, the shackle, and the burning of the "R" was the Negro Emanuel, but, significantly, he did not receive any sentence of work for the colony. Apparently he was already serving his master for a lifetime—i.e., he was a slave.

From a proceeding before the House of Burgesses in 1666 it appears that as early as 1644 that body was being called upon to determine who was a slave. In 1666 the records of the House report that in 1644 the Assembly "adjudged" a certain mulatto "no slave" even though he had been bought "as a Slave for Ever." No reasons are given as to why he was freed, but we do know that his master was surprised, for he petitioned for recompense. The Assembly refused the request, however, contending that it was not a public obligation to relieve those buyers who made poor purchases. In any case, it is clear that even this Negro served a term the length of which—twenty-one years—was unheard of for a "Christian servant."

In early seventeenth-century inventories of estates there are two distinctions which appear in the reckoning of the value of servants and Negroes. Uniformly, the Negroes are more valuable, even as children, than any white servant. Secondly, the naming of a servant is usually followed by the number of years yet remaining to his service; for the Negroes no such notation appears. Thus, in an inventory in Virginia in 1643, a twenty-two-year-old white servant, with eight years still to serve, was valued at 1,000 pounds of tobacco, while a "Negro boy" was rated at 3,000 pounds; a white boy with seven years to serve was listed as worth 700 pounds. An eight-year-old Negro girl was calculated to be worth 2,000 pounds. On another inventory in 1655, two good men servants with four years to serve were rated at 1,300 pounds of tobacco, and a woman servant with only two years to go was valued at 800 pounds. But two Negro boys, who had no limit set to their terms, were evaluated at 4,100 pounds apiece, and a Negro girl was said to be worth 5,500 pounds.

Such wide differences in the valuation of Negro and white "servants" strongly suggest, as does the failure to indicate term of service for Negroes, that the latter were slaves. Beyond a question, there was some service which these blacks were rendering which enhanced their value—a service, moreover, which was not or could not be exacted from the whites. Furthermore, a Maryland deed of 1649 suggests slave status not only of lifetime term but also of inheritance. Three Negroes "and all their issue both male and female" were deeded.

More positive evidence of true slavery is afforded by the court records of the 1640's and 1650's. In 1646, for example, a Negro woman and a Negro boy were sold to Stephen Charlton to be of use to him and "his heyers etc. for ever." A Negro girl was sold in 1652 to one H. Armsteadinger "and his heyers . . . forever with all her increase both male and female." One investigator, Susie Ames, describes the case of two Negroes brought into the eastern shore of Virginia in 1635. Over twenty years later, in 1656, the widow of the master was bequeathing the child of one of the original Negroes and the other Negro and her children. This was more than mere servitude—the term was longer than twenty years and apparently the status was inheritable.

It is true that, concurrently with these examples of onerous service or actual slavery exacted from Negroes, some members of the race did gain their freedom. But such instances do not deny the existence of discrimination or slave status; they simply testify to the unsteady evolution of a status for the Negro. Indeed, the tangential manner in which recognition of Negro slavery first appeared in the Virginia statutes strengthens the supposition that the practice long preceded the law. In 1660, in a statute dealing with punishments for runaway servants, only casual reference was made to "those Negroes who are incapable of making satisfaction by addition of time." Apparently, everyone at the time knew what was meant by the circumlocution.

But as legal questions of status arose from time to time, clarification of the Negroes' position had to be written into law. Thus in 1662 Virginia declared that the status of offspring would follow that of the mother in the event of a white man getting a Negro with child. When Maryland in 1664 prescribed service for Negroes *durante vita* and included hereditary status through the *father*, it also prohibited unions between the races. The preamble of the statute offers a clue as to the motives behind this separation of the races. Prohibition of intermarriage is necessary because "divers free born *English* women, forgetful of their free condition, and to the disgrace of our nation, do intermarry with Negro slaves," from which fact questions of status of issue have arisen. Therefore, the law was enacted in order to prevent harm to masters and "for deterring such free-born women from such shameful matches. . . ." Interestingly enough, the South Carolinian slave code of 1712 justified special legislation for Negroes on grounds of cultural difference. "The Negroes and other slaves brought unto the people of this province . . . are of barbarous, wild, savage natures, and such as renders them wholly unqualified to be governed by the laws, customs, and practices of this province. . . ."

Regardless of the reasoning behind the singling out of Negroes, as early as 1669 the law in Virginia implicitly viewed Negroes as property. An act of that year assured masters that they would not be held responsible for the accidental death of a slave as a result of punishment because it should be presumed that no man would "destroy his owne estate." But it still would be a long while before the legal status of slave property would be finally settled. In 1705, for example, Virginia law declared slaves to be real estate, though with many exceptions. Similarly, in South Carolina slaves were first denominated real estate in 1690 and then chattels in 1740. By 1750, the law in the southern colonies settled on chattels as the proper designation of slave property.

The important point is not the evolution of the legal status of the slave, but the fact that discriminatory legislation regarding the Negro long preceded any legal definition of slavery. Equally important, in view of the commonly held view that numbers of Negroes determined the inferior status imposed upon the black, is the evidence of discrimination long before numbers were large. In 1680 Virginia enacted a series of regulations which were very close to the later slave codes in restricting the movement of Negroes, prohibiting their bearing arms, and providing capital punishment for those who ran away or offered resistance to whites. Yet it would be another twenty years before the Negroes would make up even a fifth of the total population of Virginia. In short, long before slavery was an important part of the labor system of the South, the Negroes had been fitted into a special and inferior status.

That the white man's sense of difference regarding the Negro determined the character of slavery is clearly seen if one examines the

development of Negro servitude in the northern colonies. English
men there, like their countrymen in the southern colonies, inherited
no legal basis for slavery; yet a slave status which fixed the Negro
into a permanent caste position developed in New England, even
though there the economic importance of the Negro was considerably less than in the South.[8]

So few Negroes were imported into New England during the
seventeenth century that references to their status are scattered,
but those pieces of evidence which are available suggest that from
the earliest years an especially low status, if not slavery itself, was
reserved for the Negro. One source, for example, of 1639 tells of a
Negro woman being held as a slave on Noddles Island in Boston
Harbor. Her master sought to mate her with another Negro, but,
the chronicler reported, she kicked her prospective lover out of bed,
saying that such behavior was "beyond her slavery." It is also well
known that the first Massachusetts legal code, the Body of Liberties
of 1641, permitted enslavement of those who are "sold to us," which
would apply to Negroes brought by the slave ships.

Nor was the use of Negroes as slaves unknown or undesirable to
the Puritans. One correspondent of John Winthrop in 1645, for
instance, talked of the desirability of war against the Indians, so
that captives might be taken who could be exchanged "for Moores
[Negroes], which will be more gayneful pilladge for us then [sic]
wee conceive, for I doe not see how wee can thrive untill wee get into
a stock of slaves sufficient to doe all our business, for our children's
children will hardly see this great Continent filled with people. . . ."
Moreover, he went on, "servants" will not stay but "for verie great
wages. And I suppose you know verie well how we shall maynteyne
20 Moores cheaper than one English servant." The following
year the United Colonies (Massachusetts, Plymouth, New Haven,
and Connecticut colonies) decreed, in order to save prison costs,
that contumacious Indians would be delivered up to those they had
injured or "be shipped out and exchanged for Negroes" as the case
might justify. That enslavement of Negroes was well known in New
England by the early 1650's is evident from the preamble of a

[8] This point is important because Oscar Handlin, *Race and Nationality in
American Life* (New York, 1957), Chapter I, has attempted to explain the
origins of slavery in terms of economic need. Obviously his argument cannot
stand when tested in New England. There just were too few Negroes there in
the seventeenth or eighteenth century to make an economic case for pushing the
black man into a new status of slavery as Handlin contends.

Rhode Island statute of 1652. It was said that it "is a common course practised amongst Englishmen to buy Negers, to that end they may have them for service or slaves forever. . . ."

Though the number of Negroes in New England was exceedingly small, the colonies of that region followed the same path as the southern provinces in denying arms to the blacks in their midst. In 1652, Massachusetts had provided that Indians and Negroes should train in the militia the same as whites. But this ruling apparently caused friction, for in 1656 the earlier law was countermanded by the words "henceforth no Negroes or Indians, although servants of the English, shalbe armed or permitted to trayne." Connecticut in 1660 also excluded Indians and "Negar servants" from the militia and "Watch and Ward," although as late as 1680 it was officially reported to London that there were no more than thirty "slaves" in the colony.

Edward Randolph as commissioner of the Crown reported in 1676 that there were a few indentured servants in Massachusetts, "and not above two hundred slaves in the colony," by which he meant Negroes, for he said they "were brought from Guinea and Madagascar." Yet not until 1698 did the phrase "Negro slave" appear in the Massachusetts statutes. Practice was preceding law in New England just as it had in the South. In 1690, discrimination against the few Negroes in Connecticut reached the point where all Negroes were forbidden to be found outside the town bounds without "a ticket or a pass" from either master or the authorities, the restriction applying equally to free Negroes and slaves. Furthermore, it was provided that ferrymen would be fined if they permitted Negroes without passes to use their ferries. And though as early as 1680 official reports to London were distinguishing between slaves and servants, statute law barely defined the institution of slavery. In 1704, for example, the Governor gave it as his opinion that all children born of "Negro bondwomen are themselves in like condition, i.e. born in servitude," but he admitted that no law had so provided. Legislation, he said, was "needless, because of the constant practice by which they are held as such. . . ." In 1703, Massachusetts provided that "molatto and Negro slaves" could be set free only if security was given that they would not be a charge on the community, and two years later a prohibition against sexual relations between Negroes and whites was enacted. In 1717, Negroes were barred from holding land in Connecticut.

Thus, like the southern colonists, the New Englanders enacted into law, in the absence of any prior English law of slavery, their recognition of Negroes as different in race, religion, and culture. It should be especially noted that in many instances discriminations were made against all Negroes, whether slave or free—a fact which reinforces the argument that the discrimination was a precondition for the slavery and not a consequence. Unquestionably, the coincidence of slavery with discrimination fastened still more firmly the stigma of inferiority upon the Negro, but slavery must be absolved of starting the cycle. It was the discriminatory attitude and behavior which conditioned the form slavery would take. And in the absence of any law of slavery or commandments of the Church [9] to the contrary—as was true in Brazil and Spanish America—slavery in the English colonies would mirror the discrimination practiced in the society at large. In this sense it might be proper to speak of slavery in the English colonies as the institutionalization of a folk prejudice.

Once the sense of difference between the two peoples was embodied in law, the logic of the law widened the differences. All through the early eighteenth century, judges and legislatures in all the colonies elaborated the law along the discriminatory lines laid down from the beginning. In this, of course, especially in the South, they had the added incentive of perpetuating and securing a labor system which

[9] It might be asked why Christianity in the North American colonies did not exercise an influence comparable to that exerted by the Roman Catholic Church in the South American colonies. Frank Tannenbaum in his book on the subject gives no satisfactory explanation because he erroneously assumes that the Protestant churches were uninterested in the conversion of the Negro and therefore did not bring the ameliorative influence of Christianity to bear upon the condition of the Negroes. In fact, however, several of the English churches in America did seek to Christianize the slave, but the big obstacle was the persistent belief that baptism would free the slave. Thus as late as 1723, even though several laws had been enacted carefully denying that baptism enfranchised a slave, merchants were inquiring of the Attorney General in England for his opinion on the matter. It would seem, without going into the question here, that the Protestant conception of Christianity and baptism was much more liberating and special than the Catholic, for it did not seem possible for the Protestant English to believe that a Christian, ennobled by baptism, could actually still be a slave. But regardless of the reasoning behind it, it seems clear that the churches in the English colonies, thanks to the persistence of this popular belief, actually found themselves defending slavery in order to be able to go about the job of Christianizing the Negroes. The Protestant churches, therefore, could not fulfill the same function as the Catholic Church, which, although it baptized without threatening the sanctity of slave property, could also preach the equality of all Christians, slave or free.

had become indispensable to the economy. As a consequence, the cleavage between the races was deepened and hardened.

In time the correspondence between the black man and slavery would be so perfect that it would be difficult to realize that the Negro was not always and everywhere in a degraded status. Thus began in the seventeenth century the Negro's life in America. With it commenced a moral problem for all Americans which still besets us in the middle of the twentieth century. Though started casually, thoughtlessly, and without any preconceived goal, the web became so interwoven, so complex, so tightly meshed, that John C. Calhoun could say, in 1850, slavery "has grown with our growth, and strengthened with our strength."

The full social implications of American slavery, however, were not apparent until the expansion and elaboration of the institution in the nineteenth century. For that reason our discussion of its import for the future of America should wait while we now consider the contributions of the eighteenth century to the making of the social patterns of modern America.

CHAPTER II

The Awakening of
American Nationality

THE first half of the eighteenth century, as Thomas Wertenbaker
has said, was a golden age for American culture; elegance was re-
placing mere comfort in the homes of the rich, comfort was supplanting privation in the houses of the not-so-rich; farmers and
merchants, planters and craftsmen, were building a prosperous and
productive economy. A new society, often graceful and cultivated,
following the model of western European culture, was being firmly
established on the edge of the North American wilderness. At the
middle of the eighteenth century towns like Boston, New York,
Charleston, and Philadelphia were already miniature Londons; the
frontier of forests and Indians was now a hundred miles to the west.

But within the European civilization transplanted to the New
World the seeds of a new civilization were sprouting. Paradoxically
enough, Europe's colonizing experience in the New World was
doomed by its success; in the act of flourishing, the English colonies
were also ceasing to be European. This budding of American consciousness was already in evidence before 1763; under the forcing
frame of the Revolutionary era, it would burst into flower.

1. COUNTRY COUSINS

To probe for signs of cultural independence among the arts of
colonial America—even in the 1750's—is to take on an unrewarding
task. As Franklin remarked in 1763, "After the first Cares for the
Necessaries of Life are over we shall come to think of the Embellish-
ments." America was too new, too raw, too poor to be able to train,
to teach, or to afford artists in anything like the style achieved in

contemporary Europe. Though Franklin said, "Already some of our young geniuses begin to lisp Attempts at Painting, Poetry and Musick," he would have been the first to admit that these "geniuses" were attempting little more than the transplanting of European culture to America. They hardly dared express the spirit of their own land in artistic forms. Such cultural independence could come only with the self-confidence of years.

The limited possibilities for great art imposed by the rude environment of America are suggested by a comparison of the primitive techniques of the best colonial artists—men like Feke and Copley—with the finished and polished performances of English contemporaries like Gainsborough, Hogarth, and Reynolds. To an even greater degree the same was true in musical composition and performance. Literature, too, despite a solitary oak like Franklin, was still in the sapling stage when compared with Richardson, Addison, Steele, Johnson, and Boswell, to name only the most obvious in contemporary England. The absence of a long, cultivated tradition, of schools of art, of artistic and literary communities for the exchange of learning and ideas, relegated the English colonies to the backwash of European artistic and cultural achievement.[1]

Even in architecture, where the demands of living compelled the Americans to engage in its pursuit, the European influence was overwhelming; the American emulation of English models bordered on the abject. Though the climate and weather of America were different from England's and one might have expected, therefore, some significant modifications in structure of dwellings, there was surprisingly little. Georgian architectural forms, which enjoyed enormous vogue in England, duplicated their triumph in the colonies almost without alteration. In the extant homes of the colonial gentry, like Mount Vernon, one can still see the faithful reproductions of Palladian windows prescribed in the contemporary English architectural handbooks. Similarly, in the homes of the wealthy colonials, the ornate Georgian fireplaces are of a design which might have been

---

[1] In a new field of intellectual endeavor like natural science, the Americans were not at such a decided disadvantage. The work of Franklin in electricity, for example, stands out as one of the foremost achievements of science in the first half of the eighteenth century; it was on a par with any work then being done in Europe in the field of experimental physics. In older departments of natural science, like botany and zoology, although Americans made contributions, they largely "depended upon the intellectual stimulus they received from Europe," writes Brook Hindle, *The Pursuit of Science in Revolutionary America* (New York, 1956), p. 58.

copied without change from a country house in Old England. In
time the American environment would work its alchemy upon European forms brought to the new country, but that day was still in
the future.

There were aspects of colonial life, however, in which American
consciousness of self was growing and where the future was more
than implicit. Two criteria can be utilized to throw into relief the
beginnings of a sense of Americanism or nationalism in the pre-
Revolutionary years; both will be employed in this chapter as they
were implicitly used in the last. First of all, we shall notice those
divergencies of American theory and practice from European
models, for in this we catch the first glimmerings of an emergent
American people. Secondly, we shall direct our attention to those
elements in colonial society which have persisted down into our own
time; in these we first see the outlines of modern American civilization.

2. MATERIAL FOUNDATIONS

"The economic history of the United States," one scholar has
written, "is the history of the rise and development of the capitalistic
system." The colonists of the eighteenth century pushed forward
what those of the seventeenth century had begun: the expansion and
elaboration of an economy born in the great age of capitalist expansion. The economic life of the vast majority of the million and a
half people in the colonies of the mid-eighteenth century, was still
dominated, as in the seventeenth, by the rhythm of agriculture. But
now a sizable merchant class thrived in a half dozen seaboard cities,
its trading operations being one of the great sources of the new
wealth which distinguished the eighteenth-century economy from the
seventeenth.

At mid-century the continental colonies were England's most
valuable possession. "*America* has become the fountain of our
riches," it was said in the widely circulated *Gentleman's Magazine*
in January, 1755, "for with *America* our greatest trade is carried
on." The entry bills "at the Custom-House of *London* only, shew the
great quantities of our manufactures which they consume." For
Americans themselves, the economic growth of their provinces be-
tokened a general prosperity which was the envy of Europe.

The great bulk of the accumulated wealth of America, as distinguished from that which was consumed, was derived either directly

or indirectly from trade. Though some manufacturing existed, its role in the accumulation of capital was negligible. A merchant class of opulent proportions was already visible in Boston, New York, Philadelphia, Newport, and Charleston, its wealth the obvious consequence of shrewd and resourceful management of the carrying trade. Even the rich planters of tidewater Virginia and the rice coast of South Carolina finally depended for their genteel way of life upon the ships and merchants who sold their tobacco and rice in the markets of Europe. As colonial production rose and trade expanded, a business community emerged in the colonies, linking the provinces by lines of trade and identity of interest.

The needs of business and trade compelled the colonies—and to some extent the mother country—to improve the means of inter-colonial communication in the early decades of the eighteenth century. By 1740, for example, there was a complete series of post roads running from Portsmouth, New Hampshire, to Charleston. Moreover, old Indian trails into the interior were gradually being turned into roads, penetrating the hinterlands of New York, Pennsylvania, and even newly opened Georgia. Indicative of the improvement in the possibilities for travel was the publication of the first guidebook for America in 1732. Packet ships, running on schedule, linked the major ports of the colonies, greatly facilitating the movement of goods and people in an age when land travel was everywhere the most uncomfortable mode. In the first part of the century the colonial postal service was so haphazard as to be almost worthless, but once Benjamin Franklin got a chance to work his organizing abilities upon it—that is, after 1753—it became an efficient agency for the transacting of business and served to pull the spread-out colonies closer together. Travel between some of the larger towns was sufficiently important to justify the running of stage coaches on schedule. The best known of such attempts at rapid means of communication was the "flying machine," which raced the one hundred miles between New York and Philadelphia in the unprecedented time of two days.

More important than the actual physical means of communication, which must always appear to the twentieth century as inexpressibly primitive, was the fact that as people moved along these lines of travel, meeting their fellow colonists, they could not help noticing the characteristics they held in common. "I found but little difference in the manners and character of the people in the different provinces I passed thro," commented Dr. Alexander Hamilton at the end of his tour of the colonies in 1744.

There were less tangible, but nonetheless significant, ways in which the accumulation of wealth and the improvement of communication served to bind the disparate colonials together. The upper classes of the several provinces, for instance, were joined together by ties of family. The Wendells of New York were related to the Quincys, Sewalls, and Hancocks of Massachusetts. Benjamin Smith of South Carolina was related to Abigail Smith, the wife of John Adams. When the Bayards of Philadelphia journeyed north, they were welcomed in the homes of Bayards in New York and in Boston. The socially and politically prominent De Lanceys of New York were intermarried with the equally distinguished Allens of Philadelphia. The spread of the Masonic Order, among all levels of society, in the early decades of the century also provided a medium for increased intercolonial connection. Masonic lodges were established in half of the provinces of English America by 1741. Traveling Masons were always welcomed by their brethren, and the functions of the order often brought together men who might otherwise not leave their own bailiwicks.

As business expanded, so did the lawyers. Prominent ones like John Kempe and James Alexander of New York and Andrew Hamilton of Philadelphia often had clients outside their own provinces, thereby functioning as links between provinces. Jared Ingersoll, after he assumed his seat as judge of vice-admiralty in Philadelphia, continued to maintain his widespread professional connections in his native Connecticut. Leaders of the bar like Kempe, Hamilton, and others often served as instructors of young lawyers from other provinces, thus giving a unity of outlook to the provincial bars not otherwise to be expected.

Erstwhile businessmen like Franklin of Philadelphia and Cadwallader Colden of New York maintained close communication through their common interest in the science of the day. In 1745, as an outgrowth of this interest, the American Philosophical Society was born. As its name suggests, the Society brought together those men of the American colonies who were working and thinking about things philosophical, which at that time included all of human inquiry.

It was the eighteenth century which saw the first solid beginnings of the colonial periodical press; some twenty-two weekly newspapers were started in 1713–45 in seven of the thirteen colonies. Though circulation was always small and the viewpoint strongly English, these papers served to link together the ruling circles in the various colonies. Other periodicals, aside from newspapers, also made their appearance in the thirty years prior to the Revolution. The publication of books in America was a thriving business in the late colonial era; in number of books printed, Boston was second only to London among all the cities of the British Empire. By the middle of the century, in brief, interested colonials enjoyed ample intellectual fare for their mutual enlightenment and interchange of ideas.

Quantitatively, of course, and especially when compared with modern means of mass communication, the opportunities for the transmission of ideas in the colonial era were limited and narrow. But this was equally true of Europe at this time, though we often casually assume a body of public opinion in countries like England and France. Though the American colonies were more spread out than any European country, the upper classes in the provinces in America were small and therefore easily reached by limited means of communication. Because the small upper classes set the tone of public opinion in America as they did in Europe, the means of intellectual interchange did not have to be attuned to a mass audience or to be of spectacular proportions to create a sense of unity. "Socially and spiritually, as well as in trade and politics," Carl Bridenbaugh has written in a recent study of the biggest eighteenth-century colonial cities, "the gentlefolk of all five cities came to know one another better, to exchange amenities and to sense their common bonds in the leadership of an American society."

3. A POOR MAN'S COUNTRY

An expanding economy meant increasing opportunities for economic advancement, as many Americans were quick to tell the land-hungry people of old Europe. Benjamin Franklin, America's best-known booster, wrote in 1751 that land was plentiful "and so cheap . . . that a laboring man that understands husbandry can in a short time save money enough to purchase a piece of land sufficient for a plantation. . . . " Nor, Franklin went on, need the enterprising young man worry about providing for the future of his children, for he will soon see "that more land is to be had at rates equally easy, all circumstances considered." It was the boast of another colonial that "You may depend upon it that this is one of the best poor man's Countrys in the World." Cadwallader Colden of New York thought that the opportunity for any man to set himself up as a farmer was so good in this country that little manufacturing could be expected "because of the dearness of Labor and want of hands. . . ." More than the future of manufacturing was involved; the status of the laborer was also affected. What a difference there was, Crèvecoeur observed, between the hiring of workers in England and in America. "When we hire any of these people we rather pray and entreat them. You must give them what they ask. . . . They must be at your table and feed . . . on the best you have." In the colonies, a British official concluded in 1760, "a plentiful subsistence may be . . . gained by very moderate labour, and even opulence acquired from no other stock then [*sic*] is to be found in industry and economy only. . . ."

The clearest evidence of the broad opportunities available in America, even though the economic situation was not everywhere and at all times as roseate as some commentators made out, was the remarkably wide distribution of property, especially land. Thomas Hutchinson, Royal Governor of Massachusetts, said in 1764 that in all the colonies not more than 2 per cent of the tillers of the soil were tenants. "This is the ruling passion to be a freeholder," he remarked. At another time he asserted, "Property is more equally distributed in the colonies, especially those to the northward of Maryland than in any nation in Europe." In 1755 the General Court of Massachusetts gave as its opinion that land was so abundant that any young man who wanted to could start a family without venturing a farthing—an opportunity, the legislature pointed out, which could not be matched in any country in Europe.

A broadly based property-holding class, regardless of whether it primarily held land, as in the colonial era, or chattels and real estate, as in the nineteenth and twentieth centuries, has always been the principal and ultimate shield of capitalism in America. With property widely distributed from the very beginning, our political and social institutions have been conservative about it; but in doing so they have no more than reflected the people's direct interest in private property.

Even in a new society with broad economic opportunities, the eighteenth-century colonial was actually aware of status, if only because he was a child of class-conscious Europe. One Anglican clergyman who knew American urban society and English life equally well called attention to the class demarcations visible in the colonial towns. Despite the absence of a nobility or orders of gentry, he said, "you might see a proof [of] how necessarily some difference of rank, some inequality must and ought to grow up in every society, and how Eutopian and ridiculous the contrary idea and attempt is." All through the literature of the period one finds references to "the Better Sort," the "Middle Sort," and the "meaner sort" of people.

Although it was true that breeding, ancestry, occupation, and learning played their parts in determining which "sort" one was, the final arbiter in the eighteenth century as in the seventeenth was wealth. "The only principle of Life propagated among the young People," complained Cadwallader Colden in 1748, "is to get Money and men are only esteemed according to . . . the Money they are possessed of." With property as a social escalator, the acquisition of wealth became the object of the many. "The hopes of having land of their own and becoming independent Landlords," Colden said, "is what chiefly induces peoples into America." Men purchased land as quickly as possible after their arrival, Colden continued, even though a few more years as laborers would have made life easier, "but such is the desire of being independent and of leaving a certain estate to their children that it overcomes all other Considerations."

Underlying the drive for wealth among Americans was the widespread opportunity which the new land afforded. In America, Franklin wrote, "no man continues long a journeyman to a trade, but goes among those new settlers and sets up for himself." A Philadelphia newspaper in 1776 summed up both the wide distribution of property and the rapidity of social advancement. "Is not one half of the property in the city . . . owned by men who wear *Leather Aprons?*" the paper asked. "Does not the other half belong to men whose fathers or grandfathers wore Leather Aprons?"

The fluidity of class lines in colonial America can be further illustrated in the lives of men who rose from lowly status to high rank within their communities. Most spectacular, perhaps, is the history of Anthony Lamb. In 1742 he was awaiting execution at Tyburn, England, when a last-minute commutation of his sentence sent him to Virginia as an indentured prisoner. After his service he worked in a number of occupations, eventually ending up in New York City as a respected citizen and the owner of an instrument maker's shop. His son John, also an instrument maker, ultimately rose to be included among the leading gentry of the city. He entered history as

one of the leading Sons of Liberty who sparked the Revolutionary
movement in New York. Or one might cite the case of Adino Paddock of Harwich, Massachusetts, who came to Boston in 1736 as
an apprentice to a carriage maker. In 1758 he owned his own shop
and was prominent in the Masonic Order. By 1769 he was serving
on the important Committee on the State of Public Affairs for
Boston; he was appending "esquire" to his name in 1772. At the
time of the evacuation of Boston by the British in 1776, Paddock
left the country as a Tory, with property valued at over £3,000
sterling.

Even the well-known painter John Singleton Copley experienced
in his lifetime a quick ascent from low social origins. Born the son
of an immigrant tobacconist in 1738, Copley by 1769 was earning
300 guineas a year from his painting—enough to permit him to
marry the fashionable Susannah Clarke. Though his marriage undoubtedly was a factor in catapulting him into the upper reaches of
Boston society, it was his earnings, not his marriage, which permitted him to build a sumptuous mansion on Boston's Beacon Hill
appropriate to his new status.

The relative ease with which wealth could be accumulated stimulated a materialistic drive among even those in the lower ranks of
society who would probably never live on Beacon Hill or lower
Broadway. That most Americans, whether of high or low estate,
should display this avidity for wealth was, as we have seen, clearly
a disappointment to aristocratic Cadwallader Colden. Even the
usually sanguine and democratic Crèvecoeur was disturbed by the
obvious scramble for money among the colonials. "If it is not
'bellum omnium contra omnes," he wrote, " 'tis a general mass of
keenness and sagacious acting against another mass of equal
sagacity; 'tis caution against caution. Happy when it does not degenerate into fraud against fraud!" The ambitious American, intent
on his own success, Crèvecoeur sadly noted, was harsh and even
fraudulent in his dealings with the new arrivals. The American, he
wrote, appears "litigious, overbearing, purse-proud." After 1740,
when the wars with the French provided wider and more frequent
opportunities for the piling up of wealth and the perpetrating of
highly profitable, if dubious, commercial deals, colonial incomes and
avarice scaled new heights. While British and colonial soldiers and
seamen were dying fighting the French and Indians in the forests of

the West and on the high seas, other colonials were lucratively trading with the enemy.

Although, in a general way, society in the colonies was pyramidal as it was in Europe, there were differences in more than detail. For one thing, the absence of a hereditary nobility and royalty in America meant that the social pyramid was truncated rather than pointed. But, further than this, the wide dispersion of property brought the top and bottom levels of society much closer together than in Europe. Though it is true that the pretensions of the upper classes in colonial society seemed almost without limit, the highest stratum of society was in fact quite "middle class" by European standards. Nicholas Cresswell, who was familiar with English society, thought that George Washington's father was no more than "a creditable Virginia Tobacco Planter (which I suppose may, in point of rank, be equal to the better sort of Yeomanry in England)." It was indicative of the narrow distance—by European measures— between the base and the summit of society that colonial craftsmen were to be found on every level of society, from slaves to gentry. A further measure of the middling nature of colonial society was John Witherspoon's observation that the common man in the colonies spoke better English on the average than his counterpart in England, but that the speech of the educated colonial was inferior to that of the educated Briton. Carl and Jessica Bridenbaugh, in discussing the society of Philadelphia, concluded that though the "aristocracy" of the city were "members of a privileged oligarchy, none of them could have said, with Catherine of Russia, 'Je suis aristocrate; c'est mon métier.' "

It was to be expected that egalitarian sentiments would be rife in a society in which large numbers of men possessed property and in which almost all men could read and write.[2] "The people of this Province," commented a writer in the *Pennsylvania Journal* in 1756, "are generally of the middling Sort, and at present pretty much upon a Level. They are chiefly industrious Farmers, Artificers or Men in Trade; they enjoy and are fond of Freedom, and the *meanest among them* thinks he has a right to Civility from the greatest." With manifest distaste, Comptroller Weare, a British official, observed in 1760 that in America "under forms of a demo-

---

[2] "A native American who cannot read or write is as rare an appearance as a Jacobite or a Roman Catholic, that is, as rare as a comet or an earthquake," wrote John Adams in 1765.

cratical government, all mortifying distinctions of rank are lost in common equality; and . . . the ways of wealth and preferment are alike open to all men. . . ." He might have noted that it was likely that the "common equality" prevailed because "the ways of wealth were open."

Philip Fithian noticed in the 1760's that the trend toward social equality permeated even the upper classes. Among the people of his native province of New Jersey, Fithian saw "the Level" at work. "Hence, we see Gentlemen, when they are not actually engaged in the publick service, on their farms, setting a laborious example to their Domesticks, and on the other hand we see labourers at the Tables and in the Parlours of their Betters enjoying the advantage, and honour of their society and conversation." Even in Virginia, where Fithian served as a tutor on the plantation of the aristocratic Robert Carter, he was seated daily at table with the family, and, in the absence of the master, the lowly teacher was accepted as the man of the house for ceremonials like carving and serving at meals.

Thus, in the midst of a hierarchical social pattern, there were forces at work which not only modified the pattern as compared with European models, but which led directly to an egalitarian social structure in the future. In short, the stage was already set in the colonial period for that assertion of equality which is usually associated only with the Jacksonian movement of the early nineteenth century. The Revolution would add its impetus to this gathering egalitarian sentiment which, in the first half of the eighteenth century, Europeans already recognized as one of the distinctive characteristics of American society.

4. NOT ALL COLONIALS WERE ENGLISHMEN

It is a cliché to say that all Americans are descendants of immigrants; the truly striking thing about the American population is its ethnic diversity. This diversity began in the eighteenth century. Prior to the last decade of the seventeenth century, the vast majority of those who came to America—with the exception, of course, of the Dutch living in New York and the small colonies of Swedes and Finns in the Delaware River region—were of English stock.

Toward the end of the seventeenth century, however, a trickle of non-English nationalities, impelled by the hard times in their homelands, encouraged by the English authorities, and drawn by the magnet of American economic opportunity, began to come into the colonies. The signs of this movement are still upon the land. Occasional town names like New Rochelle and New Paltz in New York and New Bordeaux in South Carolina, as well as well-known family names like Revere, Ravenal, Legaré, Faneuil, Jay, and De Lancey, still bear witness to the French Huguenots who came in the years after the revocation of the Edict of Nantes in 1685. New Bern in North Carolina and Swedesboro and Finns Point in New Jersey are memorials of other tiny groups of continental Europeans who settled in the English colonies. The exquisite eighteenth-century synagogue built by Peter Harrison in Newport and the still extant Portuguese cemetery in New York recall the small but thriving Spanish and Portuguese Jewish communities of the colonial era, just as ancient Sephardic names like Cardoza, Lopez, and de Sola Pool still remind us of their continuing influence.

The great influx of non-English immigration came in the eighteenth century with the Scots, Scots-Irish, and Germans. The latter two groups arrived in large numbers in the opening decades of the century, while the Scots were most prominent after 1750. Unlike the two larger contingents, the Scots were especially noticeable in trade. Virginia planters in the 1750's and 1760's filled their letters with complaints against the Scottish factors to whom they sold their tobacco and from whom they bought European manufactures. By the time of the Revolution, Scottish immigration was well in excess of 25,000 for the century. Surprisingly enough, considering their agelong struggle against the English, the Scots in America proved to be stanch supporters of the Crown at the time of the Revolution. However, two of the best-known patriots, James Wilson of Pennsylvania and John Witherspoon, president of the College of New Jersey and a signer of the Declaration, were both born and bred in Scotland.

The Scots-Irish came from Ireland, but, unlike the later Irish, they were overwhelmingly Protestant—Presbyterians from the counties of the north. Their ancestors had been transplanted from their native Scotland in the early years of the seventeenth century by James I in an effort to secure the Emerald Isle for Protestantism. In place names like Ulster and Orange counties (New York), Orange (New Jersey), and Donegal (Pennsylvania), the Irish origins of the first settlers are still in evidence. But the importance of the Scots-Irish in America far exceeded the few towns and counties to which they gave names reminiscent of their European origins.

Pennsylvania west of the Susquehanna was thickly seeded with
Protestant Irish; so was the Great Valley in Virginia and the
Carolina piedmont. Seeming to strike for the westernmost frontier as
a plant pushes toward the sun, these hardy, God-fearing Calvinists
made themselves into a veritable human shield of colonial civilization.
With one hand, as it were, they battled the irate landlords on whose
lands they unceremoniously squatted, while with the other they
killed Indians and pushed back the forest. From the loins of this
people have sprung some of the most eminent names in American
political history: Andrew Jackson, John C. Calhoun, James K.
Polk, and the greatest covenanter of them all, Woodrow Wilson.

While the spirited Scots-Irish were war-whooping it on the
frontier, the less dramatic but numerous Germans were also spreading through the English colonies. Their line of settlement can be
followed in the Germanic town names: Rhinebeck and Newburgh,
New York: Germantown, Pennsylvania; German Valley, New
Jersey; Hagerstown and Fredericktown, Maryland; Strasburg,
Harpers Ferry and Germantown, Virginia; Mecklenburg, North
Carolina; Orangeburg and Saxe-Gotha, South Carolina. The
greatest concentration of Germans, of course, was in southeastern
Pennsylvania, where the so-called Pennsylvania Dutch still offer
visible testimony to the migration.

The Germans were so numerous in Pennsylvania in the middle of
the eighteenth century that Franklin doubted they would ever fit
into the life of an English colony. "Why should the Palatine boors
be suffered to swarm into our settlements, and, by herding together,
establish their language and manners, to the exclusion of ours?" he
asked in 1751. Their numbers—they constituted about a third of
the population of the province—caused him to wonder why "Pennsylvania, founded by the English," should "become a colony of
aliens, who will shortly be so numerous as to Germanize us, instead
of our Anglifying them? . . ." In Franklin's irritation are the first
signs of a recurring anxiety in the history of immigration to
America—the native-born's fear of the growing number of strangers
in his midst. Nativism, along with diversified immigration, began
in the eighteenth century.

If the Germans constituted one great block of people in America
who did not speak the language of England, the Dutch in New York
were another. Almost ninety years after the English took over in
New Amsterdam, Peter Kalm the Swedish traveler, visiting Albany,

reported that although all the citizenry dressed like Englishmen, "rarely is an English word heard." About the same time, in 1743, Dr. Alexander Hamilton (no relative of the later Secretary of the Treasury) took a trip up the Hudson from New York to Albany and found that the large numbers of Dutch-speaking people on board ship almost precluded his finding a companion.

The diversity of language and custom in the colonies was held responsible by one British official for the intractable spirit of the Americans under English rule. Comptroller Weare wrote in 1760 that it was not surprising there were so many controversies between the officials of the Crown and the colonials "considering how many of the subjects of alien states are settled here, without that reverence for British government, or partiality to British interest which can be derived only from education. . . ." Because they tend to settle in their own national communities, Weare continued, "one sees and hears the religions, languages and manners of Germany, spoken and professed in the British plantations by subjects born under British government."

Thanks to the massive influx of immigrants from non-English countries, the ethnic character of the colonies was markedly altered in the course of the four or five decades before the Revolution. It has been calculated that by 1776 as much as one half and perhaps more of the population was of non-English origin. This represented more than just the beginning of a long history of diverse immigration into America; it marked the establishment of an ethnic pattern which then, as now, has set America off from England and other European countries.

As Comptroller Weare implied, this first great wave of European —as distinguished from English—immigration added to the diversity of American life in still another fashion. Each of these new peoples brought a new religion with them. It is to the Scots and Scots-Irish that Presbyterians owe their numerical importance in early America; it was through the Germans that a host of sects were introduced into America—Moravians, Lutherans, Mennonites, Amish, Schwenkfelders, and Dunkers. Though most of the French who came to America were Protestants fleeing the bigotry of Louis XIV, some were Catholics, and the bishops of the Roman Church in early America were sometimes French.

By the middle of the eighteenth century, religious diversity was already recognized as peculiarly American. To an unsympathetic visitor like Gottlieb Mittelberger, Pennsylvania in 1750 was simply a chaos of religious sects, "which cannot all be enumerated." James Reed, a missionary of the Anglican Society for the Propagation of the Gospel in North Carolina, wrote to London in 1760 that he was astounded by the "great number of dissenters of all denominations . . . particularly Anabaptists, Methodists, Quakers and Presbyterians." For a European this spectrum of religions and the numerical weakness of the Established Church were new experiences and, then as now, they served to differentiate American civilization from European.

During the eighteenth century, religion in America underwent another change which carried implications for the future. Actually, the change was twofold and, in a sense, paradoxical. One aspect of this dual change was the decided trend toward secularization, toward the playing down of the place of religion and the Church in the lives of the people. The most obvious form of this alteration was the decline of Puritanism in New England, but the growing lack of interest in religion was wider than that. Though Mittelberger was shocked at the diversity of sects in Pennsylvania, he was thoroughly horrified by the irreligion of many of the people. There are "many hundreds of adult persons," he wrote, "who have not been and do not even wish to be baptized. . . . Many do not even believe that there is a true God and Devil, a Heaven and a hell, salvation and damnation, a resurrection of the dead, a judgment and an eternal life; they believe that all one can see is natural."

In the back country of the Carolinas in the 1760's, earnest Charles Woodmason, an itinerant Anglican preacher, plodded many a weary mile looking for settlers willing to hear the word of Christ. After preaching one day to a hundred people, he reported that not a single person stepped forward to accept his offer to baptize children. "Do not find but one religious person among this Great Multitude," he wrote. The unconcern of these backwoods people for conventional church morality was implicit in one of his journal entries: "Married a couple—for the 1st Time—Woman very bigg."

By the time of the Revolution, actual church attendance probably touched the lowest point it has ever reached in American history. Dean Stokes has estimated that at the end of the colonial period there was only one church for each 900 persons in the United States; in 1939, the Federal Council of Churches found the ratio to be one to 500.

Though it is accurate to see a contraction in the popular influence of the Church during the last years of the colonial period, it should not be assumed that the intensity of religious interest fell off. Indeed, it might be said that just the opposite occurred: while the number of churchgoing people declined, the religious feelings of those who remained with the Church were actually intensified. This revitalization of the religious spirit and churches in the eighteenth century is the Great Awakening. As its name implies, the Great Awakening was a rebirth of emotion in religion; sometimes the emotion bordered on hysteria or uncontrolled ecstasy, but in general it was a recognition that religion was an emotional as well as an intellectual experience. This elementary fact had often been forgotten in the late seventeenth century as religion became increasingly rigid in its dogma, ritual, and message; the Great Awakening was a direct challenge, as it was a response, to the dry, formal, and heavily intellectual religion of the earlier period. Like a pillar of fire this rebirth of emotional intensity in religion swept through church after church from New England to Georgia in the 1740's and 1750's, its progress and heat stimulated by the impassioned evangelical preaching of men like George Whitefield, Theodore Frelinghuysen, Jonathan Edwards, and, somewhat later, John Wesley. The sermons of such preachers, by skillfully blending hell-fire and damnation oratory with a wide knowledge of Biblical literature, fired the hearts and seared the souls of those who came within listening distance.

One farmer in Middletown, Connecticut, in 1740 has left an account of what it meant to him. Farmer Nathan Cole had anxiously awaited word of the great Whitefield's coming to town. When news came that the evangelist had finally come to Middletown, Cole dropped his work, grabbed his horse and wife, and with scarcely a breath to spare raced the thirteen miles to town. There the Coles were engulfed in a crowd of several thousand equally eager farmers literally panting (from their exertions) to hear the melancholy diagnosis of the state of their souls which Whitefield was sure to make. Whitefield did not disappoint Nathan Cole, for "he looked as if he was clothed with authority from the Great God, and a sweet solemnity sat upon his brow, and my hearing him preach gave me a heart wound." Since the purpose of the evangelist was to awaken in his hearers a consciousness of sin, Whitefield achieved his purpose within Nathan Cole. "By God's blessing," Cole admitted afterward, "my old foundation was broken up, and I saw that my righteousness would not save me."

Even canny, unemotional Benjamin Franklin was not secure against Whitefield's preaching. In his *Autobiography* he tells of attending a sermon delivered by Whitefield in behalf of an orphanage in Georgia, a project of which Franklin disapproved. Because of his objections, even though he knew Whitefield would be asking for money, Franklin resolved not to contribute a copper penny. But as Whitefield "proceeded I began to soften, and concluded to give the coppers. Another stroke of his oratory made me asham'd of that, and determin'd me to give the silver; and he finished so admirably, that I empty'd my pocket wholly into the collector's dish, gold and all."

Churches were split asunder by the conflict between the new "enthusiastic" approach to religion and the staid and more thoughtful forms which had been once so characteristic of colonial Protestantism. To some old-timers, emotionalism in religion was anti-intellectual, a reversion to the sectarian chaos of the early Reformation. To the "new-lights," as they were called, the injection of feeling and emotion into religion was to revivify what had been lifeless, dull, and essentially without meaning. As Whitefield said, "How can dead Men beget living children?" Though for a while extremists on both sides seemed incapable of working out a synthesis of the two views, gradually the new view began to prevail. Religion in America lost the theological and formal cast so characteristic of the seventeenth century and regained an emotional significance for the individual reminiscent of the early Church and the Reformation. Furthermore, in the years after the middle of the century, new sects like Baptists and Methodists, because of active participation in the new movement, expanded their membership. Thus the once despised "enthusiastic" sects, as the seventeenth-century Puritans called them, took their places as major churches in America.

The Great Awakening was only the first of several great religious revivals which would wash over large areas of rural America from time to time. As a result of these periodic waves of religious emotionalism, Christian ideals and a strong moral sense were freshened and refreshened in the minds of Americans, never to be completely effaced even in the dark years of deistic questioning in the eighteenth century or of materialistic cynicism in the nineteenth. Puritanism certainly bequeathed to later generations, as we have seen, a penchant for moralism which is typically, if sometimes unfortunately, American, but the dissemination of this among the masses down through the years is as much the work of the revivals as it is of the original Puritans.

5. A PARADISE FOR WOMEN

Women in America, commented an Austrian traveler in the 1870's, are surrounded "with privileges and attentions unknown in the Old World." European wives of returning American soldiers after World War II often made the same observations upon their arrival in the United States. The origins of this special place for women in America are buried deep in the colonial era.

If the empty land of the New World acted as a magnet for the land-hungry, it was also a barrier to the delicate. Because of the hardships inherent in the settling of a wilderness, men tended to predominate over women among the passengers on the immigrant ships of the seventeenth and eighteenth centuries. For example, in a group of 10,000 indentured servants who left Bristol, England, between 1654 and 1686, there were 338 males for every 100 women. A Maryland census as late as 1755 showed that the sex ratio for whites was 113 males to every 100 females. The ratio in South Carolina in 1708 was 148 males to 100 females. Indeed, all through the colonial period, except in New England in the eighteenth century, the excess of males in America is an inescapable demographic fact. The sexes had not always been in balance in Europe, but rarely if ever had there been excesses of men. Wars, the daily occupational dangers to which men were exposed, and the weaker survival power of males biologically had combined to keep women more numerous than men. In colonial America, these social and biological forces could not operate fully since the population was heavily augmented by immigration and the rigors of the primitive life tended to keep the number of women immigrants considerably below the men. In this difference in sex ratios in Europe and America are the beginnings, at least, of the differing attitudes toward women in the old country and the new. Simply put, women in America commanded influence and prestige because they were scarce.

That the position of the colonial woman was better than that of her European sister all visitors recognized. Gottlieb Mittelberger, who was no admirer of America, commented in 1750 on the fact that "the women enjoy . . . great liberties and privileges" in Pennsylvania. He told of a servant girl who had been made pregnant by her master, but had succeeded in compelling him to marry her. The court, much to Mittelberger's surprise, took the side of the girl against her superior by offering the master the choice of marriage or a heavy fine. The German traveler was further impressed by the knowledge that in Philadelphia the "English servant women" were "as elegantly dressed as an aristocratic lady in Germany." Englishman Nicholas Cresswell dryly observed that America was a paradise for women because the chances for marriage were so good. Though on the frontier women undoubtedly worked as hard or harder than most urban women in Europe, the poorer women in America were usually much better off than their counterparts in the old country. Usually they did less outdoor work—even female indentured servants in Virginia were not expected to work in the fields—and, as Mittelberger observed, they dressed better than European women. From the beginning, the social freedom of young women, which is still in marked contrast with European custom today, was evident in America. Chaperons were too delicate a refinement for the frontier and were not taken seriously in the cities. Indeed, just because the country was raw and undeveloped, women were clothed in new importance. The wife and mother in the rude settlement on or near the frontier was more than a housekeeper; she was an indispensable part of the apparatus of survival. Since the whole family was dependent upon her for a score of necessities like clothes, spices, soap, candles, lard, vegetables, medicines, and perhaps even protection when the husband was absent, a woman was a person of value.

Even in the cities, the scarcity of labor gave an advantage to women in America; there were more jobs for women outside the home.[3] In 1733 the New York *Weekly Journal* carried an advertise-

[3] One must not, of course, overemphasize the opportunities for women to work in the colonial period. Professions like medicine, the ministry, the law, were totally closed to them; most crafts were also; even teaching, which later was to become the mainstay of female professional employment, was largely in the hands of men, though a few women did run the so-called dame's schools. Mrs. Spruill, in her study of *Women's Life and Work in the Southern Colonies* (Chapel Hill, 1938), pp. 241–42, writes that "the eighteenth century saw a decline in the vigor and self-reliance of women in wealthier families and a lessening of their influence in public matters. Because of the rural character of their lives and the general influence of the frontier, American ladies were less idle and artificial than those of England, but compared with the daring and independent matrons of the preceding century, they appear somewhat effeminate and timid."

ment which told in a few words both the stuff of which some women in colonial America were made and the fact that they were economically important. "We, the widdows of this city," it read, protest the failure to invite us to "court." "We are House Keepers, Pay our Taxes, carry on Trade, and most of us are she Merchants. . . . We have the Vanity to think we can be full as Entertaining, and make as brave a Defense in Case of Invasion and perhaps not turn Taile as soon as" some of the men. On the basis of an admittedly small sample, but one nevertheless suggestive, one authority has computed that there were proportionately more "she merchants" in the 1770's in America than in 1900. Enough records from the colonial period still survive to show that it was not an uncommon event for a widow to take over the business of her deceased husband. This was especially true of taverns, boarding houses, and shops not requiring a skilled craftsman.

Nor was it unknown for women to act for their husbands, not only in an economic or business capacity, but in a legal one as well. Many women exercised power of attorney for their spouses and were sole executrices of estates. The most renowned example of the latter is Margaret Brent of Maryland, who in 1647 acted as the sole executor of Governor Leonard Calvert's substantial estate. As all this suggests, in the eyes of colonial law the rights of women were a decided cut above those accorded to the sex under the common law of England. Women, for example, whether married or not, sued and were sued in colonial courts.

There were significant differences in the legal rights of married women in America and England. The conception of marriage in Richardson's *Pamela*—that it was a "kind of state of humiliation for women"—may have been true of eighteenth-century England, Richard Morris has commented, but "it would not be applicable to the American colonies." The American environment, for one reason or another, produced important changes in the rights of women. For example, though the common law of England took no notice of a woman's right to her property once she was married, by the end of the colonial period it was rather well established in America that a woman's property could be disposed of by her husband only with her consent and acknowledgment.[4] Under the common law of Eng-

[4] On the other hand, it should be said, women were not able to control their property completely. Husbands, for instance, frequently sued for the value of their working wives' services and collected. Richard B. Morris, *Studies in the*

land married women retained no capacity to make contracts, a disability which followed from their being incompetent to hold property. In the colonies, however, because married women did possess property rights, the law granted them contractual capacity as well. As a result, wives often transacted business for their husbands when the latter were absent.

On occasion the colonial law seemed to overstretch itself to grant rights to the wife to protect her against her husband—an approach to the conjugal relationship which neither the English common law nor its noted expositor, Blackstone, would have countenanced. The common law, for instance, working on the assumption that "their Interests are absolutely the same," would not permit a wife to testify against her husband. In some colonial courts, on the other hand, such testimony was permitted in both civil and criminal proceedings. Instances are known, moreover, where colonial courts and legislatures sought to protect widows whose husbands had not treated them properly in wills. Thus in 1714 a New Hampshire statute provided that where a husband's will proved to work an injury upon the wife, the widow should receive such proportion of her husband's estate "as if he had dyed intestate."

The superior position of women in colonial America derives from a number of circumstances. Certainly, the fact that English women enjoyed more freedom than those on the Continent has something to do with it. But it would seem that the more compelling reasons arose out of the American environment: the greater number of men than women, and the demands and opportunities of a frontier society. Taken together, these circumstances could not help but enhance the value of women in the eyes of men and hence in the view of society at large.

6. AMERICANS HAVE NEW RIGHTS

"It is . . . to England that we owe this elevated rank we possess," remarked Crèvecoeur, "these noble appellations of freemen, freeholders, citizens; yes it is to that wise people we owe our freedom. Had we been planted by some great monarchy, we should have been

History of American Law (New York, 1930), p. 126, notes that the institution of marriage in America was strongly influenced, through the Calvinist sects, by the continental and Radical Protestant tradition which taught that marriage was a contract and not a sacrament of the Church. As a consequence, "the notion of mutuability in the civil marriage lay at the root of the substantial advance in the position of the wife in seventeenth century American law."

mean slaves of some distant monarch." It was for sound historical reasons that during the Revolutionary crisis the colonials stoutly asserted their claims to the "rights of Englishmen." Yet despite the English substance at the core of the colonial political forms, the colonists were departing from the example of the mother country. Frequently these deviations were merely novel twists given to English institutions; sometimes they were new institutions called into being by the new conditions in America. But whatever the nature of the changes, by the middle of the eighteenth century the forsaking of English practices was in evidence and the American constitutional system of the future was visible.

A common political vocabulary can certainly serve to bind together a colony and a mother country. But when the meaning behind the words is different, then the stage is set for misunderstanding, recrimination, and conflict. The North and the South during the 1850's found themselves in this dangerous position; the colonists and the English in the years immediately preceding the American Revolution also fell into this predicament. Steeped as they were in the English political language, the colonials spoke in what they thought was the common intellectual coin of the Empire, neglecting to observe that the American experience had given the words a content quite different from that accepted by the Englishmen with whom they debated. That Americans and Britons were saying different things when they employed the same words did not become apparent until after 1765, but the actual differences in political and constitutional practices of the two peoples were there long before the Stamp Act.

It is true, of course, as Crèvecoeur implied, that in many respects the political institutions of England were reproduced in close detail in the colonies. By the middle of the eighteenth century, for instance, all of the mainland colonies except four were headed by a Royal Governor, appointed by the King and therefore bearing a relation to the people of the colony similar to that of the King to the British people. Moreover, each of the thirteen colonies enjoyed a representative assembly, which was consciously modeled, in powers and practices, after the British Parliament. The resemblance to the English example was carried still further in the division of the colonial assemblies into upper and lower houses in emulation of the House of Commons and the House of Lords. In both England and the colonies, furthermore, the suffrage was exercised only by property holders; in all the colonies, as in England, it was an axiom, as an act of South Carolina put it in 1716, that "none but such persons who have an interest in this Province shall be capable to elect or be elected."

Though in the letter the English and colonial constitutions were similar, in the spirit they were moving in different directions. For example, English constitutional development from the earliest years of the seventeenth century had been sometimes drifting, sometimes driving, but always moving in pursuit of the absolute power of Parliament. The most unmistakable sign of this tendency was the assertion that the King was under the law, as exemplified in the Petition of Right in 1628, the judgment and execution of Charles I in 1649, and finally the *de facto* deposition of James II in 1689. Together with this resolute denial of the divine right of kings went the assertion that Parliament was unlimited in its power; that it could change even the Constitution by its ordinary acts of legislation, just as it had created the Constitution by its past acts. By the eighteenth century, as today, the British accepted the idea that the representatives of the people were omnipotent; that, as the aphorism has it, "Parliament can do anything except change a man into a woman and a woman into a man."

The colonials did not look upon the English Parliament with such fond eyes, nor—equally important for the future—did they concede that their own assemblies possessed such wide powers. There were good historical reasons for this. Though to the English the word "Constitution" meant nothing more nor less than the whole body of law and custom from the beginning of the kingdom, to the colonials it meant a written document, enumerating specific powers. This distinction in meaning is to be traced to the fact that the foundations of government in the various colonies were written charters granted by the Crown. These express authorizations to govern were tangible, definite things. Over the years the colonials had often repaired to the timeless phrases and sonorous periods in their charters to justify themselves in the struggle against rapacious Governors or tyrannical officials of the Crown. More than a century of government under *written* constitutions convinced the colonists of the necessity for and efficacy of protecting their liberties against government encroachment by explicitly defining all governmental powers in a document.

Even before the Stamp Act was passed, James Otis of Massachu--

setts articulated the striking difference between the colonial and British conceptions of Parliamentary power and the nature of constitutions. "To say the Parliament is absolute and arbitrary is a contradiction," he asserted. Parliament cannot alter the supreme law of the nation because "the Constitution is fixed; and . . . the supreme legislative . . . cannot overlap the Bounds of it without destroying its own foundation." Here, long before the Revolution, was a succinct expression of what was to become the cardinal principle of American constitutionalism, clearly setting it off from the English in both practice and theory.

It is worth emphasizing that it was English practice which was moving away from colonial. Earlier in the seventeenth century, in the minds of jurists like Sir Edward Coke, Otis's arguments would have carried much weight, but now the mutability of the Constitution was widely accepted in England. The colonials in the middle of the eighteenth century, as we shall have occasion to notice during the Revolutionary crisis, were following the old-fashioned and more conservative line.

There was another way in which English and colonial constitutional developments were drifting apart. The intimate relation between the executive and Parliament, so characteristic of English and continental democracies today, was already taking shape in the middle of the eighteenth century. The executive was the cabinet of ministers, who were drawn from the Parliament itself; as a result there was no separation of powers, the executive and legislative branches being merely different manifestations of the same body. This development, however, did not take place in America. The existence, for one thing, of a royally appointed Governor made such a development impossible; he could not be readily supplanted by a cabinet or ministerial council. Moreover, by having written constitutions or charters, the colonies were limited to the forms provided in earlier days. Under such circumstances it is not surprising that the colonial leaders entirely overlooked what was happening in England. From their distance they remained convinced that the King—like their own Royal Governors—was the real executive. Thus, because of the peculiarly American experience, the colonists were committed to a conception of government quite at variance with the English.

An important corollary to the English doctrine of parliamentary absolutism was the assumption that the colonies were subject to the legislative power of that body. For most of the seventeenth century the doctrine was no more than an assumption, and so the colonies did not feel it. This was partly because parliamentary supremacy was achieved late in the century—in 1689—and partly because the British government, embroiled in successive wars with Holland and France, did not seek to test its authority with the colonies.

This practice of "salutary neglect," as Burke named it, provided a long period during which the colonies developed self-reliance and their own ideas of government. The representative assembly in each of the provinces was widely viewed as the focus of government, peculiarly American, and constitutionally competent for all internal legislative purposes. The sole political tie of any consequence between the colonies and England was through the Royal Governor, and in four of the thirteen provinces there was not even this connection. It was to be expected, therefore, that the colonies should grow to think of their little assemblies as bearing the same relation to the Crown as the Parliament of Great Britain. Such a conception of colonial equality with England, however, ran counter not only to the strong current of parliamentary absolutism we have already noticed; it also flew in the face of a growing movement to centralize the government of the Empire in London.

There is irony in the growing divergence between England and the colonies regarding the power of representative assemblies. No institution introduced into the New World was probably more English than the representative assembly; yet it was this very political form, transformed by the American experience, which, more than anything else, served to bring about a break between the colonies and the Mother of Parliaments.

With the franchise, as with the parliamentary power, the colonists took a typically English institution and remade it into a wedge which drove the two peoples apart. Though both England and the colonies based the franchise on property holding, in the mother country this practice produced a small electorate. In America, however, the same requirement resulted in a quite different effect. Since property was widely distributed, even the use of property qualifications identical with those in England resulted in the colonies in a large electorate, occasionally even approaching universal manhood suffrage. The studies of Robert Brown in the history of colonial Massachusetts, for example, have made it clear that in both provincial and town elections well over a majority of men—perhaps 80 per cent—could vote. When Thomas Hutchinson was defeated in Boston in

1749 he said of the 200 votes he received: "they were the principal inhabitants, but you know we are governed not by weight but by numbers." At another time Hutchinson remarked with obvious distaste: "The town of Boston is an absolute democracy. . . ." Even allowing for some exaggeration on the part of a defeated politician, these statements of a contemporary indicate that large numbers of men could vote in colonial Massachusetts.

Though some of the other colonies probably could not boast as wide a franchise as Massachusetts or other New England provinces, the franchise in the eighteenth century in all the colonies was considerably wider than is often supposed.[5] Richard McCormick, for example, has shown that in New Jersey the property qualifications were quite easy for the great majority of the adult males to meet. Indeed, he has uncovered instances where the regulations at the polls were so lax that women, boys, and even Negroes voted. In Pennsylvania, Albert McKinley has estimated, at least one half of the males in a farming area outside Philadelphia could vote, though the figure would be lower in the city itself. The same authority has calculated that almost 9 per cent of the white population of Virginia actually voted, though the number eligible may have been greater. For comparison purposes it might be observed that in 1880—at a Presidential election in an era of universal manhood suffrage—only 17 per cent of the population cast ballots. The tax lists in New York City in 1761 disclose that about 10 per cent of the population were voters in that city. In 1759 in South Carolina and 1762 in Virginia the property qualifications for voting were cut and the franchise presumably widened. The leading authority on the colonial franchise has concluded that in South Carolina one "is impressed by the breadth of the suffrage in a community which possessed so many features of economic democracy. Frequently popular elections both in church and state were open to the freeholders and taxpayers of

[5] Contrary to the usual belief that the political rights of the common man have been steadily improving through the years, it should be pointed out that the franchise in the seventeenth-century colonies was generally wider than in the eighteenth. In the early years of the Virginia colony, for example, except for Negroes, virtually universal manhood suffrage prevailed. Down to 1716, voters in South Carolina were required to possess only £10 in property at a time when a house and a few farm animals would easily surpass this value. As late as 1715 any white male who paid taxes could vote in North Carolina. Before 1702, £20 in property granted the vote to a resident of Connecticut. During the seventeenth century all freemen—a rank awarded to all who applied—possessed the franchise in Rhode Island.

the colony upon a comparatively broad basis." Furthermore, unlike
Virginians and other colonists, South Carolina voters also enjoyed
the democratic device of the secret ballot. In short, the forms of
political democracy were already beginning to appear in the colonial
period.

To many observers it seemed that the spirit of democracy or republicanism was also evident in the colonies, thereby setting the
colonials further apart from the English. "The New England Governments are all formed on Republican Principles and those Principles are zealously inculcated in the Minds of their Youth in
opposition to the Principles of the Constitution of Great Britain,"
complained Cadwallader Colden to the Board of Trade in 1763.
Comptroller Weare, in offering advice on the keeping of the colonies
in due subordination, argued in 1760 that even in the royal colonies,
where the King appointed the Governor and the Council, "the
authority of the Crown is not sufficiently supported against the
licentiousness of a republican spirit in the people, whose extreme
jealousy of any power not immediately derived from themselves,"
and whose lack of true affection for England "dispose them generally to send as representatives the most artful and factious amongst
them."

Already in the colonial period the ordinary citizen participated
in government to an extent far beyond anything in contemporary
England. As we have seen, Europeans and Americans alike conceived
of colonial politics as essentially popular and quite different from
English in this regard. It is also apparent that in this strong tendency toward political democracy in the colonies lay the genesis of
the movement for universal manhood suffrage, which was to be
characteristic of the United States in the nineteenth century.

It is somewhat paradoxical that the United States, with a long
tradition of universal suffrage, also has an equally strong tradition
of an appointed Supreme Court charged with the responsibility of
passing upon the constitutionality of legislation enacted by the
elected representatives of the people. This peculiarly American doctrine of judicial review has its roots in the colonial period. In one
sense, of course, the power of the courts to declare a piece of legislation null and void when it conflicts with the Constitution is de-
ducible, as Chief Justice Marshall pointed out in *Marbury* v.
Madison, from the conception of a written Constitution. It stems
from the belief, widely held in the colonies, that no legislative or

executive power could extend beyond the authority set forth in the charter or Constitution. As James Otis phrased it in 1761, "An Act against the Constitution is void."

But there was another colonial source from which the uniquely American doctrine of judicial review of legislation was drawn. All through the eighteenth century the Privy Council in England acted as a final court of appeals for the colonies. Early in that century, in 1728, in the case of *Winthrop* v. *Lechmere* the Council declared an act of Connecticut contrary to the law of England and therefore null and void.[6] This case and two subsequent ones in 1738 and 1745 make it clear that the Privy Council was serving as a court for reviewing colonial legislation in the light of the "higher law" of the English Constitution. From start to finish the procedure in these cases was judicial and therefore an exact precedent for the later American procedure of judicial review, which is also exclusively judicial. It might not be too farfetched to perceive in this central court of the Privy Council the germ of the later United States Supreme Court. Both the eighteenth-century English and nineteenth-century American tribunals sought to bring a variety of local legal systems into conformity with a larger constitutional framework, yet neither aimed to destroy the individual provincial or state jurisdictions.

Related to both the political and constitutional innovations of the colonials was their defense of freedom of the press against the arbitrary power of government. The trial of John Peter Zenger in New York in 1735 is justly considered a landmark in the history of freedom. Under the English and colonial law of that time, the sole responsibility of a jury in a trial for seditious libel was to determine whether the accused had in fact written the alleged libel. Whether the material was in fact libelous was left up to the judge to decide. Since, in Zenger's case, Judge De Lancey was a creature of the Governor against whom the alleged libel was directed, the results of the trial seemed a foregone conclusion. This high probability was

---

[6] It is of interest here that this decision was itself evoked by the differences between colonial and English legal practices. The case revolved around the fact that Connecticut, in common with other New England colonies, did not practice primogeniture. Because partible inheritance was contrary to the English common law, the Privy Council declared null and void a Connecticut statute which assumed there was no primogeniture. Though for a while it seemed that the decision would overturn hundreds of land titles in the colony, the Council modified its position in a subsequent case, *Clark* v. *Toucey,* and the matter was not pressed in the colonies by the Crown.

further enhanced when Zenger and his attorneys announced that they conceded Zenger's responsibility for writing and printing the article in question.

The drama and long-range significance of the case, however, turns upon the action of Andrew Hamilton, who assumed the leadership of the defense. Contending that the truth of Zenger's charges was the crux of the case, Hamilton argued that a press, unfettered by official control, was indispensable in a society claiming to be free. Truth, he said, was a legitimate, nay, a necessary defense in a libel suit. Almost casually he conceded Zenger's authorship of the offending piece. But then he turned to the jury and, in a masterful presentation, urged upon the jurors a new course. Disregarding the law and appealing to their love of liberty, Hamilton challenged the jurors to decide the larger question of whether the charges Zenger levied against the Governor were true or not. If they were, Hamilton advised, then the jury should acquit the printer. Despite its sure knowledge that it was affronting a powerful and partisan judge, the jury nobly matched Hamilton's boldness and found Zenger not guilty.

It is true that censorship of the press, and even trials for libel in which truth was not accepted as a defense, occurred after the Zenger case. But there were no more trials for seditious libel in New York for the rest of the colonial period. Moreover, the trial and its outcome produced repercussions in England. Radicals and Whigs, won over by the brilliant colonial innovation in behalf of a free press, began a campaign in support of American liberty which was to reach its full power at the time of the Revolution in the voices of Burke, Fox, John Wilkes, Dr. Price, and Colonel Barré.

Implementation of the principles of the Zenger trial was quicker in America than in England. For example, most of the states after the Revolution, though, curiously enough, not New York, included guarantees of freedom of the press in their constitutions. The principle that truth was a defense in a libel suit was established in New York law in the case of Henry Croswell in 1802 through the joint efforts of Alexander Hamilton and James Kent. The doctrine was reinforced by legislative act in 1805 and inserted, for good measure, in the state constitutions of 1821 and 1846. It was not until 1791, however, with Fox's Act, that English juries were granted the right to determine whether the writing in question was libelous or not, and it was not until 1843 that truth was accepted as a defense in a libel suit under English law.

7. "ALL OF US AMERICANS"

In the course of the Zenger trial Andrew Hamilton had chided the attorney general for his constant citing of English precedent. "What strange doctrine is it to press everything for law here which is so in England," the clever Philadelphian exclaimed. Hamilton knew full well that the law of England prevailed in the colonies, but he was playing upon the colonials' growing pride of country.

In the years after 1740 the colonials became increasingly conscious of themselves as Americans. To be sure, there were very few outright demands for independence. It would take a good number of years, during which a consciousness of kind was only dawning, before the idea of independence would be thought of, much less advocated. Nevertheless, for two decades or more before the Revolutionary crisis of the late 1760's, Americans were expressing the feeling that they were different from Europeans, that they had a destiny of their own.

Ironically enough, the most obvious manifestations of this budding sense of Americanism appear in the course of the wars with France in the 1740's and 1750's, when colonials fought side by side with the English. During most of the century-long struggle against France in the seventeenth and eighteenth centuries, Britain had not demanded that the American colonies contribute anything more than the defense of their home areas and perhaps an occasional foray into adjacent French-held Canada. But beginning with the so-called War of Jenkins' Ear in 1739, which was first waged against Spain and then (as King George's War) against France, Britain stepped up her expectations of colonial military support. In 1741 the home government succeeded in goading the colonials to assist in the mounting of an offensive against Cartagena, the great port of the Spanish Main.

In part because the enterprise was a colossal fiasco, but largely because American and European soldiers were thrown together under novel circumstances, the differences between Americans and Europeans were sharply illuminated for both sides. Admiral Vernon, the British commander of the expedition, for example, consistently referred to the colonials as "Americans." The colonials, in turn, referred to their supposed blood brothers, the English, as "Euro-

peans." The words, of course, had been used before, but never so
generally or consistently as at this time. The failure of the Cartagena expedition added its bit to the splitting apart of the two national groups. The Americans came away convinced that the English
were callous and cruel in their treatment of colonials, and the
English soldiery and officers were disgusted with what they stigmatized as the cowardice and ineffectiveness of the colonial soldier.

When the New Englanders under Sir William Pepperell succeeded
in capturing the French fortress at Louisbourg in the St. Lawrence
in 1745, the colonials' incipient pride of country burst forth. To
some it seemed to prove, as one bit of doggerel put it, that in valor

> . . . the British Breed
> In Western Climes their Grandsires far exceed
> and that New England Schemes the Old Surpass,
>   As much as Gold does tinkling Brass;
>   And that a Pepp'rell's and a Warren's Name,
>   May vie with Marlb'rough and a Blake for Fame.

With the fall of Quebec in 1759, there was loosed a flood of prophecies that the star of American destiny was in the ascendant. "A
new world has arisen," exulted the *New American Magazine*, "and
will exceed the old!" It is noteworthy, considering its nationalistic
name, that the magazine was then in its first year of publication.

Meanwhile a developing American nationality was evident—perhaps less spectacularly, but nonetheless profoundly—in other ways.
Under the influences of distance and the new environment, the
mother tongue of the colonists was undergoing change. New words
from the Dutch and Indian languages, for example, were constantly
being added to the speech of the English in America; words like
"boss," "stoop," "cruller," "crib," "scow," and "spook" came from
the Dutch. The Indian names were all over the land, and they made
America exotic for Englishmen as they still do for Europeans.

Americans also made up words, some of which reflected the new
environment. "Back country" and "backwoods" were designed to
describe the novelty of the frontier. Bullfrog, canvasback, lightning
bug, razorback, groundhog, potato bug, peanut, and eggplant are
similar colonial name tags for new natural phenomena.

Familiar English words sometimes assumed new meanings in
America. "Lumber" in eighteenth-century England meant unused
furniture, but in the colonies it was applied to the raw wood—and

so it has remained. "Pie" in England, to this day, means a meat pie, but in the colonies that was a "potpie"; "pie" was reserved for fruit pastry. Dry goods in England included all nonliquids, like corn or wheat; the colonials, however, changed the meaning to textiles only. The same alteration took place with the word "rock," which in England denoted a large mass; in America as early as 1712 it was being applied to a stone of any size. "Pond" was an English word meaning an artificial pool, but in unkempt America it came to mean any small lake. Certain words obviously attached to the English environment were lost in America, where their referents did not exist: fen, heath, moor, wold, bracken, and downs. It is not to be wondered, therefore, that in 1756 lexicographer Samuel Johnson was talking of an American dialect.

The burgeoning sense of Americanism was reflected also in the colonials' image of themselves. When Eliza Pinckney of South Carolina was presented at King George's Court in 1750, she insisted upon being introduced as an "American." That same year an advertisement in a Boston paper advertised beer as "American" and urged that Bostonians should "no longer be beholden to Foreigners for a Credible [sic] Liquor, which may be as successfully manufactured in this country." It is not the self-interest which is important here, but the fact that the advertiser obviously felt he could gain by making an appeal to a sense of American pride among his potential customers. This feeling among Americans that they were different from Europeans was put forth explicitly by a Carolinian in 1762. Speaking about the question of sending young colonials to England for their education, he said it would be most surprising if a British education should suit Americans, "because the Genius of our People, their Way of Life, their circumstances in Point of Fortunes, and Customs, and Manners and Humours of the Country, difference us in so many important Respects from Europeans. . . ." Such an education could not be expected to fit Americans, he went on, any more "than an Almanac, calculated for the Latitude of London, would that of Williamsburg."

As relations between the colonies and the mother country worsened after 1765, expressions of Americanism became more explicit and sometimes belligerent. Colonial students at Edinburgh University before 1765 commonly designated themselves as from the various provinces, but at the time of the Stamp Act, Samuel Bard wrote, he and several others began to style themselves "Americans"

and the precedent was followed by many in subsequent years. About
the same time Ezra Stiles of New Haven drew up a plan for an
"American Academy of Science," which was designed, he said, "for
the Honor of American Literature, contemned by Europeans." He
stipulated that only native-born Americans should be members. And
at the Stamp Act Congress, Christopher Gadsden of South Carolina
urged the gathered colonial leaders to take cognizance of their common nationality. "There ought to be no New England man, no New
Yorker, known on the Continent," he advised, "but all of us Americans. . . ."

The magic of the moment and the atmosphere in the new country
were so potent that John Morgan, newly arrived at Philadelphia
from London in 1765, declared, only a year later, "I consider
myself at once as a Briton and an American." Such an ambivalent
attitude must have been common among colonials in the early stage
of the crisis between the colonies and the mother country. But regardless of Morgan's own ambiguous feelings, his work in helping
to establish the new medical school at Philadelphia was hailed by
Benjamin Rush as an aid to the growing self-consciousness of the
people of America. Pointedly calling Britain an alien land, Rush
wrote Morgan that no longer would the colonial student have to tear
"himself from every tender engagement" and brave the dangers of
the sea "in pursuit of knowledge in a foreign country."

One of the most curious but very clear manifestations of a growing American awareness of differences between the peoples of the
Old and New Worlds was the widespread belief that English society
was morally inferior, even decadent, when compared with the social
character of the colonies. As early as 1735 Lewis Morris, visiting
England, wrote in his diary that he and his party "wish'd ourselves
in our own Country, far from the deceits of a court." London appeared to Ebenezer Hazard as at once a wonderful "little World"
and a "Sink of Sin." In 1767, English social conditions appeared
shocking to William S. Johnson, who found the extremes of wealth
and misery "equally amazing on the one hand and disgusting on the
other." Benjamin Rush wrote from Edinburgh in 1767 that "every
native of Philadelphia should be sent abroad for a few years if it
was only to teach him to prize his native country above all places
in the world."

Standing out against the decadence of England in the minds of
colonials and of some Englishmen was the example of America as

the hope of the world. In 1771, John Penn, who was certainly no radical, wrote that he considered Great Britain "as an Old Man, who has received several strokes of the Palsy, and tottering upon the brink of the Grave, whereas America was growing daily toward perfection." In 1745 a writer in the *Gentleman's Magazine* drew the lesson from the American success at the siege of Louisbourg that the colonials were truly in the classical tradition so dear to the men of the eighteenth century. He saw the colonists in "the great image of the ancient Romans leaving the plow for the field of battles, and retiring after their conquests to the plow again." For many Englishmen, America seemed to be utopia in actuality. But it was the Americans who above all were convinced of the moral superiority of their society. Colonials returned from Europe overflowing with tales of the iniquities they had witnessed in London or commenting on the manifest corruption of British politics. As early as 1748, Josiah Quincy was saying he was fearful that the venality of English political life would ruin the country. The self-righteousness of Americans toward Britain in the 1750's and 1760's reminds one of nothing so much as an adolescent's indignant strictures against his parent's time-worn but now suddenly recognized foibles. The American people were coming of age.

Along with adolescent carping, assertions of moral superiority, and self-righteousness in the years before 1765, there were also a few strong hints that independence was coming. The war against the French in Canada prompted some Americans to anticipate separation from England. Peter Kalm, for example, traveling through the colonies in 1748, was told that after the French were expelled from the western borders of the colonies, independence would come in a matter of thirty to fifty years. Once the "Gallicks" are removed, John Adams thought in 1755, the colonies would be able to go it alone. "The only way to keep us from setting up for ourselves," he wrote, "is to disunite us."

In 1760 and after, when the British government was wrestling with the question of whether or not the French should be expelled completely from the North American continent, there was much speculation as to the effect such expulsion would have upon the restive colonies. Though the canny Franklin blandly assured Parliament that the removal of the French would bind the colonies still closer to Britain, less suspect parties, like Comptroller Weare, pointed out that never before in history had an industrious and

favored people like the Americans hesitated to break away from
their mother country when they had the power to do so. It is highly
likely, he added, "that a thousand leagues distance from eye and
strength of government" would suggest just that "*to a people
accustomed to more than British liberty.*" Also of this opinion was
a correspondent of the *Gentleman's Magazine* in 1760. "If the
people of our colonies find no check from Canada, they will extend
themselves, almost without bounds into the inland parts. . . .
What the consequences will be," he added ominously and prophetically, "to have a numerous, hardy, independent people possessed of
a strong country, communicating little, or not at all with England,
I leave to your own reflections."

There was more behind the thought of independence than the
removal of the French threat. There was the coming to climax of
the whole history of a geographically separate and different people
in America. English traveler Andrew Burnaby noticed it in 1759
when he pointed out that the growing cities of the coast were already
turning their citizens into "great republicans" and that the farm
dwellers too had "fallen into the same errors in their ideas of inde-
pendency."

In a vague cultural sense, the colonies were ready for the parting
of the ways with Britain. What still remained was something which
would cleanly and definitely cut the political ties connecting the
two peoples. The occasion would come after 1763 when Britain
sought to find a new basis for its relations with the continental
colonies, for then the differences between the two peoples would be
translated into political terms. That is the story of the coming of
the American Revolution.

CHAPTER III

A New Kind of Revolution

On at least two scores, the American Revolution was something new under the sun. Although most of the major powers of Europe boasted overseas colonial empires, never before had a colonial people successfully rebelled against the mother country. But once it was done by the United States, the example was not ignored. Within a century after the Revolution, France, Spain, and Portugal lost portions or all of their New World empires through colonial rebellion. Nor have the echoes yet ceased. In 1945, one sour Englishman in Batavia during the rebellion of the Indonesians against the Dutch remarked, "That damned American Revolution . . . is still giving us trouble."

Despite its precedent-setting character, however, the American revolt is noteworthy because it made no serious interruption in the smooth flow of American development. Both in intention and in fact the American Revolution conserved the past rather than repudiated it. And in preserving the colonial experience, the men of the first quarter century of the Republic's history set the scenery and wrote the script for the drama of American politics for years to come.

1. CAUSES WERE CONSEQUENCES

Though the colonists had long been drifting away from their allegiance to the mother country, the chain of events which led to the Revolutionary crisis was set in motion by external factors. The shattering victory of the Anglo-American forces over the French in the Great War for the Empire (1754–63), as Lawrence Gipson has rechristened the French and Indian War, suddenly revealed how wide the gulf between colonists and mother country had become. The very fact that the feared French were once and for all expelled from the colonial backdoor meant that another cohesive, if negative,

75

force was gone. At least one friend of Britain, looking back from the
fateful days of 1776, thought that "had Canada remained in the
hands of the French, the colonies would have remained dutiful subjects. Their fears for themselves in that case," he reasoned, "would
have supplied the place of the pretended affection for this nation. . . ." What actual effect the removal of the French produced
upon the thinking of the colonists is hard to weigh, but there can be
little doubt that the Great War for the Empire opened a new era in
the relations between the colonies and the mother country.

Great Britain emerged from the war as the supreme power in
European affairs: her armies had swept the once-vaunted French
authority from two continents; her navy now indisputably commanded the seven seas. A symbol of this new power was that
Britain's ambassadors now outranked those of France and Spain in
the protocol of Europe's courts. But the cost and continuing responsibilities of that victory were staggering for the little island
kingdom. Before the war the annual expenditures for troops in
America and the British West Indies amounted to £110,000; now
three times that sum was needed to protect the western frontier,
suppress Indian revolts and maintain order. Furthermore, the signing of the peace found Britain saddled with a debt of £130 million,
the annual charges of which ran to another £4 million. Faced with
such obligations, the British government was compelled to reassess
its old ways of running an Empire, particularly in regard to the
raising of new revenues.

Before the war, the administration and cost of the Empire were
primarily, if not completely, a British affair. Imperial defense on
the high seas was in the hands of the Royal Navy, and though the
colonies were called upon from time to time to assist in the war with
France, the bulk of the fighting was sustained by British troops. In
return, the colonies had acquiesced in the regulation of their trade
through a series of so-called Navigation Acts, which were enacted
and enforced by the British authority; no revenues, however, except
those collected as import or export duties, were taken from the
colonies by Britain.

Under the pressure of the new responsibilities, the British authorities began to cast about for a new theory and practice of imperial
administration into which the colonies might be fitted as actively
contributing members. Prior to the war the government had been
willing to protect the West Indian sugar interests at the expense of

the rest of the Empire. But now, in the interest of increased revenue, the old protective duty, which was much too high to bring any return, was cut in half, thus permitting French molasses to compete with British West Indian in the English and colonial markets. In 1766, this molasses duty, in a further effort to increase revenue, was cut to two thirds of what it had been before the war. In short, the need for imperial revenues, not private interests, was now dictating legislation. The Stamp Act of 1765 and the Townshend duties of two years later were similar efforts to spread the financial burdens of the Empire among the beneficiaries of the British triumph over the French.

It seemed only simple justice to London officialdom that the colonies should share in the costs as well as the benefits to be derived from the defeat of the ancient enemy. At no time, it should be noticed, were the colonies asked to contribute more than a portion of the price of their own frontier defense. The stamp duty, for instance, was envisioned as returning no more than a third of the total military expenditures in America; the remainder would be borne by the home government. And because the colonists had difficulty scraping together the specie with which to pay such duties, the British government agreed to spend all the revenue obtained from the stamp tax in the colonies in order to avoid depleting the scanty colonial money supply. Nor were Americans heavily taxed; it was well known that their fiscal burden was unique in its lightness. In 1775 Lord North told the House of Commons that the per capita tax payments of Britons were fifty times those of the Americans. It was not injustice or the economic incidence of the taxes which prompted the colonial protests; it was rather the novelty of the British demands.

The new imperial policies of the British government caught the Americans off guard. Reveling in the victory over the French, the colonists confidently expected a return to the lax, uninterested administration of the prewar years and especially to their old freedom from any obligation to support the imperial defenses. Therefore, when the first of the new measures, the Sugar Act of 1764, became law, the American protested, but on a variety of grounds and without sufficient unity to command respect.[1] By the time of the Stamp Act in the following year, however, the colonists were ready.

---

[1] For example, although the preamble of the Sugar Act explicitly cited revenue as one of the objects of the law, only two of the colonies, North Carolina and

The essential colonial defense, from which the colonies never deviated,[2] was a denial that the British Parliament had any right in law or custom to lay taxes upon the colonies for revenue purposes. Such taxes, the colonials insisted, could only be levied by the colonial legislatures. Actually, this expression of the colonial constitutional position was as novel as the imperial policy. Never before had there been an occasion for such an assertion simply because England had heretofore confined her colonial legislation to the regulation of trade. It is true that the Pennsylvania Charter of 1681 specifically reserved to the British Parliament the right to tax the colony; but since Parliament had never used this power, the colonists had a case when they said the new British taxes were historically unknown and therefore unconstitutional. The details of this controversy, in which merit is by no means the exclusive possession of either side, do not concern us here. The important fact is not whether the Americans or the British were right in their respective readings of imperial constitutional history, but that the colonials believed they were right and acted accordingly. Regardless of the constitutional niceties involved, it is patent that the English had waited too long to assert their authority. Too many Americans had grown accustomed to their untrammeled political life to submit now to new English controls. In brief, the colonists suddenly realized that they were no longer wards of Britain, but a separate people, capable of forging their own destiny.

This conviction runs all through the polemics of the Revolutionary crisis. For underlying the constitutional verbiage which Englishmen and Americans exchanged were two quite different assumptions about the nature of the British Empire and the character of the American people. Whereas Englishmen saw America as a part of an Empire in which all elements were subordinate to Britain, the Ameri-

---

New York, denied the right of Parliament to tax them. The rest of the colonial protests were on other, nonconstitutional grounds.

[2] American history books have long expressed the view that the American constitutional argument, as described above, was not finally arrived at until after the Townshend Acts. The implication is that the colonists shifted their arguments to meet new demands from the British. However, since the publication of Edmund S. Morgan's "Colonial Ideas of Parliamentary Power, 1764–1766," *William and Mary Quarterly,* 3rd Series, V (July, 1948), such a view is no longer tenable. He has shown quite conclusively that during the Stamp Act crisis the colonial leaders already reached, in one step, their ultimate position—namely, no taxes, except duties for trade regulation, could be levied upon the colonists by the British Parliament.

cans, drawing upon their actual history, saw only a loose confederation of peoples in which there were Britons and Americans, neither
one of whom could presume to dictate to the other. The colonials,
in effect, now felt themselves Americans, not displaced, subordinate
Englishmen. Jefferson suggested this to the King himself when he
wrote in his *Summary View of the Rights of British America:* "You
are surrounded by British counsellors. . . . You have no minister
for American affairs, because you have none taken from us."
Furthermore, even after 1776 many a Loyalist exiled in Britain
found the English annoying and strange—evidence of the fact that
residence in America had worked its influence even upon those loyal
to the Crown. "It piques my pride, I must confess," wrote one ex-
patriated Loyalist, "to hear us called 'our colonies, our plantations,' in such terms and with such airs as if our property and
persons were absolutely theirs, like the 'villains' in their cottages in
the old feudal system."

The imperial view so confidently advanced by Grenville and others
of the British administration came too late; the Americans were
not interested in making a more efficient Empire to be manipulated
from Whitehall. Because of this basic conflict in assumptions, American demands continued to leapfrog ahead of British concessions
right up to the Carlisle Peace Mission in the midst of the Revolutionary War. Even ministerial assurances in 1769 that there would
be no further imperially imposed taxes [3] failed to divert the colonial
drive toward equality with Britain. The child was truly asserting
himself, and, as so often happens, the parent was reluctant to strike
him down.

Measured against the age of Hitler and Stalin, the British over-
lords of the eighteenth century appear remarkably benign in their
dealings with the colonies in the years after 1763. For it is a fact
that the colonies were in revolt against a potential tyrant, not an
actual one. Much more fearsome in the eyes of the politically sensitive colonials was the direction in which the British measures tended
rather than the explicit content of the acts. Furthermore, Englishmen could never bring themselves to enforce, with all the power at

[3] In May, Lord Hillsborough officially informed the colonial governments that
the Cabinet "entertained no design to propose to Parliament to lay any further
taxes on America for the purpose of raising revenue." At about this time, however, the British people were paying per capita taxes of 25s., though Americans
paid only 6d., according to the estimate of Lord North.

their command, what they believed was the true nature of the
Empire, that is, the subordinate position of the colonies. More than
once General Thomas Gage, commanding the British troops in
America, reported that his forces were too scattered to preserve
proper order and government in the colonies. "I am concerned to
find in your Lordship's letters," he wrote from New York in 1768,
"that irresolution still prevails in our Councils; it is time to come
to some determination about the disposition of the troops in this
Country."

Part of this irresolution was born of British confusion as to what
should be the government's purpose, as the hasty repeals of the
stamp and Townshend duties testify on the one hand, and the remarkably inept Tea Act reveals on the other. Part of it stemmed
from the fact that within their own house, so to speak, were Americans: at times Lord Chatham himself, at all times Edmund Burke,
Colonel Isaac Barré, John Wilkes, and Dr. Price, who insisted that
Americans possessed the rights of Englishmen. "The seditious spirit
of the colonies," George Grenville wryly complained on the floor of
Commons in 1776, "owes its birth to the factions in this House."

Divided as to aims and devoid of strong leadership, the British
permitted the much more united colonists, who were blessed with
superb and daring leadership, to seize and hold the initiative. Not
until the very end—after the destruction of the tea at Boston Harbor in 1773—did the patience of the British ministry run dry. By
then, however, the years of acrimony, suspicion, and growing awareness of the differences between the two peoples had done their work,
and the harsh coercive measures taken against Massachusetts only
provoked counterviolence from all the colonies. Lexington and Concord, Bunker Hill and Independence Hall, were then not far behind.

By implication, the interpretation of the coming of the Revolution given here greatly subordinates the role of economic factors.
Since the economic restrictions imposed upon the colonies have
traditionally played a large role in most discussions of the causes
of the Revolution, they deserve some comment here. Those who advance an economic explanation for the Revolution argue that the
series of economic measures enacted by Britain in the century before
1750 actually operated to confine, if not stifle, the colonial economy.
Therefore, it is said, the colonies revolted against Britain in an
effort to break through these artificial and externally imposed
limits. On the surface and from the assumptions of twentieth-cen-

tury economic life, the mercantilistic system appears severe and crippling and worthy of strong colonial opposition. But before such speculative conclusions can be accepted, they deserve to be checked against the facts.

Several historians have sought to measure quantitatively the restrictive effects of English mercantilism upon the colonial economy. Their conclusions, it can be said at the outset, are generally in the negative. For example, take the three major British limitations on colonial manufactures. On the statute books the Iron Act of 1750 appears to halt the erection of additional slitting mills in the colonies, but the fact is that many were set up after that date, regardless of the act's prohibitions, and to such an extent that by 1776 there were probably more such mills in America than in England. Nor, Lawrence Harper tells us, did the Woolens Act of 1699, designed to prevent colonial competition with a major English industry, actually inhibit American endeavors in the field, since few Americans cared to engage in the industry. True, Harper concluded that the colonial beaver-hat industry suffered from the restrictions of the Hat Act of 1773, but, as he adds, that branch of economic activity could hardly be considered an important segment of the economy. And those are the three major British efforts to "stifle" American manufacturing.

Nor can the restrictions on the settlement of the West be viewed, as some historians have asserted, as a significant motive for the Revolution. For one thing, movement into the West was never absolutely halted, and as early as 1764 the Proclamation Line of the previous year was being moved westward to permit settlement beyond the mountains. Furthermore, as Thomas Abernethy has shown, the Virginia gentry—often cited as heavily involved in western land speculation and therefore concerned with restrictions on the West—were not vitally interested in the matter economically, though the religious and political implications of the later Quebec Act, for example, did arouse them. All in all, it would appear that the western land question may have been an irritating factor, but, in view of the changing and indecisive English policy, hardly a revolution-making force.

Perhaps the most that can be said quantitatively about the burden of the whole navigation or mercantilist system in which England encased the colonies is that the regulations concerning the routing of trade added between $2.6 million and $7 million to the cost of doing business in the colonies. Over against this, however, must be placed the fact that the system did not seem a burden to the colonies. Very few objections to the navigation system appear in the voluminous literature of the crisis. In fact, so acceptable did it appear to that jealous American, Benjamin Franklin, that in 1774 he suggested to Lord Chatham that all the basic Navigation Laws be re-enacted by the colonial legislatures as an earnest of colonial loyalty. Furthermore, in October of that year, the first Continental Congress publicly declared the colonies willing to "cheerfully consent to the operation of such acts of the British Parliament, as are bona fide, restrained to the regulation of our external commerce, for the purpose of securing the commercial advantages of the whole empire to the mother country, and the commercial benefits of its respective members. . . ." In short, the navigation system was acceptable. Certainly laws the repressive nature of which no one was disturbed about can hardly be accepted as the grounds for a revolution.

No better economic argument can be made for taxation as a cause for the Revolution. Despite the tradition of oppressive taxation which the myth of the Revolution has spawned, the actual tax burden of the colonies was much heavier in the seventeenth century than in the years immediately before the conflict. On a per capita basis, taxes were five times greater in 1698 than they were in 1773. The lightness of the British taxes in the pre-Revolutionary period is also shown by the fact that the duty on molasses in 1766 was only a penny a gallon, or less than the duty the federal government imposed in 1791. As Lord North pointed out in 1775, taxation of the Americans was neither excessive nor oppressive.

From the unconvincing character of the economic explanations for the coming of the Revolution, it would appear, therefore, that the underlying force impelling the break was the growing national self-consciousness of the Americans. "The Revolution was effected before the war commenced," John Adams remarked years afterward. "The Revolution was in the minds and hearts of the people. . . ." The origins of the "principles and feelings" which made the Revolution, Adams thought, "ought to be traced back . . . and sought in the history of the country from the first plantations in America." For a century and a half the Americans had been growing up and now they had finally come of age. Precisely because the Revolution was the breaking away of a young people from a parent, the substance of the Revolution was political. The argument concerned the question of parental authority, because that is the precise point at which tension appears as the child approaches maturity and seeks to assert his independence. Unfortunately for Britain, but like so many modern parents, the mother country had long before conveniently provided the best arguments in favor of freedom. And the colonists had learned the arguments well. For this reason, the rhetoric of the Revolutionary argument was in the language of the British political and constitutional tradition.

As children enjoying a long history of freedom from interference from their parent, the Americans might well have continued in their loose relationship, even in maturity, for they were conservative as well as precocious. History, however, decreed otherwise. Britain's triumph in the Great War for the Empire put a new strain on the family relationship, and so intense was the pressure that Americans could not fail to see, as the argument increased in acrimony, that they were no longer members of the English family, but rather a new people, with their own separate destiny. Some Americans saw it earlier than others;[4] a good many saw it by 1776. John Penn, while in England in 1773, was struck by the English ignorance "with respect to *our* part of the world (for I consider myself more American than English). . . ." To South Carolinian Henry Laurens, the Boston Port Act hit at "the liberty of all Americans," not just at that of the people of Massachusetts. Once they were convinced of their essential difference as a people and that British obduracy would not melt, Americans could not accept the old familiar arrangements. Anything less than their independence as a people was unacceptable; it would take Englishmen another generation to realize that the disagreement was as deep as that.

At no time during the ten-year crisis, however, were most Americans spoiling for a rupture with England merely for the sake of a break. Indeed, no one can run through the constitutional arguments of that day without being struck with the reluctance—almost mis-

---

[4] As early as 1768 Benjamin Franklin voiced the opinion that England would have to treat the colonies as equal with herself or forgo any connection. England, he said, was supreme in everything or in nothing insofar as the colonies were concerned. He thought they were supreme in nothing. In which case, he said, "the colonies would then be so many separate states, only subject to the same king, as England and Scotland were before the Union." John Adams and Lord Camden, the English statesman, also came to this view in the course of the crisis.

givings—with which Americans reached the conclusion of independence. After attending the Continental Congress in 1774, Washington, for example, was "well satisfied that" independence was not "desired by any thinking man in all North America." And, as late as July 6, 1775—over two months after the embattled farmers made their stand at the "rude bridge"—Congress denied any "designs of separation from Great Britain and establishing independent states."

This was no heedless, impetuous overthrow of an oppressor; rather it was a slowly germinating determination on the part of Americans to counter and thwart a change in their hitherto established and accepted ways of governing. Except for the long-deferred assertion of independence, the whole corpus of Revolutionary rhetoric—and nothing lends itself more to radicalism than words—was conservative, expressive of the wish to retain the old ways. The demands made upon Britain were actually pleas for a return to the old relationship: repeal the Stamp Act, the Townshend Acts, the Mutiny Acts; restore trial by jury as abrogated by the expanded admiralty courts; remove the restrictions recently placed upon western migration. One needs only to run through that famous list of grievances in the Declaration of Independence to be forcefully reminded that what these revolutionaries wanted was nothing but the *status quo ante bellum.*

"We have taken up arms," the Continental Congress carefully explained in July, 1775, two months after Lexington, "in defense of the freedom that is our birth-right, and which we ever enjoyed til the late violation of it. . . ." These men had been satisfied with their existence, they were not disgruntled agitators or frustrated politicians; they were a strange new breed—contented revolutionaries.

2. NEW GOVERNMENTS IN OLD CHARTERS

"You and I, my dear friend," exulted John Adams to Richard Lee in 1776, "have been sent into life at a time when the greatest lawgivers of antiquity would have wished to live. How few of the human race have ever enjoyed an opportunity of making an election of government . . . for themselves or their children!" Actually, of course, the new nation was not born, like a Venus fresh from the sea, unencumbered by history. But John Adams was not exaggerating when he referred to the novelty of the opportunity. And insofar as posterity is concerned, the governments which were erected by the Revolutionary states expose, better than any treatise can, the prevailing political and constitutional views of the Revolutionary Fathers. Even more important is the fact that these early conceptions of what constituted just government continued to be accepted, in subsequent years, as the basic assumptions and ideals of American political philosophy, the economic and historical realism of John C. Calhoun to the contrary notwithstanding.

When the allegiance to the British Crown, which heretofore had been the juridical source of governmental authority in America, was dissolved, a new legal basis for government was needed. The search for one, however, was not long or difficult since it lay conveniently at hand in the familiar political philosophy of John Locke, the English theorist of the seventeenth century. In his works, the Americans had earlier found the justification for their Revolution, a version of which Jefferson had elegantly embodied in the Declaration of Independence. The Lockean conception which the Americans now borrowed was that the true origin of government was a compact among the governed. Unlike Europeans, eighteenth-century Americans can be pardoned for their ready acceptance of the Lockean theory as historically valid, since all around them they witnessed governments coming into being by virtue of agreement. The Mayflower Compact, formed at the settlement of Plymouth, was only the most formal variety of innumerable compacts by which Americans agreed to live together in the forbidding wilderness.

During the Revolutionary era, therefore, when Americans were compelled to lay down a new juridical basis for their government, they naturally turned to the compact. The Maryland Convention of 1776 could speak for almost all the states when it asserted "that all government of right originates from the people, is founded in compact only, and instituted solely for the good of the whole." For most modern Americans, the just powers of government still derive from the compact of the people.

The actual making of a compact among the people of a whole state, however, was not feasible in the eighteenth century, so the Americans introduced a political device which met the requirements of the compact theory and still made it possible to write a constitution: the constitutional convention. Today, Americans, along with most of the western world, accept the convention as a part of the natural political order, but its inception dates only from those early days of the Revolution. In Massachusetts and New Hampshire, the institution actually contained the two essential elements of the modern convention. The body was convened for the sole purpose of constitution-making, and the product of its labors was submitted to popular ratification—the people of New Hampshire requiring three versions before they were satisfied! Most of the other states insisted only on the separation of the legislative and constitution-making functions, but this was the essence of the convention principle. The reason for the insistence on separation of authority was best expressed by the town meeting of Concord, Massachusetts, in 1776: "The same body that forms a Constitution have of consequence a power to alter it, and a Constitution alterable by the legislature is no security at all to the individual."

The content of the constitutions which the new states adopted reveals a remarkable continuity with the colonial experience. That the organic law was a written document was itself a hangover from the colonial charter. Connecticut and Rhode Island did not even feel it necessary to write new constitutions; they merely dropped a few words from their Crown-granted charters and continued to be governed under them. Usually, the new constitutions included bills of rights, or guarantees of the individual against the power of government. These too had their roots in English history and the colonial experience with tyrannical and rapacious agents of the Crown. As a whole the constitutions and the bills of rights were symptomatic of that exaggerated faith of the eighteenth century in the power of documents and words to insure free government. As true children of the Enlightenment in which their country was born, Americans still exhibit enormous faith in written documents as protections of the liberties of the citizen.

During the colonial period, as we have seen, the belief had been growing that only through a separation of the powers of the three branches of government were freedom and good government to be secured. The conservatism of the American political thinkers would not permit the new state constitutions to bestow plenary power upon the legislatures—the creatures of the "people"—but neither would the memory of the recent struggles with the Royal Governors allow the executive to dominate. As Fisher Ames recalled years later in connection with the circumscribed powers of the executive: "we looked for danger on the same side where we had been used to look. . . ." Similarly, the Crown's efforts to dominate the judiciary decreed that, under the new governments, the courts, like the executive and the legislature, would be independent. Though the separation of powers, so carefully built into these first constitutions, and in the federal Constitution of 1787, has been challenged at times, notably during Reconstruction, as a principle it remains today perhaps the most characteristically American element in our constitutional system.

Probably nothing reveals more accurately the cautious, conservative political habits of these Americans than the franchise qualifications which were included in the new constitutions. Possession of real property had been a universal requirement for voting during the colonial eighteenth century, the assumption being that only propertied citizens had a "stake in society." Though, as we have seen in the last chapter, this principle was not as restrictive in practice as it sounds, it still resulted in the barring of a large number of people from the suffrage. Significantly enough, the colonial suffrage pattern was barely disturbed by the Revolution. As late as 1800 only two of the sixteen states of the Union had removed all property and taxpaying qualifications for voting. Furthermore, property qualifications for officeholding, which had been common in the colonial period, were retained in all but one of the thirteen original states after the Revolution. All of the states, for example, required representatives to hold some property, while five of them also demanded that the governor possess some minimum of property, usually land.[5] Not until well into the nineteenth century would the property basis for the suffrage and officeholding give way before the modern, democratic view that manhood was sufficient.

3. REVOLUTIONARIES CAN BE CONSERVATIVE

In the historical literature dealing with the years between 1775 and 1800, two words—"radical" and "conservative"—seem to be indispensable for describing or analyzing the political events and men of the period. Tom Paine, it is said, was a radical; James Wilson and George Washington were conservatives; James Madison was a conservative in 1787, but a Jeffersonian radical in 1794;

---

[5] It is true, of course, that some states like Pennsylvania, New York, Georgia, and South Carolina lifted their restrictions on disfranchised religious sects, notably Catholics and Jews, but such an expansion of the suffrage was numerically insignificant, though the liberal principle embodied in the enfranchisement was important.

Alexander Hamilton a conservative all the time, and so on. But it
is clear that these words do not always describe the same individual
all the time, and especially is this true of those who are called
radicals before 1776, but conservatives after the Revolution. Everyone knows, for example, that John Adams of Massachusetts was a
"radical" in 1775, as it is also known that he was a "conservative"
in 1790. Such a switch suggests that either he was inconstant in his
views or that the terms are inadequate to deal with the factual situation. A knowledge of Adams would strongly suggest that the latter
is the more likely of the two explanations.

If, however, we try to see what the terms really meant in each of
three periods—the early 1770's, the 1780's, and the 1790's—then
perhaps the continuity which runs through all three will stand out
as it does not if we think of radical and conservative as having
constant meanings. Before 1776 the term radical designated anyone
who advocated a hard policy toward Britain, even looking toward
independence, if necessary. People like Sam Adams, Tom Paine, and
John Adams would fall into this category. Conservatives, on the
other hand, included those who wished to conciliate Britain as much
as possible, to work out some accommodation whereby independence
could be avoided, if possible. Robert Morris, John Dickinson, and
Joseph Galloway, the last of whom eventually became a Loyalist,
were representatives of this group. Once the colonial connection was
broken, however, there was a new alignment; many so-called radicals
found themselves facing former comrades across ideological bar-
ricades. Tom Paine and John Adams, both at one time in hot pursuit
of independence, are classic examples of this, the years after 1776
bringing a progressively frigid atmosphere to their relationship.

Such a shift in ideological allegiances after the Revolution makes
it plain that rather than being a united party, as appeared superficially, the so-called radicals before 1776 were actually of two
persuasions in regard to their opposition to Britain. Though both
factions of the radicals opposed the Crown's efforts at imperial
centralization in London, their reasons for doing so were quite different. To one wing, which we might call the radicals, centralization
endangered local control and thereby threatened colonial freedom;
to the other wing, which we will call the conservatives, centralization
was objectionable primarily because British and not American
authorities undertook it. Before 1776 this divergence in motivation
was largely obscured or ignored under the pressure of events and

the obvious need for a united front against Britain. Once independence was declared, however, the conflict split the Revolutionary party into two factions—radicals and conservatives—who now clashed over the large question of the purpose of the Revolution and the direction in which the newly freed nation was to move.[6]

In the final analysis, the central issue between the conservatives and the radicals in the period of the 1780's was still the matter of where supreme authority was to be lodged. Now, however, it took the form of the states versus an American central authority instead of the colonies versus London. Take, for example, the attitudes of the two factions toward the question of a union of the emergent states. The Articles of Confederation, as adopted in 1781, embodied the radical position, as the Constitution of 1787 represented the conservative. The Articles of Confederation, really the first constitution of the United States, baldly exalted local government: "Each state," the second article warned, "retains its sovereignty, freedom and independence." Limiting the states almost not at all, the article established a deliberately weak government, hobbled by a plural executive and emasculated by the denial of any direct power to tax the people or the states over which it presumed to rule. To radicals like Thomas Burke of North Carolina or George Clinton of New York, such a central government was precisely that for which they had fought the Revolution. To them free government inhered in local control and the supremacy of the states.

The triumph of the radicals, however, was short-lived, for the Constitutional Convention of 1787 was dominated by conservatives. The Constitution which was produced there reflected the conservatives' belief in a central government which could support itself, enforce order, and command respect at home and abroad. In the dexterous hands of the conservatives, the weak position of the central government under the Articles of Confederation was dramatically reversed. The new Constitution provided that the "Constitution and Laws of the United States, which shall be made in Pursuance thereof . . . shall be the supreme Law of the Land . . . the Constitution or Laws of any States to the Contrary notwith-

---

[6] Looked at from this viewpoint, the shift from radicalism before independence to conservatism after, as happened in the case of men like John Adams, William Floyd of New York, and Thomas McKean of Delaware, to mention some of the Signers, is easily understood. Basically they were not radical at all; they were merely opponents of British centralization, or conservatives.

standing." Considering the boldness of the reversal, it is not surprising that when old radical Sam Adams read the new Constitution, he said, "As I enter the building I stumble on the threshold. I meet with a National Government instead of a Federal Union of Sovereign States."

And it truly was a national government. The ability of the new central government directly to tax individuals within the states and to bring them to its own system of courts was completely unknown under the old Articles. Simultaneously with the increased powers of the national government, the states were being severely restricted in their authority. No state, for example, could erect tariff barriers, issue money, enact stay laws for the relief of debtors, or deal directly with any foreign power.

The contrast in the energy of the central authorities under the old Confederation and under the new Constitution was painfully apparent in the area of military power. In 1787, Shays' Rebellion in Massachusetts was just too tricky a matter and too threatening for the Congress to aid in its suppression, though it was obviously a danger to the peace of the Union. But when the Whisky Rebellion of 1794 broke out in western Pennsylvania, the central government under the new Constitution quickly snuffed it out with overwhelming military power.[7]

Deep as their fear of strong government ran, the radicals, once the new Constitution was ratified, fell into line behind the new government. Even passionate defenders of the sovereignty of the several states like Patrick Henry and George Clinton bowed to the

[7] The dangers of employing terms like radical and conservative to cover what actually amount to congeries of ideas instead of a single attitude are most apparent in this matter of centralization. Insofar as the so-called conservatives worked for a strong central government, they were, in reality, not conserving anything; central government was unknown in the colonies. Rather it was the so-called radicals, with their accent on local government, who were conserving. Those who pushed for a strong central government were, in actuality, completing the Revolution which George Grenville had begun in 1765, for the stamp tax he offered was but an earlier version of what later would be the federal taxing power contained in the Constitution. The power was acceptable, of course, because it was carried out by Americans and not by Englishmen.

The labels "conservative" and "radical" became twisted and misapplied in this confusing fashion because historians and contemporaries focused their attentions on other aspects of their several beliefs, like the suffrage, paper money, credit, and so forth, overlooking the anomaly of denominating strong Federalists as conservatives, when their view of the central government's proper power was probably the most radical innovation in American political life at that time.

decisions of the ratifying conventions. By shunning the temptation of continued opposition, the radicals added their voices to the growing veneration of the Constitution and the beginning of a long tradition of political stability. Since those days radicals and conservatives alike have accepted the Constitution as beyond debate; no party or movement of significance has advocated scrapping it. Even on the eve of secession, southern leaders did no more than accuse the North of deliberately misinterpreting a fundamentally sound instrument of government, and they closely followed it in writing the Constitution of the Confederacy.

Though they were certainly defeated in their attempt to maintain the supremacy of the states, the radicals in the 1790's did not change the substance of their disagreement with the conservatives. The argument still concerned the proper locus of power in a free government. And, as in the days before 1776, the question which divided the two groups was still local versus foreign rule, only now "foreign" meant Philadelphia and Washington instead of London. Though unable to secure the kind of weak central government they preferred, the radicals were still free to do their utmost to prevent the new government from being any more powerful than was literally spelled out in the Constitution. For this reason the radical Jeffersonians of the 1790's filled their quiver of arguments with arrows marked "strict construction," or a literal interpretation of the Constitution.

Fisher Ames, an uncompromising Federalist from Massachusetts, was both amused and exasperated by this new stage of the old argument. "We have near twenty *antis* [former opponents of the Constitution], dragons watching the tree of liberty," he complained from Congress in 1792, "and who consider every strong measure and almost every ordinary one, as an attempt to rob the tree of its fair fruit. We hear incessantly, from the old foes of the Constitution, 'this is unconstitutional, and that is': and indeed, what is not? I scarce know a point which has not produced this cry, not excepting a motion for adjourning."

Though this was the Jeffersonian position as seen through rather clouded glasses, it was reasonably accurate; for to the Jeffersonians of the 1790's, the federal government should be rarely heard and even more rarely seen. And how reminiscent it was of those "radicals" who had said the same about English rule in the days before '76.

When weighed in the scales of such a constitutional philosophy the economic program of Alexander Hamilton quite naturally became another point of difference between radicals and conservatives. Inasmuch as the Hamiltonian plan envisioned a national bank, the assumption of a great debt to buttress the national credit, and a protective tariff to encourage manufacturing, the Jeffersonians could not fail to oppose this enhancement of the federal authority.

Moreover, the Hamiltonian program touched the sensitive nerve of the radicals' self-interest, revealing the hitherto concealed material divergence of interest which separated the two camps. Since the radicals were largely drawn from the agricultural class, they took a jaundiced view of Hamilton's ambitious efforts to expand credit, create a banking system, and encourage manufacturing through the power of the federal government. To the Jeffersonians such machinations smacked of favors paid for by the taxes of the "honest, hard-working part of the community," as Representative Jackson of Georgia complained, in order to "promote the ease and luxury of men of wealth." After a debate in the Senate over the Bank of the United States, radical Senator Maclay from Pennsylvania wrote that he made no secret, in the course of the debate, that "I was no advocate of the banking system; that I considered them as machines for promoting the profits of unproductive men."

Convinced of the evil intent of the Federalist approach to government and its favoritism to business, the Jeffersonians fought the Hamiltonian program as they would the Devil. Hamilton and his fellow Federalists, however, were no more devils than they were saints. Hamilton himself was inspired by the noble vision of a durable, wealthy, and powerful United States, the actualization of which, he was convinced, depended upon bold and imaginative measures to support the public credit, encourage manufacturing, and secure the allegiance of the wealthy and commercial classes. Almost all of the Hamiltonian program was enacted in the early 1790's and, from the vantage point of retrospect, this was most fortunate; for of the two contending economic programs, the Federalists' was the more far-sighted. The laissez-faire Arcadia of Jefferson would have been neither a strong nor a prosperous nation for long.

If the Hamiltonians won in the sense that their vision of a commercial and industrial America was gradually made fact, the Jeffersonians did not lose, either. Their ideology of opposition to business has remained as bright as the new nickels which bear the leader's head and home. The Jeffersonian platform of suspicion of business, of antimonopoly, and of opposition to government favors to the special interests has become a seemingly inexhaustible reservoir of ideals and rhetoric upon which numerous radical and democratic groups have drawn. Jacksonian Democracy, Greenbackism, Populism, the Progressive Movement, and the New and Fair Deals are only the best known of such beneficiaries of the Jeffersonian economic tradition. To a great degree the tension between the Jeffersonian ideology and the Hamiltonian facts of economic life accounts for the seemingly inconsistent history of the relation between government and the economy in America.

Tradition and the parlance of the times have it that these two parties, symbolized by the rivalry between Jefferson and Hamilton, held views separated by a wide and virtually impassable gulf. In some respects, as we have seen, this is true. Certainly, for example, in sentiment the Jeffersonians placed a larger measure of trust in the "Great Beast" of the people, as Hamilton is supposed to have described them, than did the wary and pessimistic Federalists. However, at this late date in American historiography it would be well to point out that their areas of agreement were larger and perhaps more important than either side was willing to admit in the heat and joy of political rivalry.

When the Jeffersonians captured the national government in 1800, and the confusing dust of conflict had settled, the new President admitted that the area of agreement was indeed great. For, as he observed, "every difference of opinion is not a difference of principle. We have called by different names brethren of the same principle. We are all Republicans, we are all Federalists." And in office Thomas Jefferson showed that he practiced his dictum. His administration retained the hated Bank, paid off the fearsome debt, embargoed the states in the interest of a national policy, and doubled the territory of the Union in the face of the President's and the party's doubts as to constitutionality.

In 1805, like a delayed echo to Jefferson's assertion of agreement on fundamentals, aristocratic, high-Federalist Fisher Ames of Massachusetts extended what looked suspiciously like the warm hand of conversion: "I have never yet met with an American of any party," he emphasized, "who seemed willing to exclude the people from their temperate and well-regulated share of concern in the government. Indeed," he went on, "it is notorious that there was

scarcely an advocate for the Federal Constitution who was not
anxious, from the first, to hazard the experiment of an unprecedented and almost unqualified proportion of democracy, both in
constructing and administering the government, and who did not
rely with confidence, if not blind presumption on its success." In
short, the conflict over the rule of the people was less a matter of
principle than of method. "This is certain," Ames concluded, "the
body of the federalists were always, and yet are, essentially democratic in their political notions."

That these were more than rhetorical flourishes is suggested by
the record. Ames was correct when he observed that no Federalist
envisioned government in the United States without popular participation; even the imperious Hamilton, it is worth remembering,
advocated universal manhood suffrage for the election of the lower
house of a federal Congress. Moreover, one can exaggerate the Jeffersonian Republicans' belief in the uncontrolled will of the people;
both Republicans and Federalists were in fundamental accord on the
necessity of restraints upon the people and the state in the interests
of order and liberty.

Economically, the war between them concerned rather peripheral
issues like banks and debts and never touched basic assumptions like
private property or freedom of enterprise. "The soul [*sic*] end of
Government," the ultraradical farmer William Manning wrote, "is
the protection of life, Liberty and property." Government, he continued, has only to be evenhanded; "the poor man's shilling ought to
be as much the care of government as the rich man's pound."

Seen through the lenses of a century and a half, the divergencies
of the Hamiltonians and the Jeffersonians are more a matter of
tone or temperament than of hard substance. The Jeffersonians
leaned toward the agrarians and the mass of people, but they were
no enemies of what the Federalists liked to call sound money, sound
credit, and the commercial classes. Similarly, the Federalists were
aristocratically inclined, but they also stood for popular elections,
republican institutions, and a free and open society in America. The
best government, Federalist John Adams had written in 1776 in
his handbook for conservative constitutions, *Thoughts on Government*, is "the form of government which communicates . . . happiness to the greatest numbers of persons, and in the greatest degree.
. . ." No Jeffersonian Republican, or Benthamite Radical for that
matter, wanted to go any further.

One measure of the essential agreement of the two early parties was the harmonious consequences of their furious and often vituperative battles. Contrary to the fears of both sides, the Constitution proved to be a government of the people and a bulwark of individual liberty at the same time that it was a stable and energetic national government capable of sustaining itself and the economy of the country.

The vigorous party battles of those stirring days also forged weapons which would henceforth occupy a prominent place in the armory of American politics. The states' rights doctrine of the Jeffersonians is today a respectable doctrine, commonly associated with the Democratic party, but actually employed by all who distrust, fear, or hate Washington, regardless of their opinions of those embattled agrarians who originally enunciated its virtues. Similarly, the glory, dignity, and essential supremacy of the national authority—the hallmark of Federalists, Whigs, and Republicans—has found acceptance in all camps from Populists to New Dealers. Thus, in the process of determining the significance of their Revolution and the essence of free government, that first generation of Americans defined the intellectual framework within which the subsequent politics of the country has been carried on.

4. CONSERVATIVES CAN BE INNOVATORS

Like fabled genii grown too big to be imprisoned in their bottles, wars and revolutions frequently take on a life of their own irrespective of their first purposes. The overarching considerations of survival or victory distort or enlarge the narrow and limited aims for which the conflict was begun. The Revolutionary War was one such event. Begun for only limited political and constitutional purposes, the Revolution released social forces which few of the leaders ever anticipated, but which have helped to mold the American tradition.

One such unforeseen result was the rapid and final disestablishment of the Anglican Church, heretofore the state-supported religion in all of the colonies south of Mason and Dixon's Line and in parts of New York and New Jersey as well.[8] In knocking out the props of the State from beneath the Anglican Church, the states

---

[8] This is not to say, however, that disestablishment of all churches was brought about by the Revolution. All of the New England states, with the exception of Rhode Island—still loyal to Roger Williams in this respect—continued to support the Congregational Church.

provided the occasion for wider and more fundamental innovations. Virginia in 1786, in disestablishing the Anglican Church, put no other church in its place and instead passed a law guaranteeing religious freedom. This law, with which Madison and Jefferson had so much to do, prepared the ground for the ultimate triumph of the American doctrine of separation of Church and State.

The ratification of the federal Constitution in 1788 constituted the first step in the acceptance of the principle that a man's religion was irrelevant to government, for the Constitution forbade all religious tests for officeholding.[9] Then in 1791, when the first ten amendments were added, Congress was enjoined from legislating in any manner "respecting an establishment of religion or prohibiting the free exercise thereof." These legalistic and now commonplace phrases had centuries of man's religious history packed within them; upon their implementation western Christendom reached a milestone in its long quest for a viable accommodation between man's religious conscience and *raison d'état*.

For millennia a man's religion had been either a passport or a barrier to his freedom and the opportunity to serve his State; it had always mattered how a man worshiped God. Since Emperor Theodosius in the fourth century of the Christian era, religious orthodoxy had been considered necessary for good citizenship and for service to the state. All this weighty precedence was boldly overthrown by Americans in 1789-91 when they erected a government wherein "a man's religious tenets will not forfeit the protection of the Laws nor deprive him of the right of attaining and holding the

---

[9] Just because the so-called conservatives dominated the Constitutional Convention, such religious indifference was possible. Generally the radicals during the Revolutionary era were in favor of state support or recognition of some religion. Thus in the states where the radicals dominated, religious tests were part of the Constitution: Georgia (all members of the legislature had to be Protestants); North Carolina (no one could hold office who denied "God or the truth of the Protestant religion"); and Pennsylvania (the test oath demanded a belief in one God and his rewarding and punishing, and the acknowledgment that the Old and New Testaments were "given by Divine Inspiration"). The contrast with the Constitutional Convention of 1787 is striking. The Continental Congress, which had been dominated by the radicals, always opened its deliberations with chaplain-led prayers; the Convention of 1787, however, failed to have either a chaplain or prayers, though Franklin made an eloquent plea for both. He wrote later that "the Convention except three or four persons thought Prayers unnecessary." Whereas the Declaration of Independence refers to "God" and "Divine Providence," such words are completely absent from the "conservative" Constitution—much to the mystification of modern conservatives.

highest offices that are known in the United States," as George Washington said. Americans succeeded in "building a wall of separation between Church and State," Jefferson added.

In the course of the early nineteenth century, the federal example of a strict divorce of State and Church was emulated by the individual states. At the time of the Revolution many states had demanded Christian and often Protestant affiliations for officeholding, and some had even retained a state-supported Church. Gradually, however, and voluntarily—Massachusetts was last in 1833—all the states abandoned whatever connections they might have had with the churches. The doctrine of separation has been more deeply implanted in our tradition in the twentieth century by the Supreme Court, which has declared that separation is a freedom guaranteed by the Fourteenth Amendment to the Constitution and therefore obligatory upon the states as well as the federal government. Thus the two extremes of the American political spectrum—the popular state governments and the august Supreme Court—have joined in sanctioning this doctrine born out of the Revolution by the liberalism of the Enlightenment.

It was a remarkably novel and even unique approach to the question of the relation between the State and religion. Although the doctrine repudiates any connection between the State and the Church, the American version has little in common with the practice in countries like revolutionary France and Mexico and atheistic Soviet Russia, where separation has been so hostile to religion as to interfere, at times, with freedom of worship. The American conception is not antireligious at all. Our Presidents invoke the Deity and offer Thanksgiving prayers, our armies and legislatures maintain chaplains, and the state and federal governments encourage religion through the remission of taxes. In America the State was declared to be secular, but it continued to reflect the people's concern with religion.

For the eighteenth century the American action was an audacious experiment; never before had a national state been prepared to dispense with an official religion as a prop to its authority, nor had the Church ever been set adrift without state support. In practice, in a society teeming with diverse religious sects, the American doctrine has proved to be one of the most frictionless solutions to the problem of reconciling God and Mammon which any people have evolved.

As the principle of the separation of Church and State was a kind
of social side effect of the Revolution, so also was the assertion in
the Declaration of Independence that "all men are created equal."
These five words have been sneered at as idealistic, refuted as manifestly inaccurate, and denied as preposterous, but they have, nonetheless, always been capable of calling forth deep emotional response
from Americans. Even in the Revolutionary era, their power was
evident. In 1781 the Supreme Judicial Court of Massachusetts
declared slavery at an end in that state because it "is inconsistent
with our own conduct and Constitution" which "set out with declaring that all men are born free and equal. . . ." The Reverend
Samuel Hopkins told the Continental Congress that it was illogical
to "be holding so many hundreds of blacks in slavery . . . while
we are maintaining this struggle for our own and our Children's
liberty." In 1782 William Binford of Henrico County, Virginia, set
free twelve slaves because he was "fully persuaded that freedom is
the natural right of all mankind." Another Virginian, a few years
later, freed all his slaves which had been "born after the Declaration
of Independence." Such efforts to reconcile the theory of the Declaration with the practices of life represent only the beginnings of the
disquieting echoes of the celebrated phrase.

It is wrong to assume, however, that the mere inclusion of that
phrase in the Declaration worked the mighty influence implied in
the foregoing examples; social values are not created so deliberately
or so easily. Like so much else in the Declaration, this sentence was
actually the distillation of a cherished popular sentiment into a
ringing phrase, allegiance to which stemmed from its prior acceptance rather than from its eloquence. The passionate belief in social
equality which commentators and travelers in Jacksonian America
would later find so powerful was already emergent in this earlier
period. Indeed, we have already seen its lineaments during the
colonial period. After 1776 the conviction was reinforced by the
success of the Revolution and by the words of the great Declaration itself.

It was also supported by the facts of American social life. Despite
the lowly position accorded the Negro, wrote the French traveler
Brissot in 1788, it still must be admitted "that the Americans more
than any other people are convinced that all men are born free and
equal." Moreover, he added, "we must acknowledge, that they direct
themselves generally by this principle of equality." German traveler

Johann Schoepf noticed that in Philadelphia "rank of birth is not recognized, is resisted with a total force. . . . People think, act, and speak here precisely as it prompts them. . . ." [10] And in the privacy of the Federal Convention of 1787, Charles Pinckney of South Carolina urged his fellow delegates to recognize the uniqueness of their country. "There is more equality of rank and fortune in America than in any other country under the sun," he told them.

There were other signs of what an earlier generation would have stigmatized as "leveling tendencies" in the new post-Revolutionary society. The attacks made by the Democratic-Republican societies upon the privileged Order of the Cincinnati, because it was secret and confined to Revolutionary officers and their descendants, were obviously inspired by a growing egalitarian sentiment. French traveler Moreau de Saint-Méry recalled with disgust how Americans proudly told him that the hotel custom of putting strange travelers together in the same bed was "a proof of liberty." By the end of the century old social distinctions like rank-seating in churches and the differentiating title of esquire were fast passing out of vogue. On an economic level, this abiding American faith was translated as equality of opportunity, and here dour Federalist Fisher Ames could lock arms with his Republican opponents when he averred that "all cannot be rich, but all have a right to make the attempt."

Though economic grievances seem to have played a negligible role in bringing on the Revolution, this is not to say that there were no economic consequences. The economic stimulus afforded by the war demands and the freedom from English mercantilistic restrictions which victory made permanent provided adventuresome American merchants and entrepreneurs with wide opportunities for gaining new markets and new sources of profit. The expansion of the American economy, which was to be characteristic all through the nineteenth century, was thus begun.

But even when one has added together the new constitutions, the enlightened religious innovations, and the stimulus to equality, it is quickly apparent that the social consequences of the Revolution were meager indeed. In both purpose and implementation they were

[10] Schoepf, interestingly enough, discovered in the economic opportunities available in America the source of the social equality. "Riches make no positive material difference," he wrote concerning Philadelphia society, "because in this regard every man expects at one time or another to be on a footing with his rich neighbor, and in this expectation shows him no knavish reverence, but treats him with an open, but seemly familiarity."

not to be equated with the massive social changes which shook France and Russia in later years. For the most part, the society of post-Revolutionary America was but the working out of social forces which were already evident in the colonial period.

It is significant, for example, that no new social class came to power through the door of the American Revolution. The men who engineered the revolt were largely members of the colonial ruling class. Peyton Randolph and Patrick Henry were well-to-do members of the Virginia Assembly; Washington, reputed to be the richest man in America, was an officer in the Virginia militia. The New York leaders John Morin Scott and Robert Livingston were judges on the Supreme Court of the colony, while William Drayton, a fire-eating radical of South Carolina, was a nephew of the lieutenant governor of the province, and himself a member of the Governor's Council until his anti-British activities forced his removal. Certainly Benjamin Franklin, citizen of the Empire, celebrated scientist, and long retired, well-to-do printer, was no submerged member of Philadelphia's society—or London's for that matter. Moreover, Franklin's natural son, William, was a Royal Governor at the outbreak of the Revolution. Hancock of Boston and Christopher Gadsden of Charleston were only two of the many respected and wealthy merchants who lent their support to the patriot cause. In fact, speaking of wealth, the Revolution in Virginia was made and led by the great landed class, and its members remained to reap the benefits. Farther down the social scale, in the backwoods of Massachusetts, it has been shown that the chief revolutionists in the western counties were the old leaders, so that no major shift in leadership took place there either as a result of the Revolution.

This emphasis on position and wealth among the Revolutionary leaders should not be taken as a denial that many men of wealth and brains left the colonies in the exodus of the Loyalists. Certainly few patriots were the peers of Jared Ingersoll in the law, Jonathan Boucher in the Church, and Thomas Hutchinson and James Galloway in government. But the Loyalist departure did not decapitate the colonial social structure, as some have suggested—it only removed those most attached to the mother country. The rest of the governing class remained to guide the Revolution and reap its favors. It is true that in the states of Georgia and Pennsylvania, where the radical democrats held sway in the early years of the Revolution, new men seemed to occupy positions of power. But these

men were still unknowns on the periphery of government and business, and generally remained there; they cannot be compared with
the Robespierres and the Dantons, the Lenins and the Trotskys, of
the great continental eruptions.

A convenient gauge of the essential continuity of the governing
class in America before and after the Revolution is to be found in
an examination of the careers of the signers of the Declaration of
Independence. Surely these fifty-five men are important patriot
leaders and presumably among the chief beneficiaries of the Revolution they advocated. Yet they were by no means a disadvantaged
lot. Fully 40 per cent of them attended college or one of the Inns
of Court in England at a time when such a privilege was a rarity.
An additional 21 per cent of them came from important families of
their respective colonies, or, like Robert Morris and Joseph Hewes,
were men of acquired wealth. Over 69 per cent of them held office
under the colonial regimes, 29 per cent alone holding some office
within the executive branch; truly these were not men held at arm's
length from the plums of office.

Most striking about the careers of these men is the fact that so
many of them held office before and after the dividing line of the
Revolution. Of those who held an office under the state governments
after the Revolution, 75 per cent had occupied offices before 1774,
proving, if need be, that service in the colonial governments before
the Revolution was no obstacle to political preferment for a patriot
afterward. If those who held no office before 1774 are not counted—
and several might be considered too young to be expected to have
held office—then the continuity shows up even more clearly. Eighty-
nine per cent of those who filled an office before the Revolution also
occupied an office under one of the new state governments. And if
federal office after 1789 is included, then the proportion rises to 95
per cent. Add to this the fact that other leaders, not included in
the group of signers, had similarly good social backgrounds—men
like Washington, Robert Livingston, Gouverneur Morris, Philip
Schuyler, and a dozen more—and the conclusion that the Revolution was a thoroughly upper-middle-class affair in leadership and
aim is inescapable.

A further and perhaps more important conclusion should be
drawn from this analysis of the political careers of the signers after
the Revolution. These conservative, upper-class leaders who proclaimed the Revolution suffered no repudiation in the course of the

struggle, no mass from the bottom rose and seized control of the Revolutionary situation to direct the struggle into new channels. Rather these men merely shifted, as it were, from their favored status under the colonial regimes to comparable, if not improved, positions after the Revolution.

As a colonial revolt against an alien power, such a development is not surprising. But certainly—for better or for worse—the continuity brought a degree of social and political stability to the new nation rarely associated with the word "revolution" and serves, once again, to illustrate the truly conservative nature of the American revolt.

Similarly, in the redistribution of land, which played such a crucial role in France and Russia, the American Revolution set no example of social motivation or consequence. The Crown's lands, it is true, were confiscated, and—of greater import—so were the lands of the proprietors and those of the literally thousands of Tories. But the disposition of these lands hardly constitutes a social revolution of major proportions. One can collect, of course, examples of the breakup of great estates, like the De Lancey manor in New York, which was sold to 275 individuals, or the 40,000-acre estate in North Carolina which was carved into scores of plots averaging 200 acres apiece, or the vast 21,000,000-acre proprietary lands of the Penns. But the more significant question to be answered is who got the land. And, from the studies which have been made, it would appear that most often the land went to speculators or men already possessing substantial acreage, not to the landless or even to the small holder. To be sure, much Tory land which first fell under the auctioneer's hammer to a speculator ultimately found its way into the hands of a yeoman, but such a procedure is a rather slow and orderly process of social revolution.

Furthermore, it is obvious from the Confiscation Acts in the several states and the commissioners who operated pursuant to them that the motive behind the acquisition of Tory lands was enhancement of the state revenues—as, indeed, the original resolution from Congress had suggested. Under such circumstances, pecuniary motives, not democratic theories of society, determined the configuration distribution would take. And it is here that we begin to touch upon the fundamental reason why the confiscation of the royal, proprietary, and Loyalist lands never assumed crucial social importance. Land was just too plentiful in America for these acres to matter. Speculators were loaded down with it; most men who wanted it already possessed it, or were on the way toward possession. One recent investigator of the confiscations in New York, for example, has pointed out that land there could be bought cheaper from speculators than from a former Tory estate.

Even the abolition of primogeniture in all the southern states by 1791 cannot be taken as a significant example of the Revolution's economic influence. The fact of the matter is that primogeniture had never appreciably affected land distribution, since it came into play only when the owner died intestate. Considering the notorious litigiousness of eighteenth-century Americans, it is hardly to be doubted that partible inheritance was the practice, if not the theory, long before primogeniture was wiped from the statute books. Furthermore, in almost half of the country—New Jersey, Pennsylvania, and all of the New England states—primogeniture never prevailed anyway.

As for the abolition of entail, it was frequently welcomed by owners of entailed estates, as was the case in Jefferson's Virginia, since it would permit the sale of otherwise frozen assets. These laws had not created a landed aristocracy in America and their repeal made no significant alteration in the social landscape.

Instead of being an abrupt break, the Revolution was a natural and even expected event in the history of a colonial people who had come of age. It is true that social and political changes accompanied the Revolution, some of which were destined to work great influence upon American institutions in the future, but these had been implicit in the pre-Revolutionary society. Moreover, important social institutions were left untouched by the Revolution: the class structure, the distribution of property, the capitalistic economy, the ideas of the people concerning government.

This lack of profound and widespread social and economic change is not surprising. These Americans, for all their talk, had been a contented and prosperous people under the British Crown and they were, therefore, contented revolutionaries who wanted nothing more than to be undisturbed in their accustomed ways. They are in no wise to be compared with the disgruntled lawyers, the frustrated bourgeois, the tyrannized workers, and the land-hungry peasants of the *anciens régimes* of France and Russia.

Yet, in conclusion, it is perhaps fitting to recall that America was born in revolution, for this fact has become embedded in our folk and sophisticated traditions alike. It was apparent in the self-conscious, often naïve enthusiasm displayed by American statesmen and people in support of the colonial rebellions in South America and Greece in the early years of the nineteenth century. Revolutionaries of the middle of the century, like Kossuth and Garibaldi, garnered moral and material benefits from this continuing American friendship for rebellion. European exiles and revolutionaries of 1848 were entertained at the London residence of United States Minister James Buchanan. And it is still apparent today. When Americans arrived in Batavia in 1945 during the revolt of the Indonesians against the Dutch, they found quotations from the Declaration of Independence and the Gettysburg Address scrawled on the walls of buildings. And Nasser of Egypt, at the time of the American intervention in Lebanon in July, 1958, taunted us with it. "How can the United States, which pushed off British colonialism many years ago, forget its history?" he shouted to a crowd in Damascus. "Our history books tell us that the American Revolution ended in Yorktown," Richard Nixon, Vice-President of the United States, said in 1956. "But the American Revolution will not be complete until the ideals of independence, equality and freedom which kept men fighting at Valley Forge are a reality not only for Americans but for peoples throughout the world."

An anticolonial tradition of such weight could not fail to leave its stamp upon American attitudes, as any perusal of the anti-imperialistic literature at the time of the Spanish-American War reveals. The United States has been fortunate in that its remarkably abundant natural endowment has always permitted its people to indulge in idealistic anticolonialism unhampered by the elemental economic needs which have driven other less fortunately situated peoples into imperialistic adventures. As a consequence, Americans have generally scorned colonies; even after some were acquired in 1898, the nation soon began to try to shake them off. Within a decade of the acquisition of the alien Philippines, the nation was already discussing means whereby the burden could be shifted to Filipino shoulders. Today Hawaii is following Alaska to statehood, while Puerto Rico has attained a status amounting to virtual freedom.

Long before, in the era of the Revolution, American leaders, profiting from the lessons of Britain's imperial problems, agreed in the Ordinance of 1787 and the Constitution that newly acquired territories could attain, in the natural course of events, equal constitutional status with the original thirteen states. Thus, in a single stroke, Americans sidestepped the tensions and divisions attendant upon a colonial empire and laid the enduring foundations for an expanding and united country.

Constitutional devices, however, no matter how clever or far-sighted, cannot of themselves create a new people. The forces of economics and geography can wreak havoc with the best laid plans of Founding Fathers. Whether Americans would retain their independence and become a truly united people was to be determined only by time and the people themselves.

CHAPTER IV

To Make a
More Perfect Union

BETWEEN the War of 1812 and the Spanish-American War in 1898, the great events which agitated American life were almost exclusively internal and domestic. One of the objects of this inward concentration was the taming and settling of the vast geographical reaches of the new country. This task, which was not completed until the end of the century, was not thrust upon Americans; rather it was one which they eagerly undertook. The conquest of a continent with ax, plow, and factory was at once an expression and a determinant of the American character.

Land, however, does not make a people. Indeed, when the land is of great extent, as it was in the United States, it poses serious problems for a young Republic seeking to become a united nation. In the course of the years between 1812 and the Civil War, the economic bonds and sinews of the Union were created. So well did the Americans of those years build that the Union was able to withstand the disruptive force of a rebellion of unprecedented proportions.

1. AGRARIAN IMPERIALISM

In 1800 the United States stretched no farther inland than the Mississippi River and, though its northern border was very much as it is today, on the south the American flag did not anywhere touch the Gulf of Mexico: Florida, which then extended along the coast to the Mississippi, was still in the hands of Spain—and so was New Orleans at the mouth of the river. Within the lifetime of a middle-aged man—that is, within less than fifty-five years—the

United States exploded to its present size, an increase in area of some 300 per cent.

In no case was the acquisition of new land dictated by the elemental need for *Lebensraum;* Americans always had access to more land within the United States than they could utilize. In 1820, for instance, when Americans were already moving into Louisiana, Mississippi, and Illinois—states which at that date were ".western" —the density of population in Georgia was still less than two persons per square mile. County after county in north-central Pennsylvania, which later would support thousands of people, was largely unsettled. There were still great areas of South and North Carolina which averaged no more than eighteen persons per square mile. And in 1840, when the nation was eyeing the territories of Mexico stretching beyond the Louisiana Purchase, large parts of central Illinois, southern Georgia, and western Virginia were still only at the frontier stage.

It was the West which drew them on, the West which was free for the taking, the West which was a challenge and a terror all in one. Free land, unencumbered by speculator's high prices or landlord's rents, was an irresistible magnet to native American and displaced European alike. As the world was to find out, there was nothing that could stem this drive short of the sea itself.[1]

Early in the history of the Republic, abundant land was placed at the disposal of the people long before they felt any need for it. The Louisiana Purchase, as is well known, was an accident—another of those instances where Europe's distress was America's gain. President Jefferson would have been content to buy the port of New Orleans from Napoleon, but the needs of the French ruler made it possible for the American ministers to purchase half the land between the Mississippi River and the Rocky Mountains. Though the

---

[1] Illustrative of the process whereby Americans before 1860 filled up the West was the migration of Thomas Lincoln, small farmer and father of the President. Born in western Virginia, Thomas Lincoln moved as a small boy, with his father, to central Kentucky. When he married, he settled on a farm in Hardin County in the western part of the same state, where Abraham was born in 1809. When the son was only seven the family moved to Spencer County in southwestern Indiana. By the time the future President reached his majority, Thomas was on the move again—this time to Macon County in central Illinois. Though the frequency of Thomas' moves is somewhat unusual, the shortness of the jumps is quite in keeping with frontier practice. Aside from the European immigrants, very few westering people made a dramatic leap from the East to the farthermost fringes of civilization.

Purchase doubled the size of the Republic with one stroke of the pen—and for a mere $15 million—it was only the beginning of that lust for real estate which would bring the American people face to face with salt water within a generation after Jefferson's death. As the English traveler Harriet Martineau observed in the 1830's, "The possession of land is the aim of all action, generally speaking, and the cure for all social ills, among men in the United States. If a man is disappointed in politics or love, he goes and buys land. If he disgraces himself, he betakes himself to a lot in the West."

Sometimes this hunger for land, for settlement, for speculation, for temporary squatting, for isolation—all these motives were operative—was so strong as to run ahead of the boundaries of the nation. Even though the United States had only recently acquired the enormous and empty expanse of the Louisiana Purchase, a number of Americans in the early years of the century pushed into the scantily populated lands of Spain along the Gulf of Mexico. By 1810 these hardy souls had effected a revolution against Spain in the territory then called West Florida and now included in southern Louisiana and Mississippi. With almost studied casualness, these settlers offered this generous slice of Spanish territory to the United States; and, with less reason for naïveté, President Madison accepted—but not before the administration deliberately misdated documents to cover up American governmental complicity in the *coup d'état*. Apparently swayed by the success of such intrigues against the "effete Spaniard," the President looked forward to a similar coup in the rest of West Florida—that is, as far east as Mobile. His hopes, however, garnered no fruit. Not until the War of 1812, in which Spain was conveniently the ally of Great Britain, was the United States able to wrest Mobile from Spanish Florida. The process of rounding out the southeastern border of the nation was completed in 1819, when John Quincy Adams succeeded in negotiating the purchase of the rest of what is now the State of Florida.[2]

This was only the springtime of American territorial ambitions; summer was still to come. But it was about this time that Adams, as

[2] The confident air which surrounded American thoughts on the matter of the proper borders for the country is strikingly illustrated in a quotation from a newspaper in 1819, when the purchase of Florida was being discussed. "Any man . . . must have seen that the Floridas would certainly pass into the possession of the United States. They as naturally belong to us as the county of Cornwall does to England."

Secretary of State, told a private Cabinet meeting that "the world shall be familiarized with the idea of considering our proper domain to be the continent of North America." Ever since we gained our independence, he said, "it was as much a law of nature that this should become our pretension as that the Mississippi should flow to the sea." Before long, Americans would be saying such things in public.

During the 1820's and 1830's large numbers of Americans moved into the northern portion of Mexico, and by 1835 these new settlers were strong enough to carry out a successful revolt against Mexican authority. Once again the restless, vigorous, and expansive spirit of Americans on the move and on the make proved overwhelming for a people whose ancestors had been the suzerains of Europe and the conquistadors of the New World.

The American infiltration of Texas was more than simply a revolt against Mexico; it provided the occasion for the war between the United States and Mexico in 1846.[3] The Texan Revolution, which Harriet Martineau called "the most high-handed theft of modern times," had not ended in a clear-cut victory for the Texans because Mexico refused to acknowledge the independence of the newly declared Republic even though the Mexican government was powerless to exercise control over its erstwhile subjects. This, however, did not prevent the Texans from negotiating for annexation to the United States. In 1845, as inclusion of Texas in the United States came closer to reality, Mexico agreed to full recognition of the Republic of Texas on the condition that annexation to the United States would not take place. In the light of history, Mexico had good reason to fear that annexation was merely a prelude to further encroachments upon Mexican territory. Neither the United States nor the Texans, however, permitted the Mexican concern to impede

---

[3] This was not the first time that "agrarian cupidity" had helped to push the United States into war with its neighbors. Before 1812 it was the Westerners who clamored for war against Canada and Spanish Florida in order to gain access to the lands of those colonies. The famous War Hawks of the period were almost entirely congressmen from the western states. It was in the course of the fateful Twelfth Congress (1811–12) that John Randolph of Roanoke made his celebrated attack upon the war party. "Sir, if you go to war it will not be for the protection of, or defence of your maritime rights," he said. "Gentlemen from the north have been taken up into some high mountain and shown all the kingdoms of the earth; and Canada seems tempting in their sight. That rich vein of Genesee land, which is said to be even better on the right side of the lake than on this. Agrarian cupidity, not maritime right, urges the war."

annexation. When Texas was incorporated into the American Union, the stage was set for war between the United States and Mexico.

One thorn which had long irritated Texan-Mexican relations had been the determination of the southern border of Texas. Mexico insisted that the boundary was the Nueces River; Texas, and now the United States, claimed it was the Rio Grande, the mouth of which was over a hundred miles south of that of the Nueces—the distance between Corpus Christi and Brownsville. As was to be anticipated, soon after the annexation of Texas, the armed forces of the United States and Mexico clashed in the disputed area. For this and other reasons, President Polk called upon an expansion-minded Congress to declare war against Mexico.

Though once held to be a gigantic slaveholders' conspiracy to extend the area open to slavery, the Mexican War is today likely to be viewed by historians as part of that feeling of Manifest Destiny [4] which eventually planted the American flag on the shores of the Pacific. The irresistible territorial ambitions and sense of mission which gripped Americans in this era are only credible in the language of the time. Listen to this speaker at a Democratic state convention in 1844. "Make way, I say, for the young American Buffalo—he has not yet got land enough; he wants more land as his cool shelter in summer—he wants more land for his beautiful pasture grounds. I tell you, we will give him Oregon for his summer shade, and the region of Texas as his winter pasture. Like all of his race, he wants salt, too. Well, he shall have the use of two oceans—the mighty Pacific and turbulent Atlantic shall be his. . . . He shall not stop his career until he slakes his thirst in the frozen ocean." Except for the implied interest in the acquisition of Canada, which was real enough, the future was to fulfill the orator's prophecy.

Convinced as they were of their virtues and hungry for the un-used lands of the Mexican-held Southwest, Americans could not resist, when the cost seemed so slight, taking what they craved. One journal in 1845 spoke of the American people as "the most inde-

---

[4] Historians usually credit John L. O'Sullivan, spread-eagle nationalist editor of the Jacksonian-Democratic organ *United States Magazine and Democratic Review,* for originating the phrase. In an article in 1845, justifying American claims to the Oregon territory, O'Sullivan asserted that the American claim "is by right of our manifest destiny to overspread and to possess the whole of the Continent which Providence has given us for the development of the great experiment of liberty and federated self-government entrusted to us."

pendent, intelligent, moral and happy people on the face of the earth." And Caleb Cushing asked, in affirming the annexation of territory after the Mexican War, "Is not the occupation of any portion of the earth by those competent to hold and till it, a providential law of national life?" The victory over Mexico added territory to the Union from which were created the states of California, Nevada, New Mexico, Arizona, Utah, and Texas.

While the troubles with Mexico were deteriorating into war, President Polk successfully carried through negotiations with Great Britain concerning our northwestern boundary with Canada. Unable to sustain against powerful Britain the highly inflated claims blown up by the winds of Manifest Destiny, the American government resorted to compromise. The 49th parallel, which was already the northern boundary of the Louisiana Purchase, was simply extended from the Great Lakes to the Pacific. (The original American demand of 54 degrees and 40 minutes north latitude would have set the border just below the present southern tip of Alaska!) As a consequence of the agreement with Britain and the concluding of peace with Mexico, when James K. Polk left office in March, 1849, the map of the United States looked as it does today, with the exception of a little slice of southern Arizona—the so-called Gadsden Purchase, which was acquired in 1854.

The incorporation within the United States of the immense trans-Mississippi region by the peaceful Louisiana Purchase and the violent war with Mexico opened up a treasure chest of natural resources. In that territory were to be found some of the richest wheat- and breadstuff-producing lands of the New World; pasture lands of fabulous extent which would one day support a great cattle industry; almost endless forests of superb timber; deposits of copper, zinc, lead, silver, and gold sufficient to quench the greed of a Spanish conquistador. The future triumph of American industrial power was largely foreshadowed in those gifts of nature and the westward movement.

A gargantuan territory, however, also presented problems. From a political standpoint alone, the new lands, long before they were even settled, were responsible for the sharpening of the conflict between North and South. It was over the question of the extension of slavery into the trans-Mississippi region that the long-bubbling issue of slavery finally boiled up into secession and civil war. As the West had lain at the center of the constellation of forces which

brought on the Mexican War, as it lay like a smoldering fuse among
the powder kegs of North-South suspicions and animosities.

2. MORE THAN SENTIMENT

But this is getting ahead of our story. Long before it presented
itself as an issue in politics, the West was an economic problem.
Moreover, before there was a trans-Mississippi West there was an
earlier West—the land between the Appalachians and the Mississippi—and its challenge to the new nation was both early and real.

Even before the Louisiana Purchase in 1803, the United States
far exceeded in extent every country in Europe with the exception of
the multinational empires of Russia and Austria-Hungary. As a
result and in view of the scattered character of the settlements west
of the Appalachians, the problems of communication alone were at
once enormous and vital if the new nation was to stay together. At
the time of the Revolution, Europeans had freely predicted that no
country of such dimensions could long remain united. And when one
contemplates the travel facilities of the time, the predictions have
the ominous ring of truth: one and a half weeks at best to make the
trip from New York to Pittsburgh in 1800; four days from New
York to Washington; four weeks for the trip from New Orleans to
New York. Moreover, it should be remembered that news could travel
no faster in those days than a man.

Such great distances carried economic as well as political implications. It meant that surplus goods would have only local, and
therefore limited, markets unless the interior was provided with improved communications. And so long as the market was restricted,
there would be restraints on the expansion of production and the
accumulation of wealth. In short, in the absence of adequate transportation facilities, the new nation would be held down—or at least
large segments of its population would be held down to a subsistence
level of production and consumption. Politically, the geography of
the country was a source of disunity. After the Revolution, thousands of Americans climbed the Appalachians to seek out the untouched territories of the West. With only primitive and tedious
communications to connect them with the East, the allegiance of
these Westerners was both tested and eroded by the elemental facts
of topography.

As early as the 1780's and 1790's disaffection among the transmontane settlements in Kentucky and Tennessee was acute; the people of these areas found their most expeditious routes for exporting surpluses to be the great rivers of the region: the Cumberland, the Tennessee, the Ohio, the Green, and the Kentucky, all of which ultimately drained into the Mississippi and thence to the Spanish-held port of New Orleans. The leaders of the young nation, however, well aware of such dangers to national unity, took several steps to forestall the separation of the West. The climatic stroke was the purchase, in 1803, of New Orleans and its hinterland for a thousand miles to the north.

Nor were such precautions premature. Several conspiracies to detach from the Union the men and lands of the West punctuated the history of the early years of the Republic. General James Wilkinson had been active all during the 1780's and 1790's in behalf of the Spanish power; and in 1804–6 Vice-President Aaron Burr was engaging in shadowy schemes with Wilkinson and English and Spanish agents, all of which boded ill for the territorial integrity of the country.

Though the assorted separatist conspiracies failed, there was nothing inherent in the vastness of the new country to weld it into a nation. Only improved means of communication and transport could do that, for only when a people know one another and their common land do they begin to experience that quickening of emotion and consciousness of kind called national feeling. The material foundation for the growth of a national consciousness, laid down in the first half of the nineteenth century, has come to be called the Transportation Revolution.

Historians are wary, and rightly so, of the word "revolution" when applied to social and economic change, for rarely do such alterations come rapidly and dramatically enough to justify the term. But sometimes, when the word is applied to changes measured against a long previous history, it is appropriate. Despite the fact that fifty years were required for the completion of this Transportation Revolution, those years are telescoped to but an instant of time when compared with the preceding two or three millennia during which no comparable improvements in communication were made.

The Transportation Revolution began in the last years of the eighteenth and first decades of the nineteenth centuries with the

construction of improved roads and turnpikes [5] State and local
governments and private companies were responsible for the building
of roads westward into the interior and north and south. The national government made its contribution in the form of a major east-
west artery which ultimately connected Cumberland, Maryland, with
central Illinois.

Prior to the coming of the railroad, land transport, regardless of
the quality and quantity of roads, was held down to the low efficiency
of animal power. Because of this, beginning in the 1820's with New
York's spectacularly successful Erie Canal, the construction of
canals was undertaken to link the rivers and lakes of the interior and
to connect them with seaboard ports. Down to 1816 there were no
more than one hundred miles of canals in the United States, but by
1840, when the canal-building era was at its zenith, there were over
3,300 miles in being. By water the bulky farm products of the interior could be cheaply shipped to distant markets, with consequent
stimulus to the economic growth of the newly opened lands.

The Erie Canal, running almost 400 miles into the West and connecting the Hudson River with Lake Erie, providing an incredibly
cheap means of transportation between the Great Lakes states and
New York City, was an outstanding example of the potentialities of
the inland waterway. (Francis Lieber said that it was also "a clamp
by which the west of this Union is tightly fastened to the east and
north.") Between 1817 and the 1850's the Erie Canal cut the cost
of transportation between Buffalo and New York City 95 per cent.
Feeder canals north and south extended the benefit of the waterway
to the widely scattered farmers of western and northern New York.

Canals in Indiana, Ohio, and Illinois linked the settlers of the
interior with oceanic ports, either to the north, through the Lakes
and the Erie Canal, or to the south, through the Ohio-Mississippi
rivers. The Wabash and Erie Canal, which ran between Toledo on
the Lakes to Evansville, Indiana, on the Ohio River, when completed
in 1856 exceeded even the Erie Canal in length; it was over 450 miles.

States other than those along the Lakes found that canals pro-

[5] The word "turnpike," which in the automobile age signifies a superhighway,
did not, of course, have any such meaning in the early years of the Republic. It
merely stood for a road upon which tolls were paid at stated intervals. When the
toll was paid, the pike, which had been placed across the road, was turned—
hence the name—and the traveler permitted to proceed. It is, of course, the pay-
ment for travel which has caused the word to be revived in the middle of the
twentieth century.

vided a desperately needed answer to the problems of settlement and economic expansion. Pennsylvania, for instance, attempting to duplicate New York's success, built a combined canal, railroad, and system of inclined planes to stretch from Philadelphia to Pittsburgh. The geographical obstacles in Pennsylvania were too great for that effort to be as successful as the Erie—there was no low pass through the Alleghenies such as the Mohawk River provided in New York— but parts of it were links between ports, markets, and the back country. Other canals were built north and south, following the Susquehanna River, thus providing the northern and southern parts of Pennsylvania with outlets for goods. Maryland constructed the Chesapeake and Ohio Canal, which ran beside the Potomac River into the interior of the state. The cities of Richmond and Lynchburg, on the James River in Virginia, were joined by a canal. New Jersey mixed the waters of the Delaware River and the Atlantic Ocean by digging the Delaware and Raritan Canal in 1838. With the opening of the Soo Canal, between Huron and Superior, in 1855, the Great Lakes themselves were turned into a gigantic inland waterway usable by large ships. Though England had built canals with success in the eighteenth century and even the Romans had constructed shipping canals almost two millennia earlier, the extensive canal building in the United States, compressed as it was into a mere generation, is accurately called a minor revolution in transportation.[6]

Cheap as canal transportation was, its speed was still tied to the plodding gait of the mule, just as the movement of goods overland was held down to the speed and power of the horse. The adaptation of steam power to inland water transportation was, therefore, one of the liberating innovations of the early nineteenth century. Considering the immense distances within the United States and the large number of navigable rivers in the interior, it is not surprising that the river boat was an American invention. Though originating in the East, the steamboat figured most prominently on the rivers and in the economy of the West.

The western steamboat was quite a different craft from the eastern. As a study in technological adaptation to environment, the steamboat of the West is eminently instructive. Compelled to sail

[6] Nor has the canal lost its usefulness in the age of the railroad and the truck. Some of the canals built in the early nineteenth century still function, notably the Erie and several in Ohio and Illinois. The Erie, now the New York State Barge Canal, regularly carries about 4.5 million tons of goods each year.

upon rivers which were notorious for their shallow depth (the
Mississippi above St. Louis averages less than five feet), the river
boats were designed to carry everything, including the engines,
above the waterline—hence their characteristic pile of superstruc-
ture. Charles Dickens likened them to "a child's Noah's Ark in form,
with the machinery on the top of the roof." In order to deal with the
treacherous currents and innumerable snags and bars, the boats
had to have great power—hence the constant danger of explosion.

It was not until the years 1815–17 that the full potential of the
steamboat on western waters was recognized. Within these years a
number of long trips up the Mississippi demonstrated the enormous
economic value of the western rivers. Henry Shreve, who helped to
break Robert Fulton's monopoly on steamboat construction, sailed
the *Enterprise* (1815) and the *Washington* (1817)—the latter
being the biggest boat on the river at the time—from New Orleans
to Louisville in the unheard-of time of twenty-five days. Within these
same years, one of Fulton's boats, the *Aetna*, made four such long
and rapid trips.

Prior to the introduction of steam in navigation, the western
rivers had been usable, of course, on a downstream trip, but as
arteries of trade they were almost totally useless upstream, short
of a backbreaking and costly poling against the current. For this
reason the arrival of the towering river boat at a town was more
than a picturesque social event—though it was usually that, too.
The river boat, like the later railroad, was a symbol of the great
importance of machine technology in the making of the United
States. The steamboat could, like the later railroad, make or break
an ambitious community. The fact that Cincinnati was known as
Porkopolis—because of its large shipments of hog meat—is largely
attributable to the steamboat. In the same way, cities like St. Louis,
Cairo, Memphis, Natchez, and Louisville were almost the creations
of the river boats.

Probably the technolgical device in transportation which most
truly merits the appellation "revolutionary" is the railroad. Introduced into the country at the end of the 1820's it found a secure
niche in American economic life almost from the outset; by 1860,
over 30,000 miles of track had been laid and, as events would prove,
this was only the beginning.

The economic and social consequences of the railroad can scarcely
be exaggerated. It was the first land transport vehicle in history

which could carry bulk goods in competition with water routes. Louis Hunter, seeking to compare costs of transportation during the years 1831–58, offers some figures on rates which also serve to sum up statistically the economics of the Transportation Revolution. Roughly comparable rates in cents per ton-mile were: by road, 11.66; by canal, 2.37; by railroad, 2.25; by steamboat, 1.14. Though railroad rates were often higher than those of river boat or barge, the greater speed and adaptability to topography of the railroad easily made up the difference. In many sections of the country the coming of the railroad blackened the future as well as the sky over the canal barge. Considering the fact that a farmer in 1810 was still sending his goods to market by the same means as a farmer in the days of Julius Caesar, the advent and expansion of the railroad was a revolutionary event in the economic life of the American people—as it has proved to be for any people into whose lives it has been introduced. Emerson wrote at the time, "Railroad iron is a magician's rod in its power to evoke the sleeping energies of land and water."

A measure of the importance the American people attached to canals and railroads was the support which their governments gave to such enterprises. From the work of a number of scholars in recent years it has become increasingly clear that financial assistance from state and local government was often crucial in the building of lines of transport. The best-known example, of course, was the Erie Canal, which was entirely state-built. Two other ventures in which the state assumed full responsibility for construction when private enterprise had neither the heart nor the resources for it were the Blue Ridge Railroad of Virginia and the Western and Atlantic of Georgia.

But the commonest mode of public assistance to internal improvements was the so-called mixed enterprise, in which public and private funds were pooled. For some forty years before the Civil War, Virginia employed the mixed corporation in the building of internal improvements. Three fifths of the capital in such corporations was contributed by private persons and two fifths by the state, the latter naming a proportionate number of directors, but receiving its dividends last. Between 1816 and 1861, the State of Virginia invested about $41 million in such projects.

Other states also encouraged transportation construction in concrete ways. The Missouri Constitution of 1821, for instance, explicitly stated that "internal improvements shall forever be encouraged by the government of this State," and by 1860 something like $23 million had been pledged by the state to such improvements, despite the fact that the figure was twenty-five times the state's average annual income. Pennsylvania invested over $6 million of state funds in some 150 mixed corporations, while Massachusetts spent $8 million on eight railroads in the years before 1860. The latter state continued its interest in public aid to transportation after the Civil War, building the Hoosac Railroad Tunnel at a cost of almost $29 million. Well over half of the cost of construction of the railroads of the South before 1860 came from public funds, one authority has calculated. A recent study of canal building throughout the nation reveals that 60 per cent of the almost $200 million invested in canals between 1815 and 1860 came from public funds.

Local communities were as vitally interested as the states in the support of railroad construction. Between 1826 and 1875, it has been estimated, some 315 New York cities and towns pledged almost $37 million to railroad building in the state. The city of Baltimore alone invested $20 million between 1827 and 1866, while Cincinnati topped even that figure. Towns and cities contributed almost a third of the $144 million in public aid to railroads in the South before 1860.

In the 1830's Mrs. Trollope, so critical of America in many ways, was moved to say that nothing in the American character "commands so much respect as the boldness and energy with which public works are undertaken and carried through." In this historical context, Lincoln's dictum that the "legitimate object of government" is to do for the people what they "cannot do at all or cannot do so well for themselves in their separate or individual capacities" takes on a meaning more friendly to government enterprises than usually supposed.

Apart from the improvement in internal communication, public assistance to economic enterprise during the first half of the nineteenth century has important implications. It suggests that government aids like land grants to railroads after the Civil War and even the much later Tennessee Valley Authority are quite within a long American tradition of fruitful union between public and private enterprise. More concerned about getting the job done than about dogmatic conceptions of the relations between government and the economy, the Americans of the pre-Civil War era amply demonstrated the practical streak in their economic thought.

In the building of an American nation, the transportation net was of tremendous importance. Emerson observed that "the rage of road building" was "beneficent for America . . . inasmuch as the great political promise" of internal improvements was "to hold the Union staunch" against "the tedious distances of land and water." But of all the various improvements in transportation, the railroad was the most important. Canals, roads, and steamboats, for all their advantages, were, if nothing else, severely limited in their efficiency and usefulness. Canals required water to fill them, and despite the steamboat captain's boastful jest that his light-draft ship could sail anywhere so long as there was a heavy dew, rivers were his only roads. Simply because of this limitation, if for no other, large areas of the back country never heard the deep-throated whistle or saw the tall black stacks of the river boat. The railroad, however, with its magic rails, could leap over the most desolate areas almost as easily as it followed the gentle roadbed of the river valley.

The cohesive power of transport and particularly of the railroad is dramatically evident in the years leading up to the disruption of the Union in 1861. Because settlement in Ohio, Indiana, and Illinois prior to 1825 was primarily in the southern portions, along the Ohio and Mississippi rivers, goods and people tended to flow south and north, following the natural trade artery of the rivers. When the Erie Canal was opened in 1825, the northern portions of these western states grew rapidly by shipping their goods and receiving immigrants via the New York canal and the Lakes. But even though the eastern pull of the canal was strong, it could not eliminate the powerful southward attraction of the Mississippi-Ohio route. As late as 1850, the southern-flowing rivers were carrying 2.4 million bushels of corn compared with 3.6 million bushels traveling eastward. While only 300,000 barrels of western pork was being sold in the East, 1.2 million barrels were being shipped in 1850 down the rivers to the South.

For this reason, southern leaders in the late 1840's and early 1850's looked with confidence to the West for support in the political struggle with the Northeast over the questions of the nature of the Union and slavery. Economic self-interest, they felt, would compel the West to side with the South or at least remain neutral in the event of a showdown between the sections. The southern leaders, however,

reckoned without the influence of the railroad. By 1860 and secession, when the South sought to capitalize upon its control of the
Mississippi, several thousand miles of railroad track between
Chicago and the East had effectively weakened the once-powerful
trade monopoly of the Mississippi-Ohio system. In that year over 19
million bushels of corn went to the East as compared with a mere
4.8 million to the South; pork from the West to the East was three
times what it had been in 1850, while that to the South was only a
half of the figure ten years earlier. The railroads built during the
decade thus helped to create that united front which the North and
the West presented to the secession of the South. Moreover, by
knitting together the industry of the Northeast and the breadbasket
of the West, the railroads forged a crucial economic link in the chain
of northern victory in the ensuing war; for the winning of the Civil
War was as much a matter of logistics and supply as it was of men
and military ardor.

Beside the marching tracks of the railroad swung the wires of
another invention which helped to bring about the revolution in communications in the first half of the nineteenth century. Soon after its
successful trial in 1844, the telegraph of Samuel F. B. Morse began
to weave its slim web across the nation, building markets, carrying
news, and helping to create a new people.

3. THE FACTORY COMES

A natural outgrowth of the extension of transportation and communication lines was the expansion of manufacturing; the two went
hand in hand. To be sure, during the colonial period there had been
manufacturing in America, but the so-called Industrial Revolution
cannot be said to have come to the United States until the second
decade of the nineteenth century. Before then the factory and the
industrial worker were novelties in the economy. Though no single
year can be properly singled out as the beginning of industrialization
in the United States, 1816 has a better claim than most; the first
frankly protective tariff was passed in that year. During the War of
1812, American capital and labor had been attracted into manufacturing because the hostilities cut off the usual imports from Great
Britain. In effect, the wartime interruption of trade acted as protection for the development of new industry. With the cessation of the
war in 1815, however, American manufacturers were threatened

with extinction by a flood of cheaper British goods. As a result, a strong movement for a protective tariff quickly got under way.

The sponsors of the tariff ranged in motivation from the narrow self-interest of a manufacturer to the broadly patriotic concern of a publicist like Hezekiah Niles, who hoped to render the national economy independent of British exports. The truly great breadth of the protariff forces is revealed by the fact that even old Jeffersonians like President Madison acceded to this departure from the ancient faith that once had sanctioned a tariff only for revenue. Measured against subsequent protective tariffs of the post-Civil War years, the act which was passed in 1816 was modest indeed, but it stands, nevertheless, as a convenient and accurate bench mark in the rise of American industry. From this date on, there was a growing pressure for the protection of American industry against foreign competition.

By the decade of the 1830's the factory, with its disciplined workers, its whirring machines, and its prodigious production, was sufficiently widespread to allow one to speak of the onset of industrialization. Most noticed by foreign and native observers alike were the textile mills of eastern Massachusetts, where the celebrated girl workers astounded visitors by their intelligence, their poetry reading while tending the looms, and their distinctly unproletarian appearance. The records of the period, however, make it quite clear that the girls at Lowell were exceptional both in their intellectual surroundings and in their contentment. (Realistic Herman Melville described a factory of women operatives as "the Tartarus of Maids.") Actually, most manufacturing in the United States was carried on in urban centers under conditions of low wages, stale air, poor light, atrocious housing, and tediously long hours of work under the rigorous tempo and discipline of a machine.

There was more aborning in those early years of industrialization than the slow spreading of the factory through the land. Very early in the history of the new Republic, the fundamental principle of manufacture from which would develop the mass-production techniques of modern industrialism was set forth. In 1798 a young Connecticut Yankee and former schoolteacher, who had recently revolutionized agriculture in the southern United States, contracted with the federal government to turn out 10,000 muskets in the short space of two years. Probably because Eli Whitney was well known to Vice-President Jefferson and to Secretary of the Treasury Oliver

Wolcott, the government agreed to his ambitious undertaking. But whatever the reason for the government's accepting him at his word, at the end of the contract period, no more than 500 muskets had been produced. Nevertheless, when Whitney demonstrated to his sponsors the innovation he had introduced into the manufacture of guns, instead of annoyance, additional money was forthcoming.

Whitney's new process was nothing less than the principle of the interchangeability of parts, the fundamental idea in mass production. The principle was described by President Jefferson, who realized from the outset the tremendous industrial implications of the innovation. "He has invented moulds and machines for making all pieces of his locks, so exactly equal," the President explained, "that take 100 locks to pieces and mingle their parts and the hundred locks may be put together as well by taking the first pieces which come to hand. This is of importance in repairing," Jefferson went on, "because out of 10 locks, e.g., disabled for want of different pieces, 9 good locks may be put together without employing a smith." The President might have added that the principle considerably cheapened the cost of production and, furthermore, enabled unskilled workers to manufacture items like guns, which heretofore could only be turned out by highly skilled men. It is important to observe that only machines, with their unvarying cutting of shapes and sizes, could make interchangeable parts; the most skilled mechanic depending on eye and hand could not make each piece precisely alike. Whitney, it might be added, invented not only the machinery but the production processes used in the new method as well.

For a society chronically short of labor and skills, the interchangeability of parts was a tremendous fillip to the expansion of manufacturers. Producers of goods like clocks, watches, hardware, and sewing machines, which used a number of parts in their manufacture, appreciated the advantages of the procedure and adopted it. Though a century would pass before one could talk of mass production on the scale popularized by Henry Ford and well known today, the basic technique and some good approximations of the later quantity of production were already in evidence as the nineteenth century moved into its second half.

Manufacturing, by the decade of the fifties, had spread far beyond New England; Pennsylvania and New York both led Massachusetts in goods produced and capital invested. The Census of 1860 revealed that well over half a million men and women were working in some 53,000 manufacturing establishments in the Middle Atlantic states alone, and the value of manufactured goods produced in the nation as a whole was almost $2 billion. On the eve of the Civil War, an urban working class was already in existence; it would be only a matter of time before the dominance of the farmer in American society would be seriously challenged by the urban wage earner, the by-product of the new factory.

That the shift away from agriculture was beginning as early as the 1850's is apparent from the fact that in 1860 less than sixty per cent of the labor force was still in agriculture. (Twelve per cent was in manufacturing, the rest in services and trade.) The movement away from farming and toward industry would be accelerated by the war and its aftermath. It was from this springboard of the fifties that the great industrialization of the post-Civil War era got its start.

The South, however, did not share proportionately in this prewar upsurge in industrial activity. Of the 140,000 manufacturing establishments in the nation in 1860, only 21,000, or fifteen per cent, were in the southern states, though that region contained a third of the population. Furthermore, southern production of manufactured commodities was only one tenth of the national total when the war began. In what proved to be the first of modern wars, industrial power occupied a prominent place in the balance of forces between the sections. The dire poverty of the Confederacy in the last years of the war and the poor quality of its military equipment bear ample testimony to the high price the South paid for failing to develop its industry in step with that of the North. The South could boast of having Lee and Jackson, but the North had railroads, iron mills, machine shops, clothing factories, and shipyards—as well as U. S. Grant. The Civil War, it is true, was neither won nor lost by material forces alone. But insofar as its outcome was affected by the difference between the industrial capacities of North and South, then the dogged and heroic defense of the Confederacy takes on many of the aspects of a cause that was lost from the beginning.

4. DOES LAND MAKE A PEOPLE?

"So vast is the Territory of North America," prophesied Benjamin Franklin in 1751, "that it will require many Ages to settle it fully; and, till it is fully settled, Labour will never be cheap here, where no Man continues long a Labourer for others, but gets a

Plantation of his own. . . ." Franklin's observations on the impact of empty land upon Americans was echoed by many another American in his time and later: Jefferson, Hamilton, Emerson, and Henry George are only some of the older ones. The conviction that the roots of the American character are to be found in the frontier experience has long since passed into the folk wisdom of the nation, and in our own century it has been a stock in trade of historical scholars as well.

In the waning years of the nineteenth century, the vague belief that, in some fashion or other, the frontier was a formative factor in the history of the United States was boldly cast into an academic hypothesis by a young historian from the West. The study of American history has not been the same since Frederick Jackson Turner made that presentation before the American Historical Association in 1893; only Charles A. Beard has exercised a comparable influence upon the writing of our history.

This influence has stemmed primarily from Turner's broad, but highly suggestive and challenging thesis, running all through his writings, that the settling of a new land did more to mold the character of the American people and institutions than the European heritage. "American democracy was born of no theorist's dream," he argued in one essay, "it was not carried in the *Susan Constant* to Virginia, nor in the *Mayflower* to Plymouth. It came out of the American forest, and it gained new strength each time it touched a new frontier. Not the constitution," he asserted, "but free land, and an abundance of natural resources open to a fit people, made the democratic type of society in America. . . ." Furthermore, something more than democracy issued from the forest; "the frontier," he contended, "is productive of individualism" in the American character. In his first and most famous frontier essay, he concluded "that to the frontier the American intellect owes its striking characteristics."

As a number of scholars have subsequently pointed out, Turner was generous in attributing a variety of American traits to the frontier, but it is not always clear what he meant by the frontier. Sometimes, in Turner's writings, it is an area—that is, the zone where civilization and forest meet; at other times the frontier is little more than the western part of the United States, although it is obvious that Illinois in 1850 is hardly a zone of contact between civilization and savagery. At still other places in his writings

Turner is apparently thinking of the frontier as a process—a way of life for those actually participating in the settling of vacant lands. Then, at another time, he will write of the frontier as an abundance of natural resources. As analytical tools for explaining the origins of Americans, these four definitions are of quite different orders. To lump them under the single heading of the "influence of the frontier" is to obscure rather than to clarify. "As an analytical device," Richard Hofstadter has said, the frontier thesis "was a blunt instrument." If the frontier is the cutting edge of civilization, then it clearly cannot also be the western part of the United States at a later stage of social evolution; and if it is natural resources, then it is not the process of settlement, for men may wrestle with the problems of subduing a wilderness but enjoy only a paucity of natural resources. In short, these four definitions of the same term are not only different; they are sometimes mutually exclusive.

Turner never tired of reiterating that the frontier remade the Europeans who entered it. "The wilderness masters the colonist," he explained. "It finds him a European in dress, industries, tools, modes of travel, and thought. . . . It strips off the garments of civilization and arrays him in the hunting shirt and the moccasin. It puts him in the log cabin of the Cherokee and Iroquois and runs an Indian palisade around him. . . . In short, at the frontier the environment is at first too strong for the man." But after the first adjustment, the pioneer begins to change. "Little by little he transforms the wilderness, but the outcome is not the old Europe. . . . The fact is, that here is a new product that is American." This was a most persuasive argument, but Turner was so imbued with a belief in the influence of environment that he underestimated the tough conservative character of men's cultural patterns.

Sixty years before Turner, Alexis de Tocqueville believed, much the same as Turner, that in America one could actually witness the successive stages of social evolution.[7] Upon visiting the actual frontier of Michigan, however, Tocqueville found that his assumption required serious modification. "Of all the countries of the world America is the least fitted to furnish the spectacle I came there to

---

[7] Turner wrote in his first essay on the frontier: "The United States lies like a huge page in the history of society. Line by line as we read this continental page from West to East we find the record of social evolution. It begins with the Indian and the hunter" and goes down through the various stages of development.

seek," he noted in his diary, "In America, even more than in Europe there is only one society. . . . The plane of a uniform civilization has passed over it. The man you left behind in New-York you find again in almost impenetrable solitudes: same clothes, same attitude, same language, same habits, same pleasures." To factors like widespread education, "the spirit of equality," and the very recent contact with civilized living Tocqueville attributed the "universal civilization" in America. The settlers on the Michigan frontier, he wrote, "have come with the customs, the ideas, the needs of civilization. They only yield to savagery that which the imperious necessity of things exacts from them. . . ." Tocqueville then described a cabin, deep in the virtually untouched forest, at which he visited. But, he said, if you think you are entering the abode of the American peasant, you are wrong. "You enter this cabin which seems the asylum of all the miseries, but the owner wears the same clothes as you, he speaks the language of the cities. On his rude table are books and newspapers"; he asks about events in Europe. In fact, "the wood cabin is only a temporary refuge for the American, a temporary concession made to the exigencies of the situation." As soon as possible he will reproduce his civilized life as he knew it, right in the midst of the wilderness.

Tocqueville, the observer, is a better guide to the cultural impact of the frontier than Turner, the historian. Instead of recapitulating the cultural history of the race, men on the frontier did their best to reproduce the civilization as quickly as they could when they came. More recently, Louis B. Wright, in his book *Culture on the Moving Frontier*, has shown in some detail how this was done through the seventeenth, eighteenth, and nineteenth centuries.

The most widely accepted part of Turner's frontier hypothesis is that American democracy is a unique product of the struggle with the wilderness. One of the favorite means for substantiating this point has been to point to the democratic features of the western state constitutions. Universal manhood suffrage, elected officials, and so forth, it is argued, first appeared in the western states and then spread to the rest of America. Actually, however, as one of Turner's disciples, John Barnhart, has recently shown, the constitutions of Kentucky and Tennessee—the first transmontane states to enter the Union—were both modeled after the Pennsylvania Constitution of 1790—a document which was considerably more conservative than the 1776 organic law of that state! Rarely, as Barnhart demonstrates, did these western states, for all their supposed democratic propensities, make a novel contribution to government; they merely copied from the eastern states.

From his investigations of the provisions of the state constitutions of the Ohio-Mississippi region—the so-called "Valley of Democracy" —Barnhart found only a handful of clauses which could be called original with the West. In Ohio's first constitutions, for example, out of 106 clauses, only eleven were counted as original, while fifty were very much like those in Tennessee's and nineteen like those in Pennsylvania's. Lest this be thought to be an instance of one "advanced democratic" western state copying from another, it should be noted that forty-seven of Tennessee's clauses were taken from the constitution of Pennsylvania and nineteen from North Carolina's.

To be sure, as one looks over the constitutions of the states in the first half of the nineteenth century, it is clear that democratic forms came earlier, on the average, to the new states than to the old. But since it can also be shown that an old state like Pennsylvania in 1776 wrote a constitution more radically democratic than those of most western states in subsequent years, it does not appear that democracy is uniquely a product of the West, much less of the forest.

Moreover, if we broaden our perspective a little, we cannot escape noticing that the most democratic ideas expressed anywhere in European civilization before the nineteenth century were those of the Levellers in seventeenth-century England. No one has argued, however, that their demand for universal manhood suffrage and a written constitution to protect the people against arbitrary government was a result of the frontier.

But the failure of the Levellers to gain their democratic objectives, while the pioneers in the American forest secured theirs, suggests that the influence of the frontier lay not in its evocation of democratic ideas, but in the providing of an opportunity for them to be put into practice regardless of their place or occasion of origin. This would explain why democratic forms seemed to come more slowly to eastern states than to western; the latter had a clean slate on which to write new ideas. Though Turner seems to have underestimated the conservative streak which makes men strive to perpetuate the old in the midst of the new environment, he nevertheless grasped the important fact that ideas and innovations unable to get a trial in

the older states often were put into practice in the communities
abuilding in the West.

Such a function of the frontier, though not as formative as
Turner asserted, is still important. Free land offered a chance for
political and social experiment by peaceful means, and this opportunity unquestionably aided the rapid triumph of democratic ideals
in America. But to repeat, the availability of opportunity should not
be confused with the origination of democratic ideas. Later, by looking at the experiences of other peoples who were confronted with
frontiers of empty land, we shall see that empty land does not always
produce democracy or liberty.

But there is more to be said about the democratic influence of the
frontier. Recently, two scholars, Eric McKitrick and Stanley Elkins,
have suggested that Turner's accent on the frontier as the molder of
American democracy has been not so much misplaced as merely in-
expertly elucidated. They decry, to begin with, the excessive emphasis by Turner's critics upon formal definitions of democracy, such as
suffrage qualifications, constitutional provisions, and the like. Mc-
Kitrick and Elkins would substitute a functional definition of American democracy in which the essence is taken to be concern with
political problems and the active participation in community affairs
on the part of large numbers of citizens. Under this definition, they
point out, the newness of the land, the necessity of establishing
brand-new communities in the wilderness, demanded greater participation in political activity than was true in Europe. Therefore,
they say, the empty land may be said to have contributed to the
making of a peculiarly American variety of democracy.

Moreover, with so much to be done in the raw communities of the
West, there simply were not enough trained and traditionally accepted leaders to organize and manage the new settlements. Hence
ordinary people, Everyman, had to come forward and pitch in.
As this procedure was repeated across the face of the land, the habit
of community problem solving, to use the phraseology of McKitrick
and Elkins, became fixed in the American character. From this, they
think, stemmed the American propensity for associative activity,
committee forming, writing of petitions, and the general recourse to
political and group action. This conception of the frontier is close
to Turner's; but because it does not suffer from his confusion of
definitions for the frontier, it is much more convincing.

The participation of many people in the affairs of government,

McKitrick and Elkins further point out, inevitably reinforces self-confidence and self-reliance—qualities usually associated with the frontier and the American. How the new land did this economically was illustrated by Karl Marx in the latter part of the nineteenth century. Marx's example was a letter written by a French worker who went to California. "I never could have believed," the worker wrote, "that I was capable of working at the various occupations I was employed on in California. I was firmly convinced that I was fit for nothing but letter press printing. . . ." But once "in the midst of this world of adventurers, who change their occupation as often as they do their shirt, egad, I did as the others. As mining did not turn out remunerative enough, I left it for the town, where in succession I became a typographer, a slater, plumber, etc. In consequence of thus finding out that I am fit for any sort of work, I feel less of a mollusk and more of a man."

One must be careful, however, not to romanticize the opportunities of the free land to the point of unreality. Both Turner and his followers, for example, have written of the West as a safety valve for the unsuccessful and discontented of the East. So plausible has this hypothesis appeared that laymen and academic historians alike talk of the significance for American society of the "closing" of the frontier in 1890.

But, suggestive as the safety-valve theory is, it, too, like the thesis of the frontier origins of American democracy, suffers when subjected to close analysis. For example, of the large number of historians who have undertaken concrete examinations of the validity of this thesis, almost none has found evidence that discontented and poor urban workers of the East could find a second chance in the West of the nineteenth century. Two economic historians tried to uncover examples of workers who left an industrial town like Fall River, Massachusetts, for new opportunities in the West; but, though they combed newspaper after newspaper, they found no evidence of emigrating workers. Another historian demonstrated that the cost of starting a farm in the West in the nineteenth century was in excess of a year and a half's income of the average urban worker if he was fortunate enough to work all year. Confirmation of the urban worker's inability to finance his own movement to the West was forthcoming in another study which reported that, during the 1850's in New York City, societies were formed to assist workers to make the trip to the hinterland. By implication this was evidence

that few workers were in a position to leave for the West on their
own. Finally, in what he called a "post-mortem" on the safety-valve
thesis, Fred Shannon noted that the census, especially after the Civil
War, clearly showed that the largest migration of Americans was
from the country to the city and not the other way around, as the
safety-valve hypothesis would have it.

Yet despite the avalanche of attack, adverse evidence, and the
paucity of defensive data, something is still to be salvaged from
this much-mauled thesis of Turner. Shannon, resting his case on the
census data, has vehemently argued that, rather than the country's
being a safety valve for the discontent of the city, the urban centers
were the outlet for farm discontent and surplus population. Such an
argument is going too far, however. The very existence of an empty
frontier, which in the course of the years was gradually populated,
makes it obvious that pressure on the city was reduced to the extent
that some people—especially farmers and new immigrants—went to
western farming areas instead of to the city. In this *indirect* sense,
one is justified in talking about the ameliorative effect of the frontier
on urban crowding and in preserving opportunities for city
workers. Nor should it be forgotten, though little research has been
done on this aspect of the problem, that the West—though not the
frontier—had cities; many craftsmen and small shop owners must
have migrated from the highly competitive and overcrowded cities
of the East to seek new opportunities in the towns of the West.

The fact remains, however, that once tests of data are applied to
it, the safety-valve thesis in any literal sense does not come off very
well. Not many eastern people in the nineteenth century could
actually utilize the West as a safety valve for their discontent or as
an opportunity for a new start.

But to confine our analysis of the impact of the West on America
to measurable matters is to miss the tremendous psychological import of the safety-valve conception. All through the nineteenth century, Americans believed that the West was a haven for the oppressed
and a cornucopia for the ambitious. This was the underlying reason
for the liberalizing of the land laws in the course of the century.
George Henry Evans and his Land Reformers, Thomas Hart Benton
and his Pre-emption Act, Andrew Johnson's and the Republican
party's homestead bills, all epitomized the belief that if the lands of
the West were made easy of acquisition, "every worker will be enabled
to hew out for his family a home from the virgin soil of the Great

West," as Horace Greeley put it in 1859. A form of this conviction lay behind the efforts on the part of businessmen and philanthropists in the 1850's to organize societies to help defray the expenses of the unemployed in traveling to the western lands. During the Panic of 1857, newspapers constantly urged the unemployed to go West for work. "It should be known to females out of employment," counseled a Philadelphia newspaper in 1857, "that throughout the West, there are thousands of homes and liberal pay awaiting any reputable persons who are willing to engage themselves for domestic duties." The Children's Aid Society of New York, under the imaginative and energetic leadership of Charles Loring Brace, undertook a continuous program of sending homeless children to the West. Between 1853 and 1872 some twenty thousand New York City children were placed in homes in the West. The Association for the Improvement of the Condition of the Poor, in 1858, though hostile to the idea of aided emigration for urban workers, nevertheless conceded that "The relief of our overburdened city of its pauperism, by migration to the country is a very popular idea. . . ."

And precisely because it was *believed* to be a safety valve, regardless of what it was in fact, the western frontier worked an influence upon the attitudes of Americans. It left its mark in the optimism, the belief in progress, the promise of the future and the second chance— all of which have been deeply embedded in the American character.

The influence of the doctrine is seen also in the widespread acceptance of the corollary that the closing of the frontier meant the end of an older America. "Our last frontier has long since been reached," Franklin Roosevelt said in 1932, "and there is practically no more free land. . . . There is no safety valve in the form of a western prairies to which those thrown out of work by the eastern machines can go for a new start." The view that the ending of the frontier posed new problems for the American economy found easy acceptance among a group of prominent and influential economists in the 1930's. For them the economy had lost its motive power when the frontier closed. "The Bogy of Economic Maturity," as one of their opponents phrased it, gripped a whole generation of depression economists, of whom Alvin Hansen of Harvard was the chief. These men found in the depression the final confirmation of the effects of the end of the frontier in 1890. They asked, as Hansen put it in the title of one of his books, "Stagnation or Recovery?" Only through government investment, they argued, could the natural stagnation of the economy now be overcome.

Generally, of course, these economists drew upon John Maynard Keynes for their economics, but their historical frame of reference was the work of Frederick Jackson Turner. In the remarkably widespread acceptance of the frontier hypothesis among men of affairs and humble citizens alike is a striking vindication of Lord Keynes' remark that ideas, whether right or wrong, can exert enormous social influence.[8] As a psychological force the frontier has not yet lost its power; it is still common coin in American thought. Certainly while the frontier was in being, it was powerful in fostering the belief that the American was unique and different from the European. And insofar as he believed so, he was.

Underlying most of the criticisms of Turner is the assumption that the frontier influence is in reality passive rather than active. When Turner's thesis, which is essentially a geographical interpretation of history, is cut to its marrow, it stands forth as the simple assertion that when people move into a new geographical setting they alter their mores. This proposition has been amply documented and repeatedly demonstrated for a variety of environments. An especially convincing example is *The Great Plains*, by Walter Prescott Webb, a disciple of Turner's. But even in Webb's study it is apparent that geography is less a creator of culture and more a selector of existent cultural patterns. Men found it difficult to continue to be wheat farmers when climatic and soil conditions were more suited to cattle raising. But the cattle business did not spring forth for the first time on the Great Plains—it merely flourished there after being introduced from other areas. Climate and soil prevented New England from being a cotton-producing area, but they did not dictate that Maine should grow potatoes. Geography may set the limits within which men must live, but it does not determine which of several alternatives available to man's cultural versatility actually will be pursued.

[8] Keynes wrote that "the ideas of economists and political philosophers, both when they are right and when they are wrong, are more powerful than is commonly understood. Indeed the world is ruled by little else. Practical men, who believe themselves to be quite exempt from any intellectual influences, are usually the slaves of some defunct economist. Mad men in authority, who hear voices in the air, are distilling their frenzy from some academic scribbler of a few years back. I am sure that the power of vested interests is vastly exaggerated compared with the gradual encroachment of ideas." *General Theory of Employment, Money and Interest* (New York, 1938), p. 383.

The best proof of this generalization in regard to the frontier theory can be found in an examination of the effects of empty land upon peoples other than Americans. Several peoples of the world, both in the remote and recent past, have had to wrestle with the challenge of a raw frontier. In the twelfth century, the area east of the Elbe River constituted a nearly empty frontier land for the restless Saxons of north Germany. The movement of Germans into this region was one of the great colonizing efforts of the Middle Ages; and in some respects, this frontier wrought changes in the customs of the Saxons who settled on the vacant lands. The form of village settlement, for example, changed strikingly. Serfdom declined and its burdens were considerably lightened as lords were compelled to recognize that the peasants had access to more land and opportunity to the east. Though undoubtedly there were changes in cultural patterns, they were already implicit in the old ways; they merely awaited an opportunity for expression, just as the liberalizing of francise requirements in the western United States waited upon the opportunity of a new land for realization. In sum, the empty land in Germany determined neither the direction the changes would take nor the character of them.

This is illustrated even more clearly if one compares the alleged effects of the frontier upon the character of Americans and the South African Boers. The history of both peoples is dominated by the movement into open land. There can be no question of the fierce individualism and the hatred of outside control which characterize the typical cattle-raising Boer, but his almost fanatical conservatism in matters of religion, science, education, and government are in sharp contrast with the belief in progress, education, science and liberal government which has always stood out in the complex of American national traits. Both peoples struggled with the demands of the empty lands in which they settled, but the resulting traits and cultural patterns were strikingly different because each brought its own cultural baggage into the more or less neutral frontier. New land denies vitality to certain cultural patterns, but it creates no particular ones.

One other frontier experience might be mentioned. Like the Americans, the Russians of the eighteenth and nineteenth centuries were a people constantly in contact with a frontier. While the Americans were moving west, the Russians were striking east across Russia and Siberia. Both peoples reached their respective Pacific shores about

the same time. Here, however, the similarity stops; movement into
the steppes of southern Russia and into Siberia by a people governed
by an autocrat brought no liberalization of the regime, nor did it
prepare the ground for a democratic society. The Cossacks of the
lower Don, it is true, came into being as a people in the seventeenth
century while in direct contact with the free lands of the region, and
enjoyed for a while a primitive democratic military organization. But
it was not long, despite the frontier, before an oligarchy emerged,
slowly but ineluctably changing the Cossacks into the most reactionary arm of the czarist regime. It is hard to find among the Cossacks
any signs of the frontier influence of democracy and individualism
as Turner spoke of it in America. Once again the cultural patterns
of each people remained largely unchanged even though both peoples
moved into an area of empty land.

Old cultural traits persisted on the American frontier. One scholar
has found that when Germans in colonial America moved into Pennsylvania, Maryland, and Virginia, they differed markedly from the
English colonists in farming methods, crops, and labor system. The
Germans selected clay loams in heavily wooded areas, while the English chose light, sandy uplands. Whereas the English girdled trees
and farmed among the stumps, the fastidious Germans cleared the
land completely and plowed deeply. The English, on the other hand,
merely scratched the soil and were appalled to see it run away in the
rains. Tidewater Virginians let their stock roam freely, but the careful Germans actually built their barns before they built homes. Unlike the English, the conservative Germans did not take to tobacco
cultivation, but stuck to the familiar wheat; nor did they become
slaveholders as avidly as the English. Both peoples were on the same
frontier, but the vacant land did little more than provide them with
a canvas upon which each depicted the old familiar cultural patterns. In his enthusiastic conception of the frontier as a democratiz-
ing force, Turner ignored the new lease on life given to slavery by
the free land of the West. Though the new southern states in the
early years of the nineteenth century accurately reflected in their
constitutions the national trend toward greater popular participation in government, these same constitutions were conspicuous for
their complete acceptance of human slavery at the very time the
institution was more and more viewed as contrary to the democratic
spirit.

It is apparent from any survey of frontiers throughout the world that free land offers opportunities for social advancement and wealth accumulation. But whether men will seize these opportunities often depends more upon the cultural attitudes they bring with them than upon the free land. The land, in and of itself, will not do it. The history of the Indians and the Spaniards on the American frontier is a case in point here. The availability of free land and natural resources did not spur them on to new forms of production because their cultural heritage did not include the traits which fostered such activity. But bring into this empty land the work-conscious Puritan, for instance, and then the free land takes on a different aspect; it now becomes a spur, a veritable goad to economic activity and hard work. Similarly, a people with a vigorous conception of self-government, moving into new lands, finds it natural to expand popular participation in government, as McKitrick and Elkins have shown occurred on the American frontier. But it is important to recognize that it is not the land which makes the difference; it is the cultural attitudes of the people. The frontier, rather than being the key to American development, is merely one among a number of influences which have gone into the shaping of Americans.

One of the manifestations of the western influence upon Americans was Andrew Jackson and the Democracy for which he spoke. Jackson was proudly a Westerner, and in many respects the West's *beau ideal* for most of the years between the War of 1812, in which he played so conspicuous a role, and the election of 1860, when his beloved Union was split asunder. He was also, however, more than a western figure, for he gathered to himself, almost like the symbol of Uncle Sam itself, the democratic aspirations and hopes of Americans for their country and their future. For this reason the era of Jackson was also the Age of the Great Experiment.

CHAPTER V

The Great Experiment

EVEN before the first settlers had arrived, America was an object of curiosity to Europeans; but in the thirties, forties, and fifties of the nineteenth century the United States was as interesting to Europeans as Soviet Russia was to the world a hundred years later. Scores of foreign travelers made the Grand Tour of America in those years, dutifully recording their impressions for the edification of their less fortunate, but no less curious, fellow Europeans. This was the era of Tocqueville, Mrs. Trollope, Charles Dickens, Harriet Martineau, Charles Lyell, Fredrika Bremer, and Captain Hall. And whatever else America may have been in the writings of visitors, all seemed agreed that the United States was the great experiment in democracy. To English Chartists, struggling to democratize English government, the United States appeared as "the bright luminary of the western hemisphere whose radiance will extend across the Atlantic's broad expanse and light the whole world to freedom and happiness."

It was in the course of these years that the Democratic Dogma, as Brooks Adams was to call it later, was pushed to its outer limits. The common people came into their own as political arbiters and participants; majority rule was invested with a kind of sanctity. By the time the era was over, new, popular colors had been added to the bare outline of American politics inherited from the Revolutionary Fathers. The modern party system was in being, the Presidency bore the indelible marks of Andrew Jackson and James K. Polk, and the principle of a people's administration of government had been permanently implanted in American political thought.

136

1. "LET THE PEOPLE RULE"

Even during the eighteenth century, as we have noticed, more people could vote, proportionately, in the United States than in England and other European countries. But in the years after 1815, Americans deliberately expanded the suffrage in order to rest their governments upon the consent of all the governed.

By the decades of the 1830's and 1840's this movement reached flood tide, as the states altered their constitutions in conformity with the principle that manhood, not property, was the most just basis for political rights. This was a new view, one which constituted a sharp departure from colonial and early republican theory and practice. "The pretense has been that none but the rich have a stake in society," James Fenimore Cooper wrote. But this is wrong, he insisted. "Every man who has wants, feelings, affections and character, has a stake in society." Hence he is entitled to vote. It was precisely this abandonment of the traditional assumptions regarding the suffrage which renders this period significant; goodly numbers of people had always voted in America, where property was widely distributed. Now, however, even property was removed as a limitation. Once it was conceded that the basis for the suffrage was mere citizenship, then it was possible for any group or class to advance a claim to participation in government. The floodgates of democracy were open. In due time, on this basis, women, Negroes, and eighteen-year-old youths would be accepted as voters.

The shift away from the stake-in-society conception of politics was dramatic because it was accomplished so rapidly. In 1800, only three of the fifteen states of the Union granted the vote to all white men, regardless of property; by 1860, in a Union of thirty states, all but seven states extended the ballot to all white men,[1] rich and poor alike. Property holding as a test of fitness to hold office was also discarded. Most of the new states in the early years of the century entered the Union without such requirements, while the original

[1] It is revealing that during the very period that the suffrage was being extended to new economic levels of the white population, it was being withdrawn from Negroes. At least three southern states—North Carolina, Maryland, and Virginia—withdrew the ballot from free persons of color during this period. And New York, in 1821, when property qualifications for voting were removed for white men, deliberately retained such requirements for the Negro voter. Since the new states did not extend the suffrage to Negroes at all, there was no need to withdraw it.

states gradually dropped theirs; Maryland began in 1810, Pennsylvania followed in 1838, then New Jersey in 1844, and so on.

The suffrage was only one of the several governmental innovations which embodied the upsurge in democratic ideals. Governors, for example, were now popularly elected instead of being chosen by the legislature. Maryland in 1837, North Carolina in 1835, New Jersey in 1844, and Virginia in 1850 all made changes in this direction. A large number of other offices were also made elective; indeed, it might be said that during this period the "long ballot" came into being, for a host of minor and middling offices were newly opened to election on the state and local level.

Most striking as a measure of the belief in the validity and value of a wide suffrage was the subjection of the judiciary to popular election. Between 1846 and 1853, thirteen states made various of their judges subject to the direct pleasure of the people—an extension of the democratic ideal which probably none of the Founding Fathers would have sanctioned.

The democratic faith was also extended to the making of the state constitutions. At the time of the Revolution only two states had found it necessary to submit their constitutions to the people for ratification; by the Age of Jackson, however, such a procedure was the usual practice; only an occasional state failed to seek the people's judgment on a constitution. The principle that just government derives from the consent of the governed was taken literally in this democratic age.

Faith in the infallibility of the people's judgment was the sun around which American political thought now revolved. Andrew Jackson, for example, upon retiring from the Presidency in 1837, told the people in his Farewell Address that they should "Never for a moment believe that the great body of the citizens of any State can deliberately intend to do wrong." It is true, he confessed, that they may be misled, "but in a community so enlightened and patriotic as the people of the United States, argument will soon make them sensible of their errors" and they will therefore rectify them. Martin Van Buren, Jackson's successor, was widely known for his dictum that "the sober second thought of the people is never wrong." And George Bancroft, Democratic theoretician, historian, and politician, contended that "true political science does indeed venerate the masses. . . . Individuals are of limited sagacity; the common mind is infinite in its experience. . . . Individuals are time-serving; the masses are fearless." To Bancroft the new democratic upsurge meant that "the day of the multitude is now dawned." "Democracy is the cause of Humanity," proclaimed the first number of the radical Democratic organ *The United States Magazine and Democratic Review.* "It has faith in human nature. It believes in its essential equality and fundamental goodness. It respects, with a solemn reverence to which the proudest artificial institutions and distinctions of society have no claim, the human soul. It is the cause of philanthropy." The virtues of the common man as a class were often said to be superior. At the New York Constitutional Convention of 1821, for example, it was asserted that "more integrity and more patriotism are generally found in the labouring class of the community than in the higher orders."

Such a deeply held belief in the people's wisdom was something new in conservative America; neither Thomas Jefferson nor even Tom Paine would have gone to such extremes, for both these advocates of the people saw the flaws as well as the beauty in humankind. To be sure, there still were many who would not accept the new-found democratic oracle; the Whig party in general for a while stood against such doctrine. But by the election of 1840 even the Whigs, at least publicly, were throwing their money and their oratory in the same direction as the Jacksonians—that is, in outright flattery of the people. After 1840 no political party would again dare to doubt the wisdom of the people as the Federalists and even some of the Whigs had done in earlier years. Charles Francis Adams, for example, while editing his grandfather's works in 1851, bemoaned the fact that candid political criticism was no longer possible in America. ". . . The fact is certain," he wrote, "that no leading political man" since John Adams' day "has been known to express a serious doubt of the immaculate nature of the government established by the majority." America was now committed to the dubious dogma that wisdom in politics was in direct proportion to the participation of the people.

The people did not need politicians to bolster their self-esteem; they demanded not only the ballot but access to appointive office as well. Even before Jackson's administration there was popular demand for a rotation of officers among the people. Jackson, however, gave the movement intellectual footing when, in his first annual message to Congress, he justified the removal of many old civil servants. "I cannot but believe," the new President wrote, "that more is lost by the long continuance of men in office than is generally gained from their experience." And it was true that many officeholders were superannuated in both mind and body. (Not insignificant in Jackson's motivation was the patent fact that a good number of the officeholders thought "the wild man from the West" a real danger in the White House after the incumbency of cultivated John Quincy Adams.) Moreover, many of them had come to think of their offices as a species of personal property—as Englishmen were wont to do in the eighteenth century. "In a country where offices are created solely for the benefit of the people," Jackson argued in lofty democratic tones, "no one man has any more intrinsic right to official station than another. Offices were not established to give support to particular men at the public expense."

Though the rotation of public office among the people opened the gates for an increasingly vicious spoils system, it also faithfully mirrored the American democratic philosophy that any citizen could adequately perform the work of government. Nor was this rather naïve conception of governmental work without truth. While today the tasks of government bureaus are infinitely complex and technical, in the early years of the Republic the bulk of the employees were little more than clerks, postmasters, and the like. The vast proportion of the jobs of the government could be effectively and efficiently carried on by the average citizen.

Jackson's deliberate removal of the old and the partisan from the offices of his administration brought forth a flood of aspirants for the vacancies. Thus was initiated the burden of the patronage system, the weight of which, in the course of subsequent years, has almost borne down the Presidency. Whig Daniel Webster said in 1835: "No one can deny that office of every kind is now sought with extraordinary avidity. . . ." Convinced that theirs was a people's government, the people were not hesitant in demanding their places. The policy initiated under the Democrats was continued by the Whigs in 1841, the faithful rushing "pell-mell to Washington, every man with a raccoon's tail in his hat" to identify himself as a supporter of William Henry Harrison. Such men, John Quincy Adams wrote with distaste in 1842, were "wolves of the antechamber, prowling for offices." President after President struggled hopelessly and unendingly with the "wolves" until the murder of a Chief Executive in 1881 by a disappointed office-seeker startled the American people from their unconcern. It was only then that civil service reform got an opportunity to lighten the crushing burden of the patronage.

Though the rotation system unquestionably wasted much of the Presidents' time and threatened to reduce officeholding to the work of party hacks,[2] something of value, nevertheless, came out of it. Principally this was democratization of administration on both the federal and state levels. There would never grow up in America any remote civil service which was divorced from the people or which conceived of itself as a superior caste or class, outside or above the main body of the citizenry, as, for example, occurred in Germany to the detriment of the democratic Weimar Republic. Americans made sure, in this period, that their government, like the society at large, reflected their firm belief in the equality of men. Undoubtedly, a democratic administrative structure has been a prop and a succor to the whole democratic way of life in America.

At first glance it appears incongruous that in this very period when popular control of government was at its height, the office of the President, occupied as it is by a single person, should also attain new strength and prestige. This consequence is largely the result of two men's influence upon the people and upon the office. It is true that George Washington, as the first President, did more than any other incumbent to create the mold from which the Chief Magistracy of the Republic would thereafter be cast. But if the austere and essentially aristocratic Washington bequeathed dignity, independence, and high prestige to the Presidency, it remained for Andrew Jackson and James K. Polk to make it also an expression of the democratic spirit of the American people.

It was Jackson, for instance, who first declared that "the President is the direct representative of the people" and no less capable of speaking for the people than the Congress. In practice, Jackson did not hesitate to appeal to the people to sustain policies which the Congress opposed, as, for example, when he vetoed the Bank re-

[2] Graft, "voluntary" political contributions, and assessments of government employees for the support of the party in power, as well as the placing of incompetents in posts for party reasons, all followed naturally, if undesignedly, from the Jacksonian theory and practice. It is necessary to emphasize, however, that Jackson himself was no spoilsman in the sense of using patronage as a naked device for building the party. He hated "honest" graft, assessments, and other devices which converted rotation into a party-building subterfuge. His political adviser, Amos Kendall, as Fourth Auditor of the Treasury, set forth the first—and in some respects the most stringent—rules pertaining to the work habits and standards of behavior expected of government employees.

charter bill in 1832. Polk, who with reason was often called "Young Hickory," made no secret of following Jackson's conception of the President as the Tribune of the People. "The President," Polk wrote, "represents in the executive department the whole people of the United States, as each member of the legislative department represents portions of them." As early as 1824, ardently democratic Senator Thomas Hart Benton advocated changes which would bring the President closer to the people than the cautious Founding Fathers had intended. Stigmatizing indirect election through the Electoral College as a "favorite institution of aristocratic republics," Benton urged that the people be able to vote directly for the Chief Magistrate. Jackson himself, in his first annual message, also urged the amending of the Constitution in order to permit the people to elect the President directly. Though nothing came of either Benton's or Jackson's proposals regarding election, the nomination of the President was democratized in the early 1830's. The Anti-Masonic party [3] held the first Presidential nominating convention in the United States in 1831; within a few years the two major parties abandoned the old caucus system in favor of the more popular convention.

It was Jackson who conclusively established the right of a President to control his Cabinet, even though the Congress may have legislated otherwise. At the time of his war against the Bank of the United States in 1832–33, Jackson, despite Congress' deliberate effort to make the Secretary of the Treasury responsible to the legislature, successfully compelled two Secretaries of the Treasury to resign because they would not implement his policies. Congress protested vehemently and the Senate, in an extraordinary procedure, formally censured the President. But Jackson was vindicated and the President's power enhanced when a more friendly Senate later, in a dramatic ceremony, expunged the censure from its records. Since that time all Presidents, with the exception of the befuddled Grant, have been encouraged by the example of Jackson

[3] This party began in New York State in the late 1820's, but coalesced with the Whigs in 1836. As its name suggests, its *raison d'être* was opposition to the influence of the Masonic Order after the lodges of upper New York State were implicated in the mysterious disappearance of William Morgan, a former Mason who had revealed the secrets of the order. The party easily became an anti-Jackson force, since many high Democrats, including Jackson, were Masons. In the political history of the United States, the Anti-Masonic party is noteworthy as the first third party and the first political party to set forth a platform.

to fight vigorously against any congressional efforts to control the Cabinet.

It was left to James Polk to explore the immense reservoir of power inherent in the President as Commander in Chief of the armed forces. The Mexican War, as Leonard White has pointed out, was really fought from the White House: Polk named the generals, set forth the grand strategy which won the war, cajoled and bullied the Congress into granting the necessary credits and support, and finally drew up the peace terms. All this was achieved with a minimum of consultation with or dependence upon the Congress. When faced with a much greater military challenge, Abraham Lincoln would find encouraging precedent in Polk's use of the Presidential power.

Under imaginative handling by Jackson and Polk, even an essentially negative power like the veto was made to strengthen the authority and prestige of the Presidency. For the first forty years of the Republic it was more or less assumed, from the precedent set by Washington, that the veto was merely a check on unconstitutional legislation and not a weapon which the President could use to enforce his own views. All the Presidents prior to 1829 used their negatives so sparingly that Jackson's vetoes numbered more than all those of his predecessors combined. More important, Jackson made no effort to conceal the fact that the motives behind his vetoes were at best a compound of constitutional scruple and expediency. It is true that he said he doubted the constitutionality of the Bank when he vetoed the recharter bill. But a perusal of his veto message made it clear to everyone that his opposition stemmed from his distrust of the Bank as such and not from any questions of constitutional niceties concerning an institution which, after all, had functioned for almost forty years.

The new Democratic view of the veto power was not discarded by John Tyler, the first Whig President. And even though Tyler was threatened with impeachment for daring to veto legislation which the Congress considered constitutional, the Jacksonian conception of the veto prevailed then and later. In vetoing a river and harbors bill Polk did not find it necessary to offer any justification for his act other than his mere disapproval. The power and prestige which the Jacksonian veto added to the arsenal of the President is best appreciated when it is realized that no veto was overridden by Congress until 1866.

Such an accretion of Presidential power was possible only after the President had been transformed into the Tribune of the People. Prior to that time, the unlimited exercise of the veto smacked of the royal prerogative and of the flouting of the will of the people's representatives. But once the President was accepted as a representative of the people, then the augmentation of his power, even during a period of expanding popular participation in politics, was quite possible and in conformity with democratic ideals.

Indeed, it might be said that the expansion of Presidential power during these years, as well as the increasingly popular character of the office, bear testimony to the realistic political judgment of the American people. Rather than being jealous of the power of the executive, the people seemed to recognize the vital role which strong executive leadership must occupy in any democratic polity which seeks to avoid the deadly paralysis of factionalism.[4] As a result, twentieth-century Americans enjoy an executive unparalleled in its independence and power, yet one responsive to the people's will.

2. "ALL MEN ARE CREATED EQUAL"

The democratization of politics and government was only one of the signs spelling out the Rise of the Common Man; the new democratic spirit was apparent throughout society. Dixon Ryan Fox went so far as to entitle his history of these years *The Decline of Aristocracy*. But that is a phrase which almost sacrifices accuracy to neatness. For as we have seen, it is doubtful that an aristocracy, as the term has meaning in European history, ever existed in America, much less declined. Any ruling class which may have existed in this country has always been tempered by the fact that it could lay no claim to a long tradition of wealth and power such as European aristocracies enjoyed and which is the true soil of an aristocracy.

But even if Fox's phrase somewhat overstates the situation, it does serve to accentuate the fact that in the years between 1820 and 1860, Americans made it quite clear that theirs was to be an equalitarian and open society. Earlier expressions of this sentiment

---

[4] The example of Jackson and Polk on the federal level was not lost upon the states. A number of states during these years lengthened the term of office of their governors, or otherwise strengthened the hand of the executive, thereby bringing to the division of powers more balance than the fears born of the Revolution had heretofore permitted.

had been sporadic and moderate; in the Age of Jackson it was blatantly and continuously proclaimed. "The equality of Man is, to this moment," wrote British traveler Alexander Mackay in 1842, the "cornerstone" of American society. Earlier Alexis de Tocqueville concluded that democratic societies like America were "ardent, insatiable, incessant and invincible" in their passion for equality. "They will endure poverty, servitude, barbarism, but they will not endure aristocracy."

A symptomatic expression of this strong distaste for privilege was evident in the attacks upon West Point during the mid-1830's. Tennessee, for example, in a resolution of the legislature, stigmatized the Military Academy as "this aristocratical institution." And the Ohio legislature declared that West Point was "wholly inconsistent with the spirit and genius of our liberal institutions." And so sure were Americans of their "liberal institutions," wrote Mrs. Trollope, that she "once got so heartily scolded for saying that I did not think all American citizens were equally eligible" for the Presidency "that I shall never again venture to doubt it."

The source from which the reservoir of American faith in equality was constantly being replenished was opportunity. "The United States are certainly the land of promise for the labouring class," wrote Michel Chevalier in 1834. "After landing in New York, I thought every day was Sunday, for the whole population that throngs Broadway seemed to be arrayed in their Sunday's best." Even prickly Mrs. Trollope bore witness to the opportunities of the new country. "Any man's son may become the equal of any other Man's son," she admitted, "and the consciousness of this is certainly a spur to exertion." Harriet Martineau thought she saw unlimited horizons for the lowly in America: "an artisan may attain to be governor of the state, member of Congress, even President," she said. "It is extremely seldom," Englishman Alexander Mackay observed, "that the willing hand in America is in want of employment."

The opportunities open to Americans were reflected in how well the average citizen lived. "I saw no table spread, in the lowest order of houses," Harriet Martineau recalled, "that had not meat and bread on it. Every factory child carried its umbrella; and pig-drivers wear spectacles." Michel Chevalier related the story of a newly arrived Irishman who showed his employer a letter he wrote to his family in the old country. " 'But Patrick,' said his master, 'why do you say that you have meat three times a week, when you have it three times a day?' 'Why is it?' replied Pat; 'it is because they wouldn't believe me, if I told them so.' " Other observers remarked on the notable absence of beggars. There were poor in America, to be sure, for while some men prospered others slipped and fell. And already the tenements of the burgeoning cities were open for inspection and the slum was no longer a European monopoly. But even with such qualifications, and especially when compared with European social conditions, this country opened new economic vistas for Everyman. As Emerson said, "America is another word for opportunity."

One immediate consequence of the breadth of opportunity was the looseness of class lines. We have noticed already a tendency in this direction all through American history; during the first half of the nineteenth century, however, this blurring of classes was a fact and a boast. "We have no different estates," Erastus Root told the New York Constitutional Convention of 1821, "having different interests, necessary to be guarded from encroachment by the watchful eye of jealousy. We are all of the same estate—commoners. . . ." New citizen Achille Murat said that "the lines which divide" Americans "are so delicate that they melt into each other; and that . . . there are neither castes nor ranks." European social patterns do not fit in the United States, German immigrant Francis Lieber wrote home. "In America there is no peasant. . . . He is a farmer, and may be rich or poor; that is all the difference."

In a country in which most men possessed "a competence," as Alexander Mackay put it, property was in no danger. Where acquisition of property is relatively easy, as it was in America, the demand for equality of holdings is rarely heard. It is significant that at no time, insofar as the great majority of Americans was concerned, did "equality" signify an equal division of wealth; too many men owned wealth, or soon expected to, to become involved in schemes or theories which might someday be fashioned into weapons with which to wrest from them their tangible goods. "There will be no attack on property in the United States," Harriet Martineau correctly prophesied. Because property was distributed throughout the various levels of society, no philosophy or organization fundamentally opposed to private property, be it Brook Farm or "agrarianism," was able to win the support of the American people.

3. JACKSONIAN LIBERALISM

For many Americans of the early nineteenth century the belief that the opportunities of their country were almost unlimited was most often embodied in the figure of Andrew Jackson. Born into a poor Carolina back-country family, Jackson rose to be a heroic general, an astute politician, a wealthy planter, and an exceptionally popular President of the United States. In some respects, as John Ward has pointed out, Andrew Jackson was as much a symbol of his age as he was a molding force. The people saw themselves and their aspirations reflected in him and his fabulous career. In an article entitled "The Poorest Boy May Be President," the St. Louis *Argus,* in 1837, called attention to the low social origins of Jackson. The conclusion was that the Presidency itself was "within reach of the humblest urchin that roams the streets of our villages. . . . *Liberty and Equality* is the glorious motto of our republic." Jackson's life, the popular portraits of him, the songs about him, the very cartoons which praised and ridiculed him, were suffused with the people's conception of what the leader of the rising American democracy should be. Understandably, therefore, the popular image of his personality and career was shot through with paradox. He was the gruff War Hero who struggled unflaggingly to keep the nation at peace; the Man of Iron Determination and Inflexible Purpose who loved children; the Unschooled Backwoodsman who could match wits and wield power in competition with eastern bankers and great merchants. There was enough of the Walter Mitty in most Americans to find themselves in Jackson.

Of course he was more than this. He was the first President to capture the imagination of the common people and to evoke from them unquestioning devotion while drawing almost unreasoning hatred from his opponents. An archconservative like wealthy Philip Hone of New York bore witness to both. "The President is certainly the most popular man we have ever known," he wrote in his diary in 1833. "Talk of him as the second Washington! It won't do now. Washington was only the first Jackson." The following year Hone told of meeting some friends while traveling on board ship. We talked, he said, "as is the fashion now-adays—abusing General Jackson and marveling at the undeserved popularity he still enjoys. . . ." Old Chancellor Kent of New York wrote Justice Story, "I look upon Jackson as a detestable, ignorant, reckless, vain and

malignant tyrannt." Cultivated Philip Hone was also convinced that
Jackson was a threat to the nation. "If the people continue to support him in his unwarrantable assumption of power," he wrote in
his diary, "it will be idle to talk about the republican principles on
which the government is founded." On the other hand, his supporters could be ecstatic about him. In 1839 a sonnet appeared in
the *United States Magazine and Democratic Review* in which Jackson was portrayed as more than man-sized. The sonnet began:

> Come, stand the nearest to the country's sire,
> Thou fearless man of uncorrupted heart!
> . . . Raised by the voice of freemen to a height
> Sublimer far than Kings by birth may claim,
> Thy stern, unselfish spirit dared the right. . . .

Given the tremendous appeal of Jackson, it is no accident that
during his tenure the President became the leader of his party. To
some extent this had been true in Jefferson's day, but then the
parties were much less organized and disciplined than they were
after 1828. Thus, during the 1830's, began the modern party system, both in structure and mass character.

Jackson was more than a man who occupied the Presidency and
helped to mold its character; he was also a spokesman and symbol
of a philosophy of government and economics which soon came to
dominate America. It is difficult, if not foolhardy, to try to fit into
a neat pattern so diverse a group of interests as those which went
to make up the Jacksonian movement. Some, for example, like the
radically eccentric Loco-Focos of New York, in their philosophy
were really throwbacks to the Jeffersonian agrarians, although
their habitat was urban. Others, like many businessmen of the
eastern cities and towns who were pushing for the main chance,
were vanguards of the future. Still others of the Jacksonian coalition were farmers in the old American tradition of the farmer-
speculator, covetously eyeing the vacant lands of the West. Yet,
amid such diversity of interests, there does seem to be a common
attribute which deserves to be called the Jacksonian Principle. This
was the belief in economic freedom.

When the Jacksonians talked of economic freedom, they meant
freedom of opportunity. Even radicals like the Loco-Focos and
William Leggett, the outspoken editor of the Jacksonian New York
Evening Post, had this in mind when they used their favorite slogan

of "equal rights." Indeed, the official name of the radical Jacksonian Loco-Focos was the Equal Rights party. Equal rights, however, did not mean that government should guarantee rights to all equally; rather it meant that no one should obtain rights or privileges from government which no one else enjoyed. In practice this meant that the state should not favor one class or individual over any other. If government, said Andrew Jackson, "would confine itself to equal protection, and, as heaven does its rains, shower its favors alike on the high and the low, the rich and the poor, it would be an unqualified blessing."

In Jacksonian thought, special legislation in behalf of only a portion of the community came under the heading of "monopoly." The Bank of the United States, for example, was a monopoly, not because it cornered the banking business, which it did not, but because it enjoyed a federal charter that endowed it with privileges no other bank possessed. Another example of Jacksonian reasoning was evident in Chief Justice Taney's decision in the Charles River Bridge Case of 1837.

When appointed to the Supreme Court by Jackson in 1835, Roger Taney was already notorious as an ardent supporter of the President. He had been amply tested and retested in the hottest fires of controversy, the most notable example of which was the unprecedented rejection of his appointment as Secretary of the Treasury by the Senate in 1834. It was to be expected that he would not follow in the judicial footsteps of his illustrious but Federalist predecessor, Chief Justice John Marshall.

For almost a third of a century John Marshall had used his position on the Supreme Court to build impregnable protections for property against the onslaughts of the state legislatures. Especially noteworthy were the cases of *Fletcher* v. *Peck* and *Dartmouth* v. *Woodward*, in which it was made clear that a charter or a grant by a state to a private individual or corporation was a contract within the meaning of the constitutional clause which prohibited the states from impairing contracts. Even if the grant was fraudulently obtained, *Fletcher* v. *Peck* held it was still valid and to be honored by the state which entered into it.

It was from behind this sturdy bulwark of law erected by Marshall that the Charles River Bridge Company challenged the issuance of a charter by the State of Massachusetts to a rival bridge company. Because the new bridge had, in point of fact, deprived the old bridge of much traffic and thereby virtually destroyed its value, it was asserted that the state was guilty of breaching the original contract with the Charles River Bridge Company. The property value of the old bridge was one of the rights protected by the federal Constitution, it was argued; therefore no state could impair it. It was this argument which Justice Joseph Story, Marshall's aptest pupil on the Court, followed in his dissent.

The Court under Taney, however, executed a decided modification of the Marshall-Story approach. The sanctity of private property was not impaired, despite the assertions of contemporary alarmists, but its pre-eminence as a judicial desideratum was considerably reduced. With Taney writing the decision, the Court found in favor of the new bridge and enunciated the doctrine that whenever there is some doubt as to the precise privileges granted in a charter, the benefit must be awarded to the state. "While the rights of property are sacredly guarded," Taney pointed out, "we must not forget that the community also have rights. . . ."

Taney was not unmindful of the economic importance of this principle in an age when new means of transportation were challenging old ones and legal flexibility was crucial if the expansion of the economy was to continue. "The whole community are interested in this inquiry," the Chief Justice noticed, "and they have a right to require that the power of promoting their comfort and convenience, and of advancing the public prosperity," by new methods and devices "shall not be construed to have been surrendered or diminished by the States, unless it shall appear by plain words that it was intended to be done. . . ." In this sentence were summed up the basic economic and political assumptions of Jacksonian Americans.

A later age would characterize the Jacksonian approach to economic activity as simply one of "laissez faire," citing as evidence Jackson's veto of the bill for an extension of the National Road in Kentucky. Though Polk's vetoes of internal improvements show that the attitude was persistent, the evidence of the Maysville veto of Jackson tends to oversimplify the Jacksonian conception of the government's role in the economy. We have already noticed, for instance, that during the 1830's and 1840's most of the states, many of which were dominated by good Jacksonian Democrats, were busily supplying funds for internal improvements. Moreover, it should not be forgotten that the federal government, under Jackson, appropriated far more money for roads and canals than did the previous administration of John Quincy Adams, though the earlier President was easily the nation's most ardent exponent of the principle that the federal government should underwrite economic growth. Even from the standpoint of theory, there was a body of Jacksonian opinion which encouraged governmental support of internal improvements. Improvements, wrote John Vethake, a New York Jacksonian of prominence, "like the Great Erie and Champlain Canal . . . should be paid for out of the common purse for the common benefit of all." He then went on to echo the classic Jacksonian division of constitutional labor: "If national in character, these works should be constructed by the general government; if local, by the state, county, or town to which their benefits are more especially confined. . . ." The Jacksonians certainly entertained serious doubts as to the wisdom of restrictions by the states upon business, but governmental assistance *to* business in opening up the country did not fall under such a ban. After all, it was a later Jacksonian, Stephen A. Douglas, who championed the first federal land grants to railroads.

To governmental interference in the competitive system the Jacksonians were unalterably opposed. No one, said the *United States Magazine and Democratic Review*, should be artificially assisted by government to a position of superiority over his fellow men. Men of talent, it asserted, can make their own way without such aid. Moreover, society benefits most from such abilities when they are permitted to function within "a perfectly free democratic system, which will abolish all artificial distinctions," thereby permitting "the free development of every germ of talent wherever it may exist, whether on the proud mountain summit, in the humble valley or by the wayside of common life."

This principle of free competition and individualism was followed to its logical conclusion by the radical Jacksonian editor William Cullen Bryant in his attack on the usury laws. Instead of such "fetters" on "the trade in money," he argued, there was "no reason why the laws of supply and demand, which regulate the value of all other articles," should be suspended in the case of money "and their place supplied by the clumsy substitute of feudal ignorance and worse than feudal tyranny." This was laissez faire of the purest sort. Such a pristine doctrine is no longer in fashion; indeed, it is

almost subversive; but in the context of the early nineteenth cen
tury, laissez faire was both progressive and necessary.

For decades, business in America, and more so in England, had
been enmeshed in government regulation and privilege-mongering of
one sort or another. The common practice of dispensing favors and
privileges to special interests had long ceased to be an effective device for expanding business enterprise; instead, it became a bar to
the enterprising who often could not secure the favor of government. The most obvious examples of this kind of discrimination
were acts of incorporation. Prior to 1837, incorporations were
special acts of the state legislatures, a procedure which made businessmen who desired to take advantage of the corporate form dependent upon the pleasure and honesty of a large body of men.
After that date, however, spurred by the new views then coming
forward, state after state began to enact general incorporation
laws. These statutes permitted anyone to enjoy the legal advantages
of incorporation simply by compliance with certain administrative
procedures. The corporation was thus made into a vehicle for the
future expansion of the economy; in time, the corporate form would
dominate American business. In sum, the historic function of Jacksonian laissez faire was to free private enterprise of those governmental restrictions left over from the age of mercantilism; at the
time it was liberating and progressive, but it also cleared the field
for what V. L. Parrington called the "Great Barbecue" after the
Civil War.

Business was not the only beneficiary of the new spirit of freedom
of Jacksonian America; workingmen stood to gain as well. Government has always been on the side of wealth, complained William
Leggett, the radical New York Jacksonian. "It was never wielded
in behalf of the community. . . . Thus it will be seen that the sole
reliance of the labouring classes, who constitute a vast majority of
every people on the earth, is the great principle of Equal Rights;
that their only safeguard against oppression is a system of legislation which leaves all to the free exercise of their talents and industry, within the limits of the General Law," which bestows upon
no class or group "rights or privileges not equally enjoyed by the
great aggregate of the body politic." As Theophilus Fisk, another
Jacksonian, declared in behalf of labor: "We ask no protection; we
simply desire *to be let alone.*"

It must be admitted that these remarks sound more like modern strictures of the National Association of Manufacturers against government interference than utterances of labor spokesmen. But in the early nineteenth century, laissez faire could be sound doctrine for workingmen.

Up until the 1830's, at least, the courts and the common law in America were openly hostile to labor organization. Usually any attempt on the part of workers to organize or to strike or to bargain collectively was interpreted by the state courts as a conspiracy in restraint of trade and punishable under the common law. Under this doctrine, strike after strike was broken by the jailing or fining of leaders. In 1836, for example, twenty-one tailors were fined a total of $1,150 by a New York court for having "perniciously" formed and united "into an unlawful club or combination to injure trade" and for having gone on strike. (A good annual wage for a worker employed all year round was no more than $600.)

The impact of the rising labor movement and the new accent on freedom in economic affairs were reflected in Chief Justice Lemuel Shaw's decision in *Commonwealth of Massachusetts* v. *Hunt* in 1842. Labor unions, the Chief Justice of Massachusetts announced, were legal organizations and therefore could not be construed as conspiracies or combinations in restraint of trade. That public and judicial opinion in the nation was ready for such a declaration is evident from the fact that courts in the rest of the states thereafter generally ceased to hold labor organizations contrary to the common law. Workers, like other men, were hereafter free to join together in pursuit of their economic ends. Shaw's decision and its acceptance throughout the nation constituted the legal foundation of the American labor movement; the unions, however, would have to wait another generation before social and economic conditions were such that they could strike root and grow.

4. ON THE ROAD TO DAMASCUS

Although many in Jackson's America concentrated their attention upon the economic and political sides of the Great Experiment, there were others whose horizons were wider. Indeed, sometimes it appeared that nothing except the dogmas of democracy and equality were left unchallenged throughout the length and breadth of society. The whole period was one of change. The steamboats and canals, the revolutionary railroads, the new factories, the growing cities were at once causes and symptoms of the upheaval

through which the old order was passing. The very intellectual
underpinnings of the eighteenth-century Enlightenment were being
knocked out. The ideals of that previous age—urbanity, precision,
reason—were under attack from the Romantic cult of the natural,
the simple, and the ordinary. Nathaniel Hawthorne,[5] Herman Melville, Walt Whitman, and the Hudson River school of painters were
but the New World counterparts of more celebrated European
Romantics who were revolting against the optimistic and reasonable
assumptions of the Enlightenment.

In the face of so much change and ferment, it was inevitable that
the basic institutions of society should be called into question and
challenged to justify themselves. "Education, labor, politics, debt,
war, dress, health, family life, church, prisons, the poor, the crippled
and the unfortunate," as Russell Nye has said, were all tumbled
together as fit subjects for scrutiny by a host of eager reformers.
It is not our purpose here to get involved with Amelia Bloomer and
her improvements in women's clothing or to explore the interesting if
strange customs of the Oneida Community, or to discuss the merits
of prisons which held their inmates incommunicado. Yet the fact
that reforms and reformers were so numerous and so diverse in this
period throws not a little light on the ingredients which went into
the formation of the American character.

The very act of being a reformer reveals something of one's
assumption about the world. To work for reform implies a belief in
the efficacy of making the world over, even if only in a small corner.
To Americans tomorrow always looked better than today, not because today was so miserable, but because it was so good. As one
writer in the southern magazine *De Bow's Review* put it, "To him
who has watched the progress of discovery and invention in the
different countries of Europe and America, scarcely anything now
will appear to be impossible." To be convinced that the future is
unlimited, "it is sufficient to contemplate what man has done." Nor

---

[5] Hawthorne, in the introduction to his novel *The Marble Faun*, gave expression
to some of the problems of a Romantic writer in America; his words are worth
repeating here for what they reveal about America in the 1850's. "No author,
without a trial," he wrote, "can conceive of the difficulty of writing a romance
about a country where there is no shadow, no antiquity, no mystery, no picturesque and gloomy wrong, nor anything but a commonplace prosperity, in
broad and simple daylight, as is happily the case with my dear native land. . . .
Romance and poetry, ivy, lichens, and wall-flowers need ruin to make them
grow."

was there much doubt that men, along with conditions, could be changed for the better. "I have faith," wrote Horace Mann, the great educational reformer, "in the improvability of the race—in their accelerating improvability." A workingman's newspaper in 1830 dwelt on the immense capabilities of the human mind. The railroads, canals, and other inventions of the age, the paper said, "dwindle into insignificance—into mere child's play—when brought into comparison with the intellectual and moral improvement of the people." The American commitment to simple progress was a source of real irritation to Mrs. Trollope. Of all the strictures of the Americans against the English, she remembered, "the favorite, the constant, the universal sneer that met me everywhere, was on our old-fashioned attachment to things obsolete."

It is true, of course, that belief in progress and perfectibility of man is as much an eighteenth-century article of faith as it is nineteenth. Reformers of the nineteenth century, almost by definition, were believers in natural law, natural rights, and the application of reason to human institutions, just as the men of the Enlightenment had been. As Merle Curti has noticed, the austere rationalism of English utilitarianism was well exemplified in America's Age of Reform. But in practice, nineteenth-century reform exhibited at least two important additions to that of the Enlightenment. For one thing, in the earlier period interest in reform was usually confined to a relatively small class of people who were quite divorced from the mass of the population. If the eighteenth century was an age of Enlightenment, the masses rarely shared in the glow. The reforming spirit of the nineteenth century, however, as befitted a self-consciously democratic people, penetrated the lower levels of society, as foreign observers soon discovered.

The second difference between the two periods of reform was to be found in the motivation behind the impulse. By and large the reformers of the Enlightenment were moved by reason; they attacked institutions because they were irrational, useless, or inefficient. Slavery was evil, for example, for the man of the eighteenth century, more because it was a denial of natural and economic law than because it was cruel. The abolitionist of the nineteenth century, however, opposed slavery because of its inhumanity as often as for its denial of abstract rights to the slave. Impatience with irrationality and prejudice was the animating force in most gentlemen of the Enlightenment; pity for the hungry, the oppressed, the mistreated was often the mainspring of the nineteenth-century reformer. Pity was a conspicuous element among the reformers. At best it was manifested as a compassionate humanitarianism which included within its circle of concern all mankind, high and low, white and black; at worst it was an uncritical sentimentality which would equate animal vivisection with human torture. Modern American reform has never lost that broad strain of humanitarianism which burst forth with such energy in the Era of Jackson.

In the twentieth century American faith in progress and the perfectibility of man has been tempered by realistic psychology and unpleasant economics. But deep inside himself, the modern American still feels the optimism which animated the nineteenth-century reformer. Our self-confidence may be reduced somewhat, but there are still very few Americans in the mid-twentieth century who are not convinced that in this country lies the model for the world. There may be almost continuous crises in the perilous world of today, but the old optimism, the familiar belief in a better tomorrow, we have not lost.

Indeed, so confident have Americans been regarding the future that they have willingly borne a mission in the world. The Puritan who said God "sifted a whole nation that he might send choice grain over to this Wilderness" was convinced of it. The leaders of the Revolution were sure it would mark a turning point in the history of free men. By the age of Jackson, Americans were convinced that their country was the model for the world. "The old and motheaten systems of Europe have had their day," wrote Walt Whitman in the Brooklyn *Eagle*. "*Here* we have planted the standard of freedom, and here we will test the capacities of men for self-government." Even normally hardheaded John C. Calhoun subscribed to the proposition that America was unique. "We are charged by Providence," he declared, "not only with the happiness of this great people, but . . . with that of the human race." If the American experiment should succeed, he continued, "it will be the commencement of a new era in human affairs. All civilized governments must in the course of time conform to this principle." Herman Melville summed up the attitude when he said Americans are "the peculiar chosen people, the Israel of our time."

For better or worse, America still imagines itself the Savior of the World—with less braggadocio, to be sure, but in essential form just as in the first half of the nineteenth century. It is significant, for instance, that in the two great wars of the twentieth century, the master phrasemakers of the age both gave utterance to this missionary impulse of the American people. Woodrow Wilson called upon Americans "to save the world for Democracy"; Winston Churchill lauded the New World's coming to "redress the balance of the old." Both men tapped that reservoir of missionary zeal which has been engrained in the American character for a hundred years.

Central to American belief in progress was the conviction that through the door of education the better world would be reached. To Americans of the first half of the nineteenth century, education was the key to everything: to a successful democracy, to progress, and to individual enrichment. Education, said the educator Horace Mann, is "the great equalizer of men. . . . It does better than to disarm the poor of their hostility towards the rich, it prevents being poor." "Free schools," an Ohio educator wrote in 1822, "lessen the distinction, which fortune makes, between the children of the rich and the poor. . . ." But important as educational reform seemed to Americans then, to moderns the significance of those years lies in the fact that it was then that the essential outline of the present school system in America took shape.

As enterprising Europeans who emigrated to a new and empty land, Americans have always been intensely concerned about the transmission of their values to their children. The Puritans of the seventeenth century, as we have seen, made a significant educational innovation with their town-supported schools; the eighteenth century also contributed its bit to the modern educational pattern in America by the proliferation of collegiate institutions of learning. But during the latter portion of the eighteenth and first decades of the nineteenth centuries, the enunciation of a strong belief in the value of education far exceeded the performance. Schools were permitted to decline for lack of funds and repairs; little effort was even made to insure that children would receive the rudiments of reading and writing; nothing was done to secure qualified teachers or even to provide adequate training schools for their recruitment, though the number of children was mounting.

One of the first fruits of the reforming spirit of the 1830's and 1840's was the gradual but decisive reversal of this failure to live up to the widespread belief in public education. Led by men like Horace Mann, Henry Barnard, and Calvin Wiley, a movement for the improvement of the public schools spread across the country. By the time of the Civil War the movement succeeded in building a school system which was free and open to all white children.

The essential elements of the educational structure and philosophy of today were worked out by 1860, though not, of course, practiced everywhere in the nation. Schools were to be supported by public funds and all members of the community were required to send their children to them or to some alternative school. To insure uniformity in the quality of instruction, the schools were to be placed under the supervision of a state authority. As a further safeguard for the quality of education, the state was to provide special, advanced schools—often called normal schools after the French institutions—for the training of teachers. Finally, in view of the diversity of religions and nationalities in America, instruction in the public schools would be secular and dedicated to the training of loyal citizens.

Free schools of some type always existed in all sections of the nation, not only in Puritan New England. In the nineteenth century, for example, there were a number of schools which, because of an endowment of one sort or another, were able to accept students without charge, or at least were in a position to offer instruction to children unable to pay. Rhode Island, New York, and some of the southern states for a while even supported free schools by lotteries. Some of the nation's large cities, like Boston and Charleston, boasted very good tax-supported schools. But in the days of Horace Mann, in the 1830's and 1840's, there were few systems of genuinely free public schools. The most common form of public education at that time was the so-called rate school. This was a school ostensibly supported by public funds—usually some kind of endowment—but these funds were heavily supplemented by the levy of rates or taxes upon the parents of the children who attended. Actually, of course, this was no more a free public system of education than the lottery-supported schools or the charity schools; it was neither free nor universal nor a system. "We want a COMMON and EQUAL education—also PUBLIC because it is of general concern," cried one Jacksonian radical newspaper in 1835. "It belongs to the public interest. As rational beings, it is in the INTEREST OF ALL, that ALL should be equally well educated." Because of the rate system's haphazard arrangement and support, reformers interested in a system of truly free schools worked vigorously to eliminate it.

It was not until the fifties, however, that the rate system began to be replaced by the free public school as we know it today—that is, by a system of schools open to all and supported by all. Massachusetts instituted its system as early as 1827, Vermont came along in 1850, Ohio followed two years later, Iowa in 1858, Rhode Island in 1868, Michigan and New Jersey in 1870, Indiana in 1871; the southern states achieved state-wide free schooling during Reconstruction.

The first step toward permanently secularizing the public schools was taken in New Jersey in 1844, when it was provided in its constitution that no school funds could be diverted to private educational institutions. This marked the end of the attempt on the part of Catholics in particular and religious groups in general to secure public support for religious education. The tradition of separation of Church and State and the superior logic of the great diversity of sects in America were the operative forces in the decision. By the end of the century all the old states, and all but one of the new, included clauses in their respective constitutions prohibiting the expenditure of school funds on private religious education.

The common school was conceived of—and has actually become —a device for welding a diversity of peoples into a single nation. To this day, the inculcation of patriotism and civic-mindedness in the young is more the function of the public school than of any other social institution in the United States. There the child learns to salute and make his pledge to the national flag, and studies Problems of American Democracy. Often the state legislatures prescribed that the schools provide courses—as was the case in West Virginia in 1940—"for the purpose of teaching, fostering and perpetuating the ideals, principle and spirit of Americanism. . . ."

Once the basic structure of the elementary school was hammered out, the rest of the education system, in the course of time, followed as an extension of the first principles. The first tax-supported high school, the English Classical School of Boston, was established in 1821; New York opened its first public high school in 1825. By 1860, some 320 high schools were in existence, of which 167, or over half, were located in the three states of New York, Massachusetts, and Ohio. Although the tuition academy dominated secondary education until well into the post-Civil War decades, the principle of free education for all would ultimately overtake secondary education as it had the grammar school. Moreover, in time, free college education, led by the state universities, would place a crown upon the whole system.

In a fundamental sense, of course, the American educational system, wherein a child could rise as high as his ability would permit, was a direct response to the equalitarian assumptions of the people. But the educational system was also a force in itself, perpetuating and encouraging equality within the society. This was urged at the time of its founding, and so it still remains today. Again and again, the school, above all else, has been charged with teaching the values of democracy and the virtues of equality. The last such charge was uttered by the Supreme Court in May of 1954.

For the world, as for America, the struggle for the truly public school in the Age of Jackson had important consequences. Though not all countries have necessarily accepted all our procedures, if they are democratic in philosophy they have accepted our assumptions. Most democratic nations have recognized, as Americans in the 1830's and 1840's made clear, that if the people are to take part in their own governance, then they must have access to the schools. And, for this to be true, the Americans of the early nineteenth century pointed out, the providing of schools must be recognized as a responsibility of society as a whole. It is in this sense that we can talk of the public school as a legacy from the age of the Great Experiment.

Although the objects of reform were numerous in this era of ferment, there was one which swallowed up all the rest. Ever since the early 1830's the issue of slavery had figured with increasing prominence in the talk and politics of Americans. By the decade of the 1850's it lay like a weight on the minds and consciences of almost all Americans. As an issue it proved itself capable of rending churches, disrupting an ancient political party, turning the floor of Congress into a parody of deliberative debate, and igniting civil war on the plains of Kansas. Slavery, it is clear, was not just another object for reform. It was the greatest moral and social issue confronting Americans in the age of the Great Experiment, for it divided the people as nothing else ever has. Its impact on American society then and for the future was at once devastating and enduring.

CHAPTER VI

The American Tragedy

WHEN Louis Kossuth, the Hungarian revolutionary, came to America in 1851, he was only one of many visiting Europeans who believed that America was "unequaled in general intelligence and in general prosperity," and "a glorious evidence of mankind's capacity to self-government. . . ." Some Europeans, however, could not fail to notice the fact of human slavery, which, as one English newspaper phrased it in 1845, "is a canker in the root of the seemingly fair and flourishing plant . . . and threatens to make the great republic of modern times a warning instead of an example to the world at large." The United States, John Stuart Mill tartly remarked, is a "country where institutions profess to be founded on equality, and which yet maintains the slavery of black men. . . ."

Simply because slavery was in truth a denial of American equalitarian pretensions, it increasingly dominated the affairs of the Republic. And even as it dominated the thinking of men, it was shaping Americans, both black and white, for a long time to come.

1. THE PECULIAR INSTITUTION

Slavery was an inheritance from the colonial period, and one common to all the states of the new Republic. In the course of the late eighteenth and early nineteenth centuries, however, several of the northern states found the institution at once repugnant to their conception of liberty and of little import in their economic life. Under such a combination of blights, slavery withered and died in a number of states before 1800; and in those states in the North where it did not, it was clearly on the road to extinction. Happily enough, farther south there was some promise of the same result if sufficient time were allowed. Southern leaders of the Revolution like

Washington, Madison, Jefferson, and Patrick Henry frankly
looked forward to the day when Negro slavery would be gone completely from the Republic.

The prospects for such a future were propitious in the latter
part of the eighteenth century, inasmuch as tobacco, the staple of
the slave-manned plantations of the South, was becoming an increasingly unprofitable crop. Should the economic and libertarian
forces of the period pull in the same direction long enough, it was
felt by many and hoped by even more, the anomaly of slavery among
a people who believed that "all men are created equal" would soon
cease to exist.

But toward the very end of the eighteenth century, two historical
developments combined to infuse a new vigor into American slavery.
The first and most important of these was the mechanization of
English manufacturing, or the Industrial Revolution. Among the
earliest industries to respond to mechanization was cotton textile
manufacturing, with the immediate consequence of a precipitous
increase in the demand for raw cotton, which in turn drove the
price to very high levels. Prior to the Revolution no cotton of
measurable quantities had been grown on the American mainland,
though the West Indies had long exported the snowy "wool." The
new rise in cotton prices, however, offered great incentive for the
American production of the fiber. States like Georgia and South
Carolina found that long-fiber cotton, which was readily separated
from the seed, could be grown along their littorals and coastal
islands. But efforts to expand cultivation of this sea-island cotton
to the interior lands failed. The only cotton which would grow
successfully on the uplands was a type in which the fiber tenaciously
adhered to the seed, a fact which rendered its separation a tedious
and expensive process even with slave labor.

With such economic incentive for ingenuity, it was inevitable that
soon some device would be invented which would quickly and
cheaply separate the short-fiber cotton from its seed. The inventor
and the invention arrived in 1793 in the form of Eli Whitney and
his gin. Immediately recognized as the answer to the ambitious
planters' prayers, the gin and the unflagging English demand for
cotton provided the necessary encouragement for the development
of the Cotton Kingdom on the lands of western Georgia and South
Carolina and in the new lands to the west. Intent upon reaping their
profits as quickly as possible, the planters turned to the plantation

and the Negro slave as the most expeditious means of production. Slavery was reborn, soon to flourish as never before.

By as early as the 1820's and the 1830's slavery was firmly established in the economy of the South. Even southern states like Kentucky, Virginia, North Carolina, and Missouri, which grew little or no cotton, gained a new economic interest in slavery from the fact that they found a ready market for their excess slaves in the rapidly expanding cotton states to the south. Moreover, these upper southern states continued to use Negro slave labor on their tobacco and hemp plantations.

At the same time in the North, however, slavery had either ceased to exist or was well on the way to legal extinction. This parting of the ways between the two sections of the country was freighted with ominous significance for the South and for the future of the Republic.

Though cotton cultivation certainly brought new life to the failing institution of slavery, this is not to say that the southern people thereby became a nation of slaveholders. In fact, despite the tons of paper and myriad hours of oratory expended on the slavery question in the ante-bellum years, the slaveholder was far from being the typical Southerner. The great majority of the southern white people held no slaves at all and therefore had no direct interest in or even connection with the institution. Out of a total of some 1.6 million families in the South in 1860, only 384,000 owned the four million slaves. And even those who held slaves did not possess them in the number legendarily associated with the Old South of magnolias and white-pillared mansions. In 1860, 20 per cent of the slaveholders owned only a single Negro; fully two thirds of them possessed fewer than twenty slaves each. Over 99 per cent of the slaveowners held 100 or fewer slaves. The possession of 500 or more slaves, according to the Census of 1860, was indeed a rarity, since only fourteen "millionaires" enjoyed that distinction in all of the South.

Such census statistics should destroy any lingering illusion that the planter and his hundreds of slaves were typical or even common-place figures in Dixie. Indeed, the Southerner with any slaves at all, let alone hundreds, was in the distinct minority, a curiosity amid the millions of plain people who owned no slaves at all and who, perhaps, rarely saw one. Statistically, the small yeoman farmer, work-

ing his land unassisted by the labor of black men, was the typical
Southerner in the ante-bellum era.

Furthermore, as the figures on slaveholding imply, the plantation itself was not typical either; small individually operated farms
far exceeded plantations in number. In 1850, for example, the census reported 569,000 agricultural units in the South, of which only
101,335, or 18 per cent of the total, could be classified as plantations—that is, a unit producing marketable quantities of one or
more of the five basic staples of cotton, tobacco, sugar, rice, or
hemp. If another definition of plantation is used, such as U. B.
Phillips', of a farm with twenty or more slaves, then the proportion
of plantations to farms shrinks still further, to less than one in ten.

But such figures on slaveholding and plantations, though often
cited to demonstrate the relative unimportance of slavery in the
ante-bellum South, are quite misleading if one seeks to measure the
economic significance of slavery.[1] It was the function in the economy
performed by Negro slave labor which gave slavery its crucial place
in the life of the South. For though it is true that slaves made up a
minority of the labor force, and their typical habitat, the plantation, comprised a very small proportion of the region's agricultural
units, the slaves on the plantations produced the bulk of the section's marketable surplus, for, by definition, the plantation was a
producer of surplus.

It was from the plantations that the exports came which paid for
the South's imports from the shops, factories and warehouses of
Europe; the labor of slaves provided the wherewithal to maintain
lawyers and actors, cotton factors and publishers, musicians in
Charleston, Senators in Washington, and gamblers on the Mississippi River boats. In short, it was slavery which maintained, as the
South realized, the culture and civilization of the region. Furthermore, the majority of the planters, agrarian and status-minded as
they delighted in portraying themselves, were actually adventur-
ously, and often ruthlessly, bent on profit and reinvestment. That
is, they were agricultural entrepreneurs in a capitalist society; their
central importance as a class resided not in their numbers, which
was admittedly small, but in their ability to accumulate surplus for
investment.

[1] As L. C. Gray has pointed out, the census figures can be expressed in such
a way as to give quite a different picture of the incidence of slavery in the South.
One out of every two persons in the southern population of 14 million was either
a slave or a member of a slaveholding family.

Moreover, to focus attention, as some historians have done, on the large number of slaveowners who held only a few Negroes is to obscure the more significant fact that the majority of the slaves were held in units of a size well adapted to surplus-producing plantations. In 1860, according to the calculation of L. C. Gray, 53 per cent of the slaves in the South were held in parcels of twenty or more. If ten is taken as a good working unit for staple production, as it might well be, then three quarters of the slaves fell into this grouping. As a labor force, then, the slaves, though fewer than the working white farmers, were much more important in the economy because black labor, unlike white, was heavily concentrated in the surplus-producing sector. In substance, whether considered as capital or as labor, the slave regime was central to the southern economy.

Implicit in what has been said up to now about the importance of slavery in the economy has been the assumption that it was profitable. Because the profitability of the plantation regime has been frequently questioned, more extended comment is in order here.

Unfortunately, in discussing this question commentators and historians have not always been clear as to what they are proving. Though ostensibly showing the unprofitability of slavery, they often merely show that it is less efficient than a hypothetically free labor system. Charles Sydnor, for example, an astute modern historian who questioned the profitability of slavery, was actually doing nothing more than arguing that it was less efficient than free labor. Frederick Olmsted, the well-known northern traveler in the antebellum South, was guilty of the same error in his discussions of the profits derived from bound Negro labor.

In actuality, the question of the comparative costs of slave and free labor was and is an academic one, since the issue never really threatened the South's peculiar institution. Furthermore, a labor system is so tightly enmeshed in the web of custom and habit that it is rarely, if ever, overthrown by abstract comparison with another system's profits. Especially is this true when the labor system is actually producing profits.

There are several good general reasons for believing that, for the South as a whole, the slave regime was a profitable one during the decades immediately before the War.[2] According to the computa-

[2] Specific examples of profit rates do not answer the question because we have too few of them to establish their representativeness, but they do illustrate the

tions of Thomas Govan, for instance, the value of real and personal
estate in the Southern states between 1850 and 1860 jumped from
$2.8 billion to $6.2 billion—an increment of over 100 per cent. It is
difficult to believe that such economic growth could have taken place
if slavery were unprofitable. Moreover, the ease with which the
South, as compared with the other two sections, hurdled the Panic
of 1857 suggests a sound and prosperous economy rather than one
struggling to make ends meet.

The rising price curve for slaves—often erroneously cited as a
reason why slavery would cease to show profits—is actually another proof that the South enjoyed an expanding rather than a
stagnant or contracting economy. Under a slave system, as in a
unionless free economy, a rising price for labor (wages in a free
society) is an indication that enterprise is expanding at such a rate
that the supply of labor is inadequate. The planter on old and worn-
out lands, it is true, may have found a rising price curve in slaves a
brake upon his acquisitions of labor. But for the planter on new
land, who, after all, was bidding up the price, the slave was well
worth it; only with the Negro's labor could the planter reap the
maximum advantage from the good cotton prices. Besides, even if
the price of slaves climbed too high, demand would then fall off and
the price would drop to accommodate itself to the shrunken demand.[3] In short, slavery would continue to produce profits for the

level of return on some plantations. James K. Polk's Mississippi plantation, according to John Bassett's examination, yielded annual profits ranging from 14 to 25
per cent. Elizafield, a Georgia rice plantation, produced enough wealth for its
owner to add $10,000 in real estate value and $13,000 in personal property, including slaves, in the years between 1850 and 1860. Thomas Govan has carefully calculated, from records extending over periods of from four to eleven
years during the 1840's and 1850's, that three plantations, two in Georgia and
one in South Carolina, earned average annual profits of 3.7 per cent (after a
managerial salary of $5,000 had been deducted), 6.6 per cent, and 12 per cent,
respectively.

[3] It is often argued that slavery "froze" the South's capital in labor and
thereby prevented the growth of manufacturing in that region. Whatever strictures may be laid against slavery as an economic situation, this is not one of
them. The argument that putting capital into slaves rendered it unavailable for
investment in manufacturing confuses the capital of the individual slaveholder
with that of the section. It is true that by investing his profits in additional slaves,
the planter had no excess for investment in manufacturing. But those who advance this argument forget that the southern slave trader, to whom the planter
paid over his cash for the labor, was perfectly free to put the money into manufacturing, if he so desired. The failure of the ante-bellum South to develop
manufacturing on a scale comparable with the contemporary North is therefore

economy as a whole. The fact that the prices for hiring slaves were also rising in the last decade of the ante-bellum period further supports the view that slavery was profitable. And since it was profitable, the contention that the Civil War was a needless war because slavery was on the way to extinction for lack of economic usefulness is more wishful thinking than hard fact.

But there was more to the South's defense of slavery than economics; there was also race. All the profits of all the plantations cannot explain the tenacity, the passion, with which the little people of the South—that majority of the people who held no slaves—rallied to the defense of the slave system, both before the war and in the armies of the Confederacy. Their stake in slavery is found in that institution's undoubted ability to prevent Negro domination and to provide psychological status where there was no other. For few Southerners hated the Negro so much as those whose economic position was almost indistinguishable from that of the slaves. Even non-slaveholders who happened to abhor the institution for moral or economic reasons were often silenced by slavery's undoubted ability to control the Negroes.

One such back-country farmer confessed his dilemma to Olmsted. "I wouldn't like to hev 'em free, if they gwine to hang around . . . because they is so monstrous lazy. . . . Now suppose they was free, you see they'd all think themselves just as good as we. . . ." Then came the fear of intermarriage: "how'd you like to hev a nigger steppin' up to your darter? Of course you wouldn't; and that's the reason I wouldn't like to hev 'em free; but I tell you, I don't think it's right to hev 'em slaves so; that's the fac—taant right to keep 'em as they is."

In 1860 Andrew Johnson, acknowledged spokesman for the South's little people against the pretensions of the slaveocracy, promised on the floor of Congress that in the defense of slavery all white men would be united. "When there was agitation in Tennessee, in 1856," he recalled, "I saw that the non-slaveholder was the readiest man to rise up and join the master in extirpating, if necessary, this race from existence, rather than see them liberated and turned loose upon the country."

When all is said and done, then, profits and fear of the black man

---

not traceable, in any direct sense, to the prevalence of slavery. Rather it would seem to be bound up with the general profitability of agriculture and the outlook of an agriculturally oriented people and society.

offer the most succinct explanation as to why the South, in the full
glare of nineteenth-century humanitarianism, hugged to its bosom
the moral anachronism of slavery.

2. ALL SLAVES ARE BLACK

In the minds of many modern Americans, the Negro is pictured
as a man who was once a slave and one, moreover, who was essentially content in that status. This reading of the past has more than
academic import, for, intended or not, it partially determines the
subordinate status assigned the Negro in modern American culture.
Other races, it is said, would not and could not have remained content in so degraded a status. But the Negro, the argument goes, is
truly inferior simply because he has proved to be so adaptable to
an inferior status.

There are a number of arguments which have been advanced to
establish the essential contentment of the Negro in slavery, but perhaps the most persuasive is the fact that during the war, when the
men were away from the plantations, there were very few slave revolts in the South. Indeed, all through the history of slavery, it can
be added, the number of slave revolts was remarkably small. True,
over two hundred revolts have been uncovered by diligent research,
but even that number is insignificant when it is recalled that they
spread out to something like two a year in an area the size of western
Europe and among a servile population of two to four millions.
Furthermore, many of these revolts were nothing more than temporary labor stoppages under a system which did not provide a
means whereby dissatisfaction with immediate working conditions
could be registered.

Furthermore, even the most celebrated instrument of protest, the
Underground Railroad, heroic as its "conductors" and "passengers"
were, tells us little about the attitude of the majority of the slaves.
At most, according to the Road's sympathetic historian, an
average of 2,000 slaves escaped annually between 1830 and 1860;
compared with the millions held in bondage, these runaways are
numerically and economically inconsequential.

In the same way, the sporadic suicides, self-mutilations by a
sensitive slave, or the murder of a baby by a slave mother may illustrate the extremes to which some were driven by slavery, but they
afford us little insight into the feelings of the many. Most unsatis-
factory in shedding light on the Negro's conception of slavery are

the reminiscences of the slaves themselves. Taken down long after freedom was attained, suffused with the romantic haze of years, or written by militant Negro abolitionists, they merely inform us of the variety of reactions to the system, but tell us little of the response of the slaves in general.

Actually, the arguments summarized above and rejected as inadequate reveal more about those who advanced them than about the attitude of the Negroes toward bondage. In looking for militant opposition to slavery, historians, northern and southern alike, were viewing slavery through their own stereotypes. Both used the same test for the Negroes' reaction to slavery—militant revolt. When the rebellions did not occur in the profusion expected, the liberal historian exaggerated those he did find; the Southerner, on the other hand, concluded that the Negro was content in slavery. But because the criterion of revolts was unrealistic from the outset, it revealed little about the Negro's attitude toward his status.

Widespread revolts were just not to be expected under the conditions of southern slavery. Psychological and physical obstacles to revolt were virtually insuperable. For example, the inevitable human element in slavery—the paternalistic, reciprocal relationship obtaining between many masters and their slaves—created bonds which greatly reduced the possibilities of successful or widespread revolt. E. F. Frazier, the Negro sociologist, for example, has observed that in many abortive conspiracies it was the faithful house slave who, to save his master, gave away the plot. Furthermore, the very rural, often frontier character of the South rendered any large-scale, organized revolt almost an impossibility, though individual, localized revolts could and did take place.

Those very areas, moreover, most susceptible to antislavery influences from the North—the border states—were also the localities where the treatment of the slave was traditionally most humane and consonant with the reciprocal loyalties of a big family. In such areas pressure for revolt was relatively weak, and distaste for violence against a good master was greatest. Moreover, it was in these same border states that the Underground Railroad was most active—a fact which meant, perforce, that the most aggressive and capable leaders were drawn off, leaving the least capable to cope with the formidable obstacles to organized revolt.

Finally, slavery must have seemed to many Negroes raised within its confines a part of the natural order, with which they might not be satisfied, but toward which they were incapable of militant and aggressive opposition because of their long acculturation.

But revolts are not the only criteria which can be used for the detection of dissatisfaction with slavery. Any standards which are used, though, must take into consideration the limitations which slavery imposed on the Negroes' ability and opportunities to express discontent. Once we cease to look for revolts as the major test of dissatisfaction under slavery, then we can find important evidence of widespread discontent.

The slave songs, for example, as the expression of a whole people, reveal much about the inner reactions of the Negroes to their lot. Rarely can a song of real exaltation be found; but the words of discouragement, dissatisfaction, and melancholy appear in profusion: "Nobody knows de trouble I've had"; "Why don't you give up de world?"; "My Father, how long?"; "We'll soon be free, de Lord will call us home." Sometimes the songs made direct reference to the burdens and anxieties of slavery, as in "O run, nigger, run, for the patrol will catch you"; "[Plantation] Bell da ring"; "Go in the wilderness"; then, finally, there are the many songs which bemoan the separation from loved ones—certainly a reflection of the realities of slavery.

Additional evidence that the Negroes were generally discontented with slavery is found in the fact that they escaped when a real opportunity to do so was presented to them. During the war, thousands of slaves deserted the plantations as the federal troops approached, seeking refuge and freedom within the Union lines. Moreover, over 200,000 Negroes, most of whom were former slaves, voluntarily joined the armed services of the Union to make war on the slave South.

Another indication of the widespread discontent under slavery is the superstitious reverence and awe in which the Negroes held the name of their emancipator. This sentiment was prevalent among former slaves even before Lincoln suffered his martyr's death and while they still had not tasted much of the sweets of freedom. It might also be added that southern slaveholders themselves testified to the Negro's desire for freedom when they acknowledged that manumission was the greatest boon a master could bestow upon a faithful Negro.

When these signs of pervasive discontent are taken together with the sporadic revolts, the conspiracies, the runaways, and the individual acts of defiance, a pattern of mass dissatisfaction with slavery is the inescapable conclusion. Contrary to the apologetics of southern slavery and modern myths, the Negro was no more a natural slave than other men.

In an earlier chapter we have already seen that the close association between the stigma of slavery and the Negro began early in the history of American society. The reinvigoration of slavery during the nineteenth century rendered that original attachment even more close. The most obvious measure of the stigma which had been fastened upon the Negro race by the middle of the nineteenth century was the legal status of the southern free Negro, of whom there were about 250,000 in 1860.[4]

The freedom of Negroes was entirely dependent upon their ability to maintain it; all men of black or brown skin in the South were presumed to be slaves unless their freedom papers or custom could prove the contrary. With zealous slave catchers not always careful to notice the limits of their authority, the tendency of the law was strongly in the direction of slavery. Indeed, sometimes the special criminal law for free Negroes created avenues for a return to bondage, as in Maryland, where punishment for first offenders included sale outside the state for a term of years—and some so punished apparently never returned to freedom.

But even if the blacks could prove their freedom, the quality of their liberty was strained. They could not travel in the same cars, live in the same hotels, or attend the same churches as whites; in some states, like North Carolina, they were excluded from the slaves' church meetings as well. Economically their job opportunities were limited by law and custom; and though political opportunities and privileges were denied them, they were taxed the same as whites, where additional taxes were not levied upon them.[5]

[4] There were also about a quarter of a million free negroes in the North in 1860. There they were subjected to as severe social discrimination as in the South, but legal discrimination was much milder.

[5] Despite such restrictions on their economic opportunities, free Negroes in the South, particularly in cities like Charleston and New Orleans, owned considerable amounts of property. Estimates of the property run to several millions of dollars, including, in some cases, ownership of Negro slaves. The life of one free Negro, that of William Johnson of Natchez, has been documented by the publication of his diary in 1951, edited by W. R. Hogan and E. A. Davis. Johnson was born a slave in 1809, was emancipated in 1820, and soon became a respectable barber for whites. His business flourished in Natchez, where he employed several other free Negroes in his barber shop and earned enough to lend

In a society justifying slavery as the proper status for the Negro race, there was little place for the free Negro; he was a pariah. As the defense of slavery in terms of race mounted through the 1850's, southern legislation increasingly reflected this view in a most literal fashion. In most states of Dixie, for instance, all newly manumitted Negroes were required to leave the state, an additional price thus being exacted from them for their liberty. Tennessee, Texas, Louisiana, and Maryland, in the last years of the slave era, enacted legislation designed to facilitate the enslavement of these anomalous persons. Arkansas actually passed legislation in 1859 to compel the emigration, on pain of enslavement, of all free Negroes in the state.

Unless he accepted the protection of slavery, the southern free person of color was visited with all the responsibilities of freedom and precious few of its privileges and immunities. Is it any wonder, then, that free Negro William Bass petitioned in 1859 for permission to submit to a master? His position as free Negro, he wrote, "is more degrading, and involves more suffering in this State, than that of a slave, who is under the care, protection and ownership of a kind and good master." As a free person of color, he continued, he "is preyed upon by every sharper," has little money, though ablebodied and capable of working. Moreover, he "is charged and punished for, every offense," whether guilty or not, "committed in the neighborhood."

For all his inferior position, however, the free Negro was feared in the South, for he always stood as a potential nucleus around which servile insurrection might organize. It was for this reason that the southern states in the 1840's and 1850's increased the obstacles to manumission, often to the point of prohibition. Some states, as we have seen, endeavored to hound them out of the community completely. South Carolina and five other southern states decreed, in their unassuageable anxiety, that free Negroes who came into port as ships' crew members had to spend the time of their sojourn in jail.

But the enduring impress of slavery was most deeply felt by the Negro who was a slave, and in 1860 over four million of the 4.3 million Negroes who lived in the South were held in bondage. To all

money and invest in local enterprises. He often employed white men on his farm and even owned several Negro slaves. He was murdered in 1851 by a white man, who could not be convicted, though three trials were held, because the only witnesses to the slaying were Negroes—and they could not testify against a white man. At his death, Johnson was worth at least $25,000.

intents and purposes, therefore, the image in which the Negro beheld himself, and in which white men beheld him, was largely determined by his actual status under slavery.

Unlike the Indian who was enslaved, the Negro entered American slavery stripped of his native culture. Even anthropologists like Melville Herskovits, who maintain that some African cultural traits survived in America, cannot list more than a handful of minor customs of speech and dress to buttress their case. The culture of the Negroes was inevitably limited to that which slavery provided and which a slave status permitted them to absorb from the white men with whom they lived and worked.

The Negro's very demeanor and family pattern were conditioned by slavery. Under the duress of the whip he learned the need for deferential behavior; recognized that he must present a happy visage to his master, and that to appear too smart or too ready around white folks was dangerous. Married with a ceremony which pointedly omitted any perpetual vows, since all unions were dissolvable upon the sale of one of the partners, Negroes were conditioned to look upon marriage as a fiction which carried little meaning beyond the salving of the white man's conscience. One slave preacher, for instance, married couples "until death or *distance* do you part." Indeed, the slave family not only possessed very little spiritual or legal cohesion; it lacked even an economic bond. The master, after all, not the father, was responsible for the support of the wife and children. Under such circumstances it is remarkable that there was as much unity in the slave family as there was.

Habits of work, responsibility, and self-respect were geared to a low standard by slavery. Compelled to work, though deriving very little direct benefit from it, and exercising little responsibility in it, the slave easily became shiftless, careless, and irresponsible. Because many masters feared that if their slaves learned a skilled trade they would become "uppity" and hard to handle, the Negro was usually discouraged from improving himself. One Charlestonian, for example, spoke of the "baneful effects" of hiring out slaves because it produced in them an unwillingness "to return to the regular life and domestic control of the master." Laws in most of the southern states prohibited the teaching of reading and writing to slaves; and though some planters did not obey the law, there were many who did not need it to remind them that even a partly educated slave could be at least difficult and at most dangerous. In the clearer air of the eighteenth century, Southerner Thomas Jefferson recognized the moral crippling which slavery inflicted upon the Negro. "That disposition to theft," he wrote, with which they "have been branded must be ascribed to their situation, and not to any depravity of their moral sense."

Perhaps the most enduring monument to slavery and its effects upon the Negro was the elaboration of the doctrine of Negro inferiority. As we have seen, this belief began as early as the seventeenth century; but during the last decade of the ante-bellum period, the doctrine was dressed up in pseudoscientific garb and elevated to the position of a principal argument in justification of a labor system the world's morality had outgrown. "The Negro races stand at the lowest point in the scale of human beings, and we know no moral or physical agencies which can redeem them from their degradation," wrote Dr. J. C. Nott, the South's leading ethnologist in the 1850's. "It is clear," he concluded, "that they are incapable of self-government, and that any attempt to improve their condition is warring against an immutable law of nature." Slavery's boldest and learned apologist, publicist J. D. B. De Bow, contended that the physical differences between Negro and Caucasian rendered them morally and politically different. The "physical differences between the two races," he wrote, are so great "as to make what is wholesome and beneficial for the white man, as liberty, republican and free institutions, etc., not only unsuitable to the negro race, but actually poisonous to its happiness."

The disabilities which slavery imposed on the Negro made proof of the black man's inferiority deceptively easy. As a slave the Negro was trained to be an inferior; then this very inferiority was used to support the argument that he was incapable of improvement. Only an occasional example of a successful free Negro could refute this circular reasoning, but such evidence was so limited that it could easily be dismissed as exceptional. In modern America, with its continuing discrimination against the Negro, a variety of this vicious circle persists, still confusing the thinking of Americans on the nature and potentialities of the black man.

3. BUT ALL WHITE MEN ARE NOT FREE

Though unquestionably the Negroes felt the impress of slavery more profoundly than any other Southerners, the whites of the region were also touched by an institution which was central to their way of life. This was true despite the fact that the bulk of the white people had no immediate connection with the "peculiar institution."

By far the largest class of white men were yeoman farmers, of whom perhaps as many as 80 per cent, according to Frank Owsley, owned their own land—a happy situation not duplicated in the twentieth-century South. Generally prospering in the expanding southern economy of the fifties, the common man of that section was quite remote from the conventional poor white conjured up by the fertile imagination of the abolitionists of that day or dwelt upon by the southern "realists" of our own.

But with all due respect to these independent, hard-working, God-fearing farmers of the Old South, their numerical superiority does not overbalance the influence exerted by the slaveholding class. Through the possession of black labor, the small class of slave-owners actually dominated the economic, political, and intellectual institutions of the whole white South. And by virtue of this fact the South's civilization was increasingly shaped to fit the needs of the slave system.

In the fundamental matter of land distribution, for example, the owners of slaves tended to command the richest soil areas—a situation which was at once an explanation and a consequence of their prominent position in the Old South. It is true, as some southern historians have made clear, that the elbowing out of the yeoman by the slaveholder was not absolute, for these historians have shown that the two classes often held adjacent farms. But the contention that the slaveholders and nonslaveholders generally held lands of equal quality is hard to accept in the face of other evidence. It has been shown, for example, that on 300 selected holdings in Alabama and Mississippi, the cash value of the land per acre increased as the size of the holding. Thus in farms of one to fifty acres, the value per acre was $7.20; but in farms of 501 to 1,000 acres the value was $19.81 per acre, over twice as much. Furthermore, on a broader scale, as is well known, areas of the South having a high concentration of slaves coincided remarkably well with the richest land areas, e.g., along the Mississippi River Delta and in the so-called black belts stretching across central Georgia and Alabama.

The superior position of the slaveholder consisted of more than his having the best land; his class were more often landholders than were the nonslaveholders. In 1860 in the Georgia black belt, for instance, 92 per cent of the slaveowners were also owners of land, but only 58 per cent of the nonslaveholders were. Even in eastern Tennessee, generally thought to be the stronghold of the non-slaveholders, 92 per cent of the holders of slaves owned land, while only 55 per cent of the slaveless farmers were so fortunate. About the same proportions for the two classes obtained in the cotton-growing western part of the state. As a matter of fact, these proportions of land distribution among slaveholders and nonslave-holders held generally for all the states studied by Frank Owsley and his students at Vanderbilt University. It seems clear, therefore, that the great bulk of the landless folk in the South were nonslave-holders.

Such a distribution of the land further emphasizes what was obvious to the travelers and commentators of the period, namely, that to rise in southern ante-bellum society one needed slaves; the source and measure of wealth in this highly commercialized agriculture were not merely acres, but land worked by Negroes. In this situation lies the weakness of considering the plain folk the backbone of the ante-bellum South, as the historians of the Vanderbilt school are wont to do. Significance in a capitalistic economy, as we have observed before, is measured by wealth accumulation, not by numbers of persons.

Even southern white men remote from the plantation, like urban wage laborers, felt the effects of slavery. Negro bondage, for instance, must bear a good share of the responsibility for the fact that labor organization in the South lagged behind that in the North. In the South, "the courts were openly antagonistic to striking workers," Richard Morris has written, because many southern officials believed "that strike action, like anti-slavery agitation, was an attack on their 'peculiar' institution." And where official attitudes played no part, the success of a strike was always threatened by the omnipresent possibility that slaves could be hired to break it as happened at the Tredegar Iron Works at Richmond in 1847.

In still other ways, nonslaveholders were involved in the protection of slavery. It was the yeomen who held no slaves who were expected to make up the slave patrols which acted as the rural police of the slave society. Furthermore, the law prescribed severe penalties for any white Southerner who seemed to threaten the slave system. Heavy fines awaited the man who traded with slaves or taught them to read or write. In several states a white man was liable to capital punishment if he encouraged or aided a slave to escape. All the southern states declared it a felony to write or say anything which directly or indirectly might lead to rebellion or discontent among the Negroes. Even fraternization between a white man and another man's slave could catch the former in the tangles of the law.

Finally, it should not be forgotten that because the defense of slavery required Negroes to be incompetents in the law, justice sometimes miscarried. For example, when Professor George Whyte of William and Mary was poisoned by his nephew, the culprit could not be convicted because the principal witness against him was a Negro, legally incapable of testifying against a white man.

Since the law was so solicitous of the peculiar institution, it comes as no surprise that slaveholders dominated the political life of the South. This is not to say, it should be quickly added, that the South was ruled by a hereditary aristocracy or anything like it. That is no more than a hoary legend which ignores the many leaders of the region, like Alexander Stephens, Albert Gallatin Brown, Andrew Johnson, and Joseph Brown, who came from the very bottom of southern society. Indeed, the bulk of the Cotton Grandees of the late ante-bellum South were self-made men rather than sons of wealthy planters or aristocrats.

But regardless of their social and economic origins, the slaveholders dominated the political leadership of the South, especially on the national stage. Because slavery was wealth and because slavery was race, the peculiar institution lay at the core of southern politics, determining issues and influencing men in relation to itself, just as it ran like a dark thread through the fabric of the economy. Whereas in the 1830's and 1840's the South enjoyed two major political parties, by the middle of the fifties there was only one. The need to defend slavery at all costs destroyed the once powerful Whig party of the South. The great planters had long been more Whiggish than Democratic, but the tendency of northern Whigs to be antislavery by 1850 pushed more and more of the southern Whig planters into the once detested Democracy. At one time in the South—during the 1830's and 1840's—nonslaveholders and slaveholders had strongly disagreed over matters like the National Bank, the tariff, Andrew Jackson, and popular government, but the growing necessity to defend slavery finally overrode all these differences. In the name of racial solidarity, the issue of slavery covered over class antagonisms and gave a new, but false, unity to southern political thought. Ever since those days Southerners have been deprived of an adequate two-party system to express the diversity of their interests and political objectives.

Since the preservation of slavery was now the South's litmus test of acceptable politics, it was hardly to be expected that the frankly but mildly antislavery Republican party could receive a hearing in the Cotton Kingdom. And this despite the fact that the only antislavery principle of which the Republicans were guilty— opposition to the extension of slavery into the territories—was one in which most small southern farmers had no direct economic interest. So finely meshed was the political screening in the South in 1860 in behalf of slavery that Abraham Lincoln's name never appeared on a ballot in ten of the eleven states which were to make up the Confederacy. For millions of southern voters the compulsive defense of slavery and the fear of the Negro effectively restricted their choice of candidates as compared with that enjoyed by voters in the rest of the nation.

It should not be forgotten, however, that this political identification of the nonslaveholders with the interests of the slaveholders was freely undertaken, for it was carried out within the context of almost universal white manhood suffrage. To the majority of Southerners, the acquisition of slaves and the augmentation thereof were obviously a *summum bonum*, a recognized and desirable avenue of upward social movement. If the coin of economic and political advancement was slave ownership, few whites in the South thought the coinage base. But it was precisely this popular acceptance of slavery which made the institution the determinant of the contours of southern life.

If political freedom of choice was circumscribed by the demands of slavery, other fields of thought could not escape either. Already we have noticed that slavery saddled the southern people with a belief in the racial inferiority of Negroes which has persisted into our own time. Slavery also seemed to require the repudiation of one of the South's most precious gifts to America: the Jeffersonian, humanistic belief in the equality of all men.

In the waning years of the eighteenth century, the great Virginians had defended slavery only as an unwelcome inheritance from the past—necessary but evil. By the 1830's, the South was prepared to defend it as both necessary and good. "But let me not be understood as admitting," John C. Calhoun said in 1837, "even by implication, that the existing relations between the two races in the slaveholding States is an evil:—far otherwise: I hold it to be a good, as it has thus far proved itself to be to both and will continue to prove so if not disturbed by the fell spirit of abolition."

Caught in the contradiction between equality and slavery, the South chose slavery. Particularly was Jefferson's disquieting Declaration singled out for attack and scorn. "Is it not palpably nearer the truth to say," asked Chancellor Harper of South Carolina, "that no man was ever born free and that no two men were ever born equal, than to say that all men are born free and equal?" "It is as much in the order of nature," he further wrote, "that men should enslave each other, as that other animals should prey upon each other." For many Southerners the paradox of the Declaration of Independence and slavery was sufficiently embarrassing for them to want to forget it. After 1840, the Democratic party, out of deference to southern sensibilities, ceased to include the manifesto of its founder in its platform.

The suspicious profusion in which the defenses of inequality were advanced betrayed the moral conflict within the mind of the South. As early as the 1830's, Senator Pickens of South Carolina had conceded that "the truth is, the moral power of the world is against us. It is idle to disguise it." By mid-century the conflict of values had taken on excruciating sharpness. For by that time few nations of western European civilization still tolerated, much less defended, human slavery. It was true that semicivilized and reactionary Imperial Russia persisted in retaining serfdom, but that only further threw in embarrassing relief the anachronistic nature of American slavery. If a whole people can suffer an inferiority complex, the people of the South certainly acquired one during that period in which they felt compelled to repudiate the Declaration of Independence and the morality of the nineteenth century.

During the forties and fifties, with the moral condemnation of slavery growing ever stronger outside the South, the demand for conformity and repression of dissent within the South became more frantic and insistent. Slowly the region was retreating into a pattern of life increasingly divergent from that of the rest of the nation. The South at one time had been the home of abolitionist societies, radical political clubs, and deistic thinkers, but now it was turning increasingly hostile to all thought which seemed to threaten the stability or survival of the slave system.

Reformers found an uncongenial atmosphere south of Mason and Dixon's line, because it was well known that reformers interested in temperance, women's rights, international peace, and so forth, frequently maintained close ties with abolitionists. Taking cognizance of these interconnections, one North Carolina editor boasted that the southern press "has uniformly rejected the isms which infest Europe and the Eastern and Western states of this country." Southern scientist Henry Ravenal urged the South to "shrink intuitively from all the novel and revolutionary notions which are infecting the masses of Europe and the free states of the North." Nor was it an accident that out of the 130 co-operative utopias established in the United States between 1800 and 1860, only two of them were in the South. The liberal fringes of religious life were snipped off too. By 1860 the Unitarian Church had all but disappeared from the South—a casualty, in large part, to the fact that most of its ministers were antislavery. "Scratch a reformer and you'll find an abolitionist" was the southern response to the intellectual and social ferment of the age of Emerson and Amelia Bloomer.

Where the ideas of the nineteenth century were congenial to southern ante-bellum values, they spread extravagantly. Though the novels of a romantic like Sir Walter Scott were popular in North and South alike, it was in the latter section that he became a literary idol. Upon his death Richmond newspapers were edged in black. Only in the South were knightly joustings held in full pseudomediaeval armor and regalia. It was from Scott's books that Southerners lifted the word "southron," which they self-consciously applied to themselves. The romantic picture of the organic, status society of the Middle Ages, which Scott dwelt on in several of his novels, seemed to shore up southern conservative ideas on society and slavery. Hence, south of the Ohio, Scott found a welcome place denied to contemporaries like Dickens and Shelley, who mixed their romanticism with urban, humanitarian, and irreligious beliefs largely foreign to the South.

Though in the main most Southerners supported slavery and were prepared to sacrifice their freedom of thought in its behalf, coercion and even bloodshed were still needed to provide that degree of uniformity which the peculiar institution seemed to require.

Southern postmasters in the 1830's, for example, were given the power to remove abolitionist literature from the mails. Between 1830 and 1860, southern life was punctuated with numerous raids and mobbings of abolitionists and antislavery printers and speakers.

Northerners resident in the South were suspect merely on the ground of their nativity. For example, two northern teachers living in South Carolina were asked to leave town by a local committee, with the town's newspaper justifying such a manifestation of xenophobia in the following fashion: "Nothing definite is known of their abolition or insurrectionary sentiments," the paper conceded, "but being from the North and therefore necessarily imbued with doctrines hostile to our institutions their presence in this section has been obnoxious and at any rate suspicious." Even a proslavery, though Northern-born, educator, President Barnard of the University of Mississippi, was compelled to leave the South because of suspicion arising out of his nativity.

Nor were native Southerners exempt from coercive action. A college student who was discovered in Tennessee with abolitionist literature was given twenty lashes as a warning. An antislavery man in western Virginia in the 1850's was stripped, tied to a tree, and beaten until he agreed to sell his property and leave the state. Though violence of this kind could be duplicated in the North during the 1830's, by the last decade of the ante-bellum period denial of civil liberties to abolitionists in the free states was over. But in the South such restrictions increased and were actually extended to include anyone suspected of unorthodox sentiments, antislavery or otherwise.

Increasingly aware that southern ideas were different from those commonly accepted in the North, southern newspapers sought to insulate the section from outside ideas by calling for the purging of textbooks used in southern schools. They also urged the establishment of new colleges in the South in order to keep southern students out of the northern institutions, meanwhile suggesting that southern boys refrain from going North for their education. Southern xenophobes rejoiced when dozens of southern students left their northern schools in protest against the John Brown raid in 1859. A Professor Hedrick at the University of North Carolina was dismissed because he admitted that he intended to vote for Free-Soiler and Republican John C. Frémont in the election of 1856. The Raleigh *Standard* justified such tactics by writing "If there be Frémont men among us, let them be silenced or required to leave. The expression of Black Republican opinion in our midst is incompatible with our honor and safety as a people."

The South retreated within itself in the area of religion. In his book *Freedom of Thought in the Old South,* Clement Eaton attributes, in part, the growth of a narrow religious orthodoxy and the decline of Jeffersonian deism in the South of the 1830's and 1840's to the exigencies of the defense of slavery. "Only by a narrow and literal interpretation of the Scriptures," Eaton writes, "could slavery be given the high moral sanction of the Church." By the middle of the 1840's, southern and northern Baptists and Methodists could no longer remain in the same national organizations, so sectional churches were formed.

The significance of these efforts at conformity lies not in the force which may or may not have been employed; that is irrelevant. The important point is that on the whole the southern people during these years acquiesced in the suppression of free speech, free press, free assembly, and the free circulation of ideas in the name of slavery and the society which flourished upon it.

In this is to be seen the tremendous impact of Negro slavery upon the white South; the immediate victim was the liberalism of the eighteenth-century Virginians who had done so much to create a free Republic. The long-range consequence was a heritage of mob violence and extralegal sanctions in support of racial superiority —a heritage which has cast a pall over southern justice ever since. Truly history, in the form of slavery, laid a terrible curse upon the South, and by the middle years of the nineteenth century its exorcising was more difficult than ever before. But unhappily for the future of the region and the nation, the best the leaders of the South could do was to call the curse a blessing. This was the South's and the nation's tragedy.

The central place which slavery occupied in southern life has a direct bearing upon the coming of the Civil War—that culmination of the long history of slavery in America. If one is not concerned with the morality of owning slaves, then the fact that southern leaders were mainly slaveholders and defenders of slavery is no more worthy of comment than the fact that northern leaders usually possessed more land or money than their fellows and ardently defended property. But by the middle of the nineteenth century, for most people of the North and of western Europe, slaves were not property, but human beings. For slavery not only manifestly denied the American creed of equality; it was at variance with the prevailing values of western Europe.

It is true that at one time Northerners and Europeans held slaves without moral qualms. For this reason, some writers have argued that Northerners and Europeans were hypocritical to belabor the South for its continued adherence to slavery. But this kind of argument misses the point that morals change over time; what was quite acceptable morally in the seventeenth or eighteenth centuries was no longer so in the nineteenth. To many people of the North, southern slavery was not an economic question, which the Southerners insisted it should be, but a moral issue transcending economic interests. The more the support of slavery was made the test of loyalty to the South, the more the region was estranged from the rest of the nation and the world of the nineteenth century.

Under such circumstances, it was not surprising that Southerners should begin to think of themselves as a separate people with their own culture and way of life. In an important sense, therefore, slavery and the agricultural setting in which it flourished constituted the primary "cause" for the Civil War.

Incidents like the Kansas-Nebraska Act, "Bleeding Kansas," the Osawatomie Massacre, the beating of Senator Sumner, the Dred Scott decision, the John Brown raid, all played their parts in the drama by providing occasions for the hardening of the differences between the sections. But underlying all of these circumstances and events was the broad and fundamental fact that a people who adhered to a slave system in the middle of the nineteenth century inevitably became a people different from those Americans who did not. As Calhoun said at the end of his life, it was "difficult to see how two people as different and hostile can exist together in one common Union." The various incidents of the 1850's fed the rising fires of southern nationalism, until in 1860–61 the South demanded self-determination. "When you deny to us the right to withdraw from a Government which . . . threatens to be destructive of our rights," Jefferson Davis told the Senate in 1861, "we but tread in the path of our fathers when we proclaim our independence, and take the hazard." The Civil War was actually the War for Southern Independence.

4. THE AMERICAN DILEMMA

Slavery furnished more than the basis for southern nationalism; it also aroused a powerful counterforce in the North. Though the abolition movement was a part of the general reform impulse of the 1840's and 1850's, the broader antislavery movement which culminated in the Republican party was almost as much a consequence of the South's interminable search for total security for its "peculiar institution" as it was the result of the reform movement.

Apart from the restrictions on freedom in the South, which were demanded in the name of slavery, southern leaders also insisted that the North co-operate in the preservation of slavery. The Fugitive Slave Act of 1850, which the South had won as a concession in the Compromise of that year, was an example of this. Under the new law the cards were heavily stacked in favor of the slave catcher. Jury trials for runaways were eliminated in the act because free-state juries were notoriously partial to escaped slaves. In a further effort to aid in the return of fugitives, the act prescribed that any commissioner who adjudged a Negro defendant a bona fide slave was to receive double the ordinary fee for his services.

Considering the proclivity of slave catchers for seizing any Negro and returning him or selling him into slavery, this law appeared to many in the North as an endeavor to extend the southern limitations on freedom into virgin fields. As a consequence, in many of the free states the act became a nullity. Then when the South, with the Kansas-Nebraska Act, further insisted upon northern support for the extension of slavery into areas where it had heretofore been prohibited, and to which it was obviously unsuited, a new political party sprang into being. This new Republican party was dedicated to halting the seemingly endless demands which the South advanced in behalf of slavery.

Prior to the advent of the Republican party in 1854–56, the opposition to slavery had come primarily from abolitionists, reformers who, out of deep moral conviction, hated slavery more than they loved the Constitution or the Union. William Lloyd Garrison, arch-priest of abolition, said he would gladly permit the Constitution to be scrapped and the nation permanently divided if only Negro slavery could be ended in the United States. "No Union with Slaveholders" was the abolitionists' slogan. To such reformers slavery was a moral cancer consuming the essence of America, as it was also an insufferable injustice to the Negro; to achieve its extirpation no price was too costly, no pain too great.

Despite the fact that the abolitionists were amazingly active and provocatively articulate, they never won acceptance among most Americans either north or south of the Ohio. Northerners, it is true, ceased to mob abolitionist speakers by the late 1840's, but most of the people in the North would have little to do with such radicals. Part of this glacierlike hostility stemmed from the abolitionists' unabashed repudiation of the Constitution. Since slavery found sanction and legality in that document, abolitionists like Garrison called it "a covenant with death and an agreement with hell." After expressing such unconcealed contempt for the most venerated of American symbols, the abolitionists could not but fail in their attempt to galvanize the latent American belief in equality.

But if the abolitionists were unsuccessful in their efforts to arouse the North to a crusade against slavery, they did bequeath martyrs and heroes, like Owen Lovejoy, John Brown, Sojourner Truth, and many others, to the radical tradition of America. They also left an ideological Pandora's Box. For in their argument that there was a higher law than a Constitution which sanctioned slavery, they were preaching the dangerous doctrine that resistance to unjust laws is morally permissible.

The abolitionists were not the first or the last Americans to justify lawbreaking in the name of a higher morality. The speakeasy visitor of the prohibition era did it; so did the proslavery Southerner when he hurled abolitionists' printing presses into the river; so does the segregationist in the South today. This slippery principle that laws may be broken if they flout popular or moral opinion is fraught with danger to a government of law. In the service of noble causes, it has served to right injustice, resist tyranny, and protect the individual; in defense of base causes, it is naked mob rule, denial of individual rights, and the end of government by law. In both instances, however, it is distinctly and historically American.

Where the abolitionists failed, the Republican party was notably successful. Gunnar Myrdal, in his monumental study of the Negro in America, has described what he calls the American dilemma— the conflict between the traditional egalitarian creed and the actual treatment accorded the Negro. Already in the 1850's the moral conflict was dividing Americans against themselves. In the South

the dilemma was resolved, or at least covered over, by the outright
denial of the principle of equality; the Declaration of Independence
was called, among other things, a tissue of "glittering generalities."
But in the North, equality was increasingly accepted as a moral
imperative. The newly formed Republican party now incorporated
the disquieting Declaration of Independence in its appeal to Americans. Lincoln advised in 1858, "let us discard all this quibbling
about this man and the other—this race and that race, and the
other race being inferior. . . . Let us discard all these things, and
unite as one people, throughout this land, until we shall once more
stand up declaring that all men are created equal." At another
time he said, "in relation to the principle that all men are created
equal, let it be as nearly reached as we can." [6]

Though the Republicans seemed to subscribe to all kinds of
divergent political and economic ideas, they were united in their
opposition to the spread of slavery.[7] This is not to say, however,
that they were abolitionists. On at least two counts the average
Republican differed from an abolitionist. For one thing, very few
Republicans, though they opposed slavery, believed in social equality for Negroes. Lincoln spoke for many of his fellow Republicans
when he said during the debates with Douglas in 1858 that he was
not in favor of social equality for Negroes. The Negro, he said, "is
not my equal in many respects—certainly not in color, perhaps not
in moral or intellectual endowment. But in the right to eat the

[6] The irony inherent in the transfer of Jefferson as a party idol from the
Democrats to the Republicans was not lost upon Lincoln. When asked in 1859 to
participate in a Republican celebration of Jefferson's birthday, he noted that the
new party now claimed the Sage of Monticello, "while those claiming political
descent from him have nearly ceased to breathe his name everywhere." It was in
this letter that Lincoln made his famous remark that the Republicans, unlike the
Democrats with their defense of slave property, "are for both the *man* and the
dollar; but in cases of conflict, the man before the dollar."

[7] The heterogeneity of the Republican party was not much different from that
of most American political parties of importance. But in 1860, Howell Cobb, the
Georgia statesman, pointed out that the heterogeneity also emphasized its essential antislavery bias. "The Black Republican party had its origin in the antislavery feeling of the North," he told his constituents. "The fact that it was
composed of men of all previous parties, who then and still advocate principles
directly antagonistic upon all other questions except slavery as it exists in the
fifteen Southern States, was the basis of its organization and the bond of its
union. Free-trade Democrats and protective-tariff Whigs, internal improvement
and anti-internal improvement men, and indeed all shades of partisans, united in
cordial fraternity upon the isolated issue of hostility to the South, though for
years they had fought each other upon all other issues."

bread, without leave of anybody else, which his own hand earns," Lincoln added, "he is my equal and the equal of Judge Douglas, and the equal of every living man." In short, slavery was an evil because it denied the dominant American value of equality of opportunity. On this great issue, radical abolitionists and conservative Whigs, nativists and Jacksonian Democrats, could join hands in the formation of a new antislavery party.

The second point on which the Republicans differed from the abolitionists was in the lengths to which they would go to oppose slavery. The abolitionists were willing to pull the Union down about their ears if it would end slavery. The Republicans, however, were conservatives who cherished the Union and fully endorsed the safeguards which the Constitution bestowed upon slavery in the South. They would not scrap the Constitution in a frantic effort to eliminate slavery, much as they might abominate the institution.

But when, as Lincoln said, slavery seemed about to expand into areas heretofore prohibited to it, then a stand had to be taken against it. And, in such a setting, a stand could be made without repudiating the Constitution or the sanctuary which slavery enjoyed in the South. For it had always been held—at least before the Dred Scott decision—that Congress could constitutionally prohibit slavery in the territories.

Many modern historians and some contemporaries like Daniel Webster have called the opposition to the extension of slavery into the territories a trivial reason for bringing the nation to the brink of civil war inasmuch as the area was unsuited for plantation culture. But once the constitutionally conservative character of the Republican party and the American people is acknowledged, then the titanic struggle over slavery in the western territories takes on a deeper meaning. Everywhere else, slavery rested on the bedrock of the Constitution; only in this narrow, constitutional sphere could the great moral issue of slave versus free labor be fought out by a people convinced of the sanctity of their Constitution.

With the formation of the Republican party, the breakup of the Union became unavoidable. The new party's very reason for being stood athwart the South's drive for the expansion of slavery, and its almost immediate popularity in the more populous and growing North stood as a warning to the slave states that in time an antislavery government would gain power in Washington.

By the late 1850's the only alternatives to disruption of the

Union, given the alignment of parties and the hardening sectional attitudes, were that the North should become a slaveholding area or that the South should cease to be one. The first possibility, despite some wild predictions by Southerners like George Fitzhugh and some politically inspired warnings by Northerners like Lincoln and Seward, was out of the question. The second was equally unlikely when weighed against the profits of slavery and the anodyne which the institution provided for southern racial fears.

Tightly wrapped in their own cultural assumptions, Northerners and Southerners were now incapable of compromise. All that was left was mounting recrimination. The North was here more often the aggressor because the force of European moral opinion was on its side; for the same reason the South could not help but be apprehensive. But because the South dominated the largest and oldest political party in the country, it was also defiant.

When in 1860 the South's political ascendancy seemed about to end, the region turned to secession as the final salvation for its peculiar institution and the civilization which was built around it. Secession, though, could serve as an answer to the South's problem only if the rest of the nation agreed. As it turned out, the new Republican party proved to be not only antislavery but strongly nationalistic.

Thus the immediate consequence of slavery was a terrible and costly war between the North and the South. At bottom, all the issues between the sections, whether of an incidental nature, like the John Brown raid, or of a broad character, like the conflicts over the tariff or the homestead bill, were in fact and in logic reducible to the question of slavery. To the men at the time and to an increasing number of modern historians, without the issue of slavery to divide the two sections, there would have been no Civil War.

Once the war came, however, it brought to an abrupt close one period of American history and opened the door to another of a much different order. The Civil War was not only a testing of the American people as a nation; it was a watershed in their history.

CHAPTER VII

Bringing Forth a New Nation

THE disruption of the American Union in 1861 has been explained in many ways, but, viewed against the perspective of European civilization as a whole, it was primarily the work of two of the most powerful forces then abroad in the world. One, as we have seen, was the rising tide of reform; the other was the elemental emotion of nationalism.

In the middle of the nineteenth century, nationalism was spreading like a fever through the ancient body of Europe; in America it seized the imaginations of the people, too, leading them into the most costly and bloody war of the century. For two decades the southern people had been growing in the conviction that their culture, entwined about the institution of Negro slavery, made them a separate nation. The election of 1860 precipitated this feeling into secession from the Union and an experiment in nationhood. But developing alongside this southern nationalism was another, one which insisted that the Union was eternal and indissoluble. Of this brand of nationalism, Abraham Lincoln was the Bismarck, as Jefferson Davis was the Kossuth of the South. It was Lincoln who with "blood and iron" sustained and cemented the loose confederation of the Fathers and created a new nation.

"Again and again it has been proved," wrote Heinrich Treitschke, the German nationalist, "that it is war which turns a people into a nation, and that only great deeds, wrought in common, can forge the indissoluble links which bind them together." Americans then and now would be loath to subscribe to this iron philosophy, but the driving force of the new nationalism which

189

the War for the Union released suggests that it was an apt description of the making of the new America. "Before the War our patriotism was a fire-work, a salute, a serenade for holidays and summer evenings . . ." Ralph Waldo Emerson commented in 1864. "Now the deaths of thousands and the determination of millions of men and women show that it is real."

The War for the Union was a turning point in American history. After it Americans lived in a different nation, one in which freedom and equality now applied to all men, one in which the unity of the nation was beyond dispute, and one in which the power of the national government was supreme. The price of this change, however, was the ruthless denial of the southern people's aspiration for nationhood.

1. A PEOPLE'S WAR

"We cannot escape history," Abraham Lincoln told his fellow Americans in 1862. "We of this Congress and this Administration will be remembered in spite of ourselves." Many other Americans of that generation were aware of the portentous times in which they lived. To George Ticknor of Boston it seemed in April of 1861 as if "the heather is on fire" throughout the North. After weeks of indecision and doubt, the commitment to war brought a sudden release of tension and a surge of patriotism. "I am proud of my country and my grand heroic brethren," exulted newspaperman Edmund Stedman in the fall of 1861. "The greatness of the crisis, the Homeric grandeur of the contest, surrounds and elevates us all." Within a matter of weeks, it seemed to a woman in New York, the whole nation had been transfigured by the guns which battered Fort Sumter. "How long it is since Sumter!" she wrote. "I suppose it is because so much intense emotion has been crowded into the last two or three weeks, that the 'time before Sumter' seems to belong to some dim antiquity. It seems as if we never were alive till now; never had a country till now."

Upon veterans the conflict left a never-to-be-forgotten imprint. "The war was . . . a very extraordinary war," recalled M. W. Tyler after half a century. "Nothing like it ever occurred before, and I doubt if anything like it will ever happen again." Twenty years after he left the Union Army, Oliver Wendell Holmes, Jr., said: "through our great good fortune in our youth our hearts were touched with fire. It was given us to learn at the outset that life is a profound and passionate thing."

American emotional involvement in the great struggle has hardly abated in subsequent generations. During the years between 1862 and 1900, for example, over 480 short stories and novels were published about the war and its effects. One historian has counted 512 novels on the Civil War alone published between 1862 and 1948. Another literary measure of the war's impact over the years is the fact that the two best-selling novels in the whole history of American fiction are *Uncle Tom's Cabin* and *Gone With the Wind*—one concerned with the great issue which brought on the war, the other dealing with the consequences of the war. New serious and semi-popular books on the war appear each year—over one hundred appeared in 1957—and clubs and societies devoted to exploring the history of the struggle are but further testimony to the unending fascination which that war still holds for Americans. What town or village in the states which fought in the war does not have its monument to the soldiers who fell in defense of the Union or the Lost Cause? Not even World War II, with its far-flung battle fronts and its intensity of moral purpose, has found a deeper place in the American heart and memory.

All wars pluck men from their families, but this War for the Union touched so many homes with the fear of death that it seemed a new kind of war. Edward Dicey, the English journalist traveling in the United States in 1862, met a woman who said she never knew anyone in the Army until a year earlier; but now, she said, she had sixty friends and relatives in the Union forces. Nor was this, Dicey added, an uncommon experience. The records of the war reveal that almost three million men served in the federal forces—about 15 per cent of the total population—and an even greater proportion stepped forward to defend the Confederacy. Lincoln's call for 500,000 volunteers in May of 1861 was answered by 700,-000. Throughout the war the bulk of the Union Army was made up of volunteers, not draftees, since conscription procedures were neither efficient nor popular. "I very much doubt," commented Anthony Trollope in 1862, "whether any other nation ever made such an effort in so short a time. To a people who can do this it may be granted that they are in earnest. . . . The strong and unanimous impulse of a great people is seldom wrong."

The examples of supreme devotion to the cause were, as always,

provided by the men in the armies. The soldiers of the Army of the
Potomac knew very well that there were shirkers at home who were
safe and often growing rich and fat; but they also believed the
Union represented a cause worth dying for. "Well, if new men
won't finish the job," wrote one of Grant's veterans in Virginia in
1864, "old men must, and as long as Uncle Sam wants a man, here
is Ben Falls." Two months later Falls was dead at Spotsylvania
Court House. The so-called Invalid Corps, made up of thousands
of wounded veterans, bore testimony to the sense of involvement
felt by many of the soldiers. Though entitled to a discharge, these
men chose to serve their cause and country in noncombatant duties,
such as guarding prisoners and communications. When the crucial
election of 1864 arrived, the majority of the soldiers in the field
did not vote for their old commander, McClellan, and his Peace
Platform, but cast their ballots overwhelmingly for "old Abe" and
a continuance of the war.

"The longer I lived in the country," Dicey decided in 1862, "the
more I learned how deep the feeling of the North was; it was like
all English feeling, and came slowly to the surface." The war's outcome seemed to be a responsibility weighing upon all, and each felt
he had to meet it in his own way. When asked by his father why he
insisted upon enlisting in 1862, sixteen-year-old Theodore Upson
of Indiana replied simply, "Father, we must have more soldiers.
This Union your ancestors and mine helped to make must be saved
from destruction. I can go better than some others. I don't feel
right to stay at home any longer." A much older man, Henry Hitchcock of St. Louis, told General Sherman that he joined in 1864
because "I could not stay at home and let other men do the fighting
and run the risks while I was safely making money and enjoying
the fruits of their toils. . . ." In Massachusetts an Irish immigrant
begged for admission to Ben Perley Poore's battalion. "The prosperity of this country is my prosperity," he argued, "its life is in
danger and I feel that I ought to en-list to save it."

The heroic activities of southern women in support of their cause
are legendary, but equally prodigious were the exertions of northern
women, notably in support of the Sanitary Commission. This forerunner of the Red Cross and the USO contributed in money and
services at least $25 million to the Union troops. The wives and
mothers of the soldiers as well as men too old to fight were outstanding in the organization and conduct of the Sanitary Fairs

which were held in the large cities to raise extra funds for "the boys" at the front.

It was inevitable that the emotion released by the war should express itself in politics. It was no accident that all the Presidents between Abraham Lincoln and Theodore Roosevelt—with the single exception of Democrat Grover Cleveland—had served as officers during the war. Moreover, the party of the Union became the party of most Americans for almost three quarters of a century. It was twenty years after the war ended before the first Democrat, Grover Cleveland, entered the White House. Indeed, between the election of Lincoln in 1860 and that of Franklin Roosevelt in 1932, only two Democratic Presidents occupied the Executive Mansion. This is especially noteworthy when it is remembered that for sixty years after the Revolution of 1800, the Democracy, the party of Jefferson and Jackson, had continuously held the keys of 1600 Pennsylvania Avenue, with only brief interruptions during Harrison's and Taylor's terms. The War for the Union shattered the once popular Democracy and left it with the taint of treason. Only another and equally profound revolution could restore the people's confidence in the party of Jefferson and Jackson—and Jefferson Davis.

2. A BUSINESSMEN'S GOVERNMENT

When historians like Charles A. Beard and Louis Hacker, with a penchant for economic explanations, referred to the war as "the Second American Revolution," they had in mind the triumph of the northern business interest. They thought they could discern in the American struggle an analogy with the historic European bourgeois revolutions, such as took place in France in 1789. Neither the long previous history of the United States nor the years immediately prior to 1861 bear out this interpretation, however.

The impetus for war, as we have seen, came from the South, not from the North; the agrarians, not the bourgeoisie, risked war to gain their ends. Northern business had not been throttled by the admitted southern domination of the three branches of the federal government, and the census returns promised that even this domination would soon end. Moreover, business had received substantial aid from even the southern-dominated governments. Indeed, one of the justifications southern leaders advanced for secession was the alleged favoritism shown to northern shipping and manufacturing interests by the federal government. It is true that many northern

manufacturers wanted a higher tariff, that some businessmen
wanted a sounder monetary system, and that northern farmers
wanted the public domain thrown open to free settlement, but the
failure to obtain these wishes constituted neither a threat to
northern prosperity nor a reason for a war against the South.
Quite the contrary, as a number of recent studies have shown,
northern businessmen were prominent among the leaders of the
conservative forces in the North during the winter of 1860–61,
working to compromise the conflicting demands of the sections and
to heal the widening split in the Union.

The evidence for the contention that the war was a "revolution"
is to be found in the events after 1861, not in those during the pre-
secession years. To argue, as Beard and Hacker and others tend
to do, from the results of the war back to the cause is to fall into
the logical error of *post hoc, ergo propter hoc.*

But even if the Beard-Hacker analysis is weak as an explanation
for the coming of the war, it does serve to remind us that along with
the war came a new attitude toward business. With the South gone
from the Congress, the business bias of the new Republican party
was quickly translated into legislation. As John Sherman of Ohio
put it, "those who elected Mr. Lincoln expect him . . . to secure
to free labor its just right to the Territories of the United States;
to protect . . . by wise revenue laws, the labor of our people; to
secure the public lands to actual settlers . . . to develop the internal resources of the country by opening new means of communication between the Atlantic and the Pacific." In the course of the
first Lincoln administration, all these economic demands and more
were met.

For the first time since Jackson killed that "Monster," the Bank
of the United States, the federal government essayed to bring some
order into the currency chaos. For decades the circulating medium
of the nation had been composed of good, solid gold and silver coins,
issued by the federal government, on the one hand, and a host of
paper "bills" issued by private banks on the other. This paper
money was completely unregulated by the federal government and
its backing varied from nothing except faith to virtually complete
correspondence with gold. Receivers of such money could rarely be
sure of the real value of such paper bills unless they were the issue
of banks in a state like New York where the laws prescribed backing
for note issue.

The National Bank Acts of 1863 and 1864 were designed to bring some stability into this situation. First, they authorized the establishment of National Banks which could issue paper money only against holdings of United States government bonds. (In a time of national deficit spending, this was also a clever device to sell bonds and simultaneously maintain their price.) Second, in order to eliminate the unreliable paper money of the private banks, and to provide a truly national currency, a prohibitive tax was placed upon the bills of banks not subscribing to the new act, a measure which compelled all note-issuing banks to become national. The result was a new uniformity in the nation's banking and currency structure and a valuable contribution to the industrial expansion of the postwar years.

The pre-eminence of an exclusively northern political party in the councils of government was also proclaimed by the passage of the first frankly protective tariff in twenty years. Then, in the course of the war, the tariff was raised to its highest point yet in the history of the nation. Its continued rise in subsequent years proved to be one of the chief gifts of the Republican party to the rapid industrialization of the nation's economy.

Another, if minor, fillip to the progress of industrialization was the passage, in 1864, of the Contract Labor Law, which facilitated the importation of foreign skilled labor into the expanding factories of the North. Although this law was repealed in 1868, the practice which it protected continued for another twenty years before organized labor was able to have it declared illegal.

Two other pieces of legislation further demonstrate the economic benefits which the North derived from the South's secession and reveal the close linkage between the new Republican government and the economic expansion of the subsequent decades. For almost ten years the country had been expecting the federal government to help in the construction of a transcontinental railroad, but sectional rivalries over the proper route had barred any action. In 1862, with the South gone, the matter was easily settled—the northern way—and the federal government committed itself to generous aid for the building of the road. With the Homestead Act of the same year, northern farmers were at last granted free land— up to 160 acres—a privilege for which their spokesmen had been contending for fifteen years. Though it is possible to exaggerate the amount of public lands awarded to actual settlers as compared

with land speculators, there can be little question that the act, in
its openhandedness with the national resources, constituted an
ominous forecast of the free-and-easy attitudes of the years to
come.

It might well be said that in general the economic legislation of
this first Lincoln administration set both the tone and the content
of the Republican party program for the next forty years. And as
a program it provided a climate in which the new entrepreneurs of
the Gilded Age flourished mightily.

But if the war brought new support to the side of business and
enterprise in the North, it visited just the reverse upon the South.
As the battlefield of the war, the Confederacy bore the burden of
the destruction which inevitably accompanies any war. But this was
more than an ordinary war. It was a struggle by one people to
destroy the other as a nation. As such, the mere defeat of armies
could not be enough; the people of the South would have to be
shown, by the most relentless of military attrition, that they as a
people were incapable of resisting the power of the United States.

The truth of this was not clear to many Northerners at the beginning of the war, when the capture of Richmond was viewed as
the main goal of the Union armies. To western generals like Grant
and Sherman, however, it soon became apparent that only through
a systematic destruction of the southern economy would the South's
will to resist be broken once and for all. Grant first tested the immense military potentialities of "living off the country" at the time
of Vicksburg in 1863; the value of the innovation was amply
demonstrated by Wilson's raid into Alabama, by Sherman in his
devastating march through Georgia and the Carolinas, and by
Sheridan's destruction of supplies and communications in the
Shenandoah Valley of Virginia. This was total war against the
people and economy of the South, and, largely because of it and
the increasing effectiveness of the blockade, the Confederacy was
prostrate and helpless before the conqueror in less than two years
after Vicksburg.

The price of such a military policy in suppressing a rebellion,
however, is high; the South returned to the Union an impoverished
section. The emancipation of the slaves alone wiped out perhaps
$2 billion in capital, and the loss of property through deliberate
destruction and war was no less. In 1860 the value of property in
the South had been calculated at $4.4 billion; in 1870, even though

five years of peace intervened, the figure had declined to $2.1 billion. During these same ten years the wealth of the North had grown by 50 per cent.

When the war broke out, contrary to what some have argued, the ante-bellum South was no decadent civilization tottering to its ruin. Growing in wealth, proud of its culture, and flushed with confidence—too much so, as it turned out—the South was a flourishing region in 1860, brimming with promise for the future. The end came abruptly and terribly in the War for Southern Independence; rather than being a funeral pyre for a moribund culture, the war was a *Götterdämmerung*. And like an earlier Twilight of the Gods, the ante-bellum South lived on in legend as it had never lived in reality. But the destruction of the ante-bellum civilization did much more than create a legend; it introduced social and economic problems which have burdened the people of the region well into our own time.[1]

The emancipation of the slaves confronted the South, before all else, with an economic problem of great magnitude. The labor of the former slaves had to be brought to bear upon the land if the region was to recoup its losses—indeed, if it was to survive. The problem was complicated, though. Theoretically, the former slaves might have been turned into farmer-proprietors by giving them land. Thaddeus Stevens, the leader of northern Reconstruction, for example, was of this mind, for he advocated the division of the great plantations among the Negroes and the landless whites of the South.[2] Very few Northerners found this an acceptable solution,

[1] It is difficult to determine what role the destruction of property played in the slow recovery of the South. The very rapid recovery of West Germany after the enormous devastation wrought by World War II, for example, suggests that destruction *per se* is not always the determining factor. In ante-bellum days, stock raising was a significant part of the South's small-farmer economy, as it is once again today. The war, however, wrecked that ante-bellum diversification. It was not until 1900 that the number of livestock in the states of the former Confederacy reached the number for 1860. On the other hand, staple crops like tobacco and cotton reached 1860 levels of production by 1880. It appears that changes in farm labor and farm organization were more determining than the wide destruction.

[2] Though few of the Reconstruction leaders of the North gave much thought to the problem of the freedman's economic status, Thaddeus Stevens did. In March, 1867, for example, he pleaded with the Congress to grant each freedman forty acres of land and a small purse of money, the wherewithal to be obtained from the confiscation of the large estates of the South. "Homesteads to them [Negroes]," he said, "are far more valuable than the immediate right of suffrage, though both are their due." The only other political effort to give the Negro a

however, and for racial and social reasons, if nothing else, no
Southerner endorsed it as even a possibility. Thus, at the very outset, it was in effect determined that the great majority of the
Negroes would have to begin their life under freedom dependent
upon others—their former masters, in fact—for the land which
would permit them to make a living.

But even with the Negro as a dependent cultivator, the economic
hurdles were not yet surmounted. The landowners, critically short
of capital and cash, usually could not afford to hire gangs of
freedmen as field workers. The makeshift solution which most readily
suggested itself was what a later age would call sharecropping. By
parceling out his otherwise useless land to the Negroes and taking a
share of the crop, a planter could bring his acres to production
without having to find sufficient cash to pay hired labor. The Negro,
in turn, was given an opportunity to work land under his own
supervision and perhaps to sell enough of his share of the crop to
be able eventually to buy his own land.

On the surface, this system seemed to signal the breakup of the
plantation economy. In all but appearance, however, it was the same
old plantation, and even sometimes with the same owner, worked
now, however, in small family plots instead of in gangs as under
slavery.

But the real problem of the white farmer immediately after the
war was not landlessness, but lack of capital. This dearth of ready
cash occasioned the other innovation in southern agriculture born
from the war's dislocations. In order to obtain seed, supplies, and
equipment with which to work his land, the farmer gave a lien or
legal claim on his crop to the local merchant who supplied him.
Under this lien system, as it came to be called, the merchant with
his indispensable credit moved to the center of the farmer's life. He
was able to use his financial stake as a lever to compel the farmer
to produce cash crops only, or, worse yet, a single crop like cotton,
thus helping to saddle the region with one-crop agriculture and all
its attendant evils. Furthermore, credit buying by the farmer encouraged extravagance on his part and fraudulent manipulation of
the records on the part of the merchant. The net result was that

---

stake and opportunity in the postwar South was that of South Carolina during
the Radical ascendancy. The proposal was to buy up land for the former slaves,
but the plan never got beyond the beginning stages. Some Negroes did own their
own land, particularly in the Sea Islands off Georgia, where they had seized it
during the war, but the vast majority of the freedmen were landless.

the farmer often found it difficult to extricate himself from the mounting burden of debt fostered by his dependence upon the merchant. Once caught in a cycle of increasing debt, many small landowners of the South lost their land to their creditors and sank into tenancy.

The hope had been that sharecropping and crop lien would be only temporary crutches while the Southern farmers recovered from the disastrous effects of the war. But things did not work out that way; neither system distinguished itself as a training ground for self-reliance, much less a ladder for upward social mobility. Instead, tenancy grew in the South; by 1900 over 45 per cent of the region's farmers, both black and white, were tenants—about double the ante-bellum proportion. In large part, of course, this increase was attributable to the inclusion of the freed Negro in the farming statistics, but it was still a realistic acknowledgment that the postwar South was economically much worse off than before the war.

Though the scars upon the land left by the war were gradually covered over and even the animosities engendered by the conflict softened through the years, sharecropping and crop lien did not pass away. Each census after the War for Southern Independence showed an increase in the number of tenants in the South, and not until the latter days of the New Deal was this trend reversed. Thus when President Franklin Roosevelt referred to the South as "the nation's economic problem No. 1" he was giving belated acknowledgment that the war was more than just a chapter in the history books.

3. A NATIONALIST'S DREAM

The destruction of the southern economy was only the most tangible result of the War for the Union. More importantly for the nation as a whole, victory for the Union signified the reintegration of the national state which almost half a century of bitter and relentless agitation over slavery had disrupted. "The war is over," young Theodore Upson wrote in his diary in June of 1865, "and the Union is saved!" The Union, however, was a quite different one from that which Upson fought to preserve. The day was now past when even a northern President like Franklin Pierce would refer to the United States as "the general agent," "the creature of the States." The doubts which assailed President James Buchanan as to the power of the federal government to suppress secession had been laid to rest with a finality only military victory can command. In 1869, the Supreme Court, reading the war bulletins as well as the election returns, declared that the Union was "indestructible," the principle for which the North had gone to war. Never again would any state—even during the extreme segregation crisis of the 1950's —imagine that secession was a constitutional remedy for state grievances.

The repudiation of the doctrine of secession before the judgment seat of war, however, was only the first of the new and tightening bonds of Union. The armies which the North mobilized in the course of the war were like enormous forcing rooms for the quick flowering of nationalistic feeling. Men from different parts of the North, and even from areas of the South, mingled with one another in the common cause of the nation's survival. Natives and immigrants, especially Germans and Irishmen, were thrown together in a way which emphasized their common loyalty. Not since the Thirty Years' War in seventeenth-century Europe, Ella Lonn has written, had so cosmopolitan a group of Europeans been assembled in one army. "The heterogeneity of the northern Army was one of its most marked characteristics. . . . Not one of the three hundred regiments which marched out from New York was without one or more Teutons. Besides the companies of Germans from Cleveland, men of that nationality from the lake city served in twenty-two mixed Ohio regiments . . . as well as in regiments of Michigan, Missouri, Illinois, Indiana, and Pennsylvania, and in the American Fleet."

Often the service of the immigrant marked his transition from alien to citizen, and, more important, to acceptance as a fellow American. Bruce Catton in his superb history of the Army of the Potomac tells of Mike Scannell of Massachusetts, who, when called a "damned Yankee," was touchingly flattered. He replied to the astonished rebel: "Well, it is twenty years since I came to this country, and you are the first man who ever called me a Yankee." The hearty response of the Boston Irish to the call to the Union colors won them a place of new respect in the eyes of many old Bostonians; for years thereafter, anti-immigration agitation would find the going considerably tougher.

Though often having only a vague notion of the issues behind the conflict, the immigrant soldier nevertheless seemed to sense the implications which the war carried for the future of his adopted country. "We are having a war here in America," a young soldier wrote to his mother in Ireland. "The Southern states want to have a flag of their own and as many slaves as they can buy or steal. The North wants to keep the old flag and the country as Washington left it, and not to have slavery go any further; so they have gone to war about it, and I have enlisted and hope to fight for right and the country." One German, who arrived in New York City in 1860 and was dead in Virginia in 1864, wrote home about his decision to enlist. "I am a volunteer soldier in the Army of the United States to fight the rebels of South America for a sacred thing. All of America has to become free and united and the starry banner has to fly again over the new world."

Though it is true that the vast majority of the soldiers and sailors of the Union were volunteers, it should not be forgotten that the war introduced the first conscription act ever passed by the federal government. Never before had the central government stretched its hand so intimately into the very homes of the citizenry. This experience, which Southerners also knew under the Confederacy, was a precedent for the extensive and necessary use of the draft in the two great wars of the twentieth century.

The living monument to the profound nationalistic influence of the Army was the Grand Army of the Republic. In intent and in practice, this immense veterans' organization was the bridge which spanned the years between the emotions aroused by the War for the Union and the humdrum existence which stretched out afterward. The several hundred thousand veterans who joined this self-proclaimed incarnation of the cause of the Union were living testimony to the continuing significance of the war experience. Almost fanatical in its devotion to the welfare of the men who had served in the Union cause, the G.A.R., in subsequent years, proved itself to be a measure as well as a symbol of the deep well of national feeling which the war had uncovered.

4. THE TWILIGHT OF THE STATES

The sheer magnitude of the emergency which confronted the Lincoln administration in 1861 and after worked a permanent transformation upon the powers of the federal government. In part this was the inevitable consequence of the ever-increasing demands of a hard-fought war extending over far-flung battlefields and along a thousand miles of seacoast. But it was also a result of the fact

that the new Republicans and their President were bearers of a new
nationalism which envisioned a central government of power and
authority. Before the war was over, these two forces would completely overthrow the limited federal government which the Lincoln
administration inherited in 1861. In its place would be a United
States government truly supreme over the states that once called
themselves sovereign.

The sinews of war cost money, and in mere monetary terms the
salvation of the Union was an expensive proposition—one which
prompted changes in governmental financial policies. Federal expenditures skyrocketed from $66.5 million in 1861 to $474.8 million in 1862 and on up to the unprecedented level of $1,297 million
in 1865—a peak not equaled until the entrance of the United States
into the First World War. Under such conditions it was inevitable
and imperative that the financial powers of the federal government
would expand accordingly. For the first time in the history of the
country, the government of the United States resorted to the
printing press for money despite the fact that the Constitution
specifically limited the federal government to the "coining" of
money. Almost $400 million in greenbacks were issued by the federal
government to lubricate the economic machine. More than that, as
we have seen, this new kind of federal government, this government
with energy, went on to revamp the banking and currency structure
of the nation, in the course of which it taxed out of existence the
instrumentalities of the states. Never again would state bank notes
be of any significance in the American economy. Currency affairs
were now firmly in the hands of the national government, and the
road from here to the Federal Reserve System and even to a managed currency was both clear and straight.

Unlike the Confederate Congress, which failed to lay adequate
taxes, the United States in the very first year of the war greatly expanded the sources of internal revenue. Most important in this regard were the imposition of new and higher excise taxes and the
laying of a tax on personal incomes for the first time in American
history. The latter measure, never tested in the Supreme Court
before it was repealed in 1873, brought in almost 20 per cent of the
total federal revenue in 1865.

Though some of the new fiscal instruments, such as the income tax
and fiat money, were repealed after the war emergency, the American people had seen the federal government in its full panoply of

power. The sight was not forgotten by Greenbackers, Populists, and other reformers in later years when they looked about for authority and weapons with which to attack the social and economic ills of the nation.

Nor did the swollen war expenditures shrink back to the trifling $66 million of the ante-bellum years. New obligations like veterans' pensions kept the federal budget and its bureaucracy far above the prewar level, and over the subsequent years they grew steadily.

Nor was the high protective tariff, which had come in with the war, repealed. Furthermore, contrary to the situation before 1860, there now were few statesmen who doubted the constitutionality of protection; only expediency could be the objection. Thus another hotly disputed constitutional issue of the ante-bellum years—psychologically now so far in the distance—was rendered obsolete by the decisive verdict of the sword, which cut so many cords running into the past.

One of the most flagrant repudiations of state sovereignty by the central government was the acceptance of West Virginia into the Union. Though the Constitution clearly provides that no territory may be taken from a state without its consent, the western counties of Virginia were severed from the Old Dominion, never to be returned. The trick was turned by the creation of a rump government of Virginia Unionists who "agreed" to the secession of the western portion of the state. Lincoln had his doubts about the constitutionality of such a procedure, but, like Thomas Jefferson before him at the time of the Louisiana Purchase, he brushed them aside in the interest of the Union cause.

The most dramatic example of the way in which the war and the nationalist ideology of the Republican party continuously created the opportunities and necessity for enlarging the powers of the federal government at the expense of the states is provided by the handling of the delicate question of slavery. For decades the mark of a true friend of the Union was the refusal to question the legitimate existence of slavery in the southern states. All supporters of the Union, North and South alike, agreed that slavery was wrapped in the protecting folds of the Constitution itself and embedded in the compromises which the Founding Fathers had been compelled to make in 1787. Though, as Howell Cobb of Georgia shrewdly pointed out, the sole issue which united the Republican party was opposition to slavery, even this antislavery party conceded that there was no constitutional warrant for federal interference with the "peculiar institution" in the states of the South. The most the Republicans wanted to do was prohibit its spread to the territories. The secession of the South, however, removed the party's and the nation's scruples on the question of interference with slavery in the South.

This radical alteration in the nation's attitude toward slavery is all the more remarkable because it took place so rapidly.[3] Early in the war, in 1861, Union generals in the field, like Frémont and Butler, began to accept runaway slaves who entered their lines as either free men (Frémont's position—which was quickly countermanded by Lincoln) or as contraband of war (Butler's method), and therefore no longer the property of their masters. Seeking to formalize such penalizing of the slaveholders in rebellion, the Congress, in August, 1861, passed the Confiscation Act, declaring forfeit all claims to slaves actively engaged in aiding the rebellion. Almost a year later, Congress made it clear that the war was to be the occasion for striking at slavery more widely. The Act of July, 1862, provided that the slaves of all persons committing treason or supporting the rebellion were henceforth and forever free. The act also put an end to the Army's practice of returning fugitive slaves to their masters, unless the masters were adherents to the Union cause.

The growing movement to extend the federal power over the matter of slavery reached its crescendo in 1862. In April a goal was achieved for which the abolitionists had battled for twenty years: slavery was abolished in the District of Columbia. Then, in June, slave property was extinguished in the territories without compensation to the owners. Since the Supreme Court in the Dred Scott decision had denied Congress' power to end slavery in a territory, this latter action was palpably unconstitutional—but this was a

---

[3] The antislavery attitude of the Republican party and administration was visible before the Emancipation Proclamation, but only occasionally. During the secession-crisis winter of 1860–61, for example, the President-elect and his party steadfastly refused to accept any compromise which countenanced slavery in the territories. "Let there be no compromise on the question of extending slavery," Lincoln instructed his followers in December, 1860. "If there be, all our labor is lost, and, ere long, must be done again. . . . Stand firm. The tug has to come, and better now than anytime hereafter." Another instance occurred in February of 1862, when the administration permitted N. P. Gordon, a slave trader, captured the year before, to be executed—the first slave trader to be executed in the forty-year history of American prohibition of the foreign slave trade.

new era and a new government. The final act which brought this mounting antislavery pressure before the conscience of the nation and the attention of the world was the enunciation, in September, of the preliminary Emancipation Proclamation. And, significantly enough, it was under the guise of a war measure that this conclusion to a generation of agitation was achieved.

In his Proclamation, Lincoln reaffirmed his belief in the Declaration of Independence and the equality of all men, but he also extended the federal power, as the Congress had done earlier, over the most sacrosanct domestic institution in the United States. At one time men had come to blows regarding the power of Congress to control slavery in the territories, even though the territories were the creatures of the federal government. But now a nationalistic President and Congress did not scruple to end the hallowed institution in the allegedly sovereign states themselves.

Actually, at the time of its issuance, Lincoln's Proclamation did not free a single slave, since its terms applied only to those slaves held by masters in rebellion. Nevertheless, the edict marked a turning point in the history of bondage in America. It was not long thereafter that the Thirteenth Amendment, abolishing slavery throughout the Union, was started on its way to the states. Who could have predicted, three short years before, that such was to be the fate of the guarded and cherished institution of slavery? Riding on a tidal wave of nationalism, the antislavery crusade had ruthlessly swept away a $2 billion investment belonging to almost half a million Americans. As has been said, this was one of the greatest confiscations of private property in Anglo-Saxon history. That Union of "Liberty and Power" which old John Quincy Adams had worked to create and had yearned to see had finally come to pass.

The abolition of slavery did not, however, exhaust the flood of moral energy set free by the War for the Union; its tide did not ebb until freedom for the Negro and power for the federal government were firmly engrafted upon the Constitution itself. Whereas the Thirteenth Amendment to the Constitution put an end to the issue of slavery in American life, the Fourteenth opened a broad new horizon of governmental power. This single amendment, with the possible exception of the commerce clause, has done more to bury states' rights and to exalt the federal power than any other single amendment or clause in the Constitution.

Although obviously enacted to secure protection for the newly emancipated slave,[4] the power of the amendment has been felt in a dozen fields of American life. The courts have measured against it every conceivable variety of state law from slaughterhouse regulation to wages and hours legislation and on to segregated education. The use by the courts of the celebrated due-process clause of the amendment has been so protean and ingenious as almost to defy summary. This handful of words has been the basis for voiding dozens of state efforts at social reform as well as for justifying federal interference in the administration of justice within the states.

What is more, in the hands of the Supreme Court almost the whole Bill of Rights of the federal Constitution has been made an obligation of the states solely upon the authority of the due-process clause of this fecund amendment. In short, a host of domestic institutions and concerns, once strictly and admittedly within the domain of the states, have been slowly but inexorably transferred to the jurisdiction of the federal authority. Furthermore, the Fourteenth Amendment permanently made the civil rights of racial minorities a federal interest. This was accomplished not only by the due-process clause but also by the provision which threatened the state with loss of congressional representation if they counted Negroes in their population but did not grant them the vote. (Within three years, as we shall see in the next chapter, the Fifteenth Amendment was to make such enfranchisement mandatory throughout the nation.) This unprecedented interference with the suffrage, even indirectly, was yet another example of the subordination of the once-sovereign states to the burgeoning central leviathan. In the same amendment, in order to overturn completely and for all time the Dred Scott decision and its denial of citizenship to the Negro, citizenship was declared to be dependent upon place of birth. In this way it was placed beyond the discretion and authority of the states.

Although not directly connected with the forces of nationalism and freedom which the war fostered, the transformation of the office of President during Lincoln's term is certainly attributable to the war. As Woodrow Wilson observed, the Presidency is whatever the incumbent can make of it, and Abraham Lincoln was personally a

---

[4] For years, under the influence of Charles A. Beard, historians have unfortunately confused the benefits business corporations derived from the amendment with the motivation for its origin. Jacobus tenBroek, *Antislavery Origins of the Fourteenth Amendment* (Ithaca, 1949), has put it back where it belongs: blood and flesh of the antislavery movement.

strong leader and a committed nationalist. It seems indisputable, nevertheless, that the trials of the war provided the necessary conditions for him to clothe the first magistracy of the Union in new power.

In the course of the war the President stretched his war powers to their outer limits. We have already seen how that power was used to abolish slavery in the Confederacy, a usage of the power undreamed of before 1860, except in the nationalist brain of John Quincy Adams. Lincoln also suspended the writ of habeas corpus, suppressed free speech and press, declared a blockade of the southern ports without a declaration of war (despite the fact that four justices of the Supreme Court thought his action unconstitutional), spent money in the early months of the war without congressional authorization, and raised federal troops without an enabling act from Congress. As the federal armies advanced, he undertook to reconstruct the rebellious states and to provide for their return to the Union. "I conceive," he explained to Senator Chandler in 1864, "that I may in an emergency do things on military grounds which cannot be done constitutionally by Congress."

Not even in the days of Andrew Jackson had there been a President so willing to act without waiting for congressional guidance or approbation. Indeed, it might not be far wrong to see in much of the truculence of the legislative branch during Reconstruction a natural reaction to the four years of executive dominance which Lincoln exercised in the name of the War for the Union. In time of war, regardless of the cautious, circumspect men who were to occupy the White House in later years, that office would not be the same after Lincoln had sounded the almost bottomless pool of its power.

5. A NEW WORLD POWER

That the Union emerged from the war more powerful and united than before came as a surprise to many observers in London and Paris. The end of the United States had been widely predicted. The subtitle of Edward Freeman's study of federalism, published in 1863, was suggestive of English upper-class prophecies: "From the Foundation of the Achaian League to the Disruption of the United States." And in the same year, the British Chancellor of the Exchequer, William Gladstone, declared that the southern leaders "have made a nation. We may anticipate with certainty the success of the Southern States as far as their separation from the North is

concerned." The French Emperor, Louis Napoleon, all through the
early years of the war toyed with the idea of recognizing the Confederacy, but the failure of the British to do so stayed his eager
hand. He did not hesitate, however, to take advantage of American
internal preoccupations to establish a French puppet regime in
Mexico in defiance of the Monroe Doctrine.

All such anticipations of the downfall of the Union were reversed
by the military victories of 1864 and 1865. With the capitulation of
Lee, there could be no longer any doubt of the Union's survival, nor
of its awesome military might. Within a year of Lee's surrender, the
French agreed to withdraw their forces from Mexico. Europe was
beginning to feel the first stirrings of that military power, sprung
from a united people, which twice in the twentieth century would
come to redress the balance of the Old World.

"In the glare of our civil war, certain truths . . . have been
brought out with extraordinary sharpness of relief," wrote James
R. Lowell in 1865. One, particularly for Europe, "has been the
amazing strength and no less amazing steadiness of democratic
institutions." That steadiness was most obvious in the signal fact
that in the midst of a war which threatened the very existence of the
Republic, an election involving the fate of the administration itself
was held on schedule. There could be found no better example of
democracy as an orderly process of government carried out by
leaders who believed in the wisdom of the people. At the beginning
of the war, Lincoln had said that it would show "that among free
men there can be no successful appeal from the ballot to the bullet."
Northern victory had assured this. The years following would test
whether any nation "dedicated to the proposition that all men are
created equal" could make that principle work.

CHAPTER VIII I

Dawn Without Noon

IN MAY of 1954, many Americans suddenly realized, despite the fact that almost ninety years had passed since the War for the Union, that the sounds and clashes of that struggle were still echoing. The Supreme Court's decision that Negroes are entitled to equal status with whites in the public schools of the nation was but the latest of the efforts, beginning as far back as the time of Appomattox, to find for the Negro in America a place consistent with the national heritage of freedom and equality.

For a full two hundred years the character, the status, and the future of the great majority of black men in America were defined and molded by the institution of slavery. Then abruptly, within the course of four years of war, this customary and legal guide to race relations was completely swept away; white and black men alike had to set about establishing a new relationship. The determination of what that relationship should be has been slow, unsteady, and at times agonizing. Today, almost a century after the enunciation of the Emancipation Proclamation, it has still not been finally determined; it is still capable of arousing deep-seated emotions among Americans.

1. EQUALITY BY FORCE

The first attempts to carve out a place for the black man in a white-dominated America were undertaken in the dozen years after 1865, which have since come to be called the Reconstruction period. That era, despite the cataclysmic character of the War for the Union, is best understood as a continuation of the history of the previous thirty years. The conflicts of the Reconstruction period are deeply rooted in the previous generation of sectional struggle

over the issue of Negro slavery. The war, it is true, removed slavery
from the congressional debates as effectively as it destroyed it in the
South, but it failed to reconcile the opposite moral values which lay
behind the two sections' conceptions of what slavery was and what
the Negro was.

Many of the northern Radical Republicans, for example—men
like Ben Wade, Charles Sumner, Thaddeus Stevens, William Fessen-
den, and John Bingham—had been in Congress during the antislavery struggle in the 1850's. They were still there when the Reconstruction of the former Confederacy was begun. For such men,
the experiences of the years of antislavery and nationalistic agitation made it unthinkable that the South should be restored to the
Union untouched by the fires in which they themselves had been
tempered. And what was true of the leaders was true of thousands
of ordinary men of the North whose lives were permanently altered
by the moral fervor of the antislavery crusade and the emotionalism
of the great War for the Union.

But the South, too, had a history by which its people had been
molded. The Southerner's image of the Negro was shaped by the
slave past, and its contours were shaken not at all by the rhetoric
of the antislavery North or by the guns which finally destroyed the
"peculiar institution." When the South came to legislate a status
for the freedman, it would understandably draw upon the experience
under slavery.

Under such circumstances, the cessation of hostilities between the
sections brought not peace, but a political cold war, one which was
more full of hate, bitterness, and misunderstanding than the hot war
which preceded it. Since neither section had been able to transcend
its historically derived conceptions about the nature of the Union, it
was hardly to be expected that either would be able to rise above its
history when dealing with the emotionally charged question of the
freed Negro.

As the war overturned American thinking about slavery and the
nature of the Union, so the Reconstruction re-educated the American people on the place the Negro should occupy in the United
States. When the war ended, the position of the newly freed black
man was ambiguous throughout the nation. In the North, though
he was a citizen, society discriminated against him, and he was denied
the ballot in all states except New York and five in New England.
Moreover, as a measure of the North's attitude, within the previous

five years the people of several northern states had overwhelmingly refused to extend the vote to Negroes. In the South, the Negro's ambiguous position was summed up in the fact that he was neither a slave nor a citizen.

But within half a decade, under the driving will of the Radical Republicans all this was reversed. The adoption of the Fourteenth and Fifteenth Amendments to the Constitution signified that the Negro was now to be a full citizen, equal in civil rights and voting privileges with white men. Insofar as modern Americans take pride from this inclusion of the Negro in the American dream of equality and opportunity, then it is to the Radicals that they are indebted. For it was solely because of the Radicals' control over the South that the requisite number of states were brought to ratify the two amendments. If not written into the Constitution then, when the conservative South was powerless to resist and the North was still imbued with its mission of reform, then the principle of Negro equality would probably never have been included in the national charter. This achievement of the Radicals is at least as much a part of the legacy of Reconstruction as the better-known corruption and the imposition of alien rule.

The accomplishment of the Radicals is especially noteworthy because the obstacles were so formidable—not only in the South, but in the North as well. We have already seen that few states in the North in 1865 were prepared to grant Negroes the privilege of participating in the government. The North did, however, believe that the war had put a final end to Negro slavery. It was when that decision seemed to be challenged by the vanquished South that the equalitarian Radicals were presented with an opportunity to enlarge the area of the Negro's rights and privileges.

During the first year after Appomattox, there were a number of accounts from the defeated region to the effect that the former slaves were not being accorded their just rights. Even a reporter as friendly to the South as Benjamin Truman, President Johnson's personal observer, returned from his tour of the region with the impression that "even the greatest men of the South . . . believed that the Emancipation Proclamation was wicked and at least a mistake and a scourge to society." [1] Visitors less friendly to the

[1] Southern leaders were not loath to publicize their reluctance to see the end of what they considered the most workable solution to the question of the Negro. The Governor of Mississippi told the legislature in 1865: "Under the pressure of

South, like Republican Carl Schurz, found that "although the freedman is no longer considered the property of the individual master,
he is considered the slave of society and all independent state legislation will share the tendency to make him so. . . ." It was the so-
called Black Codes passed by the newly elected legislatures of the
southern states which seemed to offer the most accurate forecast of
the future the South envisaged for the Negro.

Drawn up to take the place of the now defunct slave laws, the
Black Codes were a compound of the old slavery statutes, northern
apprenticeship and vagrancy laws, and British West Indian legislation dealing with emancipated slaves. Considering the history of
slavery and the molding of the Negro under that institution, those
parts of the Codes which fell short of equality before the law or of
complete freedom are understandable, and on such grounds they
have been defended. But seen in the light of northern experience and
aspirations, the laws appeared to be a halfway station back to
slavery.

It is true that the new laws expanded the rights of the freed
Negro in permitting him to hold property, to sue and be sued, to
make contracts, to marry, and so on. But it is equally true that the
laws discriminated against black men. Negroes, for example, could
testify in court only when their own race was involved, they could
not carry firearms, and in several states restrictions were placed on
their renting or owning land. Even more important, perhaps, was
the fact that the laws required the freedman to work and forbade
him to leave his job, thereby denying to him an important, if not
indispensable, ingredient of freedom, namely, economic mobility.[2]
When these provisions are coupled with the knowledge that servitude
without pay was often the penalty for infraction of the Codes, it
was only a short step to believing, as did many Northerners, that

Federal bayonets, urged on by the misdirected sympathies of the world . . . the
people of Mississippi have abolished the institution of slavery. . . ."
  [2] It has been argued that such provisions were necessary in order that economic
production might be gotten under way again; that the Negro would not work
unless compelled to. This argument falls to the ground, however, when it is
recognized that the Codes were never put into any extensive practice (the United
States military authorities and the Freedmen's Bureau suspended them and the
later Radical state governments repealed them); yet the Negro certainly went
to work and production increased. Such a defense of the Codes only serves to
underscore the fact that the laws were actually devices to use the power of the
state in the securing of a cheap, tractable, and convenient labor supply and not
for the purpose of introducing the Negro to freedom.

the laws were in effect re-establishing slavery. The people of the North were also aware that the Codes left the Negroes at the mercy of their white employers, since judges and juries were always white. Even under the slave regime, the self-interest of the master, at least, had assured a measure of justice for the black man in the white man's courtroom or in the sheriff's office.

If the Black Codes reflected the influence of slavery on southern thinking about the Negro, the northern reactions to the laws were the result of the emotions left over from the long antislavery crusade. For many Northerners the Codes seemed to demonstrate that the South was trying to do by subterfuge what it was unable to do on the battlefield—preserve slavery.

Those Northerners who could not be especially aroused against the South by stories of atrocities against Negroes were often moved by tales of outrages against southern white Unionists. Here, too, it seemed as if the South was refusing to accept the verdict of the war. "Hour after hour the democracy here are becoming more bold, more insolent, more proscriptive," wrote one Virginian Unionist in 1866. "Under democratic rule again," he warned, "hell would be a Garden of Eden compared to the Southern States. . . ."

Under the skillful management of the Radical leadership, the unsettling reports of conditions in the South, the Black Codes, and the pleas of southern Unionists appeared as insulting mockeries of the North's wartime sacrifices and the long years of antislavery activity. This was the first step in the Radicals' effort to convince the people of the North that southern institutions needed federal renovation.

But before the Radicals could take advantage of the North's newly aroused concern and act against the South, it was necessary that Lincoln's plan for the rapid restoration of the Union be set aside. The President's plan, which his successor Andrew Johnson adopted, was deliberately lenient to the defeated South in order that the Union as it was in 1860 might be restored as speedily as possible. In pursuit of this aim, the Presidential policy left the disposition of the status of the Negro in the hands of the southern states.

By the end of 1865, all of the former Confederate states had completed the requirements under this plan and awaited only the resumption of their seats in Congress to put the final seal upon their restoration to the Union. Since southern representation in Congress would have rendered impossible any further federal interference in the affairs of the South, the Radicals, who now controlled Congress, refused to seat the southern representatives.

By thus holding the southern states in a condition of constitutional suspended animation, the Radicals hoped to be able to work a social and political revolution upon the institutions of the region. Thaddeus Stevens, the leader of the Radicals in the House, made no secret of his aims. In January, 1866, he candidly told the House that he did not want the southern states returned to the Union until the Negro had been made a good citizen under the tutelage of northern missionaries. "I do not want them [the Southern states] to have the right of suffrage," he declared, "before this Congress has done the great work of regenerating the Constitution and the laws of this country according to the principles of the Declaration of Independence."

The goals of this revolution, as they unfolded in the next few years, included Negro equality, Negro suffrage, and a Negro-based Republican party in the South. Though only part of his ambitious program was apparent in 1865–66, there could be no doubt even then of the Radicals' desire to protect the Negro in his rights as a free man. In the spring of 1866, the Congress passed the Civil Rights and Freedmen's Bureau bills, both of which employed the federal power to insure the Negro's equality before the law and his equality of treatment in public places. The President's veto of these bills and the South's adamant opposition to them were answered by a new demand upon the defeated region. The Radicals now demanded as the price of readmission to the Union—in line with Stevens' statement in January—the ratification of the newly written Fourteenth Amendment to the federal Constitution.

Aside from its remarkably nationalistic tone, which we have already noticed, the Fourteenth Amendment proclaimed the equality of all Americans, black and white. Beginning by declaring that all persons born in the United States are citizens (thereby including Negroes), it went on to forbid any state to "make . . . any law which shall abridge the privileges or immunities of citizens of the United States," or to "deprive any person of life, liberty, or property, without due process of law," or to "deny to any person within its jurisdiction the equal protection of the laws." The amendment was submitted to the states, both northern and southern, in June, 1866, but its sweeping affirmation of equality was obviously directed first of all against those states which had been lately in rebellion.

The categorical and peremptory refusal of ten of the former Confederate states to ratify the amendment was a turning point in the history of Reconstruction. One cannot be sure, of course, what would have happened if the southern states had acted differently. We do know, though, that in the case of one state, Tennessee, whose ratification Congress accepted, readmission to the Union followed immediately, and Tennessee was not molested by congressional Reconstruction thereafter. If the other ten states had similarly been restored to the Union, then, presumably, there could have been no Radical Reconstruction as we know it simply because southern representation in Congress in concert with President Johnson could have stopped any such efforts. But even if the southern states were not restored to the Union, ratification of the amendment would have removed the primary justification for the later imposition of military rule. For it was in order to secure the necessary ratifying states that Congress later moved to the military subordination of the South. By refusing to ratify, the southern states gained little if anything, since it should have been obvious, given the temper of the country as revealed in the election triumph of the Radicals in 1866, that some effort to realize the equalitarian spirit of the times would succeed sooner or later.[3] By their intransigence, the southern states presented the Radicals with a lever with which to overturn the social structure of the Southland.

Viewed from the perspective of almost a century, the requirement that the southern states ratify the Fourteenth Amendment does not appear revengeful or vindictive,[4] but neither does it seem con-

[3] It is interesting to note that the governors of Louisiana, Arkansas, and Virginia recommended ratification of the Fourteenth Amendment to their legislatures, but, of course, their advice was not heeded.

[4] Many historians, led by J. G. Randall, have come to refer to the Radicals as Vindictives. Such a simplistic view of the Radical motivation, however, obscures the remarkable lack of revenge displayed by the victors. Virtually no reprisals were taken against the South for the rebellion, despite the fact that the President of the United States was assassinated by a southern sympathizer. Probably never before in the history of any nation which had just suppressed a great rebellion could it be said, as was true of the United States, that not a single leader of the rebels was executed, or even tried for treason. Only one, Jefferson Davis, was imprisoned for any length of time, and he was released after two years. None of the military leaders was held even momentarily, though a good number of them, like Lee, had left the federal service to join the Confederacy. The greatest economic blow levied against the South was the abolition of slave property without compensation, but this was not the work of the Radical Reconstruction. The evidence which is usually brought against the Radicals to show their vindictiveness does not support the charge so much as it demonstrates their interest in

siliatory, few social revolutions, however, are easy to swallow. The amendment struck at the two most cherished canons of southern thought: states' rights and the inferiority of the Negro. The proud South was the prisoner of its history, and once again, as in the 1850's, it came up against the North's equally historical sense of mission and reform. And once again the North possessed the preponderance of power.

After the election of 1866 the North's support of the Radical program could be doubtful in no one's mind. The people of the North seemed prepared to go along with the social revolution which the Radicals were planning for the South. Moreover, they were apparently quite willing to have it apply to themselves, too, for the Fourteenth Amendment was ratified by over three-quarters of the northern states within the first year. The Radical election victory was overwhelming, even though President Johnson had embarked upon an unprecedented campaign against the Radicals and their program. New York returned a majority for the Republicans double what it had given Lincoln in 1864; New Jersey, traditionally Democratic, sent a majority of Republican congressmen; Pennsylvania elected eighteen Republicans and only six Democrats to the Congress; Michigan and Iowa returned solid Republican delegations. Only three border states, Delaware, Kentucky, and Maryland, went Democratic. All told, the Republicans secured 143 seats in a House of 192, enough to override any veto of the unfriendly President. The people of the North were solidly behind the Radicals' assertion that restoration of the Union must wait upon the South's acceptance of the equality of rights for Negroes.

"They have deliberated, they have acted," exclaimed Congressman James Garfield in February, 1867, when the ten southern states refused to ratify the Fourteenth Amendment. "The last of the sinful ten has, with contempt and scorn, flung back into our teeth the magnanimous offer of a generous nation. It is now our turn to act." Armed with the victory at the polls, the Radicals now took their most extreme step. They placed the recalcitrant ten under military rule and, in addition to ratification of the Fourteenth Amendment,

---

effecting a revolution in southern thinking and mores. Such enforced changes are admittedly painful, but hardly vindictive when viewed dispassionately. To persist in forcing through such changes is not any more vindictive than to redistribute Japanese land after World War II or to insist that anti-Semitism be prohibited in Germany.

the southern states were required to extend the suffrage to the Negro and to revise their constitutions so as to grant equality to black men.

Since the northern states would soon be asked to grant suffrage to the Negro, it is instructive to set forth Thaddeus Stevens' justification for such a proposal. In placing his arguments before the Congress in January, 1867, Stevens candidly appealed to the three great principles for which the North had fought the war: the Negro, the Union, and the Republican party. "There are several good reasons for the passage of this bill," he began. "In the first place, it is just. . . . Have not loyal blacks quite as good a right to choose rulers and make laws as rebel whites? In the second place, it is a necessity in order to protect the loyal white men in the seceded States." With Negro suffrage, Stevens believed, pro-Union men in the southern states, both black and white, would constitute majorities, "control the States, and protect themselves." The final reason he offered was that "it would assure the ascendancy of the Union party. . . . I believe that on the continued ascendancy of that party depends the safety of this great nation."

To compel the South to accept Negro suffrage was to ask of that region more than the North at that time appeared willing to give.[5] But the North's opposition to Negro voting was deceptively weak, as the rapidity with which the Fifteenth Amendment was ratified demonstrated. In February, 1869, less than two years after Negro suffrage was imposed upon the South, the Fifteenth Amendment was on its way to the states. Ratification, with the assistance of the now Radicalized southern states, was achieved within thirteen months thereafter. By a combination of persuasion and emotion in the North, and ruthless suppression in the South, the Radicals had completed their revolution. In the eyes of the national Constitution the former slave was now a full citizen, equal before the law and in possession of the ballot.

2. HOW BLACK WAS BLACK RECONSTRUCTION?

But, it will be said, the price the South and the nation paid for this ideal of equality was outrageously high. And because the history

[5] As late as 1868, only four states outside of New England and New York granted the suffrage to Negroes: Nebraska, Iowa, Minnesota, and Wisconsin. Colorado and Connecticut had rejected Negro suffrage in 1865; Ohio and Kansas did so in 1867; Missouri and Michigan in 1868.

of Reconstruction in the South has been so overlaid with myth and
emotion, it is necessary at this point to digress somewhat in an attempt to put that unhappy decade into some perspective.

There is a myth of Reconstruction history to which most Americans, Northerners and Southerners alike, give credence. In brief
outline it goes something like this. In 1867, a vengeful Congress
placed the southern states under a military despotism which supported by its bayonets an alien regime in each of the states, composed of white adventurers—the carpetbaggers and scalawags—and
their ignorant Negro allies. For a decade thereafter, the story continues, these regimes looted the treasuries of the southern states, impoverished the region with high taxes, denied the southern white
people any say in their own governance, and spread terror throughout the Southland. Not until the withdrawal of federal troops in
1877, it is said, did this nightmare end and decency in government
return to the South. As in most myths, there is some truth in this
one; but a balanced picture of Reconstruction is quite different.

For one thing, though it is common to think of Reconstruction as
lasting the ten years from 1867 to 1877, the actual duration of the
military and Radical regimes varied considerably from state to
state. Democratic or conservative governments came to power in
Virginia and North Carolina as early as 1870 (in fact, Virginia
never experienced a true Radical civilian government at all); in
Georgia in 1871; in Texas, Arkansas, and Alabama in 1874; in Mississippi in 1876. Only South Carolina, Florida, and Louisiana depended upon the withdrawal of federal troops in 1877 for the
overthrow of their Radical government. In brief, Radical Reconstruction, including the military phases as well as the civilian, lasted
as short as three years in two states and as long as ten years in only
three.

Because it is so often assumed that Radical Reconstruction was
synonymous with military rule, the role of the Army in the South
during this period must be precisely understood. Under the congressional plan of Reconstruction as set forth in the acts of 1867,
the South was divided into five military districts, each under a major
general. It was the responsibility of these generals to oversee the
establishment of registration lists for voters for the constitutional
conventions and the election of new governments in the states of
their districts. Once this was accomplished, civil governments based
on the new constitutions would assume power. Generally, the ending

of military rule roughly coincided with the date at which Congress admitted the state to the Union. Thus military rule ended in 1868 in all of the southern states except Virginia, Texas, and Mississippi, and in those states it was over in 1869 or 1870. (Only in Georgia was military rule ever imposed again.) Often, it must be admitted, the Radical civil governments required or utilized the aid of militia and sometimes the federal troops to support their regimes, but this does not mean that an extraconstitutional government was in power. For the greater part of Radical Reconstruction, then, the southern states were under civil, not military, government, and, in most cases, these were governments which conservative white Southerners could influence with their votes. Indeed, it was by losing elections that many of the Radical governments fell into conservative hands before 1877.

But even when the southern states were under the military, it should not be assumed that the government was corrupt, oppressive, or unfair toward the whites. Contrary to the usual conception of the military occupation of the South, the number of troops actually stationed in the whole region was very small. No more than 20,000 men were involved in the whole "occupation," of whom fully 7,000 were concentrated in the two states of Louisiana and Texas. No garrison, except those in Richmond and New Orleans, which contained 1,000 each, numbered more than 500 men. The relative weakness of the military force, of course, is a measure of the southern acceptance of northern control.

Though weak in man power, the military was supreme in law. In fact, the whole machinery of government and law was at the disposal of the Army; its authority was final. But the acquiesence in this on the part of the Southerners—for there was no organized opposition—is weighty testimony to the relative fairness of the administration. "It would be hard to deny that, so far as the ordinary civil administration was concerned," William A. Dunning, the authority on Reconstruction and no friend of the Radicals, has written, "the rule of the generals was as just and efficient as it was far-reaching. Criticism and denunciation of their acts were bitter and continuous; but no very profound research is necessary in order to discover that the animus of these attacks was chiefly political. . . ." There is good reason for believing, he continued, "that military government, pure and simple, unaccompanied by the measures for the institution of Negro suffrage, might have proved for a time a useful aid to

social readjustment in the South, as preliminary to the final solution
of political problems."

Even later, when the federal troops intervened in the South, it was
with care and with a concern for fairness to the whites. President
Grant in 1871, much disturbed by the attacks of the Ku Klux Klan
upon Negroes, prevailed upon Congress to pass an act to aid in the
suppression of the violence. Only once, however, did the President
invoke the broad powers which Congress granted; this was in the
famous incident of the nine counties of South Carolina in 1871. But
even in this instance, Grant was careful enough to have the Attorney
General investigate the situation in the area before he acted, and the
President withdrew his order for one county when he found he was
mistaken as to the disorders and conditions there.

In the prosecution of Southerners for infractions of the so-called
enforcement acts, passed in 1870–71 to assist in the suppression of
opposition to Negro suffrage, the federal courts tried hard to be
fair. Out of the hundreds of cases against whites for infringements
of these laws, there were relatively few convictions. One authority,
William W. Davis, a Southerner, has estimated that only about 20
per cent of the cases under the acts resulted in conviction; and
about 70 per cent of them were dismissed or nolle-prossed. "The
Federal courts," Davis has written, "insisted on reasonable testimony, and the judges, with some notorious exceptions, were generally fair in their rulings." Moreover, he added, "White judges were
inclined toward leniency in judging the white man prosecuted under
the force acts on the testimony of black men." In summary, then, it
would seem that justice was obtainable for the white man even during the grimmest days of so-called Black Reconstruction.[6]

Perhaps the explanation most commonly offered for the ascendancy of the Radicals and the Negroes in southern state governments
is that the conservative whites were disfranchised at the same time
the Negroes were enfranchised. As a literal and nonquantitative
statement, this is true, but as an explanation it will not hold water.
At no time were sufficient whites deprived of the ballot to permit the

[6] Even a work as critical and penetrating as W. J. Cash, *The Mind of the
South,* published as recently as 1941, contains exaggerated presentations of what
happened during Reconstruction. "For ten years the courts of the South were in
such hands that no loyal white man could hope to find justice in them as against
any Negro or any white creature of the Yankee policy; for twenty years and
longer they continued, in many quarters, to be in such hands that such justice
was at least doubtful."

Negroes and Northerners to take over the governments of the southern states by default.

Before the numbers involved can be discussed, the two different kinds or phases of disfranchisement must be understood. The first was during military rule, when Congress stipulated that those who had deserted federal office for the Confederacy or had voluntarily given aid to that cause were to be denied the suffrage and office-holding. Though it is impossible to obtain a completely accurate record of the number disfranchised under this rule (thousands of whites, for example, refused to register as a form of protest, but they are sometimes counted as disfranchised), the figure usually accepted is 150,000 for the whole South. This is to be compared with a total registration for whites in 1868 of about 630,000. Regardless of the size of the figure, under this disfranchisement only two elections were held, that for the choosing of the delegates to the state constitution conventions and that for the selection of the officers of the new governments created under the constitutions. After that, the qualifications for voting would be those decided upon in the conventions and written into the new constitutions. And that was the second phase of disfranchisement.

Again, contrary to the usual opinion, the states, on the whole, in their Radical-dominated conventions were not as ruthless in disfranchisement as one might expect. And those which were, found that their disabling clauses were removed before ratification. In the end, only Louisiana, Alabama, and Arkansas actually enforced suffrage and officeholding restrictions against whites; the other seven states placed no legal obstacle in the way of white voting. Finally, it should be noted that the number of southern leaders upon whom the disabilities of the Fourteenth Amendment were visited was greatly reduced as early as 1872. At that date no more than 750 Southerners, those who had occupied high office under the United States in 1860–61 and had deserted to the southern cause, were still barred from officeholding. The disabilities against these men were not removed until the time of the Spanish-American War.

In view of the foregoing, it is illusory to look to white disfranchisement for an explanation of the electoral successes of the Radicals in the southern states. Rather it has to be sought in the fact that many whites did not vote, either in protest or because of indifference, while many Negroes did, either from understanding of the issues or from compulsion from their white and Negro leaders. It should not be forgotten, in this regard, that the proportion of Negroes in the southern states was uniformly greater at that time than it is now. Three states, for example—Louisiana, South Carolina, and Mississippi—contained a majority of Negroes, and one would expect, everything being equal, to encounter a Negro-Radical majority in those states. Moreover, a comparison of the number of Negroes registered in 1868 in each of the southern states with the number of Negro males over twenty-one as listed in the Census of 1870 discloses that only in Alabama was the actual number of Negro registrants out of line with the potential number as counted in the census. In all the other states the registration figures are plausible and not the result of obvious padding or fraud.

This is not to suggest that fraud did not occur in Reconstruction elections any more than it is meant to convey the impression that New York City elections at this time were innocent of fraud; undoubtedly there was much in both places and on both sides of the political fence. The purpose here, rather, is to show that there is solid justification for the strong showing which the Radicals made at the polls and that it is not to be casually attributed to the "counting out" of the whites. As a matter of fact, even under military-run registration in 1868, white voters outnumbered Negro voters in Georgia, Virginia, Texas, and North Carolina, a fact which rather effectively demolishes the argument that military reconstruction disfranchised the white majorities. Yet, of the two phases of disfranchisement, this was the stricter.

Looming over all discussions of Reconstruction, whether by Southerners or Northerners, is always the question of Negro domination. Surely, in the fear-ridden mind of the South, the unforgettable evil of Reconstruction was the participation of the Negro in government. Actually, though, aside from the exercise of the suffrage, which will be left until later, the Negro played a relatively minor political role in the Reconstruction of the southern states. Indeed, so limited were the number of offices available to Negroes that some of the Negro leaders, one southern authority has written, complained to their white mentors that their race was getting too few plums of office. Often northern whites who came to the South did not look with favor upon Negroes in office, and Southerners who collaborated with the Radicals, retaining, at least in part, their Southern-born attitudes on race, were chary of permitting too many Negroes to hold office.

Negroes, of course, did hold some offices under Reconstruction; in fact, outside of the position of Governor, which no Negro held in any state, black men filled each executive office at one time or another. In only one state, however, was a Negro a member of the Supreme Court; that was in South Carolina. The vast majority of Negro officeholders, however, were local officials like county superintendents of education and justices of the peace.

Contrary to the legend, Negroes did not dominate the legislatures of the southern states. The popularity of James S. Pike's sensational and partisan book, *The Prostrate State,* a contemporary description of the South Carolina legislature, has fostered the erroneous conclusion that such a body was typical of Radical regimes. In truth, Negroes were a majority in the legislatures of South Carolina and Louisiana only, and even there not for all the sessions of the period. Negroes were also a minority in all of the constitutional conventions called under the military, except, again, in the instance of South Carolina, and in Louisiana, where the whites and Negroes were equally divided. (South Carolina and Louisiana stand out in this regard because each contained a large and old city in which lived numbers of free Negroes who had some education and experience outside of slavery.)

Perhaps if there had been Negro domination, Reconstruction in the southern states would have been milder, for in both the conventions and the legislatures of the states the Negro members were the opposite of vindictive toward the whites. "I have no desire to take away any rights of the white man," said Tom Lee, delegate to the Alabama Constitutional Convention in 1867, "all I want is equal rights in the court house and equal rights when I go to vote." Even in the Negro-dominated legislature of South Carolina, there was no disfranchisement of whites beyond that prescribed for officeholding in the Fourteenth Amendment. Whenever the question of amnesty for Confederates came up in the United States Congress, where several Negroes sat during Reconstruction, the Negroes were usually found on the side of leniency toward the white man.

The South Carolina convention was extreme and unrepresentative of its sister conventions when it sought to ban terms of opprobrium like "Nigger" and "Yankee." South Carolina was also out of line with the other states when it provided for racially integrated schools; only two other states followed that example. For the overwhelming majority of Southerners, Reconstruction did not involve

the mixing of races in the public schools. Nor did it mean the legal-
ization of intermarriage between the races; the ante-bellum statutes
prohibiting such unions were retained by the Radical regimes. The
Negroes, in the main, wanted equality, not dominance.

Among the advantages which Radical Reconstruction brought to
the southern states were the new constitutions which the Negroes
and Radical whites wrote in each of the states. These organic laws
stand up well upon comparison with earlier and subsequent ones in
the South. As E. M. Coulter of the University of Georgia, and no
friend of Reconstruction Radicals, has written, "The Constitutions
finally turned out were much better than the Southerners had ever
hoped for: in fact, some of them were kept for many years after the
whites again got control of the governments." Generally they were
"more democratic than the documents they supplanted, made so by
increasing the electorate through Negro suffrage, requiring the total
population as the basis for representation, reducing the terms of
office, and by adding such principles as homestead exemptions and
non-imprisonment for debt." The constitutions also provided for
"free education for all and favored the economic development of the
South," Coulter concludes.

Unquestionably, the evil most often charged against Reconstruction was the extension of the suffrage to a people the overwhelming
majority of whom had only recently emerged from the dependent
status of slavery. It is true that Negro suffrage in the South, aside
from the intense fears it stirred up in the whites, was conducive to
fraud, deception, and, at the very least, thoughtless voting. But
viewed through the glasses of hindsight and with the recognition
that universal suffrage is fundamental to a democratic society, the
enfranchisement of the Negro appears considerably less "radical"
today. The insouciant manner in which the suffrage was proffered to
former slaves and the universality of the extension are certainly
open to question, but the elementary justice of some form of Negro
suffrage cannot be denied by any sincere advocate of democratic
government.[7]

[7] It should not be thought that illiteracy was one of the legitimate arguments
against Negro suffrage. Thousands of southern whites enjoyed the franchise even
though they could neither read nor write. In 1880, for example, white illiterates
averaged over a quarter of the population in Georgia, Alabama, and North
Carolina. J. T. Trowbridge, the journalist, who made a tour of the South in
1865–66, concluded that the Negroes should be granted the suffrage. "They
are," he wrote, "by all moral and intellectual qualifications, as well prepared for

Unfortunately, on the matter of the suffrage, neither white Southerners nor northern Radicals were prepared to adjust their conception of the Negro to reality. Though some free Negroes were obviously capable of voting intelligently in 1865, as Lincoln, for example, recognized, and most Negroes would be after the mentally crippling effects of slavery had had a chance to be outgrown, few Southerners could shed their blanket view of the Negro as an incompetent. "The fact is patent to all," a South Carolina convention of whites asserted in 1867, "that the Negro is utterly unfitted to exercise the highest functions of the citizen." The South would not change. "Left to itself," southern historian Francis Simkins has concluded, "the region would not have accorded the Negro the vote or other manifestations of equality. . . ."

On the other hand, the Northern Radicals, fearful that the South, once back in the Union, would deny the vote to all Negroes, and especially desirous of creating a large number of new Republicans, went to the other extreme and decreed universal Negro suffrage. This solution, however, overlooked the obvious disabilities which slavery had temporarily stamped upon a majority of the Negroes and seriously underestimated the tenacity of the historically ingrained racial feeling of the whites. Today the only comfort which can be drawn from the thoughtless and opportunistic policy of the Radicals is that it did provide a means for the inclusion of the Negro in the electorate, even if the means almost smothered the ideal with disrepute.

Radical Reconstruction in the South left a more permanent monument than the Negro's transient experience in public office and a nobler one than the southern white's nightmares of racial amalgamation. This was the laying of the foundation of southern free public education. Almost all of the Reconstruction conventions and legislatures erected or revived systems of free public education —a not insignificant manifestation, it might be noted parenthetically, of the Radical propensity for making over Dixie in the image of the North. In most of the southern states, these Reconstruction efforts in behalf of public education remained after 1877 to be-

---

it as the mass of poor whites in the South." In a good number of states of the Union at this time, even immigrants were granted the vote prior to their acquisition of citizenship. The only valid argument against universal Negro suffrage, it would seem, was the lack of independent experience which was inherent in the Negro's former slave status.

some the bases upon which post-Radical governments built their
school systems. Though the South had always had some free schools
and even some local public-school systems, free education as it was
known in the North by the 1850's began in the South only after
the War for Southern Independence.

The other educational achievement of Radical Reconstruction
in the South was the conversion of the whites to the view that Negro
education was not only desirable but a necessity. This was largely
the work of the Freedmen's Bureau. Prior to Radical Reconstruction in Georgia, for example, as Mildred Thompson has pointed
out, the postwar government provided public education only for
whites. Education for the Negroes was viewed as a waste of effort
and perhaps even dangerous. All over the South in 1865–67,
northern whites who attempted to instruct Negroes were subject
to attack and violence. The blazing Negro schoolhouse of this period
was the predecessor of the later burning cross.

Despite such opposition, the Freedmen's Bureau succeeded in
establishing Negro schools before 1867. At its height, the Bureau
operated over 4,000 primary schools, 74 normal schools, and 61
industrial schools for Negroes. George Bentley, a recent historian
of the Bureau, concludes that by 1867 Negro and white alike in the
South had come to accept the necessity for public education of the
former slave. "Certainly in this respect," Bentley observes, "the
Bureau had performed a commendable service for the Negroes, for
the South and for the nation."

By the time the reader has gotten this far in the "other side" of
Reconstruction, he is probably somewhat annoyed at the absence
of references to the well-known corruption and fraud so much a part
of the conventional picture of the period. He is convinced that this
noisome aspect will be conveniently forgotten. There is no denying
the disreputable character of all too many of the Radical state
governments. Certainly the history of Louisiana, South Carolina,
Florida, and Alabama during this period provide rather painful
examples of what corruption can be and what government should
not be.

But again it is necessary to emphasize that the total picture is
not all dark. Mississippi, for example, under Radical Republican
rule enjoyed a government as administratively honest as most
Democratic ones, and in some ways decidedly more honest. "The
only large case of embezzlement among the state officers during the

post-bellum period," writes James Garner, the historian of Mississippi Reconstruction, "was that of the Democratic state Treasurer in 1866." Mildred Thompson, writing about her native state, says that in comparison with states like Alabama and South Carolina, Georgia under Radical Reconstruction "shows a marked moderation in her government, a lesser degree of reconstruction evils, less wanton corruption and extravagance in public office, less social disorder and upheaval. In Georgia," she concludes, "Negroes and carpet-baggers were not so conspicuous, and conservative white citizens were better represented."

Though Virginia escaped entirely the period of Radical Reconstruction which other southern states endured after the cessation of military rule, she did not escape extravagance. In 1869, the first and last election under military rule brought the defeat of the Radicals in a free polling. But under the conservatives who then took office, Virginia contracted as staggering a public debt as those run up in the Radical-dominated states. Even the usual stories of the high taxes imposed by the Radical governments in the various states are susceptible of a different interpretation when put into some perspective. In 1870, for instance, when the average tax rate for the southern states was 15 mills, that of Illinois was 45.

The fraudulent dealings of the Radical regimes appear less exceptional and noteworthy if they are placed within the context of the times. For instance, it is instructive to realize that after the end of Reconsruction, each of the conservative Democratic governments in Georgia, Alabama, Virginia, Mississippi, Louisiana, and Tennessee had treasurers or other officials who absconded with or embezzled state funds, the individual defalcations often running to half a million dollars. Then, of course, the years of Reconstruction also included the Tweed swindles in New York City, in which perhaps over $100 million was robbed from the public treasury. And on the national level, the frauds and stealings carried out under the unseeing eye of President Grant serve to round out the picture.

Though not at all excusing the Radical frauds, the corrupt climate of the times does make it clear that the Radical pilferings were little more than particular instances of a general postwar phenomenon. And once this fact is grasped, it becomes apparent that it is not corruption which has fastened disrepute upon these short-lived regimes, but the fact that Negroes participated in them. "Corruption and extravagance increased the intolerance with which the Negro regimes were regarded," Southern historian Francis Simkins has written, "yet even if these regimes had shown exemplary statesmanship they would have been unacceptable to white Southerners as long as Negroes comprising any part of them were regarded as political equals."

3. CASTE WILL OUT

The tragedy of Reconstruction is that it failed. Rather than liberating the South from its fear of the Negro, Reconstruction exacerbated it; instead of re-establishing a two-party political system, it further fastened a benumbing single party upon a region which once had led the nation in political creativity. Yet neither that section nor the North was alone responsible for the failure; both have to bear the national burden—the South for its intransigent conservatism, the North for its bungling idealism.

As is apparent today, it was imperative in those first years after Appomattox that a way be found whereby the nation and the Negro might confidently look forward to the former slave's full and equal participation in American life. But the unique opportunity of those first years was squandered. Neither Southerners nor Northerners were capable of disenthralling themselves, as Lincoln had counseled; both continued to act within their historically determined attitudinal patterns. Lincoln himself, for that matter, failed to grasp the crucial nature of the postwar era, so far as the Negro was concerned. His plan for the rapid restoration of the southern states indicated that he was quite prepared to throw away the single opportunity for realizing the equalitarian precepts of the Declaration of Independence to which he so often referred. And though the Radicals succeeded in enshrining in the Constitution their vision of equality for all, thereby illuminating the path the nation was ultimately to follow, they were woefully unequal to the complicated and delicate task of implementing their vision. Having failed to meet the problem of the Negro at its inception, Americans have been compelled to grapple with it in each succeeding generation down to our own day.

The inability of the Radicals to translate their equalitarian ideals into reality through the use of force [8] brought an end to the

---

[8] At the risk of seeming to condone the often cynical methods employed by the Radicals in the South, the principle behind Reconstruction deserves some attempt at a defense. It is a common argument that force cannot change ideas or

first phase of the search for a place for the Negro in America. During the years which followed, the South was left free to work out for itself what it considered the Negro's proper niche. Contrary to popular conceptions of Reconstruction and its aftermath, the South was neither united nor decided on what that position should be. The evolution of the region's place for the Negro would take another generation.

The southern leaders and people in 1867 had been extremely doubtful about the wisdom of Negro suffrage; but when Reconstruction came to a close, they did not move to eliminate the Negro from southern politics. Instead there was a substantial period during which the South freely experimented with Negro voting. In states like Mississippi and South Carolina, where the Negroes were a majority, a policy of bringing them into the Democratic party was tried. During the 1880's in South Carolina, for instance, several Negro Democrats sat in the legislature. A Negro was nominated by the Mississippi State Democratic Convention of 1877 for the office of secretary of state, and it was not unusual in that state for fusion tickets to be set up in black counties with Negro candidates. Such moves, however, were scattered instances, rather than general conditions; most Negroes remained in the Republican party.

But as Republicans the Negroes in the South after 1877 continued to vote and to hold office, though, naturally, when they threatened the supremacy of the whites, fraud, violence, and intimidation were used to right the balance. Negroes served in the South Carolina legislature right down to 1900, usually elected, of course, from predominantly Negro districts; during the 1880's and 1890's black representatives sat in the legislatures of North Carolina,

---

dissolve prejudices, and that, therefore, from the outset Reconstruction flew in the face of experience. It is true that ideas are best changed by sincere, inner conversion, but this is not always possible; and weak as enforced conversion may be as a foundation on which to build sympathy and understanding, it is sometimes the only alternative. In both Japan and Germany after 1945, the western powers, notably the United States, undertook to impose certain concepts and forms of democratic life upon the defeated peoples. The only essential difference between these efforts to change people's minds by compulsion and that of Reconstruction was in method; the modern effort was, all things considered, intelligently and efficiently handled. The principle, however, was precisely the same as that which animated Radical Reconstruction in the South. It would seem that only those who oppose the principle of forcible democratization of Germany and Japan can consistently condemn the leaders of Radical Reconstruction for trying to solve by force, albeit ineptly, the problem of the black man in a white America.

Mississippi, and Tennessee, Negroes also represented the South in
Washington after Reconstruction. Between 1877 and 1900, Negro
representatives and senators from the South appeared in every
Congress of the United States except the Fiftieth (1887–89). The
Fifty-first Congress (1889–91), for example, counted three Negroes,
one each from North Carolina, South Carolina, and Virginia.[9] All
this came to an end, however, at the turn of the century, a pivotal
date in the nation's search for a place for the Negro.

The first permanent law for segregating Negroes from whites in
railroad cars was passed as early as 1881 in Tennessee, but it is
erroneous to assume, as many have done, that the so-called Jim
Crow laws went onto the statute books contemporaneously with
the withdrawal of federal troops. Aside from bans on intermarriage
and the initiation of legal segregation on trains, the large body of
discriminatory legislation which is known in the South today was
unknown before 1898.

Before that date the mingling of whites and Negroes in public
places was often quite unrestricted. In 1878, Thomas Wentworth
Higginson, scion of a prominent Boston family, abolitionist, and
former officer in a Negro regiment in the war, toured South Carolina
to see the results of the resurgence of white conservative rule. He
found the Negroes traveling on first-class cars, serving on the police
force, and generally mingling with the whites in public places.
Almost twenty years later in 1897, when a move was afoot to enforce segregation on railroad cars, a Charleston editor, by implication, indicated how little segregation there was in South
Carolina. "Our opinion is that we have no more need for a Jim
Crow system this year than we had last year, and a great deal less
than we had twenty and thirty years ago." Such a system, he said,
"would be a needless affront to our respectable and well behaved
colored people." One anonymous Northerner, writing in the *Atlantic
Monthly* in 1882, was told by the head of a racially mixed school
in the South that "mixed schools" would come to the South. The
author himself became convinced "that there will soon be mixed
schools, for white and colored children, in many parts of the South.
There are already a few such schools." Southern leaders acknowl-

---

[9] All during these same years, the North sent no Negro representatives at all,
though it is only fair to add that the number of Negroes in that section was then
very small. Not until 1929 did the first northern Negro sit in the Congress of
the United States.

edge this possibility, he went on, and "they are not disturbed by the prospect."

Writing in *Harper's Monthly* three years later, Charles Dudley Warner, on a visit to the South, noted that "In New Orleans the street cars are free to all colors; at the Exposition white and colored people mingled freely. . . ." A Negro clergyman, he reported, assisted at the services of the major white Episcopal church in that city. He was told by one Negro woman that in Mobile the Negroes had their votes courted by white politicians, and served in minor municipal offices and on the police force. Even the whites' Opera House, this woman told him, was turned over to the Negroes for an exhibition which the whites also attended.

To many visitors from the North, the South in the mid-eighties seemed to be making great strides in the direction of relaxation of racial discrimination. Part of this impression was merely a reflection of increasing northern sympathy for the southern point of view now that the emotion-packed years before 1865 were receding. But a substantial part was obviously a mirroring of the true situation. The end of Reconstruction and the restoration of white rule had not resulted in the erection of a wall between Negroes and whites in the South.

But those who thought they detected a trend toward equality were destined for disappointment. Instead of expanding the realms of equality for the Negro, the South ultimately developed a pattern of race relations which clearly marked the Negro as a second-class citizen. The 1880's was a period when the racial pattern was still in flux, but already there were several signs pointing in the direction the South would go. For example, though there were very few laws requiring segregation, discrimination certainly existed, particularly in hotels, theaters, and on trains. And already in the 1880's, the ugly practice of lynching was spreading ominously. Between 1882 and 1903, almost 2,000 Negroes were lynched in the southern states, as against 567 white persons.

It was the Farmers' Revolt, coming to a head in the early 1890's, which finally brought the balance down on the side of increased restrictions on the Negro. The first form this took was the legal elimination of the Negro from southern politics. Aside from the small farmer's ever-present fear and hatred of the Negro, the aroused agrarian movement had new and compelling reasons for wanting to see the Negro deprived of the vote once and for all. The

farmers believed, and sometimes rightly so, that the Negro vote
was often mobilized against them, corruptly or otherwise, by the
conservatives and the business interests against which they were
fighting. Nor were these conservative leaders reluctant, if it served
their purpose, to accuse the newly formed farmers' party of splitting the white vote and thereby endangering white supremacy. The
complete removal of the Negro from politics, the farmers reasoned,
would permit the whites to fight out their differences untroubled by
the explosive and confusing issue of white supremacy. A further
impetus to the elimination of the Negro from politics was given
by politicians like "Pitchfork Ben" Tillman of South Carolina and
James Vardaman of Mississippi, who were eager to use the poor
man's Negrophobia as a handy vehicle to power.

The movement to eliminate the Negro voter permanently and
constitutionally was led by the Mississippi Constitutional Convention of 1890, and the pattern arrived at there became the model for
the rest of the southern states. During the nineties and the opening
years of the new century, a veritable parade of southern constitutional conventions literally wrote an end to Negro participation in
southern politics. To circumvent the prohibitions of the Fifteenth
Amendment and yet eliminate effectively the bulk of the Negro
voters, the conventions resorted to ingenious subterfuges. Poll taxes,
complicated balloting procedures, and literacy tests were among
the devices employed to strike Negroes from the registers.

Because the mass of poor white farmers had always harbored
deep fears of the black man, these new constitutional provisions
were only a translation into law of their own emotions and attitudes. But such legal narcissism exacted a price. The procedures
adopted to exclude the Negro from the suffrage also operated to
disfranchise thousands of poor, untutored white men who could not
surmount any of the hurdles. White registration under the new
Louisiana constitution, for instance, dropped 39,000 from what it
had been only three years before under the old constitution; Negro
registration fell over 125,000. But even this contraction in the
white electorate—the reversal of a century of uninterrupted suffrage expansion—seemed worth the candle if it meant the elimination of a threat to white supremacy.

Under the momentum of these political changes, the southern
states at the turn of the century began to issue a flood of legislation
narrowing the Negro's sphere of activity and carefully defining his

place in southern life. Segregation of the races was decreed on streetcars (only Georgia had such a law in the nineteenth century), in waiting rooms, in hospitals, in housing, in prisons, at drinking fountains, and even in telephone booths (Oklahoma, 1915). Rather than reflecting the mores, as is so often argued in extenuation, these laws tended to create "customs," for no such rigid and petty separation of the races had existed in the South before.

The segregation proposals came as a distinct shock to many Southerners, who were outspoken in their opposition. One South Carolina editor in 1898, voicing his opposition to legally enforced segregation on trains, attempted to ridicule the principle by carrying it out to what he thought was an absurdity. "If there must be Jim Crow cars on the railroads, there should be Jim Crow cars on the street railways," he wrote. "Also on passenger boats . . . if there are to be Jim Crow cars, moreover, there should be Jim Crow waiting saloons at all stations, and Jim Crow eating houses. . . . There should be Jim Crow sections of the jury box, and a separate Jim Crow dock and witness stand in every court—and a Jim Crow Bible for colored witnesses to kiss. It would be advisable also to have a Jim Crow section in county auditors' and treasurers' offices for the accommodation of colored taxpayers." But, as C. Van Woodward has dryly observed, "What he intended as a *reductio ad absurdum* and obviously regarded as an absurdity became in a very short time a reality. . . . All the improbable applications of the principle suggested by the editor in derision had been put into practice—down to and including the Jim Crow Bible."

The southern solution to the problem of the races was to be a caste system for the black man in a society "dedicated to the proposition that all men are created equal."

4. THE SOUTH KNOWS THE NEGRO BEST

The gradual solidification of the Southern Way for the Negro did not take place in a vacuum. The South's erection of a system of caste for its black people was largely possible because of the encouraging attitude of the North. As the fervor of reform died down during the last two decades of the century and more materialistic considerations captured the nation's interest, the North came to accept the South at its own evaluation as the section which best knew the Negro and his capabilities.

How far the North traveled toward the acceptance of a caste

position for the Negro is seen in two interpretations of the Fourteenth Amendment by the Supreme Court in 1883 and 1896. At the time of both decisions, it should be emphasized, the Court was composed almost entirely of northern Republicans. For example, when the Court handed down its decision in the Civil Rights Cases in 1883, only one Democrat—from California—and only two Southerners, both of whom were Republicans, were on the bench. In 1896, when the Court decided *Plessy* v. *Ferguson* on separate but equal railroad facilities, there still were only two Southerners. And, ironically enough, one of them, Justice Harlan of Kentucky, was the sole dissenter, as he had been in the earlier Civil Rights Cases.

The Court made it clear in its 1883 decision that the South would have a free hand in determining the civil rights of Negroes, the provisions of the Fourteenth Amendment notwithstanding. The Civil Rights Act of 1875—the statute at issue before the Court— provided that innkeepers, theater owners, hotel managers, and the like must accord equal treatment to members of all races. The Court held the act unconstitutional on the ground that the Fourteenth Amendment, upon which authority the statute rested, was only a limitation upon state-enforced discrimination and did not empower the federal government to prohibit discrimination on the part of individuals.[10] Though Harlan's biting dissent exposed the narrowly legalistic reasoning of the Court, his voice was a lone one in a nation longing for surcease from moral crusading.

At the end of the century, in the Plessy decision, the Court demonstrated its further willingness to move in step with the South on the question of segregation. The Court ruled that a Louisiana law which required separate railroad cars for the races was no contravention of the protections of the Fourteenth Amendment so long as the facilities for Negroes were equal to those for the whites. Yet the Court had promised, upon the occasion of the Civil Rights

[10] Justice Bradley, in writing the opinion of the Court, gave utterance to the growing northern disillusionment and weariness with the problems of the Negro. After a man has been released from slavery, Bradley said, "there must be a stage in the progress of his elevation when he takes the rank of mere citizen, and ceases to be the special favorite of the laws, and when his rights as a citizen or a man, are to be protected in the ordinary modes by which other men's rights are protected." As Harlan pointed out in his dissent, this argument missed the whole point; it was not that the Negro was asking for more than other men; he was pleading to be treated in the same way as other men, which was all the law presumed to do.

Cases thirteen years before, that any state action looking toward discrimination would fall under the ban of the amendment.

With the 1896 decision, the Court opened the way for the deluge of segregation statutes which soon separated the races in many areas of southern life. As a further indication of the close approximation of northern and southern conceptions of the Negro's place, it should be noted that both of the Court's decisions were viewed in the North as national, as against sectional, approaches to the rights of Negroes.

Only a southern Justice of the Court and a former slaveowner—John Marshall Harlan—saw the betrayal inherent in the decisions. In a ringing affirmation of the constitutional meaning of American freedom and citizenship, he appealed to the spirit as well as the letter of the Fourteenth Amendment. "The white race deems itself to be the dominant race in this country," he observed. "And so it is, in prestige, in achievements, in education, in wealth and in power. . . . But in view of the Constitution, in the eye of the law, there is in this country no superior, ruling class of citizens. There is no caste here. Our Constitution is color blind, and neither knows nor tolerates classes among citizens. . . . The law regards man as man, and takes no account of his surroundings or of his color when his civil rights as guaranteed by the supreme law of the land are involved." He then went on to warn his brethren: "In my opinion, the judgment this day rendered will, in time, prove to be quite as pernicious as the decision made by this tribunal in the Dred Scott case." [11]

By the end of the nineteenth century, molders of public opinion in the North had begun to look at the Negro through southern eyes. "I do not see," commented E. L. Godkin, editor of the liberal weekly, *The Nation*, "how the Negro is ever to be worked into a system of government for which you and I would have much respect." The history of the Negro race "leads to the belief," concluded Professor Albert B. Hart, himself the son of abolitionists, "that he will remain inferior in race stamina and race achievement." President Eliot of Harvard said in 1907 that if the number of

[11] The one major example of northern dissent from the increasingly restrictive view of the Negro's place was the enactment of civil rights statutes in some fifteen northern states during the 1880's and 1890's. This was after the Supreme Court declared the federal Civil Rights Act unconstitutional. These state laws, of course, had no effect in the South, and even in the North they were only rarely invoked and supported.

whites and blacks in Boston was nearly equal, "we might feel like
segregating the one from the other in our own schools. It may be,"
he added, "that as large and generous a work can be done for the
Negro in this way as in mixed schools. . . ."

In 1890, Henry W. Grady, publicist and spokesman for the business-minded New South, journeyed to Boston to deliver his last
great oration. His speech, "The Race Problem in the South," was
a spirited defense of the Southern Way, of the need for the South
to be free to work out its own solution to the Negro question.
"Hardly had he finished," reported the Boston *Herald* in describing the reaction of the predominantly Republican gathering, "when
the audience rose en masse and joined in one great cheer." Boston,
the very cradle and nursery of militant abolitionism, had capitu-
lated to the South at last.

Even Negroes found merit in the southern position. Certainly it
would be false to argue that Booker T. Washington and the
masses of his people who followed his leadership agreed entirely
with the southern conception of the black man's proper place in
American life. But it is equally certain that Washington's view of
the Negro was a limited one, summed up in his celebrated analogy
of the fingers of the hand. "In all that is purely social we" (meaning
whites and Negroes) "can be as separate as the fingers, yet one as
the hand in all things essential to mutual progress." Moreover, the
unprecedented praise which white Southerners heaped upon his
Atlanta Exposition Address of 1895, in which he set forth his conception of the Negro's place, betrays how closely his position coincided with that of the white South. His whole philosophy of race
relations was a retreat from the militant cry for equality and opportunity which had been the outlook of the earlier leader of the
race, Frederick Douglass.

It has often been argued that Washington was being only realistic
when he set forth a limited role for the Negro at that time. Be that
as it may, the fact remains that, though he did not explicitly condone caste, Washington was, by agreeing to work within it, putting
the ultimate stamp of approval upon the southern image of the
Negro.

By the time of the First World War, it appeared that the American solution to the question of the races was strikingly parallel, if
not similar, to that of South Africa. One South African, Maurice
Evans, coming from his homeland to look at the American South,

could only exclaim, "How often the very conditions I had left were reproduced before my eyes, thousands of miles melted away and Africa was before me." It seemed only natural that America, with a similar racial composition and therefore many of the same problems, would travel along the road with South Africa and move ever closer to total separation of the races. But, as we of the mid-twentieth century know, this did not happen; today, as South Africa seems to be hurtling toward racial catastrophe, America edges closer to the ideal of equality and racial tranquillity.

Not until late in the twentieth century—in the 1930's—was there a noticeable reversal of the progressive solidification of a caste place for the Negro. But the reversal did come because many Americans, Northerners and Southerners, never lost sight of the American dream of justice and equality, which the Radicals of Reconstruction had securely fixed in the Constitution itself. Like ceaseless waves beating at a seemingly immutable cliff, these amendments have eaten slowly—sometimes almost imperceptibly—into the structure of social and political inequality which had been built around the Negro in America. Ultimately—and not so far off now, it is safe to predict—these legal instruments forged during Reconstruction will be the means whereby the American urge to equality and justice for all will be translated into reality.

The advent of the Negro as a free man was only a part of the new shape the postwar America was assuming. Material forces of great potency were already at work during the war, and in subsequent years industrialization emerged as one of the molders of a new society. The sources of this new force demand some explanation.

CHAPTER IX

Machines, Men, and Socialism

Sometimes men living through an epoch of great change are so intent upon the immediate problems of their time as to be oblivious to the momentous tides swirling about them. David A. Wells, American economist and publicist, however, was not of this breed. Writing in 1889, he fully recognized that man's control "over the forces of Nature" had progressed so far that man "has been able to do far more work in a given time, produce far more product" per worker, and "reduced the effort necessary to insure a comfortable subsistence in a far greater measure than it was possible for him" to do twenty or thirty years before. Wells, in short, had put his finger on the quintessence of the industrial revolution which followed the Civil War. The years between 1865 and 1914 witnessed one of the great industrial expansions of all time; America emerged from that period the arsenal of two world wars and the prime industrial power of the planet.[1]

In the course of such a movement, however, the United States perforce underwent profound social change. The first to feel the new forces were the people who worked in the factories. The labor unions which they organized grew in importance and power along with industry, and the form they assumed was in many respects a reflection of the American environment in which they developed.

---

[1] The rate of American industrialization was not especially high; the annual rate, for example, was lower than that of either the U.S.S.R. or Canada. But the absolute increase in American production up to 1929 far exceeded that of any of the major industrial powers of the world. Most important of all, of course, is the further fact that the volume of United States production exceeded that of any other country by the opening of the twentieth century.

1. REVOLUTIONARY CHALLENGE

Between 1860 and 1914, the population of the United States tripled, while the number of workers in manufacturing increased five and one half times; the value created by manufacturing rose almost twelve times; and the capital invested in industry multiplied twenty-two times. In 1890, for the first time the value of manufactured goods surpassed that of agricultural commodities, although farm production was then at an all-time high and rising every year. By the turn of the century, the United States was already an industrial nation.

As industry expanded, railroad lines were flung across the nation at a prodigious rate. In the first thirty years of railroad construction, roughly between 1830 and 1860, some 30,000 miles of track had been laid. Within eight years after the surrender of Lee at Appomattox, the trackage was twice what it had been in 1860. By the end of the century, the United States railroad net was greater than that of all Europe: almost 200,000 miles of steel rails binding a continental empire, a people, and a market. Here, too, David Wells spelled out the implications of the new order, observing in 1885 that it cost less than seven tenths of one cent to transport a ton one mile on the average American railroad. "To grasp fully the meaning and significance of these figures," he pointed out, one has merely to realize that a ton of goods "can now be carried on the best managed railways for a distance of a mile, for a sum so small that outside of China it would be difficult to find a coin of equivalent value to give a boy as a reward for carrying an ounce package across a street. . . ."

Fundamental to the revolution in production was geography. Too often the largess of nature within the confines of the territory of the United States is overlooked in accounting for American success as an industrial power. For even the most advanced techniques cannot make up for fuel deficiencies and scarcity of resources. The French lack of good coal resources and the consequent limitation placed upon industrialization is a case in point.

The resources of the United States can only be described in Gargantuan terms: tremendous quantities of all the major minerals needed for industrialization—coal, iron ore, copper, minor metals like zinc and gold and silver, and huge quantities of the newly discovered black gold of oil; agricultural lands of virginal richness,

extending across a continent; an invigorating climate of sufficient
diversity to permit long growing seasons for fiber crops like hemp
and cotton and food crops like sugar; forests providing ample
lumber for a booming industry.

Superimposed on this geographic foundation of plenty was a
framework of political unity which permitted goods to circulate
freely. Once Americans mastered the techniques of rapid transportation and the integration of raw materials with finishing processes, the diversity of the sprawling territory and its resources
would provide new markets and sources of supply unhindered by the
political or linguistic barriers which, for example, hindered a France
in the eighteenth century and a Germany as late as the middle of
the nineteenth century.

But fundamental as geography and resources may have been, in
and of themselves they offer no dynamic explanation for the rapid
industrialization of the postwar years. The resources had lain un-
used for centuries and the climate was unchanged for millennia,
while a people of a nonindustrial culture—the Indians—occupied
the territory. Americans themselves, for that matter, had lived in
parts of the country for upward of two centuries before they
brought to life the bounty of nature buried beneath the soil. The
explanation for the new quickening of industrial activity is not
to be found in the raw materials; it must be looked for in the history of the people.

The War for the Union provided a good part of the impetus to
industrial expansion. That conflict not only permitted capital accumulation, through fraud—as with Vanderbilt's shipping deals—
and service, but it created government markets for basic industries
like iron, munitions, food, clothing, shoes, and transportation. The
war contractor became a well-known figure in Washington as firms
vied with one another for government orders. As in later wars, the
spending of the citizen's money by the government had a more immediate and far-reaching effect than when the citizen was left on
his own to spend or not as he chose. Federal expenditures ran
around $65 million annually in the years immediately before 1860;
during the war, they reached a high of $1,296.8 million in 1865;
by 1870, the figure stabilized around $300 million.

We have already seen how the war provided an opportunity for
the passage of legislation favorable to northern business—measures
like banking and currency stabilization, the protective tariff, aid

to the building of a transcontinental railroad, and others. With the cessation of hostilities, support for certain types of business enterprises continued to be offered by the federal government, the most outstanding example being the aid given to railroad construction. Though governmental contributions to internal improvements were certainly not novel in America, never before were they made on such a lavish scale as after 1860.

The federal and state governments, not to mention the municipalities scattered throughout the country, all seemed to feel, if one can judge from their actions, that to aid in the construction of railroads was to participate in the destiny of America. The governmental contributions were enormous for a nation where good government had often been equated with frugality. Cash loans totaling over $150 million were made to railroads by the federal, state, and local governments. In addition, a number of states and cities granted tax exemptions to railroad companies as an encouragement to construction—a concession, incidentally, which brought savings of at least $12.6 million to the railroads. State and local governments purchased at par almost $149 million worth of railroad securities, which, it has been conservatively estimated, returned the railroads about $50 million more than they could have realized from the sale of the securities to private purchasers. Foremost among the aids of government were the 134 million acres of public lands granted to some seventy railroads by the federal government and the 48.9 million acres granted by nine states. These gifts of land, if brought together, would comprise an area larger than the United Kingdom, Spain, and Belgium combined. Depending on how one estimates the value of these lands, the railroads received between $130 million and $500 million as an outright gift.

Beyond a doubt, the aid from the community in the construction of the railroads was substantial, but one can overemphasize its effect on total railroad building. For instance, the trackage of the roads receiving the federal grants of land comprised only about 8 per cent of the total in the country. Furthermore, after 1871 the policy of land grants, begun as far back as 1850, was discontinued. Even a transcontinental railroad like the Great Northern was constructed without any federal land grants, and many another, though less ambitious, railroad in the later years of the century could say as much.

Nor should it be casually supposed that land grants and other aids from government were necessarily fraudulently acquired or even socially undesirable. For one thing, there was a *quid pro quo:* the railroads furnished the government with transportation at reduced rates. Furthermore, the loans which the government made were almost completely repaid, with interest, although, it must be added, not until the federal government went to court. From a social standpoint there was a sound basis for the assistance. A substantial part of the lands granted to the railroads acquired worth only because the railroads built through to them; by rendering the lands accessible to settlers, the railroads largely created their value.[2] Though this point can be exaggerated, it carries especial weight in regard to those trans-Mississippi states and territories where transportation of bulk items was almost wholly dependent upon the railroad.

A recognition of such facts, however, should not obscure the important point that the aids of government were indispensable to the construction of many, if not most, of the western roads. It is inconceivable, that canny private investors, particularly in the first decades of the railroad age, would have put their money into rails running through dry and empty plains, obviously bare of both freights and markets. But such prudent men would take a different attitude if their investments were guaranteed, as they often were, by state or local governments or supported by federal land grants and loans.

In the end, though, the part which government played in the powerful thrust of industrialization after 1860 cannot be accurately measured or accounted for in dollars, acres of land, or legislative enactments. There was also something much more subtle. It was the warm, reassuring attitude of sympathy in which government in America bathed business enterprise. Such a friendly atmosphere was eminently conducive to investment and entrepreneurship, and was probably worth as much as all the gifts and laws put together. The degree of government beneficence displayed toward business is measured by the outright hostility and suspicion displayed toward labor. Recall, for example, the massive federal intervention in the

[2] In actuality, of course, the government "gave" nothing when it made land grants. It was the homesteader who bought land from the railroads who made the contribution to railroad construction. Generally, he paid a higher price when he bought from a railroad than he would have had the land been purchased from the federal government.

great railroad strike of 1877, and in the labor troubles at Coeur d'Alene and Pullman and Chicago later in the century. Remember too the notorious use made by the federal courts of the Sherman Antitrust Act to hamstring labor organization—what John Peter Altgeld was to call "government by injunction." [3] Economic historian Joseph Schumpeter has argued that capitalistic enterprising is a delicate flower, easily discouraged and impeded by governmental threats and interference. If this be so, then the late nineteenth century in America was a veritable hothouse for such flora.

This rapid and successful expansion of the industrial machine was also encouraged by the great influx of immigrants in the postwar era. Before the war, the annual immigration was measured in thousands; in the years after, it was often counted in millions. In the decade of the eighties, for example, over five million newcomers entered the United States, becoming eager workers and avid customers of American business. In any balance sheet of the nation's industrial assets, the manpower of these strangers to America must be included.

But this second wave of industrial expansion in American history was a product of things as well as of people. The hundreds of inventions of the period were, in some cases, of fundamental importance to the expansion of industry: the Bessemer process in steel, for instance, which made this versatile metal usable on a wide scale for the first time; the Siemens-Martin process, which permitted even poor ores to be converted into steel; refrigeration, which laid the foundation for a nationwide meat-packing industry; the telephone, the electric lamp, the internal combustion engine, and so on. A catalogue of major inventions of the period would almost be a list of the great industries which sprang up in the new age. And along with such spectacular inventions went numerous improvements, adaptations, minor gadgets, like the typewriter, which, by being widely adopted, allowed the machine to sink deep into the everyday life of Americans.

[3] At the time of the coal strike of 1902, President Theodore Roosevelt learned how dependent the business leaders had become upon governmental defense of their interests. In a letter to a friend, T. R. told how the coal operators with whom he had been mediating refused to deal with the union and even "in at least two cases assumed an attitude toward me which was one of insolence. . . . One of them demanded outright and several of them hinted that they were going to demand that I use the United States Army in their interests. . . . They kept referring to Cleveland's course in the Debs' riots as offering a parallel, which was of course either ridiculous or dishonest on their part. . . ."

The machine has always been welcome in America; [4] indeed it is almost a symbol of American industry. Europeans frequently poke fun at the American's preoccupation with gadgets, contraptions, and machines; they even imply it reveals our lack of human concern. But there is historical reason behind the American's machine-mindedness. As a country chronically short of labor, America has generally welcomed machines because it has needed them; where labor costs are high, employers readily turn to machines in order to save on their wage bills. This willingness to use machines is, in turn, closely related to the high standard of living in America. Machines spelled high productivity of labor, and the key to any rising standard of living is increased production per worker. The wider the acceptance of the machine, the greater the possibility of a rising wage for the individual worker.

The American addiction to the machine was apparent to foreign observers fifty years ago. In the fall of 1902, Alfred Mosley, an enterprising English businessman, succeeded in bringing the secretaries of twenty-three major British trade unions to the United States for the purpose of studying the "secret" of American productivity. The reports of these delegates from the trade unions are suffused with admiration for the advantages machines afforded the American as compared with the British worker. "The number of labour-saving appliances in use for almost everything is perfectly astounding," said G. D. Kelley of the Lithographers. "American employers believe that machines rather than men or women ought to be driven," concluded T. A. Flynn of the Tailors, "and the clever workman who, by invention or suggestion, enables his employer to carry out this ideal is encouraged in a manner delightfully real and sincere."

The close connection between this interest in machinery and an improving status for the worker was clearly seen by W. C. Steadman. "The American workers do not work any harder than their English brethren," he observed, "the tendency being to use improved machinery of the latest type, and should a new machine be put in today and a better one come out tomorrow that will turn out more work it will be put on one side for the latest and the best, no mat-

[4] In 1789 the rector of the Swedish Churches in Pennsylvania told the American Philosophical Society: "Machines for abridging human labour are especially desired in America as there can be no competition between them and the arms of industrious labour, while these have full employ on her extensive land; which must be the case for ages."

ter what the cost." This is in contrast with the situation in England, he noted, where we "use machinery to decrease wages, in America it means more wages and shorter hours, and workmen are encouraged by their employers" to make suggestions and improvements. Another delegate, after contrasting American employers' readiness to adopt new machinery with the English employers' continued use of obsolete machines, went on to say: "I don't pretend to think that the American employer loves his workmen more than does the British employer, but he recognizes" that up-to-date machinery "pays, while the other does not."

Though Americans were interested in using machines, they did not always have to invent them; many basic inventions, like the Bessemer and Siemens-Martin steel processes and the internal combustion engine, were of European origin. This fact serves to remind us that American industrialization, coming late in the century, enjoyed the signal advantage of being able to tap the accumulated industrial and technological experience of the European nations, particularly England's.

European assistance to American industrialization amounted to more than technology. An underdeveloped country at that time, the United States had access to the accumulated capital of the whole western world, and the movement of European capital into America was substantial. By the conclusion of the nineteenth century, $3.4 billion of European capital was tucked away in American enterprises. When the First World War broke out, American industry had absorbed over $7 billion of the Old World's capital. Thanks to the international tranquillity of the nineteenth century and the marvelous interchangeability afforded by the gold standard, American industry experienced a minimum of difficulty in borrowing the savings of the hard-working Victorian bourgeoisie. At any other time in history (for that golden age of peace and free exchange was of relatively brief duration), the process of American industrialization would have been more like the strenuous capital accumulation of the Russians and the Indians in the twentieth century. The advantages which accrued from the ability to tap other people's savings are graphically demonstrated in a comparison of national savings. It has been estimated that Americans saved between 11 and 14 per cent of their national income as against probably well over 20 per cent saved by the British during their rise to eminence. It is believed that Soviet Russia has been

compelled to set aside more than 20 per cent of the national income
in order to finance her industrialization. Americans, it would appear, had it considerably easier than other countries.

When one has set down all the possible factors which might account for this surge of industrialization, there still seem to be some
missing ingredients. One of importance is the very spirit of the
people themselves. What made them work; what made them strive
for wealth, status, improvement? For certainly these qualities are
as necessary as mineral wealth or salubrious climate. Was it the
Puritan past, the remarkable mobility of American society, which
offered incentive to all, the unexampled opportunities for the industrious, the speculative streak which ran through all Americans
ever since Columbus took a chance? It would be hard to say, but
certainly they all aided in sparking that drive for work and activity
which then, as now, is the trade mark of the American. Also among
the people were the entrepreneurs—not merely the capitalists who
supplied the money, but those men who possessed a genius for industrial production and who, by throwing together the resources of
a nation, the labor of millions, and the capital of the western world,
built American industry.

Who were these entrepreneurs; what made them tick; how was it
that they so dominated the American economy during those years?
This is neither the place nor yet the time to answer such important questions, since historians have only just begun to explore the
question of the crucial role of the entrepreneur in economic growth.
We can do little more than set forth some of the less controversial or obvious features of the entrepreneurs who dominated late-
nineteenth-century America.

Some time ago, in an investigation of major industrial leaders
like Rockefeller, Vanderbilt, Guggenheim, Armour, Carnegie, and
others, Charles A. Beard attempted to generalize about the social
origins of the entrepreneurs. As a class he found them coming from
the lower strata of society, sons of farmers, generally rather poorly
educated, and often foreign-born, as in the case of Carnegie. As a
group, he thought the giants were representative of a new class of
men come to economic power in America.

More recent investigations, however, using a broader sampling,
have arrived at a much different picture. Whether one looks at a
sample of fifty-one railroad presidents, as Thomas Cochran did, or
at the successful businessmen who appear in the *Dictionary of*

American Biography, as C. Wright Mills did, the conclusion is inescapable that these industrial leaders were not men who came up from the bottom. The level of education, for example, which they attained was far above that of most people of their day. Over 50 per cent of those born between 1820 and 1879 attended college in an age when high school was still the exception for most Americans.

In another study William Miller found that 70 per cent of those born between 1850 and 1879 came from upper- or upper-middle-class families. Moreover, as against Beard's findings, almost 48 per cent of them had fathers who had been businessmen, and only 21.5 per cent came from farm families. Something like 90 per cent of these men were native-born. The conclusions of a study of three hundred executives of important firms in the 1870's can serve as a summation of all these investigations. The authors found that the typical entrepreneur was "American by birth, of a New England father, English in national origin, Congregational, Presbyterian or Episcopalian in religion, urban in early environment," and "born and bred in an atmosphere in which business and a relatively high social standing were intimately associated with his family life. Only at eighteen did he take his first regular job, prepared to rise from it, moreover, not by rigorous apprenticeship begun when he was virtually a child, but by an academic education well above average for the times." In short, the men who were getting to the top, even in the 1870's—that alleged era of self-made men—had not been poor farm boys or uneducated immigrant lads starting at the bottom, but instead men who had been given rather exceptional opportunities to make the race to the top.[5]

When, however, we turn from the social origins of these men to their personality traits, generalization is much less easy, even if one confines himself to the best-known leaders. Vanderbilt may have been ruthless and gruff, uneducated and uncultured, but Carnegie was

[5] The social origins of the top business leaders of today seem to be about the same, according to Mabel Newcomer, *The Big Business Executive, the Factors That Made Him, 1900–1950* (New York, 1955), p. 149. "The typical executive of 1950," Miss Newcomer concludes, "is a native American, the son of a small, independent business man. His family's income was moderate. . . . His parents managed to put him through college, with such contributions as he himself made to his own expenses through part-time employment, mostly in summer." She notes that a college education is, in some ways, a better way to the top than inherited wealth. And because college education is so accessible, the opportunities for a poor boy's reaching the upper levels of business leadership seem to be greater now than fifty years ago.

subtle and articulate; Rockefeller was taciturn but commanding, quiet but implacable. The common factor eludes us.

One characteristic which does stand out as almost universal is their passion for their work. In a study of forty-three careers of well-known captains of business, Chester Destler discovered that only two of them actually retired in order to rest; the others either never retired or had to be compelled to for one reason or another. Numerous stories of their application to their job come to mind; some are almost noble, many are close to being sordid, but all demonstrate that the job was the thing. Rockefeller's attention to detail was legendary; at one point he indignantly inquired of a subordinate where a few hundred missing bungs from the oil barrels were, for he had detected a discrepancy in the routine accounts. At another time he painstakingly revised the number of drops of solder used in sealing oil cans in order to save the expenditure of a single extra drop. More human perhaps is the picture of J. J. Hill, the railroad magnate of the Great Northern, getting down from his train one bitter Minnesota winter's night to help his men shovel snow from the tracks.

The strike for the main chance is common among the life histories of the giants; often it appears early in their careers. William A. Clark, for example, later of the copper trust, plunged into the wilds of Montana with a load of tobacco, confident that he could sell the weed at monopoly prices to the miners there. Collis P. Huntington, subsequently of Central Pacific fame, built up his San Francisco grocery business by beating his competitors out into the Bay to meet the supply ships from the East.

Though lust for wealth was a part of the thinking and most likely the mainspring of all great entrepreneurs, one would be settling for half a man if he thought that this was all there was to them. To work so hard and so unflaggingly as they did for an additional million or two after the million mark had long been passed is not explicable in terms of simple greed. Instead, Rockefeller's urge to bring order out of chaos in the oil industry, Harriman's dream to encircle the world with his rail and steamship lines, or Ford's ambition to produce a cheaper and better automobile than anyone else suggests that a mechanism more human than profit was driving them. These men were looking for adventure, for challenge; they were men playing "the Great Game," as Allan Nevins has called it. Perhaps for the latter portion of the nineteenth century this was the equivalent of war for which William James was seeking. Though it was hardly "moral," as James hoped it would be, it was still peaceful, invigorating, and undeniably productive.

Diverse as these men may have been in personality, there can be little question as to the means which they employed. Of forty-three noted leaders of business whom Chester Destler studied, thirty-six used monopoly or near monopoly to gain their ends. Thirteen used political corruption, sixteen of them mulcted their own companies for their personal advantage, and twenty-three charged exorbitant rates if the traffic would bear it. There is no way of knowing to what extent this example was followed by lesser-known entrepreneurs, but there seems no reason to believe they were significantly more scrupulous about methods.

It is one thing to note how the entrepreneurs built their empires; it is another to make an ethical judgment on their practices. Most recently, the so-called Robber Barons have come in for more spirited defense than at any time since the days of William Graham Sumner.[6] But to defend the methods of these leaders on the ground that the job was done, as some historians have, is to be guilty of justifying the ends by the means. But to go even further, as Allan Nevins has, to justify them and their methods on the ground that the industrial power they built enabled the United States to win two world wars is to commit the more grievous crime of excusing men in the name of consequences they never intended. Such a procedure drains the whole matter of any moral content. Furthermore, to plead the extenuation of the climate of business ethics of the time, as still others have done, is to lose sight of the fact that there were, after all, many men who, objecting to the ruthless claw-and-fang tactics of the titans, were quick to point out the undesirable aspects of it. Besides, were not the workers who objected to the low wages and antiunion tactics of the great combines a part of the climate of opinion? All of which suggests that perhaps the question cannot be answered in purely moral terms.

The most we can say is that the industrial machine was built and that the social and human cost was high. But then perhaps we must also ask ourselves whether any nation has transformed its way of

[6] *The Saturday Review*, February 6, 1954, carried a lively debate on the subject of the Robber Barons between the man who popularized the term—Matthew Josephson—and Allan Nevins, who has been foremost in defense of the gentlemen in question.

life at any time in history without exacting a frightful human toll. Compared with the social costs in the England of the nineteenth century and the Russia of the 1920's and 1930's, the American industrial revolution was cheaply done.

2. THE INDUSTRIAL LEVIATHAN

To many Americans who lived through the era of the trusts, it seemed as if industrialization was synonymous with what Louis Brandeis stigmatized as "Bigness." For at the same time that industrialists pushed for a free, highly competitive economy in conformity with the most theoretical postulates of capitalist economics, in their daily work they were busily engaged in building ever larger, oligopolistic industrial empires. This consolidation of small units of production into larger ones, this concentration of control in business, has manifested itself wherever the factory has taken root: in newly emergent Japan with the Zaibatsu, in Imperial Germany with the cartels, in rising America with the "trusts," and in the older industrial nations like France and Britain. The forms of such concentration have varied widely, from actual mergers to mere loose agreements to divide the market, as in pools and cartels. But the purpose behind them has always been the same—the control of the market and the elimination of competition. Here was the paradox, for only with competition was industrial capitalism able to function as it was expected to—as both a producer of the maximum amount of goods and a system of fair distribution. When industrial capitalism forsook competition, it soon failed to fulfill its promise as a system of production and distribution. When that happened, political attacks upon the system were not far away.

One of the great consolidation movements of American industry took place in the 1890's and the early years of the twentieth century—the era of the Sugar Trust, the Beef Trust, the Steel Trust, the Oil Trust, and the Money Trust. Symbolic of the era is the United States Steel Corporation, organized in 1901 as the first billion-dollar corporation in history. At the moment of its creation, this fusion of some 200 companies in the steel and iron business controlled 60 per cent of the production in the whole industry. So effective was its control that the price of steel rails in the country was stabilized for over a decade at $28 a ton.

During the latter half of the nineteenth century, a number of other industries provided examples of consolidation. In the cotton goods industry, for example, between 1850 and 1905 the number of factories remained substantially the same, but the value of the production per establishment rose over 600 per cent. The agricultural machinery industry underwent an even more dramatic concentration; over half of the companies disappeared from independent production at the same time that the value of output of each of the remaining establishments increased almost 3,300 per cent! Examples not quite as eye-catching, but equally as indicative of the spread of concentration, could be named for other major industries of the country. Even a relatively new industry like electrical machinery manufacturing showed a 400 per cent increase in production per establishment in the course of the twenty-five years before 1905.

The same tendency was observable in railroading. In 1910, 67 per cent of the total trackage in the United States was owned by only fifty-four giant companies, each of which had over 1,000 miles of track. The prime individual example of railroad consolidation was that afforded by Edward Harriman. Obsessed with the idea of dominating the railroads of the country, he succeeded, by the time of his death in 1909, in building an empire of rails which extended from the west to the east coasts, from the North to the South; only death deprived him of Manchurian lines that he hoped to link with his American roads through Pacific steamboat routes which he also owned. His best-known effort at cornering the railroads of the country was made in conjunction with J. J. Hill, when they created the Northern Securities Company, a holding company controlling almost all the railroads west of the Mississippi. This affront to competition, however, was dissolved by order of the Supreme Court in 1904.

Consolidation of enterprises was only one sign of the maturing character of the American economy; the growth of investment banking was another, and, like consolidation, it tended to attenuate competition. As Werner Sombart has pointed out in regard to European capitalism, the advent of the investment banker signalizes the last stage of a maturing capitalism. Only after a long period of capital accumulation, and at a time when the size of individual firms has grown beyond the resources of self-financing, does the financier assume a crucial importance in the economy.

By the 1880's and 1890's the investment banker, with pools of capital at his disposal, was in ever-mounting demand from railroads requiring financial reorganization and from firms buying up competitors or marketing large security issues. It was then that the House of Morgan began to acquire its world-wide renown, attaining an almost mythical eminence as a symbol of financial power. Morgan successfully managed the reorganization of several important railroads, notably the Southern, in the late nineties, as well as gathering the necessary capital for the creation of the mammoth U.S. Steel Corporation in 1901. In the Panic of 1893, J. P. Morgan enjoyed the unexampled prestige of being appealed to by the President of the United States for assistance in saving the credit of the government itself.

The central position of the banker in the economy was officially recognized in 1912 with the appointment of the Pujo Committee of the United States House of Representatives for the investigation of what was popularly known as the Money Trust. The committee found that a small group of financiers, numbering Morgan of New York and London, and Kidder, Peabody of Boston, among them, "have . . . been more destructive of competition than anything accomplished by the trusts. . . ." By controlling the credit and capital supply in the nation, these bankers, the committee report went on, "strike at the very vitals of potential competition in every industry that is under their protection," and if they are permitted to continue, they "will render impossible all attempts to restore normal competitive conditions in the industrial world. . . ."

The Pujo Committee reported that the House of Morgan and its affiliated banks—the First National and the National City—held 341 directorships in 112 corporations having aggregate resources of over $22 billion. Such concentration of control and power, though neither complete nor absolute, was, nevertheless, highly suggestive of the distance the American economy had moved from the economist's ideal of perfect competition. Certainly, only halfhearted competition could be expected among firms each having members of the same banking house sitting on the boards of directors. In this and other ways it was clear that the penetration of finance into industry was muting competition in America.[7]

Industrial concentration, no matter whether it took the subtle forms of finance or the ruthless form of driving a competitor to the

---

[7] Nor has the problem ended in our own time. In 1951–53 the federal government presented a five-million-word case against the leading investment houses of the country, charging a conspiracy among them to restrain competition. The case was dismissed, however, in September, 1953, as unproved.

wall, presented a challenge to society; such aggregations of wealth and economic power in relatively few hands could be dangerous as well as beneficent. Just as the essence of the art of politics is balancing freedom with authority, so in an advanced capitalist state the essential economic problem is balancing efficiency and maximum production against protection for the consumer. Once competition is forsaken in pursuit of the economic advantages of great combinations, the built-in protections of theoretical capitalism cease to be operative. It is therefore necessary to work out institutions of control which will protect society but at the same time not shackle the enormous productive power and efficiency which seem to be inherent in concentration. The social need for some control over the concentration of economic power became so glaring and insistent by the end of the 1880's that all the major political parties in the country included antitrust planks of one sort or another in their platforms. For as Henry Demarest Lloyd summed it up in 1884: "If the tendency to combination is irresistible, control of it is imperative."

The American people in the years before 1914 arrived at two different solutions to the question of industrial concentration, both of which are still operative today. The first one is symbolized by the Interstate Commerce Commission, created in 1887 as an answer to the economic power of the railroads. In the railroad-building era after the Civil War, towns and shippers had vied to attract the revolutionary iron horse to their locality only to find that it was a genie which could destroy them. Often in a monopoly position, the railroads did not hesitate to use their power. Higher rates for a short haul than for a long one were common; under-the-counter refunds for one shipper and not for another were frequently used as devices to reward the big shipper. Setting rates as high as the traffic would bear was virtually standard procedure for any railroad worth its salt.

Though protests against such cavalier treatment of the consumer and shippers had been heard as early as the 1870's, no satisfactory answer to the problem was worked out until the Interstate Commerce Act of 1887, an act which signaled a significant departure from the laissez-faire ideals of the day. Ordinarily, in accordance with the textbooks on classical economics, Americans had relied upon competition as the regulator of prices and the restraint on monopoly. The railroad, however, was not easily or generally amenable to such control. It was not feasible, for example, to build competing roads when the traffic was limited. Besides, the initial cost of a railroad was so tremendous as to be a major obstacle to the free entry of competitors into the industry.

In view of such theoretical considerations and the more practical one of actual injustice to the consumers, the federal government revived an old mercantilistic practice—that is, a regulatory body which would undertake continuous supervision of the industry. This was the Interstate Commerce Commission. It is true that for two decades after its creation the Commission was almost totally ineffective in regulating rates or anything else about railroading, but the new principle had been set forth; in time the powers were forthcoming in profusion. The Interstate Commerce Act of 1887, therefore, marks the beginning of the federal government's interference in the operation of the capitalist economy through the agency of the now familiar regulatory commission.

The second device which Americans brought to bear upon the irresponsible power of industrial concentration was not only novel but unique when compared with the experience of other industrial countries.[8] The philosophy behind the Sherman Antitrust Act of 1890 was that the federal government should act to re-establish and preserve competition throughout the economy. This was to be done by the issuance of dissolution orders and, after the passage of the Clayton Act in 1914, through punitive and criminal penalties.[9] To this day—as the daily newspaper with its accounts of antitrust suits reveals—the primary means for controlling industrial concentration and monopoly in America resides in the antitrust statutes. Such an approach is uniquely American, since no other industrial country has put prohibitions against interference with competition into statutory law. "The Sherman and Clayton Acts," Franklin Roosevelt observed in 1944, "have become as much a part of the American way of life as the due process clause of the Constitution."

3. THE RECONSTRUCTION THAT TOOK

Although the industrialization of the United States after 1865

[8] *The New York Times,* July 5, 1957, reported that the lower house of the Parliament of West Germany approved on July 4 a new anticartel law, which, in effect, would be the first antitrust law in Germany.

[9] Not until the passage of the Federal Trade Commission Act of 1914 was the principle of the regulatory commission—first applied to railroads in 1887—made applicable to industrial combines, and then only in a tangential manner.

is usually taken to be a northern phenomenon, in reality it was nationwide, affecting even the agrarian South. In ante-bellum days, the intellectual and economic leaders of the South had repeatedly called for a union of mill and cotton on the soil of Dixie. But it was only when the old plantation-slave system lay shattered that the South turned to manufacturing with anything more than the most preoccupied interest. The industrial movement received the blessing of the rising leaders of the New South—men like Henry Grady of Georgia, "Marse Henry" Watterson of Kentucky, General Bullock of Georgia, and Daniel Tompkins of North Carolina who saw the future of the South intimately linked with the triumphant business interests of the North. Why shouldn't the South, they reasoned, have industries protected by tariffs and railroads built by government subsidies; why shouldn't the South overcome its agrarian weakness by girding itself in the iron power of industry as the North had done? Eagerly the ordinary folk of the South followed their new leaders. Many a small back-country cotton mill in the 1880's acquired its initial capital from numerous small contributions of the plain people desirous of setting up a new industry in their depleted farming region. Moreover, poor hill farmers and their wives and children were only too ready to supply the muscle necessary to man the machines of the new dispensation.

In the early years of the twentieth century, the cotton manufacturers of the North could not fail to see the handwriting on the wall; the South was the coming center of cotton milling. New England may have won the war, but it lost the economic struggle. In 1915, fully 60 per cent of cotton manufacturing in the United States was carried on in the South. By that time many a northern mill was moving south, drawn by the region's special advantages: proximity to the raw material, cheap, unorganized labor (primarily white because Negroes were employed in the mills only as menials), ample coal for power, and a mild climate which saved on fuel bills.

But the South was compelled to pay a price for this ascendancy in cotton manufacture. The southern mill town, set down in a rural locale, was really a miniature manorial estate, in which the workers were not only beholden to the company for their jobs, but for the roof over their heads, the food on the table, the recreation of their off hours. Unlike in the North, where towns and cities were usually the mill sites, the southern mills created the towns, leaving no area of independence for the individualistic farmers who became the new factory hands.

Often the whole family became enmeshed in the system: where father's earnings were not sufficient, mother would enter the factory along with the children. It was not unusual for half the working force in mills before 1900 to be made up of women, and in some mills children comprised a quarter of the employees. Working and sanitary conditions in the southern mills were as bad as they have been traditionally everywhere at the beginning of an industrial revolution. The sweatshops of the North, so abominated in southern literature and propaganda before the war, had now come to the land of Dixie.

Though cotton milling was the most dramatic example of the increasing tempo of industrialization in the South, it was not the only one. Steel and iron manufacture and coal mining became major industries in the middle and lower South during the years before the First World War. The opening up of the tremendous oil reserves of Texas at the turn of the century signaled the beginning of the industrialization which has transformed the state in recent years. Sulphur and other chemical production expanded in Louisiana, and lumbering flourished in virtually all of the forested southern states. Though always centered in the South, tobacco manufacturing shot forward after 1865, especially as the cigarette became increasingly popular.

By the time the First World War broke out in Europe, the American South had been "northernized" to a degree only hoped for by the most ambitious of Reconstructionists. Moreover, this was permanent change, for the northern industrial way had been voluntarily accepted by the South. As Tom Sawyer knew, such an internally motivated conversion is the most efficacious kind.

Actually, of course, this was no more than a beginning. The introduction of the factory barely penetrated the surface of southern life; for the great majority of the people, both black and white, the land and the seasons were still the center of their lives as they had been for their fathers. But for the future, the industrializing of the South was a portent; it signified the beginning of the integration of the South into the nation. The decisive break with the agrarian tradition had been made; the re-creation of the South in the image of the North was begun. With the factory came the city, both of them slowly remolding the rural South as they have been remaking

American civilization in general. Today, for the first time since the South began to drift apart from the rest of the nation, these new social forces are pulling that region once again into the main current of American life.[10]

4. DOLLARS MEAN SUCCESS

The spread of the factory throughout the land lent further credence to the old belief that in America opportunities were almost unlimited and that material success was a sign of virtue. Indeed, for someone like Horatio Alger, Jr., the virtues of money-making were already assumed, and he exulted in the wide opportunity for success. "In this country, fortunately," he wrote, "there are few places where an industrious man cannot get a living, if he is willing to accept such work as falls his way. This willingness often turns the scale and converts threatening ruin into prosperity and success." Andrew Carnegie, of course, was one of the most articulate preachers of the cult of success of the period, as well as its most widely known exemplar. It was John D. Rockefeller's opinion that no matter how poor some persons might be, they possessed "infinite possibilities. They have but to master the knack of economy, thrift, and perseverance and success is theirs."

Though Americans since at least the days of Benjamin Franklin had talked of how to get ahead in a world organized around money-making, it was not until the industrial age that the teaching of the secrets of material success became a thriving business itself. The publication of handbooks in the art of success became very popular; of the success books printed before 1900, four fifths of them appeared after 1865, and 80 per cent of them were published in the northeastern section of the country, where industry and commerce— and the opportunities for success—were centered.[11]

[10] As recently as 1880, only 12.7 per cent of the cities in the nation were located in the South; in 1950, over 28 per cent of urban communities were to be found there. The impact of urbanization on a controversial problem like desegregation, for instance, can hardly be exaggerated.

[11] As was to be expected, a variety of the Horatio Alger myth—work-hard-and-you-will-be-successful—ultimately filtered into juvenile literature, too. The effort in 1955–56 to unearth the true author of the famous story *The Little Engine That Could*, as reported in *The New York Times Book Review*, April 8, 1956, turned up the fact that the tale was an oral tradition of the 1880's and 1890's before it actually appeared in print. This would place it in the center of the success-story era. The fable teaches the moral that if one tries hard enough, success in any endeavor is thereby assured.

The popularizing of the "bitch goddess success," as William James caustically phrased it, was the job of others besides publicists and businessmen. Clergymen, particularly Protestants, were prominent in the prescribing of the proper avenues for the attainment of earthly rewards. Their recipes usually included a heavy dose of conventional morality and "right" living. Russell Conwell, of "Acres of Diamonds" fame, was a Baptist minister; Lyman Abbott, who followed Henry Ward Beecher in the pulpit of Brooklyn's Plymouth Church, published *How to Succeed* in 1882. The founder of the Christian Endeavor Society, Francis E. Clark, was a Congregational minister and the author of two self-help books, one published in 1884 and another in 1885. The ultimate in what one writer has called "the partnership between God and Mammon" must have been reached when Episcopal Bishop Lawrence concluded, "Godliness is in league with riches."

In hard fact, of course, the road to success in industrial America was not an easy one—as the social origins of the entrepreneurs rather convincingly inform us. But limited as the opportunities were, they were there; after all, a minority of the entrepreneurs *were* from farm homes and 10 per cent of them *had* been immigrants. Certainly Europeans were impressed by the opportunities for advancement available to the average citizen and worker in America. All but one of the twenty-three British workers who came to the United States in 1902 with the Mosely Industrial Commission felt that the opportunities to rise in Britian were inferior to those in this country. As Mr. Cox of the Steel Workers Union put it, "If I were just starting life . . . with my present knowledge, I would go to America." "The road to comparative wealth" in America, added Mr. Flynn of the Tailors, "is more easy to find, and the possibilities it leads to are boundless." The American social escalator was not infallible, but it was apparently working well enough for the world to believe in it.

This worship of success, this striving for wealth and position, so typical of the period, left its mark upon Americans. Insofar as it taught that all men could succeed, it served to enhance the American belief in social equality and actually assisted in maintaining the open society. By extolling hard work, the Alger myth made all labor honorable and undermined any lingering aristocratic snobbery about the degrading character of honest labor. But on the other hand, such worship of success reinforced the sometimes crude materialism which has been a part of the American character since colonial times.

In yet another way the cult of success affected subsequent American history. One of the ingredients of the cult has been the image of the businessman as an enemy of privilege and a friend of the common man.[12] The high degree of acceptance which this idea received from Americans in general is to be measured in the failure of the anti-business protest movements of the era, like Greenbackism, Populism, and Socialism, to name only the most prominent ones. The interests of the business community have been so closely identified with the cult of success that popular disenchantment with the singular virtue of the businessman has usually been of short duration. Brief periods of popular distrust of business leadership, such as during the Progressive and the New Deal eras, have been preceded and followed by long periods of adulation.

Indeed, in our time, it is clear that that part of the American Dream which promises success to every poor, hard-working, frugal American boy still lives. Each year, for the last dozen or so, the Horatio Alger Award has been solemnly presented to business leaders who have made the long stride from rags to riches, and paperback reprints of Horatio Alger's stories may once again be purchased by the upward-looking masses.

5. THE WORKERS' RESPONSE

To say that the labor movement was affected by the industrialization of the postwar years is an understatement; the fact is, industrial capitalism created the labor movement. Not deliberately, to be sure, but in the same way that a blister is the consequence of a rubbing shoe. Unions were labor's protection against the forces of industrialization as the blister is the body's against the irritation of the shoe. The factory and all it implied confronted the workingman with a challenge to his existence as a man, and the worker's response was the labor union.

There were labor unions in America before 1865, but, as industry was only emerging in those years, so the organizations of workers

---

[12] The popular image of the businessman, as reflected in folklore, however, has never been a favorable one. But then, in middle-class America, the makers of folklore are not the dominant class. Kenneth Porter, in an article "The Business Man in American Folklore," asks, "Whoever heard of the really *good* business man in American folklore, other than in Jim Fisk's Robin-Hood role?"

were correspondingly weak. In the course of the years after Appomattox, however, when industry began to hit a new and giant stride,
the tempo of unionization also stepped up. It was in these decades,
after many years of false starts and utopian ambitions, that the
American labor movement assumed its modern shape.

Perhaps the outstanding and enduring characteristic of organized
labor in the United States has been its elemental conservatism,
the fantasies of some employers to the contrary notwithstanding.
Indeed, it might be said that all labor unions, at bottom, are conservative by virtue of their being essentially reactions against a
developing capitalism. Though an established capitalist society
views itself as anything but subversive, in the days of its becoming
and seen against the perspective of the previous age, capitalism as
an ideology is radically subversive, undermining and destroying
many of the cherished institutions of the functioning society. This
dissolving process of capitalism is seen more clearly in Europe than
in America because there the time span is greater. But, as will
appear later, organized labor in the United States was as much a
conservative response to the challenge of capitalism as was the
European trade union movement.

Viewed very broadly, the history of modern capitalism might be
summarized as the freeing of the three factors of production—land,
labor, and capital—from the web of tradition in which medieval
society held them. If capitalism was to function, it was necessary
that this liberating process take place. Only when these basic factors
are free to be bought and sold according to the dictates of the profit
motive can the immense production which capitalism promises be
realized. An employer, for example, had to be free to dismiss labor
when the balance sheet required it, without being compelled to retain
workers because society or custom demanded it. Serfdom, with its
requirement that the peasant could not be taken from the land, was
an anachronistic institution if capitalism was to become the economic ideology of society. Conversely, an employer needed to be
unrestricted in his freedom to hire labor or else production could not
expand in accordance with the market. Guild restrictions which
limited apprenticeships were therefore obstacles to the achievement
of a free capitalism.

The alienability of the three factors of production was achieved
slowly and unevenly after the close of the Middle Ages. By the nineteenth century in most nations of the West, land had become ab-

solutely alienable—it could be bought and sold at will. With the growth of banking, the development of trustworthy monetary standards, and finally the gold standard in the nineteenth century, money or capital also became freely exchangeable. Gradually, over the span of some two centuries, the innovating demands of capitalism stripped from labor the social controls in which medieval and mercantilistic government had clothed it. Serfdom as an obstacle to the free movement of labor was gradually done away with; statutes of laborers and apprenticeships which fixed wages, hours, and terms of employment also fell into disuse or suffered outright repeal. To avoid government interference in the setting of wage rates, the English Poor Law of 1834 made it clear that the dole to the unemployed was always to be lower than the going rate for unskilled labor. Thus supply and demand would be the determinant of wage levels. Both the common law and the Combination Acts in the early nineteenth century in England sought to ensure the operation of a free market in labor by declaring trade unions to be restraints on trade.

Like land and capital, then, labor was being reduced to a commodity, freely accessible, freely alienable, free to flow where demand was high. The classical economists of the nineteenth century analyzed this long historical process, neatly put it together, and called it the natural laws of economics.

To a large extent, this historical development constituted an improvement in the worker's status, since medieval and mercantilist controls over labor had been more onerous than protective. Nevertheless, something was lost by the dissolution of the ancient social ties which fitted the worker into a larger social matrix. Under the old relationship, the worker belonged in society; he enjoyed a definite if not a high status; he had a place. Now he was an individual, alone; his status was up to him to establish; his urge for community with society at large had no definite avenue of expression. Society and labor alike had been atomized in pursuit of an individualistic economy. Herein lay the radical character of the capitalist ideology.

That the workingman sensed the radical change and objected to it is evident from what some American labor leaders said about their unions. Without rejecting the new freedom which labor enjoyed, John Mitchell, of the Mine Workers, pointed out that the union "stands for fraternity, complete and absolute." Samuel Gompers' culogy of the social microcosm which was the trade union has the same ring. "A hundred times we have said it," he wrote, "and we say it again, that trade unionism contains within itself the potentialities of working class regeneration." The union is a training ground for democracy and provides "daily object lessons in ideal justice; it breathes into the working classes the spirit of unity"; but above all, it affords that needed sense of community. The labor union "provides a field for noble comradeship, for deeds of loyalty, for self-sacrifice beneficial to one's fellow-workers." In the trade union, in short, the workers could obtain another variety of that sense of community, of comradeship, as Gompers put it, which the acid of individualistic capitalism had dissolved.

And there was another objection to the transformation of labor into an exchangeable commodity. The theoretical justification for the conversion of the factors of production into commodities is that the maximum amount of goods can be produced under such a regime. The increased production is deemed desirable because it would insure greater amounts of goods for human consumption and therefore a better life for all. Unfortunately for the theory, however, labor cannot be separated from the men who provide it. To make labor a commodity is to make the men who provide labor commodities also. Thus one is left with the absurdity of turning men into commodities in order to give men a better life!

"Labor is a commodity of a peculiar sort," John Mitchell pointed out. "It is a part of the very being of the man who sells it. The commodity sold is a human creature, whose welfare in the eyes of the law should be of more importance than any mere accumulation of wealth on the part of the community." For the very same reason, Samuel Gompers bestowed the label "Labor's Magna Carta" upon Section 14 of the Clayton Act, which specifically denied that labor was a commodity.

Seen in this light, the trade union movement stands out as a truly conservative force. Almost instinctively, the workers joined labor unions in order to preserve their humanity and social character against the excessively individualistic doctrines of industrial capitalism.[13] Eventually, the workers' organizations succeeded in halting

---

[13] V. I. Lenin, that archetypical radical, was well aware of the basically conservative origins and character of the trade union movement. In his *What Is to Be Done?* (1902), he contrasted trade unionism with revolutionary socialism. "The history of all countries shows," he wrote, "that the working class, exclusively

the drive to the atomized society which capitalism demanded, and in doing so, far from destroying the system, compelled it to be humane as well as productive.

The essential conservatism of the labor movement is to be seen in particular as well as in general. The organizations of American labor which developed in the course of industrialization were conspicuous for their acceptance of the private property, profit-oriented society. They evinced little of the radical, anticapitalist ideology and rhetoric so common among European trade unions. Part of the reason for this was the simple fact that all Americans—including workers—were incipient capitalists waiting for "the break." But at bottom it would seem that the conservatism of American labor in this sense is the result of the same forces which inhibited the growth of socialism and other radical anticapitalist ideologies. This question will be dealt with at some length at the end of this chapter.

"The overshadowing problem of the American labor movement," an eminent labor historian has written, "has always been the problem of staying organized. No other labor movement has ever had to contend with the fragility so characteristic of American labor organizations." So true has this been that even today the United States ranks below Italy and Austria in percentage of workers organized (about 30 per cent as compared, for instance, with Sweden's 90 per cent). In such an atmosphere, the history of organized labor in America has been both painful and conservative. Of the two major national organizations of workers which developed in the latter half of the nineteenth century, only the cautious, restrictive, pragmatic American Federation of Labor lived into the twentieth century. The other, the Knights of Labor, once the more powerful and promising, as well as the more deviant in policies, succumbed to Selig Perlman's disease of fragility.

Founded in 1869, the Noble Order of the Knights of Labor recorded its greatest successes in the 1880's, when its membership rolls carried 700,000 names. As the A.F. of L. was later to define the term for Americans, the Knights did not seem to constitute a legitimate trade union at all. Anyone who worked, except liquor dealers, bankers, lawyers, and physicians, could join, and some thousands of women workers and Negroes were members in good standing of this

by its own efforts, is able to develop only trade-union consciousness," that is, combining into unions, etc. Socialism, however, is the product of the intellectuals.

brotherhood of toilers. But the crucial deviation of the Knights from the more orthodox approach to labor organization was its belief in worker-owned producers' co-operatives, which were intended to make each worker his own employer. In this way, the order felt, the degrading dependence of the worker upon the employer would be eliminated. "There is no good reason," Terence V. Powderly, Grand Master Workman of the order, told his followers, "why labor cannot, through co-operation, own and operate mines, factories and railroads."

In this respect the order repudiated the direction in which the America of its time was moving. It expressed the small-shopkeeper mentality which dominated the thinking of many American workers, despite the obvious trend in the economy toward the big and the impersonal. As the General Assembly of 1884 put it, "our Order contemplates a radical change, while Trades' Unions . . . accept the industrial system as it is, and endeavor to adapt themselves to it. The attitude of our Order to the existing industrial system is necessarily one of war." Though the order called this attitude "radical," a more accurate term, in view of the times, would have been "conservative" or "reactionary."

In practice, however, the Knights presented no more of a threat to capitalism than any other trade union. Indeed, their avowed opposition to the strike meant that labor's most potent weapon was only reluctantly drawn from the scabbard. The Constitution of 1884 said, "Strikes at best afford only temporary relief"; members should learn to depend on education, co-operation, and political action to attain "the abolition of the wage system."

Though the order officially joined in political activity and Grand Master Workman Powderly was at one time mayor of Scranton, its forays into politics accomplished little. The experience was not lost on shrewd Samuel Gompers, whose American Federation of Labor studiously eschewed any alignments with political parties, practicing instead the more neutral course of "rewarding friends and punishing enemies."

In a farewell letter in 1893, Powderly realistically diagnosed the ills of his moribund order, but offered no cure: "Teacher of important and much-needed reforms, she has been obliged to practice differently from her teachings. Advocating arbitration and conciliation as first steps in labor disputes she has been forced to take upon her shoulders the responsibilities of the aggressor first and, when hope of arbitrating and conciliation failed, to beg of the opposing side to do what we should have applied for in the first instance. Advising against strikes we have been in the midst of them. While not a political party we have been forced into the attitude of taking political action."

For all its fumblings, ineptitude, and excessive idealism, the Knights did organize more workers on a national scale than had ever been done before. At once premature and reactionary, it nonetheless planted the seeds of industrial unionism which, while temporarily overshadowed by the successful craft organization of the A.F. of L., ultimately bore fruit in the C.I.O. Moreover, its idealism, symbolized in its admission of Negroes and women, and more in tune with the mid-twentieth century than the late nineteenth, signified its commitment to the ideals of the democratic tradition. For these reasons the Knights were a transitional type of unionism, somewhere between the utopianism of the 1830's and the pragmatism of the A.F. of L. It seemed to take time for labor institutions to fit the American temper.

In the course of his long leadership of the American Federation of Labor, Samuel Gompers welcomed many opportunities to define the purposes of his beloved organization. But probably none tried his soul so much as that day in 1914 when Morris Hillquit of the Socialist party questioned him before the United States Commission on Industrial Relations. In the course of the colloquy, the sharp contrast between the highly philosophical and theoretical aims of the Socialists and the stubbornly unphilosophical, practical spirit of the Federation's eminent leader was spread upon the record for all to see.

After sparring for a while, Hillquit asked "whether the American Federation of Labor and its authorized spokesman have a general social philosophy or work blindly from day to day?" Obviously nettled, Gompers refused to answer on the ground that the question was an insult. Finally, when Hillquit withdrew the words "blindly from day to day," the trade union leader launched into a recital of the A.F. of L.'s aims, carefully avoiding any theoretical formulations. It sought, he said, to "accomplish the best results in improving the conditions of the working people, men and women and children, today and tomorrow and tomorrow—and tomorrow's tomorrow; and each day making it a better day than the one that had gone before."

Pressed by Hillquit for some measure of what "better" meant, Gompers irascibly replied that anyone knew, without benefit of philosophy, that a wage of $3 a day was better than one of $2.50 and an eight-hour day superior to one of twelve. To Hillquit's leading suggestion that $4 and seven hours were even better, the union chief readily agreed, saying, "the best possible conditions obtainable for the workers is the aim." But Hillquit's effort to expose the philosophical poverty of the union's aims and Gompers' stubborn defense of cautious, practical unionism can best be appreciated the way it happened:

> Mr. Hillquit: Yes, and when these conditions are obtained—
> Mr. Gompers: (interrupting) Why, then we want better.
> Mr. Hillquit: (continuing) You will strive for better?
> Mr. Gompers: Yes.
> Mr. Hillquit: Now my question is, Will this effort on the part of organized labor ever stop until it has the full reward for its labor?
> Mr. Gompers: It won't stop at all.

Hillquit, working hard to convince Gompers that labor and socialism had common aims, pushed his questioning still further. The old cigarmaker, however, knew what he was doing.

> Mr. Hillquit: Then, the object of the labor union is to obtain complete social justice for themselves and for their wives and for their children?
> Mr. Gompers: It is the effort to obtain a better life every day.
> Mr. Hillquit: Every day and always—
> Mr. Gompers: Every day. That does not limit it.
> Mr. Hillquit: Until such time—
> Mr. Gompers: Not until any time.
> Mr. Hillquit: In other words—
> Mr. Gompers: (interrupting) In other words we go further than you. (Laughter and applause in the audience.) You have an end; we have not.

In the final words of Gompers, "You have an end; we have not" are summed up the great gulf which separated successful trade unionism in America from socialism. Dedicated as Gompers obviously was to organized labor and more specifically to the A.F. of L., he did not permit utopian idealism to influence his clear-eyed view of the American scene. The almost mystical identification with all workers which both the Knights and the Socialists exhibited had no analogue in the American Federation of Labor, which confined itself to the welfare of craft workers and the preservation of that group's position as the elite of the working class. Any other course, the Federation felt, would bring disintegration to the labor movement. This was business unionism, neither idealistic brotherhood nor belief in the unity of the proletariat.

"The trade unions are the business organizations of the wage-earners," Gompers explained in 1906, "to attend to the business of the wage-earners." Later he expressed it more tersely: "The trade union is not a Sunday school. It is an organization of wage-earners, dealing with economic, social, political and moral questions." As Gompers' crossing of swords with Hillquit demonstrated, there was no need or place for theories. "I saw," the labor leader wrote years later, in looking back on his early life in the labor movement, "the danger of entangling alliances with intellectuals who did not understand that to experiment with the labor movement was to experiment with human life. . . . I saw that the betterment of workingmen must come primarily through workingmen."

In an age of big business, Samuel Gompers made trade unionism a business, and his reward was the survival of his Federation. In a country with a heterogeneous population of unskilled immigrants, reviled and feared Negroes, and native workers, he cautiously confined his fragile organization to the more skilled workers and the more acceptable elements in the population. The result was a narrow but lasting structure.

Though never ceasing to ask for "more," the A.F. of L. presented no threat to capitalism. "Labor Unions are *for* the workingman, but against no one." John Mitchell of the United Mine Workers pointed out. "They are not hostile to employers, not inimical to the interests of the general public. . . . There is no necessary hostility between labor and capital," he concluded. Remorselessly pressed by Morris Hillquit as Gompers was, he still refused to admit that the labor movement was, as Hillquit put it, "conducted against the interests of the employing people." Rather, Gompers insisted, "It is conducted for the interests of the employing people." And the rapid expansion of the American economy bore witness to the fact that the Federation was a friend and not an enemy of industrial capitalism. Its very adaptability to the American scene—its conservative ideology, if it was an ideology at all—as Selig Perlman has observed, contained the key to its success. "The unionism of the

American Federation of Labor 'fitted' . . . because it recognized
the virtually inalterable conservatism of the American community as
regards private property and private initiative in economic life."

This narrow conception of the proper character of trade unionism—job consciousness, craft unionism, lack of interest in organizing the unskilled, the eschewing of political activity—which Gompers
and his Federation worked out for the American worker continued
to dominate organized labor until the earthquake of the depression
cracked the mold and the Committee for Industrial Organization
issued forth.

6. NOBODY HERE BUT US CAPITALISTS

"By any simple interpretation of the Marxist formula," commented Socialist Norman Thomas in 1950, "the United States, by
all odds the greatest industrial nation and that in which capitalism
is most advanced, should have had long ere this a very strong socialist movement if not a socialist revolution. Actually," he correctly
observed, "in no advanced western nation is organized socialism so
weak." Nor was this the first time Socialists had wondered about
this. Over fifty years ago, in the high noon of European socialism,
Marxist theoretician Werner Sombart impatiently put a similar
question: *"Warum gibt es in den Vereinigten Staaten keinen
Sozialismus?"*

The failure of the American working class to become seriously
interested in socialism in this period or later is one of the prominent
signs of the political and economic conservatism of American labor
and, by extension, of the American people as a whole. This failure
is especially noteworthy when one recalls that in industrialized countries the world over—Japan, Italy, Germany, Belgium, to mention
only a few—a Socialist movement has been a "normal" concom-
itant of industrialization. Even newly opened countries like Australia and New Zealand have Labour parties. Rather than ask, as
Americans are wont to do, why these countries have nurtured such
frank repudiators of traditional capitalism, it is the American deviation from the general pattern which demands explanation.

In large part, the explanation lies in the relative weakness of
class consciousness among Americans. Historically, socialism is the
gospel of the *class-conscious* working class, of the workingmen who
feel themselves bound to their status for life and their children after
them. It is not accidental, therefore, that the major successes of

modern socialism are in Europe, where class lines have been clearly and tightly drawn since time immemorial, and where the possibility of upward social movement has been severely restricted in practice if not in law. Americans may from time to time have exhibited class consciousness and even class hatred, but such attitudes have not persisted, nor have they been typical. As Matthew Arnold observed in 1888, "it is indubitable that rich men are regarded" in America "with less envy and hatred than rich men in Europe." A labor leader like Terence Powderly was convinced that America was without classes. "No matter how much we may say about classes and class distinction, there are no classes in the United States. . . . I have always refused to admit that we have classes in our country just as I have refused to admit that the labor of a man's hand or brain is a commodity." And there was a long line of commentators on American society, running back at least to Crèvecoeur, to illustrate the prevalence of Powderly's belief.

The weakness of American class consciousness is doubtless to be attributed, at least in part, to the fluidity of the social structure. Matthew Arnold, for example, accounted for the relative absence of class hatred on such grounds, as did such very different foreign observers as Werner Sombart and Lord Bryce. The British union officials of the Mosely Commission, it will be recalled, were convinced of the superior opportunities for success enjoyed by American workers.

Men who are hoping to move upward on the social scale, and for whom there is some chance that they can do so, do not identify themselves with their present class.[14] "In worn-out, king-ridden Europe, men stay where they are born," immigrant Charles O'Conor, who became an ornament of the New York bar, contended in 1869. "But in America a man is accounted a failure, and certainly

[14] Fifteen years ago, when *Fortune* magazine asked a sampling of Americans what class they belonged to, some 47 per cent said, "middle class" and only 15 per cent answered, "lower or working class." That these striking results can be misinterpreted if they are taken to mean that Americans do not recognize classes was shown by Richard Centers, *Psychology of Social Classes* (Princeton, 1949). Centers presented his sample with a choice of classes, including "working class," instead of leaving the question open-ended, as was done in the *Fortune* poll. Under these conditions 51 per cent of his sample selected "working class." Repetitions with two other samples yielded substantially the same results. Centers' data indicated that Americans, when pressed, *do* recognize classes in their society. But the *Fortune* data showed that Americans instinctively hold to the ideal of a society with a great middle class.

ought to be, who has not risen above his father's station in life." So long as Horatio Alger means anything to Americans, Karl Marx will be just another German philosopher.

The political history of the United States also contributed to the failure of socialism. In Europe, because the franchise came slowly and late to the worker, he often found himself first an industrial worker and only later a voter. It was perfectly natural, in such a context, for him to vote according to his economic interests and to join a political party avowedly dedicated to those class interests. The situation was quite different in America, however, for political democracy came to America prior to the Industrial Revolution. By the time the industrial transformation was getting under way after 1865, all adult males could vote and, for the most part, they had already chosen their political affiliations without reference to their economic class; they were Republicans or Democrats first and workers only second—a separation between politics and economics which has become traditional in America. "In the main," wrote Lord Bryce about the United States of the 1880's, "political questions proper have held the first place in a voter's mind and questions affecting his class second." [15] Thus, when it came to voting, workers registered their convictions as citizens, not as workingmen. (In our own day, there have been several notable failures of labor leaders to swing the labor vote, such as John L. Lewis' attempt in 1940 and the C.I.O.'s in 1950 against Senator Taft.) To most workers, the Socialist party appeared as merely a third party in a country where such parties are political last resorts.

Nor did socialism in America gain much support from the great influx of immigration. It is true that many Germans came to this country as convinced Socialists and thus swelled the party's numbers, but they also served to pin the stigma of "alien" upon the movement. Even more important was the fact that the very heterogeneity of the labor force, as a result of immigration, often made animosities between ethnic groups more important to the worker than class antagonism. It must have seemed to many workers that socialism, with its central concern for class and its denial of ethnic antagonism, was not dealing with the realities of economic life.

[15] It is interesting to note that this generalization, though apparently true as applied to labor, does not fit the farmer, who, historically, was a farmer before he was a voter. Is it for this reason that his economic interest has sometimes taken precedence over his political allegiance, as in the Populist movement, and in the farm bloc of the twentieth century?

In the final reckoning, however, the failure of socialism in America is to be attributed to the success of capitalism. The expanding economy provided opportunities for all, no matter how meager they might appear or actually be at times. Though the rich certainly seemed to get richer at a prodigious rate, the poor, at least, did not get poorer—and often got richer. Studies of real wages between 1865 and 1900 bear this out. Though prices rose, wages generally rose faster, so that there was a net gain in average income for workers during the last decades of the century. The increase in real wages in the first fifteen years of the twentieth century was negligible—but, significantly, there was no decline. The high wages and relatively good standard of living of the American worker were patent as far as the twenty-three British labor leaders of the Mosely Commission were concerned. The American is a "better educated, better housed, better clothed and more energetic man than his British brother," concluded the sponsor, Alfred Mosely, a businessman himself.

But America challenged socialism on other grounds than mere material things. Some years ago an obscure socialist, Leon Samson, undertook to account for the failure of socialism to win the allegiance of the American working class; his psychological explanation merits attention because it illuminates the influence exercised by the American Dream. Americanism, Samson observes, is not so much a tradition as it is a doctrine; it is "what socialism is to a socialist." Americanism to the American is a body of ideas like "democracy, liberty, opportunity, to all of which the American adheres rationalistically much as a socialist adheres to his socialism—because it does him good, because it gives him work, because, so he thinks, it guarantees him happiness. America has thus served as a substitute for socialism."

Socialism has been unable to make headway with Americans, Samson goes on, because "every concept in socialism has its substitutive counterconcept in Americanism." As Marxism holds out the prospect of a classless society, so does Americanism. The opportunities for talent and the better material life which socialism promised for the future were already available in America and constituted the image in which America was beheld throughout the world.[16] The

---

[16] In *Toward a United Front* (New York, 1933), pp. 49–51, Samson has an amusing and provocative page or two on the similarities between utterances of American statesmen and the slogans of socialism. One concerns President

freedom and equality which the oppressed proletariat of Europe craved were a reality in America—or at least sufficiently so to blunt the cutting edge of the Socialist appeal. Even the sense of mission, of being in step with the processes of history, which unquestionably was one of the appeals of socialism, was also a part of the American Dream. Have not all Americans cherished their country as a model for the world? Was not this the "last, best hope of earth"? Was not God on the side of America, as history, according to Marx, was on the side of socialism and the proletariat?

Over a century ago, Alexis de Tocqueville predicted a mighty struggle for the minds of men between the two giants of Russia and the United States. In the ideologies of socialism and the American Dream, his forecast has been unexpectedly fulfilled.

Industrialization was a new and potent force in American life; even when only emergent, it was reshaping the face of America. The factory, in league with the city, would eventually transform the America of Jefferson and Jackson. But these were not the only forces at work in the years after 1865—the wave after wave of immigrants which washed over America also left their impress on the American.

Hoover's avowal that America would abolish poverty. "Who has ever heard a responsible spokesman of European capitalism announce that it is the aim of, let us say, the French or the English 'system' to 'abolish poverty'?" asks Samson. "Normally, phrases such as this are uttered by spokesmen of the working class. Socialism is, normally, the philosophy of the working class."

CHAPTER X

Out of Many, One

THOUGH historians have long celebrated the ancient *Völkerwanderung* of the German tribes in the last centuries of the Roman Empire, during the nineteenth and early twentieth centuries the outpouring of peoples from the land mass of Europe and Asia dwarfed all previous mass migrations. In little more than a century, between 1820 and 1930, over 62 million people uprooted themselves from their native lands to seek a better life in the newer lands around the globe.

Almost two thirds of these enterprising souls came to the United States. No other country even approached America as a goal, the next most popular, Canada, receiving only a little more than 10 per cent of the world's migrants. If this meant that America was the promised land for the majority of the emigrants, it also meant, as George Santayana has pointed out, that in the process the United States was set apart psychologically from Europe. "The discovery of the new world exercised a sort of selection among the inhabitants of Europe," he wrote. "The fortunate, the deeply rooted, and the lazy remained at home; the wilder instincts or dissatisfactions of others tempted them beyond the horizon. The American is accordingly the most adventurous, or the descendant of the most adventurous, of Europeans."

In yet another way immigration helped to make the United States different from Europe and, for that matter, from any other new country. Other new countries like Australia and Argentina, it is true, are as much the product of immigration as the United States, but all such countries were peopled by a very narrow range of nationalities. For example, over 80 per cent of the immigration to Australia has been from the British Isles (not including Ireland); 74

273

per cent of people migrating to Canada came from the United
States and Great Britain; almost four fifths of Argentina's immigrant population derived from Italy and Spain. Only in America
were many nationalities mixed together. Though no one of the
peoples involved in the building of America contributed more than
one seventh of the total alien population, five (Germans, British,
Irish, Austro-Hungarian, and Italian) have each contributed more
than a tenth of the immigrants; two others, the Russians and the
Scandinavians, have made up 8.5 and 6.2 per cent respectively. In
short, the diversity of peoples has been much more than a mere
sprinkling; it has involved great blocs of nationalities.

1. THE WIDENING STREAM

From its inception, America has been the frontier of Europe and
the goal of those who were bold enough to take a second chance. All
through the seventeenth, eighteenth, and nineteenth centuries, people
flowed to the New World—direct responses to the economic, military,
or religious troubles convulsing the Old World. During the seventeenth century, for example, the religious and economic discontent
in England drove people to New England and the Chesapeake colonies; in the early eighteenth century, economic discontent in Ireland
and Germany introduced the leaven of Scots-Irish and Germans into
the English stock of America. But between 1820 and 1920, by far
the greatest and presumably the last of the great waves of Europeans flooded to America; in that single century, 38 million came
to the United States.

If one charted the annual arrivals of this last wave of immigrants,
the graph would assume a pattern of peaks and valleys—but until
1914, the trend would always be upward. Along this over-all upward
trend, however, two major peaks would stand out: one in the 1850's
and another in the five years between 1905 and 1910.

The dates of these two peaks can serve as convenient markers for
differentiating between the so-called old and new immigration. Unfortunately, these terms are somewhat misleading, since they apply
to the European geographic origins of the immigrants rather than
to time of arrival. But their widespread use makes them convenient
nonetheless. The first peak is associated with the old immigrants—
that is, those who came primarily from northern and western
Europe: England, France, the Low Countries, Germany, and Scan-
dinavia; the second with the new immigrants, the great peasant

peoples of eastern and southern Europe: Italians, Greeks, Poles, Russians (including Jews), and Slavs in general. The usage "old" and "new" has some justification in that before 1880 the peoples of southern and eastern Europe were almost unknown on the immigrant ships which put in at Castle Garden in New York. As late as the decade 1881–91, in fact, these peoples constituted only a little over 18 per cent of the immigrants from Europe. But in the 1890's the immigrants from northern and western Europe, though they continued to come in substantial numbers, were almost lost in the masses of people who now spilled out of the lands east of the Elbe River and south of the Alps.

The actual numbers of immigrants coming into the United States in the early years of the twentieth century were almost unbelievable. In the years before 1880, the annual arrivals had never reached half a million, and only once before the end of the century did their numbers exceed three quarters of a million. After 1896, however, when the numbers of immigrants from eastern and southern Europe for the first time surpassed those from the north and the west, annual immigration frequently topped the million mark. In each of six different years before 1915, over a million new Americans arrived; in fact, between 1902 and 1914, more than half a million immigrants poured into the country every single year, and in most of the years the figure was above three quarters of a million. In the space of those twelve years, the total number of immigrants far exceeded all the new arrivals between 1820 and 1880—the peak period for the old immigration.

It is not within the scope of this book to inquire into the forces which impelled this movement of peoples to America; that subject is is more properly European than American. But the image in which the simple European peasant beheld the United States was largely the product of the millions of immigrants who came and saw the mountains, the plains, the cities, the farms, and, above all, the people of America. And the pull which brought still more immigrants was compounded from what these newcomers saw and heard in the new land.

Thousands of letters from America, written by the recently arrived to their home folk, or more often to the local newspaper in the old country, gradually filled out an image of America in which opportunity, equality, and hope for the future were writ large. "This is a free country and nobody has a great deal of authority

over another," wrote one Swede from Illinois in 1850, "There is no
pride and nobody needs to hold his hat in his hand for anyone else.
This is not Sweden, where the higher classes and employers have the
law on their side so that they can treat subordinates as though they
were not human beings." To Johann Schmitz forty years later, as he
eagerly told his brother about America, the hat was still a symbol
of what the new country stood for. "And what is nicer yet is the fact
that this is a free land. No one can give orders to anybody here, one
is as good as another, no one takes off his hat to another as you
have to do in Germany." To a Norwegian in Minnesota in 1866, it
seemed that the lack of occupational distinctions was the great
attraction of America. "The principle of equality has been universally accepted and adopted," he wrote extravagantly, after the
manner of the newly arrived. "The artisan, the farmer, and the
laborer enjoy the same degree of respect as the merchant and
the official."

The material satisfaction which the immigrant often experienced
in America were sometimes exaggerated when he wrote back to those
who had feared to take the risk of emigration. (And did not such
an accent on material possessions contribute to the European's
notion of America's commitment to materialism and worship of
quantity?) "Generally our animals are larger here than they were in
our home parish in Norway," boasted one immigrant from Minnesota in 1859. "Our cows milk very well, and the milk and cream are
richer here than they were in Norway. . . . No bolts are used in
our irons; we heat them by putting them on a stove lid, and they
are much better for ironing than those we had in Norway." [1]

Some emigrants to America returned home, for one reason or another, giving Europeans an opportunity to see and hear with their
own senses what America was like, for not infrequently the returned
ones showed traces of their sojourn in America. One Italian landlord, for example, complained that "the men who come back from

---

[1] Not all letters home were in praise of the new Canaan. J. N. Bjorndalen in
Wisconsin wrote to his parents in 1844 to warn them against the tendency of
his fellow migrants to play up the beauties of the new world: ". . . almost all
reports and letters received in Norway from America are good," he observed
drily. "But this is very wrong; only about a third part of these letters is true.
People only write down accounts of the good, although they themselves have had
no experience of it. . . . I do not advise any of my relatives to come to
America. If you could see the conditions of the Norwegians in America at present,
you would certainly be frightened; illness and misery are so prevalent that many
have died. . . ."

America walk through the streets as if they were our equals. . . ."
Theodore Saloutus, in writing about the repatriated Greeks who had
lived in America, remarked that these former Americans upon their
return were frequently in the vanguard of progress in the old country. They brought practicality, industry, and orderliness to the
Greek villages to which they returned. Often they inspired their
fellow Greeks to be up and doing; they unconsciously stirred up
in their neighbors a discontent with present conditions. "They bring
back a more democratic spirit," one Greek labor leader told Saloutus. "They know more about machines. . . . They often encourage
sports. . . . The returned Greek-Americans are staunch defenders
of America."

Edward Steiner, that romantic chronicler of the immigrant, wrote
that landlords and manufacturers in Europe told him the Americans
"have trained" the returning emigrants in the habits of industry
and "that we have quickened their wits. . . ." Even those Americans
who by the twentieth century were becoming apprehensive as to
where the new tide of immigration was leading could not escape
being aware of the changes in the returning European after a sojourn in the United States. One haughty Bostonian remarked to
Steiner that the returning aliens "carried themselves so differently
from those who came over. . . ." One Slavic woman, on a visit from
America, added her mite to the building up of a realistic picture of
life in the United States when she said that, contrary to European
impressions, American women worked hard. But, she added, they
were not required to submit to beatings by husbands.

"America has been a blessing to us," a Hungarian statesman was
reputed to have admitted. "Had Columbus not discovered it, Europe
would still be in servitude and had it not been rediscovered by our
peasants, they would not have had a chance to get their necks from
under the yoke." This image of America as the hope of the oppressed, as the home of the common man, as the opportunity for the
industrious, was implanted and nurtured in the European heart and
mind by the immigrants who came to America and stayed—and even
by those who elected to return. Like most mirrors, this one held by
the immigrants contained flaws and distortions, but it was sufficiently accurate to satisfy most of those who acted upon the reflection of America it cast.

A vast reservoir of good will, of hope, of aspiration, was thus
created in the worn-out, hard-bitten soul of Europe. America was

rich, America was good, America was hope, America was the future. In a democratic age when the feelings and votes of the common people are taken into account, this warm feeling toward America possesses hard value as well as soft sentiment. Makers of American foreign policy have had this good will as something upon which they could depend and build—and, unhappily enough, squander. It was the gift of the immigrant and of the America which he found here.

2. HEWERS OF WOOD AND DRAWERS OF WATER

Ever since the first trying years at Jamestown, America has been wheedling people from Europe in order to put their magical labor to work upon the natural richness of the new country. This seemingly unquenchable thirst for men's labor has lain at the root of the broad welcome which America has accorded the workers of the world. For, despite their excursions into nativism, Americans in the nineteenth century were as grateful for the new hands and muscles as John Smith had been two hundred and fifty years before.

An indication of this appreciation is evident in the various efforts to calculate the value which the immigrants added to the nation's wealth. Just after the Civil War, the United States Treasury solemnly and prudently declared each immigrant to be worth $800 in the ledger of the national economy. The estimate was raised appreciably by Representative Levi Morton of Indiana in 1880. Scorning a recent government calculation of the immigrant's contribution, Morton asserted that the true value was beyond computation. "Mr. Chairman, what estimate can we place upon the value to the country of the millions of Irish and Germans to whom we largely owe the existence of the great arteries of commerce extending from the Atlantic to the Pacific and the results of that industry and skill which has so largely contributed to the wealth and prosperity of the country?" As late as 1892, by which date many Americans were having sober second thoughts about the westering human stream which never stopped, a writer in the *North American Review* was still blessing the alien's gift of labor. "By reason of this incoming, our almost limitless resources have been partially developed, forests leveled, railroads built, and canals dug . . . and the wilderness has been made to blossom. . . ."

As a class, the immigrants were "hewers of wood and drawers of water" in America; moreover, in proportion to their numbers they performed more of the nation's work than did the native-born. As one friend of the immigrant pointed out in 1893, though the foreign-born population in 1870 comprised "One-seventh of the entire population," it performed "something more than one-fifth of all the work." In 1880, this same writer went on, foreign-born workers constituted almost a third of the labor force, even though immigrants made up only 13.3 per cent of the total population.

Such disproportion is not the consequence of exploitation so much as it is the result of the peculiar age distribution of the immigrant population. The great majority of the immigrants came to the United States in the prime of life—in the working years between fourteen and forty-five. For example, four-fifths of the immigrants in 1900 fell within this age range, though less than three fifths of the native population did. Nor were Americans blind to the economic value of this age grouping. "Thus, immigration brings to us a population of working ages unhampered by unproductive mouths to feed," commented economist John R. Commons in 1906. "Their home countries have borne the expense of rearing them up to the industrial period of their lives," he thriftily pointed out, "and then America, without that heavy expense, reaps whatever profits there are on the investment." Europe was a kind of labor "farm" where workers were conveniently and cheaply raised to full size before they entered American industry.

For an America ever reaching out for more and more labor, the ratio of the sexes in the immigration which came after the 1880's was better than could have been expected. The older immigrant nationalities had often come in families, a mode of migration which tended to distribute the sexes more or less evenly. The new peoples, however, emigrated more often as single men, or married men who had left their families behind. For instance, in the decade of 1901–10, almost 70 per cent of the newcomers were men; whereas in the decade 1850–60, less than 60 per cent were. But it is significant that in both periods there was an excess of men, which, when taken together with the favorable age distribution, meant that immigration provided much more productive labor than was to be expected from any normal increase in population.

Though it is true that the labor of the typical immigrant, especially after 1880, was not skilled, this should not cause us to overlook the skills which the immigrant added to the wealth of America. Emigrants from industrialized and commercial northern and western Europe were noteworthy in this regard, particularly

the Germans who came in the 1840's and 1850's. This nationality
dominated cabinetmaking and pianomaking in New York City, for
example. Even entrepreneurs in the latter industry, like Steinway,
were immigrants. Germans were also prominent as skilled bakers,
tailors, and shoemakers in New York. Englishmen, coming from a
technically advanced society, often came, both before and after the
war, as skilled workers, such as machinists, mechanics, and ship-
building workers. In the years after 1865, the backbone of the
American glass industry was made up of skilled Belgian workers.

The skills which these workers brought, however, comprised only
a part of the immigrant's contribution to American industrial development; common, unskilled labor was the more important addition. But if important, such labor was also lowly. As an unskilled
worker, the immigrant, severely limited in his choice of occupation,
most often found himself in jobs at the bottom of the ladder, sometimes in occupations which no native, except perhaps a despised
Negro, would accept. Before 1860, the Irish were especially conspicuous as unskilled workers. In the Boston of the 1850's, for example, they bore virtually the same relation to the culture of that
city as the Negro slaves did to the contemporary South: both constituted the broad base on which rested an elegant civilization. Of
all the employed Irish in Boston in 1850, 62 per cent were working
as laborers or as domestic servants; in 1855, the state census revealed that 98 per cent of New York City's 20,000 common laborers
were immigrants. After the war, the story of the unskilled is essentially the tale of the immigrant in general, so we shall save that
until later.

But before 1860, the economic importance of the immigrants was
not confined to industry. Many of the newcomers helped to level the
forests and plow up the black earth of the western prairies. By
1860, immigrants in a new state like Minnesota constituted at least
one fifth of the inhabitants of forty-nine of the sixty-four counties;
in brand-new, sparsely settled counties, the immigrants sometimes
made up a majority. Even in an older state like Illinois, by then two
generations in the Union, immigrants, especially Germans, comprised 20 per cent or more of the population in something like one
fifth of the counties. Germans were also numerically prominent in
portions of Iowa, where in eight or nine rural counties in 1860,
every fifth person was an immigrant.

Wisconsin before 1860 was the most indebted to the immigrant for its agricultural growth. Immigrants comprised almost a quarter of the state's one million inhabitants at the outbreak of the war, with the Germans surpassing the total for the English, Canadian, Norwegian, and Irish. In twenty-two of the state's fifty-eight counties immigrants constituted a third or more of the population, and in some of those counties they were a clear majority.

Although at the end of the nineteenth century most of the immigrants were becoming industrial workers upon arrival in America, many thousands continued to push out to the new lands of the Far West and the Great Plains. Immigrants of older ethnic groups, like Germans and Scandinavians, for example, continued to be drawn to the traditional settlements of their nationalities,[2] but now some of the "new" nationalities were beginning to become prominent in agriculture. Italians, for instance, in 1910 were the most conspicuous immigrant people in thirteen of the sixteen California counties which reported 20 per cent or more immigrant population. The foreign-born made up 21 per cent of the population of the State of Washington in 1910; almost another quarter were second generation immigrants. Eastern Europeans like Finns and Russians were prominent in several of the rural counties, while in others "old immigrants" like Norwegians, Germans, and Swedes were important.

On the Great Plains of Middle America in the twentieth century, the immigrant still occupied a conspicuous place in agriculture. Though Nebraska is rarely thought of as the goal of immigrants, in 1910 six counties in that state reported that the foreign-born made up one fifth or more of their population. Two agricultural counties, Colfax and Cuming, in the center of the state, counted almost three quarters of their populations as first- and second-generation immigrants, mostly from Germany and Austria.

Though by the twentieth century the immigrant played only a small part in the drama of settlement and agriculture, in some Midwestern states, like the Dakotas, he was the star. The foreign-born in South Dakota, for example, comprised 20 per cent of the 1910 population in no less than seventeen counties; indeed, in three of these, one out of every three persons was an immigrant. Two thirds

[2] For example, as late as 1910 both Wisconsin and Illinois still counted one fifth of their populations as foreign-born, with Germans and Scandinavians predominating over all other ethnic groups. In at least nine Wisconsin counties Germans made up over a majority of the immigrants, and in each of these counties the foreign-born were more than 20 per cent of the total population.

of the inhabitants of all but three of these seventeen counties were first- and second-generation immigrants. Even more significant insofar as influence went was the fact that individual nationalities tended to cluster together. For example, three quarters of the foreign-born in three counties were Russians (actually Germans who had emigrated from Russia). In three other counties, Norwegians made up more than half the immigrant population.

If Wisconsin in the first half of the nineteenth century was largely the creation of the European peasant, the rich state of North Dakota was the product of the immigrant at the very end of the century. In 1910 the foreign-born comprised 27 per cent of the people of the state, and another 43 per cent were children of immigrants. There was not a single county in which the foreign-born comprised less than 15 per cent of the population, and there were twenty-eight counties in which they constituted more than a quarter. The 40,000 first-generation Norwegians were the largest ethnic group, with Russians (actually German-speaking people) running second with 32,000. The latter, in conformity with their traditional cultural exclusiveness even in Russia, were highly concentrated in five or six counties, where they often made up more than two thirds of the foreign-born population.

Important as the immigrant was in agriculture, the fact remains that the typical immigrant in the years after 1890 was a worker in a factory or mine. In 1910, only 14 per cent of the foreign-born were in agriculture and forestry, but 43.5 per cent were engaged in manufacturing. When the Congressional Immigration Commission of 1907 investigated the economic impact of immigration, it discovered that the labor supply in industry after industry was dominated by the foreign-born. In basic industries like iron and steel making, coal mining, construction work, copper mining and smelting, and oil refining, the foreign-born, on the average, comprised over 60 per cent of the labor force. Labor in cotton-goods manufacturing, once the province of native-born farm girls, as at Lowell in the beginning of the nineteenth century, was now almost 70 per cent foreign-born. By 1910, the clothing industry, even though always sprinkled with foreign workers, was drawing almost three quarters of its operatives from immigrant groups.[3] In terms of quantity of

[3] Certain industries, it should be noted, were conspicuous for their small percentages of foreign-born: boots and shoes counted only 27.3; collars, cuffs, and shirts, 13.3; cigars and tobacco, 32.6; and glass, 39.3.

labor, it is evident from such figures that American industry would have expanded at a much slower pace if the muscle and brain of the immigrant had not been available.

All through our history, opponents of the immigrant have pointed to the working foreigner as the thief of the native worker's job. Undoubtedly the immigrant replaced a native-born worker, but it usually was a displacement which benefited the latter. "When the foreigner came in," observed one writer in the *North American Review* in 1892, "the native engineered the jobs, the former did the shoveling. The American in every walk and condition of life . . . has been the 'boss' ever since. The foreigner plows and sows, the native reaps . . . one digs the canals, the other manages the boats; the one burrows in the mines, the other sells the product, and so on through all the various occupations."

Though the effect of the immigrant upon the native's occupational status is often described as a wedge or upward thrust, it is more accurately visualized as the filling of an economic vacuum. Before the native worker could move up the occupational ladder of the national economy, his place had to be taken by new workers coming in at the bottom—and these new workers were the immigrants. Rather than being a wedge pushing the native into a better job, the immigrant was himself sucked into the industrial system by the vacuum created by the upward movement of the natives. But regardless of the analogy employed, it is clear that the native's rise would have been much slower if there had not been an inflow of unskilled immigrant labor at the bottom.

The Immigration Commission found conspicuous examples of this occupational effect in the bituminous and anthracite coal industries and in iron and steel manufacture. In bituminous coal, for example, all white-collar jobs, the Commission's report stated, "are occupied by native American or older immigrants and their children, while the southern and eastern Europeans are confined to pick mining and to unskilled common labor." The same phenomenon was observed in six different communities in which glass manufacturing was the major industry. Sometimes, as in the case of the glass industry, the very survival of the industry was dependent on the new immigrants. Native and "old" immigrant workers were attracted to other industries, and unless cheap "new" immigrant labor had been available, an industry like glassmaking would have been hard put to secure sufficient labor.

This tendency for the older nationalities as well as the natives to move up on the occupational scale was also apparent in other spheres. Indeed, it was the usual thing for older nationalities in America to move up a notch socially as newer groups came in at the bottom. The process was discernible not only in industry but, as we shall see, in politics as well. Thus the flow of immigrants into this country has acted as a reinforcement of the social fluidity of the society. And mobility, it should not be forgotten, is broader than vertical motion through the social structure; it also includes horizontal movement across the face of the land. Both forms of movement have been highly characteristic of Americans, and immigration has been a stimulus to both.

When the peasants and farmers of eastern Europe took places in American factories and mines, they exerted an economic influence beyond the supplying of labor. Largely unskilled in even the elementary crafts of America's industries, these peasants provided an incentive for manufacturers to increase the mechanization of their processes. Because they were unable to obtain sufficient skilled labor, many employers were willing to mechanize so that they might utilize the cheap unskilled labor which was pouring into the country. "A large number of illustrations of this tendency might be cited," two authorities in the field of immigration have stated. "Probably three of the best, however, are the automatic loom and ring spindles in the cotton-goods manufacturing industry, the bottle-blowing and casting machines in bottle and other glass factories, and the machines for mining coal." The Immigration Commission made the same observation regarding the introduction of technological improvements in glass manufacturing.

The whole process was an interacting one. As an employer hired unskilled peasants to fill out his labor requirements, he was encouraged, if not compelled, by this addition to utilize machinery in tasks these people were not trained to do. Once the machines were installed, the employer acquired a vested interest in continued use of such unskilled labor, and so expanded his use of machinery until the whole cycle spiraled up to maximum mechanization. This practice of employing machinery in tandem, as it were, with the vast supply of unskilled labor became so common that one prominent economist was prompted in 1906 to complain that America was sacrificing skills to profits. "Were it not for immigration," John R. Commons argued, "American industries would ere now have been compelled to give more attention to apprenticeship and the training of competent mechanics." [4] Though America did not actually become as devoid of mechanics as Commons feared, certainly the stimulus of the new immigration contributed to that widespread use of machinery which so impressed visitors like the labor leaders of the Mosely Commission in 1902.

To bring together in this way the evidence for the importance of the immigrant in the industrial expansion of America is to run the danger of making the tail wag the dog. For, contributory as immigration was, it neither created the jobs nor provided the initial stimulus for the enormous expansion of industry which America experienced during the latter years of the nineteenth century. Immigration was a consequence, not a cause, and the proof of this is readily observable in the relation between immigration and the business cycle.

As one would expect, the rise and fall of immigration closely correlated with the ups and downs of the business cycle, but the important detail in this relationship was that the decline in the business cycle always preceded a drop in immigration. Within six months after a downturn in business, Harry Jerome has shown, the influx of foreigners fell off. From this it is apparent that the causal factor was business conditions, not the flow of foreign labor. It was the discouraging news from America in a recession and the consequent fall-off in remittances to the old country [5] which stanched the flow of people from abroad. Similarly, it would be the encouraging letters and fat money orders which would broaden the stream at a

[4] Sometimes, because of the immigrant, the geographical distribution of industries was given a special and unpredictable twist. Industries like the manufacture of cigars and tobacco, silk, and men's and women's clothing were located, the Immigration Commission pointed out, in close proximity to iron and steel and anthracite coal centers. The explanation of this development was that the consumer industries were following the cheap woman and child labor available in the homes of the immigrant men employed in the basic industries.

[5] A measure of the "pull" which America exerted upon immigrants is found in the fact that well over three quarters of the immigrants landing in the years 1908–10 gave "joining relatives" as their reason for coming. Authorities on immigration also emphasize the importance of remittances in financing and encouraging emigration to America. Even such a small ethnic group as the Greeks, according to Theodore Saloutus, sent back $4.6 million in 1910 and $8.2 million in 1914. Italians in the single year of 1907, it has been estimated by one authority, sent back $85 million. Not infrequently, a single money order from an immigrant might contain more hard cash than the peasants in an eastern European village could hope to see in a lifetime.

brighter time, The economic opportunities of America were created
here; the flood of peasants was primarily a response to that attraction.

3. IMMIGRANTS HAVE VOTES

For many Americans today the impress of the immigrant on
American civilization is summed up in the political boss and the big
city machines. Though the political influence of the immigrant undoubtedly can be exaggerated, it was certainly powerful; and during
the nineteenth century, as the immigrant ships set ashore their
cargoes, it was increasingly noticed. "One of the functions of the
Irish race in America," one observer wrote in all seriousness in 1894,
"is to administer the affairs of American cities." Cities as far apart
in miles and character, he went on, as New York, Omaha, New
Orleans, San Francisco, Pittsburgh, and St. Louis, not to mention
eleven others, were "among the cities led captive by Irishmen and
their sons" in the arena of politics. Indeed, as early as the 1880's,
Irish mayors were being elected in New York and Boston and other
cities where the Celts had thickly settled. Nor were the Irish alone
in their new-found opportunities for political activity and careers.
Perhaps the best known of the early Germans in politics were Carl
Schurz of Missouri and Gustav Schleicher of Texas, both of them
refugees from the abortive 1848 uprising in Germany. Later in the
century, in 1893, John Peter Altgeld became Governor of Illinois,
the first naturalized citizen to do so, and then went on to become a
power in the national Democratic party, kept, however, from the
Presidential nomination in 1896 by his foreign birth.

Not until after the First World War were representatives of the
second great wave of immigration, the "new immigrants," prominent
in politics. Then Italians like Pastore of Rhode Island, DiSalle of
Toledo, La Guardia and Marcantonio of New York, and a Czech
like Anton Cermak of Chicago made the headlines. In 1949, Joseph
Mruc became the first Pole to be mayor of Buffalo. It is only since
the Great Depression that any significant federal recognition by way
of choice appointment has been granted these newer immigrant
groups. The first Italo-American was appointed to the federal bench
in 1936, but the first Polish-American did not receive that recognition until Truman's administration.

In politics, as in industry, the bottom slowly rose to the top as
the immigrant learned the ways of America and mastered the levers

of political power. For basically, an immigrant group's achievement of prominent political office was a function of its numbers and its political organization. Immigrant leaders attained high elective office through the bloc voting of their nationality, such as occurred with the Irish and Germans; prominent appointive office was achieved when a nationality was recognized as a potent political force, as has recently been the case with Italians and Poles in the federal judgeships. In time, and for the same reasons, even disadvantaged and almost politically friendless groups like the Puerto Ricans and Mexicans, it can be predicted, will receive similar appointments.[6]

It would be a mistake, however, to assume that the influence of the foreign-born at the polls has been confined to the election of ethnic brethren. Even before 1865, for example, national issues were occasionally decided by the votes of immigrants, for in some states the franchise preceded citizenship; even where it did not, fraud or at most a five-year wait bestowed the ballot upon the newcomer. That the foreign vote may well account for the election of Abraham Lincoln in 1860 was suggested some years ago by William A. Dodd. The election, Dodd showed, was won in the Northwest, but only narrowly, and "by the votes of the foreigners whom the railroads poured in great numbers into the contested region." As Dodd wrote, "The election of Lincoln, and, as it turned out, the fate of the Union were thus determined not by native Americans but by voters who knew least of American history and institutions." Subsequent elections like those of 1884 (the year of "Rum, Romanism, and Rebellion") and 1916, when Woodrow Wilson did not carry a single state in which Catholics were important because of dissatisfaction with his Irish and Mexican policies, demonstrate the tendency of immigrant groups to vote in accordance with their national origins.

Even in our own time, as Samuel Lubell has shown in his book *The Future of American Politics*, the clan voting of the immigrant is often determinate. Looking into the districts and the precincts,

[6] Most recently, judging from a news item in *The New York Times*, May 4, 1957, p. 43, the political effects of immigration were to be seen in the midst of the controversial desegregation issue. Two senators in the Texas legislature carried out a thirty-six-hour filibuster against a bill which would delay the desegregation of the schools in that state. One of the two senators, Henry Gonzalez, was of Mexican descent and the other, Charles Kazan, was the son of Lebanese immigrants. Both men represent districts in southern Texas, where Mexican immigrants are numerous.

Lubell found time and again that the ethnic nerve of the voters was much more sensitive than the economic or political. For example, though the lower-income levels of the population tended to support Roosevelt in both 1936 and 1940, sometimes economic self-interest foundered on the rock of nationality. "Roosevelt's heaviest losses" in 1940 "came in German-American and Italo-American wards," writes Lubell, for by that election the President's hostility toward Hitler and Mussolini had become overt. On the other hand, Lubell shows, high-income Jews—not likely to support F.D.R. on economic grounds—registered strong support for Roosevelt in 1940 under the sting of Hitler's anti-Semitism. When ethnic background and low income pulled in the same direction, as it did for Buffalo's Polish-Americans in 1940, "the vote for Roosevelt was prodigious." Polish wards went Democratic nine to one, with some precincts reaching twenty to one, to give the President "his heaviest pluralities in the whole country." [7]

According to Jack Redding's account in his behind-the-scenes book, *Inside the Democratic Party*, Truman in 1948 was greatly indebted for his victory to the votes thousands of immigrants gave him in return for foreign policies like the Marshall Plan, the Truman Doctrine, and the Berlin airlift. Truman even carried German-American wards that had gone Republican under F.D.R.

Mr. Lubell, together with Eric Goldman, has done American political history a distinct service by showing, as Lubell has phrased it, that "the hard core of isolationism in the United States has been ethnic and emotional and not geographical." Too often it has been assumed that the isolationist politics of the Middle West are a function of that section's distance from ocean-borne menaces. Now it has been shown by Lubell and Goldman that it is the German background of many of the citizenry of the region which largely accounts for the reluctance to accept an internationalist foreign policy in the twentieth century. The truth of this proposition is suggested also by the relative absence of isolationist sentiment in the Middle West when the State Department directs its barbs at countries other than Germany.

[7] Lubell also shows the immigrant effect on a broader scale. In 1940, F. D. R.'s majority dropped 7 per cent from 1936. There were twenty counties in the country where his loss exceeded 35 per cent; of these counties, nineteen were predominantly German-speaking in background. Another thirty-five counties showed a drop of 25–35 per cent in the Roosevelt majority; in all but four of these, Germans were "first or second strongest nationality of origin."

Lubell is careful to point out, nonetheless, that emotional attachment to the homeland is not the sole cause of the isolationism of the Germans and other nationalities. Just as often, perhaps, it is the fruit of the cultural isolation in which the immigrants often live. What this often meant in fact is illustrated by an incident told by Joseph Dorfman in his biography of Thorstein Veblen. The economist's mother was so insistent upon maintaining the Norwegian language and culture that none of her children was even aware that she knew English until they were almost adults. Though the case of Veblen's mother was undoubtedly extreme, many immigrants were so culturally isolated—Lubell cites the excellent example of the German-speaking Russians of isolationist North Dakota—as to be effectively walled off from just those influences which were making other Americans more international in outlook. As a result, the immigrants often remained at least as isolationist as most Americans had been in the nineteenth century. But whether it was emotional attachment to the homeland or cultural insulation which fostered the opposition to internationalism, it arose out of the immigrant background.

The isolationism of many immigrants is one side of the foreigners' influence upon the foreign policy of the United States; the other is almost the opposite, since it involves the attempt to prescribe action for American policy. For even when cut off from American culture, the immigrant still retained, quite naturally, an interest in the country of his birth. Since immigrants also vote in America, this sentimental connection with the homeland can, and often does, influence the determination of American foreign policy. The appeals made to the Italians and the Irish by the opponents of the Versailles Treaty in 1919, to the Germans in 1939–41 by the isolationists, or to the Poles by the Republicans after Yalta in the late 1940's are all cases in point. Harold Ickes in his recently published diary reveals that Roosevelt in early 1938 told him that the embargo on arms to Loyalist Spain could not be lifted because to do so "would mean the loss of every Catholic vote next fall. . . ." Certainly, large numbers of Jewish voters make it necessary for our government officials to think twice in working out a policy toward Israel or the Arab world. Because no other country contains as large or as diverse a population, the United States in its conduct of foreign affairs is confronted with difficulties which are unique and more complicated than elsewhere.

4. MELTING POT OR SALAD BOWL?

As immigration reshaped the economy and politics of America, it also remolded other aspects of society. For instance, the immigrant was intimately involved in the growth of the city, that social development which loomed over all others in the late nineteenth century. Increasingly, as the century approached its end, the city became the destination of the immigrant just as it was the goal of a growing number of native farm boys seeking to exchange the plow for the lathe.

Most contemporaries were well aware that the typical new immigrant was a city dweller. But he was more than that: he was a dweller in a big city. At the turn of the century, one half of all the foreign-born lived in the 160 cities of 25,000 population or more. For some nationalities the proportions were even higher: three quarters of the Russians—mainly Jews—and almost two thirds of the Irish and Italians lived in cities of such size. Though less than one fifth of the American people as a whole lived in the big cities (100,000 or more population), almost two fifths of the immigrants did. The clustering of foreigners in the great city is even more striking when it is recognized that one third of the second-generation stock also lived in the thirty-eight cities of over 100,000 population, though only one tenth of the old native population lived in those cities.

This conjunction of the city and the foreigner aroused sinister thoughts in the minds of Americans still wedded to the farm—and most natives in the early years of the twentieth century still lived in a rural environment. Always suspicious of the city anyway, the rural man became more so as he saw tenement piles and ramshackle company towns crowded with people whose customs, religions, and looks differed from his own. Moreover, the immigrants, as city dwellers, with all that that word connoted to the rural mind, absorbed from the rest of America more than the share of suspicion and distrust which their foreign origin alone could be expected to evoke. In short, by being urban as well as foreign, the large numbers of immigrants tended to enhance social tensions, thus further impeding the quick acceptance which every immigrant hoped to find in his new homeland. The most obvious manifestation of these tensions, as we shall see later, was nativism.

For the history of American urbanization, the nationality ghettos of the big cities were certainly the immigrants' most obvious contribution. But these conglomerates of the foreign-born, large and obtrusive as they often were, should not completely overshadow the contribution which the immigrant made to the building of new cities. Such new towns were quite different from those which in the earlier days of the Republic were hacked out of the forest or founded at the juncture of trade and travel routes. The immigrant cities were a direct product of America's expanding industry and large numbers of newcomers, brought into being by the clustering of immigrant workers around a new ore mine or a new steel mill.

These towns were the frontier of the new industrial expansion. The hard and soft coal areas of Pennsylvania, West Virginia, Alabama, Ohio, and Illinois all gave birth to a number of such towns, as did the iron ore ranges of Minnesota and the copper mining sites of Michigan. The Immigration Report of 1910 told of one steel town, West Seneca, New York, located just outside Buffalo; only ten years old, it already had a population of 20,000, of whom four fifths were immigrants. Another such newly founded town was Hungary Hollow, Illinois, in which 15,000 Bulgarians were employed in the steel mills in 1910. Charleroi and Kensington, Pennsylvania, and Ford City, Ohio, were examples of new immigrant cities springing up around the glass factories located there.

Whether one looks at the old cities which were being swelled by the new additions from abroad or at the new ones which were being created by the newcomers, the irony still remains: the spectacular urbanization of America at this period was in large part the product of European peasants.

When the people of one culture move into another, they often have to shed layer after layer of old habits and ways of thought, much as one peels an onion. To some extent this was true of the Europeans who came to America, and especially so of those peasants who exchanged their rural life for an American city. But the danger inherent in the peeling of an onion—that so many layers will be removed that nothing is left—was no threat to the immigrants; most of them retained a number of their traditional habits.

Few of the immigrants, for instance, divested themselves of their religion or church,[8] and because they did not, they enriched the

---

[8] Part of this, as Will Herberg has pointed out, is inherent in the nature of American culture. Though demanding much of the newcomer, it has not demanded uniformity of religion. "The newcomer is expected to change many

unique religious heritage of America. The churches which the immigrants brought with them have increased the diversity of sects in America so that in the 1950's, with something like 235 distinct religious bodies in this country, at least sixty are the direct result of immigrants.

The heterogeneity of nationalities carved new sects out of old denominations, as well as creating entirely new churches. The Lutherans, for example, split into a dozen national churches; the Mennonites have thirteen varieties; the Eastern Orthodox Church is divided into nine national sects. A host of minor sects have been spawned by the diversity of immigrant nationalities—churches like the Armenian Orthodox Church in America, the Assyrian Jacobite Apostolic Church, the Free Magyar Reform Church of America, and three varieties of German Dunkers. "The tendency toward conformity with the new civilization is, strangely enough, responsible for much of the denominationalism of America," explains H. Richard Niebuhr. "It separates various generations of immigrants from each other so effectively that new schisms result." Recent immigrants, finding "themselves ill at ease among their partly Americanized kindred . . . feel compelled to organize new denominations which will be truer to the Old World customs."

Though the variety of sects is uniquely American, it is not as sociologically significant as the fact that all religion in the United States is divided into three great segments. As Will Herberg has recently pointed out, "By and large, to be an American today means to be either a Protestant, a Catholic, or a Jew. . . . Unless one is either . . . one is a 'nothing'; to be a 'something,' to have a name, one must identify oneself to oneself, and to be identified by others, as belonging to one or another of the three great religious communities in which the American people are divided."

Of these three "great communities," two are the creation of the immigrants. Without the immense nineteenth-century emigration to the United States from Ireland, Italy, Poland, and other Catholic countries, the Roman Catholic Church in America would still be merely a missionary church among the heretics as it was in the eighteenth century. The same is true of Judaism, the third of the religious divisions of Americans. It has been raised to its present

---

things about him as he becomes American—nationality, language, culture," Herberg observes. "One thing, however, he is *not* expected to change—and that is his religion." *Protestant-Catholic-Jew* (New York, 1955), p. 35.

importance solely by the large numbers of German and Russian Jews who swelled the tiny Spanish and Portuguese colonies of the seventeenth and eighteenth centuries.

Immigrants have not only fleshed out the substance of the Roman Catholic Church, but one nationality—the Irish—has long dominated the leadership—a consequence, in large part, of the Celts having gotten here "fustest with the mostest." Even today, the hierarchy is topheavy with Irish names.

But the immigrant influence upon the Church extends beyond leadership. It would seem that the Irish domination has been largely responsible for the prudishness or puritanism which is so strikingly characteristic of the American branch of the Roman Catholic Church. In America, as in Eire, the Church has taken an excessively prudish attitude on matters concerning nudity, sex, and marriage.[9] It is true, of course, that Catholic doctrine on birth control and sexual behavior is universal rather than national, but this fact does not prevent a national tinge from showing. Thomas Sugrue, the well-known American Catholic layman, speaks of "The intensely sentimental Catholicism of Spain; the fiercely Puritanical Catholicism of Ireland; the relaxed and affectionate Catholicism of Italy. . . ." It is difficult, for instance, to imagine an American church dominated by a French or Italian hierarchy indulging in the present American Church's ban on motion pictures and books which too realistically depict the natural, if sometimes lascivious, relations between men and women.

It would be misleading, however, to leave the impression that the Catholic Church was alone among the immigrant churches in ex-

[9] An example of the great concern for modesty is afforded in a recent handbook for Catholic parents, *Parents, Children and the Facts of Life,* by Henry V. Sattler, bearing the imprimatur of the Bishop of Paterson. "Teach children a routine in dressing and undressing which will expose them as little and as briefly as is reasonably possible. Teach them also to avoid too much curiosity about their own sex." Seán O'Faoláin, in an essay in J. A. O'Brien, *The Vanishing Irish* (New York, 1953), p. 121, tells of his experience in the Irish Church: "Since my boyhood I have heard my elders fulminating about keeping company, night courting, dancing at the crossroads, V necks, silk stockings, late dances, drinking at dances, girls who take part in immodest sports (such as jumping and hurdling), English and American books and magazines, short frocks, Bikinis, cycling shorts, and even waltzing which I have heard elegantly described as 'belly-to-belly dancing.' Perhaps the most extreme example of this kind of thing was to hear woman described from a pulpit to a mixed congregation as the 'unclean vessel.'" Mary Laverty, in the same collection, also tells of the excessive prudery of the Irish clergy.

hibiting a puritanical streak. Protestant immigrant sects also displayed such attitudes, and none of them, let it be said at once, traced
their descent from the original Puritans. A number of the immigrant
churches, particularly branches of the Lutheran Church, attempted
to regulate courtship habits, marital duties, and social pastimes
like dancing, drinking, and card playing—usually in the direction of
minimizing pleasure. Marcus Hansen tells the story of a group of
Scandinavians in Wisconsin in the 1850's who, after a Sunday of
picnicking, drinking, and dancing, were vehemently attacked the
next day in the native American press for their un-American and
un-Christian behavior. Though stunned by the unexpected assault,
the immigrants were even more taken aback when their ministers defended the criticism. The clergymen explained that though such
revels were permissible in Norway and were not sinful, in the new
country they only drew reproaches and hostility from Americans;
therefore the Church must disapprove. Such spontaneous puritanism, as Hansen called it, was not uncommon in the churches of
the immigrants as the leaders and members sought to make their
peace with disapproving neighbors.

"The process of Puritanization can be followed by anyone who
studies the records of a congregation or the minutes of a synod,"
Hansen tells us. "Discipline became more and more strict. One after
another, social pleasures that were brought from the Old World
fell under the ban. Temperance and Sunday observance were early
enforced; then card playing and dancing were prohibited. Simplicity
in dress and manner of living became prime virtues."

There was another reason for the puritanism of the immigrant
churches. Rather than see the community lose its identity in the
American environment, the Church instinctively threw up protective
barriers. Activities like dancing, card playing, and drinking, which
could serve as vehicles for American encroachment, were banned or
discouraged by the churches. Originally intended to preserve the old
ways, the strict moral code remained even after its *raison d'être* had
passed away. Thus, in a roundabout fashion, these aliens—so divergent from their neighbors at the outset—ended by accepting
and further advancing that brand of morality called puritanism
which so often has been considered typically American.

To many ethnic groups, the silent terror of being in a new land,
thousands of miles from native roots, strengthened rather than
weakened the loyalty to and dependence upon the old religion. They

could not help but contrast their firm religious beliefs with the indifference they found among the natives. "I think," one disgusted Norwegian preacher wrote from Wisconsin, "that the largest faction here in the West consists of veritable heathens who neither have been baptized nor have learned to know Christianity." Certainly, for the Irish, the ancient Church proved to be confessor, teacher, counselor, social director, almsgiver, and even political leader for a people ignored by the institutions and scorned by the citizens of the new land. The Lutheran Church of the Germans and Scandinavians of the Middle West performed a similar if less pervasive function.

From such bonds of intimacy, born of the immigrants' needs, sprang an attachment between the people and their Church which no American tradition of secularism or indifference could disrupt or seriously impair. It may not be far wrong to attribute the greater church attendance and religiosity of Americans in the twentieth century, as compared with the eighteenth, to the great immigration of the intervening century.

If the immigrant reinforced the Puritan strain in the American tradition, he also enhanced the conservative streak which runs all through American culture. In politics, religion, and economics, as we have seen, the weight of the immigrant has been thrown into the scales in favor of the traditional, the tried, the accepted. Even where he was not innately conservative, his cultural isolation has meant loss of contact with the stream of ideas which were changing America, and he has appeared as a conserver of old ways. At other times, the immigrants deliberately eschewed the new, as when they shunned Populism in politics and secularism in religion, and sought their security in conformity with the dominant patterns of American life. For even when the immigrant was prepared to mingle with the native Americans, he wanted nothing more than to be like them, to take the *status quo* as a bench mark by which he could maintain his bearings in novel surroundings.

In 1908, at the height of the last great surge of immigration, a naïve and sentimental play about American immigrants, written by an English Jew, captured the imaginations of American theater-goers. Played before numerous audiences throughout the country, *The Melting Pot* of Israel Zangwill also ran through many editions in book form. Its title has been immortalized as the classic description of the immigrant's reception and future in America. "There she lies, the great Melting Pot," exclaimed the hero, David Quexano.

"East and West, and North and South, the palm and the pine, the pole and the equator, the crescent and the cross—how the great Alchemist melts and fuses them with his purging flames!"

But, one is tempted to ask, is this really what happens to the immigrant in America? Do the various national traits "melt and fuse" to form a new American culture when it is clear that many of them remain untouched and persistent? Some traits, to be sure, do disappear after a while. After one or two generations most of the sharply deviant contours are worn down to the common pattern, the brassy earrings, the large mustachios, the garlicked breath, and the atrociously accented English being replaced by appropriate American substitutes. But true as that may be, it does not make a melting pot, for the dropping of old habits for new is not fusion or melting.

As we have already seen, some habits from the old country were not discarded; in those instances the children of immigrants even into the third and fourth generations retained their differences. In view of such failure to melt and fuse, the metaphor of the melting pot is unfortunate and misleading. A more accurate analogy would be a salad bowl, for, though the salad is an entity, the lettuce can still be distinguished from the chicory, the tomatoes from the cabbage.

Contrary to the conception implied by the figure of the melting pot, American civilization is not homogeneous and uniform; it is diverse and pluralistic. The evidence is all around us: in the varieties of languages, of foods and restaurants, of religions and festivals, of newspapers and books, of costumes and dances, of literatures and theaters. Though some immigrant habits and mores are undoubtedly lost in America, many others are not; and they remain, not fusing into a new cultural synthesis, but persisting as living remnants of many cultures, spicing and enlivening the broader stream of American life. As a result of these resistant, undigested bits of foreign ways within America, our culture is probably more colorful, more cosmopolitan, more diverse than any other people's since the days of Trajan and Hadrian and up until the creation of modern Israel.

5. WHO ARE AMERICANS?

With strange and different foreigners spreading throughout the country, congregating in the cities, voting with political machines, pushing their way into farms and factories, it was to be expected that there would be a reaction on the part of the native population. Nor is it surprising that the two great outbursts of antiforeign sentiment—1830–60 and 1890–1914—should coincide with the two peaks of immigration. Always it was the numbers of these newcomers which worried the older Americans.

The earlier of the two anti-immigrant movements, that of the nativists, or Know-Nothings as they came to be called in the 1850's, was directed primarily against the growing influence of the immigrant in politics and the sudden upsurge of the Roman Catholic Church, for which immigration was largely responsible. Despite the ugly turn which the anti-immigration movement in the 1830's took when it resorted to mob violence against Catholics and immigrants, the principal purpose animating the nativist movement of the 1850's was the elimination of the foreigner as a political force. For this reason the key planks of the Know-Nothing party were the extension of the waiting period for naturalization from five to twenty-one years and the exclusion of the foreign-born from public office. At no time, in contrast with later movements, did the Know-Nothings seek a restriction upon the flow of immigrants into the country. There were compelling economic reasons why this was so—the need for labor being among the most important—but the fact remains that Know-Nothingism, no matter what else it stood for, was not a restrictionist movement.

Indeed, the nature of the Know-Nothing movement is far from simple. Americans are often tempted, if by nothing more than their reverence for their alien ancestors, to look upon the nativist or Know-Nothing response to immigration as a tale of simple bigotry. But a critical examination of the movement, only a sketch of which can be given here, suggests that something more was involved than just the corroding influence of intolerance.

The history of nativism in Massachusetts offers a good example of the complex character of the nativist reaction to the immigrant. The nativists of Massachusetts in the 1850's were really a coalition of two quite dissimilar groups—old-line Whigs, who were concerned over the growing numbers of Irish in the state, and liberal Whigs and Democrats interested in counteracting the conservative policies of the dominant Democratic party. Since the Irish were almost invariably Democrats, and conservative, it was possible for the conservative Whigs and liberal Whigs and Democrats to join in a common front against the conservative Democrats and Irish, albeit for different reasons. To the social reformers and liberals, many of whom disliked the bigotry of the out-and-out nativists, joining the Know-Nothing or American party was justifiable in the interests of reform as the only practical means for welding together the divided opponents of the conservative Democratic party. The stratagem worked and the American party was swept into office in 1855.

That this was more a victory for reform than for biogotry is shown by the events which followed the election. The Know-Nothing legislature did not enact any nativist legislation, but it did pass a series of reform laws: protection for runaway slaves and free Negroes, improvements in the educational and jury systems, and expansion of the rights of women. Viewed against such a background, it does not seem so strange that a dedicated antislavery and reform leader like Massachusetts' Senator Henry Wilson was willing to be associated with the Massachusetts Know-Nothings.

Not all nativists, of course, can be properly fitted into this pattern,[10] but those who do, demonstrate that the native reaction to the immigrant was more than a simple fear of the new and the different; sometimes it was recognition that the foreigner was innately conservative and an obstacle to reform.

Underneath the political manifestations of native anxiety regarding these outlanders was the undeniable fact that the immigrants were different. Their dress was queer, their language was either unknown or wrongly accented, their religion was sometimes saturated with bloody memories of the religious strife of the sixteenth century, and, perhaps most disturbing of all to the natives, their pleasures, like lager beer gardens and St. Patrick's Day revelries, seemed to be at wide variance with what was considered moral in America. One German church worker traveling in America, for example, was told by immigrants that "we can't work with Americans; they are too good for us. They regard us as the greatest sinners if we drink a glass of beer or have a fete on Sunday afternoon."

Regardless of the distaste which these strangers seemed to arouse

[10] In the South, for instance, Know-Nothingism was genuinely conservative, using as its appeal the Southerner's fear that the immigrant endangered the institution of Negro slavery. It is ironic that in Massachusetts the typical immigrant was an Irish Catholic; from this it was generalized that the immigrant was politically conservative. In the South, however, the immigrants heard from most were the handful of antislavery Germans in Texas and those in the North; consequently, the typical immigrant in the minds of Southerners seemed to be an enemy of the "peculiar institution."

in Americans, Know-Nothingism failed to attain any of its goals, the movement declining even more rapidly than it rose. Moreover, the immigrants' enthusiastic support of the Union cause in 1861 smothered the last traces of public nativism for a generation. Not until the new wave of immigrants began to dash upon American shores in the last decade of the century was there any significant revival of anti-Catholic and antiforeign sentiment comparable to that of the 1830's and 1850's.

The counterpart of the Know-Nothings at the end of the nineteenth century was the American Protective Association. This organization was more anti-Catholic than anti-immigrant, but, since the two were so closely connected in the public mind, no real distinction was made between them. The A.P.A. was notorious for its half-truths and lies about the evil and subversive propensities of the Roman Catholic Church. Such blatant bigotry, however, was more a throwback to the worst in nativism than a new approach to the immigrant's influence in America.

A broader, though much less organized, movement than the A.P.A., and one which was destined to achieve its goal, also developed in the early years of the new immigration. This was a movement to restrict both the numbers and the kinds of people who could enter the United States—an approach to the immigrant which was new to American thought. The first concrete step in this direction was taken in 1882, when Congress, responding to the fears of Californians and others, prohibited the future immigration of Chinese.

During the remaining years of the century, a number of broadly based groups and organizations displayed mounting concern over the possible changes and dangers the rising flood of immigrants would inflict upon American society. Businessmen, for instance, though torn between their economic self-interest in cheap immigrant labor and their worry over social disturbances sparked by foreigners, began to speak out in favor of some kind of restriction on immigration. Labor leaders were similarly of two minds on the subject, but by the late nineties organized labor was taking a stand in favor of cutting down on immigration. T. V. Powderly, of the Knights of Labor, did so in 1892, and he was followed by the A.F. of L. in 1897.

The whole movement was given intellectual underpinning by men like Professors John W. Burgess of Columbia and N. S. Shaler of Harvard, President F. A. Walker of M.I.T., and Senator Henry

Cabot Lodge of Massachusetts. For years these learned gentlemen
and others like them preached the gospel of the Anglo-Saxon heritage of Americans, warning in elegant tones against the degradation
which awaited the country if the immigrant tide—particularly that
part of it originating in eastern and southern Europe—was left un-
checked.

Anglo-Saxonism, moreover, was popular as well as academic. It
was apparently accepted, for example, by the nativist Junior Order
of United Mechanics, which boasted 224,000 members in 1914. The
order's chaplain told a House committee that he wanted to see that
type of immigrant "to come from which we came . . . I glory in my
kinship," he remarked. "My father on one side, was a German, my
father upon the other was an Englishman. . . . That is the kind
we can absorb. . . . They belonged to that independent race . . .
who . . . came with the idea already imbedded in their hearts and
minds of the beauties of self-government."

To achieve the dual purpose of limiting numbers and at the same
time discriminating between desirable and undesirable peoples, the
advocates of restriction hit upon the literacy test. Thanks to the
popular educational systems of the nations of northern and western
Europe, immigrants from those countries would be able to pass such
a test, but those people from the more backward countries of eastern
Europe would not. The literacy test provided just the right mesh to
satisfy the ethnic bias of the restrictionists.

Three times measures providing for a literacy test were driven
through Congress by public concern over the ability of America to
absorb so many different kinds of people. And each time they were
vetoed. Woodrow Wilson spoke for his predecessors when he told the
Congress in his veto of 1915 that the literacy tests represented a
"radical change in the policy of the Nation." Heretofore, he pointed
out, we have kept only incompetents, the sick, and the anarchistic
from our shores. "In this bill it is proposed to turn away from tests
of character and of quality and impose tests which exclude and restrict; for the laws here embodied are not tests of quality or of
character or of personal fitness, but tests of opportunity. Those
who come seeking an opportunity," he told the Congress, "are not
to be admitted unless they have already had one of the chief of the
opportunities they seek, the opportunity of education. The object
of such provisions," he correctly observed, "is restriction, not selec-

tion." But the vetoes were only temporary holding actions; the literacy test became law in 1917 over Wilson's second veto.

The arguments in support of restriction did not stop with educational tests. Some leaders, like Madison Grant, New York patrician and president of the Museum of Natural History, injected the dangerous doctrine of race into the question of the immigrant. "Mental, spiritual and moral traits," Grant asserted in 1916, "are closely associated with the physical distinctions among the different European races. The Alpine race [i.e., eastern Europeans] is always and everywhere a race of peasants. . . . The Nordics are, all over the world, a race of soldiers, sailors, adventurers, and explorers, but above all, of rulers, organizers and aristocrats in sharp contrast to the essentially peasant character of the Alpines."

Racist views like Grant's were not confined to the study or select company; variants of them were a part of acceptable discourse at the seat of government. "Our capacity to maintain our cherished institutions stands diluted by a stream of alien blood, with all its inherited misconceptions respecting the relationship of the governing power to the governed," contended Congressman Albert Johnson, chairman of the House Committee on Immigration in 1927. Heretofore the Negro had been the primary target of racist thought, but under the impact of the new immigration such thinking was applied to the newcomers as well. In substance, one of the byproducts of the nativist response to immigration was the popularizing of racist thinking in America.

The final step in the restriction of immigration was taken in the twenties. After a generation of discussion about racial characteristics and the ability of American society to assimilate certain nationalities, it was to be anticipated that restriction would not limit itself to a mere reduction in numbers. To be sure, a severe reduction of numbers was provided for in the 1924 law; no more than 150,000 could enter the country within a single year, though as recently as 1921 over 800,000 had come in. But more significant than the large cut in numbers was the law's effort to deal with the question of western versus southern European immigration, always the central concern of restrictionists and racists. The law provided that each of the world's nationalities should be granted an annual quota of immigrants, the number of which should bear the same relation to the total of 150,000 which each nationality within the United States bore to the total population.

Superficially at least, a theory of American culture was evident here. It assumed that the people of the United States had attained the proper ethnic mixture and no further change was desirable; immigrants were to come into the country in proportion to the numbers already here. If examined a little more closely, the measure also revealed a decided ethnic bias against the eastern and southern Europeans. This was clear from the original version of the act, which used 1890 as the base year for the calculation of the proportions—a date, it will be remembered, when the number of "new" immigrants was very small. But even the final provisions, which dispensed with base years, displayed favoritism toward the Teutons and Celts, for the method of calculation tended to discriminate against the Slavic and Mediterranean peoples. For purposes of setting quotas, the total population of the United States was to be broken down into countries of origin, regardless of how far back the first generation came over. This was a procedure which obviously favored the northern and western Europeans, since they had been the earliest immigrants and by 1920 would count the most descendants.

Today, a generation after the first acceptance of reduction and restriction, Americans seem wedded to the policy, for even the most recent revision of immigration legislation, the McCarran Act of 1952, has retained the national-origins feature of the 1924 law. Despite this continued acceptance of the restrictionist attitude, however, it must not be hastily assumed that the American people have completely repudiated the broad welcome which they have historically extended to the strangers from "the palm and the pine, the pole and the equator, the crescent and the cross."

One has only to compare American policy, even at its most restrictive, with that in other new countries if one wants to appreciate the relative breadth still inherent in United States immigration practice. New countries of the British Commonwealth like Canada, Australia, and New Zealand have from the beginning tended toward national exclusiveness in accepting immigrants. More recently, frankly restrictive legislation has reinforced this tendency. Canada, in its basic immigration statute of 1910, for example, placed northern Europeans and Americans on a "preferred" basis, and permitted southern and eastern Europeans to enter only as servants and farmers, or for special occupational reasons. Both Australia and New Zealand have been most assiduous in banning Asiatics from their soil, and both countries have also raised bars against non-Britishers as well. In fact, the Undesirable Immigrants Exclusion Act of 1919 of New Zealand prohibits the landing of any person not of British birth and parentage, unless in possession of a special permit.

The Latin American countries have not been notably restrictive on grounds of ethnic origin, but they have sought to exclude certain occupational groupings, such as commercial and industrial workers. The emphasis in their policies, if one can generalize about several disparate countries at once, is on encouraging agricultural workers, and sometimes actually prohibiting, as in Mexico, the immigration of persons intending to enter commerce.

When compared with other nations, then, and for all their concern over the deleterious consequences of cultural mixture, Americans have accepted the new meaning which the immigrant has given to the national motto. "E Pluribus Unum" once referred to thirteen separate political states; today it might well stand for the peoples who came to America and here achieved unity through their cultural diversity.

The immigrant flood was only one of the three powerful social forces which were transforming America in the years after Appomattox. The other two were the factory and the city, industrialization and urbanization. The former we have already canvassed; it now remains to turn to the city.

CHAPTER XI

Alabaster Cities and Amber Waves of Grain

SEEN in the broad perspective of man's history, at least as anthropologist V. Gordon Childe contemplates it, the "Urban Revolution" dates from the sixth millennium before Christ. But, as that phrase has meaning for moderns, the Age of the City in the life of western man was the nineteenth century of the Christian era. In the course of that century, throughout the world of European civilization, millions of farmers and peasants forsook their land to stream into the strange man-made world of the city. As a result, in the middle of the twentieth century, for the first time in human history, the typical heir of European culture is a dweller in the city. Today countries as diverse in history and geography as England and Australia are highly urbanized. Seventy per cent of the population of England and Wales live in cities of 20,000 or more; over half of the people of Australia live in cities of 100,000 or more.

Though situated on the geographical periphery of European civilization, the United States also passed through the urban revolution of the latter half of the nineteenth century. Cities, to be sure, were not unknown in America before that time; almost from the first settling there had been a few like Boston, New Amsterdam, Charleston, Philadelphia, and Newport. But for almost two centuries they were little more than good-sized towns comprising no more than a small proportion of the population. As late as 1850, for example, less than 13 per cent of Americans lived in cities, of which only nine contained more than 50,000 people.

After 1865, however, the pace of urbanization noticeably quickened; by 1920, the census could report that over half the American

people, for the first time in their history, lived in cities. At that time
W. B. Munro, a lifelong student of urban institutions in the United
States, wrote, "The City of today is responsible for most of what is
good, and for most of what is bad, in our national life and ideals."
Since then, the spread of the city has been reinforced rather than
checked; for in 1950, 60 per cent of Americans lived in cities. "Cities
like sex," commented one authority in 1945, "are here to stay."

1. THE LURE OF THE CITY

The causes for the expansion of cities are complex, but they are
all firmly rooted in man's ceaseless effort to wrest more than mere
subsistence from nature. For in a quite literal sense, the birth of
cities has always been dependent upon the soil; urban life is not
possible until the return from agriculture is sufficient to permit some
men to be freed from the eternal search and labor for food. This
elementary step in human social evolution was first taken some
8,000 years ago in the New Stone Age, when agricultural technique
was first systematically used. What was necessary thousands of
years ago has continued to be essential at every subsequent stage in
the rise of urban civilization; always the migration of men from the
land to the city has been bound by the iron hoops of agricultural
productivity.

Because of this fundamental relation between the barren city and
the life-supporting soil, an urbanized society, as we use the term
today, was not technically possible before the nineteenth century.
For it was not until that century that agricultural technology and
technique were sufficiently productive to permit the majority of men
to be released from the interminable tilling of the soil. As recently
as 1787 in the United States, it required nine farm families to feed
one urban family. The impressive advances in agricultural productivity since then are graphically summed up in the fact that in 1945
eight urban families were being handsomely supported by a single
farm family.

The force which drew countrymen from their farms to the city was
economic opportunity. Sometimes this amounted to no more than a
little better life than a farmer was able to eke out of a worn-out
tenant's plot; sometimes it was a wide-open door to fame and fortune for a man whose talents were lost in a rural environment.

That the growth of cities in the nineteenth century is primarily
associated with industrial expansion is shown in a general way by

the following table, showing percentage increase of urban population each decade.

1860–1870	59.3	1910–1920	29.0
1870–1880	42.7	1920–1930	27.3
1880–1890	56.7	1930–1940	7.9
1890–1900	36.4	1940–1950	18.2
1900–1910	39.3		

From even a cursory inspection of the table, it is obvious that the rate of urbanization in the United States has been slowly falling off. But a closer look reveals that this decline has not been smooth; instead, it has been punctuated by interruptions or dips in the line of fall. Three such dips stand out: 1870–80, 1890–1900, and 1930–40. Each of these decades was characterized by a severe depression. Since after each of these decades urbanization increased—as, for example, in the 1940–50 decade, where it doubled the rate of the 1930's—it is apparent that the fall-off is due to the lack of economic opportunity in the city.

Though basically the growth of cities is the result of people moving in from the farms, that does not tell the whole story. The eternal problem of the city is the inability to supply the population with food and the factories with raw materials. Even when agricultural productivity has risen greatly, the growth of the city is still held in leading strings to the efficiency of transport. Until the steam locomotive came upon the scene in the nineteenth century, it was difficult to imagine a society in which most of the people did not live on the land; the mere transportation of the quantity of food and goods necessary to sustain them was beyond the capacity of the horse and the boat. As the way of life of a whole society, urbanism in the nineteenth century was new in man's experience, and the railroad was not the least of the several social and technological changes which made it possible. Indeed, it is possible to visualize urbanism as a new constellation of social forces—increasing agricultural production, surplus rural population, and the mechanized factory—held together by the loadstone of the railroad.

But when one has set down the economic and technological forces which undoubtedly account in large part for the growth of urbanism in America, one causal factor remains unmentioned—what A. M. Schlesinger has aptly called "the lure of the city." Always and paradoxically, the city to rural folk was repellent because of its "sinfulness" and strangeness; yet at the same time, its lights, its noises, its gaiety, its variety, its mystery were irresistible. Hamlin Garland relates in the story of his youth that he never forgot, while performing the dreary chores of the farm, the wonder of the town drugstore and its soda fountain, and above all the bustle of people and activity. For many who knew the city, its gregariousness was worth more than anything the isolated farm could promise or provide. This was illustrated in a story common in the 1890's when Americans were beginning to inquire into the "lure" which the city exercised. An Irish woman, starving in the city, was given work and a home out in the country. But in a matter of weeks she was back in her old haunts and miserable circumstances. When asked why she left her job to starve in the city again, she replied, "Paples is more coompany than sthumps."

Both the economic pull and the lure of the city were evident in the novels of the time depicting the farm boy's trek to the bright lights. "Generally speaking," concluded G. A. Dunlap, after studying over a hundred novels concerned with the newcomer to the city, "he came to find there more favorable surroundings or enlarged opportunities."

2. THE SEEDTIME OF THE CITY

In our table of urban increase after 1865, the decade of the eighties stands out as having the largest increment of population. The reasons for this are not hard to discover, for the decade was one in which city-building forces seemed to converge. The economy in general and industry in particular, after finally pulling itself out of the long depression of the seventies, was now hitting its stride. At the same time, mounting rural discontent over falling farm prices and ever-increasing waves of immigration provided hundreds of thousands of people for the building of cities.

The urban expansion in that decade is impressive. The census, for example, reported that 101 cities of 8,000 or more population doubled their size during the eighties. Examples of the growth of individual cities were sometimes not far short of spectacular. Birmingham, Alabama, for example, skyrocketed from 3,000 in 1880 to over 26,000 ten years later; El Paso multiplied itself thirteen times. Kansas City, Kansas, increased its population by 1,000 per cent, and even a large city like its namesake in Missouri jumped from 60,000 to over 132,000. Minneapolis achieved perhaps the most incredible expansion of any large city, rising from 47,000 to over

164,000. Omaha was not far behind, for it reached 140,000 in 1890, though in 1880 its population was only 30,500. In a somewhat smaller class, but remarkable for its rate of growth, was Duluth, which leaped from 3,300 to 33,100 in the course of these ten years. Two other Middle American cities deserve mention for their rapidity of growth: Sioux City, Iowa, which climbed over 500 per cent to reach almost 38,000, and Wichita, Kansas, which jumped from less than 5,000 to 23,000 ten years later.

Though the Middle West was the center of urbanization in this decade, the Far West also made tremendous strides in city building. Spokane, Washington, for example, grew from a mere 350 to 20,000, Tacoma jumped from 1,100 to 36,000, and Seattle recorded a growth of 1,100 per cent. Fresno, California, rolled up an eight-fold increase and Denver, though a good-sized city of 35,000 in 1880, more than tripled itself by 1890.

The same census which reported the expansion of the city also documented the depopulation of the rural communities. Almost 40 per cent of the 25,746 townships of the nation in 1880 reported a drop in population in 1890. The Midwest, as the center of urban growth, was also the region of striking examples of rural decimation. Almost 50 per cent of Indiana's townships, for instance, showed a decline in population for the 1880's, though the state as a whole grew in numbers. Fifty-four per cent of Illinois' and 58 per cent of Ohio's townships lost people in a decade when the states as a whole were increasing in population. In Michigan, the Census of 1890 reported almost 7,500 fewer farmers than in the previous return, though the population of the state had climbed almost half a million.

In New York and New England, the historic springs of Middle Western settlers, two thirds and more of the townships of New England and New York reported fewer people in 1890 than in 1880. It was said that in a single county in New York, 400 empty farmhouses were to be seen. Over 1,440 abandoned or vacant farms were counted in New Hampshire by the state commissioner of agriculture.

By 1910, the urban population fell only a little short of comprising half of the nation: 46 per cent. One has only to look beneath such a broad statistic to recognize that a good part of the nation was much more urbanized than even that figure suggests. Almost 85 per cent of the people of New England and over 70 per cent of the inhabitants of the Middle Atlantic states made their homes in towns and cities. In the tier of states which stretched from Pennsylvania to the Mississippi, north of the Ohio River—the area which was becoming the heart of industrial America—over 50 per cent of the people were classified as urban folk. Fifty-five per cent of the people living in the three states which faced the Pacific Ocean were living in cities. Indeed, the decade between 1900 and 1910 saw the Pacific coastal states set the pace of urbanization for the rest of the nation, as the Midwestern states had done in the 1880's. Whereas the country as a whole increased its urban population by only 35 per cent, the three Pacific states more than doubled their city dwellers in the first ten years of the twentieth century.

The most dramatic manifestation of urbanization is the great city—urban centers which counted 100,000 or more in population. By 1910, almost 45 per cent of the people of the Middle Atlantic states lived in a relatively few great cities, and a third of the population of the Pacific coastal states did. It was also in 1910 that the census recognized twenty-five so-called Metropolitan Districts, which, in reality, were twenty-five large cities surrounded by contributory and contiguous smaller cities and towns. In effect, the Metropolitan District was an acknowledgment that many small cities which were contiguous were actually providing an environment very close to that of a great city. It also provided a new measure of the extent to which America had become urbanized; in 1910, over 22 million people, out of a total of 92 million, lived in these twenty-five Metropolitan Districts.[1]

As the great city and the metropolis developed, the urban satellite soon followed. "Dormitory cities" out from the industrial city began to appear as early as the 1880's; in that decade Brookline, Massachusetts, was already being termed the "bedroom" of Boston. In 1884, when a branch line of the Pennsylvania Railroad was run out, Chestnut Hill assumed the same relationship to Philadelphia and, about the same time, Lake Forest became Chicago's "dormitory." More recently, whole counties have taken on this function for the great metropolis of New York: Essex in New Jersey, Nassau on Long Island, Fairfield in Connecticut, and Westchester in New York.

There were other kinds of satellites, too. Small industrial towns

---

[1] The movement into the urban conglomerate continues today. In 1951, almost a quarter of the people of the nation were living in *eight* of the largest of these great urban centers; in 1910, the same percentage of the population was spread among twenty-five such districts.

surrounding a great city and drawing on its labor pool were increasingly evident. Pittsburgh, for example, was rimmed with little steel towns in the years after 1880: Homestead, Duquesne, McKeesport, Aliquippa, and Ambridge. Graniteware manufacturing towns like Granite City, Alton, and East St. Louis, all in Illinois, grew up across the Mississippi from Missouri's great city of St. Louis. A somewhat different type of industrial satellite was the town established by the company to house its workers and to enable it to exert a greater control over the employees. Pullman, Illinois, and Gary, Indiana, just outside Chicago, were examples of these.

The rapidity with which the city spread across America, engulfing more and more of the people, was only the exterior of the Urban Revolution. Its deeper significance was to be sought in the kind of environment the city provided.

3. MEN MAKE CITIES

Eager as many a countryman appeared to be to get to the city, the physical aspects of the object of his trek must have often been disillusioning upon arrival. The Census of 1880 contains a wealth of data on the unsavory countenance of the American city, and almost any random selection from it calls up pictures of primitive conditions. Take, for example, the report on sanitation in the old and established city of Philadelphia. "The custom almost universally practised of turning sink-and-slop water on the ground," the report said, "allowing it to flow across the sidewalks, and stagnate in the street-gutters, has such a pernicious influence upon the atmosphere that one feels an indescribable sense of relief in going to the park or moving out of town, where the air is not laden and polluted with the fetid vapors and foul odors everywhere prevailing in Philadelphia." It was further said that across the river in New Jersey, Camden emptied the night soil from its privies upon the "gathering grounds of the public water supply." Manufacturing wastes were run into the Delaware River without check from the Camden side, and on the other bank Philadelphia emptied its sewers into the same waters. This was the very same river, it should be added, from which Philadelphia drew a good part of its drinking water.

Such lack of concern over sanitation was more typical than exceptional in American municipalities in 1880. Indianapolis, with a population of over 75,000, did not have more than 10 per cent of its homes equipped with water closets; the night soil removed from the city's thousands of privies was emptied into the White River. In Baltimore, with a population of over 330,000, there were "no sewers to speak of . . . all chamber slops," the census reported, being "deposited in cess-pools or privy-vaults." As might have been anticipated, the city's 80,000 cesspools, thanks to the porous soil, constituted a menace to the wells of drinking water. A sampling of thirty-five wells and springs showed that twenty-three were "filthy" in the official opinion, and all the rest in bad or suspicious condition, except for a single one, which was classed as "good."

Paved streets were so rare, even in the large cities, that they might be classified as municipal luxuries. Though Minneapolis, for example, contained almost 47,000 people and 200 miles of streets, none of the streets was paved and the sidewalks were nothing but pine planking. "One of the serious drawbacks" of a great city like New Orleans, the census recognized, was the fact that less than one fifth of its 500 miles of streets were paved, though its population exceeded 200,000. Heavy rains turned the streets into "almost impassable mire" and during a drought the same streets were "extremely dusty." Although Atlanta, Georgia, was approaching a population of 40,000, only three of its 100 miles of streets were paved; the rest were only dirt roads.

Gradually, during the remainder of the century, brick paving crept over the streets of American cities, but it was not until the twentieth century that asphalt, the paving of the great cities of Europe for half a century, could rival brick. It was largely the advent of the bicycle and then the automobile which provided the stimulus for laying a smoother and quieter pavement in the cities of America.

Americans have never distinguished themselves, except perhaps for the TVA, by their social planning; for the most part, social institutions have been left to develop freely and under the stimulus of individual interest. Only later, if at all, do Americans get around to shaping them to the various needs of the people. This attitude was particularly evident as the cities of the nineteenth century began to mushroom across the nation. Occasionally a city, like New York in 1810, actually worked out a plan for its future growth, but usually the cities grew as they would, without plan and without guidance.

Very few of the municipal governments made any provision for recreation in the growing cities, even though it should have been obvious that the new urban environment was almost devoid of the old rural facilities for play. New York, it is true, set an admirable example in the 1850's with its great Central Park, which became the wonder of American municipal life. But few other cities were so thoughtful or farsighted. Several big cities like Newark and Jersey City in New Jersey, Allegheny and Pittsburgh in Pennsylvania, Brooklyn in New York, and Cleveland in Ohio actually devoted more of their areas to cemeteries than they did to recreational parks. Whereas New York led the list with 19.8 per cent of its land given over to parks, Newark could spare less than 1 per cent, though 1.7 per cent was taken up with cemeteries. Only four of the cities of 100,000 population in 1880 devoted more than 5 per cent of their acreage to recreation.

One of the distinguishing features of urban living was the high density of population, a fact which must have been painfully apparent to anyone who walked along the crowded streets and saw the closely packed tenements bulging with humanity. In 1890, the average number of persons per dwelling in the United States was 5.45, but for New York City the average was 18.52. For Cincinnati it was 8.87; for Boston, 8.52; for Chicago, 8.60; for Hartford, 8.12. In Montana, the ratio was 4.9.

The tenement, which was largely responsible for the city's higher density, came to New York as early as the 1830's, attaining the distinction of a problem in the 1850's.[2] By the 1890's, land-use maps for New York afforded ample testimony of the almost incredible coverage of the land by the dumbbell style of tenement. This type of housing, first introduced in 1879 as a "sanitary" improvement, received its name from the shape of the floor plan, the slim indentations on the side forming a narrow air shaft between the otherwise closely set buildings. The design was eagerly taken up by landowners anxious to squeeze the maximum of rent from their city footage, and soon, as one writer has said, the tenement "spread over Manhattan

[2] The apartment house for the middle and upper classes did not arrive until the 1870's and 1880's, even though the tenement for the poor was long in evidence and the "flat" had been accepted in Paris for a hundred years. To New Yorkers and Bostonians of the upper classes, the apartment had a flavor of French immorality about it. "It was no easy matter for the French-trained [Richard Morris] Hunt . . . to persuade respectable New Yorkers to take advantage of the apartment house," two recent historians of American building have written. "They were as provincial as the rest of the country at the time and were convinced that the 'French flat' would lead to a breakdown of the American family."

Island like a scab." For acre after acre the poor of the city were crammed into these airless, unsanitary, unattractive firetraps. Other cities, like Boston, followed the example of New York and introduced the dumbbell; some cities, like Philadelphia, did not, but other types of multiple dwellings in row after monotonous row served much the same purpose of utilizing every precious foot in an overcrowded city.

The result of such lack of planning and unconcern for beauty and attractiveness was a dull and uninteresting urban face. Lord Bryce, for example, when traveling in the United States in the 1880's, thought that only eight or nine cities in the whole country displayed any distinction or charm. The rest, he wrote, "differ from one another only herein, that some of them are built more with brick than with wood, and others more with wood than brick. In all else they are alike, both great and small." And then he went on to describe the result of the miserable amount of imagination expended on city planning. "In all the same wide streets, crossing at right angles, ill-paved, but planted along the sidewalks with maple trees. . . . In all the same shops, arranged on the same plan, the same Chinese laundries with Li Kow visible through the window, the same ice cream stores, the same large hotels . . . the same street cars passing to and fro with passengers clinging to the door-step, the same locomotives ringing their great bells as they clank slowly down the middle of the street."

For most of the nineteenth century, the size of the city was rather rigidly limited by the slow-moving horse-drawn trolley or omnibus. It was not until the 1870's that American cities were freed from this leash on their growth through the introduction of new means of rapid transit. New York tried the elevated steam train, which had the distinct drawback of spraying oil and live ashes on passers-by below, and of being economically feasible in only the very largest of cities. Nevertheless, Kansas City, Brooklyn, Chicago, and Boston, in their desperate search for rapid urban transportation, followed the New York example. At the same time, several cities, like Philadelphia and Chicago, were experimenting with the cable car, a device first used in San Francisco on its steep hills.

The real break-through in the transportation bottleneck, however, came toward the end of the 1880's when Richmond, Virginia, successfully introduced the electric trolley. This vehicle initiated a minor revolution in urban transportation, for it was practical in both large and small cities and it was relatively swift without being dangerous. In short order the trolley became the typical mode of urban transit; by 1895, there were over 10,000 miles of trolley tracks in the cities of the nation. Though even the greatest metropolises used the trolley, they also employed the electrically driven subway and elevated railway, Boston beginning its subway in 1895 and New York in 1905. But it was the noisy but efficient trolley that dominated the main streets of America's cities and towns right up until the Second World War. By then, because the multiplicity of automobiles rendered the trolley's lack of maneuverability a traffic obstruction, it was condemned to extinction.

Transportation was only one of the problems which were unknown on the farm but assumed weighty proportions in the city. Garbage and waste disposal, for instance—a relatively simple matter on the farm—posed formidable tests of man's ingenuity and knowledge of chemistry once the city concentrated the refuse of thousands of people. It would be decades before garbage and sewage disposal was no longer a pressing problem of the city. Though in the humid sections of the nation the location of potable water was only a minor chore of settlement, in the city it became a desperate search, and aqueducts of the cities were pushed farther and farther into the back country, as they still are today, in a ceaseless quest for sufficient and pure water. Similarly, danger from fire, theft, and bodily harm increased many times as men exchanged the comparative isolation of the farms for the swarming dangers of the city.

4. BUT CITIES ALSO MAKE MEN

Though it was not until 1920 that most Americans lived in cities, urban values had long set the tone and defined the aspirations of American culture. Indeed, the history of the latter part of the nineteenth century, as we shall have occasion to see a little later, can be written in terms of the gradual spread of urban life until it pervaded the uttermost crannies of society. But for the moment it would be well to pause and try to point up those differences which have traditionally drawn a line between life in the city and life on the farm. The rural man has instinctively recognized this line, and when he has crossed it he has known himself to be in a different world. Sociologically and psychologically, what does it mean when one goes from the country to the city?

One can exaggerate the differences between urban and rural life, to be sure. It is true that the "city" is not a single type of environment, but actually a *range* of environments. A city of 3,000 people, for example, is obviously quite a different social milieu from one of three million, as any New Yorker will be quick to point out to the booster from Zenith.

Despite this, however, there are sound reasons for treating all cities as essentially a single environment. The primary reason is that all cities have more in common with one another than any of them do with the countryside. This is best illustrated by the differences in the occupations in cities as against those which are found in the country. All occupations, except farming, flourish in the city; only one, farming, exists in the country. In 1930, for example, 99.5 per cent of the agriculturally employed population lived in communities of less than 2,500 people—i.e., in areas which did not meet the census definition of a city. It does not take much imagination to recognize that, from this fact alone, the city and the country must be considerably different. Think of the complexity of life, of habits, of work which results from an environment in which a great variety of occupations is to be found, as compared with the simplicity which inevitably follows where there is mainly only one. Furthermore, all cities, even the tiniest, are knit together by their aspirations. They want to be like big cities, not like the countryside. This ambition, which is sometimes exhibited as boosterism, inevitably sets the city psychologically apart from the country. As Oswald Spengler pointed out, the city "is a place from which the countryside is henceforth regarded, felt, and experienced as 'environs,' as something different and subordinate."

Finally, it can be pointed out that the number of small cities— say, below 10,000 population—which because of their size might be thought to blur the clean line between city and country make up only a small proportion of the population. In 1910, for instance, people in towns of 10,000 or less made up only 9 per cent of the population, when the total urban ratio was something like 45 per cent. In short, though a sharp line such as the census draws with its minimum of 2,500 may be difficult to accept, there can be little question that, as between the city and the country in general, the social gulf is much wider than that between any given city and another.

"The man of the land and the man of the city are different essences," Spengler wrote. "First of all they feel the difference, then they are dominated by it, and at last they cease to understand each

other at all." Whether there are "essences" may be debatable, but
there can be little doubt that the city transforms the countryfolk
who come to make their homes there. Harriet Arnow, in her novel
The Dollmaker, has brilliantly described some of these changes, as in
this passage: "Slowly her hand dropped from the doorknob, and she
turned back to Clovis. It wasn't the way it had used to be back home
when she had done her share, maybe more than her share of feeding
and fending for the family. Then, with egg money, chicken money, a
calf sold here, a pig sold there, she'd bought almost every bite of
food they didn't raise. Here everything, even to the kindling wood,
came from Clovis."

As the novel makes quite clear, much more than a loss of wifely
independence was involved in the move from the Kentucky hills to
industrial Detroit. Privacy was lost through the thin walls of the
city apartment; the impersonalities of the city permitted cheating
at the store, both by the customer who did not know the merchant
and by the storekeeper because he was not known by the purchaser.
The social pressure to "adjust" to the new ways, the rift between
parents and children because their rates of accommodation differed
and because the children were now subjected to novel influences like
the movies, the Girl Scouts, and the soap operas, are all oddly
reminiscent of the immigrant's struggle to adjust to and understand
his new world. Actually, of course, the similarities are not so odd;
to go from the farm to the city was as much a movement out of one
culture into another as to come from Europe. The Kentucky farm
folk of *The Dollmaker* were no more prepared than European immigrants for the frightening kitchen gadgets, the chlorinated water,
the work hours unrelated to the sun, and the absence of greenery
which urban life involved.[3]

As the city and the country differed in their material aspects, so
they differed in, what was perhaps more important, the habits of

[3] A story by the nineteenth-century Spanish writer Leopoldo Alas suggests
that the city has had the same effect on rural people wherever it might be. In
Alas' story Dona Berta, the heroine, came for the first time to Madrid after a
long life in a remote rural area. "Contemplating Madrid when it was deserted
reconciled her somewhat to it. The streets seemed less hostile, more like the
small, narrow lanes she knew; the trees more like the 'real trees.' . . . She was
afraid of the multitude . . . but most of all, she was afraid of being run down,
trampled, crushed by horses, by wheels. . . . The trolley looked like a cautious
monster, an insidious serpent to her. She imagined that the guillotine was
something like those hidden wheels that slid like a knife along the two iron lines."
Great Spanish Stories (New York, 1956), p. 193.

mind of the people who lived there. As Robert MacIver has pointed out, the fact that there are no farmers in the city serves to produce a quite different outlook on life among city people as compared with rural. For the latter, he writes, "there is no sense of a common and vital dependence on the aspects of the seasons and the vagaries of the weather. There is no sense of a common earth, a common fortune and a common fate. . . . There are no impressive signs to call out at the same moment those universal comments and reflections which make man feel kin to man—the devastation of the storm, the flow of the sap, the fall of the leaf." Unlike rural men, the urban dwellers are diverse in origins, in interests, in occupations, in their whole lives. Where the rural family is relatively isolated, the urban family is closely involved with many other people; yet the breadwinner is outside the home site for most of the daylight hours. Even recreation in the city is conditioned by the environment; sports are for spectators, not participants.

Relieved in large part from the pressure of competition by the fact of his isolation, the rural man lives a relatively simple, outdoor life in contrast with the competitive, indoor, anxious search for prestige and position which the highly mobile and social environment forces upon the city dweller. Rural life, to be sure, like nature itself, changes through time, but in contrast city life races; people are constantly moving in and out; businesses are succeeding and failing; the very face of the city itself, man-constructed as it is, is also man-destroyed.

This very fluidity of urban existence induces a change in the character of the countryfolk who come under its influence. "The city calls more for alertness, the quick mind that responds to the changing occasion" than does the farm, McIver has concluded. "What is seen superficially in manners is revealed more profoundly in morals. 'Urbanity' belongs to the city." It is the rural community which holds fast to the old morality, to the traditional ways; it is the city which is so used to change that it accepts it with equanimity. But the city pays a price for this, too. The corollary of the urban man's repudiation of the social anchor of tradition is an increased burden of anxiety. Insofar as the environment of the city loosens the hold of religion, the family, and traditional morality, to that extent it undermines the social forces which sometimes are all that keep men steady in times of stress.

Essentially the city is movement—vertically and horizontally.

The ladders of social mobility, like the means of horizontal transportation and hustle and bustle, are concentrated within the city: the Church, the government, education, the law, the courts, the army, the arts, journalism, and so forth. The very hierarchy of occupations in the city, of which there is no counterpart in the country, encourages and too often compels a struggle for movement in which many rise and many fall. And if, as sociologist Louis Wirth has observed, "mobility is an index of metabolism," then the city is almost consuming itself in its own activity.

It would seem to follow, then, that as the nation becomes progressively urbanized, the competitiveness of the city will add its considerable weight to that historic American drive to excel, to keep up with the Joneses, to rise in the social scale.

But if the city has encouraged the drive to excel, it at least has provided the opportunity. Toward the end of the Dark Ages, as cities began to reappear upon the map of Europe, the hallmark of the emergent city was freedom; "*Stadtluft macht frei*" was the urban slogan of the twelfth century. In the twentieth century, one urban planner still finds the essence of the city to be its air of freedom. "In our industrial society, the city represents a particularly precious form of freedom—freedom of choice of work," Charles Ascher wrote in 1945. "If one skill becomes obsolete, there are facilities to learn another and the chance to practice it. Father can work in a mill, son in a filling station, daughter in an office."

The site of all past civilizations, as the word itself implies, has been the city, and so it is today. Uniformly, literacy has been higher in cities than in country districts, just as it has been greater in urbanized New England than in the rural South. At one time in the 1890's it was calculated that American cities produced twice as many names in *Who's Who* as the proportion of urban people warranted. One student investigated the origins of 6,000 French men of letters for the five centuries prior to 1895 and found that cities produced thirteen times as many prominent figures in proportion to the population as did the country districts. Then, as now, it is obvious that the city, wherever it is found, is the center of art, the theater, the newspaper, publishing—indeed, the center of all endeavors concerned with the printed and written word or the transmission of ideas.

Cities are also paradoxes. "Their rapid growth and large size testify to their superiority as a technique for the exploitation of the earth," two sociologists have written, "yet by their very success and consequent large size, they often provide a poor local environment for man." And that "poor local environment" is something else besides inadequate housing, noise, filth, crime, and crowded conditions, though they are bad enough. It also includes psychological factors like competitiveness, anxiety, insecurity, and loneliness.

"In the city there is little or no sense of neighborhood," wrote Josiah Strong, a crusading clergyman of the 1890's. "You may be separated from your next neighbor by only a few inches, and yet for years never see his face or learn his name. Mere proximity does not imply social touch." This phenomenon, which all who have lived in the city immediately recognize as typical, is perhaps the most paradoxical aspect of the city. It seems, almost, as if there is a social law that decrees that the more people there are in a city, the slighter the contact among them. To young men just arriving from the country, Strong remarked, "the first thing that is impressed on them is their own utter loneliness, which often seems unendurable." In such loneliness a sociologist like Sorokin has located the cause for the consistently higher suicide rate of the city—a rate, incidentally, which has steadily increased in the United States as urbanization has proceeded. In 1860, the suicide rate per 100,000 was 3.18; in 1922, it was 11.9.

But it is not only in regard to suicides that the city is a greater threat to human life than the country. For the most part, a person born in the city could not anticipate living as long as he might, had he been born on a farm. For example, the parents of a baby boy born in a city in 1901 could expect him to attain the age of forty-four, but farm parents of a male child would be able to look forward to slightly more than ten additional years of life for their offspring. Since the turn of the century, the spread between rural and urban life expectancies has narrowed, but it is still there.

It is only fair to add that the city as distinguished from industrialization may not be responsible for the short life expectancy of city dwellers; there is evidence, for example, that it is industrialization which is the true cause. But since it is almost impossible to separate industry from its natural habitat, and since no cities are without some industry, we are justified in concluding that between the twin forces of the factory and the city, men are robbed of several years of life.

A similar difficulty in separating the influence of the factory from that of the city is met with when we deal with rural urban differences in birth rates and family sizes. It is well known that the birth rate is lower and the family size smaller in cities as compared with rural communities.[4] But it is also well recognized that family size and birth rate decline as income increases, and since it is equally acknowledged that wealth is more highly concentrated in cities than in rural areas, we cannot know whether the downward changes in these indices are the result of rising incomes or of the environment of the city. It is logical to assume, nonetheless, that the urban milieu plays some part, if only because the children in the city constitute an economic loss rather than an asset as they do on the farm. Moreover, contraceptive knowledge and equipment have usually been more available in the city than in the country.

The precise causal factors, however, are not so important as far as American civilization is concerned. More significant is the fact that these population and mortality trends are closely associated with urban life. If the United States continues to fall under the influence of the city—as everything seems to suggest it will—then these urban characteristics will become increasingly descriptive of American life as a whole.

It is not necessary, however, to speculate about the future effects of urbanization and industrialization; the past impact is spread upon the record for all to see. One of the first areas to feel the alchemy of industrial and urban change was agriculture.

5. THE HAND THAT FEEDS IS BITTEN

The broad foundation on which both industrial and urban expansion rested in the nineteenth century was the great improvement in farming—an event which agricultural historian Carl Taylor has called "as significant in its effects as the Industrial Revolution" in England a century before. Between 1865 and 1900, a mountain of foodstuffs and raw materials poured from the farms of America. Wheat production climbed from 152 million bushels in 1866 to 500 million in 1880 and then soared up to 675 million in 1898. The out-

[4] Urban fecundity has been so low that for most of the last fifty years cities in the United States have failed to reproduce themselves. Only the influx of immigrants and countryfolk has kept cities growing. In 1930, for example, the net reproduction rate for cities was 88.0, where 100 represents bare replacement of the population. The rate at that time for rural-farm population was far above replacement: 159. Only since World War II has the urban reproduction rate gone above 100. Before 1900, the birth rate of cities was lower than that of rural areas, but the net reproduction rate was above 100.

put of corn exceeded even these levels: 730 million bushels in 1866, 1,500 million in 1880, and 2,330 million in 1898. Though the Civil War had all but extinguished cotton production in the United States, the snowy fiber made a spectacular comeback; in 1898, something over 11 million bales or 4 billion pounds were grown in the American South.

The torrent of production was of such proportions that even the rapidly expanding population of the United States could not absorb it; it gushed out to engulf the world. Whereas in the 1850's the United States exported about 19 million bushels of wheat and 33 million pounds of beef products, by the late 1870's the annual exportation of these agricultural commodities increased sevenfold. Yet this was only the beginning of the flood of food and fiber which surged across the face of the world from the American cornucopia, the crest not being reached until the opening years of the twentieth century. In 1901, the wheat surplus of the country was 234 million bushels; in 1906, the exports of beef products exceeded 731 million pounds; and it was not until 1910 that the exportation of pork products fell below an annual rate of one billion pounds. It almost seemed as if the grim prognostications of old Robert Malthus were being smothered in foodstuffs.

Such production, however, was only possible because the American farmer, in the years between 1870 and 1900, transformed raw nature at an unprecedented pace. It was as if the cover of half a continent was ripped off in those thirty years. Between 1870 and 1900, 225 million acres of improved land were added to American farms, or 37 million acres *more* than had been put to the plow in all of the two and a half centuries since Jamestown was settled.

The beginnings of this incredibly rapid opening of the lands of the country go back to the years of the War for the Union. The passage of the Homestead Act in 1862, for example, permitted the rapid transfer of enormous quantities of public lands into private hands, both directly to settlers and otherwise through fraud. Similarly the land grants to railroads immediately after the war resulted in millions of acres of government lands being thrown on the market for private exploitation.

The great spurt in agricultural expansion is only partly explained by the increase in the amount of land opened up to cultivation; of equal importance was the coming of the machine to the farm. Like the opening of the land, the mechanization of agriculture was pushed by the war. With perhaps a million farmers in the Union armies at a time when the nation's demand for food was increasing, those left behind on the farms were compelled to turn to machinery. The success of machines, particularly reapers and threshers, in producing a greater wheat crop than during peacetime assured the future use of such labor-saving instruments.

Through the remaining four decades of the century, man power was generally replaced by horse power as the thresher, grain drill, hay mower, corn and fodder cutters, and other machines came into wider and wider use. Furthermore, as other machines were invented and introduced, they too brought the superior power of the horse to the service of the farmer. By as early as 1880, four fifths of the wheat grown in the nation was cut by machine; in the 1880's and 1890's, a mechanical corn harvester also came into use, to be followed soon by a corn binder.

Some of the machines were enormous savers of time and labor. One government witness before the Industrial Commission of 1901 testified that in the mid-nineties a bushel of corn could be shelled by a steam sheller in one and a half minutes; by hand it used to take 100 minutes. When farmers reaped, bound, and threshed by hand, the witness reported, it took 160 minutes for each bushel of wheat; with a combine, the same tasks were completed with only four minutes of human labor. In the 1880's and 1890's, great steam tractors were rumbling over the flat, open prairies of the Dakotas and the bonanza farms of California as men tried to harness steam power to the needs of agriculture. Though the cotton belt enjoyed no significant harvesting improvements, the productivity of the southern farmer was nevertheless increased by the growing use of mechanical planters, stalk cutters, and fertilizer distributors.

After 1860, the recourse to machinery in agriculture steadily advanced. The Census of 1850 reported that $6.8 million was invested in farm implements and machinery; in 1880, the figure had risen ten times; and by 1900, it was $101.2 million. Furthermore, such figures, rather than overestimating the increase in the use of farm machinery, actually tended to minimize it, since prices of farm implements fell during the years after 1865. As in industry, the key to the expansion of agricultural production was improved technology and the intensification of capital.

Unquestionably the greatest stimulus to production in the latter half of the nineteenth century was the ever-widening market. Within the nation, the railroad net, with its progressively finer mesh, provided improved marketing facilities for farm goods, while fresh arrivals of immigrants meant new stomachs to be filled and bodies to be clothed by the produce of the farms. But the growth of American agricultural production outran even the rapidly expanding national market. As early as the 1880's, American wheat was flowing like water into the remote crevices and valleys of western and central Europe. "Austrians and Hungarians stood aghast," William Trimble has written, "to see it sold even in the markets of Trieste and Fiume, the long-time places of exportation." In 1900, 34 per cent of American wheat, 10 per cent of the corn, and 66 per cent of the cotton crop was exported. A witness before the Industrial Commission of 1901 estimated that "about one-fourth of the total agricultural production of the country is exported."

The immediate effect of the entrance of American farmers into the world agricultural market was near catastrophe for many European countries. Despair settled over the farms of Europe as prices and land values plummeted. Between 1871 and 1891, for instance, the price of wheat fell 27 per cent in Germany and about 30 per cent in Sweden. In the face of such a decline in farm income, many European farmers were ruined and pressed down into the status of agricultural laborers; many sought relief by flight to El Dorado itself, the source of their misery. Landlords also felt the pressure from American fecundity. Rents on the large estates of Prussia fell 20 to 30 per cent; land values in the United Kingdom tumbled almost 50 per cent between 1874 and 1894. Under such conditions, it is not surprising that Dr. Alexander Peez, the Austrian statesman, spoke of the enormous American grain exports as "the greatest economic event of modern times," comparable in significance with the influx of American gold in the sixteenth century which produced the Price Revolution.

This second Price Revolution to emanate from America was only possible because another revolution, one in communications, was under way. Thanks to the telegraph, the improved marine steam engine, the submarine cable, and the steady decline in rail and shipping rates, the separate national economies of the North Atlantic basin were being integrated into a single intercontinental market. Thanks to the rapid and tightly knit system of international communications and transport, the expanding industrial economy of Europe was able to look to America as the breadbasket of its industrial and urban population. To America, the creation of an international market for its agricultural output meant that the United States would be able to balance the payments on its own imports. Between 1873 and 1900, the United States enjoyed a favorable balance of trade every year save two. That it was agriculture which made this possible is shown by the fact that in all those years farm commodities made up three quarters or more of total American exports. This was the farmer's contribution to the acceleration of American industrialization.

But if the commercialization of agriculture ensured favorable trade balances for the economy as a whole, for the farmer it meant loss of control over his market. The price of wheat, for example, was now determined by forces outside America, since the almost instantaneous communications and the cheap, efficient transportation made world supply and demand the determinant of prices. A poor harvest in America, which in earlier days might at least have had the mitigating consequence of higher prices, now might mean nothing of the sort; a bumper crop in faraway Russia or in distant India could just as easily drive the price down.

Indeed, American farmers soon found that the expansion of the world's agricultural production, of which America's was but a part, brought a steady fall in farm prices all through the 1880's and 1890's. Entrance into a world market, as far as the farmer was concerned, meant that there was no longer any possibility that he or his government could exercise any significant control over farm prices at all. Unfortunately, this fact was never clear to the American farmer, if one is to judge from the protest literature he issued; he always held the trusts, the grain elevators, the railroads, and Wall Street chiefly responsible for his falling income. It was only after the farmers had wrestled with these local devils that they turned, in the twentieth century, to the fundamental source of their woes: the impersonal, almost mysterious interaction of world supply and demand over which no trust and no monetary policy ruled. But before we deal with the farmers' efforts to ameliorate the impact of the market, it may be worth while to indicate what that impact was.

6. THE FARMER COMES OF AGE

Despite the idyllic image of the independent subsistence farmer conjured up by agrarian philosophers like Thomas Jefferson and John Taylor of Caroline, the commercialization of agriculture was

as inevitable as time. As early as 1776, Adam Smith had shown
that economic efficiency and material abundance followed specializa-
tion and the division of labor. Once this principle was learned in
industry, it was foreordained that farming would pick it up, too.
For after all, idealize him as one might, the fiercely independent
frontiersman who, in addition to raising his own food, also built his
home and made his own furniture and tools, while his wife made the
family's clothes, candles and soap, and whatnot, lived a hard life of
never-ending toil. And even when his years of work were done, his
home was still crude, his furniture makeshift, his clothes coarse, and
his diet monotonous. Under such conditions, the farmer and his wife,
when new markets became available, were only too happy to see their
home industries transferred to the factory, the products of which
could now be purchased with the cash obtained from the sale of a
commercial crop.

For a number of years before the Civil War, this transfer of home
industries to the factory had been in process. By the end of the century, the vast majority of the farmers had given up the home manufacturing of their ancestors and concentrated their labor and talents
on the raising of one or two cash crops. In substance, the farmer had
become a businessman, producing and selling a commodity in an in-
tricately interconnected market of exchangeable commodities.

The effect was to change the farmer's way of doing business. "The
old rule that a farmer should produce all that he required and that
the surplus represented his gains, is part of the past," observed the
Chicago *Prairie Farmer* in 1868. "Agriculture, like all other business, is better for its subdivisions, each one growing that which is
best suited to his soil, skill, climate, and market, and with its pro-
ceeds purchase his other needs." Later, in 1904, the *Cornell Countryman* frankly declared the Jeffersonian Arcadia outmoded. "Now the
object of farming is not primarily to make a living, but it is to make
money. To this end it is to be conducted on the same business basis
as any other producing industry."

On a wider scale, commercialization changed the patterns of agricultural production. For example, with the creation of a national
railroad net, eastern farmers were brought into competition with
the virgin and richer farm lands of the West. For New England this
often resulted in the wholesale abandonment of farms; in other areas,
such as New York and Pennsylvania, the only recourse was a shift to
perishable crops like dairy products and vegetables, which were out

of the reach of western competition. Thus, for some, the wider
markets meant increased opportunities; for others, it meant economic death or drastic shifts in old habits. In all cases, the impersonal but powerful forces of the market were narrowing the
freedom of choice available to the heretofore free-wheeling, individualistic farmer.

Attention to the problems and changes which commercialization
bestowed upon the American farmer must not obscure the fact that
most of the material advantages he sought were actually forthcoming. "This is a new age to the farmer," George Holmes, a statis-
tician for the Department of Agriculture, told the Industrial
Commission in 1901. "He is now, more than ever before, a citizen of
the world. Cheap and excellent books and perodical publications load
the shelf and the table in his sitting room and parlor. He travels
more than he ever did before, and he travels longer distances. His
children are receiving a better education than he received himself,
and they dress better than he did when he was a child. They are more
frequently in contact with town and city life than he was."

Yet this was apparently not enough. Eight years after Holmes
testified, and still during a period of farm prosperity, President
Theodore Roosevelt told the Congress, "It would be idle to assert
that life on the farm occupies as good a position of dignity, desirability and business results as farmers might easily give it if they
chose. One of the chief difficulties," the President said, "is the failure
of country life, as it exists at the present, to satisfy the higher social
and intellectual aspirations of country people."

Contradictory as these two summaries of the farmers' life are,
they actually symbolize the consequences of commercialization. On
the one hand, the farmers enjoyed the variety and cheapness of
goods which the market and expanding industry placed at their
disposal; but on the other, they were discontented and insecure because, as mere cogs in the great machine of the market, they were
exposed to every shock which the system sustained. Though involvement in the market brought sweets, it also demanded hostages to
fortune.[5]

[5] Even mechanization, lamented the president of the Grange when he appeared
before the Industrial Commission, seemed to bring too few advantages to the
individual farmer. Asked whether it was not true that mechanization reduced
production costs, he replied, "It has reduced the cost of production to some extent, but what is strange to say, in those cradling days [that is, before the
mechanical reaper] it appeared to be as easy for the farmer to pay his lawful

Moreover, it was a fact that the more the farmer savored the delights of the larger world, the more meager farm life appeared to him. One manifestation of this was the steady depopulation of the countryside in the later decades of the century; another was President Theodore Roosevelt's call in 1908 for a Country Life Commission. It was the President himself who asked, "How can the life of the farm family be made less solitary, fuller of opportunity, freer from drudgery, more comfortable, happier, and more attractive?" Such a question was itself a severe indictment of what life on the farm was. And when the Commission had completed its inquiry, it reported in the same vein as the President's charge: "agriculture is not commercially as profitable as it is entitled to be for the labor and energy that the farmer expends and the risks that he assumes" (no one seemed willing to admit that the farmer was now a producer in a market in which the supply was far outrunning the demand) "and . . . the social conditions in the open country are far short of their possibilities." One of the striking evils of farm life, named again and again in the hearings, was heavy drinking. The commissioners concluded in their report that "Intemperance is largely the result of the barrenness of farm life, particularly the lot of the hired man." In brief, farming was hardly the wholesome, satisfying existence Americans had thought it was; the problem of "How you gonna keep 'em down on the farm" long antedated any visit to Paree.

If a taste of the fleshpots of Egypt had rendered the farmers discontented with the agrarian life Jefferson and others had taught them to prize, it had not always been so. It is true that the apotheosis of the independent, hard-working, simple but honest farmer had always been an ideal rather than an actuality, but once there had been more truth than distortion in it. Richard Hofstadter is perfectly right when he argues that American agriculture has always been tainted with the search for the main chance; has always been highly enterprising, even speculative, rather than static and traditional. But when he further declares that the "United States failed to develop . . . a distinctively *rural* culture," he is using European agricultural mores as the norm. To do that is quite misleading, for the agrarian ideal of America, the truth of which Hofstadter seems to deny, took the independent, forward-looking, free *American*

---

debts then as it is now, and if you put that question to 100 farmers, I venture to say that 99 of them would say, 'much easier.'" Moreover, he regretfully observed, with all the mechanical aids, the farmer seemed to work as long as ever.

farmer as its typical figure, not the tradition-directed European
peasant. The putative father of the myth, Thomas Jefferson, certainly thought of his idealized yeoman as struck from a far different
mold from that which shaped the downtrodden European peasant.
None of the agrarian philosophers were singing the praises of European peasants; they were celebrating the progressive American
farmer as they knew him in the fields of America.

It is true, as Rudolph Heberle pointed out in 1929, that "The
agricultural population in the United States . . . is mobile to a
high degree if compared with the country population of Europe. The
facility with which the American farmer changes from one farm to
another has always astonished the European observer." But if the
occupational mobility of the city and the country in America is
compared, then the relative stability of farm life is quite apparent.
Only 22.5 per cent of the businessmen of Minneapolis, for example,
followed their fathers' occupation, but 63.7 per cent of the sons and
daughters of Minnesota farmers did so. In short, compared with the
European, the American farmer was mobile; but compared with the
city dweller, he was traditional, secure, conservative, and steady.

According to agricultural historian Paul Johnstone, so it was in
the years before 1860. The farm home, he says, was a "Gibraltar of
security," and because "no one was far from hardship and none had
excess of ease," poverty did not bring loss of self-respect. Moreover,
"when opportunity was not at hand, it could be found just over
the horizon." At one time, then, there had been hard substance to the
dream of Arcadia, and though farmers, like most Americans in the
nineteenth century, contended for a foothold on the ladder of social
advancement, this does not deny the independence and security
which farming brought to its practitioners in the years before 1870.

But in subsequent years the pervasiveness of the commercial spirit
gradually reduced the truth of the ideal to microscopic proportions.
The rhetoric has remained, however, for even today the virtues of
farm living are said to be almost miraculously regenerative. "The
big farm produces crops," asserted Roger M. Kyes, businessman and
later Deputy Secretary of Defense, "the small farm produces men."
Compare this with the statement from W. H. Harvey, *A Tale of
Two Nations*, a popular Populist novel of 1894: "As the country
makes the body better than that developed in the city, so also, even
in a greater degree it does the mind and soul. It is man-making." The
Country Life Commission Report of 1909 contains many such ex-

amples of a continuing belief in the special powers of agricultural life. An assistant secretary of agriculture, who appeared before the Industrial Commission, offered the opinion that "the undesirable class [of immigrants] does not usually go out on the farms; they can not stay on the farm without becoming pretty good people."

At the same time that the farmer-businessman was aspiring to be a part of the glittering civilization of the urban world, that civilization was stretching out to encompass him. Even in such a minor aspect of life as reading matter, the farmer found himself accepting the urban view of things. Before 1860, the fiction printed in farm journals almost invariably concerned the vicissitudes of rural life and the villain was usually a city slicker. By the turn of the century, however, the great national farm magazines—and they were the main ones—carried fiction of the same type and locale as the urban periodicals. Rural folk, like the people of the city, were now reading stories based on urban assumptions and depicting the life of the city. In the twentieth century, the telephone, the mass newspaper, the mail-order catalogue, the automobile, improved highways and roads, rural free delivery, the radio, the movies, and, most recently, television have advanced still further the farmer's emulation of urban ways. And where the farmer himself might be slow to respond to such stimuli, his more worldly-wise and adaptable children added to the pressure.

As early as 1896 one sociologist noted, with obvious regret, the insidious influence of the city upon the sheltered life of the farm. "The isolated farmer and his family have begun to be affected by the strain of modern life in a deplorable way," complained Frank Giddings in his textbook in sociology. "They are no longer ignorant of the luxuries of the towns and the simple manner of life no longer satisfies them. The house must be remodeled and refurnished; the table must be varied; clothing must be 'in style,' and the horses, carriages and harnesses must be more costly." By the early decades of the twentieth century, urban values had penetrated the countryside to such an extent that it was no longer possible to talk of a sharp division between urban and rural life; there were now only varying degrees of urbanism.

7. THE FARMER AS POLITICIAN

Though few farmers objected to the material benefits which the commercialization of agriculture bestowed upon them, a great many

of them protested the steady fall in farm prices which accompanied
it. All during the last decades of the nineteenth century farm prices
fell at a faster rate than prices in general—a fact which persuaded
many farmers that they were victims of a conspiracy as well as an
economic squeeze.

In an endeavor to stay the steady deterioration of the farmers'
economic position, a number of farm organizations sprang into existence in the 1870's and 1880's. Some, like the Patrons of Husbandry, began as farmers' fraternal and social clubs, but soon
shifted to being pressure groups advocating the regulation and control of railroads and grain elevators. Others, like the Agricultural
Wheel and the various Farmers' Alliances of the 1880's, were, from
the outset, deliberate attempts at meeting the challenge of declining
farm prices in an economy which was increasingly dominated by big
business. These latter organizations also attacked the railroads for
their high rates and the trusts for their exorbitant prices, but no
purely economic pressure group seemed capable of improving the
farmers' worsening position.

As a result, in 1892 the aroused farmers turned to politics as a
way out; the People's party was born. In its first election that year,
the Populist party, as it was also called, made surprising gains at
the expense of the two major parties. James Weaver, the Presidential candidate, captured over a million votes, and in local contests
Populists were elected to five U.S. Senate seats, ten congressional
seats, and three gubernatorial chairs—a substantial achievement for
the first important third party since the rise of the Republicans in
the mid-1850's.

The platform of the People's party throws considerable light on
the changes through which American agriculture was passing. As an
industry develops, James Malin has pointed out, it first concerns
itself with the problems of production and only secondarily and at a
later time with the problems of distribution. By the last decade of
the nineteenth century, at about the time of the Populist protest, the
industry of agriculture had more than surmounted the problems of
production; more goods were being put out by American farms than
the world could absorb. It was now the distribution of these surpluses which constituted the major problem confronting the agricultural industry.

In a dim way, the Populist revolt recognized this fact. Its major
farm planks, for example, dealt with matters of distribution like

prices (inflation through paper money or free silver), transportation (railroad rate regulation and so forth), and credit (the subtreasury plan, whereby a farmer could borrow government funds at
a low interest rate against his stored crop). But these same planks,
especially those regarding prices and credit, also greatly encouraged
production, a fact which in itself revealed the confusion in the
economic thinking of the Populists. The weakness or error in Populist economics was not its heretical and inflationary demands, but
rather the failure to acknowledge the fundamental problem of overproduction. For the most part, Populist remedies for the farm situation were directed at the symptoms and not at the disease.

That this was not because of general ignorance on the subject is
apparent from the writings of contemporaries. C. Wood Davis, for
example, writing in *Forum* in 1890, put his finger directly upon the
real cause. Between 1870 and 1890, he showed, the population in
the United States rose 30 per cent; but during the same period, the
number of farms went up 51 per cent, the number of bales of cotton
increased 90 per cent, and the acres of land devoted to corn and
wheat jumped 50 per cent. "The logical conclusion," Davis pointed
out, "is that the troubles of the farmers are due to the fact that
there are altogether too many farmers" and too great production of
farm commodities.[6]

But that kind of analysis was not for the Populists. *Coin's Financial School*, the leading Populist tract, and a veritable Bible of
free-silver agitation, only ridiculed the overproduction diagnosis.
Coin (the fictitious teacher of free-silver principles in the pamphlet)
said "that overproduction could not be claimed so long as tens of
thousands were going hungry; and that the only overproduction
admitted by all, was millionaires." To which can only be added
E. L. Godkin's remark that "Of the world outside," the farmer
"knows and cares nothing."

Though the Populists were blind to the role the surplus played in

[6] Davis proved to be a remarkable prophet in an area where the future has
often confounded the seer. In a subsequent article in *Forum* that year, entitled
"When the Farmer Will Be Prosperous," he predicted a turn for the better by the
end of the nineties—almost the precise years in which it did come. His major point
was that it was dependence upon the foreign market which made agricultural
prices and income so unstable, and that when American consumption caught
up with production there would then be an equilibrium between supply and
demand which would assure the farmer a decent living. In its essentials, this
prediction was about what happened after 1900 and before 1914, when the
balance was shattered by the abnormal demands of the European war.

the making of their problems, an investigation of the focal points of
Populist strength further supports the argument that overproduction was the mainspring of much of the farmers' unaccustomed
radicalism. For example, wheat-producing Kansas, Nebraska, and
North and South Dakota gave a third or more of their votes to the
Populist ticket in 1892; but equally agricultural Iowa, Illinois, and
Wisconsin cast less than 5 per cent of their votes for the People's
party candidates. The difference may be explained by the differences
in the diversification of crops in the two groups of states. In the
latter group, the development of dairying and corn-hog production
had done much to stabilize farm income, since the farmers there were
less dependent upon the foreign market. As a result, there was less
economic pressure to drive them to radical political measures.

Though cotton might be expected to play the same role in the
South as wheat in the Midwest, the election results do not clearly
bear out this assumption, probably because the race question complicated, where it did not stifle, the growth of a third party in that section. Nevertheless, cotton states like Texas, Alabama, Georgia, and
Mississippi were conspicuously more Populist in their voting than
more diversified and noncotton states like Kentucky, Virginia, Tennessee, and North Carolina.

It is surely no accident that the withering away of the farmer's
militancy at the opening of the twentieth century was accompanied
by a decline in the agricultural surplus. Whereas in 1897–1901 the
United Kingdom purchased 72 million bushels of wheat and 74 million bushels of corn each year from the United States, in 1910–14
that country's average annual importations of these crops were only
27 million and 10 million respectively. Germany's annual importation
of American corn fell more than 80 per cent, and bacon imports
dropped over 95 per cent between 1900 and 1910. Despite this decline in foreign purchases, however, American farm prices in general
rose almost 90 per cent between 1899 and 1910. It would seem that
in those years before the outbreak of World War I, industry and
agriculture in the United States had finally reached an equilibrium
in which the farmer and those he fed and clothed were relatively
satisfied.

The happy future promised by this equilibrium, however, was
shattered by the intrusion of the First World War. Agricultural
acreage and production were pushed far out of line with the domestic
market, and the way was paved for the prolonged farm depression

of the 1920's and 1930's and the everlasting surplus problem which still perplexes the country. But Americans of the 1950's can at least salvage hope from the 1910–14 experience; if once there were no forbidding farm surpluses, perhaps that happy circumstance may return in the future.

8. STANDING JEFFERSON ON HIS HEAD

As a political movement, the farmers' revolt was full of meaning for the future of American politics. Unfortunately, much sentimentality has been expended in depicting the Populist-Democratic defeat of 1896 as the farmers' last stand against the overpowering and ruthless forces of industrialism and the money power. Though this view has a measure of truth in it, Populism is more accurately viewed as a manifestation of a transitional phase in the history of American agriculture. Populism was at once the last gasp of the agrarian myth and the coming of age of the farmer as businessman.

As befits a leader who stood at the juncture of two eras in the history of the American farmer, William Jennings Bryan in his famous "Cross of Gold" speech in 1896 appealed to both the old and the new farmer. Proudly he called the farmer "as much a business man as the man who goes upon the Board of Trade," only to fall back upon the tried and true agrarian creed that if the farms are destroyed, "the grass will grow in the streets of every city in the country." This confusion as to the commercial farmer's actual role in the economy was also apparent in Populism's overtures to urban labor.

The farmer as a son of toil had always been celebrated by the agrarian tradition; after all, did not the farmer labor with his hands, was not his bread earned in the sweat of his brow? [7] And true to the tradition, the platforms of the angry farmers proclaimed the unity of all labor. "The interests of rural and urban labor are the same, their enemies are identical," asserted the St. Louis platform of 1892. The Omaha platform of the same year endorsed several labor demands like the eight-hour day and opposition to Pinkerton police,

[7] Though the farmer was becoming more and more involved in the market during the 1890's, his socioeconomic role could be confusing even to a Columbia University professor. C. E. Emerick, writing in the *Political Science Quarterly* in 1897, wrestled with the question in this manner: "The farmer, it is true, is to some extent a capitalist—and to some extent, also, by coordinating capital and labor, he acts as entrepreneur. But the farmer is by distinction a laboring man. . . ."

as well as declaring a secondary boycott of the Rochester clothing
manufacturers, against whom the Knights of Labor were then striking.

But all this was thinking with rhetoric rather than with realities;
it was appealing merely to the common American heritage of Jeffersonian and Jacksonian symbolism and not to the hard facts of
economic life. Clear-eyed Samuel Gompers of the American Federation of Labor saw the emptiness behind the words and, though
touched by the idealistic sentiments, he could not overlook the economic gulf which separated the farmers and the urban workers. The
People's party, he wrote in the *North American Review* in 1892, is
not a labor party, and "in the nature of its makeup" it cannot ever
be a party "in which the wage-earners will find their haven. Composed, as the People's Party is, mainly of *employing* farmers without
any regard to the interests of the *employed* farmers of the country
districts or the mechanics and laborers of the industrial centres,
there must of necessity be a divergence of purposes, methods, and
interests." The union of such forces, he concluded, is "impossible,
because it is unnatural."

The validity of Gompers' analysis was reflected in discussions of
the "farm labor problem" which were already a feature of the farm
journals in the 1880's. The farmers were employers for the most
part, and the deeper the commercial spirit invaded agriculture, the
more profoundly the farmer accepted the assumptions of a businessman and alienated himself from the working man who worked for
wages, whether he was on the farm or in the factory.

After the debacle of 1896, the business side of the schizoid farmer's
movement was dominant; thereafter we hear little of the Jeffersonian
rhetoric but much of parity, export debentures, equity fees, and
crop allotments. Rather than being the last stand of the farmers,
1896 was the first step in their road to success. In business-minded
America, the farmer as an entrepreneur and salesman has been much
more successful in gaining the ear of the government and the nation
than he ever was as a latter-day agrarian philosopher.

Naïve and unrealistic as Populism's appeal to urban labor may
have been, the new and radical demands in the new party's platforms
constituted a turning point in the history of modern American political reform. Populism brought to a national audience a bushel of
new solutions to American problems; some were bizarre, but most
were long overdue and of interest to all Americans, not just farmers.

In addition to obviously agrarian proposals like the subtreasury plan and free silver, and labor planks like the eight-hour day, the platform also went on record in favor of the graduated income tax; the public ownership of railroads, telephones, and telegraphs; the direct election of senators; and the initiative and referendum, to name only the best-known.

The important point is that underlying several of these reforms was the clear assumption that government was charged with responsibility to regulate the economy. As an idea, of course, this was not new, but before the Populists it had never been linked so effectively with popular aspirations and problems, and never before had it been actively championed by so many Americans.

The Populist views of the responsibilities of government in the economy were doubly important because, in 1896, the Democratic party was inoculated with the virus. Though dedicated Populists like Henry D. Lloyd and Tom Watson fulminated against the alliance with the Democrats in that year, the alliance was the beginning of the triumph of Populism's philosophy of government. It was also the signal for a decisive shift in the ideology of the Democratic party and ultimately of the nation itself.

For a century the party of Jefferson and Jackson had carried high upon its banners the legend "That government is best which governs least." In the years before 1860, the party had pushed its states' rights—laissez-faire philosophy to such an extreme that when the War for the Union was won, the new nationalism of the people denied national power to the Democracy for nearly a generation. And then, when a Democrat did assume the Presidential power, he turned out to be a firm believer in the old tradition. When Grover Cleveland was presented with a bill appropriating a small amount of money for the relief of drought-stricken farmers in Texas, he needed only to consult traditional Democratic doctrine to decide to veto it. In his veto message Cleveland appealed to the "limited mission" of government and the necessity "that the lesson should constantly be enforced that though the people support the Government the Government should not support the people." Staunchly adhering to his party's ancient faith, even in the face of the Green Uprising of the 1890's, Cleveland earned the deep-seated disgust of dirt farmers and urban intellectuals everywhere, but especially in his own party.[8]

[8] To see how far Cleveland lagged behind Populist sentiment, one has only to compare his statement with one uttered by the Populist Governor of Kansas in

During the last years of Cleveland's second administration, the deep dissatisfaction with the laissez-faire heritage of the party impelled many Democrats to look toward a union with the Populists. There had always been important points of contact between the two parties. The Populists, for example, also revered Jefferson and Jackson, although for somewhat different reasons. For many Democrats the virtues of these heroes were largely associated with their championing of local govenment and limitations on the federal power. The Populists, on the other hand, conveniently overlooked that part of their heroes' thinking and loved them for their espousal of the agrarians and for their opposition to monopoly. But such a convenient historical memory was nothing new for Americans when they employed their history for contemporary purposes. It was ironical, though, that the author of the Kentucky Resolutions and the author of the Maysville veto should be stood on their heads and made into symbols of national power. And it approached humor when hard-money Andy Jackson was expected to buttress free silver and cheap money.

Despite the Populists, advocacy of an interventionist national government, the Democratic party, at its convention in 1896, took on the leadership of the farmers' revolt and the issue of cheap money. In doing so, the party underwent a historic change of course. For though it is true that the Democratic platform of that year said little about most of the other Populist demands, the party's obvious willingness to use the power of the national government to manipulate the currency supply and its denunciations of the National Banks amply demonstrated that a new philosophy animated its members. Moreover, during the campaign the Democratic standard bearer, William Jennings Bryan, by strongly supporting labor unions and denouncing court injunctions against labor, further revealed the party's departure from the ancient tenets of economic liberalism. In fact, the overwhelming defeat of the Cleveland forces at the convention could be interpreted in no other way than as a

---

1893. "The Government must make it possible for the citizen to live by his own labor. . . . If the Government fails in these things, it fails in its mission. . . . What is the State to him who toils if labor is denied him and his children cry for bread? . . . The people are greater than the law or the statutes, and when a nation sets its heart on doing a great and good thing, it can find a legal way to do it." The close similarity of this statement with many utterances in and out of government during the early days of the New Deal is striking and at least partly explained by the fact that depression stalked the land in 1893 and 1933.

sharp slap at the ancient laissez-faire tradition of the party. Like a
snake sloughing off its old skin, the Democratic party was shaking
itself free of its fear of the national government—a fear it had inherited from Jefferson and the ante-bellum leaders of the South who
had dominated the party for so long. The process was to be pushed
still further by Woodrow Wilson in the next century and brought to
completion by Franklin Roosevelt and Harry Truman.

It would be misleading, however, to leave the impression that the
Democratic party was the sole vehicle of this sea change in the
American conception of the federal government. Both the Republican
party and the nation at large took up the new view. The Populist
agitation, for all its focus on the farmers' problems, had galvanized
the reform spirit throughout the country.

The proof of this is to be read in the series of Populist measures,
once denounced as either subversive or outlandish, which, by other
hands, were translated into law in the years between 1900 and 1914.
The power of the I.C.C. to regulate railroads was greatly strengthened in 1906 and 1910; postal savings banks were established in
1911; the income tax and the direct election of senators came in
1913. Also in 1913 the Populist demand for a flexible currency and
the end of the National Banking System was achieved with the establishment of the Federal Reserve System. Even the Populist's favorite
measure, the subtreasury plan, can be said to have been put into law
with the passage of the Warehousing Act of 1916. In an important
sense, therefore, the farmers' revolt was the forerunner of the much
more successful Progressive movement which followed. Populism not
only provided the stimulus but, as enacted legislation testifies, it
sometimes set the goals.[9]

The transformation of the American farmer into a businessman
was only the most obvious result of the industrialization and urbanization of the nation. Ancient and established institutions like the
Church and the home were also being transformed by the forces of
the new era.

---

[9] A less admirable inheritance from the Populist movement has also been
noticed by several writers. "It is not too much to say," writes Richard Hofstadter,
"that the Greenback-Populist tradition activated most of what we have of
modern popular anti-Semitism in the United States." And Eric Goldman in
Rendezvous with Destiny has also called attention to the Populists' denunciation
of the "Jewish Money Power" as the true beginnings of popular anti-Semitism in
America. The Populist novel, *A Tale of Two Nations,* shows this aspect of
Populism quite clearly.

CHAPTER XII

New World A-Comin'

"THE generation which was beginning to take shape and character when I came of age," President W. J. Tucker of Dartmouth wrote concerning the years after 1865, "was to have the peculiar fortune, whether to its disadvantage or to its distinction, of finding its own way into what we now call the 'modern world.'" In the years between 1880 and 1915, industrialization and urbanization, like two gigantic hands touching the spinning clay on a potter's wheel, refashioned the contours of American society; institutions with long lineage and stability like the Church and the home were shaken and altered. To an American who was alive in 1870, the world of forty years later lost many of its familiar bench marks. This was so for more profound reasons than the fact that the automobile was beginning to appear in the streets or because two brothers had kept some pieces of wood and iron in the air for a few minutes.

More than this, the new world of the city and the factory confronted the American Dream with a spiritual challenge which almost overwhelmed it. But when the challenge had been met, the America which emerged, despite its industrial and urban character, remained in spirit remarkably like the old, still loyal to the old tradition of equality, humanitarianism, individualism, and socal justice. For, like the political Revolution of 1776, the Progressive movement of the early twentieth century was distinguished almost as much by what it conserved as by what it introduced.

1. JESUS VERSUS RICARDO

To the rural mind the city was tantalizing; it was both attractive and repulsive, good as well as evil. "Every city has been a Babylon, and every city has been a New Jerusalem," Plymouth Church's

Reverend Lyman Abbott said, "and it has always been a question whether the Babylon would extirpate the New Jerusalem or the New Jerusalem would extirpate the Babylon." To many in the 1880's and 1890's it seemed that Babylon had won out.

Looking about him in 1887, the Reverend Josiah Strong saw "great perils threatening our Christian civilization, such as wealth, its worship and its congestion, anarchism and lawlessness, intemperance and the liquor power, immigration and a superstitious Christianity," and all of them, he noticed, "are . . . massed in the city. And not only so, but in the city every one of these perils is enhanced." And so it seemed to others more worldly. A friendly foreign visitor like Lord Bryce was appalled at the corruption in municipal government which gnawed away at the self-respect of Americans and threatened the continuance of democracy itself. Continue as you are, he told some Americans, and "you will set us liberals back in Europe five hundred years."

The churches could not long escape what Strong later aptly called "the Challenge of the City." From the beginning the roots of religion had penetrated deep into the consciousness of Americans; since the Revolution several great revivals had broadened the popular base of Protestantism. But in the year which followed the Civil War, there was an almost palpable recession of religious interest under way among a broad class of Americans. "Everybody knows," a churchman told the students of Andover Theological Seminary in the mid-1880's, "that the Protestant Churches, as a rule, have no following among the workingmen." Attending church in Chicago, dressed as a working man, Princeton Professor Walter Wyckoff noticed that "I was conspicuously lonely as a representative of the poor." His fellow workers admitted to him that in their rural homes they had been regular in church attendance, but that "the habit had dropped completely from them upon coming to live in town." One worker said, "The rich folks build their churches for themselves, and they keep them for themselves, and I ain't never going to interfere with that arrangement." And the richly decorated urban churches, with their high-priced pews and sedate air, bore him out. A survey made in Pittsburgh in 1888 revealed that though business and professional men made up only 10 per cent of the population, they constituted 60 per cent of the membership of the Protestant churches.

Many churches stood empty and unused amid the congested working-class districts of the great cities. Between 1868 and 1888,

for example, although nearly 200,000 people moved into the part of
New York City below 14th Street, seventeen Protestant churches
moved out, their places being taken by only two Roman Catholic
churches and a single synagogue. One minister complained that "to
the mass of workingmen Sunday . . . is a day for labor meetings,
for excursions, for saloons, beer-gardens, baseball games and ca-
rousals," rather than a time to attend church. It was notorious that
the urban citizenry were increasingly breaking the Sunday laws which
rural-dominated state legislatures imposed upon them. It came as no
surprise, therefore, that in the 1880's three markedly urban states,
New York, Massachusetts, and California, relaxed or abandoned
their Sunday laws. Among the cities of the nation a retreat from the
old-time religion was in full swing.

Contrary to the opinions of some shortsighted churchmen, the es-
trangement of the urban working class from Protestantism was
something more than a shift in interest or an increase in human depravity. At bottom it stemmed from the failure of the churches to
adapt themselves to the altered face of American society. Because,
historically, Protestantism in America, like the nation at large, was
rural, the Church was bewildered by the city; nothing in its history
prepared it for the problems now thrown up by urbanization. Long
accustomed to class relations remarkably free of conflict, the
Protestant churches, suffused with the Calvinist ethic of individual
achievement and responsibility, could not easily understand an era
characterized by class warfare, ruthless monopolies, and the squalor
of tenement-filled cities. Moreover, many of the urban workingmen
were immigrants and Catholics and therefore beyond the appeal of
the Protestant churches.

The churches were suspicious of, when they were not openly hostile
to, the new urban proletariat, who bore slight resemblance to the
steady, conservative farmers of an earlier America. "You can count
on the ends of your fingers all the clergymen who take any interest in
the labor problem," Terence Powderly of the Knights of Labor complained in 1892. The workers, Samuel Gompers of the A.F. of L. said
a little later, "have come to look upon the Church and the ministry
as apologists and defenders of the wrongs committed against the
interests of the people simply because the perpetrators are the pos-
sessors of great wealth." The Reverend Washington Gladden was
told by one worker in the 1880's that the reason he and his fellows
did not attend church was that it seemed to be a place for employers

only. "Of course," he admitted, "the manufacturers can and should dress better than the laborer; but when we see them so full of religion on Sunday, and then grinding the faces of the poor on the other six days, we are apt to think they are insincere." Nor was Henry Ward Beecher's remark that any workingman worth his salt could support a family on a dollar a day, providing he did not drink or smoke, conducive to the increase of workingmen in the Protestant churches.

All men of the cloth, however, were not Beechers either in moral obtuseness or income. (Beecher was reputed to have an income in excess of $20,000 a year when he uttered his dictum.) The implications of the great railroad strike of 1877, in which thousands of workers ran amuck destroying trains, roundhouses, and yards in angry protest against a wage cut, were not lost on a minister and philanthropist like Charles Loring Brace of New York. "There is something always impressive," he wrote at that time, "in these blind, passionate movements of the laboring classes for the larger share of the goods of life. . . . The great problem of the future is the equal distribution of the wealth. . . . I believe myself that, in general, the laboring classes do not receive their fair share. Strikes are one of their means of getting more. . . ." In later life, the well-known exponent of the social gospel, Washington Gladden, recalled that it was in the late 1870's and early 1880's that his attention was first drawn to the impending social conflict between capital and labor. Hard-fought strikes of the 1880's, he remembered, "brought very strongly before my mind the critical character of the relations between the men who are doing the work of the world and the men who are organizing and directing it." Because the growing hostility between capital and labor was tearing Protestantism apart as it was rending the nation, churchmen were soon compelled to seek out explanations and remedies in places which were far removed from theology or their usual social circles.

Instinctively almost, leading churchmen appealed to the universal character of Christianity as an antidote to the social cleavage. "Christianity, from the nature of it," Samuel Loomis told the students at Andover Seminary in 1886, "cannot remain the religion of classes; it must be the religion of the whole people or none." The churches will never re-establish contact with the urban masses, Washington Gladden cautioned in the same year, until they recognize that these " 'masses' are composed to a large extent, of . . .

wage earners," and the churches must "adjust their theories and
their methods" to that fact if they wished "to see daylight shine
through this dark problem of church neglect." The new social setting was "most disturbing" to the popular "influence of the church,"
W. J. Tucker recalled in reviewing the period. "The study of the
enlarged and more complicated economy was thus necessary if the
church was to maintain or recover its influence." Unless the Church
is successful in its appeal to the working class, Samuel Loomis
warned, the workers, "perishing in their blindness, will involve all
Christendom in common ruin."

As tension between workers and employers was successively built
up, discharged, and built up again in bitter strikes such as those of
1877, 1886, 1892, and 1894, an increasing number of Protestant
clergymen found it difficult to reconcile the doctrines of Jesus with
the impersonal and ruthless functioning of a laissez-faire economy.
"Jesus Christ knew a great deal more about organizing society,"
Washington Gladden wryly commented, "than David Ricardo ever
dreamed of knowing, and the application of his law to industrial society will be found to work surprisingly well." The historic alliance
between religion and business which began with the Calvinists was
coming under searching scrutiny. Many churchmen, Gladden noted,
were recognizing that the doctrine of laissez faire not only meant
"let well enough alone . . ." but also "let ill enough alone!"

But the clergymen of the new view were well aware that mere exhortation and appeal to Christian principles could not be expected
to undermine this sacrosanct shibboleth. Inasmuch as capital has
combined, Gladden told a labor audience in 1886, then let the workers "combine, and let the people say Amen." In 1893, Josiah Strong
insisted that even though real wages may have been rising in the last
decade or so, the more basic question was whether the laborer was
"receiving his just dues." And he concluded that the rampant
poverty and destitution in the cities made it clear that the worker
"has not had his due share, and ought not to be satisfied until
justice is done him." During the Homestead strike of 1892, several
religious journals recognized, almost for the first time, the claims
of labor to a fair hearing. The *Christian Union* called the disturb-
ance a part of "the transition from an aristocratic to a democratic
industrial organization."[1]

[1] But the conversion of large numbers of clergymen, it should be noted, was
a slow process. As late as 1892, a survey revealed that the overwhelming majority

In 1887, a number of Episcopalians in New York City organized the Church Association for the Advancement of the Interests of Labor, which gradually spread to other cities of the nation. Five years later, the Baptists, led by Walter Rauschenbusch, established the Brotherhood of the Kingdom, pledging themselves to—among other things—"obedience to the ethics of Jesus." Significantly, the purpose was the re-establishment of the true meaning of the Kingdom of God and "to assist in its practical realization in the world."

The most obvious and earliest sign that the churches were acting to establish contact with the urban masses was the so-called institutional church—that is, one which performed social services for its members. "Too long has Rome been allowed a practical monopoly of the humanitarian agencies of religion," declared the Cincinnati Conference of the Methodist Church in 1889. One Congregational church in Connecticut took up the new humanitarian and social work with such zeal that fashionable people called it "the church for ex-drunkards." Despite the appellation, membership grew. A wealthy urban church like St. Bartholomew's in New York assumed the burdens of the new duty, building an elaborate parish house in 1891 at a cost of $400,000, most of the sum being donated, ironically enough, by the Vanderbilts. St. Bartholomew's was only one of a large number of Episcopal churches which built parish houses for the new activities among the urban masses. Among the Baptists, Russell Conwell's Temple in Philadelphia, built in 1890 at a cost of a quarter of a million dollars, offered a wide variety of athletic, literary, and benevolent activities.

The institutional church pushed its activities out into the city itself. Volunteer women went out into the streets and into the tenements to seek out the deserving poor; co-operative ventures among several churches were initiated in order to provide church services to those working people who had no nearby churches. It was in these years that youth organizations like Christian Endeavor (Congregational), Epworth League (Methodist), and the Brotherhood of St.

---

of Congregational ministers in Massachusetts believed that the discontent among the working population bore "little or no effect upon the attitude of the working-men toward the churches." And in 1886, at the time of the Haymarket bombing, the *Congregationalist* belligerently advised, "when anarchy gathers its deluded disciples into a mob, as at Chicago, a Gatling gun or two swiftly brought into position and well served, offers, on the whole, the most merciful as well as effectual remedy."

Andrew (Episcopal) were started. In short order these organizations undertook projects among the working class.

While the laboring class's lack of interest compelled some Protestant churches to replant their roots in the cities, the urban challenge brought forth a new church, conceived in the city itself. Imported into the United States from England in the 1870's, the Salvation Army by the 1880's was by far the largest Protestant denomination active in the slums and streets of the cities of America. Deliberately shaped to help lighten the soul-crushing burdens of discouragement, intemperance, and poverty, the Army performed a host of services ranging from cheap ice in summer to warm lodgings in winter. The Army's work with the poor was essentially humanitarian and only secondarily theological; before it exhorted, it fed the hungry and clothed the naked. Without ever forgetting the spiritual message they carried, the "slum angels" and other workers of the Army brought genuine compassion into the lives of the poor. Such realism and sympathy were repaid with success.

Much as the urban friars of the thirteenth century had stirred up the ire of indolent and uninterested priests of the medieval Church, the Army in the early years aroused the enmity of the staid and established churches. A popular story summed up the success the Army enjoyed and the ecclesiastical hostility it provoked. When asked by his vicar whether he liked the Salvation Army, a bishop replied, "Well, I cannot say that I do, but to be honest I must confess I believe God does." As the leaders of the Army well knew, the sensationalism of the drum and the soup kitchens, when coupled with unremitting and practical humanitarianism, constituted the Army's most compelling appeal to the working class. "The Salvation Army in no sense desires to become respectable," declared Ballington Booth, the son of the founder and the head of the American branch in 1893. "We are not going to give up the ungloved hand for the kid glove; the drum for the church bell; the cornet for the piano or organ."

By the opening of the twentieth century, the Army, once hounded and even despised by the older churches, had won a place as an institutional church born to the manner, ideally suited for the work of adapting Christianity to the new conditions of the city. "I have long recognized the Salvation Army as one of the most potent, if not the most potent, force for the betterment of mankind now at work for the safety of mankind," concluded Governor Albert Cummins of Iowa in 1904.

Once the churches embarked upon the path of attempting to square social practices with the ethics of Jesus, the institutional church and the Salvation Army proved to be merely halfway stations along the way; much more thoroughgoing renovations of religious thought were to follow. Some of the impetus came from outside the churches. Economist Richard Ely of Johns Hopkins, with his influential *Social Aspects of Christianity*, directed attention to the religious implications of the contemporary social situation at the same time that he revealed the underlying religious thought animating much of the growing literature of discontent. The same could be said about *Social Reform and the Church*, a book by another economist, John R. Commons, in which, among other things, it was said that "the object of sociology is to teach us to love our neighbors." Pressed by empty churches on the one hand and appalled by the gulf between Christian ethics and social practice on the other, many Protestant clergymen began to listen to academicians like Commons and Ely and ministers like Gladden. As churchmen studied economics, talked with workers, and visited slums, a theological and philosophical basis for a new mission of the Church gradually emerged. The social gospel, as a later generation would call it, was being hammered out on the anvil of social realism.

Although in the past the theological seminaries had been rather unresponsive to the play of social forces, in the last decade of the nineteenth century they took the lead in propagating the new ideas. In his autobiography, William Jewett Tucker confessed that as a lecturer at Andover Seminary in the 1880's he had deliberately taken on a "Lectureship on Pastoral Theology" which no one else wanted in order that he might widen its content. "It became," he recalled, "an open door through which I had free access to those special problems which were confronting the Church. It became entirely logical, under the construction put upon this lectureship, to emphasize the new and enlarged functions of the church in modern society." Moreover, his *Outlines on Social Economics*, distributed in the late 1880's, inspired many a pastor already in his pulpit. "I am growing more and more interested in the sociological problem," one minister in Topeka, Kansas, wrote Tucker in 1889, "I am coming to believe that the second service of the Church should be

directed to this line of work, and I have a church here that is
ready to follow in this departure from the old traditional conception of what constitutes proper church work." Washington Gladden
lectured at Yale in 1886 on "The Relation of the Church and Ministry to Socialism." In 1892, seven seminaries initiated professorships
or lectureships in social ethics; two years later, such courses were
added in three more theological centers. And in the same year a
professor of sociology was added to the staff of the Episcopal
Theological School in Cambridge. During the summer of 1895,
Oberlin sponsored a conference for clergymen at which the theme
was "The Causes and Proposed Remedies for Poverty." Not only
was the conference directed by an economist, John R. Commons, but
it featured Socialists and labor leaders among its speakers.

The doctrine of the social gospel achieved its most eloquent expression in the personality and prolific writings of Walter Rauschenbusch of Rochester Theological Seminary. Over and over again his
books appealed for a recognition of the social mission of Christianity. "The chief purpose of the Christian Church in the past
has been the salvation of individuals," he wrote in *Christianizing
the Social Order* in 1912. "But the most pressing task of the present
is not individualistic. Our business is to make over an antiquated
and immoral economic system; to get rid of laws, customs, maxims,
and philosophies inherited from an evil and despotic past; to create
just and brotherly relations between groups and classes of society"
and thereby make it possible that men might "live and work in a
fashion that will not outrage all the better elements in them. Our
inherited Christian faith dealt with individuals; our present task
deals with society."

Constantly striving to show the social implications of the Christian message, Rauschenbusch declared, "The purpose of all that
Jesus said and did and hoped to do was always the social redemp-
tion of the entire life of the human race on earth." Under this interpretation, the obligation of the Christian ministry was clear and
inescapable. "The ministry must apply the teaching functions of the
pulpit to the pressing questions of public morality," he wrote in
1907. In practice this meant to Rauschenbusch that "Every step
taken in industrial life to give the employees some proprietary
rights in the business, and anything placing owners and employees
on a footing of human equality, would deserve commendation and

help." The Church, in short, in the estimation of Rauschenbusch, should range itself on the side of the working class.

Though many rural churches of Protestantism escaped the fire of the new doctrine, and even whole denominations like the Presbyterians were slow to react, the year 1914 found the social gospel permeating the major denominations of Protestantism. The Methodist "Social Creed," setting forth in 1908 a variety of goals for the amelioration of labor conditions, was one of the outstanding fruits of the movement. Included in the Creed were such purposes as "a living wage in every industry," "abolition of child labor," "the highest wage that each industry can afford," and "the recognition of the Golden Rule . . . as the supreme law of society and the sure remedy for all social ills." That same year the Federal Council of Churches of Christ in America was formed by thirty-three Protestant denominations. Since the Council drew its statement of social principles almost verbatim from the Methodist Social Creed, it stood as tangible evidence that the Protestant churches were now willing to commit themselves to the realization of the principal demands of the working people.

The new social outlook of the churches was evident in the report which the Federal Council of Churches issued in 1920 upon completing its investigation into the national steel strike of 1919. The report, for all its endeavor to achieve objectivity, was animated with sympathy for the strikers, as it was heavy with indignation at the callousness of the employers. Protestantism had come a long way since the days of Henry Ward Beecher, half a century before.

The acceptance of the social gospel spelled the transformation of American Protestantism. At one time thoroughly saturated with the individualism of the frontier and the Calvinist ethic, the Protestant Church became, in the words of W. J. Tucker, "as conspicuously the agency of 'social service' as it had been the 'means of grace' in the work of individual salvation." Heretofore a prime support of the doctrine of laissez faire, the churchmen were now included among its sharpest critics—as many clergymen still are in modern America.

With the triumph of the social gospel, Protestantism not only profoundly altered its social outlook but regained much of its lost prestige among the people. There was a period, John Mitchell, president of the United Mine Workers, commented in 1913, "when it was taken for granted that clergymen . . , were unable to comprehend trade unionism." But today, he continued, "many of the denominations as such, and the prevailing opinion among clergymen as individuals, have pronounced for unions. . . ." Under such circumstances, he went on, "it may be regarded as an accepted fact that the church is today emphatically on the side of union labor." Another group, social workers, once critical of the churches' aloofness from the social issues of the day, had returned. In 1905, it was reported that three quarters of the social workers in the American Institute of Social Service were "faithful church members."

So completely and pervasively was the social gospel accepted that it has become, in the words of a European religious historian, "the distinguishing characteristic of American Christianity." It is true that since the late 1930's the primacy of interest which the social gospel previously enjoyed has been somewhat reduced by the rise of neo-orthodoxy. But the core of the social doctrine is still a powerful force in American theology. To illustrate this, one has only to recall that Reinhold Niebuhr, though the best-known neo-orthodox theologian, is also a member of the executive committee of the Americans for Democratic Action. Even those who do not consider themselves exponents of the social interpretation of Christianity now recognize, as F. E. Johnson put it in 1940, that "there is no necessary incongruity between what has been called the Social Gospel and the basic concerns of traditional Christianity; that, on the contrary, a vigorous social ethic is vital to orthodoxy, while our liberal social Christianity needs to discover its roots in the historical Christian faith."

In conquering the churches, the social gospel extended its influence through society at large. By helping to heal the widening breach between the working class and the rest of society, by demanding a fair share of American abundance for the worker, the social gospel was instrumental in halting the dangerous drift toward class division so imminent in the 1880's and 1890's. Rather than being an "opiate of the people," as Karl Marx had described religion, the churches in industrial America consciously ranged themselves on the side of the poor and the downtrodden, striving to achieve social justice for all. In doing so they threw a formidable obstacle in the path of socialism in the United States.

On the other hand, a Protestantism shot through with the social gospel is a veritable hothouse of reform movements and social protest; it can no longer be an automatic defender of the *status quo.* Indeed, considering the transcendent standard by which society is judged under the social gospel, those who apply such a yardstick can never be satisfied. After the advent of the social gospel, it was possible to advocate social reform in the language of religion. It is not accidental that reform leaders like Woodrow Wilson and Franklin Roosevelt used religious phrases to clothe their pleas for reform. Religious allusions, for example, frequently occurred in the speeches of Franklin Roosevelt. The New Deal, he said in 1934, "is as old as Christian ethics, for basically its ethics are the same. . . . It recognizes that man is indeed his brother's keeper, insists that the laborer is worthy of his hire, demands that justice shall rule the mighty as well as the weak." By broadening the definition of Christianity to include justice for all members of society, the ministers of the social gospel made it possible to harness the long religious heritage of the people in behalf of the realization of the American Dream of justice, equality, and opportunity.

Whereas the urban effect upon Protestantism was at first shattering and only later beneficial, upon Roman Catholicism at first it was not apparent at all. This was true if only because the Catholic Church in America, flourishing largely among the poor immigrants of the cities, required little instruction in the degradation of poverty and the squalor of tenement living. Those Protestant clergymen who were beginning to be concerned over their own churches' alienation from the people were frankly envious of Rome's appeal. "The Catholic Church," remarked Samuel Loomis in 1887, "is emphatically the workingman's church. She rears her edifices in the midst of the densest populations, provides them with many seats and has the seats well filled." Richard Ely, the economist, complained in the middle eighties that Protestant ministers had difficulty being fair to labor, though this was not true of Catholic priests. "It is not a difference of good will," Ely emphasized, "so much as a difference of knowledge. The Catholic revealed an acquaintance with the movements of the masses—the Protestant ignorance." When President Theodore Roosevelt discussed his proposed arbitration commission with union leader John Mitchell during the coal strike of 1902, Mitchell asked, as Roosevelt reported it, that "a Roman Catholic prelate" be put on the body "as the great mass of miners were Roman Catholics." Obviously these Catholic workers trusted their churchmen.

350 Out of Our Past

But, for all its centuries of diverse historical experience in social adjustment, the Roman Church was only less unprepared for the new era than Protestantism; it too had to adapt as industrialization transformed society. Because the seat of Catholic authority was in Rome, it was not until 1891, with Leo XIII's encyclical *Rerum Novarum*, that the American Church could speak with authority in the idiom of the industrial age. In that justly famous document, the Church, in the words of the Pope, now came out in favor of the "dignity of labor," "the equality of rich and poor," the undesirability of child labor, the need for protections of the worker in industry, and "the employers' moral obligation to pay fair wages."

Even with such an invitation to social reform through religion, the Catholic Church in America, with notable and rare exceptions like Father Edward McGlynn and Archbishop Ireland, was slow to respond. One historian, writing of Boston in the urban age, observed that "the Archdiocese of Boston failed to send a single priest into the army of social reform, which recruited so many Protestant ministers during the period 1880–1900."

By the time of the First World War, however, adjustments in Catholic official attitudes were beginning to appear. In 1917, Father John A. Ryan was granted permission to establish the *Catholic Charities Review*, a request which had been denied him only a few years earlier. Immediately after the war, the four bishops composing the leadership of the National Catholic War Council issued a "Program of Social Reconstruction," in which the meaning of Leo's great encyclical on labor was spelled out for postwar America. In short order there followed the formation of the National Catholic Welfare Council and its Department of Social Action which issued, in 1920, a collection of church social documents, significantly entitled *Church and Labor*. Thus Catholicism, even within the relatively rigid limits imposed by the international character of its authority, endeavored, like Protestantism, to shape itself to deal with the challenge of the new era.

As has been implied, social Christianity constituted much more of a psychological wrench for Protestantism than for Catholicism. The latter, after all, having attained intellectual maturity within the social and historical context of the predominantly agrarian economy of the High Middle Ages, was never very friendly toward rationalistic capitalism. Unlike Calvinistic Protestantism, Catholicism did not especially prize thrift, frugality, hard work, sobriety, and wealth accumulation, which were so helpful in the growth of capitalism. As American Protestantism and Catholicism drew together in social ideology in the course of the early twentieth century, they moved farther away from the ethic of work and saving which had nurtured the expansion of capitalism and contributed to its enormous productive capacity. As modern American economist Kenneth Boulding has pointed out, "the 'lost gospel'—the old gospel of individualism, of self-help—is in many respects a sound one. Indeed, the middle-class nature of Protestantism is testimony to its long-run success." It was Protestantism which taught the middle class the virtues of "hard work, thrift, family limitation, productivity and frugality. . . . There is hardly any better overall recipe for economic development, whether for the individual or for a society." But, Boulding observes, "the old doctrines are discredited in the churches today." And, it should be added, it was the old gospel which supplied the energy to run the great engine of American production. One wonders what effect a reversal of that historic religious economic ethic will have upon capitalism's great achievement of production. And if it does interfere with productivity, what effect will that have on the American promise of abundance for all?

2. BE IT EVER SO SMALL

If the forces of the new era widened the domain of religion, they had the opposite effect upon the family and the home. In both a literal and figurative sense, the home shrank, working a significant alteration in the position of women and children in American society.

The initial force, of course, was industrialization. Wherever that process has taken place, whether in Europe, Asia, or the United States, it has demanded the labor of women and children. Even before 1860, tens of thousands of women stood before machines in the factories of New England and the Middle Atlantic states. Indeed, in that year women held, proportionately, more jobs in manufacturing than they did in 1900—a fact which illumines their important role in the beginnings of industrialization. But our concern here is not with the significance of women in the process of economic growth, but with the effect of industry upon the status of women. In this regard, the noteworthy fact is that as industry spread across the face of the nation in the 1880's and after, the number of women

in the labor force grew steadily. Whereas in 1870 only 14.8 per cent
of the women over sixteen years of age were gainfully employed, in
1900 the figure was up to 20.6 per cent; by 1910 it was 24.3. It
should be noted that the flow of women into the labor force between
1860 and 1914 far exceeded the increase in the number of women
in the country. Thus during the 1880's, though the feminine population grew about 28 per cent, the number of women workers jumped
over 50 per cent.

Though the factory provided many of the occupational opportunities for women in this period, it was by no means the only one.
In service industries like domestic service, telephone and telegraph,
nursing, and teaching, women far outnumbered men. In business
offices, that holy of holies of the American male, the woman worker
became increasingly in evidence as the new invention, the typewriter, was widely introduced. It is true that the number of women
in the professions was quite small, but Lord Bryce in the 1880's
noticed that American women "have made their way into more of
the professions more largely than in Europe." In fact, he wrote, "it
is easier for women to find a career, to obtain remunerative work of
an intellectual as of a commercial or mechanical kind, than in any
part of Europe."

Undoubtedly, what opportunities there were in the professions
for women are to be attributed to the opening of higher education
to the sex. By the end of the century the battle for women's education had been won, largely by the establishment of women's colleges
with curricular and educational standards deliberately raised to
the level of the best men's institutions. Unlike the older men's colleges, which were founded by churches, a number of the women's
colleges, like Vassar (1861), Smith (1870), Wellesley (1870), and
Bryn Mawr (1885), were founded upon fortunes derived from industry and commerce. For this reason it might be said that the
woman's college was doubly symbolic of the decisive role industrialization played in changing women's place in American society.

By providing opportunities for work outside the home, industrialization served to weaken the dependence of women in the family
upon the breadwinning father. It was now possible for women to begin to experience the wider world. In 1903, Mrs. Bessie Van Vorst,
a matron of society who wished to sample the life of a working
girl, took a job in a Pittsburgh pickle factory. After only a day or
two of the deadening drudgery of the factory, Mrs. Van Vorst

could continue no longer and was compelled to stay away from work for two days. At the end of that time, however, she began to want to go back to work—exhausting as she knew it was. "Two days of leisure without resources or amusement make clear to me," she explained afterward, "how the sociability of factory life, and freedom from personal demands, and escape from self can prove a distraction to those who have no mental occupation, no money to spend on diversion. It is easier to submit to factory government . . . than to undergo the arbitrary discipline of parental authority." This was one form of independence which industrialization offered to women.

The other kind, which was more material than spiritual, was equally important in accounting for women's leaving the home. As a girl worker in a woolen shirt mill in Perry, New York, put it, "My father gives me all the money I need, but not all the money I *want*. I like to be independent and spend my money as I please." Though as a matter of hard fact few women workers were in such a fortunate economic situation at home, it is nevertheless true that financial independence for women was a significant by-product of industrial expansion. Certainly in many a home the father's pre-eminence was shaken when it was possible for the daughters and even the wife to support themselves against his actual or potential tyranny. And over the years the number of married women in the labor force has steadily increased. In 1890, only 13.9 per cent of working women were married; fifty years later, the figure was 36.4. As early as 1898, the day nursery, indispensable for the working mother, assumed significant proportions, for in that year the National Federation of Day Nurseries met for the first time.

In an even more obvious fashion, urbanization was cutting the home to smaller dimensions. The private house, so common in the rural and small-town environment, was given up in the great city where land was measured by the square foot instead of the acre. In New York City, for instance, the number of private houses annually constructed dropped from 1,300 in 1886 to a mere 40 in 1904. The multifamily dwelling, the tenement or the apartment house, had become the typical home of the urbanite. And as the physical dimension of the home shrank, so did the family size, despite the fact that public morality frowned upon contraception and federal and state laws prohibited the circulation of information about techniques. In the single decade 1890–1900, the average num-her of persons in families declined in over three quarters of the cities of 25,000 population or more.

This falling off of the urge to procreate was particularly noticeable among upper-class educated women—that is, among those most affected by the new forces. One New York City woman physician in 1904 asserted that "having a family is not an American ideal. Among my patients I find that the majority do not want any children; certainly not more than one." Urban resistance to childbearing received national attention in 1903, when President Theodore Roosevelt publicly denounced "the man or woman who deliberately avoids marriage, and has a heart so cold as to know no passion and a brain so shallow as to dislike having children." Such a person, the President declared, "is in effect a criminal against the race, and should be an object of contemptuous abhorrence by all healthy people."

The exhortation of even a President, however, was not strong enough to overcome contrary forces. Only 53 per cent of the members of the Vassar College classes of 1867 to 1897 were married, it was reported in 1915. And an investigation of 17,000 alumnae of eight women's colleges and coeducational Cornell turned up the fact that by 1918 less than 40 per cent of them had married. Educational and occupational opportunities newly available to women were making them independent in their choice of husbands, and many apparently had doubts as to the desirability of matrimony at all.

The questioning of the hallowed institution of matrimony extended even to those who were married. Foreign observers of American society have generally been impressed with the close internal bond of the family in the United States, yet, paradoxically, marriages in this country have usually been less durable than those in Europe. As industrialization and urbanization grew apace after 1870, the divorce rate in America was not only higher than Europe's, but it rose higher each decade. For instance, between 1870 and 1880, the population as a whole increased some 30 per cent, but divorces rose almost 80 per cent. In the following decade, the number of divorces increased three times as fast as the population. At the end of the century, the American states were granting seventy-three divorces for each 100,000 of the population as compared with ten awarded in Australia, two in England, thirty-two in Switzerland (the highest in Europe), and twenty-three in France.

At that time, as now, divorce more frequently occurred among urban than rural families and, as the United States has become increasingly urban, marriages have more frequently ended in divorce. The divorce rate in 1955 was more than twice what it was in 1900.

Though a high divorce rate obviously betokens great marital instability throughout the society, it nevertheless can be interpreted more favorably. A long duration for marriage is by no means a conclusive measure of marital happiness; on the contrary, a long-lived marriage may merely conceal unrelieved misery. The ready availability of divorce makes it reasonably certain that long marriages are also happy marriages. Since it is the institution of marriage which has provided the principal agency for the limiting of women's place in society, liberalization of divorce laws has been a demand of the woman's movement, and its attainment has been an important step in the achievement of freedom for women. The truth of this is borne out by the fact that in the late nineteenth century almost two thirds of the divorces were granted to wives; in the twentieth century the proportion is even greater.

On the farm, children were a source of labor and an integral part of the working unit of the family. This situation was altered, however, in the city. Inasmuch as there were few household and no farm tasks which the children could perform, nor any meadows and woods in which they could amuse themselves, the position of children in the urban family changed. Furthermore, because industry could make good use of child labor, society was confronted with the urgent necessity for protecting youngsters against economic exploitation. As early as 1880, the census reported that one million children between the ages of ten and fifteen years were gainfully employed; within ten years, the number increased 75 per cent.

"Responsible citizens often say that they do not believe in play," H. S. Curtis, an authority on the adaptation of children to urban life, wrote in 1917, "and that the child ought to work, but these people fail to realize, apparently, that the work of children has disappeared, and the choice is not between work and play, but between play and idleness." Though hard to believe today, before 1885 there were no public playing places for children in any city of the country. At that date, a women's philanthropic society, seizing on an example witnessed in Germany, dumped heaps of sand at two places in the streets of Boston. The children's response to this rather belated recognition of their instinct for play was sufficiently encouraging for three piles to be put out the following year; from such beginnings the practice spread to other localities and cities.

But it was a long way from piles of sand to organized playgrounds. At the end of the century, the actual number of cities which had progressed to supervised play facilities added up to no more than a baker's dozen. The movement, however, gained impetus in 1899 when the New York Board of Education set up thirty-one playgrounds attached to the public schools. The providing of supervised play areas for city children was adopted by other cities. In 1906, the Playground and Recreational Association of America was founded and by 1915 over 430 cities maintained playgrounds for their children.

But playgrounds in the city are far removed from country meadows; the play habits of children were compelled to change to fit the limits of the city. "Most of the traditional games of the world have grown up under conditions of plenty of space and plenty of time," James Gulick has pointed out. "Relatively few games can be found that are useful where 500 children are turned out for a ten-minute recess into a yard where 50 can play comfortably." A game like "monkey-chase," developed in a Connecticut orchard and requiring a grassy running space, "could not bear transplanting to the city." On the other hand, a gambling game like "craps . . . is a typical city game, invented by the children of the city. . . . Craps is the almost inevitable outgrowth of modern city conditions; it bids fair to become the national game of the tenements." As Gulick noted, it can easily be played in a limited space, it is quiet, and it is well suited to limited time; "it can be played in five minutes or five hours. It adapts itself to any number of players, five, ten, or any indefinite number."

The belief in play as an important part of the life of the child has paralleled the growth of the city. In 1917, H. S. Curtis observed that the playground was only the most primitive contribution of the Play Movement. The next stage was one which was only beginning in the United States, he wrote, but had already captured much attention in Europe. "It is built on the assumption that play is essential to development of children and that it must be furnished to every child every day." On this philosophy are founded the kindergarten, the nursery school, and the progressive approach to education, all typically urban devices which first assumed significant proportions during the first years of the twentieth century.

3. THE NEW WOMAN

In offering new opportunities to women outside the home, industrialization constituted one of the silent but potent forces behind the so-called feminist movement. It is true that the forging of the intellectual weapons for women's emancipation long antedated the factory, for the celebrated declaration of feminine "independence" was announced at Seneca Falls, New York, in 1848. But from a social standpoint, it was only with the increase in economic opportunities resulting from the spread of the factory that the movement of women out of the traditional home assumed noticeable proportions.

The term "emancipation," however, when applied to the women's movement is misleading. Although it is perfectly true that women have been subordinate to men during most of history, it is equally true that they have shared in the rewards and perquisites of power, prestige, and wealth as no other "oppressed" group ever has. Women as wives and mistresses, rulers and leaders, as intellectuals and salonières, have always been a "force in history," to use Mary Beard's phrase. In contrast to minorities like Negroes, Jews, and Indians, women have been included in the innermost circles of the ruling males, enjoying advantages, protection, and succor usually ruthlessly denied a subject class. Thus, as Mrs. Beard has observed, when a bill was introduced in the New York legislature in 1848 to grant married women greater property rights, it "was drawn by a member of the legislature who was eager to safeguard the rights of his wife, and it was vigorously pressed by another member equally eager to protect the interests of his daughter." In substance, just because women are a sex, they have been vouchsafed a measure of equality customarily withheld from an inferior class—namely, marriage with the master class. In fact, to render the paradox of women as subordinates even more involved, what for the normal minority group represents the achievement of complete equality, that is, marriage with the dominant class, for the feminine "minority" has been the avenue whereby women's most complete subjection has been effected.

Though in certain realms, like employment and voting, a superficial similarity existed between the status of women and that of other disadvantaged social groups, the truly influential role of women in history, Mary Beard showed, has been obscured. The

nineteenth century feminists did their propaganda job in behalf of
their sex's rights with such superb thoroughness that the world
now accepts a view of woman's historical impotence that is more
myth than fact. Almost obsessed with the need for proving the disabilities visited upon women by men, the feminists drew a picture
of female subordination which was far removed from the realities
of the past or of their own day. Men have done their bit in the
creation of the myth by forgetting to include women in their histories.

For this reason, the women's movement of the nineteenth century,
rather than being an emancipation of the sex, is more accurately
viewed as an extension of the opportunities for women. This widening of the social base of "woman as force in history" was accomplished in two ways. One we have already noticed: the expansion
of women's work through the growth of industry and urbanization.
The other was less obvious but no less important. Because the home
in the city was smaller and managed with relative ease, the woman
who did not work in the factory or at the office was almost compelled to seek diversion outside the narrow confines of the family.
In *One Woman's Life*, Robert Herrick described the changes which
came over the home life of a married woman in the city. Milly, the
heroine of the novel, lived an easy life in a small apartment, with
one child and a servant or two who did most of the work. Hers was,
writes Herrick, "much like the lives of many thousands of young
married women in our transition period." She just did not have
"enough to do to occupy her abundant energy and interest in life.
. . . And modern life had also so skillfully contrived the plebeian
machinery of living that there was little or nothing left for the
woman to do, if she were above the necessity of cooking and wash-
ing for her man." Such generalizations, of course, apply almost exclusively to women of the middle class. But that does not weaken
their importance, since the movement for women's rights was almost
entirely the work of middle-class women.

The smallness of the home was only one factor which gave more
time to women of the city; many of the time-honored chores of the
housekeeper were being lightened or eliminated. Gradually more
and more household tasks, once considered *de rigueur* for the home-
maker, left the home to be performed commercially. Cheap ready-
made clothing was commonplace in the city by the middle of the
nineteenth century, and in the years after the Civil War what sew-

ing had to be done could be facilitated by the mechanical home sewing machine. In 1853, six companies produced 23,000 such machines, but twenty years later their combined production exceeded half a million. The indispensable duty of daily cooking, which was more often a heavy chore than a wifely delight, was made somewhat pleasanter and easier by the commercial sale of gas for fuel and illumination. During the 1880's, the commercial laundry began to assume a prominent place in the lives of many middle-class women, thereby relieving them of a great part of the drudgery of housekeeping.

As far as the art of cooking was concerned, food preparation was simplified by packaged cereals like Quaker Oats and Wheatena, which supplanted the rural cornmeal mush. Home-baked bread, though always tasteful and a fond memory of former rural residents, was time-consuming in a household burdened with a bewildering variety of tasks. Women eagerly supported the expansion of the baking factory in the 1880's and 1890's, thereby hastening the removal of one more ancient chore from the urban home. At about the same time, canned vegetables were taking a prominent place on urban tables. "Housekeeping is getting to be ready made, as well as clothing," commented one woman, with a measure of exaggeration, in *Good Housekeeping* in 1887. Commercially produced ice, first widespread in the seventies, removed dependence on changes in the weather and systematized the most satisfactory means for the preservation of food.

The well-organized transportation system of an urban-industrial society made it possible for the first time for menus to have variety and style. The frontier and rural character of this country, if in no other way, was always impressed upon foreign visitors by the deadly monotony of the popular American diet. Farm cookery, nostalgia to the contrary notwithstanding, always leaned heavily upon the frying pan, and in winter fresh fruits and vegetables were unknown on the farm table. The variety of foods available in the city a large part of the year encouraged diversification in menus and titillated palates in a manner either unthought of or impossible in the country regions. A gauge of this new and, one might add, gratifying interest in food was the establishment of cooking schools in the mid-1870's. Within three years after it opened in 1874, the New York Cook School counted 1,200 students. During the 1880's, cookbooks began to appear in profusion for the first time, with perhaps the acme being reached in 1896 by Fanny Farmer of the Boston Cooking School, whose book was destined to assume in short order the proportions of a classic.

Many thousands of middle-class American women soon discovered, as did Milly Rindge in Herrick's novel, that the restricted urban home afforded married women new leisure for outside activities. Women's organizations grew as the cities grew. Though some of these groups were made up of workingwomen, many were composed of middle-class women released from the drudgery of the home and searching for avenues of social expression. Though organizations like the Daughters of the American Revolution, United Daughters of the Confederacy, Colonial Dames of America, and United States Daughters of 1812—all founded in the 1890's—are obvious reflections of a resurgence of nationalism, they are also indicative of this growing surplus of female social energy. What one might call economic organizations of women were also formed during these years. The American Association of University Women, organized in 1881, and the National Association of Deans of Women, founded in 1891, mirrored the increasing participation of middle-class women in higher education. The great range of women's organizations is suggested by three which differed widely in purpose and membership: the National Consumers' League (1899), The Junior League (1901), and the National Woman's Trade Union League of America (1903).

The number of such societies of women were the wonder of foreign visitors. When Lord Bryce tried to explain why American women have "an average of literary taste and influence higher than that of women in any European country," he gave as one of his reasons "the leisure which they possess as compared with men."

These organizations, however, should not be thought of as so many sponges sopping up excess womanly energy and time, but serving no social purpose. On the contrary, their impact on society was scarcely short of astounding. For though the mention of a woman's club brought a smile to most masculine faces in the early twentieth century, as it does in our own post-Hokinson era, the clubs were actually enormously effective in the 1890's and later. Many a town or city owed its library, children's playgrounds, or a charming park to the efforts of the local woman's club. Frequently, there were no other civic organizations in the town.

The club movement achieved such power and prestige that in

1901 an act of Congress awarded the General Federation of Women's Clubs a national charter. Then in 1904, the president of the Federation, Mrs. Sarah Decker, pushed the clubs into high gear as social improvement agencies with her famous remark: "Ladies . . . Dante is dead . . . and I think it is time that we dropped the study of his inferno and turned our attention to our own."[2] The General Federation as one measure of women's exodus from the home is impressive; by 1914, over a million women were members.

The Women's Christian Temperance Union was another major woman's organization which was obviously a direct response to changes in the home and in the social milieu. Under the leadership of Frances Willard, the W.C.T.U., with a quarter of a million members, became a school on a national scale for the education of women in social affairs and the need for social reform. Despite its title, the W.C.T.U., after the middle 1880's, was active in a number of reforms unconnected with the evil of drink. The power of the W.C.T.U. was put behind movements for the protection of working-women, for laws raising the age of consent, for kindergartens, for the training of girls for domestic service, and for the realization of international peace through arbitration. Frances Willard herself was a member of the Knights of Labor and an important figure in the early history of the Populist party, as well as an experimenter with vegetarianism, phrenology, and theosophy.

The work of the W.C.T.U., like the organization itself, is symbolic of the radiating effects of the emergence of women from what feminist Charlotte Perkins Gilman called the "smallest, oldest, lowest" work of the world—that of the home. Just as the espousal of the temperance cause by women ultimately helped to bring prohibition to America, so the women's attacks on the peculiarly urban evil of prostitution stimulated legislation in an aspect of social life which had heretofore been virtuously skirted. The Mann Act of

[2] Since it is commonly held that the woman's movement was essentially a suffrage lobby, it is relevant here to point out that the General Federation of Women's Clubs did not officially discuss the suffrage issue until 1910 and that even the W.C.T.U. was brought to accept the suffrage plank only after a bitter campaign by Frances Willard. The suffrage aspect of the women's movement has been omitted in the text because it is so well known and because it has unfortunately obscured the larger and fundamentally more important aspects of the popularization of women's opportunities. Many women in the 1890's and after who were interested in a wider sphere for women felt, like Ernestine Geyer in Herrick's *One Woman's Life*, "Things aren't done in this world by voting about 'em."

1910, sometimes called the White Slave Act, was one such measure on the federal level. Though Americans could never bring themselves to consider regulated prostitution, the agitation stirred up over the "social evil" resulted in a massing of information on the subject which, in turn, permitted the eradication of the grosser evils of the trade, such as recruitment through the seduction of innocent girls, and forcible submission. Moreover, for the first time, the causal connection between sweatshop working conditions and recruitment into commercial vice was so plain that none could blink it away.

The manner in which industrialization added a new depth to the literature of the woman's movement is illustrated in the voluminous writings of Charlotte Perkins Gilman. Her first major work, *Women and Economics*, published in 1899 and widely circulated in the United States and abroad in subsequent years, was a powerful and reasoned case for the economic independence of women if they were to achieve true freedom on a broad scale. Ever mindful of the needs of society, Gilman stressed the loss which society sustained when the peculiar creative talents of women were denied expression.

The significance and nature of these talents were apparent in the diversity of work undertaken by a growing number of women in the nineties and the early years of the twentieth century. In a field like social work and industrial relations, women like Florence Kelley of Chicago, Mary Simkhovitch of New York, and Vida Scudder of Boston not only distinguished themselves, but incidentally offered a striking example of the interacting effects of the new social forces. Once the social conditions of an urban, industrial society permitted women to participate fully in the work of the world, their energies and abilities, in turn, could be utilized for making the raw, new society a better place for human habitation.

4. NEW POLITICIANS WITH OLD PRINCIPLES

That hurricane of reform called Progressivism, which blew through all levels of American political and social life in the years between 1900 and 1917, was many things, but above all it was a response to the challenge of the city and the factory, an attempt to bring to heel the untamed forces which had almost reduced the American Dream to a mockery.

For three decades the voices of protest—the labor unions, the churches, the Populists, the publicists, the utopian novelists—had been increasing in number and growing in volume, but the orgy of corruption and chicane, the piling up of corporate and individual wealth, continued while the squalor of the cities spread and the poverty of the farms deepened. The decade of the nineties, which experienced the deepest depression up to that time, brought fresh examples of class cleavage and class hate: the bloody struggle between workers and Pinkerton police at Homestead in 1892; the deliberate starving of the Pullman employees in 1894; the clashes between federal troops and striking railway workers in Chicago; the pitiful march of Coxey's Army of unemployed, dramatizing the workers' desperate need for work. While thousands of workers struggled to keep their jobs or to eke out an existence on a reduced wage, the New York *Tribune* reported in 1892 that there were "only 4,047 millionaires" in the country. It truly seemed as if American society had been riven into the many poor and the few rich; that the ideal of an America of equality of opportunity for all, of social justice, of decency in government, had become a nightmare in which the ideals had been inverted as in some kind of social Black Mass.

Progressivism changed all this; its advent was like a bright spring day after the bleak, depressing, soul-crushing days of February. Hope and spiritual uplift seemed to flood back into the hearts of Americans, even if the country was not actually transformed into a paradise. It seemed worth living in America again now that, even in the age of the city and the factory, men and women were trying to breathe life into the American Dream.

In 1907, in the midst of the Progressive ferment, sociologist E. A. Ross published *Sin and Society*, a book which, in its brief compass, set forth the underlying philosophy of the new reform movement and illumined the way in which the forces released by industrialism had transformed the old question of good and evil. Under the heading "New Varieties of Sin," Ross dramatically directed attention to the necessity of re-evaluating moral responsibility in an age when no man was an island unto himself. "Modern sin," he wrote, "takes its character from the mutualism of our time. . . . Nowadays the water main is my well, the trolley car is my carriage, the banker's safe my old stocking, the policeman's billy my fist. My own eyes and nose and judgment defer to the inspector of food, or drugs, or gas, or factories, or tenements, or insurance companies. I rely upon others to look after my drains, invest my savings, nurse my sick, and teach my children." Unfortunately, he continued, when all men are so interdependent and the web of connection is at once tight and far-flung, the moral focus becomes blurred, and no one assumes responsibility for the evil he commits. "The modern high-power dealer of woe wears immaculate linen, carries a silk hat and a lighted cigar, sins with a calm countenance and a serene soul, leagues and months from the evil he causes. . . . Modern sins are impersonal. . . . The hurt passes into that vague mass, the 'public' and is there lost to view." In a less complex society one could know and trust those upon whom one depended, but in this new order, though the dependence was infinitely enhanced, personal knowledge of people was in inverse ratio.

The reformers of the early twentieth century to a greater or less degree appreciated the new morality imposed by social change. Sometimes, as we shall see, their awareness was translated into legislation designed to meet the problem; sometimes the problem was beyond legislation. But in any case, an increasing army of reformers and writers in the first decade of the twentieth century threw a flood of light upon the social results of the factory and the city—results which were threatening to overwhelm, if not destroy, the old America.

Foremost among such publicists were the so-called muckrakers, who for a decade and in dozens of books and magazines unmercifully pricked the American conscience. Lincoln Steffens, for example, disgusted by the corrupt political machines in the cities and states of the nation, probed and questioned until he was able to reveal in his *Shame of the Cities* and *Shame of the States* the unholy alliance between business wealth and corrupt politics. The complacency of the nation was shattered by David Graham Phillips' sensational report on "The Treason of the Senate," in which some of the biggest names in "the greatest deliberative body in the world" were charged with and convicted of history's most heinous crime.

Before, during and after the exposures of corruption, movements were afoot to bring some decency and reform to a number of cities and states. Reformers like Samuel Jones of Toledo and Tom Johnson of Cleveland showed that cities could be run honestly if they were divorced from the extraneous and often corrupting influence of state and national politics and if knowledgeable men could be encouraged to run for office. New forms of local government were created to deal with the special problems of the cities. The commission form of municipal government and the city-manager plan date from these years between the late 1890's and 1910. Both were attempts to fit government to the novel and complex requirements of urban life. By our own time, several hundred American communities have adopted some form of the commission-manager system in order to bring businesslike operation into the running of their urban machinery.

Out of the determination to break the grip of machine politicians and corporate wealth upon government, the Progressives took up the fight for new devices of popular government. Because corrupt or reactionary legislatures often impeded efforts at reform, the new leaders turned to the initiative, recall, and referendum as the means whereby the people might "initiate" legislation themselves, remove from office those who had betrayed their trust, and pass on controversial legislation which seemed too vital to entrust to the judgment of indifferent legislatures. The adoption of the Australian or secret ballot (it was provided by the government instead of by the political parties, as had heretofore been the case) threw one more obstacle in the path of corruption at the polls. None of these devices, nor all of them together, it must be admitted, made saints out of politicians or eliminated the political machine, but politics was a more honorable profession when the Progressives were finished than it had been for two generations.

The squalor and congestion of the city also came in for sensational exposure at the hands of Progressives like Jacob Riis, Jane Addams, Florence Kelley, and Mary Simkhovitch. Addams' Hull House in Chicago and Lillian Wald's house on Henry Street in New York became bywords among the many poor who received warm shelter and sympathy there and at other settlement houses. Under the insistent prodding of Riis' exposures, the legislature passed new tenement laws providing for decent living conditions among the poor. At long last "the scab" of the dumbbell tenement began to recede from New York City.

The poverty, sickness, and degradation which woman and child labor brought in their train also came under vigorous attack. Robert Hunter's *Poverty* and John Spargo's *The Bitter Cry of the Children* trenchantly brought home to even the most hardened reader the painful details of what persistent poverty, inadequate housing, and urban living were doing to the mothers and the future of the nation. The workers' acclaim and the nation's headlines were

captured by Louis D. Brandeis when he convinced the Supreme
Court, that fountainhead of conservatism, in his monumental
sociological brief in the case of *Muller* v. *Oregon* in 1908, that the
regulation of hours and conditions of work for women was not a
denial of the liberties guaranteed in the Fourteenth Amendment.
State after state in the course of the Progressive era enacted legislation to protect women and children in their working conditions.
Toward the end of the period, the federal government stepped in
to prohibit child labor completely, but the act was struck down by
the Supreme Court.

It was the great corporations, however, which undoubtedly drew
most of the Progressives' fire, for from that direction seemed to
arise the greatest threat to a democratic society. Grown to enormous proportions, ramifying throughout the economy, these industrial combines appeared to have made themselves masters of all
America. "Some of the biggest men in the United States . . . are
afraid of somebody, are afraid of something," Woodrow Wilson
said. "They know that there is a power somewhere so organized, so
subtle, so watchful, so interlocked, so complete, so pervasive, that
they had better not speak above their breath when they speak in
condemnation of it." This concern of the Progressives was translated into a wave of state and national legislation which endeavored
to throw up protections against concentration of economic power.
Many of the states, for example, set up within their boundaries
regulatory commissions and stringent rules for corporations. The
so-called Seven Sisters Acts, pushed through the New Jersey legislature by Governor Woodrow Wilson, transformed that state from
the haven of corporations to one of the Union's strictest monitors
of industrial behavior.

On the national level, laws in 1903, 1906, and 1910 supplied the
Interstate Commerce Commission with weapons which for the first
time enabled it to tame the railroads' power to do evil. The Clayton
Antitrust Act of 1914 set forth a long array of objectionable,
monopolistic procedures by corporations with criminal and civil
penalties attached to them. In substance, it sought to plug up the
holes in the old Sherman Act of 1890. As a further safeguard, the
Federal Trade Commission was created in 1914 to serve as a kind
of watchdog over the practices of the business world, empowered to
publicize corporate activities contrary to the public interest and to
take the delinquents to court.

As an agency which carried on a continuous policing of the amoral world of business in the interest of the consumer and free enterprise, the F.T.C. was helping to create a new morality for the corporation. Indeed, the whole corpus of regulatory legislation of the Progressives looked in that direction. Insofar as business morals have improved since the days of the nineteenth-century Buccaneers of Business, this is the result of the new police and the new climate of opinion encouraged by the Progressive movement.

And as Richard Hofstadter has observed, there was certainly an improvement in business responsibility during the Progressive years. At the opening of the twentieth century, he writes, "thoughtful American businessmen, pressed by the threat of union organization, condemned my muckrakers, and smarting under the comparisons with the most efficient managers of Europe, began to address themselves to poor working conditions and employee morale, and to the reformation of their haphazard shop methods. Between 1900 and 1910, 240 volumes on business management were published. . . . The emerging business schools, nonexistent in the country before 1898, provided numerous new agencies for discussion, education, and research in the field of management. Employers began to study personnel problems, consider devices for cutting fatigue and improving work conditions, and launched in some cases upon their own welfare and pension programs and profit-sharing schemes."

The passage of legislation for inspection and certification of the purity of food and drugs by government was a similar realistic avowal that in a modern industrial-urban society it was no longer safe to depend upon personal reputations or personal knowledge as a guarantee of the wholesomeness of food or the therapeutic value of drugs. The laissez-faire precept, *caveat emptor*, was too callous and too dangerous now.

Long convinced that the great corporations were dependent for their power as well as for their excessive profits on the protective tariff, the Progressives undertook to knock out that prop of monopoly. Unsuccessful in their first assault in 1909, they did better in 1913, when the Wilson administration succeeded in substantially cutting the tariff for the first time since it had begun to rise in 1861.

In the Tariff Act of 1913, the Progressives included a tax on corporate and personal incomes. This tax was a symbol of the new

attitude. In taxing incomes according to the ability to pay, the
Progressives were taking notice of the highly interdependent nature of their society. At a time when a man's income was a direct
consequence of his individual labors, a graduated tax might have
appeared unjust. But for a society wherein the amassing of wealth
was totally dependent upon the co-operation of many men and
institutions, this was not the case. No matter how sycophantic one
might be, it was difficult to argue that the "great American fortunes" were the result of individual exertions. They were truly social products, taxable by society. The income tax symbolizes, as
nothing else does, the new industrial age. Rooted in the realities of
the society, it was at the same time the principal equalizer of the
great disparities of wealth which seemed to be at once an evil and
an integral part of industrialism.

But Progressivism was more than merely a random response to
the insistent problems of the new social order. Implicit in the disgust which the Progressives felt for the corruption and power lust
of the Gilded Age and fundamental to the reforms which they advocated was a vague vision of what America should be. It was
against this vision that the Gilded Age was measured and found
wanting; it was for the achievement of this dream that the reforms
were pushed.

The vision was not new, however; it was not a product of the
emergent new society. Though the Progressives were overwhelmingly
city men and dealing with urban problems, they espoused ideals
developed in an earlier and rural period of the nation's history. For
seen in terms of goals rather than means, the Progressives embraced
the same large purposes for which the Jeffersonians and the Jacksonians fought: equality of opportunity, opposition to monopoly,
humanitarianism, and belief in democracy. Like so much else in the
American experience, the Progressives were more a conservative than
an innovating force. Though it is true that to one who had lived
through the Gilded Age, Progressivism seemed radical and novel,
to one who sees it against the backdrop of an earlier era in American thought, it was but a latter-day Jeffersonianism.

But it was a Jeffersonianism shaped to fit the demands of a new
society. In this lay the Progressives' strength, their weakness, and
their lasting contribution to modern America. A philosophy well
rooted in the American past strengthened them because it drew upon
the common heritage; it weakened them because it circumscribed

their reform efforts within the limits of a philosophy derived from a vastly different social context. But the philosophy bequeathed to modern Americans an outlook which spoke up strongly for freedom, equality of opportunity, and individualism despite all the social and economic forces which pulled in the opposite direction. That these ideals are still relevant to America is largely the result of the Progressives. They poured hard substance into ideals which at the time seemed outmoded in a world of factories and cities.

If Populism was the instinctive and ill-considered reaction of troubled farmers to the onrush of urbanism and industrialism, Progressivism was the urban middle class's recognition that the misgovernment, poverty, and class hatred of the new society must be eliminated. But whereas the farmers' response grew out of the elemental impulse of self-preservation, the Progressives were goaded to reform by no such force. Indeed, as city people, they were a rising, not a declining, class in the new society. Certainly it was not economic discontent which drove the Progressives to undertake their reforms. The first decade of the twentieth century was noteworthy for its prosperity; indeed, the single recession of the period, the Bankers' Panic of 1907, affected most people as little as its title suggests. In short, one looks in vain for an economic spur to such a perversive age of reform.

The springs of the reforming spirit are rather to be found in the sudden feeling that the vital juices of America were being drained away in the sewer of the Gilded Age. The ground had long been prepared for this spiritual rebirth, but for some reason it was not until 1900 that the slow accretion of protest, the gradual heightening of social sensitivity, coalesced into a swell of reform. [3]

[3] In his recent book, *Age of Reform* (New York, 1956), pp. 148–72, Richard Hofstadter offers a multifaceted explanation for the bursting forth of reform after 1900. No summary here can more than suggest the many forces Hofstadter sees coming together around the turn of the century. Among the things he points to are the status revolution in the professions which came to a head in the form of protests against business and commercial dominance in the society; the impact of the cheap, mass periodical press which permitted the sensationalism of the muckrakers to be effective on a wide scale; the spur to labor organization and agitation because of the relative decline in real wages after 1900; the interest of "respectables" in returning to politics in order to regain prestige lost during the Gilded Age; and the growth and threat of industrial combination and trusts in the late 1890's and early 1900's. On the other hand, his argument that rising prices account, in part, for the onset of Progressivism is not convincing at all. A period of rising prices is an anodyne to businessmen's reform impulses and not a stimulant; yet Progressivism, as all admit, was largely a

The pith of Progressivism then, and its importance for Americans today, are to be found in the same fact. As a philosophy Progressivism was a revitalization, a restatement of traditional American ideals; in substance it was the application of Christian morality and Jeffersonian principles to the twentieth century—an effort to shape society to the dimensions of an ideal. In short, it was moral. Indeed, unless one accepts the moral nature of Progressivism, one misses the heart which vivified the body of the movement. It was a supreme effort to bring back into American public life decency and old-fashioned concern for morality and humanitarianism. In a sense, it was an attempt to make Americans worthy of their history. "We stand in the presence of a revolution—not a bloody revolution," Woodrow Wilson said in 1912, "but a silent revolution, whereby America will insist upon recovering in practice those ideals which she has always professed, upon securing a government devoted to the general interest and not to special interest."

Pervasive as moral concern was among the vast majority of Americans who espoused Progressivism, in some it amounted almost to a confession of guilt for having delayed too long in redeeming the Promise of America. Only a repressed feeling of guilt can account for much of the utter sentimentality with which some of the muckrakers and social workers portrayed the conditions of the poor. The sense of guilt was laid bare in a poem "Tortured Millions," published in the celebrated muckraking magazine *McClure's*. After reciting the personal gains which the poet enjoyed at the cost of the workers' degradation, the poem closes with these lines:

> O thou Eternal Law, I wish this was not to be.
> Nay, raise them from the dust and punish me.

It was for just such attitudes, though admittedly less explicitly expressed, that Lloyd Morris aptly described Jane Addams, the social worker, and Emma Goldman, the radical, as "sentimentalists with swollen consciences," an epithet which is applicable to other Progressives as well.

Such feelings of guilt are closely related to the Protestantism which was the religion of most Progressives. By virtue of the absence

---

businessmen's movement. Though not all of Hofstadter's forces are new in the late 1890's, and so do not clearly reveal themselves as causes for the reform outburst in 1900 and after, his analysis of the coming of the Progressive movement is the most penetrating so far.

of recognized expiatory channels like confession and penance, self-accusatory guilt is peculiarly Protestant. But the Protestant source of Progressivism runs deeper; it is to be found in the soul-searing experience through which the Protestant churches had been passing for nearly a decade and a half. Richard Hofstadter calls Progressivism "a phase in the history of the Protestant conscience, a latter-day Protestant revival. . . ." In a real sense, Progressivism was the social gospel in practice.

Though not all historians would subscribe to the accent on the religious sources of early twentieth-century reform implied here, the religious understratum to the social protests of the 1880's and 1890's is too pervasive to be ignored. Recall, for example, the deep religious conviction and phraseology in such influential and supposedly secular works as Henry George's *Progress and Poverty* and Edward Bellamy's *Looking Backward*. Or, as an even more striking example, the American Economic Association's rejection, at its founding in 1885, of the "doctrine of laissez-faire" because it is "unsafe in politics and unsound in morals. . . ." At about the same time Richard Ely, the secretary of the Association, was telling the members that what "we wish to accomplish . . . lies in the direction of practical Christianity. . . ." The existence of a Christian Socialist movement in the 1890's similarly testified to the religious element which underlay the incipient reform movement. That the mass of people also felt the contradictions between Christian ethics and their society is apparent from the fabulous success of a third-rate novel like Charles Sheldon's *In His Steps; What Would Jesus Do?* Published in 1897, the novel quickly became one of the greatest best sellers of all time, well over two million copies being sold in America alone.

Sheldon's book, coming late in the nineties, was a bridge between the new religious upsurge of that era and the Progressive movement which followed. The novel concerns a minister and his church who decide to carry on their daily lives according to their understanding of the precepts of Jesus. All decisions were to be weighed in the scale of "What Would Jesus Do?" In the course of the book, those who follow this principle sound and act like the Progressives of a later day. They show concern for the plight of the workers; they display a recognition of the role of the environment in shaping people's actions and thoughts. Those who are well-to-do exhibit a sense of guilt for their money; respectable people are encouraged to participate in politics as their duty to society; railroad regulation is demanded; settlement houses are established; and several of the characters display the isolationism of the later Progressives by preferring missionary work at home rather than in foreign lands.

The Progressives, for their part, often gave voice to a religious sentiment. In his autobiography, Frederick Howe, the prominent Cleveland Progressive, wrote that, though he discarded his strict religious upbringing early in life, it constituted only an outward divestment. "From that religion my reason was never emancipated," he recalled, ". . . early assumptions as to virtue and vice, goodness and evil remained in my mind long after I had tried to discard them." Such a persistence of religious values, he concluded significantly, "is, I think, the most characteristic influence of my generation." Among the national political leaders of Progressivism, the religious element in their language and thought has often been noticed. "If I did not believe that the moral judgment would be the last and final judgment in the minds of men as well as at the tribunal of God," Woodrow Wilson said, "I could not believe in popular government." And who needs to be reminded of William Jennings Bryan's intense religious nature? Or that when Theodore Roosevelt thundered at the Progressive convention, "We stand at Armageddon and we battle for the Lord," the nearly hysterical delegates burst into perfervid singing of "Onward, Christian Soldiers"?

The intimate connection between political Progressivism and the social gospel can be traced down to even finer links. Both Theodore Roosevelt and Woodrow Wilson as Presidents consulted on their social programs with Walter Rauschenbusch, the nationally known exponent of the social gospel. And Robert La Follette, the other great national Progressive leader, was powerfully influenced both in his youth and later by his friendship with John Bascom, another prominent clerical advocate of social Christianity.

Though Americans of a later and more cynical age frequently look upon Samuel ("Golden Rule") Jones with bemused tolerance, his firm conviction that Christianity was practical is of central importance to an understanding of the moral impulse of Progressivism. A well-to-do manufacturer in Toledo in the 1890's, Jones quickly earned the soubriquet "Golden Rule" because of his saintlike and consistent application of that ethical rule of thumb. In his factory, for example, the sole regulation he insisted upon was that single precept of Jesus. As tangible witnesses to his conviction, he built for the entertainment and enlightenment of his employees Golden Rule Park and Playground and Golden Rule Hall. First elected mayor of Toledo in 1897 on the Golden Rule Platform, he was still in office at his death in 1904.

Jones enjoyed the support of all classes of society even though his radical approach to government earned him powerful and relentless enemies. (The day he died, it is said, the Toledo street car companies' stocks jumped twenty-four points!) Moreover, naïve and innocent as his thought sometimes appears, Jones attracted to himself both as friend and leader some of the most sophisticated men of the time, notably Brand Whitlock, who became Jones's mayoral successor, Frederick Howe, and Tom Johnson of Cleveland. What humble folk and men of affairs alike responded to in Jones were his idealism and his faith in the goodness of men and the teachings of Jesus. Jones, like many another Progressive, exemplified Santayana's definition of an American—"an idealist working on matter."

Years later, Brand Whitlock wrote that most men never realized what Golden Rule Jones taught, "namely that, above all the laws men make with political machines . . . there is a higher law, and that the Golden Rule is a rule of conduct deduced from that law. . . ." For most Progressives it was always clear that their fight was a moral one, a struggle of good against evil.

It should also be said that the moralistic outlook of the Progressives was a long-term weakness, if a short-term strength. Tending to see the world in black and white, the average Progressive battled against monsters he could not really lick, or else he contented himself with only the illusion of victory. Thus many of the reform measures of the era, like the Federal Trade Commission, the anti-trust laws, and the initiative and referendum, soon proved themselves inadequate to deal with the complexities of economic and political life. Though, as we shall see later, there were Progressives of an increasingly relativistic strain of thought, most of them displayed a highly moralistic approach to the world, such as religion in America has exhibited ever since the Puritans. Being highly moral, Progressivism was often also absolute. In this regard, it was a throwback to an earlier and simpler America, for by the opening years of the twentieth century a relative morality was the coming thing.

The social ethics of Protestantism were but one of the sources of the new reformers' moral purpose; the other was derived from the political idealism of the early Republic. Jefferson's vision of America was just as much the ideal of the twentieth-century reformer as it had been of Democrat Andrew Jackson, Republican Abraham Lincoln, and Populist Tom Watson. "I hear men talk about following in the footsteps of Jefferson," Progressive John Peter Altgeld said in 1902. "Why, Jefferson was the great radical of his day! He referred everything back to the people; he wanted everything left in the hands of the people. . . . Were Jefferson alive today, his voice would be heard from ocean to ocean demanding that the people themselves must own the monopolies." Rather than discard the presumably outdated Jeffersonian image of America, the Progressives proceeded to update it, thereby salvaging for the twentieth century the Jeffersonian vision of a free and open society in the New World.

The shibboleths and touchstones of the Jeffersonian-Jacksonian tradition ran all through the electrifying campaign speeches of Woodrow Wilson in 1912. As he himself said, "The New Freedom is only the old revived and clothed in the unconquerable strength of modern America." His New Freedom was little more than the equality of opportunity which permeated Jacksonian Democracy. The purpose of government, Wilson said, was "to set business free," in order that it might "follow its own right laws." "I stand," he declared, "as the party behind me stands, for regulated competition of a sort that will put the weak upon an equality with the strong."

Competition and individualism, so close to the heart of the earlier agrarian creed, still were meaningful slogans to the leaders of Progressivism. "The supreme task of the American people," Progressive Senator Albert Cummins of Iowa told the Senate in 1908, "is stimulating, fostering and protecting the competitive factor in American business." To Charles McCarthy of Wisconsin, the right-hand man of Senator Robert A. La Follette, Progressivism meant the "beginnings of a new individualism." In the forefront of the radical wing of Progressivism was John Peter Altgeld of Illinois, the pardoner of the Haymarket anarchists. Yet in the 1890's, he told a group of students: "This is an age of individual achievement. . . . If you are sent out to bring something, bring it, and not an explanation. If you agree to do something, do it; don't come back with an explanation. Explanations as to how you came to fail are not worth two cents a ton. Nobody wants them or cares for them."

Long before the Progressive era, Jefferson, in a plea for unity in American society, had said, "We are all Republicans, we are all

Federalists." But for all their admiration of Jefferson, the Populists had ignored his counsel of harmony, boasting instead of their class allegiance. The Progressives, on the other hand, placed themselves above and outside of classes, presuming to speak for Americans without reference to economic interest. In this respect Progressivism was a vehement denial of the cleavage into classes which the economic strife of the preceding Gilded Age had seemed to portend for the American future. In part this lack of class consciousness resulted from the movement's drawing its members from almost all classes. If small businessmen were the special darlings of the Progressive program, farmers, laborers, and consumers were nonetheless members of the family. Even the rich were not excluded, for, as George Mowry has noted, "few reform movements in American history have had the support of more wealthy men."

But there was more to it than that. Lack of class consciousness sprang from a long American tradition in favor of social unity and in opposition to class divisions. "It was essential," Theodore Roosevelt wrote at the time of the coal strike of 1902, "that organized capital and organized labor should thoroughly understand that the third party, the great public, had vital interests, and overshadowing rights in such a crisis. . . ." "I should be ashamed of myself if I excited class feeling of any kind," Woodrow Wilson told an audience in 1912. "The government of our country cannot be lodged in any special class. . . ." When Robert La Follette was attacked for setting class against class, one of his newspaper supporters in Wisconsin rushed to his defense. "We challenge . . . his enemies to cite one line in which Bob La Follette has ever arrayed class against class, one speech in which he has not been as concerned for the civic-minded rich man as for the poor. . . ." In speaking for the people as a whole, the Progressives were refurbishing a sense of social unity inherited from an earlier America and one which the corrosive acid of capital and labor strife had almost obliterated.

On the surface it might appear that Progressivism and socialism would have much in common. Both were direct responses to the challenge of industrialization and urbanization. But their conceptions of the good society were as far apart as the continents which spawned them. Where socialism sought to exacerbate class division, Progressivism tried to heal it; where socialism denied the validity of private property, Progressivism attempted to strengthen it; where socialism looked forward to the co-operative society, Progressivism sang the praises of the individual.

Yet simply because both movements grew from the same soil, the triumph of Progressivism marked the end of a significant Socialist movement in the United States. It would not be far wrong to see in the reform movement of the early twentieth century one of the most formidable obstacles to the growth of socialism in America. Nor is it accidental that the high point of socialism's popularity in this country was reached in 1912, the same year Progressivism captured the national government. Never again would any Socialist or Communist candidate receive as large a percentage of the votes as Eugene Debs did in 1912.

Like a safety valve on a steam engine, the reforms of the Progressive era seemed to draw off the popular pressure for drastic social change which had been building up during the many years of untrammeled industrialism. With that release of pressure, socialism lost its only chance for power. "The accomplishments of the Interstate Commerce Commission are the greatest triumphs of modern times in scientific government," moderate Progressive Samuel Untermyer concluded in 1911. "It saved us from government ownership of the Railroads, as the like regulation of Industrial Corporations will save us from Socialism." Especially conscious of this role of Progressivism was Theodore Roosevelt. Irritated by the attacks made upon him by the coal operators during the strike of 1902, he asked testily, "Do they not realize they are putting a very heavy burden on us who stand against socialism; against anarchic disorder?"

No better summation of that blending of the old ideals with the new social forces can be provided than a statement of Fred Howe in 1907. He began by reiterating the old Jeffersonian goals of American reform. "The great problem now before the American people is, how can opportunity be kept open; how can industry be saved from privilege; how can our politics be left to the unimpeded action of talent and ability?" But then he acknowledged that these old goals must be achieved through new means. "This is the problem which the city has to solve, even more than the state or the nation. For in the city the life of the future is to be found." Snipping here, pasting there, the Progressives fitted the old American Creed to the new conditions of an industrial and urban society in a more than tolerable fashion. Despite their name, the Progressives stand forth as true exemplars of American conservatism.

It would be misleading, however, in pointing out the dominant conservative aspects of Progressivism, to lose sight of those elements in the movement which were novel. From what has been said about the reforms of the Progressives, it is apparent that the Jeffersonian principle of the limited state found no analogue in Progressive thought. The seeds of the welfare state which were beginning to sprout in Populism grew under the forcing frame of Progressivism, to reach full flower in the hothouse of the New Deal. Populism buried the limited state, once and for all; no Progressive endeavored to resurrect it.

There was yet another new element which Progressivism introduced into American thought. Although most Progressives were naïvely but strongly absolutistic in their morality, there were also a number of intellectuals in the movement who were discarding that outlook. Though small in number, these Progressives developed a view of the ancient problem of evil which was conspicuously relativistic and social. For "we now see, or begin to see, if vaguely," Brand Whitlock remarked, "that, except in metaphysics, there is no such thing in our complex life as an absolute good or an absolute bad, and to the problem of evil we begin to apply the conception of economic influences, social influences, pathological influences . . . most of us know little or nothing about." From Golden Rule Jones, Whitlock had learned that criminals "were all people, just folks, and that they had so much more good than bad in them, that if some way could be devised whereby they might have a little better opportunity to develop the good, there was hope for all of them." Corruption, the apathy of the citizenry, and "poverty, vice, crime and disease," Frederick Howe concluded, "are due to causes economic and industrial. They are traceable to our institutions, rather than to the depravity of human nature." Herbert Croly, the high priest of Progressive ideology, observed, "Jefferson believed theoretically in human goodness, but in actual practice his faith in human nature was exceedingly restricted." The Progressives went far beyond Jefferson in seeing men as essentially good and merely corrupted by environment.

The origins of this moral relativism can be traced to the new environment of the city. In a rural society, the milieu is provided by nature; it is given, like an axiom in a geometry book—something one

assumes. Under such conditions, it made sense for men to believe
that each individual was the master of his future; that his destiny
was a more or less direct consequence of his own moral choices. The
advance of the city and the onslaught of industrialism, however, destroyed that uncomplicated and illusory sociology. In the industrial
city, the framework in which men worked out their morality was
socially created, put together by the hands of man, not the hands of
God. The evil which flourished in this environment was easily conceived of as the creation of men's collective action; from this it
would follow that no one man was responsible for the evil which he
personally committed. Hence someone like Golden Rule Jones refused
to believe that the criminals and prostitutes with whom his office
brought him into contact were truly responsible for their transgressions. Nothing was any longer absolute, not even evil.

If moral relativism now became increasingly commonplace in the
upper intellectual reaches of society, men farther down on the scale
would soon recognize that "we are all in the same boat together."
Under the pressures of the Great Depression, this acknowledgment
that man possessed only limited moral and economic independence
would come completely out into the open as economic debacle
dragged down good and evil men into common ruin.

CHAPTER XIII

The Third American
Revolution

TWICE since the founding of the Republic, cataclysmic events have
sliced through the fabric of American life, snapping many of the
threads which ordinarily bind the past to the future. The War for
the Union was one such event, the Great Depression of the 1930's the
other. And, as the Civil War was precipitated from the political and
moral tensions of the preceding era, so the Great Depression was a
culmination of the social and economic forces of industrialization
and urbanization which had been transforming America since 1865.
A depression of such pervasiveness as that of the thirties could happen only to a people already tightly interlaced by the multitudinous
cords of a machine civilization and embedded in the matrix of an
urban society.

In all our history no other economic collapse brought so many
Americans to near starvation, endured so long, or came so close to
overturning the basic institutions of American life. It is understandable, therefore, that from that experience should issue a new conception of the good society.

1. "HUNGER IS NOT DEBATABLE"

The economic dimensions of the Great Depression are quickly
sketched—too quickly perhaps to permit a full appreciation of the
abyss into which the economy slid between 1929 and 1933. The value
of stocks on the New York Exchange, for example, slumped from
a high of $87 billion in 1929 to a mere $19 billion in 1933. Wholesale prices dropped 38 per cent by 1933 and farm prices seemed
almost to have ceased to exist: they were 60 per cent below the low

level of 1929. Within less than three years, realized national income
plummeted to almost half of what it had been in the last boom year;
and the same was true of industrial production. The human cost of
this catastrophic breakdown in the complicated industrial machine,
Fortune magazine estimated in September, 1932, was 10 million
totally unemployed or 25 million people without any source of
income.

To worsen matters, the industrial stagnation was accompanied
by a spreading fever of bank failures. First here and there, then all
over the country, the banks began to close their doors in the faces of
their depositors. By the beginning of 1933, the financial self-
confidence of the nation reached a dangerously low level, requiring
the new administration of Franklin Roosevelt, as its first official act,
to order the closing of all banks. In all, more than 10,000 deposit
banks failed in the five years after 1929. If the banks, the custodians
of the measure of value, proved to be unsound, men might well wonder what was left to cling to as the winds of disaster gained in fury.

Unnerving as the failure of the banks undoubtedly was, for most
people the Great Depression became starkly real only when unemployment struck. No one knew whom it would hit next; the jobless were
everywhere—in the cities, in the towns, on the farms. Their help-
lessness, their bewilderment, were often written in their faces, reflected in their discouraged gaits, and mirrored in their run-down
dwellings. John Dos Passos reported seeing the unemployed of
Detroit in 1932 living in caves scooped out of giant abandoned sand
piles. Though it was said that no one would be allowed to starve,
Fortune, in September, 1932, suggested that some had already. The
magazine counted the millions of the unemployed and told of families subsisting on a single loaf of bread for over a week or of going
without food for two or three days on end. Discarded and spoiled
vegetables or wild dandelions were the substance of meals for some
families. Other reports in 1933 told of at least twenty-nine persons
who died of starvation in New York City. Moreover, thousands must
have died from diseases which gained an easy foothold in weakened
and underfed bodies; but these unfortunates were never counted.
Food, casually consumed in good times, suddenly became the focus
of existence for thousands. In their desperation some urban folk
actually tried to wring their food from the barren soil of the city. In
Gary, Indiana, for example, 20,000 families were raising food on
lots lent by the city; Robert and Helen Lynd reported that in

Middletown in 1933, 2,500 of the town's 48,000 people eked out their food budgets with relief gardens.

The spreading unemployment generated new and deep-seated fears. When the unkempt veterans of the First World War camped in Washington in 1932, demanding a bonus to tide them over their joblessness, a fearful and unsure President had them dispersed by troops armed with tear gas. And when Congress in that same year voted a 10 per cent cut in government salaries, President Hoover sent a secret message urging that the enlisted men of the Army and the Navy be excluded from such decreases so that in case of domestic troubles the federal government would not be compelled to rely upon disgruntled troops.

Nor was it only the federal government that felt uneasy in the presence of the specter which was stalking the land. Malcolm Cowley, in an eyewitness account, described how the trucks bearing the disillusioned veterans out of Washington were quickly sped through town after town, the local authorities fearing that some of the unemployed veterans would jump off and become burdens on already overtaxed communities. Cowley tells of one citizen in Washington, not a marcher at all, who was hurriedly bundled into a truck by mistake and could not get off until he reached Indianapolis!

Driven by their desperation, some Americans began to talk of violence. Mutterings of revolution and threats to return with rifles were heard among the bonus marchers as they left Washington. Out on the farms, the dissatisfaction of the veterans was matched by sullen farmers who closed the courts and disrupted mortgage auctions to save their homes. The ugly turn which the discontent could take was revealed by the arrest of a man in Wisconsin in 1932 on suspicion of having removed a spike from the railroad track over which President Hoover's train was to pass. In that bleak year it was not uncommon for the President of the United States to be booed and hooted as he doggedly pursued his ill-starred campaign for re-election. To Theodore Dreiser, as the cold night of the depression settled over the land, it seemed that Karl Marx's prediction "that Capitalism would eventually evolve into failure . . . has come true."

Even for the Lords of Creation, as Frederick Lewis Allen was to call them, the Great Depression was an unsettling and confusing experience. "I'm afraid, every man is afraid," confessed Charles M. Schwab of United States Steel. "I don't know, we don't know,

whether the values we have are going to be real next month or not."
And in the very early months of the Roosevelt administration,
Harold Ickes, attending a dinner of the Chamber of Commerce of
the United States, could sense the pitiable impotence to which the
nation's industrial leaders had sunk. "The great and the mighty in
the business world were there in force," he rather gleefully noted in
his diary, "and I couldn't help thinking how so many of these great
and mighty were crawling to Washington on their hands and knees
these days to beg the Government to run their businesses for them."

But it was the unspectacular, the everyday dreariness of unemployment that must have cut the deepest and endured the longest
as far as the ordinary American was concerned. The simplest things
of life, once taken for granted, now became points of irritation. "I
forget how to cook good since I have nothing to cook with," remarked one housewife. Children lost their appetites upon seeing the
milk and mush "that they have seen so often." Even the rare treat
of fresh meat could not awaken an appetite long accustomed to
disappointment and pallid food.

The routine entertainments of the poor were casualties to unemployment. "Suppose you go to a friend's house and she gives you
a cup of tea and something," the wife of an unemployed worker told
a social worker. "You feel ashamed. You think, now I got to do the
same when she comes to my house. You know you can't so you stay
home." Shifts in entertainment patterns among the unemployed were
revealed in a study made of some 200 families in New Haven. Before
the breadwinner lost his job, some 55 per cent went to the movies;
once unemployment hit, however, only 16 per cent did. In the days
when work was to be had, only 13 per cent found recreation in "sitting around the house," but now 25 per cent did so. With the loss of
their jobs, 12 per cent of the men admitted they "chatted and
gossiped" for recreation, although none of them did when they had
work.

Unemployment's effect upon the family was often more profound
and far-reaching. In recounting the case history of the Raparka
family, one sociologist wrote that when Mr. Raparka "lost his job
in the fall of 1933, he dominated the family. Two years later it was
Mrs. Raparka who was the center of authority." Again and again
social workers chronicled the alteration in the father's position in
the family during a period of unemployment. Humiliation settled
over many a father no longer able to fulfill his accustomed role in

the family. "I would rather turn on the gas and put an end to the whole family than let my wife support me," was the way one unemployed father put it. One investigator found that one fifth of her sample of fifty-nine families exhibited a breakdown in the father's authority, particularly in the eyes of the wife. For example, one wife said, "When your husband cannot provide for the family and makes you worry so, you lose your love for him."

Fathers discovered that without the usual financial power to buy bikes or bestow nickels, their control and authority over children were seriously weakened and sometimes completely undermined. In one family where the father was unemployed for a long time, his role was almost completely taken over by the eldest son. The father himself admitted: "The son of twenty-two is just like a father around the house. He tries to settle any little brother-and-sister fights and even encourages me and my wife." In the same family, a younger son who was working summed up his relationship to his parents in a few words. "I remind them," he said, "who makes the money. They don't say much. They just take it, that's all. *I'm* not the one on relief." In such circumstances, it is no exaggeration to say that the massive weight of the depression was grinding away at the bedrock of American institutions.

The ties of a home struck by unemployment were weak and the opportunities for fruitful and satisfying work were almost totally absent in 1932–33. *Fortune* reported in February, 1933, that something like 200,000 young men and boys were traveling around the country on railroad trains for lack of anything better to do. Tolerated by the railroads because of their obvious poverty and lack of jobs, the boys were often suffering from disease and malnutrition. The authorities in Los Angeles asserted, for example, that 25 per cent of those coming into the city needed clinical attention and 5 per cent required hospitalization. During a single season, one railroad announced, fifty such footloose boys were killed and one hundred injured. From Kansas City it was reported that girl wanderers, dressed in boy's clothing, were on the increase. To many such young people, now grown, the Great Depression must still seem the most purposeless, the most enervating period of their lives.

What Robert and Helen Lynd concluded for their study of Middletown in 1935 can be applied to America as a whole: ". . . the great knife of the depression had cut down impartially through the entire population cleaving open lives and hopes of rich as well as poor. The experience has been more nearly universal than any prolonged recent emotional experience in the city's history; it has approached in its elemental shock the primary experiences of birth and death."

2. THE END OF LAISSEZ FAIRE

Perhaps the most striking alteration in American thought which the depression fostered concerned the role of the government in the economy. Buffeted and bewildered by the economic debacle, the American people in the course of the 1930's abandoned, once and for all, the doctrine of laissez faire. This beau ideal of the nineteenth-century economists had become, ever since the days of Jackson, an increasingly cherished shibboleth of Americans. But now it was almost casually discarded. It is true, of course, that the rejection of laissez faire had a long history; certainly the Populists worked to undermine it. But with the depression the nation at large accepted the government as a permanent influence in the economy.[1]

Almost every one of the best-known measures of the federal government during the depression era made inroads into the hitherto private preserves of business and the individual. Furthermore, most of these new measures survived the period, taking their places as fundamental elements in the structure of American life. For modern Americans living under a federal government of transcendent influence and control in the economy, this is the historic meaning of the great depression.

Much of what is taken for granted today as the legitimate function of government and the social responsibility of business began only with the legislation of these turbulent years. Out of the investigation of banking and bankers in 1933, for example, issued legislation which separated commercial banking from the stock and bond markets, and insured the bank deposits of ordinary citizens. The stock market, like the banks, was placed under new controls and a higher sense of responsibility to the public imposed upon it by the

---

[1] A complementary and highly suggestive way of viewing this trend away from laissez faire, of which the events of the 1930's are a culmination, is that taken in K. William Kapp, *The Social Costs of Private Enterprise* (Cambridge, Mass., 1950). Kapp observes that for a long time private enterprise had shifted the social costs of production—like industrially polluted water, industrial injuries, smoke nuisances and hazards, unemployment, and the like—onto society. The decline of laissez faire has, in this view, actually been a movement to compel industry to pay for those social costs of production which it has hitherto shirked.

new Securities and Exchange Commission. The lesson of Black Tuesday in 1929 had not been forgotten; the classic free market itself—the Exchange—was hereafter to be under continuous governmental scrutiny.

The three Agricultural Adjustment Acts of 1933, 1936, and 1938, while somewhat diverse in detail, laid down the basic lines of what is still today the American approach to the agricultural problem. Ever since the collapse of the boom after the First World War, American agriculture had suffered from the low prices born of the tremendous surpluses. Unable to devise a method for expanding markets to absorb the excess, the government turned to restriction of output as the only feasible alternative. But because restriction of output meant curtailment of income for the farmer, it became necessary, if farm income was to be sustained, that farmers be compensated for their cut in production. Thus was inaugurated the singular phenonomen, which is still a part of the American answer to the agricultural surplus, of paying farmers for *not* growing crops. The other device introduced for raising farm prices, and still the mainstay of our farm policy, came with the 1938 act, which provided that the government would purchase and store excess farm goods, thus supporting the price level by withdrawing the surplus from the competitive market. Both methods constitute a subsidy for the farmer from society at large.[2]

Though the Eisenhower administration in the 1950's called for a return to a free market in farm products—that is, the removal of government supports from prices—very few steps have been taken in that direction, and probably very few ever will.[3] A free market was actually in operation during the twenties, but it succeeded only in making farmers the stepchildren of the golden prosperity of that decade. Today the farm bloc is too powerful politically to be treated so cavalierly. Moreover, the depression has taught most Americans

[2] On the day that the first AAA was declared unconstitutional, a Gallup poll revealed that, although the nation as a whole did not like the AAA, the farmers of the South and Midwest did. As a result, invalidation of the act by the Court did not mean the end of such a policy, but only the beginning of a search to find a new way of accomplishing the same end. Hence there were successive AAA's, whereas, when NRA was declared unconstitutional in 1935, it was dropped, primarily because neither business nor labor, for whose interests it had been organized, found much merit in its approach to their problems.

[3] As reported in the *New York Times,* July 2, 1958, forecasts for the fiscal year 1958–59 see government subsidies to agriculture reaching $6 billion—an all-time high.

that a free market is not only a rarity in the modern world but sometimes inimical to a stable and lasting prosperity.

Perhaps the most imaginative and fruitful of these innovations was the Tennessee Valley Authority, which transformed the heart of the South. "It was and is literally a down to earth experiment," native Tennesseean Broadus Mitchell has written, "with all that we know from test tube and logarithm tables called on to help. It was a union of heart and mind to restore what had been wasted. It was a social resurrection." For the TVA was much more than flood and erosion control or even hydroelectric power—though its gleaming white dams are perhaps its most striking and best-known monuments. It was social planning of the most humane sort, where even the dead were carefully removed from cemeteries before the waters backed up behind the dams. It brought new ideas, new wealth, new skills, new hope into a wasted, tired, and discouraged region.

At the time of the inception of the TVA, it was scarcely believable that the "backward" South would ever utilize all the power the great dams would create. But in its report of 1956, the Authority declared that the Valley's consumption of electricity far exceeded that produced from water sites: almost three quarters of TVA'S power is now generated from steam power, not from waterfall. In large part it was the TVA which taught the Valley how to use more power to expand its industries and to lighten the people's burdens. Back in 1935, Drew and Leon Pearson saw this creation of consumer demand in action. "Uncle Sam is a drummer with a commercial line to sell," they wrote in *Harper's Magazine*. "He sold liberty bonds before, but never refrigerators."

Measured against textbook definitions, the TVA is unquestionably socialism. The government owns the means of production and, moreover, it competes with private producers of electricity.[4] But pragmatic Americans—and particularly those living in the Valley—have

---

[4] The extent of the intellectual change which the depression measures introduced can be appreciated by a quotation from President Hoover's veto in 1931 of a bill to develop a public power project in what was later to be the TVA area. "I am firmly opposed to the Government entering into any business the major purpose of which is competition with our citizens." Emergency measures of such a character might be tolerated, he said. "But for the Federal government deliberately to go out to build up and expand such an occasion to the major purpose of a power and manufacturing business is to break down the initiative and enterprise of the American people; it is destruction of equality of opportunity amongst our people; it is the negation of the ideals upon which our civilization has been based."

had few sleepless nights as a consequence of this fact. The TVA does its appointed job and, as the recent fight over the Dixon and Yates contract seemed to show, it is here to stay. It, too, with all the talk of "creeping socialism," has been absorbed into that new American Way fashioned by the experimentalism of the American people from the wreckage of the Great Depression.

Undoubtedly social security deserves the appellation "revolutionary" quite as much as the TVA; it brought government into the lives of people as nothing had since the draft and the income tax. Social security legislation actually comprises two systems: insurance against old age and insurance in the event of loss of work. The first system was completely organized and operated by the federal government; the second was shared with the states—but the national government set the standards; both were clear acknowledgment of the changes which had taken place in the family and in the business of making a living in America. No longer in urban America could the old folks, whose proportion in the society was steadily increasing, count on being taken in by their offspring as had been customary in a more agrarian world. Besides, such a makeshift arrangement was scarcely satisfying to the self-respect of the oldsters. With the transformation of the economy by industrialization, most Americans had become helpless before the vagaries of the business cycle. As a consequence of the social forces which were steadily augmenting social insecurity, only collective action by the government could arrest the drift.

To have the government concerned about the security of the individual was a new thing. Keenly aware of the novelty of this aim in individualistic America,[5] Roosevelt was careful to deny any serious departure from traditional paths. "These three great objectives—the security of the home, the security of livelihood, and the security of social insurance," he said in 1934, constitute "a minimum of the promise that we can offer to the American people." But this, he quickly added, "does not indicate a change in values."

Whether the American people thought their values had changed is not nearly as important as the fact that they accepted social

---

[5] Characteristically enough, as his memoirs show, President Hoover had long been interested in both old-age and unemployment insurance, but always such schemes were to be worked out through private insurance companies, or at best with the states—never under the auspices of the federal government. "It required a great depression," he has written somewhat ruefully, "to awaken interest in the idea" of unemployment insurance.

security. And the proof that they did is shown in the steady increase in the proportion of the population covered by the old-age benefit program since 1935; today about 80 per cent of nonfarm workers are included in the system. Apart from being a minimum protection for the individual and society against the dry rot of industrial idleness, unemployment insurance is now recognized as one of the major devices for warding off another depression.

It is true, as proponents of the agrarian life have been quick to point out, that an industrialized people, stripped as they are of their economic self-reliance, have felt the need for social insurance more than people in other types of society. But it is perhaps just as important to recognize that it is only in such a highly productive society that people can even dare to dream of social security. Men in other ages have felt the biting pains of economic crisis, but few preindustrial people have ever enjoyed that surfeit of goods which permits the fat years to fill out the lean ones. But like so much else concerning industrialism, it is not always easy to calculate whether the boons it offers exceed in value the burdens which it imposes.

For the average man, the scourge of unemployment was the essence of the depression. Widespread unemployment, permeating all ranks and stations in society, drove the American people and their government into some of their most determined and deliberate departures from the hallowed policy of "hands off." But despite the determination, as late as 1938 the workless still numbered almost ten million—two thirds as great as in 1932 under President Hoover. The governmental policies of the 1930's never appreciably diminished the horde of unemployed—only the war prosperity of 1940 and after did that—but the providing of jobs by the federal government was a reflection of the people's new conviction that the government had a responsibility to alleviate economic disaster. Such bold action on the part of government, after the inconclusive, bewildered approach of the Hoover administration, was a tonic for the dragging spirits of the people.[6]

[6] It was the misfortune of Herbert Hoover to have been President at a time when his considerable administrative and intellectual gifts were hamstrung by his basic political philosophy, which, instead of being a guide to action, served as an obstacle. Much more of an old-fashioned liberal than a reactionary, and deeply attached to the Jeffersonian dogma of the limited powers of the federal government, Hoover was psychologically and philosophically unable to use the immense powers and resources of his office in attacking the urgent threat of unemployment. Back in 1860-61, another President—James Buchanan—had been

A whole range of agencies, from the Civil Works Administration (CWA) to the Works Progress Administration (WPA), were created to carry the attack against unemployment. It is true that the vast program of relief which was organized was not "permanent" in the sense that it is still in being, but for two reasons it deserves to be discussed here. First, since these agencies constituted America's principal weapon against unemployment, some form of them will surely be utilized if a depression should occur again. Second, the various relief agencies of the period afford the best examples of the new welfare outlook, which was then in the process of formation.

Though in the beginning relief programs were premised on little more than Harry Hopkins' celebrated dictum, "Hunger is not debatable," much more complex solutions to unemployment were soon worked out. The relief program of the WPA, which after 1935 was the major relief agency, was a case in point. In 1937, *Fortune* magazine commented on "the evolution of unemployment relief from tool to institution"—a recognition of the importance and duration of relief in America. "In 1936, the federal government was so deeply involved in the relief of the unemployed," *Fortune* contended, "that it was not only keeping them alive, but it was also giving them an opportunity to work; and not only giving them an opportunity to work but giving them an opportunity to work at jobs for which they were peculiarly fitted; and not only giving them an opportunity to work at jobs for which they were peculiarly fitted, but creating for them jobs of an interest and usefulness which they could not have expected to find in private employment." The statement somewhat distorts the work of the WPA, but it sums up the main outlines of the evolution of the relief program.

The various artistic and cultural employment programs of the WPA are excellent examples of how relief provided more than employment, though any of the youth agencies like the Civilian Conservation Corps or the National Youth Administration (it

paralyzed in the midst of a national crisis by his limited conception of the federal power, but in that instance his inaction was palliated by the fact that his successor was to take office within less than three months. Hoover, however, wrestled with the depression for three years, and all during that trying period he stoutly held to his rigid intellectual position that federally supplied and administered relief would destroy the foundations of the nation. Never has an American President, including the two Adamses, defied overwhelming popular opinion for so long for the sake of his own ideals as Herbert Hoover did then; and never has a President since Buchanan fallen so quickly into obscurity as Hoover did after March 4, 1933.

subsidized student work) would serve equally well. At its peak, the
Federal Writers' Project employed some 6,000 journalists, poets,
novelists, and Ph. D.'s of one sort or another; unknowns worked
on the same payroll, if not side by side, with John Steinbeck, Vardis
Fisher, and Conrad Aiken. The $46 million expended on art—that
is, painting and sculpture—by the WPA in 1936–37 exceeded the
artistic budget of any country outside the totalitarian orbit—and
there art was frankly propagandistic. *Fortune*, in May, 1937,
found the American government's sponsorship of art singularly
free of censorship or propaganda. The magazine concluded that "by
and large the Arts Projects have been given a freedom no one
would have thought possible in a government run undertaking. And
by and large that freedom has not been abused." During the first
fifteen months of the Federal Music Project, some fifty million
people heard live concerts; in the first year of the WPA Theater,
sixty million people in thirty states saw performances, with weekly
attendance running to half a million. T. S. Eliot's *Murder in the
Cathedral*, too risky for a commercial producer, was presented in
New York by the Federal Theater to 40,000 people at a top price
of 55 cents.

"What the government's experiments in music, painting, and the
theater actually did," concluded *Fortune* in May, 1937, "even in
their first year, was to work a sort of cultural revolution in
America." For the first time the American audience and the
American artist were brought face to face for their mutual benefit.
"Art in America is being given its chance," said the British writer
Ford Madox Ford, "and there has been nothing like it since before
the Reformation. . . ."

Instead of being ignored on the superficially plausible grounds of
the exigencies of the depression, the precious skills of thousands of
painters, writers, and musicians were utilized. By this timely rescue
of skills, tastes, and talents from the deadening hand of unemployment, the American people, through their government, showed
their humanity and social imagination. Important for the future
was the foresight displayed in the conserving of artistic talents
and creations for the enrichment of generations to come.

The entrance of the federal government into a vast program of
relief work was an abrupt departure from all previous practice, but
it proved enduring. "When President Roosevelt laid it down that
government had a social responsibility to care for the victims of the

business cycle," *Fortune* remarked prophetically in 1937, "he set in motion an irreversible process." The burden of unemployment relief was too heavy to be carried by local government or private charities in an industrialized society; from now on, the national government would be expected to shoulder the responsibility. "Those who are on relief and in close contact otherwise with public matters realize that what has happened to the country is a bloodless revolution," wrote an anonymous relief recipient in *Harper's* in 1936. The government, he said, has assumed a new role in depressions, and only the rich might still be oblivious to it. But they too "will know it by 1940. And in time," they will "come to approve the idea of everyone having enough to eat." [7] Few people escaped the wide net of the depression: "Anybody sinks after a while," the anonymous reliefer pointed out. "Even you would have if God hadn't preserved, without apparent rhyme or reason, your job and your income." That the depression was a threat to all was perhaps the first lesson gained from the 1930's.

The second was that only through collective defense could such a threat be met. By virtue of the vigorous attack made upon the economic problems of the thirties by the government, the age-old conviction that dips in the business cycle were either the will of God or the consequence of unalterable economic laws was effectively demolished. As recently as 1931, President Hoover had told an audience that some people "have indomitable confidence that by some legerdemain we can legislate ourselves out of a world-wide depression. Such views are as accurate as the belief that we can exorcise a Caribbean hurricane." From the experience of the depression era, the American people learned that something could and ought to be done when economic disaster strikes. No party and no politician with a future will ever again dare to take the fatalistic and defeatist course of Herbert Hoover in 1929–33.

As the enactment of the Employment Act of 1946 showed, the prevention of depression now occupies top listing among the social anxieties of the American people. The act created a permanent Council of Economic Advisers to the President, to keep him con-

---

[7] The providing of work relief instead of the dole did more than fill hungry stomachs; it re-established faith in America and in one's fellow man. "I'm proud of our United States," said one relief recipient. "There ain't no other nation in the world that would have sense enough to think of WPA and all the other A's." The wife of one WPA worker was quoted as saying, "We aren't on relief any more—my man is working for the government."

tinuously informed on the state of the economy and to advise him
on the measures necessary to avoid an economic decline. And the
Joint Committee on the Economic Report does the same for
Congress.

Today political figures who indignantly repudiate any "left-
wing" philosophy of any sort readily accept this inheritance from
the depression. "Never again shall we allow a depression in the
United States," vowed Republican candidate Eisenhower in 1952.
As soon as we "foresee the signs of any recession and depression,"
he promised, ". . . the full power of private industry, of municipal
government, of state government, of the Federal Government will
be mobilized to see that that does not happen." Ignoring the fact
that as a prospective federal official he had promised more than he
could deliver, he innocently and accurately added, "I cannot pledge
you more than that." Sensing the tremendous importance of the
matter to the American people, Eisenhower made substantially the
same statement three other times—at Yonkers, Peoria, and Pittsburgh. At Yonkers he said that he had "repeated this particular
pledge over and over again in the United States" and that he and
his associates were "dedicated to this proposition. . . ."

In the White House, Eisenhower continued to reflect this underlying and persistent fear that a depression would once again stride
through the land. According to the account in Robert Donovan's
semiofficial *Eisenhower: The Inside Story*, at session after session
of the Cabinet during the recession of 1953–54, it was the President
who stressed the urgency of the economic situation. It was he who
constantly prodded Arthur F. Burns of the Council of Economic
Advisers to prepare plans with which to forestall a serious drop in
the economic indicators. Indeed as late as June, 1954, just after
Burns had delivered an optimistic report on the condition and
future of the economy, as Donovan tells it, "The President . . .
was still concerned about whether the administration was doing
enough. Even though it jarred the logic of some members of the
Cabinet, he insisted, everything possible must be done to restore
vigor to the economy. It was important, the President said, to
produce results and to err on the side of doing too much rather
than too little."

In the midst of the recession of 1957–58, Vice-President Nixon,
speaking on April 24, 1958, specifically repudiated the Hoover approach of permitting the economy to right itself without govern-

ment intervention. "Let us recognize once and for all," he told his audience, "that the time is past in the United States when the Federal Government can stand by and allow a recession to be prolonged or to deepen into depression without decisive Government action." Though Eisenhower was obviously worried that hasty measures might bring on further inflation, on May 20, in a public address, he agreed with the Vice-President that the government had "a continuing responsibility . . . to help counteract recession." In the same speech the President enumerated concrete measures already taken, such as extension of unemployment benefits, speeding up of defense and civilian procurement, acceleration of government construction projects, and the easing of credit by the Federal Reserve.

The Republican administration's evident acceptance of the new obligations of government in the economy is strikingly suggestive of the shock which the depression dealt conventional economic thought in America.

3. REVOLUTION IN POLITICS

In passing through the dark valley of the depression, Americans discarded more than conventional economics; they also revised their political preferences. Like downswings in other times, the depression of the thirties spawned a number of ephemeral political aberrations like the Share the Wealth of Huey Long, the oldsters' rebellion led by Dr. Francis E. Townsend, and the soured Populism of Father Coughlin's crusade for Social Justice. But the most portentous shift in popular political thought was the Roosevelt Revolution— the raising of the Democratic party to the predominant position in American political life. What the War for the Union did for Republicans, the Great Depression achieved for the Democrats; and ever since, they have been making as steady use of the tattered shirt as the Republicans did of the bloody shirt. It has worked, too; even in the mid-fifties, as the election of 1956 demonstrates, there are more Democrats than Republicans in the country. For despite the re-election of Eisenhower, the Republicans lost both houses of Congress, an unprecedented failure for a party with a winning President. The grip of the depression on the American psyche has barely loosened a full generation after 1933.

This massive shift in popular opinion from the Republican to the Democratic party was a direct result of the wide range of social groups to which the Democratic administration offered succor and recognition. Midwestern farmers, for example, had always been deemed safe within the Republican fold, but after the AAA program they eagerly joined the Roosevelt coalition. And as late as 1948 it was clear that many were still there, for the farmers held the key to Harry Truman's unexpected victory that year. Numerous relief payments to workers, labor legislation, and the benevolent interest of the President himself succeeded in tying the working classes of the city more firmly and in greater numbers than ever before to the wheels of the Democratic chariot. Not until the election of 1956 was there any noticeable breach in the solid Democratic allegiance of the big cities. Even then what breaks appeared seemed to be attributable more to the charismatic effects of Ike than to any massive shift in party allegiance.

Perhaps the most unexpected result of the revolution was the transfer of the Negro vote from the Republicans, where it had lain for three generations, to the Democrats. Like so much else in the twentieth century, this change in the Negro's voting habits is closely linked to the growth of industrialization. For almost half a century after the end of slavery, about 90 per cent of the Negro population of the country lived in the South; in 1910, for example, the figure was 89 per cent. But with the expansion of northern industry during the First World War, there was an increasing demand for skilled and unskilled labor. For the first time in American history, large numbers of Negroes, attracted by the new opportunities in northern industry, left the South. In the seven years after 1916, it has been estimated, as many as a million Negroes migrated northward. Northern industrial centers experienced enormous increases in their Negro populations between the censuses of 1910 and 1920. In Akron, Ohio, for example, the increase was over 780 per cent; in Cleveland, 307 per cent; and in Detroit, the automobile industry attracted enough new workers to swell the Negro population by over 620 per cent. This emigration from the South continued through the twenties. Whereas in the Census of 1920 15 per cent of the Negro population lived outside the South, in 1930 20 per cent of the Negroes made their homes in the North and the West. In the course of the single decade of the twenties, the Negro population in the North jumped over 64 per cent, while it grew in the South by only 5 per cent. So massive was this new migration, much of

which came out of the Deep South,[8] that in 1920, for the first time
in the history of the nation, the statistical center of the Negro
population reversed its historic southwestern course and shifted
north and east.

In moving out of the South the black man divested himself of two
distinguishing social and political characteristics. In the South
the Negro was typically rural and usually disfranchised, despite
the Fifteenth Amendment. Once in the North, the Negro became
primarily a city dweller, and he was permitted to exercise the vote.
The new urban setting of the Negro, of course, was dictated by the
industry which drew him northward. In 1930, over 88 per cent of
the northern Negroes and 82 per cent of Negroes in the West lived
in cities; by contrast, 68 per cent of the Negroes in the South lived
on the land. The concentration of Negroes in northern cities was
even greater than these figures suggest; one third of them lived in
only four northern cities. The conjuncture of the ballot and urban
concentration created a formidable Negro voting power for the
first time in the North. It is not surprising, therefore, that the
election of the first Negro congressman outside of the South—that
of De Priest in 1929—occurred in Chicago only a decade after the
massive migration to the North. Not much before that date were
there enough northern Negroes to compel politicians and parties to
take them into account.

What party allegiance they would assume, however, was determined by other considerations. As Mark Hanna, the powerful
Republican boss at the turn of the century, said, "I carry the
Negro vote around in my vest pocket." He did; and other Republican bosses before and after him could say the same. To tell the
truth, where could the Negro find sympathy but in the Republican
party, the party of the Emancipator? As the Negro leader Frederick Douglass is supposed to have warned his followers: "The
Republican party is the ship; all else is the sea." Was it to be ex-

[8] Heretofore most Negro migration, which rarely exceeded 10,000 annually,
had come from the states of the upper South. The new migration, however, was
significant in that it was drawn from the lower South. Between 1900 and 1910,
for example, a mere 2,000 Negroes left South Carolina for Pennsylvania; in the
following decade, 16,196 did. Only 781 Negroes left Alabama for Ohio in the
ten years before 1910; in the subsequent decade, 17,500 made the trip—and so
it went in state after state in the Deep South. The significance of this movement
of Negroes out of the area of their greatest concentration, of course, has had a
profound effect on the future of the Negro in the South and has enhanced the
prospects for greater racial amity in that region.

pected that the black man could look for support from the Democracy, the party of the Southern white man? Well, at least not until
Republican promises on behalf of the black man had worn thin
enough to force his looking elsewhere.

During the optimism of the Progressive period, a few middle-
class Negroes and intellectuals did talk of playing off the Democrats
against the inertia-ridden Republicans. Some Negro leaders, for
example, urged support of Woodrow Wilson in 1912 on the ground
that he was untainted with the "lily-white" practices of which both
Taft and Theodore Roosevelt were plainly guilty. Disillusionment
for those Negro leaders, however, was fast in coming. True to his
southern training and the southern bias of his party, Wilson in
office quickly introduced segregation into the federal service in
Washington. Thus it turned out that Progressivism, in both its
Democratic and Republican forms, failed to include the Negro in
its vision of a better America. The incipient movement for a two-
party system for Negroes was halted for another two decades.

In the depths of the depression, even though there was some dissatisfaction with Hoover among Negro leaders, it is clear that the
rank-and-file black voter clung to his Republican faith. The name
Franklin Roosevelt carried no magic for Negroes in 1932. In the
black wards of Chicago that year, Roosevelt picked up only 23 per
cent of the vote—a ratio smaller than Al Smith's in the prosperous
year of 1928. It was the same among the Negroes in Cleveland;
Detroit Negroes awarded F. D. R. only a little more than a third of
their votes.

By 1936, however, the somersault had been executed. At that
election Chicago's Black Belt gave Roosevelt 49 per cent of its
votes; the Negroes of Cleveland went all out for the President—62
per cent—even though in 1932 they had awarded Hoover 72 per
cent of their ballots. Roosevelt garnered almost two thirds of the
Negro vote in Detroit, and the four Negro wards in Philadelphia
each gave him a majority of 5,000. The swing to the Democrats had
been forecast in 1934, when the first Democratic Negro congressman in American history was elected from Chicago. Between 1936
and 1940, exactly half of the eighteen Negroes elected to state
legislatures were Democrats. Though a tendency has been developing among some Negro leaders since the Second World War to be
more critical of their new Democratic allies, Samuel Lubell reported that in the election of 1950 there was "less of a break among

Negroes than among any other major group in the Roosevelt Coalition." Despite the fact that civil rights had become a supercharged issue in the country at the time of the 1956 elections, Negroes, particularly in the North, continued to adhere to their recent Democratic conversion.[9]

What brought about this dramatic reversal? Part of the answer, of course, lies in the demographic facts of migration, but, as the Negro voting in 1932 demonstrates, the really operative force was the Roosevelt administration's recognition of the Negro. It is most interesting that very little of the Democratic appeal to the Negro before 1940 can be illustrated in pronouncements or even in particular pieces of legislation. Only rarely does one find in the literature of Franklin Roosevelt and his New Deal such self-conscious appeals to the Negro as, say, in Harry Truman's Fair Deal or Henry Wallace's Progressive party.

There are several reasons for this. Primary, of course, is the fact that these other two movements developed after the Roosevelt regime had already given the Negro a bigger and higher platform from which to articulate his demands. Moreover, because F. D. R., as a working politician, was always conscious of his party's southern wing, he would rarely antagonize the Southerners on the race issue alone. Furthermore, Roosevelt as a leader was only tangentially aware of the Negro as a special case, as a minority to be singled out for exceptional treatment or concern. It was Eleanor Roosevelt, not Franklin, who went out of her way to be racially democratic and to concern herself with minority problems.

Nonetheless, the Roosevelt administration in its relatively undramatic fashion did much for the Negro, and this too stemmed from both the character of Franklin Roosevelt and the underlying philosophy of his administration. Just as the federal government found a place for the artist, so its humane outlook could not exclude the Negro. Thus if white men were to be given relief work, so must Negroes; and if so, then why not on an equal basis? "We are going to make a country in which no one is left out," the President said in another connection. And there was nothing to suggest that he had any mental reservations about race when he said it. Besides,

[9] In a postelection survey of the Negro vote, *The New York Times,* November 11, 1956, p. 60, reported that "the party of Lincoln still has a long way to go to regain the politico-racial domination that it held so firmly from post-Civil War days until Franklin D. Roosevelt smashed it twenty years ago."

although F. D. R. would do little publicly to antagonize his southern allies on the race question, his political perspicacity told him that in the North his power was heavily dependent upon city machines, many of which could or did benefit from Negro votes.

From the very outset the Democratic regime in Washington accepted the black man. Negroes were sprinkled through almost all its agencies either as advisers or as employees in a lesser capacity. The administration consulted and bestowed office upon nonpolitical Negroes (the Republicans had generally used Negroes as political appointees) like William H. Hastie, later to be the first Negro federal judge; Robert C. Weaver, the economist; and Mrs. Mary Bethune, the educator. When low-cost housing went up, Negroes got their share; Negro youths were welcome in the CCC and the NYA just as the whites were, though in the former the races were segregated. Recreational centers, hospitals, and schools were built for Negroes with federal money. Evenhandedly distributed federal relief funds were a gift from heaven to the black man, who was traditionally "hired last and fired first." As one Negro newspaperman told Samuel Lubell, "The really important thing about WPA is that it is a guarantee of a living wage. It means Negroes don't have to work for anything people want to give them." In the votings conducted by the AAA among farmers and those supervised by the National Labor Relations Board among workers, Negroes were treated the same as white men, even though in the South these same black men were excluded from political elections. In short, the Roosevelt administration took a number of concrete steps toward accepting the Negro as a full citizen—a simple innovation of portentous consequences. It would be difficult hereafter for any party in power to do less.

All the credit for converting the Negro from his Republicanism, however, should not go to positive acts of the Democratic administration; the objective economic and social environment also deserves some. Negroes, for example, began to secure jobs in a greater variety of occupations than ever before; under the impact of the depression, some employers were willing to hire Negroes for the first time, if only because the black worker accepted lower wages. Moreover, the C.I.O. unions now began to organize Negro workers on an equal basis with whites. To accomplish this end, Negro organizers were sent among the steel, maritime, and auto workers, and, when the permanent Congress of Industrial Organizations was

formed in 1938, a clause in the constitution prohibited any constituent union from discriminating on grounds of race. The startling
improvement in the Negro's position in the thirties could not help
but redound to the benefit of the party in power.

By 1940, the capturing of the Negro vote by the Democrats was
an accomplished fact, and the party platform of that year, using
the word "Negro" for the first time, boasted of its friendship for
the black man. "Our Negro citizens," the platform proclaimed,
"have participated actively in the economic and social advances
launched by this Administration." It would not have been an exaggeration, for once in the history of political platforms, if it had
been noted that this was about the first time since the 1870's that
any party could truthfully say half as much.

4. REVOLUTION IN LABOR

The change wrought in the political affiliations of Negroes by
the depression was as nothing compared with the catalytic and
subversive effect it worked upon the labor movement. And, analogous
to the change in the preference of the Negro voter, the alteration in
the position and power of labor was indebted to the action of the
Roosevelt administration, the Democratic Congress, and the new
social atmosphere of the depression era.

During the prosperity of the twenties the labor movement had
gone into a decline rare in the history of unionization. The usual
tendency had been for membership to rise in prosperous times and
to decline in bad. But whereas in 1920 organized labor could claim
its largest membership to date—some five million workers—by 1929
barely three million could be counted. Thus labor entered the depression under the handicap of declining membership. But instead
of killing off many unions, as depressions had done earlier, the depression of the thirties seemed to stimulate a new and aggressive
organizing spirit among the workers. In the light of the later tremendous expansion of union membership, it might be said that the
depression created a class consciousness among American workingmen for the first time sufficient to permit large-scale unionization.

Despite the fact that the vast majority of unionized workers
were then in the American Federation of Labor, that body was not
destined to be the instrument of the new unionization. The Federation was too cautious, too saturated with Samuel Gompers' commitment to craft forms of organization and his fear of governmental

interference, to be able to capitalize on the unrest among the workers. It is true that some Federation leaders like John L. Lewis of the Miners and Hillman of the Clothing Workers were pressing hard for new organizing drives among the workers of the still unorganized great industries of the country like textiles, steel, rubber, automobiles, and aircraft. But such men were a small minority in the Federation.

The deepening of the economic slump, however, did open crevices in the Federation's high wall of tradition. At the 1932 convention in Cincinnati, John L. Lewis convinced the convention to go on record in favor of state unemployment systems. To the old-timers in the Federation this was a serious and dangerous departure from Gompers' inflexible principle of "voluntarism"—that is, no government interference on either side in the match between capital and labor. Lewis also cajoled the delegates—apparently bewildered and shaken by the enormity of the economic crisis—into accepting the principle of a legislatively limited working day—a further repudiation of Gompers' principles.

Then came the opening notes of the Rooseveltian performance, foremost among which was the National Industrial Recovery Act. This measure contained a labor clause—the well-known 7a—which guaranteed to workers the right of free choice of union and committed the employers to dealing with such unions. Spurred by this government encouragement, both spontaneous organization and A.F. of L.-affiliated unionization surged forward. More than 1,100 federal and local unions in the mass production industries of automobiles, aluminum, and rubber were brought into being by 1935; union membership for these industries shot up from less than 11,000 in 1933 to over ten times that figure in 1935. President Green of the A.F. of L. announced that between 60,000 and 70,000 workers had been added to the Federation in Akron alone in 1933, most of them in the rubber industry. Capitalizing on Roosevelt's acceptance of section 7a, John L. Lewis told the miners, "The President wants you to join a union." The United Mine Workers, though wasting away all through the twenties, attracted 300,000 members to its rolls in the spring and early summer of 1933. The Ladies Garment Workers Union added 100,000; the Amalgamated Clothing Workers gathered in another 50,000 during the middle months of NRA's first year. At the A.F. of L. convention of 1934, the Executive Council reported "a virtual uprising of workers for union membership. Workers," the Council said with amazement, "held mass meetings and sent word they wanted to be organized."

The emphasis on craft organization and the cautious philosophy of the American Federation of Labor, however, were not equal to the task of organizing and canalizing this upsurge among the workers in the mass production industries. The craft form, where unionization proceeded along the lines of the job, rather than the factory, made no sense whatsoever in any of the great industries where the mass of workers were semiskilled or unskilled rather than skilled. Moreover, to divide the workers in a plant according to occupations resulted in endless jurisdictional disputes among the unions. Ultimately the mishandling of the organizational problem reflected itself in loss of membership. For example, though in 1934 the A.F. of L. had over 150,000 members in its 100 locals in the automobile industry, by 1936 the membership had dwindled away to 19,000. A willingness to try new forms and to include the unskilled and semiskilled, who bulked so large in the mass production industries, was urgently needed if organized labor was to benefit from the workers' new interest in unions.

The obvious failure of the A.F. of L.'s approach to the mass industries came to a head in the heated Atlantic City convention of October, 1935. Beetle-browed, leonine John L. Lewis of the industrially organized Miners raised his stentorian voice in behalf of the unorganized. "Heed this cry from Macedonia that comes from the hearts of men," he cried to the impassive leaders of labor's elite. "Organize the unorganized and in doing this make the A.F. of L. the greatest instrument that has ever been forged to befriend the cause of humanity and champion human rights." Defeated at every turn on the floor of the convention (except perhaps in his famous right hook to the nose of arch-conservative William Hutcheson of the Carpenters), Lewis and his fellow rebels, the day after the convention closed, organized the Committee for Industrial Organization. Composed of ten of the more aggressive and spirited of the A.F. of L. unions, this committee sparked the mighty organizing effort which transformed American industrial and labor relations in the next handful of years. Within a year after the formation of the C.I.O., the A.F. of L expelled the constituent unions. The split in the labor movement, destined to remain unhealed for twenty years, was a fact.

In view of the consequences, however, that split was the most promising thing that ever happened to Samuel Gompers' beloved American Federation of Labor in particular and to the American workingman in general. The C.I.O.—formed into the permanent Congress of Industrial Organizations in 1938—undertook a massive and energetic invasion of unorganized mass industries like steel, automobiles, textiles, rubber, aircraft, and lumber—all industries which had implacably resisted the union organizer for over a generation. One by one, with varying degrees of violence and resistance, they fell to the determination, the guts, and the persistence of the new unionism. In time the A.F. of L. also joined in, and by 1940 total union membership in the country had risen to 8.5 million from 3.7 million only five years earlier. Under the impact of the depression, the American labor movement had come of age.

Aside from the new and vital spirit which the C.I.O. breathed into the labor movement, its great innovation was its effective use of the industrial-union form. So successfully was this form adapted to the economic structure that the industrial union soon captured a prominent place in the once craft-dominated A.F. of L. By 1940 about a quarter of the A.F. of L.'s four million members were in industrial unions and a quarter of the C.I.O.'s workers were in craft unions. Furthermore, by organizing recent immigrants, the unskilled, Negroes, and women on a scale and with a determination never attempted by the A.F. of L., the C.I.O. revived a broad approach to unionism which had been sidetracked in America ever since the A.F. of L. had beaten out the old Knights of Labor.

The enormous expansion of unionization in the last years of the depression was not solely attributable to the novel spirit among the unions and the workers. Much of the impetus came from the new attitude of the government. We have already seen the catalytic effect the NRA had on the rush toward unionization, and it would be difficult to exaggerate that effect. When that act was declared unconstitutional in 1935, its place was taken by the National Labor Relations Act (the Wagner Act), in itself perhaps the most revolutionary single measure in American labor history.

The Wagner Act started from the same premise as section 7a of the NRA—that is, that workers should be free to choose their own unions and employers must abstain from interfering in this choice. It also required that employers accept duly constituted unions as legitimate representatives of their employees and bargain with them. The act also set up a board—the National Labor Relations

Board—whose duty it was to supervise elections for the certification of unions as representatives of a majority of the workers in a plant, and to hear complaints against employers for having interfered with union organizing. The Board was also empowered to hear complaints against employers for refusing to bargain with a certified union.

In two different ways, the act threw the enormous prestige and power of the government behind the drive for organizing workers. In the first place, it flatly declared unionization to be a desirable thing for the national economy, forbidding employers to interfere in the process of organization. Five so-called unfair labor practices were listed, all of them acts which only an employer could commit; the act listed no "unfair" practices of labor. (Actually, the courts had built up such a large body of common-law interpretations of unfair labor practices by unions that it was hardly necessary to add to them in the act.) Moreover, as an additional indication of its belief in the labor movement, the law virtually outlawed the company union—that is, the labor organization sponsored by the employer. In the second place, once a union was formed, and it had been certified by the Board as speaking for a majority of the workers, the employer, under the act, had no alternative but to recognize it as the representative of his employees. Though it is true that many employers refused to accept the constitutionality of the law—usually on the advice of their lawyers—until after the Supreme Court decision of 1937 in the Jones and Laughlin Steel case, this placing of the government on the side of unionization was of central importance in the success of many an organizational drive of the C.I.O., notably those against Ford and Little Steel.[10]

The passage of this controversial act marked, insofar as labor was concerned, an acceptance of governmental assistance which would have made old Sam Gompers apoplectic. All during his leadership of the A.F. of L., labor had consistently refused to accept (except for the war emergency) government intervention at the bargaining table of labor and business. But by accepting governmental assistance, the American labor movement not only departed

[10] Even before the Wagner Act had won the support of the Supreme Court, Presidential "pressure" and prestige helped the C.I.O. attain some of its most telling victories, like that over General Motors in February of 1937. The sensational exposure of union-busting tactics of employers by Senator Robert La Follette's investigating committee, beginning in 1936, was still another form of governmental assistance to the cause of labor.

from its own traditions, but from those of European labor as well. Although well aware of the benefits to be derived from such government support as the American movement received, labor in England and on the Continent has not abandoned its historic independence of the state. European labor unions have preferred to remain untouched by the quasi-governmental status in which the American labor movement has permitted itself to be clothed. Labor's bête noire, the Taft-Hartley Act, is an obvious confirmation of the truism that dependence on government is a knife which cuts both ways.

Another, though less important, difference between American and European labor practices is the attitude toward the union and closed shops. Largely because of the historic fragility of American labor organizations, unions in the United States have found it desirable, if not imperative, to insist that all workers in a given shop or plant join the union to which a majority of workers belong. The Wagner Act reinforced this practice by making it an unfair labor practice for an employer to refuse to sign an agreement requiring all of his employees to join the union.

European employers have rarely signed such agreements, and the Swiss, French, German, English, and Swedish labor unions have gone on record as opposing such closed or union shop agreements. Indeed, in the basic Matignon agreement between French capital and labor in 1936, the unions voluntarily agreed to management's right to hire and fire regardless of union membership. Generally speaking, labor and the courts alike in Europe have looked upon the closed shop as an infringement of a worker's right to join or not join any association he pleases. Unionism, however, is considerably stronger there than here, and the workers can be confident that the open shop is not an excuse for refusing to deal with unions at all, as it has proved to be in the United States. It still remains to be seen whether the growing movement for "right to work" (i.e., without joining a union) statutes in many American states is a reflection of the European concern for individual associative freedom or an upsurge of the old antiunionism so indigenous to America.

The Wagner Act broke new ground in labor law, going even beyond the epoch-making Norris-La Guardia Act of 1932. This latter act, passed after years of agitation and half a dozen tries on the part of labor and liberal congressmen and senators, severely restricted the use of antiunion injunctions issuing from federal courts in the course of labor disputes. So expertly was the act drawn that it overthrew in one stroke a mountain of legal obstacles to labor organization and activity which ingenious judges and lawyers had quarried out of the common law. In substance, though, the main achievement of the act could be summed up in the phrase "laissez faire in labor relations." Labor would now be free to use its full economic power, without judicial hamstringing, just as employers had always been free to use theirs. In no way, it should be emphasized, did the Norris-La Guardia Act compel, or even advise, employers to accept unions or to bargain with them.

That innovation came only with the Wagner Act. As a federal court of appeals said in 1948, "prior to the National Labor Relations Act no federal law prevented *employers* from discharging employees for exercising their rights or from refusing to recognize or bargain with labor organizations. The NLRA created rights *against employers* which did not exist before then." In this lay the revolution in governmental attitudes toward organized labor.

So lusty and powerful did organized labor grow under the new dispensation that by the time the Second World War was over, a strong movement was afoot to amend the Wagner Act in order to protect the interests of the employer and to secure the national welfare against certain powerful national unions. The result was the Taft-Hartley Act of 1947, actually but an amendment to the original 1935 act. Without entering into the details, suffice it to say that this amendment now added certain unfair labor practices of which unions might be guilty, such as the secondary boycott, and bestowed special powers upon the federal government for effectively handling paralyzing nationwide strikes. But the central core of the National Labor Relations Act was left unimpaired, as it remains today. The American people under Republican as well as Democratic regimes have reaffirmed more than once the principle that it is the obligation of the federal government to protect a worker in the free exercise of the right to join a union and that all employers must bargain collectively with a certified union.

Enormous as was the assistance which labor received from government in the form of the NLRA, there was still another piece of legislation which offered a boost to labor. This was the Wages and Hours Act of 1938, which set minimum wages and maximum hours for workers in industries engaged in interstate commerce. Since its example has been followed by several industrial states like New York, the principle of a legislative floor under wages and a ceiling

an hours has been extended beyond the constitutional limits of the
federal government's power. Because the minimum set by law was
well below the going industrial wage, the act did not affect most
workers, but it helped considerably to pull up wages in certain unorganized industries. Furthermore, it helped to narrow the wage
differences between northern and southern industries. During the
first two years of the act, nearly a million workers received increased wages under its provisions and over three million had their
hours shortened. Subsequent to that time, the minimum wage has
been progressively increased from the original 25 cents an hour to
the present (1958) $1, thereby putting a rising floor under the
nation's industrial wage scale. Furthermore, in abolishing child
labor in all industries involved in interstate commerce, the act
achieved a long-sought goal of the labor and liberal movements in
the United States. And once again, it is worth noticing, it was
accomplished through the powerful intervention of an active federal
government.

Seen against a broader canvas, the depression, together with
government support, profoundly altered the position of labor in
American society. Girded with its new-found power and protections,
Big Labor now took its place beside Big Business and Big Government to complete a triumvirate of economic power. And when it is
recognized that through the so-called farm bloc in Congress agriculture also has attained a sort of veto power on the operations of
the economic system, it is not difficult to appreciate the aptness of
John Galbraith's description of modern American capitalism as a
system of "countervailing power." Instead of competition being the
regulator of the economic system, Professor Galbraith persuasively
argues, we now have a system of economic checks and balances—
Big Labor, Big Business, Big Agriculture, and so forth—no one of
which is big enough or powerful enough to control the total economy.
Though Galbraith's argument is not totally convincing, his conception of the American economy is much closer to reality than is
the old competitive model. And insofar as Professor Galbraith's
analysis is correct, it is clear that this system of countervailing
power came into being during the depression, with the rise of Big
Government, Organized Agriculture, and Big Labor.

5. SECURITY COMES FIRST

The currently popular notion that the thirties were vastly dif-

ferent in social attitudes and atmosphere from the fifties certainly
has much to be said for it. Undoubtedly, the present interest in
large families even among the middle class contrasts sharply with
the depression era, when the birth rate plunged to its lowest level
in our history.[11] Similarly, the falling off of religious interest
during the 1930's stands out as strikingly different from the current religious "revival." After all, it was during the twenties and
thirties that compulsory chapel in the nation's colleges went
by the board either because of outright student opposition or because of student apathy. "Too passive to be atheist, the undergraduate is vaguely deist," concluded *Fortune* in 1936. Such lack
of interest has little reflection in the fifties, when the wide student
interest in religion has compelled the colleges to add new religion
courses to their curricula and sometimes, as in the case of New
York University, has prompted the establishment of religion departments where none existed before. It is equally true that the
thirties' interest, at least among college students and intellectuals,
in Marxism and radical answers to economic woes finds no analogy
in our own day.

Yet with all such differences before us—and there are others
which could be mentioned—one nevertheless has a feeling, upon
looking into the written materials from the earlier period, that
things were not so different—or at least that some of the basic
social attitudes of the fifties have traceable roots in the depression.
A longing for security—after years of depression-bred uncertainty
—was apparent not only in the accent on security legislation, but
it was also abroad in popular talk. One lad of twenty-three working
in a Midwestern bank in 1936, for example, complained to investigator Maxine Davis that his job actually made no demands upon

[11] Though it is true that the economic fears of the thirties which kept families
small are not operative today, the means for family limitation are certainly with
us still. It was during the decade of the thirties that birth control became accepted in America. Public opinion polls at the time and the rapid spread of birth
control clinics make it clear that contraceptive techniques were not only widely
practiced, but openly accepted. In 1931, for example, there were only 81 clinics
for the dissemination of contraceptive information; but in 1943, 549 were
counted, of which 166 were under public auspices, the latter being a decided
rarity in the earlier part of the decade. Furthermore, under the depression's
compelling reason for family limitation, even the heretofore adamant Roman
Catholic Church became interested in morally acceptable methods of contraception. During 1933 and 1934, for instance, at least three books, bearing the sanction of Church officials, were published in order to bring to laymen knowledge
of the recently discovered and scientifically attested "rhythm method."

him and consisted largely of his keeping his boss's seat warm. When asked by Miss Davis why he didn't get out and look for something more challenging, he answered: "Not on your life! At least I know I'm drawing my salary every Saturday morning." *Fortune's* survey of youth's opinions arrived at the same conclusion. "Security is the *summum bonum* of the present college generation," the magazine wrote in italics. "They want a hand in a . . . job that is guaranteed to be safe and permanent. The present day average undergraduate is no chancy gambler. He doesn't expect to make much money." Speaking of the young people of America, Maxine Davis concluded, "Security is their heart's desire." The Horatio Alger ideal, left limping after the social realism of Progressivism, was dealt a crushing blow by the depression. *Its* recovery was extremely doubtful.

Although the uncertainties of the atomic age have unquestionably augmented those left over from the depression, would it be farfetched to see here in the thirties the origins of what an observer like William Whyte has called the Organization Man? This is the young man of business in the 1950's who longs, not for power and wealth derived from hard work and fired ambition, but for security within the soft confines of a great corporation where, so long as he follows the rules and wears the gray flannel suit, he will receive adequate and presumably rising income until the blessed day of retirement. It is not unlikely that we of the fifties are seeing, in the Organization Man, the long-delayed flowering of seeds which the depression nurtured.

Nor was this the only similarity between the thirties and the fifties. Then, as now, the other side of the coin of economic security was the reaffirmation of the home as the safest guideline for life. Gone and unlamented were the flapper days and the sex-spiced nights of the twenties. "When I get married," a Memphis playground director told Maxine Davis, "it's for keeps. I want a wife I can count on, and who'll be sure I'll play fair, too." The dreadful uncertainties of the depression made close personal ties swell to a new importance. "Always a lover, never a husband," lamented one self-conscious youth in his diary. "God, ain't it awful? . . . To hell with that. It may fit the twenties, but it sure don't fit the thirties. . . . I ain't looking for a girl friend but a wife." In its survey of young people in 1936, *Fortune* observed that the trek to the Village in New York City which had been so popular in the twenties was now rapidly being abandoned. "Today the prospect of marriage and children is popular again. Sixty per cent of the college girls and 50 per cent of the men would like to get married within a year or two after graduation."

Such expressions can be matched almost verbatim on college campuses or at gatherings of young people today. The "togetherness" of Macy advertisements, the featuring of the familial joys in the popular magazines, the home workshops and do-it-yourself hobbies, whatever else they may signify, are obvious signs of the almost frantic quest for security in the warmth of the home fires.[12] A tremendously popular novel like Sloan Wilson's *Man in the Gray Flannel Suit* derived a large part of its appeal from the fact that readers found in it what they wanted to be told. Tom Rath's rejection of his boss's offer to become a major executive in the firm in order that he might have his week ends and evenings free with his family was reassuring to readers. It made driving ambition and worldly success pale and empty things beside the simple and soul-satisfying pleasures of the home. "Not so many years ago," William H. Whyte has written in *The Organization Man*, "it was permissible for the ambitious young man to talk of setting his cap for a specific goal—like becoming president of a corporation, building a bridge, or making a million dollars. Today, it is a very rare young man who will allow himself to talk in such a way, let alone think that way." The source of this attitude, now spreading so noticeably among middle-class Americans, can be traced back to that crisis of individualism in the 1930's. In killing off laissez faire, the chill winds of the depression seem also to have cooled the fires of the American's adventuresome spirit upon which our economic growth, our political freedom, and our social individualism have so long and so heavily depended.

[12] The do-it-yourself and psychological "encouragement" books of the fifties also had their counterparts in the depression years. The supreme best seller of 1933 was Walter Pitkin's furiously uplifting *Life Begins at Forty*. "The 30's were particularly rich in social narcotics," writes Leo Gurko in his literary history of the decade, "*Wake Up and Live, How to Win Friends and Influence People, How to Live Within Your Income, How to Make the Most of Your Life, Live Alone and Like It*, and *How to Live Without a Woman* being among the most widely publicized." Despite the decline in interest in formal religion, books on popular religion and psychology, as is true of our own era, made the best-seller lists then. "As the world of the early 30's grew more confused," concludes Leo Gurko, "the books of Emmet Fox and Harry Emerson Fosdick became immensely popular." It is tempting to add that one of Fox's books, *Power Through Constructive Thinking*, has a remarkably familiar ring in the 1950's.

If the effect of the depression was to weaken the traditional American accent on individualism in general, in particular it served to further attenuate any religious support for the timeworn doctrines of self-reliance and individual responsibility. The social gospel of the pre-1914 years, to which the churches had become increasingly converted, passed under a cloud during the prosperous twenties, for during such a period the churches tended to forget their social obligations inherited from less fortunate times.

But the descent into the depression again abruptly demonstrated to the churches the collective nature of modern society and the crucial relevance of the social gospel. A Northern Baptist Convention in 1932, for example, affirmed "That all wealth and all labor power are intended by the Creator for the highest good of all people; that from the cradle to the grave all members of the community are bound to do their best for the common good, and reciprocally are entitled to the best that the community is able to provide for its members in common; that the normal standard of living for any is that which is practicable for all. . . ." And as a kind of celestial mandate to the new Roosevelt administration, the declaration went on to say that "civil government is the sovereign agency for the promotion of the general welfare. To it belong all the rights of property and power necessary to accomplish the purpose of such an agency."

On Labor Sunday in 1937 the Federal Council of Churches, itself the first tangible fruits of the social gospel movement, publicly endorsed the Supreme Court's validation of the National Labor Relations Act. During the era of the depression, ministers moved increasingly to the fore, as they had in the 1890's, dressed in the garb of sharp social critics. For example, in 1934 a poll of some 20,000 clergymen revealed that nearly three out of five favored a "drastically reformed capitalism," while almost a third expressed themselves as supporting socialism for America. Though increasingly impelled to restore the more theological aspects of religion, American Protestantism today has not forsaken the social gospel, which was pressed upon its conscience by the depression.

6. WAS IT A NEW OR OLD DEAL?

One of the most enduring monuments to the Great Depression was that congeries of contradictions, naïveté, humanitarianism, realistic politics, and economic horse sense called the New Deal of Franklin

D. Roosevelt. As the governmental agent which recast American thinking on the responsibilities of government, the New Deal was clearly the offspring of the depression. As we have seen, it was also more than that: it was a revitalization of the Democratic party; it was the political manifestation of that new spirit of reform which was stirring among the ranks of labor and the Negro people.

In their own time and since, the New Deal and Franklin Roosevelt have had a polarizing effect upon Americans. Probably at no time before Roosevelt has the leader of a great democratic nation come to symbolize as he did the hopes and the fears of so many people.[13] Not even Jackson, in whom Roosevelt himself recognized a President of his own popularity- and hatred-producing caliber, could rival him. Over a decade after Roosevelt's death, the mention of his name still evokes emotions, betrayed by the wistful look in the eye or in the hard set of the jaw. The election of 1956, moreover, demonstrated once again that the Old Guard of the Republican party still fights the dead Roosevelt while the Democratic party wanders leaderless in his absence. This too is a measure of the political revolution he led.

For the Democratic party, Roosevelt was like a lightning rod, drawing to himself all the venom and hatred of the opposition, only to discharge it harmlessly; nothing, it seemed, could weaken his personal hold on the affections of the majority of Americans. That something more was involved than sheer popularity is shown by the example of Dwight Eisenhower. Though held in even greater popular esteem, Eisenhower has been unable to invest his party with his own vote-getting power; Republicans lose though Eisenhower wins. The difference between F. D. R. and Ike is that one stood for a program, a hope, and a future, while the other stands for himself as a good, well-intentioned man whom all instinctively trust and perhaps even admire. The one is a leader of a nation, the other a popular hero. Roosevelt is already a member

[13] According to Harold Ickes, Roosevelt was profoundly struck by the adoration which was bestowed upon him by his admirers. During the 1936 campaign, the President told Ickes "that there was something terrible about the crowds that lined the streets along which he passed. He went on to explain what he meant, which was exclamations from individuals in the crowd, such as 'He saved my home,' 'He gave me a job,' 'God bless you, Mr. President,' etc." In May, 1936, Marquis Childs published an article in *Harper's,* entitled "They Hate Roosevelt," in which he described and tried to account for the unreasoning hatred for the President on the part of what Childs called the upper 2 per cent of the population.

of that tiny pantheon of great leaders of Americans in which Washington, Jackson, Lincoln, and Wilson are included; it is difficult to believe that Eisenhower will be included. His monument is more likely to be inscribed: "The best-liked man ever to be President."

In the thirties, as now, the place of the New Deal in the broad stream of American development has been a matter of controversy. Historians and commentators on the American scene have not yet reached a firm agreement—if they ever will—as to whether the New Deal was conservative or radical in character, though it does appear that the consensus now seems to lean toward calling it conservative and traditional.[14] Certainly if one searches the writings and utterances of Franklin Roosevelt, his own consciousness of conservative aims is quickly apparent. "The New Deal is an old deal—as old as the earliest aspirations of humanity for liberty and justice and the good life," he declared in 1934. "It was this administration," he told a Chicago audience in 1936, "which saved the system of private profit and free enterprise after it had been dragged to the brink of ruin. . . ."

But men making a revolution among a profoundly conservative people do not advertise their activity, and above all Franklin Roosevelt understood the temper of his people.[15] Nor should such a statement be interpreted as an insinuation of high conspiracy— far from it. Roosevelt was at heart a conservative, as his lifelong interest in history, among other things, suggests. But he was without dogma in his conservatism, which was heavily interlaced with genuine concern for people.[16] He did not shy away from new means and new approaches to problems when circumstances demanded it. His willingness to experiment, to listen to his university-bred Brains Trust, to accept a measure like the TVA, reveal the flexibility in his

[14] For example, one of the most recent short evaluations of the New Deal, by a most knowledgeable historian, Arthur Link, concludes as follows: "The chief significance of the reform legislation of the 1930's was its essentially conservative character and the fact that it stemmed from a half century or more of discussion and practical experience and from ideas proposed as well by Republicans as by Democrats." *American Epoch* (New York, 1955), p. 425.

[15] It is significant that only once during the 1932 campaign, according to Ernest K. Lindley, did Roosevelt call for "a revolution"; and then he promptly qualified it to "the right kind, the only kind of revolution this nation can stand for—a revolution at the ballot box."

[16] When an economist suggested to F. D. R. that the depression be permitted to run its course and that then the economic system would soon right itself—as Frances Perkins tells the story—the President's face took on a "gray look of horror" as he told the economist: "People aren't cattle you know!"

thought. Both his lack of theoretical presuppositions and his flexibility are to be seen in the way he came to support novel measures like social security and the Wagner Act. Response to popular demand was the major reason. "The Congress can't stand the pressure of the Townsend Plan unless we have a real old-age insurance system," he complained to Frances Perkins, "nor can I face the country without having . . . a solid plan which will give some assurance to old people of systematic assistance upon retirement." In like manner, the revolutionary NLRA was adopted as a part of his otherwise sketchy and rule-of-thumb philosophy of society. Though ultimately Roosevelt championed the Wagner bill in the House, it was a belated conversion dictated by the foreshadowed success of the measure and the recent invalidation of the NRA. In his pragmatic and common-sense reactions to the exigencies of the depression, Roosevelt, the easygoing conservative, ironically enough became the embodiment of a new era and a new social philosophy for the American people.

"This election," Herbert Hoover presciently said in 1932, "is not a mere shift from the ins to the outs. It means deciding the direction our nation will take over a century to come." The election of Franklin Roosevelt, he predicted, would result in "a radical departure from the foundations of 150 years which have made this the greatest nation in the world." Though Hoover may be charged with nothing more than campaign flourishing, it is nevertheless a fact that his speech was made just after Roosevelt's revealing Commonwealth Club address of September. Only in this single utterance, it should be remembered, did Roosevelt disclose in clear outline the philosophy and program which was later to be the New Deal. "Every man has a right to life," he had said, "and this means that he has also a right to make a comfortable living. . . . Our government, formal and informal, political and economic," he went on, "owes to everyone an avenue to possess himself of a portion of that plenty [from our industrial society] sufficient for his needs, through his own work." Here were the intimations of those new goals which the New Deal set for America.

Accent as heavily as one wishes the continuity between the reforms of the Progressive era and the New Deal, yet the wide difference between the goals of the two periods still remains. The Progressive impulse was narrowly reformist: it limited business, it assisted agriculture, it freed labor from some of the shackles imposed by the courts, but it continued to conceive of the state as policeman or judge and nothing more. The New Deal, on the other hand, was more than a regulator—though it was that too, as shown by the SEC and the reinvigoration of the antitrust division of the Justice Department. To the old goals for America set forth and fought for by the Jeffersonians and the Progressives the New Deal appended new ones. Its primary and general innovation was the guaranteeing of a minimum standard of welfare for the people of the nation. WPA and the whole series of relief agencies which were a part of it, wages and hours legislation, AAA, bank deposit insurance, and social security,[17] each illustrates this new conception of the federal government. A resolution offered by New Deal Senator Walsh in 1935 clearly enunciated the new obligations of government. The resolution took notice of the disastrous effects of the depression "upon the lives of young men and women . . ." and then went on to say that "it is the duty of the Federal Government to use every possible means of opening up opportunities" for the youth of the nation "so that they may be rehabilitated and restored to *a decent standard of living* and ensured proper development of their talents. . . ."

But the guarantor state as it developed under the New Deal was more active and positive than this. It was a vigorous and dynamic force in the society, energizing and, if necessary, supplanting private enterprise when the general welfare required it. With the Wagner Act, for example, the government served notice that it would actively participate in securing the unionization of the American worker; the state was no longer to be an impartial policeman merely keeping order; it now declared for the side of labor. When social and economic problems like the rehabilitation of the Valley of the Tennessee were ignored or shirked by private enterprise, then the federal government undertook to do the job. Did private enterprise fail to provide adequate and sufficient housing for a minimum standard of welfare for the people, then the government would build houses. As a result, boasted Nathan Straus, head

[17] Social security is an excellent example of how, under the New Deal, reform measures, when they conflicted with recovery, were given priority. In siphoning millions of dollars of social security taxes from the purchasing power of the workers, social security was a deflationary measure, which must have seriously threatened the precariously based new economic recovery. For this reason and others, Abraham Epstein, the foremost authority in America on social security, denounced the act as a "sharing of poverty."

of the U.S. Housing Authority, "for the first time in a hundred years the slums of America ceased growing and began to shrink."

Few areas of American life were beyond the touch of the experimenting fingers of the New Deal; even the once sacrosanct domain of prices and the valuation of money felt the tinkering. The devaluation of the dollar, the gold-purchase program, the departure from the gold standard—in short, the whole monetary policy undertaken by F. D. R. as a means to stimulate recovery through a price rise—constituted an unprecedented repudiation of orthodox public finance. To achieve that minimum standard of well-being which the depression had taught the American people to expect of their government, nothing was out of bounds.

But it is not the variety of change which stamps the New Deal as the creator of a new America; its significance lies in the permanence of its program. For, novel as the New Deal program was, it has, significantly, not been repudiated by the Eisenhower administration, the first Republican government since the reforms were instituted. Verbally, it is true, the Republican administration has had to minimize its actual commitments to the New Deal philosophy, and it tends to trust private business more than the New Dealers did—witness, for example, its elimination of the minor governmental manufacturing enterprises which competed with private firms. But despite this, the administration's firm commitment to the guaranteeing of prosperity and averting depression at all costs is an accurate reflection of the American people's agreement with the New Deal's diagnosis of the depression. Nor has the Republican party dared to repeal or even emasculate the legislation which made up the vitals of the New Deal: TVA, banking and currency, SEC, social security, the Wagner Act, and fair treatment of the Negro. The New Deal Revolution has become so much a part of the American Way that no political party which aspires to high office dares now to repudiate it.

It may or may not be significant in this regard (for apothegms are more slippery than precise) but it is nonetheless interesting that Roosevelt and Eisenhower have both been impressed with the same single sentence from Lincoln regarding the role of government. "The legitimate object of Government," wrote Lincoln, "is to do for a community of people whatever they need to have done but cannot do at all or cannot do so well for themselves in their separate or individual capacities." Twice, in 1934 and again in 1936, F. D. R.

in public addresses used this expression to epitomize his own New
Deal, and Robert Donovan in his officially inspired book on the
Eisenhower administration writes that this same "fragment of
Lincoln's writing . . . Eisenhower uses time and again in describing his own philosophy of government." Between Lincoln and Eisenhower there was no Republican President, except perhaps Theodore
Roosevelt, who would have been willing to subscribe to such a free-
wheeling description of the federal power; in this can be measured
the impact of the New Deal and the depression.

The conclusion seems inescapable that, traditional as the words
may have been in which the New Deal expressed itself, in actuality it
was a revolutionary response to a revolutionary situation. In its
long history America has passed through two revolutions since the
first one in 1776, but only the last two, the Civil War and the
depression, were of such force as to change the direction of the
relatively smooth flow of its progress. The Civil War rendered a
final and irrevocable decision in the long debate over the nature of
the Union and the position of the Negro in American society. From
that revolutionary experience, America emerged a strong national
state and dedicated by the words of its most hallowed document to
the inclusion of the black man in a democratic culture. The searing
ordeal of the Great Depression purged the American people of their
belief in the limited powers of the federal government and convinced
them of the necessity of the guarantor state. And as the Civil War
constituted a watershed in American thought, so the depression
and its New Deal marked the crossing of a divide from which, it
would seem, there could be no turning back.

Critical Bibliographical Essay

THE works cited herein make no pretense of exhausting the literature on the subject, nor do they include all those I have read, but they do represent the principal materials from which I have drawn my factual data and my ideas. Books cited or discussed in the body of the book are not incuded here, nor have I listed the more obvious collections of printed sources used.

I. THE BEGINNINGS

For the colonial period as a whole, I have relied heavily on Herbert L. Osgood, *The American Colonies in the Seventeenth Century* (3 vols., New York, 1904–7), and Charles M. Andrews, *The Colonial Period of American History* (4 vols., New Haven, 1935–38). The early chapters of Ralph H. Brown, *Historical Geography of the United States* (New York, 1948), have been the source of my generalizations about the nature of the land.

Louis Hacker's provocative *Triumph of American Capitalism* (New York, 1940) has sparked much of my thinking, though my conclusions are much different from his. The essay on the businessman in France by John Sawyer in William Miller, ed., *Men in Business* (Cambridge, 1952), is the basis for my remarks contrasting the American and French businessman. The significance of the absence of a feudal past in America is set forth with verve by Louis Hartz in *The Liberal Tradition in America* (New York, 1955). Richard Morris, *Studies in the History of American Law* (New York, 1930), Chapters I and II, discusses the departures from European property law. For the efforts to establish quasi-feudal regimes in the colonies, I have drawn on John Johnson, *Old Maryland Manors* (Baltimore, 1883); Clarence Rife, "Land Tenure in New Netherlands," in *Essays in Colonial History Presented to Charles McLean Andrews by His Students* (New Haven, 1931); and Samuel G. Nissenson, *The Patroon's Domain* (New York, 1937).

Though John Winthrop's *History of New England from 1630–1649*, edited by J. Savage (Boston, 1853), is a partisan account by a leader of the oligarchy, it is a mine of information on the early history and mores of the Puritan settlement. At the other end of the seventeenth century,

Cotton Mather's *Magnalia Christi Americana* (Hartford, 1820) performs the same function and the additional one of including many sources for Puritan thought and action in the course of the century. An excellent collection of Puritan writing is Perry Miller, *The American Puritans* (New York, 1956), in paperback edition.

The writings about the Puritans bid fair to exceed even the great output of the notoriously prolific Puritans themselves. The dean of such commentators is undoubtedly Perry Miller. As anyone familiar with his work must recognize, my interpretation of the Puritans is heavily indebted to his books: *Orthodoxy in Massachusetts, 1630–50* (Cambridge, Mass., 1933); *The New England Mind: Seventeenth Century* (Cambridge, Mass., 1953); and its sequel, *From Colony to Province* (Cambridge, Mass., 1953). Two of the number of works belaboring the Puritans deserve to be mentioned here if only because they have done so much to produce an opposite reaction in me: James Truslow Adams, *The Founding of New England* (Boston, 1926), and the first part of Vernon L. Parrington's *Main Currents in American Thought* (New York, 1930). Both these books represent the high-water mark of the effort to give scholarly clothing to the popular impression that the Puritans were a narrow-minded, repressed, antidemocratic people.

A less partisan approach to the Puritans was already begun in the 1920's with Kenneth Murdock's *Increase Mather* (Cambridge, Mass., 1926), which did much to rescue that divine from, among other things, Parrington's imputations of ignorance. The 1930's saw a number of historians step forward to take a second and fresher look at the Puritans: Herbert Schneider, *The Puritan Mind* (New York, 1930); Samuel Eliot Morison, *Puritan Pronaos* (New York, 1936), and his *Harvard College in the Seventeenth Century* (Cambridge, Mass., 1936). Though I have not always followed Professor Morison's almost total defense of the Puritans, his influence on my handling of them has been great. Clifford K. Shipton, "A Plea for Puritanism," *American Historical Review*, XL (April, 1935), 460–67, is a direct answer to James Truslow Adams. Ralph Barton Perry's *Puritanism and Democracy* (New York, 1944) is broader in scope and more temperate than Morison's work, and seeks to relate the Puritans to the democratic ideal in America. Not all recent treatments of the Puritans, however, have been favorable, as both the title and content of Thomas J. Wertenbaker's *Puritan Oligarchy* (New York, 1947) demonstrate. Three very recent works on the Puritans which have stimulated my thinking have continued the trend toward greater appreciation of the Puritans: Chard Powers Smith, *Yankees and God* (New York, 1954); Raymond Stearns, *The Strenuous Puritan: Hugh Peter* (Urbana, Ill., 1954); and Alan Simpson, *Puritanism in Old and New England* (Chicago, 1955). These last three books, it should be noted, treat Puritanism as primarily a religion; the tendency to play down the religious element has not been revived appreciably since Adams and Parrington. Perry Miller, *Roger Williams* (Indianapolis, 1953), and Mauro Calamandrei, "Neglected Aspects of Roger Williams' Thought," *Church History*, XXI (September, 1952), 239–58, have thrown much new and important light on this controversial Puritan.

The nature of the Puritan's outlook on life has been singled out by a number of writers for special treatment. Henry Bamford Parkes, "Morals and Law Enforcement in Colonial New England," *New England Quarterly*, V (July, 1932), 431–52, was an attempt to test the implications of Charles Francis Adams' famous essay, "Some Phases of Sexual Morality and Church Discipline in Colonial New England," *Proceedings* of the Massachusetts Historical Society, 2nd Ser., VI (1891), 477–516. Parkes found the Puritans purer than Adams implied. Edmund Morgan in "The Puritans and Sex," *New England Quarterly*, XV (December, 1942), 591–607, and in *The Puritan Family* (Boston, 1944) carried the investigation further and on a broader front. He has enlisted in the rehabilitation of the Puritans—and on the side with the weight of the evidence, it seems to me. Percy Scholes, an English musicologist of note, in *The Puritans and Music in England and New England* (London, 1934) has made a firm case in their favor which, in my opinion, Cyclone Covey, "Puritanism and Music in Colonial America," *William and Mary Quarterly*, 3rd Ser., VIII (July, 1951), 378–88, has not been able to shake, though he deliberately attempts to. Though Emil Oberholzer, *Delinquent Saints* (New York, 1956), is no apologist for the Puritans, his thorough monograph offers ammunition to both sides in the controversy regarding Puritan morals.

The seminal essays on the relation between Puritanism and capitalism are Max Weber, *The Protestant Ethic and the Spirit of Capitalism* (New York, 1930), and R. H. Tawney, *Religion and the Rise of Capitalism* (New York, 1937). Much water has passed under the historiographical bridge since these studies, but no writer on Puritanism has yet succeeded in ignoring the connection they descried between Puritan morality and economic growth. Bernard Bailyn, *The New England Merchants in the Seventeenth Century* (Cambridge, Mass., 1955), is noteworthy for its clear demonstration of the acceptance by the merchants of Puritan doctrine as well as the undermining which economic activity worked upon the Zion in the wilderness. I am much indebted to Frederick B. Tolles, *Meeting House and Counting House* (Chapel Hill, N.C., 1948), for the incisive pointing up of the similarity in Quaker and Puritan ethics as they bear on wealthmaking. Edward B. O. Beatty, *William Penn as Social Philosopher* (New York, 1939), and the essay on Penn in Joseph Dorfman, *Economic Mind in American Civilization* (2 vols., New York, 1946), present a jaundiced view of Penn with which I do not completely agree, but they are important. Lois K. Mathews, *The Expansion of New England* (Boston, 1909), is the standard study on the outward movement of the Puritans.

Three studies on the relation between Puritanism and democracy, aside from Ralph Barton Perry's, mentioned earlier, need to be cited here, for from them I have drawn many of my data on the subject: Herbert Osgood, "The Political Ideas of the Puritans," *Political Science Quarterly*, VI (March, 1891), 1–28 (June, 1891), 201–231; H. Richard Niebuhr, "The Idea of Covenant and American Democracy," *Church History*, XXIII (June, 1954), 126–35; B. Katherine Brown, "Freemanship in Puritan Massachusetts," *American Historical Review*, LIX (July, 1954), 865–83.

All who write on the history of seventeenth-century Virginia are indebted, as I am, to the various studies of P. A. Bruce: *Economic History of Virginia in the Seventeenth Century* (2 vols., New York, 1896), *Institutional History of Virginia in the Seventeenth Century* (New York, 1910), and *Social Life of Virginia in the Seventeenth Century* (2nd ed., Lynchburg, Va., 1927). The last book, however, has been superseded by Thomas J. Wertenbaker, *Planters of Colonial Virginia* (Princeton, 1922), and Louis B. Wright, *First Gentlemen of Virginia* (San Marino, Calif., 1940). The best recent study of the colonial South is Wesley Frank Craven, *The Southern Colonies in the Seventeenth Century, 1607–1689* (Baton Rouge, 1949).

The literature on the history of slavery is enormous. Frank Tannenbaum's *Slave and Citizen* (New York, 1947) prompted my thinking about the contrast between American and Brazilian slavery; Gilberto Freyre, *Brazil: An Interpretation* (New York, 1945) and *The Masters and The Slaves* (New York, 1946), and Donald Pierson, *Negroes in Brazil* (Chicago, 1942), continued the process. The standard history of American slavery is U. B. Phillips, *American Negro Slavery* (New York, 1933); I have used it with profit for this early period. Oscar and Mary Handlin, "The Origins of the Southern Labor System," *William and Mary Quarterly*, 3rd Ser., VII (April, 1950), 199–222, was the starting point for my thinking about the origins of racism, though my conclusions are now quite opposed to theirs. I found much important material in James C. Ballagh, *A History of Slavery in Virginia* (Baltimore, 1902); J. R. Brackett, *Negro in Maryland* (Baltimore, 1889); Susie Ames, *Studies of the Virginia Eastern Shore in the Seventeenth Century* (Richmond, 1940); John Russell, *Free Negro in Virginia, 1619–1865* (Baltimore, 1913); Lorenzo Greene, *Negro in Colonial New England, 1620–1776* (New York, 1942); and B. C. Steiner, *History of Slavery in Connecticut* (Baltimore, 1893).

II. THE AWAKENING OF AMERICAN NATIONALITY

In varying degrees I have drawn upon a number of works dealing with the eighteenth-century colonies. Lawrence Gipson, *The British Empire Before the American Revolution* (Caldwell, Ida., 1936), presents in the first three volumes a masterly survey of the colonies around 1750. Max Savelle, *Seeds of Liberty* (New York, 1948), is an excellent survey of the colonial mind. The long, meaty introductory chapters on the economic, social, and political character of the colonies in Clinton Rossiter, *Seedtime of the Republic* (New York, 1953), have been both stimulating and informative. James Truslow Adams, *Provincial Society, 1690–1763* (New York, 1927), a volume in the History of American Life Series, provided me with much detailed information, as did Evarts B. Greene, *Revolutionary Generation, 1763–1790* (New York, 1943), the next volume in the series. Greene's earlier book, *Foundations of American Nationality* (New York, 1922), was the springboard for a good part of this chapter. The quotation pointing up the contemporaneous growth of capitalism and the American colonies is from G. O. Virtue, "Capitalistic Aspects of the Colonial Economy," in *Explorations in Economics* (New York, 1936). The sources for my generalizations about colonial architecture are Fiske Kimball's highly respected *Domestic Architecture of the American Colonies and of the Early Republic* (New York, 1922) and the more recent and most readable Hugh S. Morrison, *American Architecture from the First Colonial Settlements to the National Period* (New York, 1952). The only book dealing in any comprehensive way with colonial scientific interests is the recent Brooks Hindle, *The Pursuit of Science in Revolutionary America, 1735–1789* (Chapel Hill, N.C., 1956).

The standard history of the family in America is the old, but still useful, Arthur Calhoun, *A Social History of the American Family* (3 vols., Cleveland, 1917–19). There is a great need for a synthetic study of the family in America before 1900. Herbert Moller, "Sex Composition and Correlated Culture Patterns of Colonial America," *William and Mary Quarterly*, 3rd Ser., II (April, 1945), 113–53, is somewhat prolix, but its data are valuable. A number of studies on the position of women in the colonial period are available. I have drawn upon Elizabeth Dexter, *Colonial Women of Affairs* (Boston, 1924); Mary Benson, *Women in Eighteenth Century America* (New York, 1935); and Julia C. Spruill, *Women's Life and Work in the Southern Colonies* (Chapel Hill, N.C., 1938). Richard B. Morris has a most valuable discussion of women's legal rights in his *Studies in the History of American Law*, already mentioned. Edmund Morgan, in his *Virginians at Home* (Williamsburg, Va., 1952), tried to do for the southern colony what he did for New England, but with less success.

My sources for the distribution of immigrants have been the standard Albert B. Faust, *The German Element in the United States* (2 vols. in one, New York, 1927), and Charles A. Hanna, *The Scotch-Irish* (2 vols., New York, 1902). Ian C. C. Graham, *Colonists from Scotland: Emigration to North America 1707–1783* (Ithaca, N.Y., 1956), is especially noteworthy for its rescuing of the important Scottish immigration from being lost in the mass of Scots-Irish. My understanding of the Great Awakening has been enhanced by reading Leonard J. Trinterud, *The Forming of an American Tradition. A Reexamination of Colonial Presbyterianism* (Philadelphia, 1949), and Perry Miller, *Jonathan Edwards* (New York, 1949), which, like everything Professor Miller touches, throws new light and meaning on our religious history. William Sweet, *Religion in Colonial America* (New York, 1942), is a standard but important book by an eminent authority. Several of my quotations from contemporaries during the religious revivals have been taken from Merrill Jensen's valuable collection of sources, *American Colonial Documents to 1776,* which is Vol. IX of *English Historical Documents,* edited by David C. Douglas (London, 1953–56).

The best general treatment of the political connections between England and the colonies is Leonard Labaree, *Royal Government in America* (New Haven, 1930). I have relied upon Charles Grove Haines, *The American Doctrine of Judicial Supremacy* (New York, 1914), and Joseph Henry Smith, *Appeals to the Privy Council from the American Plantations* (New York, 1950), for my treatment of the judicial relations of the colonies with Britain. Richard B. Morris's chapter on the Zenger trial in *Fair Trial* (New York, 1952) has been the main source for my handling of that incident. Robert E. Brown's *Middle Class Democracy and the Revolution in Massachusetts, 1691–1780* (Ithaca, N.Y., 1955) emphasizes convincingly the democratic practices in colonial Massachusetts. Brown's work and Richard McCormick, *The History of Voting in New Jersey* (New Brunswick, N.J., 1953), and Charles Sydnor, *Gentlemen Freeholders* (Chapel Hill, N.C., 1952), all support the contention that the suffrage was more widely open than many historians have heretofore believed. Actually, the standard authority on the colonial suffrage, Albert McKinley, easily lends himself to this "new" interpretation. I have made much use of his *The Suffrage Franchise in the Thirteen English Colonies in America* (Philadelphia, 1905). Even earlier than McKinley, J. Franklin Jameson in "Virginia Voting in the Colonial Period (1744–1774)," *Nation,* LVI (April 27, 1893), 309–10, showed that colonial voting was not inconsiderable when compared with voting in 1880.

The sources for social attitudes and structure in the pre-Revolutionary era are primarily the writings of travelers and colonials. The *Works* of that indefatigable American Benjamin Franklin are filled with comments on the society of the new country. The *Letters of Cadwallader Colden* in *Collections* of the New-York Historical Society, Vols. 52–56, 67–68, are valuable for the opposite reason: Colden was most unsympathetic with the American aspirations of his day. *Gottlieb Mittelberger's Journey to Pennsylvania in the Year 1750 and Return to Germany in the Year 1754* . . . (Philadelphia, 1898) contains much interesting information because the German is so unfriendly to America. The same can be said about Comptroller Weare, "Observations on the British Colonies on the Continent of America," in *Collections* of the Massachusetts Historical Society for the year 1792, 1st Ser., Vol. I. Michel Guillaume St. Jean de Crèvecoeur, *Sketches of Eighteenth Century America,* is a mine of information, but not always to be taken without qualification. His *Letters of an American Farmer* is, of course, a classic, but subject to the same limitation. Like Franklin, *Letters of Benjamin Rush,* edited by L. H. Butterfield (2 vols., Princeton, 1951), offer material from an enthusiastic American. *American Husbandry* (New York, 1939), a famous agricultural treatise of the period, written anonymously and edited by Harry J. Carman, has information on social conditions as well as agriculture. *The Carolina Backcountry on the Eve of the Revolution,* edited by Richard J. Hooker (Chapel Hill, N.C., 1953), contains interesting material on religious activities in the journal and other writings of Charles Woodmason, an Anglican itinerant preacher. I have also used *The Journal and Letters of Philip Vickers Fithian, 1773–1774,* edited by H. D. Farish (Williamsburg, Va., 1943), and Per Kalm, *The America of 1750,* edited by Adolph B. Benson (2 vols., New York, 1937). *Gentleman's Progress; the Itinerarium of Dr. Alexander Hamilton, 1744,* edited by Carl Bridenbaugh (Chapel Hill, N.C., 1948), offers much material on the state and attitudes of the colonies north of Maryland.

More and more, historians have been turning to an investigation of the growth of American nationality in the years before 1776. One of the most provocative, and one which I have followed closely, is Albert J. Harkness, Jr., "Americanism and Jenkins' Ear," *Mississippi Valley Historical Review,* XXXVII (June, 1950), 61–90. Much material, incidentally, in this connection is to be found in William Sachse, *The Colonial American in Britain* (Madison, Wis., 1956). Two books of Michael Kraus have pioneered in showing the growth of an American consciousness in the midst of an Atlantic civilization: *Intercolonial Aspects of Colonial Culture on the Eve of the Revolution* (New York, 1928) and *The Atlantic Civilization: Eighteenth Century Origins* (Ithaca, N.Y., 1949). Carl Bridenbaugh's *Cities in Revolt* (New York, 1955), a continuation of his earlier *Cities in the Wilderness* (New York, 1938), argues convincingly for the point that an American feeling was growing fast in the cities of the mid-eighteenth century. Many of my conclusions on this subject are indebted to his work. His small book *Myths and Realities; Societies of the Colonial South* (Baton Rouge, 1952) argues the same point from a somewhat different angle. Bridenbaugh's study of the *Colonial Craftsman* (New York, 1950) also contains information on the nature of society. Though Leonard Labaree's *Conservatism in Early American History* (New York, 1948) does not go along with the newer views on the mobility within colonial society, his book cannot be overlooked, for it is a corrective to those who would ignore the rigidities in the social stratification. My paragraph on linguistic changes in American English was derived from H. L. Mencken's *The American Language* (4th ed., New York, 1936). See also Albert H. Marckwardt, *American English* (New York, 1958).

III. A NEW KIND OF REVOLUTION

For the periods before and after the Revolution, the writings of the important participants are a mine of information on attitudes. I have explored with profit the standard published works of John Adams, Benjamin Franklin, Fisher Ames, Alexander Hamilton, Thomas Jefferson, George Washington, and Benjamin Rush. *The Correspondence of General Thomas Gage* (2 vols., New Haven, 1933) highlights the irresolution of the British Ministry and dispels the colonial illusion that military power was being exerted against them before 1774.

The debate about the causes for the Revolution has spawned a tremendous literature; only representative samples can be mentioned here. To Charles H. Lincoln, *Revolutionary Movement in Pennsylvania, 1760–1776* (Philadelphia, 1901), perhaps belongs the honor of first presenting in scholarly fashion the thesis that the Revolution was an internal struggle between classes as well as a revolt against British control. Carl L. Becker, *History of Political Parties in the Province of New York, 1760–1776* . . . (Madison, Wis., 1909), pushed the same argument. In addition to showing the class divisions over revolution, A. M. Schlesinger, *The Colonial Merchants in the American Revolution, 1763–1776* (New York, 1918), also bore down hard on the economic causes for the coming of the break with England. Louis Hacker set forth the most blatant economic explanation for the Revolution in "The American Revolution: Economic Aspects," *Marxist Quarterly,* I (January–March, 1937), 46–67, and in Chapters 10–12 of his later *Triumph of American Capitalism.* Earlier Charles M. Andrews in his *Colonial Background of the American Revolution* (New Haven, 1924) argued that the Revolution was an outgrowth of the colonial experience and not a consequence of English economic restrictions. In his later work, *The Colonial Period of American History,* IV, 425–28, Andrews set forth a blistering denunciation of the Hacker school of thought regarding the influence of British mercantilism. I have followed the Andrews point of view. John C. Miller, *Origins of the American Revolution* (Boston, 1943), comes closer to Andrews' view, but does not repudiate the economic. Most recently, Lawrence Gipson, *The Coming of the Revolution, 1763–1776* (New York, 1954), argues for the long-term causes, but because of the chronological limits of his book he does not go into the matter. Relatively unique among modern explanations for the coming of the Revolution is Robert E. Brown, *Middle Class Democracy in Massachusetts and the Revolution* (Ithaca, N.Y., 1955), wherein it is contended that the Revolution was an effort to preserve democracy against British tyranny. Merrill Jensen, "Democracy and the American Revolution," *Huntington Library Quarterly*, XX (August, 1957), 321–41, in its repudiation of Brown's thesis sums up my own objections. I do not, however, go along with Jensen in subscribing to a democratic versus aristocratic struggle after the Revolution.

My disbelief in any fundamental economic explanation for the coming of the Revolution stems from a number of works; foremost is Lawrence Harper, "The Effect of the Navigation Acts on the Thirteen Colonies," in R. B. Morris, ed., *Era of the American Revolution* (New York, 1939), a superb piece of quantitative historical investigation. I have accepted A. C. Bining's conclusions in *British Regulation of the Colonial Iron Industry* (Philadelphia, 1933). The *coup de grâce* was dealt one aspect of the economic explanation for the coming of the revolution by O. M. Dickerson, *Navigation Acts and the American Revolution* (Philadelphia, 1951). Thomas Abernethy, *Western Lands and the American Revolution* (New York, 1937), shows that British limitations on westward expansion had no appreciable effect on Revolutionary sentiment. Edmund S. Morgan, "The American Revolution: Revisions in Need of Revision," *William and Mary Quarterly*, 3rd Ser., XIV (January, 1957), 3–15, is an excellent summary of the changing interpretations of the Revolution and stresses the need for more local studies.

For my interpretation of the coming of the Revolution I have also used Edmund and Helen Morgan, *Stamp Act Crisis* (Chapel Hill, N.C., 1953); Charles R. Ritcheson, *British Politics and the American Revolution* (Norman, Okla., 1954); Vincent Todd Harlow, *The Founding of the Second British Empire, 1763–1793* (London, 1952), to name only the most recent studies. Much detailed information was obtained from the old, but full, William E. H. Lecky, *A History of England in the Eighteenth Century* (8 vols., London, 1878–90). For the political and constitutional ideas of the era I have used Randolph G. Adams, *Political Ideas of the Revolution* (Durham, N.C., 1922). Charles H. McIlwaine, *The American Revolution: A Constitutional Interpretation* (New York,

1923), and Robert L. Schuyler, *Parliament and the British Empire* (New York, 1929), are the two protagonists in the debate over the constitutional nature of the Empire—McIlwaine supporting the colonists, Schuyler maintaining that the Parliament had plenary power over the colonies.

Though in interpreting the period after the Revolution historians have been taking sides for some time, the factual, detailed investigations upon which judgments may be based are few. Charles A. Beard's *An Economic Interpretation of the Constitution* (New York, 1935), originally published in 1913, can be said to have opened the debate by arguing that the period between 1776 and 1789 was characterized by a struggle between economic classes for control of the central government. His *Economic Origins of Jeffersonian Democracy* (New York, 1915) continued this line of argument into the Federalist-Jeffersonian era. Merrill Jensen's *The Articles of Confederation* (Madison, Wis., 1940), and *The New Nation: A History of the United States During the Confederation, 1781–1789* (New York, 1950), have attempted, unsuccessfully to my mind, to support the Beardian case. The evidence and methodology in Beard's first book have been devastatingly criticized by Robert E. Brown, *Charles Beard and the Constitution* (Princeton, 1956). My understanding of the Jeffersonian Democratic-Republicans has benefited from reading E. Wilder Spaulding, *New York in the Critical Period* (New York, 1932); Eugene Link, *Democratic-Republican Societies, 1790–1800* . . . (New York, 1942); and Elisha Douglass, *Rebels and Democrats* (Chapel Hill, N.C., 1955), though I do not agree with their general acceptance of fundamental divergence of philosophy between the Jeffersonians and Federalists. *The Journal of William Maclay* (New York, 1927); William Manning, *Key to Liberty* (Billerica, Mass., 1922); and Charles Warren, *Jacobin and Junto* (Cambridge, Mass., 1931), are writings of Republicans which I have used with profit. *The Records of the Federal Convention of 1787* (4 vols., New Haven, Conn., 1911–37), edited by Max Farrand, are a prime source for the conservative view in this period. I have followed J. P. Warren, "The Confederation and Shays' Rebellion," *American Historical Review,* XI (October, 1905), 42–67, in emphasizing the conservatives' concern over lack of central power in the Articles of Confederation.

The starting point for all subsequent studies of the social implications of the American Revolution is J. Franklin Jameson, *The American Revolution Considered as a Social Movement* (Princeton, 1926). Criticism of Jameson's thesis has been piecemeal rather than total, though Frederick B. Tolles attempted a comprehensive review in "The American Revolution Considered as a Social Movement: a Re-Evaluation," *American Historical Review,* LX (October, 1954), 1–12, but without doing justice, it seems to me, to the large amount of evidence against Jameson's position. C. S. Crary, "Forfeited Loyalist Lands in the Western District of New York—Albany and Tyron Counties," *New York History*, XXV (July, 1954), 239–258, and Harry Yoshpe, *Disposition of Loyalist Estates in the Southern District of the State of New York* (New York, 1939), emphasize the absence of any significant redistribution of land through revolutionary seizures. A critical reading of Robert O. DeMond, *Loyalists in North Carolina During the Revolution* (Durham, N.C., 1940), leads to much the same conclusion. Lee M. Newcomer, *The Embattled Farmers* (New York, 1953); Robert J. Taylor, *Western Massachusetts in the Revolution* (Providence, 1954); and Allan Nevins, *The American States During and After the Revolution 1775–1789* (New York, 1924), all supplied information and insights which have contributed to my conception of the so-called Critical Period.

Three authorities have been the main source for my generalizations regarding constitutional changes after the Revolution: Walter F. Dodd, *Revision and Amendment of State Constitutions* (Baltimore, 1910); Fletcher Green, *Constitutional Development in the South Atlantic States, 1776–1860* (Chapel Hill, N.C., 1930); and, most detailed of all, W. C. Webster, "Comparative Study of the State Constitutions of the American Revolution," *Annals* of the American Academy of Political and Social Science, IX (1897), 380–420. I also used the authoritative source collection, F. N. Thorpe, ed., *The Federal and State Constitutions* (7 vols., Washington, 1909).

The old but still valuable Philip Schaff, "Church and State in the United States," in *Papers* of the American Historical Association, II (1888), 391–543, has been most influential in my thinking about the American doctrine of separation of Church and State. Evarts B. Greene, *Religion and the State* (New York, 1941), was of great value, as was A. P. Stokes's monumental *Church and State in the United States* (3 vols., New York, 1950). Leo Pfeffer, *Church, State and Freedom* (Boston, 1953), is argumentative, but important.

Of social commentary, the most valuable for my interests was Johann Schoepf, *Travels in the Confederation*, translated and edited by Alfred J. Morrison (2 vols., Philadelphia, 1911). J. P. Brissot de Warville, *New Travels in the United States* (2 vols., London, 1794), and *Moreau de St. Méry's American Journey, 1793–1798*, Kenneth and Anna M. Roberts, editors (Garden City, N.Y., 1947), also supplied some data.

My conclusion that the American Revolution was a conservative one was prompted by reading the last chapter of Clinton Rossiter's *Seedtime of the Republic* (New York, 1953) and Daniel Boorstin's provocative *The Genius of American Politics* (Chicago, 1953). The same idea was advanced in Friedrich Gentz's essay, first published in 1800, *The French and the American Revolutions Compared,* translated by John Quincy Adams (Chicago, 1955).

IV. To Make a More Perfect Union

The history of the westward movement and the diplomacy of Expansion have been well dealt with in general volumes upon which I have drawn liberally: Ray Billington, *Westward Expansion* (New York, 1949); Thomas A. Bailey, *A Diplomatic History of the American People* (3rd ed., New York, 1947); Albert Weinberg, *Manifest Destiny* (Baltimore, 1935), which is a superb study of the ideas Americans have used to justify their expansion; Roy F. Robbins, *Our Landed Heritage* (Princeton, 1942), a comprehensive account of the evolution of land policy; and Helene Zahler, *Eastern Workingmen and National Land Policy, 1829–1862* (New York, 1941).

There are a number of surveys of the economic history of the United States; I have found Edward Kirkland, *A History of American Economic Life* (3rd ed., New York, 1951), the most stimulating. More detailed for this period and covering much more than its title suggests is George Rogers Taylor, *Transportation Revolution, 1815–1860* (New York, 1951). Louis Hunter, *Steamboats on the Western Rivers* (Cambridge, Mass., 1949), is indispensable. I have followed Henry Clyde Hubbard, *The Older Middle West 1840–1880* (New York, 1936), in the discussion of the importance of the railroads linking the West and the East.

The recognition that government was closely concerned with economic development in the pre-Civil War years has been one of the newest interpretations in the historical literature. Oscar and Mary Handlin, *Commonwealth, A Study of the Role of Government in the American Economy: Massachusetts, 1774–1861* (New York, 1947), and Louis Hartz, *Economic Policy and Democratic Thought: Pennsylvania, 1776–1860* (Cambridge, Mass., 1948), were among the first of such studies, though they sometimes see more than was there. More convincing, but narrower in conception since they deal only with aid to internal improvements, have been the studies of Carter Goodrich: "The Virginia System of Mixed Enterprises, A Study of State Planning of Internal Improvements," *Political Science Quarterly,* LXIV (September, 1949), 355–87; "The Revulsion Against Internal Improvements," *Journal of Economic History,* X (November, 1950), 145–69; "Local Planning of Internal Improvements," *Political Science Quarterly,* LXVI (September, 1951), 411–45. The whole literature on the subject has been admirably summed up and critically appraised in Robert A. Lively, "The American System: A Review Article," *Business History Review,* XXIX (March,

1955), 81–96. The evidence on governmental support of canals is from a mimeographed paper by Jerome Cranmer, "Canal Investment, 1815–1860," delivered at the Conference on Research in Income and Wealth at Williams College, September 5, 1957.

The standard treatments on the labor movement of the pre-Civil War years are John R. Commons *et al., History of Labour in the United States,* Vols. I and II (New York, 1918), and Norman Ware, *Industrial Worker, 1840–1860* (New York, 1924). I have also used Caroline F. Ware, *Early New England Cotton Manufacture* (New York, 1931), and Hannah Josephson, *Golden Threads* (New York, 1949), for the Lowell girls. For my treatment of Eli Whitney I have relied upon Jeannette Mirsky and Allan Nevins, *The World of Eli Whitney* (New York, 1952), which is a remarkable job of integrating original sources into a smoothly flowing text.

All discussions of Turner's theories must begin with the collection of his essays, *The Frontier in American History* (New York, 1921). The literature about Turner and his theories is simply too large even to list here; a good sample of it is contained in the bibliography to Ray Billington's *Westward Expansion.* John D. Barnhart's *Valley of Democracy* (Bloomington, Ind., 1953) is the most recent of the pro-Turner studies which try to apply empirical data to some of the master's ideas. To my mind it does not come off, though it offers much detailed information on the building of new states. Benjamin F. Wright, "Political Institutions and the Frontier," in Dixon R. Fox, ed., *Sources of Culture in the Middle West* (New York, 1934), is one of the earliest criticisms of Turner's thesis as it relates to democracy in the West. The best and most penetrating over-all critique of Turner's ideas is contained in two articles of George W. Pierson, "The Frontier and Frontiersmen of Turner's Essays," *Pennsylvania Magazine of History and Biography,* LXIV (October, 1940), 449–78, and "The Frontier and Our Institutions," *New England Quarterly,* XV (June, 1942), 224–55. The long quotation from Tocqueville's letter on his observations in Michigan is from Pierson's magnificent *Tocqueville and Beaumont in America* (New York, 1938). Richard Hofstadter, "Turner and the Frontier Myth," *American Scholar,* XVIII (Autumn, 1949), 433–43, sums up the anti-Turner literature. The most important support for Turner's ideas on democracy and the frontier comes from Stanley Elkins and Eric McKitrick, "A Meaning for Turner's Frontier," *Political Science Quarterly,* LXIX (September, 1954), 321–53; (December, 1954), 565–602.

The safety-valve thesis has come in for very extended empirical investigation. Foremost in this regard is Carter Goodrich and Sol Davison, "The Wage Earner in the Western Movement," *Political Science Quarterly,* L (June, 1935), 161–85, and LI (March, 1936), 61–116.

The weakness of the factual data for believing that a safety valve was working is demonstrated unintentionally in Joseph Schafer, "Was the West a Safety Valve for Labor?" *Mississippi Valley Historical Review,* XXIV (December, 1937), 299–314, which was intended as an answer to Goodrich and Davison. Studies which also offer evidence for disbelieving in the safety valve include Rufus S. Tucker, "The Frontier as an Outlet for Surplus Labor," *Southern Economic Journal,* VII (October, 1940), 158–86; Clarence Danhof, "Farm-making Costs and the 'Safety-Valve': 1850–1860," *Journal of Political Economy,* XLIX (June, 1941), 317–59; Carl N. Degler, "The West as a Solution to Urban Unemployment," *New York History,* XXXVI (January, 1955), 63–84; and Fred A. Shannon, "A Post-Mortem on the Labor-Safety-Valve Theory," *Agricultural History,* XIX (January, 1945), 31–37.

My thinking about the implications of the frontier for the making of American character has been stimulated by Fred A. Shannon's *An Appraisal of Walter Prescott Webb's The Great Plains* (New York, 1940), though I do not agree with all of Professor Shannon's strictures against Webb. Needless to say, I have read Webb's *The Great Plains* (Boston, 1931) with great profit. For my summary of comparative frontiers I have used James G. Leyburn, *Frontier Folkways* (New Haven, 1935); section 4, Chapter VII, of the *Cambridge Economic History of Europe,* Vol. I (Cambridge, 1941); James Westfall Thompson, *Feudal Germany* (Chicago, 1928); Richard Shryock, "British versus German Traditions in Colonial Agriculture," *Mississippi Valley Historical Review,* XXVI (June, 1939), 39–54. W. D. Wyman and E. B. Kroeber, *The Frontier in Perspective* (Madison, Wis., 1957), contains several essays on the frontier influence in lands outside the United States.

V. THE GREAT EXPERIMENT

As at perhaps no other time in our history, the United States in the three decades before 1860 was scrutinized by foreigners; their impressions are contained in literally dozens of books, many of which I have perused in writing this chapter. Beyond all others, that of Alexis de Tocqueville, *Democracy in America* (2 vols., New York, 1948), is the most critically perceptive. Harriet Martineau, *Society in America* (2 vols., New York, 1837), and Achille Murat, *A Moral and Political Sketch of the United States of North America* (London, 1833), are among the most friendly, while Frances Trollope, *Domestic Manners of the Americans,* edited by Donald Smalley (New York, 1949), is probably the most acid. The writings of two Americans should also be mentioned here: James Fenimore Cooper, *The American Democrat* (New York, 1956), which was an American's answer to the strictures of European conservatives upon the western democracy, and Philip Hone's

Diary, edited by B. Tuckerman (2 vols., New York, 1889), which offers the views of a home-grown conservative in Jacksonian America.

Leonard White's long-needed and most readable study of administrative history of the period, *The Jacksonians* (New York, 1954), has been my main authority for the treatment of the changing character of the government. I have supplemented it with reading in J. Mark Jacobson, *The Development of American Political Thought* (New York, 1932); Charles Merriam, *A History of American Political Theories* (New York, 1909); Clinton Rossiter, *The American Presidency* (New York, 1956); and Fletcher Green, *Constitutional Development in the South Atlantic States, 1776–1860* (Chapel Hill, N.C., 1930).

The most stimulating and comprehensive treatment of the Jacksonian era is Arthur M. Schlesinger, Jr., *Age of Jackson* (Boston, 1945). Joseph Dorfman, "The Jackson Wage-Earner Thesis," *American Historical Review,* LIV (January, 1949), 296–306, and Chapter III of Richard Hofstadter, *The American Political Tradition* (New York, 1951), have put forth the major objections to Schlesinger's accent on the nature of the so-called labor support for Jackson. See also Bray Hammond's review of Schlesinger's book in *Journal of Economic History,* VI (May, 1946), 79–84. My interpretation of Jacksonian economic thought follows Hofstadter more closely than Schlesinger. John Ward, *Andrew Jackson, Symbol for an Age* (New York, 1955), is a stimulating analysis of the image of Jackson in popular literature; Marvin Myers, "The Jacksonian Persuasion," *American Quarterly,* V (Spring, 1953), 3–15, does a similar job on the Jacksonian self-image and image of social forces.

I have derived much insight into Jacksonian ideas from the handy collection of sources edited by Joseph Blau, *Social Theories of Jacksonian Democracy* (New York, 1954). William Leggett and the radical Loco-Focos are analyzed and put into historical perspective in Richard Hofstadter, "William Leggett, Spokesman of Jacksonian Democracy," *Political Science Quarterly,* XLVIII (December, 1943), 581–94; and Carl N. Degler, "The Locofocos: Urban 'Agrarians,' " *Journal of Economic History,* XVI (September, 1956), 322–33. Theodore Sedgwick, Jr., a supporter and friend of Leggett, has edited *A Collection of the Political Writings of William Leggett* (2 vols., New York, 1840). The economic implications of Jacksonian ideas are admirably dissected by one who is unconvinced of their soundness on finances in Bray Hammond, "Free Banks and Corporations: the New York Free Banking Act of 1838," *Journal of Political Economy,* XLIV (April, 1936), 184–209, and "Banking in the Early West: Monopoly, Prohibition and Laissez-Faire," *Journal of Economic History,* VIII (May, 1948), 1–25. Obviously, I have followed Hammond in this regard. The long-needed biography of the great Jacksonian spokesman, Thomas Hart Benton, by William Chambers, *Old Bullion Benton* (Boston, 1956), is somewhat weakened by a rather uncritical acceptance of the Schlesinger view of the war against the Bank. I have used with great profit Carl B. Swisher's *Roger B. Taney* (New York, 1935) and Benjamin F. Wright, *The Contract Clause of the Constitution* (Cambridge, Mass., 1938), in dealing with the Charles River Bridge case.

My generalizations and quotations on the reform movement as a whole have been drawn primarily from Alice Felt Tyler, *Freedom's Ferment* (Minneapolis, 1944), a survey of the movement; Russell Nye's recent short biography, *William Lloyd Garrison and the Humanitarian Reformers* (Boston, 1955); Merle Curti, *Growth of American Thought* (New York, 1943), Chapters XII, XIV, XV; Arthur Ekirch, *The Idea of Progress in America, 1815–1860* (New York, 1951); George D. Lillibridge, *Beacon of Freedom; the Impact of American Democracy upon Great Britian, 1830–1870* (Philadelphia, 1955); and the source collection of Irving Mark and Eugene L. Schwaab, *Faith of Our Fathers* (New York, 1952).

There is a crying need for a synthetic treatment of the ideas and forces behind the educational revival of the 1830's and 1840's. In lieu of that I have rested my conclusions on the standard works now available: Ellwood P. Cubberley, *Public Education in the United States* (Boston, 1919); Paul Monroe, *Founding of the American Public School System* (New York, 1940); Sidney Jackson, *America's Struggle for Free Schools* (Washington, 1941), which really deals only with a few states; and B. A. Hinsdale, *Horace Mann and the Common School Revival in the United States* (New York, 1900).

VI. The American Tragedy

The best over-all treatment of the ante-bellum South in one volume is Clement Eaton, *History of the Old South* (New York, 1949); it is written by a Southerner with a national outlook. Vol. V in the ten-volume History of the South, Charles S. Sydnor, *The Development of Southern Sectionalism, 1819–1848* (Baton Rouge, 1949), is a model study and is in striking contrast with the subsequent volume in the series, Avery Craven, *Growth of Southern Nationalism, 1848–1861* (Baton Rouge, 1953), which is largely focused on the national scene and deals hardly at all with developments in the South. The much older and more popular book of William A. Dodd, *Expansion and Conflict* (New York, 1915), also by a Southerner, I have found suggestive and informative. Though my assumptions regarding slavery and the Negro are quite different from those of U. B. Phillips, in substance my conception of the "Central Theme of Southern History" is his. His essay of that name can be found in the collection, *The Course of the South to Secession,* edited by E. M. Coulter (New York, 1939). From a somewhat different angle, Jesse T. Carpenter's *The South as a Conscious Minority, 1789–1861* (New York, 1930) has been influential with me. Robert R. Russel, *Economic Aspects of Southern Sectionalism, 1840–1861* (Urbana, Ill., 1922), endeavors to explain the growth of southern self-consciousness in terms of economic interest, but I think it unconvincing.

The subject of southern Negro slavery seems to be perennially interesting if one is to judge from the number of words devoted then and now to its discussion. The unquestionably basic work on the subject of southern economics and one upon which I have relied is Lewis C. Gray, *History of Agriculture in Southern United States to 1860* (2 vols., Washington, 1933). The best-known worker in the vineyard of slavery history is U. B. Phillips; the fruits of his scholarship are *American Negro Slavery* (New York, 1933, though first published in 1918) and *Life and Labor in the Old South* (Boston, 1929). Phillips has come in for increasingly severe criticism for his very mild strictures against slavery as a system and his southern-born callousness to the moral crippling to which slavery subjected the Negro, but the facts and details of his books still repay study. Recently a modern scholar, northern in birth and orientation, has essayed to write a general institutional history of slavery within a more modern framework of anthropological and sociological knowledge. Kenneth Stampp, *The Peculiar Institution* (New York, 1956), is now the best treatment of slavery, but it sometimes romanticizes the Negro and tends to see harshness and guilt in the slaveowner. Allan Nevins, *Ordeal of the Union* (2 vols., New York, 1947), in Chapters XIII and XIV of Vol. I has a good brief account of the practice of slavery and its economics, but is sometimes highly charged with moral indignation. The classic sources on the ante-bellum South are the journalistic accounts of the acute northern observer Frederick Law Olmsted: *Journey in the Seaboard Slave States* (2 vols., New York, 1904), and *Journey in the Back Country* (New York, 1861). I have also used the reissue of his *Cotton Kingdom,* edited by Arthur M. Schlesinger (New York, 1953). The collection of sources *Plantation and Frontier* (2 vols., Cleveland, 1909), edited by U. B. Phillips, is indispensable. That great southern nationalist of the 1850's, J. D. B. De Bow, edited a broad-ranging compendium of sources on the South of that decade which I have used: *Industrial Resources of the Southern and Western States* (3 vols., New Orleans, 1852–3).

Specialized studies in aspects of southern slavery and economics in the ante-bellum period abound, and I have relied upon a number of them. Though Phillips and a good number of other scholars have argued that

slavery was unprofitable, the balance is now shifting; Thomas P. Govan,
"Was Plantation Slavery Profitable?" *Journal of Southern History,* VIII
(November, 1942), 513–35, though tentative in conclusion, convinced me
in the affirmative. Stampp in his recent book and Robert W. Smith, "Was
Slavery Unprofitable in the Ante-bellum South?" *Agricultural History,*
XX (January, 1946), 62–64, also conclude that slavery was profitable.
Especially persuasive in showing how profitable slavery was and richly
documented is A. H. Conrad and J. R. Meyer, "The Economics of
Slavery in the Ante-Bellum South," *Journal of Political Economy,* LXVI
(April, 1958), 95–130. Robert R. Russel, "Economic History of Negro
Slavery," *Agricultural History,* XI (October, 1937), 308–21, and "The
General Effects of Slavery Upon Southern Economic Progress," *Journal
of Southern History,* IV (February, 1938), 34–54, have been important
in delineating the importance of slavery in the economy. I have also
drawn data from, though not always agreeing with, the conclusions in
Alfred H. Stone, "Free Contract Labor in the Ante-Bellum South," and
Walter F. Fleming, "Slave Labor System in the Ante-Bellum South,"
both of which are in Vol. V. of *The South in the Building of the Nation*
(10 vols., Richmond, 1909–13).

The most important new interpretation of the character of southern
society is the work of the so-called Vanderbilt school, led by Frank
Owsley. Though L. C. Gray a long time ago recognized the importance
of the nonslaveholder in the southern economy, only since Owsley
has any systematic study been made of that class. The pioneer study
was Frank and Harriet Owsley, "The Economic Basis of Society in
the Late Ante-Bellum South," *Journal of Southern History,* VI (February, 1940), 24–25; a broader study, drawing upon the work of
his students, is Frank Owsley, *Plain Folk of the Old South* (Baton
Rouge, 1949). I have also used James C. Bonner, "Profile of a Late
Ante-Bellum Community," *American Historical Review,* XLIX (July,
1944), 663–80; and Herbert Weaver, *Mississippi Farmers, 1850–1860*
(Nashville, 1945). Though I have not followed the Owsley group in as-
signing a central role in the southern economy to the yeoman, I have found
its picture of general prosperity a convincing one. My criticisms of the
Owsley school have been sparked by the involved but penetrating work
of Fabian Linden, "Economic Democracy in the Slave South," *Journal
of Negro History,* XXXI (April, 1946), 140–89. Other studies on plantation life and economy I have used with profit include Weymouth T.
Jordan, *Hugh Davis and His Alabama Plantation* (University, Ala.,
1948); John Spencer Bassett, *Southern Plantation Overseer as Revealed
in His Letters* (Northampton, Mass., 1925); Frederick Bancroft, *Slave-
Trading in the Old South* (Baltimore, 1931); and Charles S. Sydnor,
Slavery in Mississippi (New York, 1933).

The most extreme case for the rebelliousness of the Negro in bondage is made in Herbert Aptheker, *American Negro Slave Revolts* (New York, 1943); the evidence in R. A. and A. H. Bauer, "Day to Day Resistance to Slavery," *Journal of Negro History*, XVII (October, 1942), 388–419, suffers like that in Aptheker's book from lack of representativeness. The standard authority on the underground railroad is Wilbur H. Siebert, *Underground Railroad from Slavery to Freedom* (New York, 1898). B. A. Botkin has edited a collection of slave reminscences: *Lay My Burden Down* (Chicago, 1945). Two Negro scholars have written remarkably objective studies of their own people which I have used: E. Franklin Frazier, *The Negro in the United States* (New York, 1949) and John Hope Franklin, *From Slavery to Freedom* (New York, 1947), a history of the Negro in America. There are many studies of the free Negro under slavery, as there are many individual state studies of slavery. I have used John Hope Franklin, *Free Negro in North Carolina, 1790–1860* (Chapel Hill, N.C., 1943); J. M. England, "The Free Negro in Ante-Bellum Tennessee," *Journal of Southern History*, IX (February, 1943), 37–58; and L. P. Jackson, *Free Negro Labor and Property Holding in Virginia, 1830–1860* (New York, 1942).

Three studies, though largely unconcerned with slavery historically, throw much light on the impact of slavery on the Negro: Abram Kardiner, *The Mark of Oppression* (New York, 1951), which discusses the long-range psychological effects of slavery; Gunnar Myrdal *et al.*, *The American Dilemma* (2 vols., New York, 1944), a wide-ranging study of the Negro in America; and Melville Herskovits, *The Myth of the Negro Past* (New York, 1941), which shows, unintentionally, how weak is the case for persistence of African culture in America. Miles Mark Fisher, *Negro Slave Songs in the United States* (Ithaca, N.Y., 1953), though it tries to show, by analyzing the slave songs, that the Negro longed for Africa, proves just the opposite by the paucity of evidence. For my discussion of slave songs I have used the compendium of William F. Allen, *Slave Songs of the United States* (New York, 1929, first published in 1867). For the reaction of Negroes during the war, I have followed Bell I. Wiley, *Southern Negroes, 1861–65* (New Haven, 1938).

That the South was not ruled by an oligarchy is demonstrated in Fletcher Green, "Democracy in the Old South," *Journal of Southern History*, XII (February, 1946), 3–23, but the pre-eminence of the issue of slavery is admitted. The effects of slavery upon the urban white worker are delineated in Richard B. Morris, "The Measure of Bondage in the Slave States," *Mississippi Valley Historical Review*, XLI (September, 1954), 219–40. I am greatly indebted to Clement Eaton's superb volume *Freedom of Thought in the Old South* (Durham, N.C., 1940) for much of my description of the constrictive intellectual effects of slavery; other studies leading in the same direction are his "Mob Violence in the Old South," *Mississippi Valley Historical Review,* XXIX (December, 1942), 351–70; and Charles S. Sydnor, "The Southerner and the Laws," *Journal of Southern History,* XI (February, 1940), 3–23, which, while denying the Southerner is any more prone to lawlessness than other Americans, admits that slavery encouraged extralegal action. See also H. M. Henry, *Police Control of the Slave in South Carolina* (Emory, Va., 1914), and Kenneth M. Stampp, "The Fate of the Southern Antislavery Movement," *Journal of Negro History,* XXVIII (January, 1943), 10–22. Rollin Osterweis broke new and important ground when he showed the intellectual connection between slavery, romanticism, and nationalism in *Romanticism and Nationalism in the Old South* (New Haven, 1949); I have learned much from this work.

Southern defenses of slavery have been set forth in detail, though without much critical analysis, in William S. Jenkins, *Pro-Slavery Thought in the Old South* (Chapel Hill, N.C., 1935). Winifred Carsel, "The Slave-holders' Indictment of Northern Wage Slavery," *Journal of Southern History,* VI (November, 1940), 504–20, and Harvey Wish, *George Fitzhugh, Propagandist of the Old South* (Baton Rouge, 1934), set forth the counterthrust of the South. I have also used collections of the proslavery writings of Southerners: *Pro-Slavery Argument* (Philadelphia, 1853), and E. N. Elliott, ed., *Cotton Is King and Pro-Slavery Arguments* (Augusta, Ga., 1860).

The distinction I make between antislavery and abolition is derived from a reading of a number of studies of the period. Outstanding in this regard is Dwight Dumond, *Antislavery Origins of the Civil War in the United States* (Ann Arbor, Mich., 1939), and Russel B. Nye, *Fettered Freedom: Civil Liberties and the Slavery Controversy* (East Lansing, Mich., 1949). Theodore C. Smith, *Liberty and Free Soil Parties in the Northwest* (New York, 1897), and Julian P. Bretz, "The Economic Background of the Liberty Party," *American Historical Review,* XXXIV (January, 1020), 250–64, offer much material on the growth of northern opposition to slavery on grounds other than morality. The same is apparent in Charles B. Going's biography of *David Wilmot Free Soiler* (New York, 1924). The standard treatment of the antislavery movement, including abolition, is Gilbert H. Barnes, *Antislavery Impulse, 1830–44* (New York, 1933).

The view that slavery could not expand after 1860 has been most vigorously stated in Charles W. Ramsdell, "Natural Limits of Slavery Expansion," *Mississippi Valley Historical Review,* XVI (September,

1929), 151–71. The question of which of the sections was more aggressive is canvassed in C. S. Boucher, "In Re: That Aggressive Slaveocracy," *Mississippi Valley Historical Review,* VIII (June, 1921), 8–79, in which the South is said to have been more divided than aggressive; and in Russel B. Nye, "The Slave Power Conspiracy: 1830–1860," *Science and Society,* X (Summer, 1946), 262–74, in which the South's defense of slavery is seen as a threat to liberty and therefore aggressive, though not as a deliberate conspiracy. My own view is closer to Nye's than Boucher's. Southern historian Thomas Govan, in "Was the Old South Different?" *Journal of Southern History,* XXI (November, 1955), 447–55 is one of the recent writers who sees slavery as the determining cause of the ante-bellum South's culture and the ensuing war.

The literature on the coming of the Civil War is so voluminous and controversial that it has to be discussed in detail or not discussed at all. Since space does not permit the former course, the latter will have to be taken. Two surveys of the literature, however, can be noted: Howard K. Beale, "What Historians Have Said about the Causes of the Civil War," in Social Science Research Council, *Theory and Practice in Historical Study: A Report of the Committee on Historiography* (New York, ca. 1946), which deals with a host of writers and neatly categorizes them; and Thomas J. Pressley, *Americans Interpret Their Civil War* (Princeton, 1954), in which several major historians are critically dissected in detail.

VII. Bringing Forth a New Nation

The standard survey on the Civil War and one which I used frequently is J. G. Randall, *Civil War and Reconstruction* (Boston, 1953); the bibliography in this new edition is brought up to date and is invaluable. In *Roots of American Loyalty* (New York, 1946), Merle Curti has several good chapters on the making of a new nation. The popular literature resulting from the war is listed in R. W. Smith, "Catalogue of the Chief Novels and Short Stories by American Authors dealing with the Civil War and Its Effects, 1861–1899," *Bulletin of Bibliography,* XVI (September–December, 1939), 193–94; XVII (January–April, 1940), 10–12 (May–August, 1940), 33–35 (September–December, 1940), 53–55 (January–April, 1941), 72–75, and delightfully discussed and analyzed in Robert Lively, *Fiction Fights the Civil War* (Chapel Hill, N.C., 1957).

Reminiscences and reporting on the war are voluminous. A handy compendium which I have used is *The Blue and the Gray,* edited by Henry Steele Commager (2 vols., Indianapolis, 1950). I have also quoted from Theodore Upson, *With Sherman to the Sea* (University

Station, La., 1943); Mason W. Tyler, *Recollections of the Civil War* (New York, 1912); William T. Lusk, *War Letters* (New York, 1911); *Letters of a Family During the War for the Union* (2 vols., New Haven, 1899); *Touched with Fire; Civil War Letters and Diary of Oliver Wendell Holmes, Jr., 1861–4,* edited by Mark DeWolfe Howe (Cambridge, Mass., 1946); Henry Hitchcock, *Marching with Sherman* (New Haven, 1927); John Beatty, *Memoirs of a Volunteer, 1861–3,* edited by H. S. Ford (New York, 1946). Anthony Trollope's *North America* (New York, 1862) is interesting in the light of his mother's earlier criticisms of the North. Another Englishman, Edward Dicey, also portrayed the North sympathetically in *Six Months in the Federal States* (London, 1863). Bruce Catton's *A Stillness at Appomattox* (Garden City, N.Y., 1954) is already a minor classic in its genre of portraying the impact of the war upon the soldiers who fought it.

My thinking about the military aspects of the war has been greatly influenced by reading General J. F. C. Fuller's lively and controversial *Grant and Lee* (London, 1933) and *The Generalship of Ulysses S. Grant* (New York, 1929). Ella Lonn's *Foreigners in the Union Army and Navy* (Baton Rouge, 1952) is the basis for my statements on the importance of the immigrants; Mary Dearing, *Veterans in Politics, the Story of the GAR* (Baton Rouge, 1952), and Wallace Evan Davies, *Patriotism on Parade* (Cambridge, Mass., 1955), supplied information for my description of the G.A.R. Frank Owsley's disenchanted treatment of *King Cotton Diplomacy* (Chicago, 1931) is the standard authority on the diplomacy of the Confederacy.

The immediate economic consequences for the South are set forth in James L. Sellers, "Economic Incidence of the Civil War in the South," *Mississippi Valley Historical Review,* XIV (September, 1927), 179–91. The adjustments in southern agriculture are handled admirably in Fred Shannon's *The Farmer's Last Frontier* (New York, 1945) and in more detail in the first four chapters of Robert Preston Brooks, *Agrarian Revolution in Georgia, 1865–1912* (Madison, Wis., 1914). I have also used Oscar Zeichner, "The Transition from Slave to Free Agricultural Labor in the Southern States," *Agricultural History,* XIII (January, 1939), 22–32, and Marjorie Mendenhall, "The Rise of Southern Tenancy," *Yale Review,* XXVII (Autumn, 1937), 110–29.

The standard study on *The Social and Industrial Conditions in the North During the Civil War* is by Emerson D. Fite (New York, 1930), but it is little more than a hodgepodge of facts. My conception of the Lincoln administration's economic policies was aided by reading Reinhard Luthin, *The First Lincoln Campaign* (Cambridge, Mass., 1944), which stresses the economic elements in Lincoln's appeal more than I do. J. G. Randall, *Lincoln, the Liberal Statesman* (New York, 1947), in which the title essay is the last, tries to make Lincoln into a Manchesterian liberal, but without complete success. The lack of northern business interest in war is clearly set forth in Philip Foner, *Business and Slavery* (Chapel Hill, N.C., 1941), and in Ollinger Crenshaw, "Rural and Urban Voting in the Election of 1860," in Eric F. Goldman, ed., *Historiography and Urbanization* (Baltimore, 1941). The relative lack of interest in the tariff is demonstrated in Richard Hofstadter, "The Tariff Issue on the Eve of the Civil War," *American Historical Review*, XLIV (October, 1938), 50–55. Paul W. Gates, "The Homestead Law in an Incongruous Land System," *American Historical Review*, XLI (July, 1936), 652–81, and Fred Shannon, "The Homestead Act and the Labor Surplus," *American Historical Review*, XLI (July, 1936), 637–51, show that free land went more to speculators and the corporations than to bona fide settlers. The history and significance of the Contract Labor Law has been carefully analyzed by Charlotte Ericksen in *American Industry and the European Immigrant, 1860–1885* (Cambridge, Mass., 1957). My thinking about the nationalistic character of the Republican party has been much stimulated by William A. Dunning, "The Second Birth of the Republican Party," *American Historical Review*, XVI (October, 1910), 500–518. I am greatly indebted to J. G. Randall, *Constitutional Problems Under Lincoln* (New York, 1926), for my understanding of this aspect of administration policy.

VIII. Dawn Without Noon

The basic collection of sources on Reconstruction is Walter F. Fleming, ed., *Documentary History of Reconstruction* (2 vols., Cleveland, 1906–7), upon which I have drawn often. Herbert Aptheker, ed., *Documentary History of the Negro People in the United States* (New York, 1951), contains a section on the Reconstruction period in which the selections are designed to show the Negro's positive contributions. The view of a moderate Northerner in the years immediately after the war is J. T. Trowbridge, *The South: A Tour of Its Battlefields and Ruined Cities* (Hartford, 1866). The two contradictory reports of the South's reaction to defeat are Carl Schurz's, to be found in his *Speeches, Correspondence and Political Papers*, edited by Frederic Bancroft (6 vols., New York, 1913), and Benjamin Truman's *Report* in Senate Executive Documents, 39th Congress, 1st Session, No. 2. The history of Reconstruction in Mississippi is told by a Negro Republican in John Lynch, *Facts of Reconstruction* (New York, 1913). It is highly suggestive in regard to the possibilities of Negro-white collaboration before the debacle of the Grant regime aborted them. For a long time the standard account of an "eyewitness" of South Carolina Reconstruction was James S. Pike's *Prostrate State* (New York, 1874), but recently Robert F. Durden, *James Shepard Pike* (Durham, N.C., 1957), has shown it to he superficially prepared and animated by a desire to embarrass the Grant regime. One carpetbagger of unquestioned liberal views has revealed his efforts in the South in Louis F. Post, "A Carpetbagger in South Carolina," *Journal of Negro History*, X (January, 1925), 10–79. I have found John William de Forest, *Union Officer in the Reconstruction* (New Haven, 1948), invaluable for visualizing the day-to-day problems of a conscientious Northerner dealing with ignorant ex-slaves in a society trying to live under a new dispensation. Though reports of Georges Clemenceau, later Premier of France and then a Washington correspondent, in *American Reconstruction, 1865–1870* (New York, 1928), deal with events at the capital, they offer a European view of the Radicals' efforts to remold the South.

Though the writing on Reconstruction has been enormous and, since 1900, largely favorable to the southern point of view, Claude Bowers, *The Tragic Era* (Cambridge, Mass., 1929), has probably done more than any other book to delineate the view now so commonly accepted regarding the enormities of Reconstruction. William A. Dunning's *Reconstruction, Political and Economic 1865–1877* (New York, 1907) and *Essays on the Civil War and Reconstruction* (New York, 1898) are still important, but they are marred by the then prevalent attitude of seeing the Negro as incapable of taking a place as a full citizen. I am indebted to several of the works on Reconstruction which Dunning's students completed: C. Mildred Thompson, *Reconstruction in Georgia* (New York, 1915); James Garner, *Reconstruction in Mississippi,* (New York, 1901); J. G. de R. Hamilton, "Southern Legislation in Respect to Freedmen, 1865–1866," and W. W. Davis, "Federal Enforcement Acts," both in *Studies in Southern History and Politics* (New York, 1914).

Soon after the students of Dunning completed their investigations of individual states, re-evaluations of some of them began to appear; a pioneer in looking at Reconstruction from a positive point of view was Francis Simkins and Robert H. Woody, *South Carolina During Reconstruction* (Chapel Hill, N.C., 1932). R. W. Shugg, *Origins of Class Struggle in Louisiana* (University, La., 1939), covers the 1850's as well as the Reconstruction and sees the latter period as much more than a conflict between southern whites on the one hand and northern carpetbaggers and Negroes on the other. Vernon L. Wharton, *The Negro in Mississippi, 1865–1890* (Chapel Hill, N.C., 1947), stresses the achievements of Negroes in that state and plays down the so-called atrocities of the era. James S. Allen, *Reconstruction: The Battle for Democracy* (New York, 1937), though the work of a dedicated Marxist with an ax to grind, is important for its canvassing of the Negro's attempt to get land for himself after slavery. The role of the Negro school in early

Reconstruction is carefully and fairly treated in Henry Swint, *Northern Teacher in the South, 1862–1870* (Nashville, 1941). The most recent treatment of Reconstruction as a whole, E. M. Coulter, *The South During Reconstruction, 1865–1877* (Baton Rouge, 1947), fails to build upon the new turn taken in Reconstruction studies and so continues the essentially biased attitude toward the Negro so common in earlier studies. I have relied for much of my information regarding disfranchisement on two articles by William A. Russ, "Negro and White Disfranchisement During Radical Reconstruction," *Journal of Negro History*, XIX (April, 1934), 171–92, and "Registration and Disfranchisement Under Radical Reconstruction," *Mississippi Valley Historical Review*, XXI (September, 1934), 163–80. The approach historians take toward Thaddeus Stevens seems to be dependent on things other than evidence: Richard N. Current's *Old Thad Stevens* (Madison, Wis., 1942) is a good example of one which puts the worst construction on many of the things Stevens did and said; Ralph Korngold, *Thaddeus Stevens* (New York, 1955), sees him as pure gold; there is still a need for a critical but objective biography of the leader of Radical Reconstruction.

Understandably, the reinterpretation of Reconstruction has been led by Negro scholars, notably W. E. B. Du Bois. His "Reconstruction and its Benefits," *American Historical Review*, XV (July, 1910), 781–99, was followed by Alrutheus A. Taylor's pedestrian but informative volumes *Negro in South Carolina During Reconstruction* (Washington, 1924) and *Negro in the Reconstruction of Virginia* (Washington, 1926). By the time Du Bois wrote his over-all study of the period, *Black Reconstruction* (New York, 1935), derived largely from his winnowing of the Dunning and other studies, he had become a Marxist, and this pathbreaking book is seriously marred by his attempt to fit Reconstruction history into the mold of the class struggle. Two of several articles on the reinterpretation of Reconstruction to which I am indebted are Francis B. Simkins, "New Viewpoints on Southern Reconstruction," *Journal of Southern History*, V (February 1939), 49–61, and Howard K. Beale, "On Rewriting Reconstruction History," *American Historical Review*, XLV (July, 1940), 807–27. Simkins has offered concrete data for his view in Chapters 17–19 of his survey, *A History of the South* (New York, 1953). Two very good studies of the Freedmen's Bureau portray that much-maligned institution in a manner which highlights its immense aid in the rehabilitation of the South and the Negro: Paul Peirce, *The Freedmen's Bureau* (Iowa City, 1904); and George Bentley, *A History of the Freedmen's Bureau* (Philadalphia, 1955), the latter trying a little too hard to find economic motivation behind the Bureau's work. John and LaWanda Cox, "General O. O. Howard and the Misrepresented Bureau," *Journal of Southern History,*

XIX (November, 1953), 427–56, also defend the Bureau. In *Lincoln and the Radicals* (Madison, Wis., 1941), T. Harry Williams portrayed the President as fighting against the extreme Radicals before his assassination; this view has been seriously disputed in David H. Donald, *Lincoln Reconsidered* (New York, 1956). The respectable nature of some so-called scalawags has been convincingly argued in Donald's "The Scalawags in Mississippi Reconstruction," *Journal of Southern History*, X (November, 1944), 447–60.

The period after Reconstruction has been substantially reinterpreted in the work of C. Vann Woodward. His major work, *Origins of the New South, 1877–1913* (Baton Rouge, 1951), should be supplemented with his *Tom Watson, Agrarian Rebel* (New York, 1938) and *The Strange Career of Jim Crow* (New York, 1955). I am deeply indebted to these books. A number of articles in the periodical press of the time attest to the ambiguity of southern attitudes toward the Negro in the 1880's: A South Carolinian, "The Result in South Carolina," *Atlantic Monthly*, XLI (January, 1878), 1–12; T. W. Higginson, "Some War Scenes Revisited," *Atlantic Monthly*, XLII (July, 1878), 1–9; "Ought the Negro to Be Disenfranchised? Ought He to Have Been Enfranchised?" *North American Review*, CXXVIII (March, 1879), 225–83; Anonymous, "Studies in the South," *Atlantic Monthly*, L (September, 1882), 349–61, and (November, 1882), 623–33; Charles Dudley Warner, "Impressions of the South," *Harper's Monthly*, LXXI (September, 1885), 546–51, and, by the same author, "The South Revisited," *Harper's Monthly*, LXXIV (March, 1887), 634–40. Paul Lewinson, *Race, Class and Party* (London, 1932), is an early attempt to trace the gradual disfranchisement of the Negro. Francis Simkins, *Tillman Movement in South Carolina* (Durham, N.C., 1926), tells the story for one state; Albert K. Kirwan, *Revolt of the Rednecks* (Lexington, Ky., 1951), does it for Mississippi with great detail. One of the leaders of the New South is dealt with by Raymond R. Nixon in *Henry Grady* (New York, 1943), upon which I have drawn.

The North's lack of interest in the Negro as well as the declining position of the Negro are well set forth, though not without some bitterness, in Rayford Logan, *Negro in American Life and Thought: The Nadir, 1877–1901* (New York, 1954); George B. Tindall, *South Carolina Negroes, 1877–1900* (Columbia, S.C., 1952), reveals the progress and disabilities of the Negro in a key state during this period. The legal discrimination against the Negro in both North and South is chronicled in Gilbert T. Stephenson, *Race Discriminations in American Law* (New York, 1910). Somewhat unsympathetically, Samuel D. Smith tells the story of *The Negro in Congress, 1870–1901* (Chapel Hill, N.C., 1940). I have drawn my data on lynching from *Thirty Years of Lynching in the United States, 1889–1918* (New York, 1919) and J. E. Cutler, *Lynch Law* (New York, 1905), Chapters 5 and 6. The most recent biography of the great leader of the Negroes in this period is Samuel R. Spencer, Jr., *Booker T. Washington and the Negro's Place in American Life* (Boston, 1955), in which an effort is made to justify the pragmatic position Washington assumed. Paul Buck, *Road to Reunion, 1865–1900* (Boston, 1937), tells without criticism the North's growing acceptance of the inferiority of the Negro. Two contemporary accounts of conditions in the South upon which I have drawn are Maurice Evans, *Black and White in the Southern States* (London, 1915); and Albert B. Hart, *The Southern South* (New York, 1910), the latter by a Harvard professor more puzzled than indignant at what he sees.

IX. Machines, Men, and Socialism

For the expansion of American industry I have relied upon a number of standard surveys of economic development: Allan Nevins, *Emergence of Modern America, 1865–1878* (New York, 1927); Ida Tarbell, *Nationalizing of Business, 1878–1898* (New York, 1936); H. U. Faulkner, *The Decline of Laissez-Faire, 1897–1917* (New York, 1951). Most suggestive of all has been the contemporary *Recent Economic Changes* (New York, 1895) of David A. Wells. Charles R. Van Hise, *Concentration and Control* (New York, 1912), provided many examples of corporate concentration. I profited much from Hans B. Thorelli, *Federal Antitrust Policy* (Baltimore, 1955). The standard and unsuperseded authority on early southern industrialization is Broadus Mitchell, *Rise of the Cotton Mills in the South* (Baltimore, 1921). The statements of English workingmen on the wide use of machinery in America have been taken from A. Mosely, *Reports of the Delegates, Mosely Industrial Commission to the United States, October–December, 1902* (London, 1903).

Aside from the general acounts, I have also used for the railroads Robert R. Riegel's interesting *Story of the Western Railroads* (New York, 1926); the classic Charles F. Adams, Jr., and Henry Adams, *Chapters of Erie* (Boston, 1871); and, for financial consolidation, E. G. Campbell, *Reorganization of the American Railroad System, 1893–1900* (New York, 1938). The role of the land grant in railroad construction has received much attention; the pioneer article is Robert S. Henry, "The Railroad Land Grant Legend in American History Texts," *Mississippi Valley Historical Review*, XXXII (September, 1945), 171–94; see also the replies and criticisms in XXXII (March, 1946), 557–76. I have followed, in the main, Henry's position. T. C. Cochran, "Land Grants and Railroad Entrepreneurs," *Journal of Economic History*, X (Supplement, 1950), 53–67, calls attention to the importance of the grants in financing the roads. That the government received no financial gain from the grants is shown in Paul W. Gates, "The Railroad Land-Grant Legend," *Journal of Economic History*, XIV (Spring, 1954), 143–46. The basic work for calculating the governmental support to the roads is *Public Aids to Transportation* (4 vols. in 2, Washington, 1938–40), a governmental publication.

For my treatment of financial consolidation I have relied upon Louis Brandeis, *Other People's Money* (New York, 1914), a contemporary analysis of the findings of the Pujo Committee; George W. Edwards, *The Evolution of Finance Capitalism* (London, 1938); and the somewhat sensational Lewis Corey, *House of Morgan* (New York, 1930).

The literature on individual entrepreneurs and businesses is voluminous and of very uneven quality. The classic indictment of the great business leaders of the period is Gustavus Myers' indignant *History of the Great American Fortunes* (New York, 1936), first published in 1910. In the same vein is the famous Matthew Josephson, *Robber Barons* (New York, 1934). An attempt at rehabilitating one of the most notorious leaders is Allan Nevins, *John D. Rockefeller* (2 vols., New York, 1940). Keith Sward's *Legend of Henry Ford* (New York, 1948) is caustic in the older tradition. Much more sympathetic is Roger Burlingame, *Henry Ford* (New York, 1955). A number of leaders are popularly dealt with in Stewart Holbrook, *Age of the Moguls* (Garden City, N.Y., 1953). With humor and irony Oscar Lewis describes the activities of Crocker, Stanford, Huntington, and Hopkins in *The Big Four* (New York, 1946). Another railroad giant receives sympathetic treatment in Stewart Holbrook, *James J. Hill* (New York, 1955). Some of the giants have left expressions of their aims; I have used John D. Rockefeller, *Random Reminiscences of Men and Events* (New York, 1916); Henry Ford, *My Life and Work* (New York, 1926); and Andrew Carnegie, *Autobiography* (Boston, 1920).

My generalizations about the social origins of the entrepreneurs of the period depend upon a number of studies: C. Wright Mills, "The American Business Elite: A Collective Portrait," *Journal of Economic History*, V (December, 1945), 20–44; William Miller, "American Historians and the Business Elite," *Journal of Economic History*, IX (November, 1949), 184–208; F. W. Gregory and I. D. Neu, "Industrial Elite in the 1870's," in William Miller, ed., *Men in Business* (Cambridge, Mass., 1952); and Thomas C. Cochran, *Railroad Leaders, 1845–1890* (Cambridge, Mass., 1953). The kinds of business practices engaged in by the giants are categorized in Chester McA. Destler, "Entrepreneurial Leadership Among the 'Robber Barons'; A Trial Ballance," *Journal of Economic History*, VI (Supplement, 1946), 28–49. The social impact of the age of the entrepreneurs is set forth in Irving

Wyllie, *Self-Made Man in America* (New Brunswick, N.J., 1954). I learned about other aspects of the same subject from R. Richard Wohl, "The 'Rags to Riches Story': An Episode of Secular Idealism," in Richard Bendix and Seymour M. Lipset, eds., *Class, Status and Power* (Glencoe, Ill., 1953); and Sigmund Diamond, *Reputation of the American Businessman* (Cambridge, Mass., 1953), in which it is shown that by the end of the century the businessman had become in popular thought an ordinary man instead of a genius beyond the emulation of the common herd. See also K. W. Porter," The Business Man in American Folklore," *Bulletin of the Business Historical Society,* XVIII (November, 1944), 113–30.

For the labor movement as a whole, I have used in varying degrees Norman Ware, *The Labor Movement in the United States, 1860–1895* (New York, 1929), which despite its title is a history of the Knights of Labor only; Foster Rhea Dulles, *Labor in America* (New York, 1949); Philip Foner, *History of the Labor Movement in the United States* (2 vols., New York, 1947–55). The two books which have sparked my thinking on the conservative nature of the labor movement are Karl Polanyi, *The Great Transformation* (New York, 1944), and Frank Tannenbaum, *A Philosophy of Labor* (New York, 1951). Selig Perlman, *A Theory of the Labor Movement* (New York, 1928), uses conservative in the conventional sense of "friendly to property."

The writings of some of the labor leaders are invaluable for understanding the assumptions of the movement: Terence Powderly, *The Path I Trod,* edited by H. J. Carman, H. David, and P. N. Guthrie (New York, 1940); Samuel Gompers, *Seventy Years of Life and Labor* (2 vols., New York, 1925), and *Labor and the Common Welfare* (New York, 1919); John Mitchell, *Organized Labor* (Philadelphia, 1903), and *The Wage Earner and His Problems* (Washington, 1913). The quotation from Gompers before the U.S. Commission on Industrial Relations is from Vol. II of the *Final Report and Testimony* (11 vols., Washington, 1916). Louis S. Reed, *Labor Philosophy of Samuel Gompers* (New York, 1930), was also helpful.

In considering the failure of socialism, several works on the movement proved enlightening. The foremost study of the leader Eugene V. Debs is Ray Ginger, *Bending Cross* (New Brunswick, N.J., 1949). Howard Quint, *Forging of American Socialism* (Columbia, S.C., 1953), which deals only with the early years, and David A. Shannon, *Socialist Party of America* (New York, 1955), both discuss the limited appeal of the movement and I am indebted to both of them. Norman Thomas' thought on the subject is contained in *Socialist's Faith* (New York, 1951). The failure of other radical movements like anarchism and the International Workers of the World to attract large segments of the

American working class is canvassed or illuminated in Paul F. Brissenden, *The I.W.W.* (New York, 1919), and John S. Gambs, *The Decline of the I.W.W.* (New York, 1932); Chester McArthur Destler discusses anarchism in *American Radicalism, 1865–1901* (New London, Conn., 1946). The limited nature of the demonstrative behavior of labor is clearly set forth in Donald L. MacMurry's *Coxey's Army* (Boston, 1929). Sidney Hook essays an answer to the question "Why Has Socialism Not Been More Successful in the United States," in Donald D. Egbert and Stow Persons, eds., *Socialism and American Life* (2 vols., Princeton, 1952). The answer of Leon Samson is contained in his *Toward a United Front* (New York, 1933). The classic study on social movement is Pitirim Sorokin, *Social Mobility* (New York, 1927), which I have used with profit. The differences between the American and the European worker are recognized in Robert W. Smuts, *European Impressions of the American Worker* (New York, 1953), and in the observations of contemporaries like James Bryce, *The American Commonwealth* (3rd ed., 2 vols., New York, 1901); H. G. Wells, *The Future in America* (New York, 1906); and Matthew Arnold, *Civilization in the United States* (Boston, 1900).

X.   OUT OF MANY, ONE

The great source for the distribution of immigrants is the census reports after 1850. Even in a relatively early census like that of 1860, it is possible to carry investigation of immigrant population to the county level. For the twentieth century I have used the very complete and detailed Census of 1910. For the early years of the twentieth century, the *Report* of the United States Immigration Commission (41 vols., Washington, 1911–13) contains a wealth of data, though rather unorganized. I have used extensively the more convenient *Abstracts of Reports of the Immigration Commission* (2 vols., Washington, 1911). Though valid criticisms of bias have been brought against the conclusions of this report, its data are still unsurpassed for the period. Isaac Hourwich, *Immigration and Labor* (New York, 1912), is an early attack on the conclusions of the Commission; Chapter V of Oscar Handlin, *Race and Nationality in American Life* (Boston, 1957), is the most recent. I am much indebted to William S. Bernard *et al.*, eds., *American Immigration Policy: A Reappraisal* (New York, 1950), for comparisons of American immigration policy with that of other countries.

In recent years a number of collections of immigrant sources have been published. One of the oldest in the broad field of immigration policy, and still valuable, is Edith Abbott, *Historical Aspects of the Immigration Problem* (Chicago, 1926). I have drawn much from Theodore C. Blegen, ed., *Land of Their Choice; the Immigrants Write Home*

(Minneapolis, 1955). George M. Stephenson published some letters of immigrants in "When America was the Land of Canaan," *Minnesota History*, X (September, 1929), 237–60, and the same was done in Henry S. Lucas, ed., *Dutch Immigrant Memoirs and Related Writings* (2 vols., Assen, Netherlands, 1955). The impact of America on returned immigrants is illuminated in Theodore Saloutus, *They Remember America: The Story of the Repatriated Greek-Americans* (Berkeley, Calif., 1956), and Merle Curti and Kendall Birr, "The Immigrant and the American Image in Europe, 1860–1914," *Mississippi Valley Historical Review*, XXXVII (September, 1950), 203–30. The rather romanticized approach toward immigration in Edward Steiner's volumes appeared at the height of the last great wave of immigration: *The Immigrant Tide* (New York, 1907) and *On the Trail of the Immigrant* (New York, 1906), and I have drawn on them.

The standard authority on immigration before 1860 is Marcus Hansen, *Atlantic Migration, 1607–1860* (Cambridge, Mass., 1940). No comparable study has been made for the new immigration, though Oscar Handlin, *The Uprooted* (Boston, 1951), does cover the period. Handlin's interest, however, is primarily in the immigrants' adjustment here, rather than the process of migration itself. More detailed and a model of its kind is his earlier work, *Boston's Immigrants, 1790–1865* (Cambridge, Mass., 1941). The New York immigrant scene is canvassed as closely, though not as strikingly, in Robert Ernst, *Immigrant Life in New York City, 1825–1863* (New York, 1949).

Aside from the immigration *Report* and special studies mentioned already, on the role of the immigrant in the economy I have used Isaac Hourwich, *Immigration and Labor* (New York, 1912), which is essentially a defense of the immigrants; while John R. Commons, *Races and Immigrants in America* (New York, 1907), like the Immigration Commission, raises questions as to their influence, but not their economic value. The same can be said of Jeremiah Jenks and W. Jett Lauch, *The Immigration Problem* (New York, 1912). Harry Jerome, *Migration and Business Cycles* (New York, 1926), is the basic work on the subject, from which I have learned much. The important role of the immigrant in the leadership of labor unions is demonstrated in P. A. Sorokin, "Leaders of Labor and Radical Movements in the United States and Foreign Countries," *American Journal of Sociology*, XXXIII (November, 1927), 382–411. The periodical literature of the day is filled with comment on the contribution of the immigrant.

For my discussion of the political role of the immigrant, I am especially indebted to Samuel Lubell's illuminating researches in *The Future of American Politics* (2nd edition, Garden City, N.Y., 1956); the same view of the connection between isolationism and immigrant background has been suggested by Eric Goldman, *Rendezvous with Destiny* (New York, 1953), Chapter XI. Oscar Handlin, "The Immigrant and Politics," in David F. Bowers, ed., *Foreign Influences in American Life* (Princeton, 1944), puts great emphasis on the conservative politics of immigrants, though ignoring the Germans in the Socialist movement. The importance of the immigrant in the election of 1860 is demonstrated in William E. Dodd, "Fight for the Northwest," *American Historical Review*, XVI (July, 1911), 774–88, but somewhat modified in Andreas Dorpalen, "The German Element and the Issues of the Civil War," *Mississippi Valley Historical Review*, XXIX (June, 1942), 55–76.

My thinking on the connection between religion in America and immigration has been greatly stimulated by Will Herberg, *Protestant-Catholic-Jew* (New York, 1955). Of a somewhat different nature, but certainly complementary, is H. Richard Niebuhr, *Social Sources of Denominationalism* (New York, 1929). My discussion on immigrant Puritanism is indebted to Marcus Hansen, "Immigration and Puritanism," in his book *Immigrant in American History* (Cambridge, Mass., 1940). On the nature of Catholicism in America, Thomas Sugrue, *A Catholic Speaks His Mind on America's Religious Conflict* (New York, 1952), is important for calling attention to the variety within the Church. Carl Wittke, "The Immigrant Theme on the American Stage," *Mississippi Valley Historical Review*, XXXIX (September, 1952), 211–32, points up another manifestation of immigrant influence and stereotype.

For the nativist movement, Ray Billington, *Protestant Crusade, 1800–1860* (New York, 1938), has long been the standard treatment, but it suffers from the failure to recognize that anti-Catholicism had a variety of roots, not all of them in the soil of bigotry. Handlin in his *Boston's Immigrants* offers a most suggestive corrective and it is substantially that which I have followed. A similar approach is taken in Harry J. Carman and Reinhard H. Luthin, "Some Aspects of the Know-Nothing Movement Reconsidered," *South Atlantic Quarterly*, XXXIX (April, 1940), 213–34; William G. Bean, "An Aspect of Know-Nothingism— The Immigrant and Slavery," *South Atlantic Quarterly*, XXIII (October, 1924), 319–34, and "Puritan versus Celt, 1850–1860," *New England Quarterly*, VII (March, 1934), 70–89. The differences between northern and southern nativism appear, by implication, in W. Darrell Overdyke, *Know-Nothing Party in the South* (Baton Rouge, 1950).

The movement for restriction of immigration is well described and analyzed in John Higham, *Strangers in the Land* (New Brunswick, N.J., 1955); the New England movement for restriction, with the focus on Boston, is treated in Barbara Miller Solomon, *Ancestors and Immigrants* (Cambridge, Mass., 1956). Much of my discussion has been taken from Higham's searching examination. Confirmation of Higham's view that business as well as labor desired limitation on immigration by the end of the nineteenth century is forthcoming in Morrell Heald, "Business Attitudes Toward European Immigration, 1880–1900," *Journal of Economic History*, XIII (Summer, 1953), 291–304. Madison Grant's racist view of the new immigrant is contained in his *Passing of the Great Race* (New York, 1916). The standard treatment of restriction is Roy L. Garis, *Immigration Restriction* (New York, 1927).

XI.   ALABASTER CITIES AND AMBER WAVES OF GRAIN

There is a wealth of material on the growth of cities in the censuses of the United States beginning in 1880, when *Social Statistics of Cities* was issued in two volumes. Thereafter the Bureau of the Census included increasing detail on cities; especially useful for comparative purposes is the *Statistical Atlas of the Twelfth Census* (Washington, 1903), in which a summary of historical changes for individual cities is to be found. The stimulating work of Lewis Mumford, *Culture of Cities* (New York, 1938), has been the beginning of my thinking on the subject of urban life. The classic statistical work is the pathbreaking Adna Weber, *The Growth of Cities in the Nineteenth Century* (New York, 1899). Two books of Josiah Strong, *New Era* (New York, 1893) and *Challenge of the City* (New York, 1907), contain statistical data and stimulating suggestions by a perspicacious contemporary. For a long time the standard historical authority has been Arthur M. Schlesinger, *The Rise of the City, 1878–1898* (New York, 1933), of which only a part, unfortunately, is devoted to the subject of the title. See also his "The City in American History," *Mississippi Valley Historical Review*, XXVII (June, 1940), 43–66. The difficulties and pitfalls of interpreting history in terms of cities are well set forth in William Diamond, "On the Dangers of an Urban Interpretation of History," in Eric Goldman, ed., *Historiography and Urbanization* (Baltimore, 1941), primarily a critique of Schlesinger. I have learned much from Christopher Tunnard and Henry Hope Reed, *American Skyline* (Mentor ed., New York, 1956), which is a history of urban building in the United States.

The impact of the city on society has been primarily the province of sociology, and I have drawn freely upon a number of texts and studies in this field. A pioneer study in this area is J. G. Thomas, *Urbanization: Its Effects on Government and Society* (New York, 1927), which is suggestive but too exuberant in its pretensions to be uncritically used. More temperate is Louis Wirth, "Urbanism as a Way of Life," *American Journal of Sociology*, XLIV (July, 1938), 1–24; and Charles S. Ascher, "What Are Cities For," and Chauncey D. Harris and Edward

I. Ullman, "The Nature of Cities," in *Annals* of the American Academy
of Political and Social Science, Vol. 242 (November, 1945). I have also
used the very readable Robert MacIver, *Society* (New York, 1949);
Wilbur C. Hallenbeck, *American Urban Communities* (New York,
1951); Svend Riemer, *The Modern City* (New York, 1952); and S. A.
Queen and D. B. Carpenter, *The American City* (New York, 1953).
Pitirim Sorokin, *Society, Culture and Personality* (New York, 1947),
has some data on the growth of cities. The city in literature is dealt
with rather unimaginatively in G. A. Dunlap, *The City in the American
Novel, 1789–1900* (Philadelphia, 1934). Pitirim A. Sorokin and Carle
C. Zimmerman, *Principles of Rural-Urban Sociology* (New York, 1929),
did much to point up for me the difference in the city and country environments.

The standard and best treatment of the history of agriculture after
the Civil War is Fred A. Shannon, *Farmer's Last Frontier* (New York,
1945), which I have relied upon. The problem of the surplus is admirably dealt with in William Trimble, "Historical Aspects of the Surplus Food Production of the United States," American Historical
Association, *Annual Report, 1918*, I, 221–40. I have also used Edwin
G. Nourse, *American Agriculture and the European Market* (New York,
1924), a searching economic analysis of the problem. The mechanization
of agriculture is told in detail in Leo Rogin, *The Introduction of Farm
Machinery . . . During the Nineteenth Century* (Berkeley, Calif.,
1931), and in the famous essay by E. E. Edwards, "American Agriculture—The First 300 Years," in *Yearbook of Agriculture, 1940* (Washington, n.d.), pp. 171–276. Some material is also to be found in Vols.
10 and 11 of the *Report of the Industrial Commission* (18 vols., Washington, 1901). See also L. B. Schmidt, "The Agricultural Revolution
in the United States," *Science,* LXXII (December 12, 1930), 585–94.
The whole question of the relation between industrialization and mechanization of agriculture is discussed and attempts made at measurement
in Pei-kang Chang, *Agriculture and Industrialization* (Cambridge, Mass.,
1949). The subject is well canvassed for America in Theodore Saloutus,
"The Agricultural Problem and Nineteenth-Century Industrialism,"
Agricultural History, XXII (July, 1948), 156–74. The failure of tenancy as a ladder to land ownership is dealt with convincingly by
LaWanda F. Cox, "Tenancy in the United States, 1865–1900," *Agricultural History,* XVIII (July, 1944), 97–105.

For my conception of the farmer under the impact of industrialism,
I have leaned heavily upon Paul H. Johnstone, "Old Ideals versus
New Ideas in Farm-Life," in *Yearbook of Agriculture, 1940,* pp. 111–
170. The differences between the American farmer and the European
peasant are brought out in Joseph Schafer, *Social History of American*

Agriculture (New York, 1936). *A Systematic Sourcebook in Rural Sociology,* edited by Pitirim Sorokin *et al.* (3 vols., Minneapolis, 1930–32), provided convenient source material on the subject, as did the *Report of the United States Country Life Commission* (Washington, 1909). See also Horace Plunkett, *The Rural Life Problem in the United States* (New York, 1910), the work of an Englishman, and the two books on New York State agricultural mores by James M. Williams, *Our Rural Heritage* (New York, 1925) and *The Expansion of Rural Life* (New York, 1931). The persistence of the myth of the idyllic life of the farmer is demonstrated in Elmer T. Peterson, ed., *Cities Are Abnormal* (Norman, Okla., 1946), and in two excellent scholarly studies of the historic connection between the democratic ethos and farming: A. Whitney Griswold, *Farming and Democracy* (New York, 1948), and Henry Nash Smith, *Virgin Land* (Cambridge, Mass., 1950).

All studies of the Populist movement begin with John D. Hicks, *Populist Revolt* (Minneapolis, 1931), which is still very useful but rather uncritical about the validity of the farmer's complaints. Carl C. Taylor, *Farmer's Movement, 1620–1920* (New York, 1953), is greater in scope but no more critical of the farmer's diagnosis of his ills. Completely untouched by romantic illusions about the farmer is Richard Hofstadter, *Age of Reform* (New York, 1956), and I am much indebted to it. I have followed the stimulating suggestions of B. H. Wilcox, "An Historical Definition of Northwestern Radicalism," *Mississippi Valley Historical Review,* XXVI (December, 1939), 377–94. I have profited greatly from the illuminating suggestions of James C. Malin, "Notes on the Literature of Populism," *Kansas Historical Quarterly,* I (February, 1932), 160–64, and "The Background of the First Bills to Establish a Bureau of Markets, 1911–12," *Agricultural History,* VI (July, 1932), 107–29. For the twentieth century I have also used Frederic L. Paxson, "The Agricultural Surplus: A Problem in History," *Agricultural History,* VI (April, 1932), 51–68, and Theodore Saloutus and John D. Hicks, *Agricultural Discontent in the Middle West, 1900–1939* (Madison, Wis., 1951). The fumbling attempt to unite labor and the Populists is traced in Chester McArthur Destler, *American Radicalism, 1865–1901* (New London, Conn., 1946), Chapters 8, 9, and 11.

XII. NEW WORLD A-COMIN'

A number of the religious and philanthropic leaders put their thoughts into print during and after the period. The autobiography of William Jewett Tucker, *My Generation* (Boston, 1919), contains much information; so does Samuel Lane Loomis, *Modern Cities and Their Religious Problems* (New York, 1887). The most vocal of the early spokesmen for a new approach to religion was Washington Gladden;

I have used his *Applied Christianity* (Boston and New York, 1886), *Social Salvation* (Boston and New York, 1902), and his memoirs, *Recollections* (Boston and New York, 1909). Josiah Strong, *Challenge of the City* (New York, 1907) and *New Era* (New York, 1893), are also important expressions of concern for religion in the midst of the city. *The Life of Charles Loring Brace* (London, 1894) edited by his daughter Emma, contains many letters of this influential New York philanthropist and minister. The two works of Walter Rauschenbusch I have used extensively are *Christianizing the Social Order* (New York, 1919, though originally published in 1912) and *Christianity and the Social Crisis* (New York, 1907). Some material is also to be found in Walter Wycoff's account of his experience as a disguised itinerant worker: *The Workers* (2 vols., New, York, 1897–98).

An important article on the urban impact on religion is A. M. Schlesinger, "Critical Period in American Religion, 1875–1900," in *Proceedings* of the Massachusetts Historical Society, LXIV (June, 1932), 523–47. Three books are standard in the field now and I am greatly beholden to all of them: Aaron I. Abell, *Urban Impact upon American Protestantism, 1865–1900* (Cambridge, Mass., 1943); Charles H. Hopkins, *Rise of the Social Gospel in American Protestantism, 1865–1915* (New Haven, 1940); and, perhaps the best of all and certainly the broadest in scope, Henry F. May, *Protestant Churches and Industrial America* (New York, 1949). May also makes a good case for the connection between the social gospel and Progressivism. Charles A. Barker's full biography of *Henry George* (New York, 1955) also emphasizes the close ties between religious idealism and the reform movement of the 1880's and 1890's. For a less popular reform movement, James Dombrowski does the same in his *Early Days of Christian Socialism in America* (New York, 1936). For the Salvation Army I have drawn upon Frederick Booth-Tucker, *Social Relief Work of the Salvation Army in the United States* (Albany, 1900), and Herbert A. Wisbey, Jr., *Soldiers Without Swords* (New York, 1955). The effect of the new movement upon Catholicism is apparent in John A. Ryan and Joseph Husslein, eds., *The Church and Labor* (New York, 1924), a collection of sources and essays. Robert D. Cross, *The Emergence of Liberal Catholicism in America* (Cambridge, Mass., 1958), nicely distinguishes between conservatives and liberals within Catholicism. Some discussion is also contained in Arthur Mann, *Yankee Reformers in the Urban Age* (Cambridge, Mass., 1954). An interesting examination of the city's effects upon religion in France is contained in Joseph Folliet, "The Effects of City Life Upon Spiritual Life," in R. M. Fisher, ed., *The Metropolis in Modern Life* (New York, 1955). *The Trends in Protestant Social Idealism* are traced by Neal Hughley (New York, 1948). The quotation from Kenneth E. Boulding is in "Religious Foundations of Economic Progress," *Harvard Business Review*, XXX (May–June, 1952), 33–40.

There is no satisfactory history of the woman's movement of the late nineteenth and early twentieth century; in the absence of this much-needed work, I have drawn upon a number of studies, some only partly or incidentally concerned with the subject. Much factual information is to be found in the two volumes in the History of American Life Series: A. M. Schlesinger, *Rise of the City* and H. U. Faulkner, *Quest for Social Justice* (New York, 1931). More contemporary than historical, but with much information on the early twentieth century, is Ernest R. Groves, *The American Woman* (New York, 1937). The same can be said of Willystine Goodsell, *A History of Marriage and the Family* (rev. ed., New York, 1934). Ideas concerning *Marriage, Morals and Sex in America* (New York, 1953) are traced by Sidney Ditzion, but with a little too much attention paid to the bizarre. Some interesting comments on the American woman at the turn of the century are to be found in Hugo Münsterberg, *American Traits from the Point of View of a German* (Boston and New York, 1902). A book which I used, but which the feminists of the period berated, was Mrs. John Van Vorst and Marie Van Vorst, *The Woman Who Toils* (New York, 1903). Arthur Mann, *Yankee Reformers in the Urban Age* (Cambridge, Mass., 1954), makes some important comments on the nature of the new woman as exemplified especially in Vida Scudder of Wellesley College. Mary I. Wood, *History of the General Federation of Women's Clubs* (New York, 1912), is an official and dull recital of activities. Economic data on women are contained in S. P. Breckinridge, *Women in the Twentieth Century* (New York, 1933), and Helen Sumner's *History of Women in Industry in the United States* (Washington, 1910), Vol. IX in *Report on the Condition of Woman and Child Wage Earners in the United States* and Vol. X, *History of Women in Trade Unions* (Washington, 1911), by John B. Andrews and W. D. P. Bliss.

I have also used a number of studies of individual women leaders; especially noteworthy is Mary Earhart, *Frances Willard* (Chicago, 1944); see also Josephine Goldmark, *Florence Kelley's Life Story* (Urbana, Ill., 1953); Rheta Dorr, *What Eight Million Women Want* (Boston, 1910); and Katherine Anthony, *Susan B. Anthony* (Garden City, N.Y., 1954). There is no biography of Charlotte P. Gilman except her autobiography, *The Living of Charlotte Perkins Gilman* (New York, 1935), though one is certainly justified. Her ideas are summarized and criticized in Carl N. Degler, "Charlotte Perkins Gilman on the Theory and Practice of Feminism," *American Quarterly*, VIII (Spring, 1956), 21–39.

My presentation of the movement for children's play is indebted to
C. E. Rainwater, *Play Movement in the United States* (Chicago, 1921);
Henry S. Curtis, *The Play Movement and Its Significance* (New York,
1917); and Luther Halsey Gulick, *A Philosophy of Play* (New York,
1920).

Several of the intellectuals of the Progressive movement have left
statements of their aims and philosophy; they were indispensable for
the writing of this section: Frederick Howe, *Confessions of a Reformer*
(New York, 1925), and his earlier book, *The City, the Hope of Democracy* (New York, 1906); Brand Whitlock, *Forty Years of It* (New
York, 1914), and *Letters and Journal of Brand Whitlock*, edited by
Allan Nevins (New York, 1936); Robert M. La Follette's *Autobiography* (Madison, Wis., 1913); the major "theoretical" work of the
movement was Herbert Croly, *Promise of American Life* (New York,
1911). A bridge between contemporary and later appraisals of the movement is Lincoln Steffens' *Autobiography* (New York, 1931), in which
he is much less sanguine about reform than he had been at the time.
Harry Barnard, *"Eagle Forgotten"; the Life of John Peter Altgeld*
(Indianapolis, 1938), clearly points up the aspiring middle-class roots
of the Progressive mind of even the most radical variety; Alfred D.
Chandler, Jr., "The Origins of Progressive Leadership," in *Letters of
Theodore Roosevelt*, edited by E. E. Morison (Cambridge, Mass., 1951–
54), Vol. VIII, Appendix III, does the same for all the leaders of the
political movement. The letters of Roosevelt open a broad window into
the mind of the most famous Progressive. *The New Freedom* (New
York, 1913), a collection of Woodrow Wilson campaign speeches in
1912, is indispensable for understanding the Democratic variety of
Progressivism. Charles McCarthy, *The Wisconsin Idea* (New York,
1912), is an exposition of the third facet of Progressivism, that of the
La Follette followers.

The literature on the Progressive movement is constantly increasing.
The first major critique of the movement was John Chamberlain, *Farewell to Reform* (New York, 1932), which is shot through with the bitter
defeatism of the liberal in the midst of the Great Depression. More
optimistic and much less interpretive is C. C. Regier, *Era of the Muckrakers* (Chapel Hill, N.C., 1932). Still true to the spirit of the Progressive era is Louis Filler, *Crusaders for American Liberalism* (New
York, 1940), but in the same year the acid pen of Matthew Josephson
touched Progressivism in *The President-Makers* (New York, 1940).
Highly critical of the movement, but brilliant in its fusion of political
and literary events and in its style, is Part I of Alfred Kazin, *On
Native Grounds* (Anchor ed., New York, 1956). Impressions of the
era, especially as drawn from literature, are to be found in Lloyd

Morris, *Postscript to Yesterday* (New York, 1947). A detailed but
important study of the Progressive mind is George E. Mowry, "The
California Progressive and His Rationale: A Study in Middle Class
Politics," *Mississippi Valley Historical Review*, XXXVI (September,
1949), 239–50. Russel Nye sees the Middle Western Progressive as more
individualistic and more Jeffersonian in philosophy than the eastern in his *Middle-Western Progressive Politics* (East Lansing, Mich.,
1951). The first half of Eric Goldman's *Rendezvous with Destiny* (New
York, 1953) is a searching and provocative analysis of the changing
ideas before and during the Progressive era; he makes much of the
relativistic approach to society and politics taken by some of the Progressive intellectuals. Though not primarily concerned with the Progressive movement, Morton White, *Social Thought in America* (New
York, 1949), throws much light on the growing relativism in the thought
of the early twentieth century. The most recent and in many respects
the best analysis of the social forces underlying the Progressive revolt is contained in Richard Hofstadter, *Age of Reform* (New York,
1956), though it tends to underplay the power of moral ideals.

Theodore Roosevelt and Woodrow Wilson as the two major political
exponents of Progressivism have been reinterpreted in recent years. A
much more jaundiced view of T. R. was taken by Henry W. Pringle,
Theodore Roosevelt (New York, 1931), than had been current before.
This view of Roosevelt as opportunistic and even somewhat juvenile
was continued in George Mowry, *Theodore Roosevelt and the Progressive Movement* (Madison, Wis., 1947). Roosevelt's inherent conservatism despite his Progressive label is emphasized in John Morton
Blum, *The Republican Roosevelt* (Cambridge, Mass., 1954), and in
Richard Hofstadter's mordant sketch in *American Political Tradition*
(New York, 1948). Woodrow Wilson has also come in for more critical
appraisal, especially from his chief biographer, Arthur Link, *Wilson*
(2 vols., Princeton, 1947–56), and in Link's more general work,
Woodrow Wilson and the Progressive Era, 1910–1917 (New York,
1954). The limits of Wilson's economic knowledge constitute the heart
of William Diamond's criticism in *The Economic Thought of Woodrow
Wilson* (Baltimore, 1943).

XIII. THE THIRD AMERICAN REVOLUTION

The impact of the depression on American life has hardly begun to
be assessed, but some general treatments were already being prepared
during the era. Most detailed, but confined to a single town, is the
critical and painstaking dissection of Muncie, Indiana, by Robert and
Helen Lynd, *Middletown in Transition* (New York, 1937). Frederick
Lewis Allen made a superficial survey of the thirties in *Since Yesterday*

(New York, 1940), which makes no pretense of being analytical. More
scholarly, but more pedestrianly written, is Clarence J. Engler, *Some
Social Aspects of the Depression, 1930–1935* (Washington, 1939), in
which the social costs of the debacle are assessed. The *Journal of Sociology*, XLVII (May, 1942), devoted its entire issue to "Recent Social
Changes" in the period 1932–42. It emphasizes the changes in the family
and in the role of government. Most recently Dixon Wecter made a
survey of the era in *The Age of the Great Depression* (New York,
1952), upon which I have relied for many facts. A rather superficial,
but lively, survey of the literary aspects of the decade is Leo Gurko,
Angry Decade (New York, 1947).

My presentation of the immediate impact of unemployment has been
drawn from several studies by sociologists and from surveys in the
periodical press: R. C. Angell, *The Family Encounters the Depression*
(New York, 1936); Mirra D. Komarovsky, *The Unemployed Man and
His Family* (New York, 1940); and E. W. Bakke, *Citizens Without
Work* (New Haven, 1940). See also "No One Has Starved," *Fortune*,
VI (September, 1932), 19–29 ff., for an ironic examination of the extent of misery in the depths of the depression; the story of the wandering youths is in *Fortune*, VII (February, 1933), 46. The eyewitness
accounts of the Bonus Army and the unemployed in Detroit are re-
printed in *The New Republic Anthology, 1915–1935* (New York,
1936), pp. 424–34. An anonymous article, "I'm On Relief," *Harper's
Magazine*, Vol. 172 (January, 1936), 200–209, gives voice to the new
attitude toward governmental responsibilities. *Fortune* surveyed the
general unemployment situation almost yearly; a detailed investigation
of one family is to be found in Vol. XIII (February, 1936), 63–68 ff.;
the survey of the arts programs is "Unemployed Arts," *Fortune*, XV
(May, 1937), 109–17 ff.

The literature on the new legislation of the period is very great. On
control of banks: Ferdinand Pecora, *Wall Street Under Oath* (New
York, 1939), by the counsel for the congressional investigation; and a
critical article, Bernard Flexner, "The Fight on the Securities Act,"
Atlantic Monthly, CLIII (February, 1934), 232–50. The history of
social security proposals which I used for background is Isaac M.
Rubinow, *The Quest for Security* (New York, 1934); the leading authority on social security at the time, Abraham Epstein, opposed the
program in "Our Social Insecurity Act," *Harper's Magazine*, Vol. 172
(December, 1935), 55–66. For an expression of the new approach to
government's role, see G. R. Leighton and Richard Hellman, "Half
Slave, Half Free; Unemployment, the Depression, and American Young
People," *Harper's Magazine*, Vol. 171 (August, 1935), 342–53. The
standard authority on the TVA is C. H. Pritchett, *The Tennessee Valley*

Authority (Chapel Hill, N.C., 1943), and I have also used the relevant portions of Broadus Mitchell, *Depression Decade* (New York, 1947), here and elsewhere in this chapter. Odette Keun, *A Foreigner Looks at the TVA* (New York, 1937), is very sympathetic, as is the contemporary Drew and Leon Pearson, "The Tennessee Valley Experiment," *Harper's Magazine,* Vol. 170 (May, 1935), 699–707. Donald Davidson presents a jaundiced but not unfair picture of TVA in the second volume of his *The Tennessee* (2 vols., Now York, 1948).

My thinking about the social values spawned by the depression has been stimulated by Dorothy Dunbar Bromley, "Birth Control and the Depression," *Harper's Magazine,* Vol. 169 (October, 1934), 563–74, and Paul Carter, *Decline and Revival of the Social Gospel* (Ithaca, N.Y., 1956). On the attitudes of youth I have used extensively Maxine Davis, *The Lost Generation* (New York, 1936), and "Youth in College," *Fortune* (June, 1936), 99–102 ff.; see also Dorothy D. Bromley and F. H. Britten, *Youth and Sex* (New York, 1938).

The altered position of the Negro is dealt with in detail in E. L. Tatum, *Changed Political Thought of the Negro, 1915–1940* (New York, 1951); Henry Lee Moon, *Balance of Power: The Negro Vote* (Garden City, N.Y., 1948); E. D. Waldron, "The Negro Exodus From the South," *Current History,* XVIII (September, 1923), 942–44; and in Gunnar Myrdal's *American Dilemma* and Samuel Lubell's *The Future of American Politics.*

For the new labor movement I have relied on Edwin W. Witte, *The Government in Labor Disputes* (New York and London, 1932), for the period of the twenties; R. R. Brooks, *When Labor Organizes* (New Haven, 1937); Edward Levinson's dramatic and very sympathetic *Labor on the March* (New York, 1938); and Leo Huberman's sensational but factual *Labor Spy Racket* (New York, 1937) for the great organizing drives. On the implications of the new labor laws I am indebted to Charles O. Gregory, *Labor and the Law* (New York, 1946); Harry A. Millis and Emily C. Brown, *From the Wagner Act to Taft-Hartley* (Chicago, 1950); and Kurt Braun, *The Right to Organize and Its Limits* (Washington, 1950).

The volume of writings about Franklin D. Roosevelt and his New Deal by both scholars and contemporaries is so huge that it cannot be surveyed here; only those items which actually went into the writing of my chapter will be mentioned. The prime source, of course, is *The Public Papers and Addresses of Franklin D. Roosevelt* (5 vols., New York, 1938). An early but very usable short treatment of his administrations in Basil Rauch, *The History of the New Deal, 1933–1938* (New York, 1944). The first volume of a projected study of the Age of Roosevelt by Arthur M. Schlesinger, Jr., *The Crisis of the Old Order*

(Boston, 1957), is rather thin but it has some material on the depression. The most rewarding memoir for my purposes was Frances Perkins, *The Roosevelt I Knew* (New York, 1946); it is both sympathetic and clearheaded. Interesting as an impression written before F. D. R. became a hero is Ernest K. Lindley, *The Roosevelt Revolution* (New York, 1933). Some impressions have also been culled from *The Secret Diary of Harold L. Ickes* (3 vols., New York, 1953–54). I found James McGregor Burns, *Roosevelt: The Lion and the Fox* (New York, 1956), informative, if sometimes overdramatic. *The Memoirs of Herbert Hoover* (3 vols., New York, 1951–2) are indispensable for putting the New Deal in some critical perspective. The essays on Hoover and F. D. R. in Richard Hofstadter, *The American Political Tradition,* are critical and illuminating.

Index

459

Catton, Bruce, 200
"Causes and Proposed Remedies for
Poverty, The," 346
Census (1850), 322
(1860), 123
(1870), 222
(1920), 394
Centers, Richard, 269n
Central Pacific Railroad, 248
Central Park, New York, 312
Cermak, Anton, 286
Chamber of Commerce of the United
States, 382
Charles I (Charles Stuart), 11, 62
Charles River Bridge Case (1837),
149–150
Chatham, Lord, 80, 82
Chesapeake colonies, 2
Chesapeake and Ohio Canal, 115
Chevalier, Michel, 145
Chicago *Prairie Farmer*, 325
Child labor, 365–366, 406
Childe, V. Gordon, 304
Children, economic exploitation of,
355, 365–366, 406
effect of industrialization on, 355–
356
play facilities for, 355–356
Children's Aid Society, New York, 131
Childs, Marquis, 411n
Chinese, immigration restrictions, 299
Christian Endeavor Society, 258, 343
Christian Union, 342
Christianity, and Negro slavery, 38n
Christianizing the Social Order, 346
Church Association for the Advance-
ment of the Interests of Labor,
343
Church and Labor, 350
Church and State, doctrine of separation of, 20, 96–97, 159
Churches, acceptance of social gospel,
347–349, 410
attendance, 18th-century, 54–55
disestablishment by Revolutionary
War, 95–97
during 1930's depression, 410
effect of industrialization on, 338–
351
founding of colleges by, 19–20
and immigrants, 291–295
reform movements, 348–349
and urban working class, 339–351
Churchill, Winston, 157

Cincinnati Conference of the Methodist Church (1889), 343
C.I.O., *see* Congress of Industrial Organizations
Cities, apartment houses, 312n
birth rate and family size, 320
dependence on agriculture, 305
dependence on transportation, 306
divorce rate, 355
"Dormitory cities," 309
dumbbell style of tenements, 312–
313
effect on dwellers, 314–320
effect of river boats on, 116
1880 Census, 310
18th-century colonial, 45
environment compared to rural life,
314–317
expansion in 1880's, 307–310
factors in growth, 305–307
governments, 364–365
growth of in 18th century, 40
growth in South, 257n
immigrant populations in, 290–291
industrial satellites, 309–310
lack of social planning, 311–312,
313
life expectancies, 319
"lure" of, 306–307
Metropolitan Districts, 309
1910 urban population, 308–309
opportunities in, 318
Pacific states, 309
paradoxical aspects, 318–319
paved streets, 311
population density, 312
problems peculiar to, 314
provisions for recreation, 311–312
rate of urbanization (table), 306
religion in, 339–351
sanitation, 310–311, 314
social fluidity, 317–318
and suicide rates, 319
tenement housing, 312–313
transportation in, 313–314
uniformity, 313
urbanization of farm life, 329
water problem, 314
Citizenship, and the Fourteenth
Amendment, 206, 214
Civil rights, and the Fourteenth
Amendment, 206
Civil rights, of Negroes, 234–235
Civil Rights Act (1875), 234

Civil Rights bill (1866), 214
Civil service, 139–141
Civil War, 189–208; business interests, northern, 193–196
destruction of southern economy by, 196–197
diversity of nationalities engaged, 200–201
economic legislation during, 194–196
effect on Presidency, 206–207
effect on slavery, 203–206
emotional impact, 190–191, 192, 193, 210
European anticipations of outcome, 207–208
and industrial capacity, 123
literature concerning, 191
monetary cost of, 202–203, 240
nationalism during, 199–201
as a people's war, 190–193
railroads affect outcome, 120
Reconstruction period after, *see* Reconstruction period
as "revolution," 193–194
slavery as cause of, 188
volunteers, 191
women in, 192–193
Civil Wars, English, 1
Civil Works Administration (CWA), 389
Civilian Conservation Corps, 389, 398
Clark, Francis E., 258
Clark, William A., 248
Clark v. *Toucey*, 67n
Clarke, Susannah, 48
Class consciousness, and political affiliations, 270
and Progressivism, 375
relative weakness in America, 268–270
Class differentiations in dress, Puritan, 10
Class structure in America, 18th-century, 44–50
19th-century, 146
European tradition, 5
and Revolutionary War, 100–102
and wealth, 4
Clayton Act (1914), 254, 262, 366
Cleveland, Grover, 193, 243n, 335–336
Clinton, George, 89, 90
Cobb, Howell, 186n, 203

Cochran, Thomas, 246
Coin's Financial School, 331
Coke, Sir Edward, 63
Colden, Cadwallader, 44, 46, 47, 48, 66
Cole, Nathan, 55
College of New Jersey, 51
Colleges, *see* Schools and colleges
Colonial Dames of America, 360
"Colonial Ideas of Parliamentary Power, 1764–1766," 78n
Colonials, ethnic diversity of, 50–53
Colonies, British limitations on manufactures, 81
navigation system imposed, 81–82
participation in English-French wars, 69–70
political institutions, 61–62
as source of wealth for England, 42
Combination Acts, 261
Committee for Industrial Organization (A.F. of L.), 268, 401; *see also* Congress of Industrial Organizations (C.I.O.)
Committee on the State of Public Affairs for Boston, 48
Commons, John R., 279, 284–285, 345, 346
Commonwealth Club address, Roosevelt, 413
Commonwealth of Massachusetts v. *Hunt*, 153
Communication, in 18th-century America, 43–45, 112
Communications, effect on agriculture, 323–324
Competition, government attempts to save, 253, 254
Competition vs. trusts, 250–254
Comstock, Anthony, 15
Confiscation Acts, 102, 204
Congregationalist, 343n
Congregationalists, 19
Congress of Industrial Organizations (C.I.O.), 265, 270, 398–399, 402
Congressional Immigration Commission (1907), 282, 283, 284, 285n
Connecticut, first school laws, 18
Negroes in, 37
Conscription, use of in Civil War, 201
Conservatism, European, 5
and immigrants, 295
of labor, 260, 262–263, 267–268

Schmitz, Johann, 276
Schoepf, Johann, 99
Scholes, Percy, 11
Schools and colleges, desegregation
  (1882), 230–231
  desegregation (1950's), 24, 287n
  and egalitarianism, 160
  founded by churches, 19–20
  19th-century, 157–160
  patriotism inculcated in, 159
  public supported, 159–160
  rate schools, 158
  and Reconstruction period, 225–226
  religious education, 159
  secularization of, 159
  in 17th-century America, 17–20
  teacher training, 158
  see also Education
Schurz, Carl, 212, 286
Schuyler, Philip, 101
Schwab, Charles M., 381
Science, 18th-century interest in, 44
Scots-Irish immigration, 51–52
Scott, John Morin, 100
Scott, Sir Walter, 180
Scottish immigration, 18th century, 51
Scudder, Vida, 362
Secession, repudiation of doctrine, 200
Secret ballot, in 18th century, 66
Sects, religious, diversity of, 53–54
  "enthusiastic," 56
  and immigration, 292
Secularization, 18th-century trend to-
  ward, 54
Securities and Exchange Commission,
  385, 414, 415
Security, as social attitude, 406–410
Segregation, of Negroes, *see* Negroes,
  segregation of
Self-government, evolution of, 20–26
Sephardic communities, colonial era,
  51
Sermons, of Puritan clergy, 16–17
Servants, in 17th-century America, 32,
  33
Seven Sisters Acts, 366
Sewell, Samuel, 11
Sex, Puritans' attitude towards, 11–14
Sex ratios, in colonial America, 57
Shakespeare, racial attitudes in plays,
  30–31
Shaler, N. S., 299
Shame of the Cities, 364
Shame of the States, 364

Shannon, Fred, 130
Shaw, Chief Justice Lemuel, 153
Shays' Rebellion (1787), 90
Sheldon, Charles, 371
Sherman, John, 194
Sherman, General William Tecumseh,
  192, 196
Sherman Antitrust Act (1890), 242,
  254, 366
Shreve, Henry, 116
Siege of Rhodes, The, 11
Siemens-Martin steel process, 243, 245
Simkhovitch, Mary, 362, 365
Simkins, Francis, 225, 228
Sin and Society, 363
"Sinner in the Hands of an Angry
  God, A" (sermon), 16n
Skills, of immigrants, 279–280
Slavery, 26–39, 161–188; abolished in
  Europe, 179
  abolition movement, 179–181, 184–
  187
  beginnings in colonies, 31–32
  as cause of Civil War, 188
  conditioning of Negroes by, 173–174
  conditioning of white men by, 175–
  183
  and the Constitution, 184, 185, 187
  cotton cultivation effects, 162–163
  culture of Negroes, 173
  dilemma of, 184–188
  discriminatory punishment, 32
  distinction between white slaves
  and Negro, 32
  doctrine of Negro inferiority, 174
  economic significance of, 164–165,
  176
  effects of Revolutionary War on, 98
  effect of secession, 203–206
  emancipation after Civil War, 197–
  198
  Emancipation Proclamation, 204n,
  205
  extension issue, 111–112, 187
  Fourteenth Amendment, 205–206
  and free land in West, 134
  Fugitive Slave Act (1850), 184
  impact on white South, 182–183
  and Indians, 31
  Industrial Revolution, effect of, 162–
  163
  Kansas-Nebraska Act, 184
  and labor organizations, 176
  and labor scarcity, 2